GRAND IMPROVISATION

AMERICA CONFRONTS
THE BRITISH SUPERPOWER,
1945–1957

Derek Leebaert

FARRAR, STRAUS AND GIROUX | NEW YORK

Farrar, Straus and Giroux
175 Varick Street, New York 10014

Library of Congress Cataloging-in-Publication Data
Names: Leebaert, Derek, author.
Title: Grand improvisation : America confronts the British superpower, 1945–1957 /
    Derek Leebaert.
Other titles: America confronts the British superpower, 1945–1957
Description: New York : Farrar, Straus and Giroux, [2018] | Includes bibliographical
    references and index.
Identifiers: LCCN 2018002520 | ISBN 9780374250720 (hardcover)
Subjects: LCSH: United States—Relations—Great Britain. | Great Britain—
    Relations—United States. | World politics—1945–1955.
Classification: LCC E183.8.G7 L35 2018 | DDC 327.73041—dc23
LC record available at https://lccn.loc.gov/2018002520

Designed by Richard Oriolo

Our books may be purchased in bulk for promotional, educational, or business use.
Please contact your local bookseller or the Macmillan Corporate and Premium Sales
Department at 1-800-221-7945, extension 5442, or by e-mail at
MacmillanSpecialMarkets@macmillan.com.

www.fsgbooks.com
www.twitter.com/fsgbooks · www.facebook.com/fsgbooks

10 9 8 7 6 5 4 3 2 1

Confirm thy soul in self-control . . .
O beautiful for patriot dream
That sees beyond the years
"AMERICA THE BEAUTIFUL,"
KATHARINE LEE BATES

CONTENTS

GRAND IMPROVISATION

INTRODUCTION

A FREQUENTLY REPEATED TALE ABOUT THE TWENTIETH CENTURY is this: At the end of World War II, the British Empire was too weak and too dispirited to continue as a global imperial power; thus a confidently prosperous, well-armed America assumed leadership of the West—and did so while creating a U.S.-led international order that we've lived with ever since. Today this story is taken for granted. The twentieth century, after all, became the American Century.

But it's a myth. Britain, heart of a historic and militarily adroit empire covering a quarter of the world's land surface, was unlikely to "hand on the baton of democracy," "liquidate" its realms, or "retreat" from a singular global presence—especially not in the alleged "thousand days" after it had played a pivotal role in winning the bloodiest conflict in history.[1] Equally unconvincing is the notion that the United States, a self-contained continental island-state, traditionally fenced off by oceans and high tariffs, should suddenly drop its insularity and transform itself into a world political-military force.

In fact, the British Empire hardly "wanted out," and the United States did not "willy-nilly" become a superpower, let alone possess the unique ability "to affect the course of events in the developing world," which remained a largely colonial one.[2] As for creating a world order, the best minds—even a decade after the Axis had been defeated—believed that anything like such an arrangement was merely "emerging" and "vulnerable."[3]

There's no doubt that at the end of World War II America was by far the world's strongest nation, with an atomic monopoly and unprecedented industrial weight. But it was still a resolutely distant superstate, hesitant to take up a commanding political and military position. In the dozen years that followed, it faced a shrewd, high-tech, deeply entrenched, Anglo-Saxon colossus whose war-hardened leaders had no intention of stepping aside or of serving as junior partners to anyone. These men continued to assert their power and even their ascendancy until at least the end of 1956, when the just-reelected administration of Dwight Eisenhower finally avowed a "declaration of independence" from British influence. It was then that the United States explicitly took over, in the words of its vice president, Richard Nixon, "the foreign policy leadership of the free world." Only at that point was Geoffrey Crowther, longtime editor of *The Economist*, a magazine attentive Americans regarded as the voice of the British establishment, compelled to admit that "Britain is no longer a Super-power."

There are few twentieth-century dramas so relevant to the world today. At no time between the aftermath of 1945 and the present have so many aspects of international life been in flux: the rise and retreat of superpowers; shifts in global currency regimes; uncertain mutual defense commitments; and severe doubts among Americans about the value of military primacy in the first place. The roots of today's turmoil spring from this epoch: Europe's qualms about U.S. reliability; the destabilization, and re-destabilization, of the Middle East; the making of the enduring tragedy of America's Vietnam War; the country's justified fears of other long-term entanglements; and fights against "terrorists" throughout the world. Moreover, an aggressively nationalistic Russia has returned to its crude Soviet-like behaviors while employing its familiar techniques of hybrid war and possession of the planet's second-largest nuclear arsenal. Again North Korea and Iran are world issues, and U.S. policy makers continue to speak of how they'll supposedly shape the future of China.

Currently, in Beijing, strategists are devoting intense effort to modeling the fall of empires. They study the fate of the Soviet Union and what caused the hammer and sickle to be hauled down from over the Kremlin on Christmas Day 1991. But they're also analyzing the destiny of the far-flung British Empire, which they presume to have been displaced almost overnight by an American one—the days of which are supposedly numbered as well.

For most of the years between 1945 and 1957, it was difficult to tell how the fate of the British Empire might affect America, except on financial matters. When Eisenhower became president in 1953, he acknowledged not only that Britain was dominant in the Middle East, as it was throughout this era, but also that it wielded a veto over U.S. decisions in Southeast Asia. And this was at a time when top U.S. officials believed that America's "biggest post-war difficulty"—perhaps more than the Soviet threat—was the inability to say no to the British Empire. In effect, serious people in Washington believed that "no acceptable foreign policy" was available to the United States if it wasn't aligned with its sprawling, problematic ally. Britain maintained the profile and the substance of a "superpower"; Eisenhower was, for the time being, candid in his awareness that global military ambitions, along with the attendant political involvements, were alien to the United States.

This book offers a new understanding of the world that arose in the years following World War II. History's largest empire was battling to maintain its standing, while an utterly novel form of global preeminence loomed from across the Atlantic. The outcome shows the changing might of nations, the illusion of trying to mold the destinies of peoples and places unknown, and the risks of attempting to maintain huge political-military edifices on shaky foundations. We see how thoughtful, informed wielders of power reached decisions while feeling besieged, and we find ourselves asking how our country may segue into some new type of its now-familiar stature in the decade ahead.

Leaders in Washington and London rarely grasped how much was out of date in their thinking as they mused upon worldwide commitments and vacuums of power, upon the indispensability of their nations and, oftentimes, of themselves. To this end, we see Winston Churchill in a very different light, after he returned as prime minister from 1951 to 1955, grumbling that the war years might well have been easier than what he then faced in trying to restore the British Empire to its former greatness. So, also, with other players, such as Eisenhower himself, President Truman's provocative secretary of state Dean Acheson, the literary diplomat George Kennan, and an already redoubtable senator Lyndon Johnson. We encounter once immeasurably influential men who've been lost to history but now regain their prominence: for instance, Truman's closest friend and adviser, doubling as the century's most powerfully placed secretary of the Treasury; and Britain's commissioner general for Southeast Asia who maneuvered for nearly a decade—while holding cabinet rank in London—to commit the United States to Vietnam. This era cannot be understood unless we appreciate these figures and what they accomplished.

Eisenhower never used the term "superpower," and it barely appears in the jargon of the time. It had been coined amid the depths of war. William T. R. Fox, a professor of international relations at Columbia University, used it in 1944 to categorize nations that possessed "great power *plus* great mobility of power." For a country to function as a superpower, it had to be able to project force most anywhere it pleased. That, in turn, required not only an utterly modern arsenal but also a tentacular espionage apparatus and a network of allies who could leverage such strengths. Fox identified the "Super Powers" of his moment: the United States, the Soviet Union, and the British Empire. But we can now see that after the war ended, neither the Soviet Union nor the United States fully met these requirements. The Soviet Union was rather more than 20 percent larger than today's Russia, with double the population. It was the most massive unitary land power ever, yet it lacked overseas reach, except through spying and subversion. The United States, for its part, had no intention of continuing to entangle itself abroad. It took years to accept the need to garrison GIs in Europe and Asia, to develop a naval presence in the Persian Gulf, and to build an intelligence capability that offered more than amateurish adventuring.

In contrast, the British Empire and Commonwealth was planetary, with deep relationships nearly everywhere, including those of secret intelligence. Britain drew upon statecraft and experience that—as many U.S. officials, businessmen, and field commanders believed—outweighed any nation's. Its elite career civil servants sat in continuing authority, from government to government. The American press wrote of Britain deploying a million fighting men across a thousand ports and garrisons. Britain led the world in jet aviation, life sciences, and civil atomic power (unquestionably the industries of tomorrow) and in 1952 became the third nuclear-weapon state. Within two years, its Army of the Rhine was the strongest military presence in Western Europe. The prewar system of global trade had collapsed, and during most of this period no substitute was built up to take its place. Yet London was still banker to much of the world, core of its largest trading area, and center of the world's diplomatic activity.

Only after its "declaration of independence" in December 1956 did the United States find itself pushing out alone into a slew of involvements across the Middle East, Asia, and Africa. The break point was to come slightly later—specifically in October 1957, when Russia launched the first Sputnik, a satellite propelled by an intercontinental ballistic missile that once and for all stripped America of its island security. There followed a string of glaringly public U.S. missile failures, and America was gripped by dread that it would not be able to catch up. Whatever happened, it was apparent that only the United States and the Soviet Union could compete at this level. Americans were primed for the call of John F. Kennedy, the magnetic young senator from Massachusetts, who was soon to thrill the nation as he evoked "a struggle for supremacy" against Moscow's "ruthless, godless tyranny." We have been driven by such dangerous zeal until today, when a new array of irrevocable decisions presses upon us.

The story that follows has not been told, and only some of its outlines may be familiar. It was a world without any American "grand strategy," and one in which most every move by Washington was a desperate improvisation. We now face another time of historic geopolitical adjustment as the kaleidoscope again spins faster. To recognize what transpired between the two most powerful democratic nations over these dozen years may help us find our way through the current predicaments.

I. THEY THOUGHT IT WAS PEACE

President Franklin D. Roosevelt and Vice President Elect Harry S. Truman,
1944: one looks weary, the other anxious.

1

THE THREE IN 1945

Britain, who thinks she saved the world, is mute in the bonds of austerity; Russia, who thinks she saved the world, sits back, enormous, suspicious, watching; and America, who thinks she saved the world, makes one think of a nervous, hysterical girl holding a hand grenade, not knowing what to do with it or when it will go off.

—Nat Gubbins, 1946, British philosopher-humorist and
   Daily Express columnist

A T 10:30 P.M. ON MAY 1, RADIO HAMBURG REPORTED THAT Hitler lay dead in the Reich Chancellery. World War II was at last coming to an end, at least in Europe, and by then over 36 million people had been consumed in that charnel house alone. There were more refugees on the move than at any time until today, some 13 million altogether, including 5 million starting to arrive in western Germany from within the nation's prewar frontiers. But Winston Churchill made no statement in the House of Commons that night. Speaking to a member of Parliament earlier in the day, he'd merely observed that the situation was "more satisfactory than it was this time five years ago," when the Nazi war machine had cornered for slaughter some 400,000 Allied soldiers on the beaches of Dunkirk.[1] Just a few days before Churchill spoke, Russian and American infantrymen had embraced along the river Elbe in northeastern Germany, cutting the Reich in two. This entailed more than Hitler's downfall. The encounter also signaled the end of Europe's primacy in world affairs.

Victory had been certain by late 1944. To decide the political division of the postwar world, the great Allied powers—the United States, the Soviet Union, and the British Empire, or "the Three," as Harry Truman would later call them—gathered early in February 1945 for seven days at Yalta, a czarist-era resort on the Black Sea in the Crimea. Churchill was then seventy, having all the demeanor of a bulldog, as the famous photographs showed. He led a British delegation of around 350 that included the lean and elegant foreign secretary, Anthony Eden, forty-seven, who was Churchill's closest political ally. General Hastings "Pug" Ismay, the prime minister's personal military assistant, was there, as were key economic advisers and half a dozen of Britain's top commanders.

President Franklin Delano Roosevelt, sixty-three, arrived bundled in a wheelchair despite the mild climate, which was due to the sheltering mountains to the north. His big frame looked frail, and he indeed had just two months to live. Accompanying him were some 350 Americans as well. They included his senior White House staff officer, Fleet Admiral William Leahy; the austere army chief of staff, George Marshall; and Edward Stettinius, the silver-haired forty-four-year-old secretary of state, who was in the third month of his seven-month tenure. Joseph Stalin, five years younger than Churchill, was the host—and around him were V. M. Molotov, people's commissar for foreign affairs; Molotov's deputy, Andrei Vyshinsky; and three of the Soviet armed forces' most senior commanders. On the fifth day, the sadistic torturer Lavrenti Beria appeared. Stalin playfully described him as "our Himmler," referencing the *Reichsführer-SS*, and it was Beria's NKVD, the dreaded People's Commissariat for Internal Affairs, that handled arrangements for the conference.

At Yalta, the principals addressed those nations and regions that would become flash points in the years ahead: a divided Germany, Iran, Greece, Turkey and the Balkans, the Middle East, Indochina, and Korea. Also discussed were swaths of the Bloodlands—the conquered and reconquered terrain between the Baltic and the Black Sea in which Hitler and Stalin, from 1933 to 1945, killed some fourteen million civilians.[2]

Historians have long contended that Yalta demonstrated Britain's waning stature among "the Three," but that's not how Churchill and the men around him saw it. They had reasons to expect the British Empire to be the presiding power over much of the postwar world. Churchill, ever the romantic, code-named the conference "Argonaut," a reference to the ancient Greek myth of Jason and his Argonauts, a band of heroes who had sailed on the beautiful vessel *Argo* into hostile lands to retrieve the Golden Fleece—a symbol of power and rightful kingship.

The British knew that their empire had neither the industrial heft of the United States nor the hordes of Red Army soldiers and flaming Marxist-Leninist ideology of the Soviet Union. Still, they believed they had other advantages, and the shock of FDR's appearance added to their confidence. General Ismay concluded Roosevelt "was more than half gaga," which was untrue, but the president looked so ill that right after the conference U.S. press officers tried to explain away the photographs in which he wanly appeared. He was having trouble with his dentures, they claimed, which affected his speech and caused his face to fall in.[3] Men who were there, however, could see for themselves. With a dying president in office—who'd sooner or later be succeeded by an obscure vice president untutored in foreign affairs—the United States would likely play only a marginal role in the months and maybe the years ahead. Moreover, as Roosevelt emphasized on the conference's second day, America's three million troops would be gone from Europe within two years of Germany's defeat.

Russia was known to have been bled terribly by the war, though the figure of 26.6 million dead was yet to be calculated by the Soviet General Staff. Yalta itself had been liberated only the previous April from the Germans, and FDR was shocked by the Crimea's war-torn landscape. He witnessed it up close during the eighty-five-mile drive over rough and winding roads from the airfield in Saki, where the American and British delegations had landed, to Yalta. Though he remained in London, Tommy Lascelles, King George VI's shrewd and influential private secretary, predicted that the Russians "will be greatly dependent on us and the USA for their financial and industrial rehabilitation."[4]

The territory of the empire and commonwealth was half again as large as that of the Soviet Union, and its population at least double. But there was another factor to consider. Most of all, Churchill was convinced that the British Empire possessed "superior statecraft and experience" in its officials and institutions, and no one around him, certainly not Lascelles or Eden, disagreed.[5] Nor, as it turned out, did the Americans. Along with other advantages, it therefore seemed plausible that the men at the center of a postwar world would be speaking in crisp British tones.

As the conference got under way, the British began sending news home via a diplomatic pouch that was couriered to London daily. The more urgent messages were sent through a secure electronic communications station aboard the Cunard Line's RMS *Franconia* anchored nearby. And one of those was a cable Churchill sent to Clement Attlee, the deputy prime minister and leader of the Labour Party, saying that he'd come upon a different Russia than he'd known previously. His own private secretary, John Martin of the Dominions Office, reported home that Stalin and the prime minister were getting on swimmingly.

The once-enigmatic dictator now appeared to see the funny side of everything. He'd taken up smoking cigars, just like Churchill, rather than cigarettes. To be sure, Roosevelt joked with Stalin at Churchill's expense, observing that the British were peculiar people who wanted to "have their cake and eat it too." But when Churchill heard such digs, he responded by just playing quietly with his cigar while Foreign Secretary Eden stared off into the distance. In the end, Eden concluded that at Yalta "the Americans had been very weak." That was Lascelles's sense as well, though he wasn't as harsh. After reading all the conference telegrams, he wrote in his diary that "the Americans have supported us loyally."[6]

Roosevelt's priorities included persuading Stalin to join the final battle against Japan and establishing direct communication between Red Army headquarters and those of General Dwight Eisenhower, who commanded the assault into Germany from the west. He accomplished both, and he also got Stalin's agreement to participate in the United Nations Organization, or "Uno," as sardonic British diplomats tended to call it, until corrected by earnest Americans who preferred a more respectful term, "the UN."

The British believed they were getting much of what they wanted at Yalta. They convinced the Americans and the Russians that after an Allied victory, France should also control an occupation zone in Germany.

This was a critical goal for the British, who couldn't risk being the only democracy on the scene when the GIs went home. They were additionally scoring successes in bilateral trade and commercial issues with the Americans, a neglected element of this conference. The industrialist Frederick Leathers, minister of war transport, reported his surprise that U.S. officials were finally adopting his views on global trade, including London's right to discriminate against foreign shipping and oil imports from non-British firms.[7]

Churchill and his advisers didn't object when Roosevelt proposed that the Three issue a "Declaration on Liberated Europe" to close the conference. It was essentially a memorandum of good intentions to build a free and peace-loving world. Not least, it underlined each power's commitment to an early democratic vote in Poland for a new constitution and government—a salient point because Britain and France had declared war on Nazi Germany in September 1939 to uphold Poland's independence. Back in London, Tommy Lascelles came to believe, as did others, that the "Liberated Europe" declaration was a historically more important achievement than the Magna Carta or the Declaration of Independence.

Skeptics within the U.S. and British delegations, such as Admiral Leahy, knew the language behind all this to be as pliant as a rubber band. Nonetheless, Churchill was pleased, despite his having vowed for decades to see Bolshevism crushed. He regarded Stalin as one of the great figures of history, and he'd blurted out, "I *like* that man," while adding, "In spite of everything I'd like that man to like me."[8] Anthony Eden had been horrified, but Churchill was a figure of prodigious emotions and had no vocabulary for a middle way.

Once home on February 19, and despite some early ambivalence, Churchill told his cabinet that Stalin was a man who could be trusted. On the twenty-seventh, he assured a cheering House of Commons in a two-hour speech that no government had ever kept its word more faithfully than the Soviet Union. Eden was more cautious, but implied his confidence in Stalin. The Argonauts had done well, and the empire's clout had been confirmed.

Or so it appeared. In fact, Stalin had already created a ready-to-be-installed puppet regime for Poland, which deemed the legal Polish government in exile (based in London) a usurper. Crack divisions of the conquering Red Army—the mightiest that ever existed—were sweeping through Poland's towns and villages to push deep within Germany's borders. Bridgeheads were being established 43 miles from Berlin, while Russia's allies in the west were still 370 miles away. No matter what had been said, prospects for democracy anywhere in Europe were slim once the Red Army and the NKVD arrived.

Churchill and Roosevelt knew this. But happiness can be defined as the perpetual state of being well deceived, and they were eager to come to terms with Stalin in any way possible.

Above all, the Americans and British needed events to be settled. For them, the war had to be final; it *had* to be followed by a just and enduring order. That meant accepting Stalin's assurances. The Americans enjoyed their own illusions, but nothing like the British, who were experiencing the hopes of despair. Self-deception within Britain's official circles arose from an ordeal of war that went back to August 1914. The second global war *must* have a conclusive settlement. The alternative of renewed war, or of a fully armed peace, was unthinkable.

Soon enough, however, Churchill found his faiths hard to justify. On February 23, as he learned more about Stalin's moves to impose Soviet-model police states on Eastern Europe, he mused to one of his staff that he might be trusting Stalin as Neville Chamberlain had trusted Hitler, and on the twenty-eighth he fumed—in private—that he was ready to go to the "verge of war" with Stalin over Poland.[9] Distressed, Churchill sent long telegrams to Roosevelt, back in the United States, about Stalin behaving contrary to the understandings reached at Yalta.[10] But the president, in his final weeks of life, could express only anxiety, concern, and disappointment.

SINCE NOT LONG AFTER PEARL HARBOR, CHURCHILL HAD BEEN RE-ceiving acute insights on American politics from Isaiah Berlin, a Russian émigré and Oxford don in his mid-thirties who'd soon be recognized as one of the century's leading historians of ideas. In 1944, Berlin was serving as an analyst in the Special Survey Section of the British embassy in Washington, where his job was to harvest intelligence and compose clever weekly commentaries to be sent to London under the name of the busy ambassador, Lord Halifax. Churchill knew the original source of these stylish essays and paid attention. On December 10, he received a report that described a desire within Congress and the Roosevelt administration "for a brand new 100 per cent American foreign policy not tied to Britain's apron strings." It was a warning that Berlin had been pressing in his dispatches for two years. A hard-boiled, businesslike approach to foreign affairs was quickly emerging, he noted. Energetic U.S. technicians, industrialists, and traders were eyeing vast new markets, "eager to convert the world to the American pattern." He urged his superiors to pay attention to America's expansive aspirations, and in the last months of the war he stated that "the world had better get ready."[11]

Influential men were indeed speaking of the need for a "Pax Americana" following the war, but what did they mean by this term that echoed Roman tyranny and British mythology? To some, such as Maine's Republican senator Owen Brewster, it entailed encouraging the nation's best businessmen and most businesslike officials to compete overseas with the savvy, well-organized British. The United States could shape the postwar world by playing to its strengths in trade and industry and by being an exemplar of democracy.

In the better drawing rooms of the northeast coast, however, other men were taking "Pax Americana" literally. Among them was Lewis Douglas, then serving at the War Shipping Administration; his brother-in-law John J. McCloy, the assistant secretary of war; and their friend James Conant, the president of Harvard. They envisioned an assertively dominant nation that would replace the British Empire, which they took, until just about now, to have been the world's foremost political and military force.[12]

It's a common tendency for a country to blame its allies for doing nothing to win a war. During this war, however, it was also frequently claimed that one's allies were doing too much to win the peace. "Never absent from British minds," as President Roosevelt himself had suggested in a briefing note for his military chiefs, "are their post-war interests, commercial or military."[13] At Yalta, one U.S. naval aide saw the British "losing a lot of sleep" in trying to outsmart the Americans at the conference table. Their goal was "not to cause us to lose the war," he allowed, "but just to lighten their burden and debt as much as they could without fighting."[14]

In another of his Washington dispatches, Isaiah Berlin reported that the political, diplomatic, and military officials he met in the capital suspected that his government was poised to create a new balance of power in the postwar world by "driving a wedge" between America and Russia.[15] As late as the spring of 1945, on the verge of victory, Tennessee's senator Kenneth McKellar, chairman of the Appropriations Committee and one of the best-informed people in Washington, would warn colleagues that Britain was ready to embark on a postwar buildup intended to make its Royal Navy dangerously larger than a demobilized U.S. fleet.[16]

On the other hand, Admiral Leahy concluded after Yalta, in his usual snapping-turtle manner, that a weakened Britain was ruined beyond repair.*

From whatever viewpoint, it was hard to evaluate the British Empire. State and the Pentagon, for instance, offered several conflicting analyses of their own. It was at least clear, by the time the Yalta Conference ended, that Churchill was growing troubled about economic prospects at home. World War II had cost Britain twice the amount of World War I. In its last terrible year, 10 million men and women out of a working population of 21.5 million were either carrying weapons or making them. Britain's economy had been stripped for the fight.

To help clarify matters, Roosevelt sent a personal emissary to see Churchill six weeks after Yalta: the wise, elderly South Carolina financier-troubleshooter Bernard Baruch, known as "Chief" to friends and employees. Churchill and Baruch liked each other. Baruch had chaired the War Industries Board during World War I, and Churchill was his opposite number when minister of munitions from 1917 to January 1919. As usual with FDR's emissaries, Baruch had carte blanche to discuss

---

*The empire was long said to be finished, as by the French and German press during 1899, when imperial troops were trounced at Magersfontein, Stormberg, and Colenso in one bloody week of the Boer War. In 1939, however, the Royal Navy was the world's largest and generally rated the best—a reason why many informed Americans believed, at the war's beginning, that the British Empire could handle the Hitler menace, along with France. Britain also possessed healthy reserves of gold and foreign currency.

what he thought necessary. He received only a single directive: he should ask the British to restore Hong Kong to China.

The tall, white-haired Baruch, with chiseled features and antebellum manners, knew a lot about Wall Street, Democratic Party politics, and advising presidents. Moreover, he had recently completed a secret White House study, *War and Postwar Adjustment Policies*, for the president. Baruch arrived in London at the beginning of April. Once Churchill had dismissed the request about Hong Kong, Baruch offered an expertly reassuring analysis to him and the cabinet. "The empire," he said, "could emerge from the war stronger than ever—physically, economically, politically and spiritually."[17] This would come from pent-up consumer demand and accumulated savings at home. He also sensed that the economy's total annual production (GDP) had risen in real terms during the war—as it did, by 15 percent. Then there was the fact that Germany and Japan were eliminated from world trade. Therefore, Britain could restore its depleted wealth by quickly modernizing its industry and profiting from its dominions, its colonies, and its vast areas of interest. It could gain commanding heights in technology and trade, with minimal U.S. assistance required.

Churchill took the message to heart and quoted Baruch's analysis to commonwealth leaders as evidence that Britain's economy would recover rapidly without much support from overseas. Its ongoing political and military weight could be assumed. But in a letter to his wife from Chequers Court, the country house of Britain's prime ministers, Churchill expressed doubts about having an equal standing with the Americans after the war. "How can you do that against so mighty a nation and a population nearly three times as large?"[18] The word "against" is telling.

ROOSEVELT DIED ON THURSDAY, APRIL 12, 1945, FROM A STROKE at his getaway in Warm Springs, Georgia. But his presence shadows the postwar ties between Britain and America for two reasons. First, his rapport with Churchill was pivotal to waging the war, and ever since their ties have been cited on both sides of the Atlantic as the ideal of fraternal cooperation. Second, Churchill, after returning in 1951 to Downing Street, longed to establish the same ties with Presidents Truman and

Eisenhower that he believed he had shared with FDR. As a result, it's helpful to have a correct understanding of that complex relationship. For instance, it's wrong to think of Roosevelt and Churchill as friends. They were more like two officers in the mess with no particular fondness in peacetime but who then bond during combat—to return to rivalry as the smoke starts to clear.

The war was about all they had in common. In fact, Roosevelt was the coldest of men—something that sharp-eyed Harry Truman, who served as vice president during the eighty-two days of Roosevelt's fourth term, understood. Roosevelt's iciness could be laced with charm, but he was a very lonely person, as his daughter confided to her mother after he died.[19] In contrast, Churchill had a gift for friendship and held deep affections across parties and types. He'd first been elected to Parliament in 1900 and was a fount of stories, memories, and insight. He immersed himself in the great drama—the "triumph and tragedy"—of a world at war.[20] But Churchill's enthusiasms could wear thin with Roosevelt. A sticking point was Roosevelt's aversion to colonialism, as seen in his views on Hong Kong—a quirky exception being his respect for the Dutch Empire, due to an ancestral fondness for the Netherlands.[21] The harmonious wartime correspondence between Roosevelt and Churchill might give an impression of intimacy and candor, but each man knew that history was looking over his shoulder, and they were both writing for the record. The "special relationship" that they are believed to have personified was, from the start, much less than it seemed.

Throughout their association, Roosevelt judged Churchill to be living in the past, believing him to be rooted in an era of subjugated colonies, of kings and queens, and of a social structure akin to that of Downton Abbey. It's an easy caricature. Churchill had no shortage of illiberal points, such as the romantic excitements he found in making war, especially against lesser-armed people in primitive places (sentiments not unknown today). Isaiah Berlin made the same mistake as did Roosevelt. He'd later write that, despite all, "Churchill remains a European of the nineteenth century."[22] Professor Berlin, however, had no familiarity with the world of technology that fascinated Churchill.

For today's technologists, Churchill is immediately recognizable. He's a modern entrepreneur: curious, excited, open to a breadth of views, eager to share the fruits of his imagination, and having nothing of the snob. He admires brains and character. There's a sense of the possible with a readiness, as needed, to tear down the old, plus an enjoyment of science fiction (in his case H. G. Wells), a common taste among high-tech innovators. He yearned to have the Massachusetts Institute of Technology replicated in Britain, and in 1958 he founded MIT's equivalent in his country—Cambridge's Churchill College, which boasts thirty-two Nobel Prize winners among its fellowship. He himself reasoned like a scientist, as shown in the eleven-page essay "Are We Alone in the Universe?," which was discovered in 2017. He also had the key entrepreneurial trait of being exceedingly flexible. That's seen in his own calling as a politician, which included switching parties two and a half times. "For Churchill," observed one of his ministers, "business never stopped."[23] Revealingly, he was usually on the outs with party leaders, as entrepreneurs tend to be with any hierarchy. And no one could be more inspiring to those around him.

In many ways, it was Churchill who best embodied Emerson's picture of America as "the country of tomorrow." This 51 percent American son of a glamorous mother from Cobble Hill, Brooklyn, spent a lifetime exploring the new, from imagining electric turbines on the Zambezi, in 1907, to catching the significance of the first atomic detonation in July 1945. Splitting the atom could displace fossil fuel, he concluded; perhaps a fragment might even yield 800 horsepower when harnessed to industry.

Churchill was always absorbed by what he called the Great Republic. He never shared the British establishment's nervous patronizing of America. The two Conservative Party prime ministers who would follow him, Anthony Eden and Harold Macmillan, were seeing themselves as ancient Greeks who needed to instruct the rising imperial presence in the subtleties of worldly ways. Their view presumed that the new Romans only valued money and power unless taught otherwise. Churchill didn't accept that. Instead, he dreamed of a future consecrated to some noble purpose, a very American quality.

Life would have been easier for Washington in the decade ahead had Churchill indeed been a nineteenth-century European. He could have been brushed aside. Instead, "that Yankee careerist," as he'd been called at home, kept exerting a pull on the American imagination.[24]

. . .

WITH ROOSEVELT GONE, HARRY TRUMAN NOW SAT IN THE WHITE House, a cocky figure who acknowledged that he knew nothing about foreign affairs, though he devoured books of history. To many Americans, Truman's salient feature was his bankruptcy as a Kansas City haberdasher. For observers in London and Moscow, his ascent confirmed their suspicions that Washington might well eschew deep political and military ties with the world.

Tommy Lascelles, however, was among the British officials who expected the Americans to be shocked out of isolationism once and for all. One reason, he believed, was that the full horror of the concentration camps was being revealed by the spring of 1945: after Majdanek was liberated in the summer of 1944 came Auschwitz in January, then Buchenwald, Bergen-Belsen, Dachau, Mauthausen, and finally Theresienstadt. Seeing such evil, he hoped, would compel the Americans to finally grasp the world's true malevolence and then ask themselves where it would stop.

On May 7, less than a month after Roosevelt's death, the Germans surrendered unconditionally, having lost a still-disputed number of seven to nine million dead. With the war in Europe at last over, Churchill and Clement Attlee brought their wartime coalition to an end fifteen days later. They then formed a caretaker government and called for a general election to be held on July 5—in effect a two-party race between Conservatives and Labour. The election occurred as scheduled, but because military ballots from around the world had to be gathered, no results could be announced until later in July. This was awkward: at Yalta, the three heads of government had agreed to reconvene following Germany's defeat. They did so from July 17 to August 2 in Potsdam—an intact, well-gardened suburb ten miles from Berlin. (In the city itself, corpses still lay among the ruins, covered only by bricks.) The Potsdam Conference, unlike Yalta, had an agenda, and it included questions of Europe's postwar borders, Poland, reparations, war criminals, and Vietnam, in French Indochina. The British, however, would begin negotiations without knowing which party had won their election.

Churchill arrived on July 15 along with Attlee and Foreign Secretary Eden, whose eldest son, Simon, an RAF navigator, had six days earlier been posted as missing over Burma. The Americans also appeared on the fifteenth, after sailing into the fortress city of Antwerp on the cruiser USS *Augusta* and then being flown by Air Transport Command to Berlin. Churchill and Truman met for the first time the following morning, at a juncture when Harold Macmillan, who was secretary of state for air in Churchill's cabinet, held the common belief in London that his country was "on an equal footing" with America.[25]

At Potsdam, under the spreading chestnut trees, Stalin was smiling and amiable, though he had already wiped Yalta off the slate by, among other steps, installing a Soviet-controlled, so-called provisional regime in Poland. Truman, for his part, had his thoughts largely on New Mexico, because the conference also overlapped with the first-ever test of an atomic bomb. That occurred on July 16 when a twenty-kiloton detonation caused an unnaturally early dawn over New Mexico's Jornada del Muerto desert and sent a mushroom cloud rising 7.5 miles into the air. Stalin was unfazed when Truman told him, on the twenty-fourth, that America now possessed a hugely destructive new weapon. Soviet spies within the Los Alamos research facility had kept the Kremlin informed. As for Churchill, he was again under Stalin's spell—delighted that Stalin had promised that there'd be democratic elections "in the countries set free by his armies."[26] Churchill, however, was also thinking of the contributions made in New Mexico by British scientists. "We put the Americans on the bomb," he mused to his friend and physician, Lord Moran, who joined him in Potsdam.[27] Whether anyone in Washington remembered was questionable.

After wide-ranging discussions, the conference had to adjourn for four days on Wednesday, the twenty-fifth, to allow Churchill, Attlee, Eden, and other key members of Britain's delegation to fly home to be present when election results were made public the following day. Churchill's party lost in a landslide. It would be Clement Attlee who'd return to Germany as prime minister. During his restless months to come, Churchill would reflect to Moran, with tears in his eyes, that he did not care if he never saw England again, "better to have been killed in an aeroplane or to have died like Roosevelt."[28] But he also admitted to Lascelles that had he stayed in office, the strain would likely have finished him.

. . .

ATTLEE, SIXTY-TWO, WAS A DECADE YOUNGER THAN CHURCHILL, the son of a solicitor, and a small, balding, faultlessly turned-out person who nevertheless conveyed a sense of the moths having been at work. His pipe, mustache, wire rims, best suit, and modest Hillman car reflected the comfortable life of middle-class southwest London. His wife would drive him on election campaigns. He had read modern history at Oxford, graduated in 1904, and been called to the bar, after which he applied his skills to social work. In World War I, as a major, he was the next-to-last man evacuated by sea from the bloody crags at Gallipoli and then was badly wounded by a British shell in what is today Iraq. He entered Parliament in 1922 and was flat and damp when speaking. He often talked in cricketing language—about sticky wickets and times to declare. No one, including Churchill, could offer a riposte after one of Attlee's epigrams of dullness. When he gave his victory speech at Central Hall, Westminster, that Thursday, he did so "without a trace of emotion," reported *The Times* (and no need to add "of London" in those days).[29]

Attlee and his party came to office with a vision of abolishing want, and they'd try to do so with a broad-scale program of nationalizing steel, coal, gas, electricity, the railroads and canals, and the central bank, the storied Bank of England. They intended to build a "welfare state," from whence the term comes, and their objective required big new amounts of domestic spending, such as for housing and health.

Attlee's first step after Labour won the election was to meet with the king. For twenty minutes on the evening of July 26, he sat at Buckingham Palace with George VI, who, as tradition demanded, invited him to form a government, at which point Attlee offered up nominees for the cabinet's key roles. To be foreign secretary, a position critical for the negotiations at Potsdam and whatever lay beyond, he identified Hugh Dalton—an Old Etonian whose father had been chaplain to Queen Victoria and who held a doctorate in economics from the University of London. Dalton had already been a Labour Party spokesman on foreign affairs and had served in Churchill's coalition cabinet. But the king didn't like the idea. "I disagreed with him," George VI wrote in his diary.[30] Instead, recognizing that this suave academic might not be the right man for the years ahead, the king suggested another choice: the sixty-four-year-old union boss Ernest Bevin, who as minister of labor had spent 1940–1945 mobilizing the nation for total war. This was not a command, per se, but a powerful hint, which Attlee seized upon, making Bevin his foreign secretary and, in time, granting him a mandate to "direct all cold war policies."[31]

It was an inspired choice. For the next five and a half years, from 1945 to 1951, Bevin would dominate all decisions concerning the British Empire's place in the world, as well as several of those concerning America's place as well. Not long after taking office, he baited one upper-class diplomat by saying, "Must be kinda queer for a chap like you to see a chap like me sitting in a chair like this. Ain't never 'appened before in 'istory."[32]

The Foreign Office can be icy to outsiders, but Bevin not only ended up in complete control of "the Diplomatic"; he also won the hearts of its mandarins as no secretary of modern times has done before or since. When negotiating, he'd bluff convincingly and use what he called "shock tactics," which meant lobbing unhappy surprises toward an opponent to get his way. When he'd stomp into the salons of the Hôtel Matignon, the residence of France's prime ministers, or up the staircase of London-derry House, the Mayfair palace of a powerful aristocrat, he was unimpressed by his surroundings. He had a right to be there, because "his people"—the working-class multitudes—had put him at their head.

There was nothing small about Bevin. He was visibly a bruiser with a bull neck and loud voice. He was squat at 240 pounds with putty-lump features and a goggling stare that gave him an aura of menace. As a press baron said of Churchill, Bevin had in him the stuff of which tyrants are made. A Conservative minister in fact once called him "the Labour Churchill." Bevin would have taken that as an insult, though he and Churchill shared an irrepressible optimism and a range of gestures. If the Nazis had invaded England in 1940, forcing the remnants of its army to fall back north of the Thames, Churchill had intended to fight on, and to rule what was left of the island, with Bevin at his side.

Like Churchill, with his man-of-the-people virtues, Bevin was at ease with Americans of various classes, a quality not shared by Attlee or Churchill's aristocratic heir apparent, Anthony Eden. In the Foreign

Office, Bevin enjoyed using an all-American expression he said he'd picked up from a U.S. general: "The difficult we do at once and the impossible we do a little slower." Churchill praised him as the "working man's John Bull."[33] Bevin could reach deep within to reciprocate. "I have never followed any man," he said during the war, "but I will follow that man."[34] Yet those were desperate days. With the peace, Bevin could revert to type: he scoffed that Churchill was at "one moment a great national leader, the next moment a Tory political crook."

Born to a forty-year-old washerwoman, his father unknown, Bevin started working at age ten as a farm laborer in Devon, then, at thirteen, was drawn to the port city of Bristol, becoming a drayman's boy, thereafter a wagon driver and a tram conductor, while taking night courses at a socialist free school. He gained a toehold in union work in his early twenties after becoming a trade representative for Bristol's struggling dockworkers. His years in Bristol were woven into an era resting ever more on trade with America, though he saw this from the bottom up. He'd soon merge thirty-one unions to build the free world's biggest labor organization, the Transport and General Workers' Union. In the 1920s, he fought off Communist attempts to subvert this creation, and in the 1930s, dismissing myopic pacifists, he urged Britain to rearm against the fascists. He could assimilate immense bodies of data to his purposes, whether in the endless negotiations of union life or in his effort to assert the British Empire's power in a world knocked off-balance. He was a man of the first Industrial Revolution—that of steel, coal, and steam—who had been politicized forever by its human costs. He thought in terms of redistribution rather than of growth. Yet he understood the material foundations of his country's world presence, and he believed America to be crucial to retaining it. And like the rest of the Labour Party, Bevin was a Zionist, until he was faced with terror out of Zion.

He had his limits, of course. Bevin was full of prejudices, and his ill will included, though was hardly confined to, the narrow-minded English middle class, New York Irish, all Germans ("I 'ates them"), plus Jewish extremists, of the sort who would try to kill him over Palestine, and Catholics, because he believed priests brought bad luck and he would mutter "black crows" should one cross his path in a soutane.[35] The milk of human kindness was thin. He nonetheless shared the socialist ideal of racial equality. In this, he differed pointedly from Churchill, who had opinions of his own on blackamoor Hottentots, slanty-eyed Orientals, "wogs" in Egypt, and, especially, sinuous Hindus.

BRITAIN'S PARLIAMENTARY SYSTEM HAS SPEEDY GOVERNMENT TRAN-sitions. With the election won and key members of his cabinet approved, Prime Minister Attlee could return to Potsdam right away, and he did so on Saturday, July 28, with Foreign Secretary Bevin at his side, this being Bevin's first time in a plane. The awaiting Americans and Russians were astounded at the reversal of fortune.

Once the new leaders of Britain's delegation arrived, the Three could resume their dealings, and the Russians encountered a difference as Stalin's foreign minister, Molotov, clashed early on with Bevin. In the 1930s, Molotov had personally signed thousands of death warrants before getting around to signing, in Moscow, the 1939 Molotov-Ribbentrop nonaggression pact with Nazi Germany, which had divided Poland for conquest. When angry, Molotov would jab his stubby little fingers downward and stutter with fury. This is how he responded to Bevin's abrasive negotiating style, as an American policy adviser would later report, telling Bevin "that other conferences had proceeded more smoothly because Churchill and Roosevelt were at them."[36] Undoubtedly.

Nevertheless, agreements were reached concerning Germany's occupation, the expulsion of German populations from the east, and the acceptance of the Soviet puppet regime in Poland. The Three closed the conference with a communiqué, but not with a final settlement, on the fate of postwar Germany. A settlement wouldn't be achieved for fifty-five years.

George Orwell, a man of the democratic Left and a keen observer of the era, expressed grave skepticism about this gathering and what was to come. Working in London as a journalist, Orwell wrote one of his essays for *Partisan Review* while, he said, "the leaders of the Big Three are conferring at Potsdam." He expected these states to split into three huge, mutually hostile camps. A month later, after the conference had ended and after Hiroshima had been destroyed, he was reporting that each superstate, as he called the Three, would end up having atomic bombs, there'd be a standoff among them, and humanity would exist on the edge of disaster.[37] He was anticipating a world that would look pretty much like *1984*.

The Americans flew out early on August 2, passing over war-wrecked German cities and landing eight hundred miles away at RAF Station Harrowbeer, near the port city of Plymouth in southwest England. Franklin Roosevelt as president had never visited Britain, despite Churchill's many invitations; nor would Truman when in office, except for this touchdown before a rendezvous at sea with George VI. Once driven to Plymouth, Truman and his party were taken by admiral's barge to the USS *Augusta*, waiting at anchor in the sound. The president's flag was broken at the mainmast, and at 12:35 Truman and two of his advisers were ferried by a U.S. Navy launch to HMS *Renown*, moored a quarter mile away. Seas were calm and weather sunny. The king met Truman atop the gangway of his battle cruiser, extended his hand, and said, "Welcome to my country." Truman inspected a guard of Royal Marines, had a private talk with the king, then took lunch in the wardroom.

The officers on deck who saluted the president saw a thin-lipped, square-looking man of five feet eight inches in a neat gray double-breasted suit, with a 35th Infantry Division insignia in the left lapel. He had a double-band gold Masonic ring on the little finger of his left hand, wore engraved rim glasses, and altogether appeared a small-city American businessman. They remembered he'd look one straight in the eye. At lunch, Truman disclosed to the king the astronomical cost of building the atomic bomb. He added that when used on Japan, as it certainly would be, perhaps man would realize war's futility. The Americans returned to their ship at 2:50, and ten minutes later sailors from the *Renown* transported the king, Tommy Lascelles, and other aides to repay the call. George VI asked Truman for an autograph "for my wife and daughters." That second visit concluded, the *Augusta* set sail an hour later for Newport News, Virginia, escorted by the light cruiser USS *Philadelphia*.

It was while they were at sea—making headway in the Gulf Stream, the crew having shifted to white uniforms for the warmer weather— that Truman got word, minutes before noon on August 6, that the *Enola*

Gay had detonated an atomic bomb over Hiroshima. He was in Washington by the time Nagasaki was destroyed on the ninth. What the press in London called "the new British-American atomic bomb" compelled Japan's surrender on August 14. From the White House, at 7:00 p.m. Eastern War Time, on a perfect summer evening, President Truman told the country that World War II at last was over.

THE NEXT MONTH IN LONDON, BEVIN WARNED THE HOUSE OF COMmons that the war had left Britain "extremely poor"—far poorer than most members of Parliament knew.[38] It was the only victorious nation to have fought both world wars from beginning to end, which meant Britain had been at war for ten of the thirty-one years from 1914 to 1945. The sacrifice was terrible.

During World War II, to judge from the figures that would soon be presented to Washington, Britain had lost a quarter of its liquid wealth, including its gold reserves, its foreign assets, and particularly its securities (acquired by the Americans at fire-sale prices). In return for its help early in the war, Washington had also extracted payment in the form of patent rights tied to innovative British technologies, including sonar, radar, and gyroscopes. Moreover, Britain had run up the equivalent of some $14 billion in debt (roughly £3.5 billion) from lenders within the sterling area, among them India, Egypt, Iraq, Ireland, and Australia, which to different degrees had been compelled to extend lines of credit during the war.*

Nonetheless, the fact that the Americans expected their former ally to pay fifty-fifty for western Germany's occupation shows some vagueness about what had been sacrificed. On its face, the British Empire and Commonwealth looked daunting. After all, the real productive capacity of Britain's economy—its capital stock—was largely intact at the end of the war. The empire had regained all the territory lost to the Axis, and at

---

*During the early havoc of the Great Depression—after the pound had left the gold standard in 1931—many countries in addition to those of the British Empire and Commonwealth (except for Canada and Newfoundland) pegged their currencies to the pound sterling, rather than to gold, or simply used British currency as their own. More than half the world's trade was conducted in sterling; Wall Street and the Chicago Mercantile Exchange usually called this arrangement the "sterling bloc."

the time a "map of the world" usually meant Mercator's famous splayed-out rendering, which influenced people's mental geography. A quarter of the map was colored in imperial red, including a swath just about "from Cairo to Cape Town," as Cecil Rhodes had envisioned. Britain dominated the Middle East, with Egypt still under its thumb. In Asia, where the Japanese had fought their way to the outskirts of Australia, British authority had returned, and in strength. In a world of 2.3 billion people, more than 600 million were subjects of the king. As for India, a colony that was still the jewel in the crown of empire, everyone recognized change would arrive. After all, India was already a founding member of the newly formed UN. But the how and when of independence remained unclear.

Foreign Secretary Bevin knew the empire's political and military strength was compromised, but he also knew the situation wasn't entirely novel. "What astounds me about the history of the British Navy is how cheaply we have policed the world for 300 years," he observed, and added, "It is a good job no one called our bluff very often."[39] Bevin, who'd prove superb at bluffing, might better have said that Britain's policing of the world, as opposed to its sea-lanes, was always a bluff, and usually called. But the point was clear. Imperial strength, for the moment, was spread very thin.

Clement Attlee, for his part, chose a different tack before the Commons that fall: he laid out the details of remarkable strength. Had the Japanese not surrendered, the empire had been set to hurl against them, even in the sixth year of an exhausting struggle, a force that included four British battleships, fourteen large and eighteen smaller steel-decked carriers, and over 1.75 million men from Britain and the same number from the empire and commonwealth. And that was just to begin with, as part of an American-led invasion. Now with the peace, Attlee was signifying, Britain could apply its resources with equal vigor to industrial enterprise and international trade while retaining its military sway.

This sort of hard power might be necessary as hopes for cooperating with Moscow faded. Russia had long been an empire in the east, ruling such lands as today's Uzbekistan and Kazakhstan. By the end of 1945, it was becoming one to its west as well—settling in to stay throughout half of Europe.[40]

. . .

TOTALITARIANISM MEANS THE BELIEF THAT NOTHING IN LIFE HAS countervailing rights against the state, and this pathology was exemplified by Stalin, the cobbler's son, former Orthodox seminarian, and mass murderer. Stalin had a brilliant grasp of intrigue and the uses of terror. The problem of Hungary, he had told Churchill, was simply one of having enough cattle cars. He meant that any difficulties posed by nationalism within the Soviet Union's empire were merely logistical ones to be solved by shipping entire races of people into the Gulag.

Leaving aside espionage and NKVD listening devices, part of the trouble with Yalta and Potsdam was Stalin's skills as a negotiator. He never wasted a word, nor raised his voice as he sat quietly at the wartime conference tables in his finely tailored field marshal's uniform. A tireless reader who was deeply knowledgeable, he'd say little until late in a discussion, then calmly offer an agreeable point or two. He was courteous, evasive, and more than ready to delay. When a request had to be refused, he always did so with regret, occasionally offering a slight smile. He had been disheartened not to be more helpful, but, alas, he was subject to pressure from hard-liners in the Politburo. He could charm so well that Churchill and Roosevelt had succumbed.

One way to think of Stalin is to recall a remark by Nikita Khrushchev, a favored killer during the 1930s purges who acted as the dictator's jovial clown before rising to the top of the Communist Party after Stalin's death. "We never knew when entering Stalin's presence," he reminisced about the Kremlin's courtiers, "if we would come out alive."[41] True, but from the early 1930s until his death in March 1953, Stalin also deliberately killed around six million people, most of them Soviet citizens deemed "enemies of the people."[42] Yet at war's end, Stalin stood stronger than ever. He had become a cult figure in the Soviet state: "Our Father," "the Divinely Anointed," and "the *Vozhd*" (roughly, Supreme Leader).

This is what the democracies now confronted, and Bevin scoffed at Molotov's excuses for Stalin's tightening grip on Eastern Europe. To show contempt, Bevin deliberately mispronounced his name as "Mowlotow." Before long, Bevin snorted that Molotov was talking "Hitler theory," adding, "You're putting your neck out and one day you'll have it chopped off." Bevin also spoke in the House of Commons about the NKVD massacres of 1941–1942, of which Molotov had known: 31,709

Polish officers, doctors, lawyers, and intellectuals had been shot, as in the Katyn Forest. Then, in January 1946, at a UN General Assembly meeting in London, Bevin provoked Deputy Foreign Minister Vyshinsky. As state prosecutor, Vyshinsky had been Stalin's chief judicial assassin during the 1930s show trials. When he accused Bevin of violating the peace by maintaining soldiers in Greece (contrary to an October 1944 agreement between Churchill and Stalin), Bevin responded by pounding the table and replying that Soviet predations in Eastern Europe were "Hitler all over again." These were inconceivable insults. Like Molotov, Vyshinsky went pale. Nothing is more offensive to a Russian than to compare his country's behavior to Hitler's. But Bevin did that rather often and while the graves of the motherland were fresh.

The Americans hesitated. A Gallup poll conducted in the fall showed that only 7 percent of U.S. voters saw foreign problems as their country's "most vital" concern, the lowest percentage since 1936.[43] And those who thought about foreign affairs didn't seem to show much spine, at least according to opinion in the Foreign Office. Life exceeded art, to recall Nat Gubbins's epigram about nervous hysteria across the Atlantic. A critic in the Foreign Office's American Department described "a certain girlishness in the part of the State Department."[44] In 1946, Washington even refused to sell army-surplus Garand rifles to Denmark, so as not to risk displeasing Stalin, and officials at State blocked the idea of U.S. and British veterans forming an "Old Comrades" association to keep up friendships. None of this was reassuring to Bevin, who, that February of 1946, told Lascelles in Buckingham Palace that he'd become convinced the Russians were out to dominate the world.

Of course, the Americans had an atomic monopoly to some unknown extent, but how that might influence the *Vozhd* and his victorious Red Army was anyone's guess. Today we know Stalin's realm had been damaged terribly by the bloodiest occupation in the history of the world, and of the yearlong famine that began in 1946, which caused well over a million more "excess deaths."[45] Those limits on Soviet strength were not apparent at the time. For Bevin and Churchill, and eventually the Americans, Stalin's tyrannical ambitions didn't look much different from those they'd just helped to crush in the Third Reich.

2

KEYNES & CO.

We saved ourselves, and we helped to save the world.

—John Maynard Keynes, 1945, on Britain's refusal to
surrender, and the price to follow

THE U.S. ECONOMY NEARLY DOUBLED DURING THE WAR, AND
America had pulled itself out of the Great Depression by an immense government demand for armaments. Yet war booms were known
to cause peace busts, as in the severe 1920–1921 recession that had followed World War I, a much less demanding ordeal for the United
States. People now feared the Depression's return, and for several years
after the peace Truman had to offer reassurances that farms, homes, and
businesses would not again be lost, nor would an unemployment rate of
25 percent return. His words were hard to accept because, three weeks
after Japan's surrender, the nation entered the worst period of labor
strikes in its history, making Truman's assurances feel hollow. They began
in New York as the city's business districts ground to a halt. Fifteen
thousand elevator operators, doormen, porters, and maintenance workers walked off the job.

In February 1946, Truman ordered the Coast Guard to seize and operate the city's striking tugboats. Two months later, almost every industry in America was enduring strikes: the steel mills, automobile factories, meatpacking plants. So too in coal mining, railroads, electrical equipment manufacturing. At least 10 percent of the U.S. workforce was on strike. The economy was getting stronger, but the costs of housing, food, and transportation were skyrocketing, while wages stagnated or fell. Truman's request to Congress for a $0.65 minimum wage (now around $5.20) went nowhere.

Americans weren't confident in their wealth and strength, as it's claimed today, and Exhibit A is their dread of a revived Depression. Nor were they "eating handsomely," as the myths say. Meat rationing ended in November 1945, but price controls continued into the fall of 1946. Truman asked Congress to keep intact the government's power to ration scarce foods, and there was a nationwide shortage even of hamburger, and little rice, food grains, or sugar.[1] Moreover, Depression-seared Americans feared government debt, which in 1946 stood at an alarming $271 billion, nearly a fivefold increase from 1941 that reached 121.70 percent of GDP. The rest of the world didn't have much faith in boom-and-bust American prosperity either.[2] That was seen in London, during December 1946, when U.S. delegates caucused with those of seventeen other nations to try to create an ambitious World Trade Organization to regulate global commerce. Yet the Americans couldn't convince anyone that their economy would remain stable. This early attempt at a WTO fizzled. The country seemed full of crazed speculators, with just deserts to follow.

The British, for their part, knew that they were in desperate financial straits, despite possessing a far-flung empire that at the time most regarded as a lucrative asset. The country's economic plight had become undeniable, and by the fall of 1945 Attlee's government couldn't avoid seeking a sizable grant or even a loan from America. Fears on Capitol Hill about debt and depression, however, made this an inauspicious time to try to wring money from Washington.[3]

During the war, arrangements like Lend-Lease, Mutual Aid from Canada, and credits largely from the sterling area had masked the extent of danger, as did the fire sale of prewar equity holdings to the

Americans. So had Churchill's driving intensity to destroy Nazism no matter the price. Through Lend-Lease, Britain had been receiving not just weapons from the United States but foodstuffs such as evaporated milk, flour, starch, dried beans, canned meat and fish, and concentrated orange juice. On August 21, Truman terminated it all. Lend-Lease was due to expire after victory in any event, but the cutoff to forty-four countries was handled precipitously, as Truman quickly recognized. Nonetheless, the war was over. Addressing Messrs. Attlee and Churchill, the *Chicago Daily Tribune* titled a sneering editorial "The Dining Room Is Closed."[4]

At this point, government ministers and Whitehall mandarins alike tried to convince themselves that Washington would still be generous.*

Each ally, the thinking went, had contributed its utmost for the common cause, with Britain even paying for 14,120,000 rounds of small arms ammunition and 282,000 grenades to supply U.S. forces. Besides, the United States was the sole country to have been enriched by the inferno, as seen in the nation's wartime growth rate. It had been the world's biggest economy since surpassing Britain's in the 1870s and had become far stronger still. In this light, Attlee and his cabinet weren't fantasizing about obtaining a sizable grant—except that Gallup polls showed it would even be difficult for Washington to offer a loan. Additionally, citizens who'd sent deer rifles and shotguns to Britain in the summer of 1940, via the American Committee for the Defense of British Homes, were petitioning Congress to get their firearms back.

A LITTLE AFTER 10:00 P.M. ON THURSDAY, AUGUST 23, 1945, JOHN Maynard Keynes, the principal economic adviser to His Majesty's Treasury, addressed an emergency meeting of Attlee's cabinet. Keynes, who'd been gazetted with a barony in 1942, was the world's most famous economist, a dubious status in today's pantheon of celebrity but then significant at a time of destruction and rebuilding. He was sixty-two and the

---

*"Whitehall" is a metonym for the center of Britain's government, where the highest levels of Parliament interact with the permanent, rigorously sieved civil service, drolly known as mandarins. In fact, it's the road that runs south from Trafalgar Square toward Parliament Square, flanked by the grand buildings of the principal departments.

protean intellectual wizard of the British liberal establishment—cool nerved and easy to notice at six feet seven inches, with white hair, a mustache, and a knack for charming a room. He had a gleam in his eyes that indicated humor. His thoughts sparkled on interests as varied as the National Gallery, ballet, Cézanne and Picasso, and his antiquarian collection of manuscripts, which included Newton's originals. He had long before entered journalistic folklore through his essays in *The Times*, such as those condemning World War I's vengeful peace, and his *General Theory of Employment, Interest, and Money* (1936) had created the terms and shapes of modern macroeconomics, to become one of the century's most influential books.

Keynes knew that Britain's efforts to save civilization had not "rendered it bankrupt," as is commonly said today.[5] "Bankruptcy" is a hard word. It doesn't lend itself to shorthand, and it didn't occur for Britain. Instead, Keynes spoke to Attlee's cabinet of the nation facing a "financial Dunkirk" and of going "virtually bankrupt." He was a master of English prose who chose metaphors carefully, and this one has been misunderstood ever since.[6] As at Dunkirk, Britain risked being exposed once more as an isolated and crippled power. But "Dunkirk" also stands for a daring recovery and quick rebounding: after a harrowing evacuation, the Royal Navy and the RAF remained intact, and the army was reequipped. Had Keynes been talking of a terminal disaster, he could have used a more conclusive metaphor, like the fall of Singapore, the cornerstone of imperial power in the Far East—until its shockingly sudden conquest by Japan in February 1942.

Keynes was warning the cabinet of calamity, but he also saw a buoyant future for his country. One way or another, astounding opportunities lay ahead. That's what he had told U.S. officials visiting London during the spring and what he would soon explain to junior officials at the embassy in Washington. If governments deftly handled the economic levers (which meant listening to him), all of Europe would boom, and Britain could equal the high U.S. standard of living.[7] Even the worst outcome, he argued, would compel "our withdrawal, for the time being, from the position of a first-class Power."[8] Note "for the time being." As he saw the situation, Britain could rally, even if that meant a halt he described as "temporary" to its imperial activities. Dunkirk, after all, was a disaster at the war's beginning, with victory to follow.

To help avert disaster, no matter what it was called, Keynes was tasked with negotiating for America's backing. Top investors make money by looking for the questions not being asked. Keynes excelled at that skill, and he had earned a fortune deploying it in the City, as London's financial district is known. It had served him well when facing the Americans during 1941 over Lend-Lease in Washington and when working with them three years later at Bretton Woods, the monetary and financial conference in New Hampshire attended by forty-four nations. But now he was to negotiate in a bitter climate of peace. He also was suffering heart trouble. A man of less self-belief would have been defeated by the magnitude of the undertaking.

Keynes was dispatched to Washington to represent the Chancellor of the Exchequer, or Treasury secretary, who agreed that Britain needed at least $5 billion in American support. He had an infectious optimism, as did Churchill and Bevin, each of whom he admired. Optimism had been an essential quality during the war years, and maybe optimism would help the British in Washington. But optimism is not just a survival mechanism. It can border on delusion.

As for America, he wasn't upbeat: he concluded that it "has *no* future in the long run."[9] The rootlessness of its people and their lack of historical awareness blocked possibilities of world leadership, which wasn't to say that Americans couldn't be supportive to Britain and its empire.

Keynes was accompanied by his devoted wife, Lydia Lopokova, a former Russian prima ballerina, and by a specialist each from the Treasury and the Board of Trade, a key administrative agency for handling commerce. The Foreign Office's senior economic adviser, Edmund Hall-Patch, came too. Unlike Keynes, Hall-Patch was a mordant pessimist who lamented the Americans' lack of "necessary experience and political maturity," and their "peasant mentality" to boot.[10] The intrepid little party took a Canadian troopship bound for Quebec City on August 27. Meetings were held in Ottawa, where the Canadians pledged to help. Then they entrained to Washington, to arrive on September 7. Keynes took a top-floor suite at the Statler (today's Capital Hilton on Sixteenth

Street), which was only a quarter mile from his offices at another hotel, the Willard, on Pennsylvania Avenue, where the wartime British Purchasing Commission still leased the ninth floor.

Keynes had little ground to maneuver in his negotiations, but he was hopeful at the start and spoke freely at the British embassy about winning a $6 billion to $8 billion grant.[11] It wasn't his own people he had to convince, however. Across the table were Fred Vinson, the secretary of the Treasury and a former Kentucky congressman; Marriner Eccles, the Federal Reserve chairman, an unsmiling Mormon who treated Britain as a company gone bust; and William Lockhart Clayton, the assistant secretary of state for economics, a new role at the department.

All debts couldn't be measured in dollars, Keynes tried to explain. Leave aside that Britain had paid for bullets, grenades, airfields, and more: its casualties in the war were greater. In fact, fatalities, not counting those of the empire, were about 400 percent heavier per capita than America's.

These arguments went nowhere. Clayton merely nodded, as did the others. A sharecropper's son from Tupelo, Mississippi, he had left school at thirteen to work as a stenographer for a cotton merchant and had become the world's biggest cotton dealer, a calling that didn't go unnoticed by his British counterparts. King Cotton was a huge American export at the time: 3.4 million bales (500 pounds gross) would be shipped out in 1946. The Houston-based enterprise he built with his brother-in-law—Anderson, Clayton & Company—was a giant brokerage operating in Europe, Egypt, India, China. And free trade was second nature to anyone associated with cotton.

At sixty-five, Clayton was a larger-than-life American internationalist businessman—of the sort who, in the postwar world, would stride the globe on behalf of eminent corporations such as IBM, Pan Am, and Esso. He had a soft southern voice, careful tailoring, and a handsome, rather rugged face and stood six feet three. He pressed the British on pledges they'd made when obtaining Lend-Lease and at Bretton Woods: first, to end their system of "imperial preference," which placed a high tariff wall around the British Empire and Commonwealth, and had preferential trading terms within; second, to make sterling freely convertible, which means the freedom to exchange a national currency for another. All was supposed to strengthen the newly vibrant liberal world economy, which was expected to follow. The term "global interdependence" hadn't arrived, but Clayton, like many Americans, believed such a fortunate condition would bring prosperity and peace. Free trade would bind the democracies. Not least, it would open the world to American exports, thereby boosting U.S. employment. For the Americans, this was a key negotiating objective, given their fears of a renewed Depression.

Keynes and his beleaguered mission team received their negotiating directives from the Treasury in London via the British embassy. The embassy is a Lutyens-designed neoclassical English country house three miles from the Statler Hotel up Massachusetts Avenue, on a hill adjacent to the Naval Observatory. The setting is impressive: grand corridors with regal portraits, an imposing double-square staircase to the ballroom, black-polished floors. But behind the scenes, at the time, was a warren of offices, one of which contained a large clanking cipher machine that spewed out top secret information on a paper roll with which recipients had to wrestle. Correspondence could be slow because the entire embassy, as well as various British delegations in Washington, all used the contraption for their most urgent and sensitive communications.

As the weeks went by, Keynes and his staff, at the end of twelve-hour workdays, would have to explain to London, via cipher, that negotiations weren't going well. Backlogs on the machine could mean that follow-up instructions wouldn't arrive for days or, at best, that they'd be waiting the following morning due to the five-hour time difference. In either case, Keynes's advice didn't seem to be heard. Repeatedly, London insisted that he had to continue to work on obtaining the grant or at least get a zero-interest loan, a similarly far-fetched idea. He offered one explanation to embassy officials for Whitehall's denseness: after the Chancellor of the Exchequer and his aides went home at night, he explained, the cleaning women were using the Treasury's machine to deliver nonsense.[12]

THE CITY OF WASHINGTON WAS EXPERIENCING ITS USUAL MID-October Indian summer, with foliage turning red and yellow and temperatures in the low seventies. Keynes's negotiations with the

Americans dragged on. By November, arguments had grown strained in overheated rooms. The Americans' terms got harsher as their experts applied a model of capital absorption rates in Latin America to help determine the proper size of an interest-bearing loan. Keynes's higher-ups in London failed to offer a plausible alternative. His heart pains returned. "We are playing for very big stakes," he warned London.[13]

Keynes had been impressed during the war by how the Americans had always managed to find "a fix" for enormous political-economic problems. President Roosevelt's use of the Lend-Lease concept to circumvent the isolationist Charles Lindbergh's America First Committee was an example. But he recognized that now, with the war over and FDR dead, no "fixes" were likely.

Washington had two objectives: to help the British with a loan that would enable self-reliance, and to prevent them, as the loan reenergized their economy, from using their regained strength to discriminate against U.S. exports. In brief, there'd be a onetime bridge (as financiers call it) toward a world economy of free trade and freely exchanged currencies. Britain was hardly bankrupt, and because the time to recover looked brief, the loan was to be a straightforward transaction on businesslike terms: a $3.75 billion line of credit, plus a write-off of most Lend-Lease obligations. The money, equal to only fifteen days of what Washington had been spending earlier in the year to fight Germany and Japan, would be interest-free for six years and then charged at 2 percent, to be repaid by the end of 2006. When they heard about the agreement, most Americans regarded these terms as characteristically generous, or foolish.[14]

Clayton and Britain's ambassador, Lord Halifax, signed the loan documents on December 6 at the State Department, housed in a flamboyant Second Empire–style building next to the White House. U.S. officials thought they had crafted a long-term financial strategy. British negotiators hoped so too, believing the borrowed dollars could last five years until their country's industrial machine was humming. Otherwise, the British regarded the terms as harsh. Interest was required, and they'd be held to their pledges on imperial preference and on making sterling convertible into gold and hard currency—in effect, the U.S. dollar. Besides, convertibility had to occur within a year of the president's signing the legislation, after it had been approved by Congress. This disturbed Keynes, who believed that such timing, in contrast to a five-year delay, was a "lunatic proposition."[15]

The core problem of sterling's convertibility was hard to imagine given that "sterling" had originally meant currency marked by a star, the most reliable of all. In theory, a nation that held cash or debts in sterling—if sterling became convertible—would immediately be able to exchange them for dollars if it were ever to lose faith in Britain's currency. Should that occur, there'd be a giant sucking sound as Britain's remaining believable assets—dollar reserves, securities, and gold—were drained out of the isles. Yet that nightmare scenario remained academic. As a result, the Americans blithely insisted that a free exchange of currencies would serve to pay for a free exchange of goods, and this was expected to happen soon, while Britain achieved a strong balance of payments.

The loan had been signed, and both parties chose to focus on the good it might do. So it was a pleasant goodbye when Keynes and Lydia called on President Truman before returning to New York, where they saw friends and then, on December 11, boarded the *Queen Elizabeth*, the world's largest ship, to sail home. The Anglo-American Financial Agreement now had to face Congress.

British officials of Keynes's generation were wary about dealmaking with Washington. They remembered how the Senate had repudiated President Woodrow Wilson's League of Nations treaty twenty-five years earlier. Who could tell what Congress might reject this time? "What our representatives say binds the British Government," Keynes reflected. "What the State Department or the Treasury or the Departments of Commerce or Agriculture may intimate in the course of our conversations with them can and does bind no one."[16]

Much was being lost in translation. Keynes had become fed up, as he told his staff, with having to educate the new political appointees in Washington who kept flowing through the U.S. government's executive ranks and then "disappeared." Like other sharp men in Whitehall, he didn't realize that assistant secretaries at State or the Pentagon, in contrast to his country's powerful, enduring, upper-level civil servants, could be independently successful businessmen, bankers, or lawyers—political players of mixed quality who'd received their positions from the White

House. That was also true of the president's high-ranking aides. When such men returned to their firms in Atlanta, New York, or San Francisco, they did not "disappear" from public affairs; they remained significant for their wealth and influence.

Another difficulty, observed a senior aide to Keynes, was that the Americans "must always be able to show that they haven't been outsmarted."[17] One senior diplomat at State believed he saw his colleagues suffering from "a strange conglomeration of neuroses and misconceptions" as they worked with the British, and he concluded an "inferiority complex" had taken hold, to use the Freudian jargon then becoming popular. A director at the Board of Trade noted a similar dynamic: "I used to be astounded at the number of times American businessmen in particular used to use the phrase 'Well, you British, you always outsmart us.' It never occurred to me that we could outsmart anybody, let alone that we could outsmart the Americans."[18] Yet many Americans suffered from this so-called complex, which was part of the problem in Congress. That was in addition to legislators wondering if they'd be abetting socialism or subsidizing imperialism, or both, by approving the loan.

DURING THE EARLY WINTER OF 1945-1946, CHURCHILL WAS TROUbled by coughs and colds. He was living mostly at Chartwell, his country house, an hour's drive southeast of London, in Kent, and he led the opposition. He kept busy writing and painting while occasionally attending the House of Commons, where his second-in-command, Anthony Eden, was doing the Conservative Party's heavy lifting. Churchill also served as chairman of the Empire Industries Association, a trade group that, as can be guessed, had strong attachments to imperial preference. Men of both parties in the Commons quietly said that Churchill, at age seventy-one, was getting old. When he stuck his tongue out at Bevin, known to be his favorite Labour minister, during a debate over pulling troops from Egypt, they shook their heads.

On January 16, accompanied by his wife and one of his three daughters, Churchill arrived in Miami Beach via the Silver Meteor from New York. He had plans to enjoy a six-week vacation at the home of his friend Colonel Frank Clarke, a Canadian shipping and timber tycoon, and he'd combine this respite with a visit to Washington, followed by a speech at Westminster College in Fulton, Missouri.

Truman, meanwhile, had to contend with the U.S. economy and was also taking steps to address a world food crisis that he said might be the worst in modern times. On February 6, he told Americans that they'd no longer be able to eat white bread. The nation wasn't a cornucopia, he explained in a nationwide broadcast. Its farmers were producing sixty-one million fewer bushels of wheat than expected, and there was also a starving world to feed. As a result, his emergency measures were intended to end the wasteful removal of the bran and the germ. Delicacies such as Wonder Bread were to be replaced, temporarily, with a wheaty, more protein-rich gray-colored substance. He offered Britain as an example worth following because, just the day before, Attlee's government had announced a return to the dark wartime loaf. Truman also warned that production of beer and whiskey was being cut, and, he added, there'd be fewer choices of meat and dairy products.

Churchill never adhered to his own country's ration laws, let alone paid attention to anyone else's. He busied himself in Miami with painting, getting a health checkup, taking a week's excursion to Havana, accepting an honorary degree from the University of Miami, and working on his speech for Westminster College.

Why there? It was the alma mater of Harry Vaughan, class of 1916, who had been a friend of Truman's since the two army lieutenants had met the following year at Fort Sill, Oklahoma. Vaughan served as Truman's military aide and had brokered the invitation. The British knew him: he'd been at Potsdam, and agents had observed him selling two of his suits on the black market. A month later, when Downing Street staffers had asked the White House to exchange a photograph of Prime Minister Attlee for one of the president, Vaughan obliged, but told them that Americans considered Churchill, not Attlee, "the first citizen of the British Empire."[19] In brief, Vaughan had a reputation that ranged from White House court jester to national menace. He exemplified the random talents thrown into high office by political patronage.

On the afternoon of March 4, a day after Churchill arrived in Washington from Miami, Vaughan accompanied him and President Truman as they boarded FDR's armored train car at Union Station, heading to Missouri. On the fifth, he sat right behind Churchill and Truman on the podium.

The speech Churchill delivered at Westminster College is known for the words "Iron Curtain," though he wasn't the first to use that loaded term. It was already percolating on Capitol Hill, and the expression has been traced to Hitler's Reich minister for propaganda, who popularized it as a geopolitical metaphor based on the device lowered at theaters in case of fire. Stalin had heard Churchill use a similar utterance, "iron fence," about Russia at Potsdam. Now Churchill repeated this variation under White House auspices, observing Europe to be divided from Stettin to Trieste. He spoke in his poetic style, one he claimed to have adopted from American oratory, with breath pauses indicated by lines in the text.

But Churchill did more in this speech than talk about an Iron Curtain. He spoke of an actual alliance with America and got into the details of what he called his "overall strategic concept." That entailed joint military planning, as in wartime, and it also included a proposal for jointly producing tanks, planes, and other weapons, something that had never occurred during the war. He pressed for bases to be shared worldwide; the use of British ones by the U.S. military, he recognized, could potentially double the reach of America's warships and bombers. Though historians have overlooked its recurring use, Churchill also spoke a line, word for word, that he'd repeat three years later at MIT, and then again in 1952 before Congress, and use in correspondence too. "Do not suppose," he said, "that half a century from now you will not see seventy or eighty millions of Britons spread about the world and united in defense of our traditions, our way of life."[20] The number came from adding fifty million of his fellow subjects in Britain with about thirty million others in the colonies and commonwealth who were white.*

Lots of Americans were shaken by his speech. Churchill had urged them to embrace a "fraternal association of the English-speaking peoples,"

---

*The word "commonwealth" generally meant "republic," and after World War I Britain's dominions headed toward independence: Australia, New Zealand, Canada, and South Africa, with an ambivalent role for the Irish Free State. In 1919, the empire began to call itself "the British Empire and Commonwealth of Nations," and a dozen years later the dominions achieved full self-government.

but this sounded like a way to get the United States to underwrite British positions in Asia, the Middle East, and who knew where else. He seemed to be talking in modern terms about England's age-old hankering for empire and power blocs. Hadn't the war been fought for a higher purpose?

The next day, in Washington, Walter Lippmann, the cerebral journalist-as-part-time-statesman, ran into Churchill's son, the thirty-four-year-old Randolph, who was drinking no more heavily than usual at lunch. Randolph had his own column in New York's *World-Telegram* and was a contributor to London's *Daily Telegraph*. He shared his thoughts with Lippmann directly. "We'll show you," Randolph said. "You don't understand the British Empire. Just let me tell you this. We dragged you into two wars and we'll drag you into the third." Lippmann didn't report the remarks, but they upset him. He believed they reflected "something of the old man."[21]

Thousands of furious letters began arriving, many addressed just to "Truman, Washington, D.C." A vitriolic cross section of them can be found in boxes at Truman's presidential library in Independence, Missouri. The gist of the letters was that America had to keep its distance from the British Empire. In London, *The Times* reacted angrily, too. "Nothing would be more dangerous," it warned two days after Churchill's speech, "than to attempt to base British foreign policy on the prerequisite of firm support from America."[22] At the Foreign Office, Bevin was contemptuous: "'E thinks 'e's Prime Minister of the world."[23]

There remained the delicate matter of how to explain Churchill's ideas to Stalin. The British ambassador in Moscow hastened to arrange an appointment. Churchill was merely speaking as a private individual, he said, to which the *Vozhd* replied, "There are no such private individuals in this country."[24]

KEYNES HAD BEEN EXHAUSTED WHEN HE RETURNED TO ENGLAND, IN December 1945. With his keen eye for the inefficient or counterproductive, he dismissed as "Foreign Office frivolities" the largesse with which his country felt compelled to "slop money out to the importunate."[25] That included helping to feed Germany, extending credits to Greece, sending (belated) famine relief to India, and contributing millions of pounds to UN reconstruction efforts in Europe. It all involved a lavishness that the Oxford economist Roy Harrod, the great man's biographer and disciple, described as reflecting "something of the pre-1939 or even pre-1914 mentality."[26] The enormous spending also included paying for a scale of military power that strained the budget.

Britain's population had been living for six years on a fruitless, starchy, monotonous diet. According to polls, half the population said they felt underfed. Physicians were treating a scourge of boils, sores, and rashes. When it came to matters of world presence, however, Britain was ready to assert its grandeur, and not just by "slopping out money" but also by staging spectacles such as the Olympics in 1948 and the coronation in 1953, both of which became riveting affirmations of strength.

The initial spectacle came soon after the first General Assembly meeting of the United Nations, which then comprised fifty-one members. The UN had convened in January 1946, at Westminster's Central Hall, in London, and in celebration on February 3 King George VI gave the first state banquet since 1939. It was held not at Buckingham Palace, which during the war had taken nine direct hits and was in need of a hot water system, but at St. James's Palace, another royal residence in London. Evening court dress wasn't required, announced the royal household, as had been mandatory before the war. White tie was acceptable. Servants wore livery, as always. There were blue-coated senior servants and red-coated junior ones. Yet life was changing belowstairs too. The royal footmen, butlers, valets, and cooks were about to organize. They'd bargain for a forty-eight-hour week and join the Civil Service Union.

The reopening of the Royal Opera House on Wednesday, February 20, also signaled a new chapter in the country's life. Confidence was palpable at the gala ballet, an extravagant new production of *The Sleeping Beauty*. Covent Garden's scarlet-and-gold opulence was polished, though no gilt was applied. As chairman of the Covent Garden trustees, Keynes had been expected to welcome George VI, Queen Mary, and the two princesses, Elizabeth and Margaret. But he couldn't. He stayed quietly in his box, suffering heart palpitations.

The event was a political statement, too, and Prime Minister Attlee, not previously known to love the ballet, attended. Churchill would have been there as well, had he not been in America, his Fulton speech just two weeks away. Bevin arrived that cold, showery night in the obligatory dinner jacket whereupon a bejeweled dowager leaped out to touch him. He had the hostesses of London at his feet; his legend of force and resolve was already taking hold. Appearing as well was Aneurin Bevan, forty-eight, the blue-eyed radical firebrand from the Welsh coal pits who was minister of health. He wore a sack suit, and he was joined by his wife, Jennie Lee—a girl from Scottish mining country, it was said—who was also a member of Parliament. She wore a red tweed coat. Yes, everyone got it. Red was the color of Britain's Labour Party, as it was of Communist revolution.

Four days later, Keynes, still weary, sailed again with Lydia to New York, accompanied by one official from the Treasury and another from the Bank of England. It was his sixth exhausting mission to America since 1941. This time he was heading to Wilmington Island, an enclave of Savannah, Georgia, to attend the first meeting of the boards of governors of the World Bank and of the International Monetary Fund, institutions he had helped establish at 1944's Bretton Woods Conference. Keynes hoped to protect the IMF from Washington's control. Azaleas bloomed and Fred Vinson, the Treasury secretary, spontaneously sang "My Old Kentucky Home" at an opening reception in the General Oglethorpe Hotel. Keynes made his case to Assistant Secretary of State Will Clayton, but Clayton had the votes of cringing Latin American delegates in his pocket, which made Keynes's efforts fruitless. After the meeting, *Time* magazine wrote, with no apparent regret, that the British "were shoved around by the U.S. at the Savannah conference until they could barely see straight."[27] Keynes left for home on March 21 to what's remembered as a glorious English spring.

AS KEYNES SAILED TO ENGLAND, THE LOAN THAT HE HAD NEGOTI-ated months earlier was moving through the Senate. At the same time, Congress was trying to reduce the national debt, hoping to put an end to New Deal habits of deficit financing. And why should America shovel more aid to Britain? legislators asked. Wasn't the money being wasted or spent unfairly? The Wine and Spirits Wholesalers association certainly thought so, alleging that Scotland's distilleries had been using grain shipments sent as emergency assistance to instead make whiskey to sell into the American market. What many people assumed, then as today, was that no one played fair with Uncle Sam. He always got suckered when looking out for others, and on matters of world trade he was never allowed a level playing field. Not least, senators dreaded that other overseas "customers," as potential borrowers were called, would want American rescue money, too.

Many newspapers also condemned the loan. The *Chicago Daily Tribune*—the country's largest-selling paper, except for a sister tabloid, the *New York News*—notoriously opposed granting aid to Britain. Its hostility toward the "Brutish Empire" was unsurpassed. In the months before the war ended, William Clark, an enterprising public affairs officer from the British consulate in Chicago, had asked himself why and in a letter to the paper's owner suggested that the *Tribune* might be pandering to its many Irish readers. To Clark's surprise, the sixty-six-year-old Robert Rutherford McCormick agreed to a meeting. No, it wasn't the Irish, said the Colonel, as McCormick was known. Instead, he recalled how he had been treated as an inferior when traveling in England as a young businessman some forty years earlier. The wounds stung yet.

This environment was heaven for a lawmaker such as Mississippi's Theodore "The Man" Bilbo, whom the Washington press corps dubbed the worst of all senators. Bilbo was a five-foot-two-inch Ku Klux Klansman and former Democratic governor from the piney woods of Pearl River County. He disclosed his knighthood in the KKK on *Meet the Press*. He was also about to publish a book, *Take Your Choice: Separation or Mongrelization*, which—by urging actual separation of the races—found mere segregation too mild for addressing the "Negro Problem."[28] Standing in the well of the Senate, he mocked the "European debt-cancellers" from World War I, who were now coming back for more.[29] Denouncing the loan was all in a day's work. Actually two days' work: in doing so, he dominated the Senate floor for the better part of forty-eight hours.

More enlightened Americans had their own concerns. In the last year of combat, for instance, Secretary of War Henry Stimson had spoken his worries aloud. "The British really are showing decadence," Stimson remarked, "a magnificent people, but they have lost their initiative."[30]

Georgia's diligent Richard Russell, for whom one of the Senate's three office buildings is named, had anxieties as well. He asked the State Department why he should support the loan. Wasn't Britain a decadent country that had involved America in two world wars? Undersecretary of State Dean Acheson had to field that one. The charge of decadence was fairly offensive, Acheson told his aides, but "of course to some extent it's true."[31]

Despite all this, support for the agreement could be found in odd places. The *Times-Herald*, Washington's biggest paper, with ten daily editions, essentially came out in favor. Its owner was McCormick's cousin Eleanor "Cissy" Patterson, the country's most powerful woman, even more so than the other Eleanor. Her views and those of the *Times-Herald* were indistinguishable. She and McCormick had both hated FDR, but on England she and her paper could be admiring. America was "an unofficial member of the British Empire," it declared in 1945, and she had endorsed Churchill in the July elections.[32]

Such public support for the Financial Agreement, and the backing of men like Clayton, allowed Keynes to conclude that Congress would nonetheless approve the money, despite all. Likelihood of a favorable decision was also helped by rising tensions with Russia. There was talk on Capitol Hill, as there'd been in 1940, of Britain's being an "outpost"—a vital bulwark against totalitarian ambitions. But Keynes didn't live to discover the agreement's fate. He returned from Savannah tired and ill, and his heart finally gave out on Easter morning, April 21, at his house in Sussex.

The loan still faced strong opposition through the spring. Speaker Sam Rayburn had to arm-twist fellow Democrats in the House. Rallying support for Britain wasn't easier in the Senate. "She's all crippled up, got one eye half gouged out and one ear bit off," said Tom Connally, the deceptively folksy Texas Democrat who chaired the Foreign Relations Committee in 1946.[33] But by May the tide had turned, and on July 15 Truman signed the Anglo-American Financial Agreement. Britain also received $1.19 billion from loyal Canada, which additionally canceled a half-billion-dollar debt from having trained RAF pilots during the war.

Will Clayton and his State Department staff expected most of the billions in debt within the sterling area to be written off too. But none of

Britain's other creditors except Australia and New Zealand would forgo a shilling, and the Financial Agreement had a clause that prohibited any of its dollars from being used to repay those debts, which meant that huge sums were still owed to India, Egypt, and additional nations in Britain's orbit. Nevertheless, an explicit purpose of the loan was to end all further requests to Washington for aid. Now the clock started ticking. Sterling was to become convertible within twelve months.

IT'S HELPFUL TO STEP BACK TO SEE THE VERY DIFFERENT WORLD FInancial system of that era. As generals are said to plan for the last war, economists plan for the last peace. Finance ministers, bankers, and politicians were determined not to relive the cascade of restricted markets and currency manipulations that had followed World War I. With Bretton Woods, currencies of industrialized nations had become connected to the dollar like spokes to the hub of a wheel. The dollar would be convertible into gold, and other currencies would be convertible into the dollar. It therefore became the centerpiece of international exchange, with sterling as second place in world banking.

Unlike today, exchange rates between currencies did not "float" in response to supply and demand. Currency par values—set in terms of their relation to the dollar as then valued at $35 of gold per ounce— could be determined arbitrarily by government officials. Ironically, that added to financial uncertainty. If people lost faith in a currency, and its actual value fell, the official price could nonetheless still be upheld by government fiat, as Britain's Treasury was doing with the pound. But such measures could not disguise the immense challenges that faced the pound. That's because it was the world's sole reserve currency, besides the dollar, and was used for at least half the world's trade—for which Britain served as the banker.

Membership in the sterling area wouldn't be defined precisely until the following year, but it embraced a vast part of the world. This included all members of the empire and commonwealth except Canada and Newfoundland (not yet confederated). It also covered all British territories, Iceland, Iraq (to which Britain owed £70,300,000), the Irish Republic, Kuwait and the Persian Gulf sheikhdoms, and Libya, plus, for the moment, Egypt, Palestine, Sudan, and Transjordan (as that kingdom would be known until 1949). They all pegged their currencies to the pound sterling, invoiced much of their trade in sterling, and deposited most of their monetary reserves in London. Britain's sterling balances had soared during the war. When Britain had bought goods and services from India, for example, payment in terms of sterling (albeit in paper IOUs) was credited to the account of the Reserve Bank of India in London. In brief, whatever affected the pound had worldwide repercussions.

The Financial Agreement was safely signed in the summer of 1946, but trade disputes only began to intensify. Big and small U.S. enterprises alike were set to compete ruthlessly with Britain and its empire. For example, the New York Cocoa Exchange weighed in first, professing its shock that the agreement hadn't pried apart the barriers of imperial preference—on which the British, despite repeated promises, were hardly budging. They had long been able to set the global price of cocoa, because 60 percent of the world's supply came from their West African colonies and because sweet-toothed Americans devoured 40 percent of the product. The exchange insisted that the price was artificially high. Angry letters to Congress flew from its dingy offices on Manhattan's Beaver Street: Hershey bars and Mars's 3 Musketeers might get too expensive to make.

Lobbying the Hill as well were purveyors of costume jewelry and artificial silk. In this case, Britain was expected to import more of the stuff. Otherwise consumers in Dorking or Leeds might forget U.S. brand names like Coro Craft and Maidenform on which millions in advertising had been spent before the war. The July issue of *Fortune* magazine—part of Henry Luce's Time Inc. publishing empire—also caused alarm with a story in which Britain's Morris Motors laid out its plans to compete against the U.S. auto giants right in America. It sounded credible. Britain was the world's largest motor vehicle exporter, and Morris was its biggest manufacturer, with cheaper production costs due to lower wages. Members of the Detroit Club took notice.

At this point, Bevin began to question whether Britain should take the loan after all, given the hooks and strings of having to accept convertibility and to drop imperial preference. Determined men on both the left and the right in Parliament already opposed the Financial

Agreement for undercutting their country's legitimate economic interests. They saw U.S. salesmen poised like greyhounds in the slip, and had no intention of jeopardizing the empire by returning to dated theories. One, for instance, was Lord Beaverbrook, the press baron and right-wing crony of Churchill's, previously known as Max Aitken. He'd started out as a Canadian cement monopolist in New Brunswick and understood firsthand what it was like to live under U.S. financial pre-eminence. It would be *appeeeeasing* the Americans to accept the money, Beaverbrook would say, through his gargoyle smile. But the alternative of not doing so was far-fetched.

Keynes had called any choice to forgo these dollars "Starvation Corner." An entire population of forty-nine million would have had to endure the most austere of war economies yet do so during peace, and with no end in sight. There'd not only be less food but little cotton for milling. Conceivably, Britain could have relied all the more on trade within the empire, fenced off with high tariffs. That's what Beaverbrook and the Empire Industries Association argued. Churchill, in turn, ended up advising his party just to abstain from voting on the loan, and he did so himself.

Bevin finally pushed the cabinet to accept the dollars. Having to underwrite the Labour Party's new welfare programs was one pressing reason. Another was knowing it would be reckless to break with the Americans on what they as a people cared about most: the success of their manufacturing, agriculture, and trade. To cross them on that would wreck his emerging political-military design. He was beginning to make real the "overall strategic concept" of alliances and interlocking weaponry about which Churchill had theorized at Fulton. Like Churchill, however, he recognized Britain couldn't go it alone, in a world once more endangered, and he was buying time to maneuver.

BRITAIN HAD PLENTY OF ASSETS THAT BEFITTED A GLOBAL POWER, as *The Times* liked to emphasize. The paper was habitually on the side of government, though that didn't always mean being for the establishment, and any important editorial was read worldwide. In the case of Britain's financial condition, *The Times* echoed the widely shared views of its Whitehall sources. The editors extolled London's unrivaled experience—"The priceless secrets of the 'know-how' as our American friends picturesquely call it"—and acclaimed its deep knowledge of men and affairs, as well as a long-refined mastery of the art of governance. "In the balance, these items total up to very many billions," said *The Times*.[34]

Other assets included the colonies, although the ruling Labour Party contained strong anticolonial feelings. Attlee, for instance, said he didn't want the British Empire to include any unwilling people. Maybe so, but many sensible observers believed the colonies were vital to Britain's renewal. For instance, Orwell—showing the perspective of a former colonial policeman—assumed Britain would shrivel without having control of India.

Until that point, most of the empire's riches had been concentrated amid expanses of otherwise useless land. The jewels were Malaya with its tin and rubber, not Sarawak or eastern New Guinea; Central Africa's copper belt, not Southern Rhodesia or the Sudan; cocoa from the Gold Coast, not Sierra Leone or Guiana. Now a huge emphasis was to be put on boosting indigenous economies—by building new railroads in Africa, for example, where new agricultural ventures would also be pulling in specialist advisers and a new generation of expatriates. The markets of dominions and colonies were becoming more important for British exports than before the war, and food and raw materials could be bought in the colonies without having to spend precious dollars. From June 1945 to September 1948, forty-one hundred new recruits to colonial service would be sent overseas, with more to follow.[35] The colonies could aid prosperity, most everyone believed, and all the more so because trade and investments were denominated in sterling.

Bevin played up these advantages while also addressing U.S. anxieties. He arranged a study of raw materials that America had lacked early in the war, and declared that it required "the full collaboration of the Colonial Governments." He then told Washington that should there be a World War III, the empire was ready to provide the copper, aluminum, nickel, tin, and other commodities that America would need to survive. It was an era when clever people on U.S. presidential committees concluded that "non-strategic materials" no longer existed.[36] Everything was vital in modern warfare, joked Bernard Baruch, except perhaps bubble gum. No one added that here too the empire had it covered. Chicago's Wrigley company tapped the sapodilla trees of British Honduras for Doublemint, Spearmint, and Juicy Fruit.

Additionally, wasn't British manufacturing far stronger than many suspected? Foreign critics might decry its enterprises as a chaotic collection of inefficient firms, with obsolescent tooling and stilted management. But *The Times* had a rejoinder here too. In late 1945, the editors compiled a book, *British War Production: 1939–1945: A Record*, advertised it for 6 shillings, 7 pence post-free, and urged readers to send it to friends overseas. If the world knew the facts of what Britain's industry had accomplished in defeating Hitler, they argued, "it would make a line of credit worth billions in the long run."[37] The editors weren't whistling in the dark. Under incredibly difficult conditions, Britain's factories had just rapidly produced some of the best weapons used in the war, and at costs that compared favorably with America's. That included not only Bren light machine guns and gyro gun sights but also high-speed De Havilland bombers and the Allies' first jet aircraft, the Gloster Meteor.

Britain was no "facade" of a superpower, as it's said today, nor were its political and military capacities, or the bounty of its empire, mere "trappings" amid "illusions of Great Power status."[38] As Baruch had predicted to Churchill, Britain's exports were about to boom beyond what anyone dared to forecast. All the same, its scarcity of hard currency—essential to buying necessities from countries that accepted only U.S. or Canadian dollars, Swiss francs, or other hard money—meant that food rations were falling below what had been endured in the war. Monthly allotments of cooking fat were cut, along with those of powdered eggs, which came from America and had to be bought with dollars. "Shell eggs," as they'd become known, were to be allocated two and a half per person per month. Nothing like this had been imagined even in 1944.

Stalin would not have been surprised by these contradictions of strengths and weaknesses in capitalism's second-largest economy. Marxist-Leninist teachings informed every aspect of his life, and he was being guided by the tenet that the old order would founder during its slumps and wars. France and Italy's big Communist parties, which had earned legitimacy by having spearheaded resistance to fascism, were set to contest elections. The economies of Europe's democracies were stagnating; their despairing citizens were hungry. Stalin felt he could await the ruin of the United States and Britain. Time was on his side.

3

ENTERING THE MIDDLE EAST

> Jesus, or perhaps Muhammad, is walking through a bazaar in the
> afternoon heat, only to encounter Satan, or Eblis, and says to him,
> "I am weary of your ill-doing." "I?" replies the Adversary indignantly.
> "What have *I* been doing?" and he dips his fingers in a sweetmeat for
> sale, putting a smidgen of sugar on the wall. A fly eats the sugar; a
> lizard leaps up and catches the fly; the stallkeeper's cat snatches the
> lizard; a British soldier's dog kills the cat; the stallkeeper kills the
> dog; the soldier kills the stallkeeper. Soon the city is burning and
> machine guns are rattling. In the midst of it all, Satan, very injured,
> shrugs and says, "I just put a little sugar on the wall."
>
> —An old imperial fable of communal conflict, as retold by the author

I N THE EARLY SPRING OF 1946, SHARP-EYED MEN AT THE MAIN
Navy Building along Washington's Mall and at the Foreign Office in
Whitehall were studying large maps of what we now call the Middle
East: an enormous sweep of the globe that extended from faraway Afghanistan to Greece and French North Africa in the west, and south
through Arab lands to the Saudi peninsula. It's the same general
region—with a few changes, such as dropping Greece, Turkey, and
North Africa while adding Uzbekistan—that U.S. Central Command
takes as its area of responsibility today. Then, as now, policy makers
believed the region to be distinct for political and military planning.

The Middle East felt alien to most Americans. They had bonds of
family and culture with Europe, and they knew something about the
Pacific Rim. The Philippines was a colony and then a commonwealth
until July 4, 1946, and for a century Americans had increasingly enjoyed

paternal ties toward China—via Protestant missions, the outreach of such universities as Yale and Harvard, and great foundations such as Rockefeller and Carnegie. They had built a flourishing trade with Asia since the era of the Yankee clipper ships, in the early nineteenth century, and by now people on Main Street could identify once-obscure places like Guadalcanal, Tarawa, Okinawa, and the Burma Road.

Americans had few such intimacies with the Middle East. Missionaries had arrived, and colleges had been established under the Ottomans, which were the origins of today's American universities in Beirut and Cairo. But the U.S. presence didn't go as deep. There was nothing equivalent to the ties to China's nominal ruler, Chiang Kai-shek, who professed Christianity, as did his imperious Wellesley-educated wife and her extended family. U.S. corporations, among them Standard Oil, had arrived in the Middle East by the 1930s, but in Depression-era America those rapacious monopolists were hated entities. Who cared about their dealings in foreign deserts? The Middle East was nearly a tabula rasa.

The British Empire held a much closer and more complex relationship with the region. Its politicians and fighting men had been involved ever since Admiral Horatio Nelson's 1798 victory over France at the Battle of the Nile. The British had occupied Aden in 1839 and Egypt in 1882, and together with France they'd carved out the League of Nations mandates after World War I—essentially colonies, with certain limitations—for Iraq, Syria and Lebanon, and Palestine. Iran had long been a semi-colony; Afghanistan's neighboring Pashtun king was on the British payroll. Imperial fortresses dotted the approaches, including Malta, which headquartered the Mediterranean Fleet. The Persian Gulf was a British lake, and treaties were enforced with its coastal sheikhdoms.

Until 1936, Egypt had effectively been part of the British Empire. By then, fascist Italy had shown its expansive designs on the Mediterranean and against Ethiopia. Massive nationalist demonstrations were occurring simultaneously in Cairo and Alexandria. Britain needed to safeguard its position in Egypt, so in August of that year, Anthony Eden, during his first time as foreign secretary, had signed a treaty pledging to withdraw British forces except those required to protect the Suez Canal.

They were limited to ten thousand troops and five hundred pilots, with the agreement to be revisited ten years hence, in 1946. The canal, after all, was recognized as an integral part of Egypt, but also as being vital to the British Empire.

Egypt's political status at war's end remained subservient. It was like that of a Central American "republic" vis-à-vis the United States, such as Nicaragua or, better yet, Panama, another ostensibly sovereign state through which a vital canal connected the seas. In all cases, U.S. displeasure could easily make itself felt—as could Britain's in Egypt. To poison matters further, Britain was heavily in debt to Egypt.

Earlier in the canal's history, by one count, London had promised sixty-six times in forty-four years to remove its soldiers—once, that is, order had been restored in Egypt. Somehow it never was, nor, after 1936, would Britain get its forces below ten thousand for years.

"Suez," as this great assembly point of imperial might was known, lay along the 120-mile waterway that runs through desert and marshland from Port Said on the Mediterranean to the port of Suez at the top of the Red Sea. It was a military reservation of about 5,400 square miles, the size of Connecticut, that included the cities of Fayid and Ismailia along the canal. Fayid was headquarters of Middle East Land Forces and was the core of the British defense system for the region; Ismailia headquartered the Middle East Air Forces. The entire stronghold contained the world's largest supply depot, a dozen airfields, railroads, power stations, harbors, firing ranges, and fields of tents and barracks. Thousands of East Africans and Mauritians served as laborers, as did about forty-two thousand Egyptians. In addition, until British forces were withdrawn from Egypt's main cities in 1947, a garrison dominated some 650 acres in central Cairo, including the largest public square, to be named Tahrir (Liberation) following the 1952 revolution. It was an area through which no Cairene could walk without permission and where British troops openly mocked the king with their filthy marching cadence, "*King* Fayrook, *King* Fayrook 'as got 'is bollooks on a 'ook."

When World War II ended, America still had no embassy in Cairo, only a legation, which voices less sovereign authority of the state. That was all the Foreign Office would allow.

Washington agreed that the British Empire was responsible for protecting the Middle East. In fact, the region's defense was one of Britain's three strategic priorities along with defending the homeland and securing sea communications. The independence of Western Europe from Russian domination wasn't on this short list: it was considered desirable but not vital, as if weighing the importance of, say, Scandinavia alone. Britain had sent its army to the Continent twice in the recent past, said Admiral Sir John Cunningham, the first sea lord, speaking of the early stages of the world wars, and "on both occasions we had suffered severely, first at Mons and more recently at Dunkirk."[1] There were overlaps of military necessity between defending the Middle East and Continental Europe, to be sure, but military planners expected the Red Army to sweep to the Channel in a World War III. That didn't mean occupied Europe was to be forsaken; it was to be reconquered, as before. Yet, according to doctrine, that couldn't happen without holding the Middle East and the imperial lifelines that ran through it.

Ernest Bevin clarified this point when he met with two American statesmen in January 1946. One was Michigan's Arthur Vandenberg, the venerable Republican Senate conference chairman who would lead the Foreign Relations Committee after his party carried both houses of Congress that fall. The other was John Foster Dulles, a key Republican foreign policy adviser, prominent lay leader of the Presbyterian church, and the senior partner at Sullivan & Cromwell, the great international law firm. Russia was making territorial claims on Iran and Turkey, Bevin lectured in his staccato speaking style, and those demands were occurring only half a year after Afghanistan had gotten its frontier lands along the Panj and Oxus Rivers snatched away in a heavy-handed treaty with Molotov. Couldn't they see that Stalin was uniting a czarist Great Russian imperial craving to master the Middle East and the Mediterranean, by way of Iran and Turkey, with the messianic passions of Communism?

Other Americans got similar tutorials. People at State and on Capitol Hill, for instance, could hear British diplomats describing Egypt as "the most important country" in that part of the world, just as Bonaparte had said. Didn't they know it lay between Asia and Europe, astride the routes to India and into Africa? Occasionally, the argument would be refined: Egypt and the Suez Canal were really like Chicago; any east-west travel would get one there. Furthermore, adjacent to Egypt was

Palestine, where conflicts of faiths could be used to subvert the Holy Land. MI5, the British internal security service that held responsibility in the Palestine mandate, and for other colonial duties, even claimed that Russian clerics in Jerusalem were acting as "Fifth Columnists."[2] Supposedly, they'd undercut government authority and then spread Moscow's influence like an oil slick into combustible Egypt.

Bevin wasn't being mindlessly antagonistic to the Russians, and he had held two forthright talks in the Kremlin with Stalin during mid-December 1945. After all, twenty-five years earlier, Bevin had done his part on the docks to prevent munitions from going to Poland to fight the Bolsheviks, and well into 1946 he'd still seek compromise with Moscow in the hope of "Left Speaking to Left." Yet enough was becoming enough, and, he insisted to the cabinet, he had to set an example of resolve for the Americans. If he didn't, "all Europe should fall" to Communism: the Red Army wouldn't even have to invade.[3] Germany barely existed as a state, and France was a broken reed.*

When Bevin argued about Europe's future being entwined with that of the Middle East, however, it wasn't easy for Vandenberg and Dulles, nor other shrewd Americans, to agree. He appeared to be reliving the nineteenth-century British-czarist rivalries that had surrounded Persia (as Iran had been known since ancient times) when the two empires had been playing their Great Game: the contest for dominance in central Asia.

Nonetheless, by the time Bevin, Vandenberg, and Dulles convened, a rough consensus was developing in Washington for a more alert, more generally engaged approach to the world. "Power vacuums" seemed to be everywhere: in a ruined Europe, in China, perhaps even in Britain, where Walter Lippmann, America's most influential journalist, detected "a partial vacuum." In those days, a malign unitary force—Soviet Communism—was assumed to be pressing on most every "vacuum."

---

*France, with a population of some forty-one million, was a great civilization but not a great power during the years of this story. At this time, it had about a one-to-one ratio of agricultural workers (compared with Britain's one to nine), and its armed forces were deeply diminished after the June 1940 surrender to Germany. Between 1946 and 1958, its Fourth Republic experienced twenty-four governments, and even the Soviet party boss Nikita Khrushchev observed in 1955 that its politicians "cannot make up their minds."

And where there's an alleged "vacuum," an enemy will be found to match it, just as today. In the months after World War II, the biggest vacuum of all looked to be in the Middle East.

DURING 1939–1945, THE MIDDLE EAST WAS THE SOLE THEATER OF land warfare in which British actions proved decisive before the full weight of U.S. power had made itself felt. Thereafter, the Americans and Britain's 8th Army fought the North African campaign of 1942–1943 to squeeze Axis forces into defeat and to stage the Allied invasion of Sicily as a stepping-stone to retaking Europe.

During the war's early years, one of Churchill's oldest friends, Walter Guinness, Lord Moyne, served as deputy resident minister in Cairo. Guinness also directed the family brewing enterprise that bore his name. In 1944, he rose to resident minister, a position of cabinet rank, and became Britain's highest official in the Middle East. By that juncture in the war, he saw U.S. commanders as overbearing and lamented that the "American idea of cooperation is that we should do all the giving and they all the taking."[4] As for Egypt specifically, all that Americans seemed to know about it was an amalgam of the bad press it had gotten from early Hebrew scribes and a modern collection of salacious smoking-room stories. But it was coming to their attention fast.

While fighting the war, Britain ran up a debt of some £400 million (then over $1.5 billion) with King Farouk's corrupt, fervently nationalist Wafd Party government. These were essentially forced loans that were extracted in the form of British IOUs for cotton, fuel, and other matériel. The British also used IOUs to employ about half a million Egyptians to build camps, procure food, and carry supplies. Moreover, as it did with other members of the sterling area, Britain enforced wartime currency restrictions in a "dollar pool": not only would sterling balances from the IOUs accumulate in London, but Egypt, like others in the pool, wasn't free to use whatever dollars it might possess to buy goods in America. Those dollars could only be used for purchases in Britain. That would augment the Bank of England's reserves of hard currency.

As the war neared its end, the Egyptians wanted their money back to cushion peacetime unemployment and to invest in their country's growth. If the British couldn't pay, bellowed Cairo's well-instructed press, then they should hand over shares of equivalent value in their many businesses within Egypt.

One was the Suez Canal Company. It was an Egyptian corporation under Egyptian law (but headquartered in Paris) with the British government as the controlling stockholder, at 44 percent. France as well as various European and Egyptian private investors held the rest. British technicians, managers, and accountants largely ran operations, while the founding documents made clear that Egypt's government owned the canal proper. This private venture was also profitable, unlike the Panama Canal, which was owned and operated by the U.S. government.

Here is the first serious reference to the takeover of the Suez Canal Company. On all these issues, Egyptians of every class composed a "smoking volcano," wrote *Al-Ahram*, the country's biggest newspaper.[5] After the war ended, King Farouk insisted that the 1936 treaty be changed to terminate the British presence. Farouk also proposed to annex the entire Anglo-Egyptian Sudan, a million square miles of terrain to Egypt's south that was administered as a British colony but with a governor-general appointed by Farouk. His demands for free trade and for freedom from imperialism resonated with Americans, most of whom would have been happy to see the British Empire disappear, as Franklin Roosevelt would have been, and even to help pry it apart. For starters, the empire impeded trade with Egypt or India.

American impatience was on display when Prime Minister Attlee visited Washington during November 10–15, 1945. For a week, the press had been saying Attlee's purpose was to discuss "the guardianship of the atomic bomb." Moscow had already denounced this trip as a conspiracy. But when he arrived at the White House, the president met him on the steps of the portico flanked by the U.S. ministers to Egypt, Saudi Arabia, Syria, and Lebanon, as well as the U.S. consul general in mandated Palestine—a testament to Washington's priorities. The two leaders did discuss the bomb, with little resolved. And America soon had an embassy in Cairo.

Meanwhile, Bevin came to see himself increasingly as an imperial statesman, more so than as a labor leader, observed the loyal, upperclass aides (nearly all Etonians) on his staff. Soon after taking office, he had declared his intention to withdraw British forces not only from Egypt's cities but perhaps from the sprawling Suez bastion as well, or the "Canal Zone" as it came to be called, though its precise boundaries were ill-defined. The prospect of quitting Egypt was the issue that had provoked Churchill, at his crankiest, to stick out his tongue at the foreign secretary in parliamentary debate.

Yet Bevin's Labour Party instincts, which told him that Egypt should be fully sovereign, were colliding with the realities of economics and politics, which showed, as he put it to the House of Commons, that "the Middle East and its oil provided a great deal of our motive power for our industry" and for merchant shipping and the Royal Navy.[6] Workmen's wages were said to be in the balance, as well as the fate of India and the Pacific dominions. If Britain lost its grip, Bevin would tell the Americans, that would virtually mean the end of England as a great power. Fittingly, Whitehall's Fuel Research Board released a report addressing the country's growing dependence on Persian Gulf oil supplies on the same day that the British handed Saladin's famed Citadel—which served as British military headquarters in Cairo—over to Egypt's army, on July 4, 1946. The two events caught the ambivalence surrounding Bevin's decisions. In the end, too much appeared to be at stake in the Middle East for Egypt to be left to its own uncertain devices.

DURING THE FINAL MONTHS OF THE WAR, STALIN, TOO, PAID INcreasing attention to the Middle East, and this is where showdowns with Russia first occurred after World War II. In his memoirs, Foreign Minister Molotov recalls watching the *Vozhd* in his Kremlin office as he moved his pipe across a small map pinned to the wall, tapped it on the thousand-mile Soviet frontier with Iran, and said, "I don't like our border right here!"[7]

At the time, Iran's northwestern Azerbaijan province shared a poorly marked mountainous border with the Azerbaijan Soviet Socialist Republic. From the Caspian through to the Black Sea, unidentified agitators in league with Red Army units were backing ethnic separatists adjacent to Soviet territory, and Red Army operatives were distributing weapons while disarming Iranian police units. This helped pro-independence

Azerbaijani nationalists to stage a well-planned coup in the historic city of Tabriz during September 1945 and to assert themselves as a state free from Tehran's control. Stalin was, in effect, trying to dismember Iran by employing a novel form of hybrid conflict known as *maskirovka*, which combines subversion, deception, concealment, and convenient deniability. It's a tactic that the Russians have turned to repeatedly since—for example, in slipping several thousand soldiers into Syria in 1983 during Lebanon's civil war, by masking them as tourists and students, or, more recently, by sending anonymous combatants into Ukraine.[8]

Sixty thousand Red Army troops were already in northern Iran, having swept down in the late summer of 1941. That's when Russia and Britain had together invaded Iran to oust a regime way too tolerant of Nazi propaganda. By 1943, these allied forces had been joined by thirty thousand U.S. military personnel, backed by thousands of American civilians with headquarters first in Baghdad, then in Basra. Their mission was to deliver four million tons of largely Lend-Lease cargo to Russia's war effort via Iran. All three allies agreed to leave Iran within six months of the peace. The Americans were mostly gone by December 1945, retaining only two small missions to train Iran's police and military, and by early 1946 the British had redeployed all but six hundred of the forty thousand soldiers they had posted originally in the south. The Russians, however, increased their presence, moving another fifteen thousand fighting men into the north.

Stalin intended to create two puppet states in northern Iran. One would be for the Azeri minority, the other for the Kurds, an ancient tribal people indigenous to western Asia. Except the Kurds spilled across several more borders. Numbers were vague, but Moscow's experts counted 1.5 million in Iraq, sitting atop British-controlled oil wells around Mosul and Kirkuk; 700,000 more in Iran; 2.7 million in Turkey; and the rest in Syria (from which the French, come early 1946, were pushed out by British forces and local nationalists).[9] Then as today, the Kurds believed themselves to be the world's largest ethnic group without a homeland, and in order to gain independence, Kurdish fighters were attacking Iranian garrisons, including along the border of Turkey and Iraq. In December 1945, the Kurdish People's Government was founded in the city of Mahabad, in northwestern Iran, and it declared itself a republic the following month, supported by Moscow. Foreign Office specialists believed Russia to be fomenting a "Greater Kurdistan."

No one in Washington or London knew if the Kurds, with their black tents and large-necked horses primed for mountain warfare, would compose a pliable Soviet client state. Already they were said by one specialist at Columbia University to be "trigger happy."[10] Red Army advisers had their doubts as well about the Kurds' willingness to comply with Soviet directives and, in fact, opposed the creation of a new tribal military force, the Peshmerga (Before Death).

In the winter of 1945–1946, the coldest in memory for Tehranis, Red Army divisions were prowling somewhere near Kazvin, nearly a hundred miles northwest of Iran's capital, with tanks and planes even closer, about a dozen miles away at Karaj. Armored columns were rumored to be moving at night. Puzzled by what they were hearing, U.S. officials who were in Moscow during December 1945, including Secretary of State James F. Byrnes, asked Stalin to explain himself. He casually replied that he feared aggression from Iran, especially saboteurs who might infiltrate to destroy oil fields around Baku, the Azerbaijan Socialist Republic's capital on the Caspian Sea. Finding that answer absurd, the Americans said they'd oppose him in the UN. "This will not cause us to blush," Stalin said with a shrug.[11]

This situation of "neither peace nor war," as Leon Trotsky had called Soviet dealings with the capitalist powers after World War I, had a certain homecoming quality for the Kremlin.

A weak and poorly armed Iran took its case against Russia to the United Nations, which was meeting in London that January. It became Item 1 before the new Security Council, which had been envisioned as a cabinet of world powers within the organization. Vandenberg and Dulles were there; nonetheless, one critic in the Foreign Office summed up the general belief that the Americans "showed signs of wilting."[12]

Stalin had also dispatched his operatives to Turkey's rugged eastern mountain provinces of Kars and Ardahan to back Georgian and Armenian nationalists near the meandering 367-mile Soviet border. The term "salami tactics" had just been coined in Hungary to describe Stalin's piecemeal slicing apart of free political parties. President Truman, the new army chief of staff, General Dwight Eisenhower, and Secretary of the Navy James Forrestal saw such bit-by-bit maneuvers at work here—and they were right. As can now be seen in Soviet records, Turkey was to be removed "as an independent player between the British Empire and the Soviet Union."[13]

In February, George Kennan, the forty-two-year-old minister counselor at the embassy in Moscow, sent a 5,327-word telegram to Washington identifying Russia as expansionist and implacably hostile.[14] The dangers were high: U.S. officials began to worry that they were heading back to war. And so Forrestal took steps to deter the Kremlin. In March, after coordinating with Truman and the State Department, he deployed the USS *Missouri*—America's mightiest battleship, painted a warlike camouflage—on a "goodwill" cruise to Turkey.

FORRESTAL WAS THE ONLY MEMBER OF FRANKLIN ROOSEVELT'S cabinet to remain for more than a year under Truman, although the new president didn't enjoy being around the driven, oddly shy New York banker. Every picture of Forrestal depicts a figure who, at a lean five feet nine, appears to be coiled and tense. Nevertheless, Forrestal made a sad effort to blend in with the Missouri boys, as the press called Truman and his poker-playing White House coterie. It didn't work, and he preferred spending his time in other ways. During a round-the-world inspection of U.S. forces in 1946, for example, he studied the six volumes of Gibbon's *Decline and Fall of the Roman Empire*—however little that eighteenth-century ironist might offer for what was happening now.

Forrestal's father, also James, had left County Cork at age nine, after the potato famine, and ended up settling in today's Beacon, New York, which at the time was a small rough-hewn town along the Hudson. The son worked for three years after high school and eventually enrolled in Princeton's class of 1915, where he became an amateur boxer and, in senior year, was voted "Most Likely to Succeed." Inexplicably, he quit before graduating. He then sold bonds for William A. Read & Company, left to serve in Naval Air during World War I, and finally returned to Wall Street to rejoin the firm that had evolved into the increasingly open-minded Dillon, Read & Co. It was known to accept Catholics, Jews, even intellectuals. He made partner and became president. Throughout, he was a man of contrasts: he had a boxing-bent face but the faultless appearance of a financier; he had a Catholic immigrant background but Episcopalian sensibilities; he had the interests of a scholar but the bravado of an ensign who'd flown the navy's wooden, death-trap 100-horsepower Aeromarine 39s. There was also a Rochesterian darkness to his life. In 1926, he married a glamorous writer for *Vogue* who slowly went mad, and through the 1930s and 1940s one heard talk about Forrestal's courage and decency in standing by her.[15]

FDR made Forrestal undersecretary of the navy in July 1940, then four years later promoted him to secretary, which was a cabinet rank, when his superior, Frank Knox, the 1936 Republican candidate for vice president, fell dead from a heart attack.[16] As secretary, Forrestal coordinated Pacific deployments with General Douglas MacArthur and landed on the beach at Iwo Jima five days into the battle. During the war's last eighteen months, he also imposed provisions against racial segregation in the navy, and thereafter in all the armed forces, appointing his friend Lester Granger, the African American executive secretary of the National Urban League, as his special adviser. No one else in government or business did anything like that.

In the two years following the war, Forrestal was Washington's closest approximation to Ernest Bevin in spearheading opposition to Stalin. Any man who could steer a securities firm through the Great Depression was likely to be persuasive, and during that postwar era Forrestal showed himself to be persuasive indeed when conveying alarms about Russia. According to John Lehman, the widely respected U.S. secretary of the navy from 1981 to 1987, Forrestal "was the real author of America's policy of containment of the Soviet Union."[17]

The writer John O'Hara was the best chronicler of his country's monied upper classes of that generation, and also a canny observer of the men who were guiding America's rise after World War II. O'Hara made one of his heroes, broken by the stress of war—Alfred Eaton in *From the Terrace*—a Princetonian (without graduating, like Forrestal) and the assistant secretary of the navy. Forrestal, in life, was an O'Hara character, in his ascent from modest prosperity to great eminence and in the fissures of his mind that would finally break him. O'Hara dedicated his one book of nonfiction to Forrestal. "Once in a while," he would write, "a man will come along who compels your admiration and trust. George Catlett Marshall was such a man in my lifetime. James Forrestal was another."[18]

ON THE AFTERNOON OF MARCH 10, A WEEK BEFORE THE *MISSOURI* sailed, Churchill—who'd just returned to Washington after speaking at Westminster College—met with Forrestal in the secretary's second-deck office at Main Navy, where the country's naval hierarchy was quartered. During their ninety minutes together, he told Forrestal that he was glad the battleship was being sent but disappointed it wasn't part of a big flotilla. Forrestal said he did in fact envision a permanent Mediterranean task force on station, and it was something he'd make a reality in August.

The *Missouri* left New York, the world's busiest port, with much publicity on the clear, brisk morning of March 22. First it sailed to Britain's stronghold on Gibraltar, the two most fortified square miles in Europe, and from there to the waters off Istanbul, in the Bosporus between the Black Sea and the Aegean. On Capitol Hill, doubts about this mission arose from both sides of the aisle. Why go in harm's way when the British, to whom Congress was considering lending an astronomical sum, should instead be doing something useful with their famous Royal Navy?[19]

The five-star admiral William Halsey, a former fleet commander in the Pacific, and known to the press as "Bull," was working on special duty for Forrestal that year. Before the *Missouri* departed, Halsey declared that his ships would now sail as they pleased in any waters of the globe, backing up Forrestal's order that the navy's spring exercises be conducted "in the Mediterranean itself."[20] Eyebrows were raised at the Admiralty, the department in Whitehall that commands the Royal Navy, over the words "in the Mediterranean itself." Except for special circumstances, as with the *Missouri*, the Foreign Office didn't permit U.S. naval vessels access to British ports around that sea.

Even before the *Missouri* anchored in the Bosporus on April 5, Red Army troops had started to withdraw from northwestern Iran. Before long, Tehran's forces retook their country's Azerbaijani provinces, whose separatist leaders retreated behind Soviet borders. The Peshmerga had lost Soviet support for their Republic of Mahabad but fought on through 1946, only to retreat at year's end into Iraq. The civilized world could breathe again, although Russia kept up political pressure on Iran. At least violence had been limited to skirmishes and executions among the locals, and as a follow-up in the spring of 1947 the Kurdish president of the republic would be hanged from a flagpole in Mahabad. Exactly why the Russians chose to withdraw from the area is debatable, but what's clear is that Stalin had no need to escalate. He could be patient as he awaited the economic collapse of the West. Stalin told disappointed Azerbaijani Communists that for the time being he intended to focus on "our liberationist policies in Europe and Asia."[21]

IN 1945, BRITISH THINKING ABOUT THE ARAB WORLD WAS STILL characterized by the romantic charms of Colonel T. E. Lawrence, "Lawrence of Arabia." The British prided themselves on knowing the languages, on embracing alien cultures, and on co-opting Arab and Iranian elites. They also seemed to have a knack for deploying odd figures who combined the roles of political officer, tourist, archaeologist, and spy, as did Lawrence and the writer Gertrude Bell, who helped create Iraq after World War I. Americans had few skills to compare, and officials in London knew it.

During the war, British military planning valued Arabs as merely useful for manual labor rather than as people who could be potent allies. The occasional tribute from a Lawrence or a Somerset Maugham to the noble qualities of the Bedouin couldn't hide the general contempt the British had for Arab peasants and city dwellers. Preparing for the postwar world, in March 1945, Foreign Office area experts organized the League of Arab States, in part to strengthen their political and economic relations with Saudi Arabia as well as with Egypt, Iraq, Lebanon, Syria, Yemen, and Transjordan. The league turned out to be a weak, lackluster coordinating body that wasn't much help in building a peace, as Bevin soon discovered.

To bolster the British position in Egypt—which meant holding on to their giant military estates—Bevin turned to Washington, though with some ambivalence, because of what he described as "the red tooth and claw of American capitalism," which he sensed was ready to take a bite out of the Middle East.[22] One way to obtain U.S. political-military support, he surmised, might be to appoint a prominent American to the board of the Suez Canal Company. Maybe that would engage Washington to pressure Farouk's government to quiet down about the ongoing presence of British troops. The State Department, however, blocked his idea. Its officials weren't about to let the U.S. government get entwined with business interests in Egypt, especially British ones. However, the Arabian Peninsula—a long-standing sphere of imperial influence—was different.

Saudi Arabia, at one-quarter the size of the United States, wasn't quite yet awash in petrodollars, and the British didn't appreciate its potential, though, for political purposes, they subsidized its monarchy to some £2 million a year. "We were surprised the Americans took such a conscious decision that Saudi Arabia was so important," Sir Donald Hawley, a diplomat in the kingdom after the war, recalled about Foreign Office opinion.[23] But the Americans had a pretty good idea what they were doing. Forrestal particularly anticipated his country's growing need for oil, as would any astute official responsible for the U.S. Navy, with its appetite for fuel. As a Wall Streeter, he was also familiar with the discoveries made by Standard Oil of California, along with its partners, before the war. These were the only fields in the Middle East where U.S. companies held exclusive extraction rights.

One Foreign Office expert, a recent chargé d'affaires in Jeddah, was open to letting the Americans "'penetrate' Saudi Arabia to their hearts' content."[24] By which he meant acceding to their economic presence. Others weren't so sure even this was a good idea. If the Americans were taking oil from the Middle East, colleagues of his then argued, Washington had better help provide security to the region. But the camel's nose could be seen within the tent. Once the Americans got interested in Riyadh's political concerns, another of the Whitehall mandarins recognized, "we cannot control the extent of penetration" elsewhere in the Middle East. That could mean meddling in Egypt, or worse. Already Bevin called U.S. involvement in Palestine "irresponsible backseat driving." The American press—observing British efforts to govern Palestine and contain the Zionist movement—wrote of an incipient "Anglo-Jewish War."[25]

PALESTINE WAS THE SINGLE MOST DIVISIVE ISSUE BETWEEN THE United States and Britain. Each had different stances toward the Zionist project in a land that, in 1946, had 1.2 million Arabs (10 percent Christian), 600,000 Jews, and 4,900 people who emphasized they were U.S. citizens. Even before the war ended, Lord Halifax, the able wartime ambassador in Washington, had advised Churchill that the Palestine mandate be dropped to avoid poisoning Britain's ties to the United States. Let the Americans take it over, he argued. That made sense to Churchill.[26] Why arbitrate religious chaos in Palestine while the Americans sat around and criticized? "Somebody else should have their turn now," he wrote in the summer of 1945, weeks before leaving Downing Street.[27] At the Foreign Office, however, a not atypical response from one mid-level diplomat was to dismiss Churchill's proposal because it would be "symptomatic of our abdication as a Great Power."[28]

After Bevin became foreign secretary, he upheld the tight restrictions on immigration to Palestine that Whitehall had enacted before the war. The purpose was to avoid inflaming the Arab majority: during the 1936–1939 Arab Revolt, the British, according to their figures, had killed more than 2,000 Arabs in combat. Arab estimates are more than twice that, but there's no disagreement that 108 rebels were hanged. Jewish deaths at the hands of Palestinian Arabs were recorded at 415. The British feared a repeat. Yet Palestine's future was now unfolding against the backdrop of the Holocaust—which Churchill, upon reading just the first detailed account of Auschwitz, called the "most horrible crime ever committed in the whole history of the world."[29]

Zionist activists in the United States had taken British officials to task over Palestine even before the war ended. Already in February 1944, Halifax had endured a tough visit from American Jewish Committee delegates aggrieved over Britain's limits to immigration and land purchases from Arab fellahin (local peasants). That spring, New York's Democratic senator Robert F. Wagner cosponsored a resolution with

Senator Robert Taft, Ohio's Republican titan, to establish a Jewish commonwealth in Palestine, but George Marshall, the army chief of staff, quashed it as contrary to the war effort. Eighteen months later, with the war over, a motion was again before the Senate: Palestine should be opened wide to immigrants. Arabs found the idea of establishing a Jewish homeland in Palestine as far-fetched as establishing an Arab homeland in California. And a parodic bill to do just that was duly introduced in the Iraqi parliament.

The opening high-profile atrocity occurred even before the war's end. In Cairo, on November 6, 1944, two Jewish gunmen shot and killed Lord Moyne and his driver, Lance Corporal A. H. Fuller, at close range. The shooters had been dispatched by Yitzhak Shamir, operations chief for the terror group known as Lehi (Fighters for the Freedom of Israel), which MI5 labeled the Stern Gang after its founder, Avraham Stern.[30] Moyne's assassination, while the British were in a death grapple with the Nazis, got worldwide attention.

The perpetrators—a twenty-three-year-old and a nineteen-year-old—were captured quickly, and Eden relayed the details of the attack to the House of Commons. Churchill was unable to speak. One MP rose to ask (using euphemisms familiar today) if torture might be applied to the captives; maybe a wider conspiracy could be uncovered in time. Jewish leaders in Palestine condemned the murder and made arrests, but here, on both sides of the conflict, began a vivid use of Nazi imagery. Eleven days after the killing, and in mourning, Churchill told the House of "a new set of gangsters worthy of Nazi Germany."[31] He ordered Britain's ambassador to have Egyptian authorities expedite the hanging of the killers, in Cairo's Bab-el-Khalk prison, which they did.

In May 1946, Arab workers in Jerusalem staged a twelve-hour general strike. They wanted freedom from British rule, and they opposed the buying of land by immigrants. One mob chanted for jihad, shouting, "Death to the Americans and British!" It was the first time "the street" took up the name of the United States, along with the usual condemnation of Britain. A hail of stones fell on British soldiers who pulled back with batons swinging and were only saved from the mob by a sudden violent rainstorm. Forrestal worried in his diary about a brewing "civil war" between Jews and Arabs. He knew something about Stalin's tactics and suspected that Russian operatives might pose as immigrants to sow further political upheaval and terror.

In Palestine, the British faced what the historian Paul Johnson concludes was the first instance of modern propaganda being combined "with Leninist cell-structure and advanced technology to advance political aims through murder."[32] Terrorists always play to an audience, and the big one here, as Zionists struggled with British authorities, was to be found among Americans. MI5 labeled it "Zionist terror"—a campaign of bombings, assassinations, and kidnappings that provoked British authorities to respond with violent, self-defeating techniques of imperial policing. Their crackdowns inflamed a wider Jewish population in Palestine and lots of observers in the United States as well—in fact, just about anyone who opposed the British Empire, whether due to colonialism, foreign aid, or the certainty that Britain would once again drag America into war. In Washington that summer, the Anglo-American Financial Agreement was nearly defeated in the House because of anger at the surge of British military action in Palestine.

During June, security forces rounded up some twenty-seven hundred Jews. Then, in July, another terrorist splinter group, the Irgun Zvai Le'umi, or Irgun (National Military Organization), led by Menachem Begin, blew up Jerusalem's King David Hotel, killing ninety-one—"an act of terror," concludes the historian Mordechai Golani.[33] Zionist terror and British reprisal continued: bridges were blown up, hostages taken, road mines laid, car bombs detonated, hand grenades thrown into barracks. A weapons cache was found hidden beneath Tel Aviv's Great Synagogue. The British brought in hundreds of their tanned desert veterans from Egypt as reinforcements and created squads of former Special Air Service Regiment commandos to attempt covert police work wearing "Jewish clothing."[34] Few observers in Britain were distinguishing between Irgun and the Stern forces, with around six thousand fighters, and Haganah, the fifty-thousand-man semiofficial self-defense organization.

MI5 also feared that terrorists were being recruited within Britain—for example, from radical Jewish youth groups in North London. Youngsters were being seduced, the intelligence people said, by appeals from hotheaded clerics and by publications, among them *Jewish Struggle*, that reprinted Irgun's calls for violence. Moreover, extremist cells within England were said to be silently awaiting activation. When the security services did apprehend Jewish terrorists, whether on British soil or in Palestine, they were surprised to discover them to be highly educated men and women, not dim-witted fanatics.

In August, the head of MI5 warned Attlee and Bevin that Zionist assassins had them and the British cabinet on death lists. Twenty-two electric-fuse-type letter bombs were mailed to senior officials in London, including to the shadow foreign secretary Anthony Eden; a twenty-four-stick dynamite bomb was planted at the Colonial Office (it failed to explode); a bomb was detonated in the Rome embassy. Tragedy was averted because the postal bombs sent to Bevin, Eden, and top officials were routinely intercepted and then disarmed by Dr. Hugh Watts, chief inspector of explosives for the Home Office. He'd collect one of the lethal packages, then be rowed in a little boat to an island in the lake of St. James's Park where he entered a concrete hut to snip the wires.[35] Meanwhile, Palestine drained £200 million from mid-1945 to the end of 1946, and embittered ties with America.

Informed Americans had a vague sense of guilt over the excuses their country had made before entering the war for not having opened its doors to rescue the doomed. Now they saw a desperate and stateless people seizing the opportunity at last to create a state of their own by battling colonial officialdom. In October 1946, Truman demanded that 100,000 immigrants be admitted promptly into Palestine. Few sympathized with Britain's predicament, and reactions to Bevin could be ugly. William Clark, who'd been with the consulate in Chicago, was now a press officer at the British embassy. He attended a dinner party in Georgetown that fall given by the Supreme Court justice Felix Frankfurter and his wife. The small, quick, and articulate jurist was known as a reliable friend of Britain's, with an honorary degree from Oxford. Yet "almost immediately," Clark recalled, he "launched into a bitter attack on Ernest Bevin whom he described as the true successor to Hitler, determined to produce a final solution by the elimination of the Jewish race."[36]

· · ·

COLLECTIVE PUNISHMENT, MASS ARRESTS BY STEEL-HELMETED SOL-
diers with tommy guns, homes destroyed, curfews, detention camps and
deportations, Jewish neighborhoods patrolled by armored cars, and
house-to-house searches: these were all "policing" methods being
employed not in 1930s Germany but by the British in Palestine. Fair-
minded Americans who scanned the headlines could be confused,
which was much of the purpose. At the same time, Irgun and the Stern
Gang drew on fund-raising in America, and explosives and ammunition
were to be found in food packages being sent to Britain.[37]

On March 2, 1946, the British declared martial law in Tel Aviv and
other Jewish areas, with Churchill, on the following day, denouncing
the terrorist "outrages."[38] A superb officer, Lieutenant General Sir Gordon MacMillan, aggressively implemented the crackdown, but Churchill,
as leader of the opposition, foresaw a losing battle. He pressed for a U.S.
peacekeeping role. If Washington wouldn't help, he said, Britain should
dump the matter into America's lap and get out.

Forrestal was at once tough-minded and naive about the situation.
He didn't oppose dividing Palestine between Jews and Arabs, yet he
objected to America's being the lead advocate in the United Nations for
the Zionist cause. His priority was U.S. defense. To this end, he worried
about securing oil supplies from Arab lands. He also feared a predicament that might entangle five thousand or maybe fifteen thousand GIs
in Palestine—thereby reigniting isolationism at home while alienating
Muslim states like Egypt, as well as others among the faithful, even
Saudi Arabia.[39] He kept asking Truman, and also New York's governor
Thomas Dewey, the powerful young Republican preparing for a second
presidential run in 1948, if it would "not be possible," as he put it in his
diary, "to lift the Jewish-Palestine question out of politics."[40] He asked
the same of the former FDR emissary Bernard Baruch, who advised
him to go slow when addressing the emotionally charged issue.

But there was no separating U.S. politics from the drama, nor could
ties to Britain be compartmentalized. Whitehall officials meanwhile
added to Washington's alarm by offering the learned reminder that
should British soldiers leave Palestine, the holy places would be left
without "impartial supervision" for the first time since the Crusades.[41]

As violence kept intensifying by early 1947, the Joint Chiefs of Staff saw no happy ending. Russia might exploit the violence, which meanwhile could only be prevented, they argued, by throwing at least 104,000 GIs into the gap. And to even deploy 15,000 of them anywhere would require "partial mobilization."[42] Moreover, said the chiefs, extremists on both sides would ruin hopes for compromise, whether that be the likes of Lehi and Irgun or, among the Arabs, followers of the Haj al-Amin al-Husseini, who held the title of grand mufti, a religious role invented by the British. Al-Husseini had fled Palestine during the Arab Revolt of the 1930s and ended up in Berlin on Hitler's payroll, at the salary of a field marshal.[43] By 1946, he had based himself in Cairo.

Forrestal kept comparing the dilemma to Ireland's war of independence, which twenty-five years earlier hadn't fractured U.S. politics, even though many Americans supported the Irish cause. Comparisons to Ireland were also made in the press—for example, by the *New York Post*, which likened Lord Moyne's murder to the IRA's earlier assassinations. Ultimately, two points about both cases remain relevant today. First, in neither upheaval was any British unit defeated. Britain just got sick of the strain, after it had worked against itself by conducting such high-visibility suppression. Second, some terrorisms become respectable, as had Ireland's. Once a state is sovereign, and begins to cooperate within the community of nations, memories will be short. That would also occur in Palestine, which is why Shamir and Begin became prime ministers while their reign of terror against civilians and soldiers is described today as "unrestrained resistance," steered, in the case of Irgun, by a "right leaning paramilitary group."[44]

THROUGH 1946, THE TENSIONS BETWEEN THE LABOUR PARTY GOVernment and the Kremlin became personal, as seen at the Paris Peace Conference, which lasted from July 29 through October 15. Foreign ministers of the Three, as well as of France and other Allied states, gathered at the Luxembourg Palace to hammer out territorial adjustments, reparations, and other vexing issues with Italy and the war's smallfry belligerents, among them Bulgaria and Romania. The open-ended haggling over minor stakes made this gathering more tedious than most, especially because the Russians fixated themselves on the presence of

British troops in Greece. Ernest Bevin headed Britain's delegation, though he didn't arrive at his hotel, the George V, until August 9, due to ill health. An evening or two later, in the palace's smoky conference hall, Molotov, with his deputy Vyshinsky sneering beside him, insulted Bevin once too often. Bevin rose to his feet, knotted his fists, and lurched in his characteristic sailor's roll toward the Soviet foreign minister, saying "I've 'ad enough of this I 'ave." While in Paris, Bevin was being surrounded by detective-bodyguards, due to a terrorist threat, and they jumped in.[45]

The "Cold War," as Orwell first called the worsening tensions, was taking shape, and Walter Lippmann helped popularize the term. His "Today and Tomorrow" column appeared three times a week in some 250 newspapers and was required reading for serious people. As he despaired over Russia, Lippmann was also thinking about the Middle East. To friends, he compared the ambitions of Soviet Marxists with those of Islamic jihadists, and he understood jihad to be the licensing of violent conquest against all unbelievers. Yet no one would think of measuring Islam's role in the world by its grand declarations, Lippmann observed, so why do so for Communist Russia?[46] Each belief system aspired to impose itself everywhere, but surely the planet was too varied a place for big parts of it to fall to either of these creeds.

With the brooding demeanor of a self-conscious sage, and writing with the added weight of being fundamentally nonpartisan, Lippmann assessed the "Mohammedan world." That meant everything from French West Africa to the Dutch East Indies, but he focused on what could be done to block Soviet inroads in the Middle East. Washington should help to divide the region's states and peoples, he concluded. To that end, U.S. decision makers had to uphold British power, induce Saudi Arabia not to act in concert with the Arab League, and "aim to turn Egypt away from the Middle East and back into Africa," thereby "breaking up Arab unity," or what there might be of it.[47]

Here's the first clear postwar manifesto of America's faith, despite all evidence, in its supposed ability to fine-tune the destinies of distant peoples and places. Lippmann was an early believer in that magic gift of effective nips and tucks, and it's a conviction that remains undiminished among policy makers today who are eager to "realign" the Middle East.[48]

At the time, however, America had yet to develop the capacities to perform such geopolitical alchemy. Special forces commandos, CIA operatives, and aid officers with millions to dispense on third-world projects hadn't yet arrived. Nor had Washington yet gotten a taste for these adventures. The bigger issue was the direction of the nation's foreign policy overall.

By the start of 1947, Washington had gone through three secretaries of state within three years. Cordell Hull, who remains the longest serving, had sat in office from 1933 through 1944, but President Roosevelt preferred to conduct affairs of state through personal emissaries. Hull's deputy, Edward Stettinius, followed. Stettinius had been U.S. Steel's board chairman for two years before joining the Roosevelt administration. He lived large and entertained foreign diplomats at his grand Greek Revival Virginia estate, with Negro spirituals and drinks served on the lawn. ("Charming people," wrote Sir Alexander Cadogan, the Foreign Office permanent undersecretary who attended one of these parties, "but so utterly different."[49]) Then Harry Truman had appointed his own man in July 1945, James F. Byrnes, a former South Carolina senator, U.S. Supreme Court justice, and wartime economic czar who had argued before the Senate that the lynching of blacks was essential to prevent the rape of white women in his native South. That America's secretary of state could profess such beliefs just came with the times. Truman dropped him after eighteen months to nominate General George C. Marshall.

Churchill called Marshall "the Organiser of Victory"—the same description that admirers in Parliament had applied to Churchill's father a lifetime before, and the only person ever so labeled by Lord Randolph's adoring son. Ernest Bevin remained to be convinced, but Marshall soon imposed his authority at the State Department. Given the cards he was dealt, Marshall brought with him a clarity of purpose not seen before or since.

4

FALSE STARTS

If the Americans are to be made conscious of anything, they
have to be shocked into consciousness.
—Ernest Bevin, foreign secretary, February 1947

O N JANUARY 9, 1947, GEORGE MARSHALL FLEW FROM NANJING
to Honolulu's Hickam Field. He had been trying for a year to resolve the decades-long civil war between Mao Zedong's Communist
revolutionaries and Chiang Kai-shek's Nationalist regime, which the
United States recognized as China's sole legal government. Several thousand U.S. aid and information experts were also in China working to
turn its political system into a representative democracy and to improve
its culture by, among other steps, distributing Hollywood movies and
Time Inc. magazines. Many in the Foreign Office ridiculed the effort,
but to the Americans this endeavor to transform China was just another
great problem that their goodwill and know-how could solve.

Marshall's steady temperament was so renowned that he was confirmed unanimously as secretary of state without any hearings just the
day before he landed in Hawaii. He had a professorial air like that of

Robert E. Lee, another Virginian, and had graduated as first captain in Virginia Military Institute's class of 1901. During World War I, he toiled as a lieutenant colonel away from the limelight constructing battle plans at the American Expeditionary Force headquarters in Chaumont, and fellow officers noticed a quieter bearing than that of General John J. Pershing, the celebrated AEF commander, or of Brigadier General Douglas MacArthur, West Point class of 1903, who won glamorous renown leading the Rainbow Division on the western front. But Marshall possessed a preternatural authority that made his presence daunting and that set him apart from other people. Following the war, as Pershing's key aide, he saw kings and presidents up close. He served in China from 1924 to 1927 and gathered a breadth of experience during the 1930s by commanding men of the National Guard and the Civilian Conservation Corps; as well as regular infantry.

Marshall was sworn in at the War Department as chief of staff on September 1, 1939, the day Hitler invaded Poland. He wore a civilian summer suit. It was an era when generals who would soon lead an army of eight million fellow citizens in total war didn't require the peacock trappings customary among the brass today. Ribbons, braid, and military pomp were for Europeans, which was why officers who testified on Capitol Hill or worked at the War Department wore mufti and why Marshall's car bore no insignia of rank. He remained chief until the war's end, selecting all of America's generals, and it was he to whom they answered: Eisenhower, Patton, Omar Bradley, Mark Clark, Hap Arnold, and the former U.S. Army chief of staff General MacArthur, too. There were men who hated Marshall, but when they spoke of him, it was in whispers.[1]

The now slightly stooped sixty-six-year-old soldier, with plain features and gray eyes, began work as secretary on January 21, 1947. From the start, Marshall faced urgencies that required him to engage with the British Empire: military cooperation was spotty; a hungry European continent had to be revived; violence was worsening in Palestine; the future of the eastern Mediterranean and the Middle East looked endangered; and, increasingly, Southeast Asia appeared open to Communist revolution.

Foreign Secretary Bevin, however, knew little about General Marshall. He therefore sought opinions from Field Marshal Henry Wilson, head of the Joint Staff Mission in Washington, and from Viscount Alanbrooke, who had commanded Britain's army during the war while serving as Churchill's key military adviser. They claimed to have been unimpressed by George Marshall's foresight but said on balance his appointment would help improve relations. Even General MacArthur's judgment was rushed to Bevin's desk from Tokyo, where, as the *Gaijin Shogun*, or "foreign generalissimo," he ruled Japan. MacArthur noncommittally said that the new secretary of state was "a good exponent of the Anglo-Saxon viewpoint."[2] Bevin also elicited opinions from the Foreign Office. The overall response was that Undersecretary Acheson, who had essentially been running the department, was doing so in a "bewildered and amateurish fashion" and that Marshall's arrival might make things worse by diverting State's flailing energies toward Asia.[3]

BEVIN FACED A MORE IMMEDIATE CHALLENGE AT THE START OF 1947 than ministerial changes in Washington: Britain's already struggling economy was imperiled, including by a coal shortage. To make matters worse, snow fell daily somewhere in the isles from mid-January to mid-March with fifteen-foot drifts pushed by a biting east wind. Roads and rails were blocked; transport between England and Scotland was severed. The army dropped supplies to snowbound farms, and German POWs were put to work shoveling. (Nearly 400,000 remained in camps scattered around the country.) Temperatures stayed in the teens, and in London the electricity was cut off between 9:00 and 12:00 and 2:00 and 4:00. A deep freeze enveloped the land. When Bevin received an Arab delegation in early February, he had to do so at St. James's Palace, to take advantage of its huge sixteenth-century fireplaces. The grime-covered Foreign Office building where he worked, across the street from the prime minister's residence, was too cold.

Otherwise Bevin would toil in the Foreign Office by candlelight in rooms with windows glazed by ice. Sitting in the gloom beneath a portrait of George III, he could look high up at a ceiling of gilded rafters. It took genius, he reflected, for a country built on an island of coal and surrounded by fish to be both cold and hungry. And it was at this point, in January 1947, that he, as one of four Labour ministers besides Attlee, made the deeply secret decision to build an atomic bomb as fast as possible.

That February was one of the most tumultuous months in his nation's long history, with world-shaking repercussions. On the fourteenth, Bevin announced that Britain would drop its mandate for Palestine and depart the following year. On the twentieth, Prime Minister Attlee declared that India would be granted full self-government no later than June 1948. Attlee also cut conscription from eighteen months to twelve. That prompted the U.S. Army's chief of staff, General Eisenhower, to conclude that there'd be fewer British professional soldiers to serve in the Middle East.[4] Then, on the gray afternoon of Friday, February 21, the embassy in Washington alerted State that Britain would be forced to end the financial, economic, and military assistance it had been giving to Greece and Turkey—and would do so by March 31. The following Monday, at 9:00 a.m., the ambassador arrived at the State Department to hand Marshall two aide-mémoire (on blue paper to emphasize importance) that formalized the point. One concerned Turkey, the other Greece, and it was the latter, all agreed, that had "utmost urgency."[5] Unlike Turkey, Greece was enduring an insurrection and British troops were upholding Athens's government.

Over the weekend, as if to heighten everyone's anxiety, news circulated that Moscow had rejected U.S. proposals for international atomic inspections, signaling to Americans that Stalin was making a rush for the bomb. At around the same time, King Farouk's government broke off negotiations over British rights in Egypt as well as in the Sudan, to which Cairo laid claim. Senior people at the State Department viewed that last development concerning Egypt as part of the growing horror being faced in the eastern Mediterranean. They assumed that Britain's announcements about Greece, Turkey, and Palestine meant that defense of the Suez Canal would be abandoned as well.[6] During February, against this geopolitical backdrop, Britain's unemployment rate quadrupled, due to calamities of weather and fuel. The Empire Industries Association reported that the loan from the United States would be exhausted by the end of 1948 if Britain maintained its rate of spending—an estimate that it revised in March to fall sooner, probably in early 1948, or even before.

Looking at all this, American editorialists began to proclaim the "liquidation" of the British Empire. So did Lippmann. More quietly, Marshall mentioned "liquidation," too. There was lots of excitement about torches being plucked from Britain's chilling fingers, of batons being handed to the United States, and even the sober Will Clayton (who had been elevated to undersecretary rank) spoke about America picking up "the reins of world leadership."[7]

Why this furor within the space of two or three weeks? All of these men had seen so much fall apart so fast: France's sudden defeat in 1940; six million quickly exterminated in the Holocaust; Germany's downfall and Hiroshima in 1945. For the British Empire to dissolve would just be the latest shock.

Time magazine added to the hype but worried that the country was "not yet mature enough to accept all its responsibilities."[8] And what *Time* said was important: it was America's foremost weekly, and its views about the economy, politics, business, and the arts shaped national opinions.

Eight years later, Joseph Jones, a former mid-level official at State (who'd previously been an editor at *Time*), would write *The Fifteen Weeks: An Inside Account of the Genesis of the Marshall Plan*, a bestselling memoir about these months in 1947. During that period, he reflected, Britain "handed the job of world leadership, with all its burdens and all its glory, to the United States."[9] This notion has been set in stone ever since. Today it's said habitually that "with the destruction at home in 1947, the British gave up trying to maintain a global empire," and that a "global political vacuum created by the collapse of the British empire" followed.[10] One reason the myth took hold is that Jones's account was published in 1955, by which time the United States was *truly* poised to take over the leadership of the West. The chronology got muddled, and people came to believe that some enormous transition had occurred years earlier, in 1947. It hadn't. The events that transpired during these weeks, which surrounded the Truman Doctrine as well as the Marshall Plan, are very different from what historians believe.

. . .

BRITISH GOVERNMENTS HAD LONG REGARDED GREECE AS ESSENTIAL to controlling Mediterranean shipping lanes. To that end, as German occupying forces retreated from Athens, in October 1944, Churchill sent in paratroopers to take over the capital. Greece by then was a poor, tired country of 7.5 million in which the Nazis had killed 7 percent of the population. With the Germans removed, Britain helped reinstall the Hellenic monarchy, which quickly found itself opposed by some twenty thousand pro-Communist guerrillas, who controlled much of the north and who swam in a sea of some quarter-million sympathizers. By the winter of 1946–1947, Greece was on the verge of full-scale civil war. The guerrillas were being supplied from "sanctuaries," a new political term, from the adjacent Balkan states, all under Communist rule. Washington grew alarmed, given recent experience with Soviet designs in Iran and in Turkey.

In February, therefore, it was easy for Marshall and Undersecretary Acheson to conclude that Greece would fall to Communism if Britain withdrew its financial aid and its remaining sixteen thousand troops. The idea of sending money to replace the British presence didn't rattle the Americans: they had already been shipping food and writing checks to Greece. But it was unnerving to think of putting U.S. boots on the ground to make up for Britain's withdrawal. For the next three weeks, starting on that dismal Friday, February 21, Foreign Office personnel waited to see, as Nevile Butler, an assistant undersecretary put it, "how far the US are prepared to go financially to keep the Soviet within bounds, and how far the Republicans will swallow their own election pledges of retrenchment."[11] The GOP, not incidentally, had just taken control of Congress on January 3 after having swept the midterm elections in November on a platform to resolve inflation, strikes, and shortages of consumer goods—not to redress foreign policy.

On March 5, Acheson asked the State-War-Navy Coordinating Committee—a precursor to the National Security Council—to explain the consequences of a British pullout from Greece. The fact that he was inquiring got to the attention of Fleet Admiral William Leahy, former head of the U.S. Navy and the country's highest-ranking military officer, who retained the White House role that he had held under FDR. Leahy was outraged. Even for Acheson to raise the question courted the prospect of directly involving the United States in the sordid intricacies of the Old World. Leahy had approved of sending the *Missouri* into the Mediterranean. Deploying GIs was a far different level of commitment. The president nonetheless kept his own counsel. On March 7, he appointed three top officials to explain to the nation's opinion leaders, particularly in business, the necessity of supporting Greece and Turkey.

This small team included Forrestal and, as a substitute for Marshall, Undersecretary Dean Acheson. But it was headed by Secretary of the Treasury John Wesley Snyder, whose presence signaled the gravity of what was unfolding. And it's essential to an understanding of these dramatic months, and to what came later, to know Snyder's significance.

SNYDER HAD BEEN A THIRTY-FIVE-YEAR-OLD COMMUNITY BANKER IN St. Louis when, in 1930, the Hoover administration appointed him—in the teeth of the Depression—to act as liquidator of national banks for the comptroller of the currency. Ten years later, in 1940, the Roosevelt administration had him running the congressionally chartered Defense Plant Corporation in anticipation of war. It was a vast, federally funded banking operation that lent $11 billion to private industry to build more than a thousand giant manufacturing enterprises (as well as to expand private ones) from which sprang, overnight, the tanks, trucks, guns, ships, and especially the planes needed to win the fight. Never had so much capital been injected so quickly into the U.S. economy. The Defense Plant Corporation bought the country at least a year's head start, perhaps two. Snyder "had a most direct effect" on victory, averred the commanding general of Army Air Forces, Carl "Tooey" Spaatz.[12]

In doing so, Snyder's "steadfast friendliness and support" ensured that he bonded not only with Assistant Secretary of War for Air Robert Lovett, and with Will Clayton (who also worked in this massive financial complex), but especially with George Marshall.[13] And it was Snyder to whom Marshall—based on Snyder's omnicompetence and unconcern about taking credit—showed a rare sentimentality. Their unique, easygoing amity provided a sheet anchor in Truman's cabinet against the gales of 1947 and 1948.

The ties between Marshall and Snyder were surpassed only by

Snyder's intimacy with Harry Truman. Elected in 1934 and then again in 1940, Senator Truman rose to prominence in 1941 by chairing the Special Committee to Investigate the National Defense Program. He had to make the enormous scope of war contracts as honest as possible. Only General Marshall favored Truman's plans. And Snyder. Behind the scenes, Synder had helped Truman establish the committee as a policing power over industry. He then helped shape the committee, and, in secret, relayed the DPC's suspicions about any malfeasance to Senate investigators. In November 1944, as vice president elect, Truman asked Snyder—who had just returned to St. Louis banking—to promise to drop everything should FDR die in office, as each believed imminent. Truman phoned Snyder late on the night of FDR's death, and Snyder became Truman's first appointment to office—as federal loan administrator. With unanimous Senate approval, Snyder took responsibility for the largest lending operations in the world.

Within two months, a job followed that was truly a make-it-or-break-it proposition for the nation. It was known colloquially as "assistant president" (not as "assistant to the president"). As director of the Office of War Mobilization and Reconversion, Snyder had to transform an economy devoted to total war into one that could uphold an era of peace. Lots of experts predicted unemployment of eight to ten million amid a brief postwar boom followed by economic collapse. Yet the widely heralded depression was averted. Industry got restructured with a speed that surpassed even that of the buildup.

Because standing up the war machine, and then dismantling it, had not happened automatically, Truman appointed Snyder to the Treasury. He became the department's first modern secretary—revamping an institution that had far more in common with the Treasury of Albert Gallatin in 1801 than the one we know today. Snyder also dominated the Federal Reserve unlike any secretary before or since. To journalists and Wall Streeters, he was "the man who holds our economic reins," and he steadied the nation's economy during an era when America was rebuilding a war-torn world.[14] Or at least he did when not advised by George Marshall to shut down the Treasury for a day so that they could go fly-fishing in Virginia. And, among other responsibilities, Snyder was second in the line of White House succession, right after Marshall.

Snyder was by far the most influential figure of the Truman administration, besides the president, and its longest-serving cabinet member. He was an overarching presence of these years who shaped the key domestic policy issues, and many international ones, too, such as Palestine, NATO, and the Korean War. Moreover, his decisions would be felt long after he and Truman left office in 1953.

TRUMAN ADDRESSED A JOINT SESSION OF CONGRESS JUST FIVE days after he assembled this stalwart trio of Snyder, Forrestal, and Acheson. He made the case directly to support Greece and Turkey, and this initiative became part of a larger policy to be known as the Truman Doctrine. Rather sweepingly, the United States pledged to uphold countries threatened by "terrorist activities," though the Russians weren't named as instigators. There was no other friend to which "democratic Greece could turn," as it confronted "terror and oppression," said the president. "Greek's [*sic*] neighbor, Turkey," similarly needed help. In the past, all this might have been provided by Britain, but no longer, he continued, because Britain was "liquidating" its role in various parts of the world.[15]

Legend has it that Truman and the State Department worked seamlessly to develop this position, and indeed Joseph Jones boasts that never before had "such efficiency in the government" been witnessed.[16] In fact, Truman's speech was heavily improvised, as shown by its having to garb U.S. involvement in a democratic crusade without pausing to ask, And then what? An overall $400 million appropriation was requested, and it seemed likely U.S. troops would follow, but the fact that Greece was run by a venal, murderous dictatorship went unmentioned.

Whitehall officials choked on Truman's statement that Britain was "liquidating" anything. They also recognized the unformed thinking. "With our better-oiled machinery," a top political adviser claimed to Bevin, "we should probably, in similar circumstances, have produced a better finished article."[17] The Russians, for their part, couldn't decide whom to blame for Truman's sudden and expansive declaration. Their usual target was Bevin and his hard-line stance against Soviet ambitions. But Kremlin propagandists increasingly described America as the "principal driving force of the imperialist camp."[18] As a result, *Pravda*, the official newspaper of the Soviet Communist Party, began to refer to the "Truman-Bevin" policy of plotting war.

Americans spoke at this point of "chain reactions." If Greece fell, or "went," well-informed people argued, so would India and the Dutch East Indies, not to mention nearby France and Italy.[19] Iran would also fall to Russia, and who knew what else, because, by implication, Britain seemed to be abandoning Suez as well.

The issue of "liquidation" aside, the British were pleased that dollars would flow to Greece and Turkey. Why should they do it all? The Chancellor of the Exchequer had been warning Attlee's cabinet through 1946 that Greece was a bad investment for taxpayers—which was the reason that Bevin had announced March 31 as the deadline for British withdrawal. It was the end of Britain's fiscal year. His negotiating style featured what he called "shock tactics," and that's what he was using here to get the hesitant Americans to pony up instead. His loyal lieutenants seem to have approved. "We have been taken for granted for too long," one of them wrote, "and it will do the American public no harm to see that our survival as a Great Power is a vital American interest."[20]

DURING 1946, BEVIN HAD BEEN INCLINED TO PULL ALL TROOPS OUT of Greece, hoping that might deprive Moscow of a source of grievance. His views had hardened since. His stance as an imperial statesman had hardened, too. In December, he had agreed with Attlee to withdraw troops from Greece, and, in cabinet during early February, he agreed again. Yet his mind was changing fast, as it had on the notion of pulling out of Egypt. The ongoing presence of British troops in Greece came to be important to him: even five thousand of them symbolized British power at the intersection of Europe and the Middle East. Moreover, in January and February the British army was urging him to push harder against the guerrillas with whatever advisers (former Special Air Service operators), infantrymen, and air assets could stay in place.

There was another factor. Despite what the Americans had been told, removing all British troops from Greece by the summer of 1947 was impossible. That was apparent once Attlee's government committed itself to evacuating all British forces from India by year's end and when it also announced plans to remove thousands of men from Egypt. Bottlenecks were likely even without shifting more large battalions of men with all their stores and heavy equipment from Greece. Above all, Bevin knew shipping, and there weren't the ships. Only in conditions of grave emergency could enough vessels have been found for a troop withdrawal of such size even by November 1947. Britain could redeploy nine thousand men between the end of March and July, as it had long planned to do, but that would still leave a big contingent in place that would be tricky to extract before April 1948—had Bevin even been inclined to do so, which he wasn't.

In truth, Bevin didn't intend to remove these soldiers. By early 1947 he was bluffing, as the weight of evidence shows. That went right past the Americans. Saying he had to extract the troops, as he did through most of 1947, was part of the shock tactics that he directed at Washington. The battalions weren't costing much, as the Foreign Office admitted two and a half years later, nor were they fully engaged in Greece's guerrilla war, because much of the manpower was concentrated around Athens to underscore political order. Marshall and Acheson cajoled and threatened Bevin to keep the troops in place, while he hemmed and hawed about supposedly having to make hard and costly decisions to oblige the Americans. His key purpose was to get U.S. aid, weaponry, and military guarantees to sustain Athens's government—and to back his own country's battalions as well.[21]

Whitehall had already designated some £70 million to £80 million to keep aiding Greece, should the jittery Americans not be persuaded to dash in with even more money. But Bevin hoped to put those pounds to better use elsewhere—such as in Africa, in Southeast Asia, in deeply subsidized Jordan and Iraq, or in the British occupation zone, which had the heaviest concentrations of Germany's industry and ruined cities.[22] He just had to get the Americans to rush emergency appropriations through Congress. Once that occurred, Bevin's staff also clarified something that they had left deliberately vague: decisions about Greece and Turkey, the Americans learned, had nothing to do with leaving Suez. There, the British forces would sit tight, and at this moment the Canal Zone contained some 169,000 personnel, including 73,000 Axis prisoners as added laborers.

Yes, the British were bluffing about pulling out all their troops from Greece, and Bevin kept doing so, telling Marshall through August that he was on the verge of withdrawing the final five to six thousand men. This was Bevin's labor unionist style: he didn't stop playing hardball until tangible winnings were in hand.[23]

But the Americans weren't entirely naive while he kept telling them that he was about to end Britain's presence. They were conducting a closely held bluff of their own against the British, as has also been unknown, and it offers two insights: how determined Washington was for those British soldiers to remain in Greece as a stabilizing force; and, at the same time, how ready the United States was even at this early date to have its fighting men oppose a Communist insurgency had the British followed through on their threat to depart.

AN ELABORATE DOUBLE GAME WAS UNDER WAY, AND THE AMERICAN bluff was this. Admiral Leahy, who knew nothing of the foreign secretary's artifice, gave an ultimatum to Britain's military chiefs: If their soldiers indeed abandoned Greece, he said, he'd need to find an equal number of U.S. troops as replacements, and they'd be taken from Germany. Leahy knew the British placed immense importance on maintaining as big a U.S. presence in central Europe as possible. "They will not be told that we actually have ready to move upon orders 5000 trained marines," he advised the president that August.[24] The marines were to be provided by the U.S. Navy; no GIs in fact needed to be diverted from anywhere, let alone Germany. This forgotten contingency plan to rush marines into Greece was code-named Operation Workdog, which is roughly how Fleet Admiral Leahy felt about having to fill in for the British Empire.

Leahy's ruse really wasn't necessary, because, as events unfolded, Bevin had already won out. British garrisons were staying, while the Americans had been induced to spend hugely to defeat the insurgency. Greece needed money, supplies, and military instructors—the first two of which the Americans delivered in abundance, and the third of which just required some two hundred advisers, because there'd be thousands of British troops remaining in place for whatever backup might be required.

Several months later, after Congress appropriated the $400 million that Truman had requested, Bevin even considered sending *more* troops to Greece in order to offset American political influence in the country.[25] By mid-January 1948, he was urging his government's defense minister that "it might be useful to put additional troops into Greece, provided that the Americans continue taking a firm line."[26] The last British units would remain into 1950, a year after the insurgency had collapsed, with counterinsurgency advisers staying on. But the Americans had been compelled to arrive long before.

NO MATTER HOW ONE LOOKS AT THESE EVENTS, BRITAIN CERTAINLY didn't "terminate assistance to Greece" in 1947, let alone yield to "financial exigencies" that compelled it "to withdraw from the eastern Mediterranean." The empire's muscle-flexing in that region hadn't even begun.

Even more far-fetched is the common belief that the United States was ever "hand-delivered the job of world policeman" during this drama, or ever thereafter.[27] What, we might ask, were the Americans to police? China? The Indian subcontinent? Southeast Asia? Africa? And with what? Instead, within the Foreign Office, Bevin described what he had accomplished as "casting the net" over the Americans. Logically enough, he'd cast it again, and farther. He had bigger fish to fry than Greece.

On September 1, while still debating troop withdrawals with the Americans, Bevin proposed an ambitious bilateral conference that would establish a joint strategy for all the Middle East from Afghanistan to North Africa. Here he was playing to Britain's strengths. Truman and Marshall accepted his idea, and what became known as the Pentagon Talks—involving top officials from the Foreign Office and State, as well as the U.S. and British chiefs of staff—were set to occur in October.

By then, the Americans were descending on Athens with their typical energy: checkbooks were opened, and communications equipment unloaded; Air Transport Command flew in aid experts and newsmen. A U.S. military planning and advisory group had gotten to work in July, and Secretary Marshall ordered it to assess the needs of the Greek army and to offer training in counterguerrilla warfare. The U.S. Navy began sending its ships at least once every six months into every Greek harbor deep enough to enter. The administration told Congress that no U.S. combat troops per se were in Greece—yet, as advisers, U.S. Army officers were allowed to accompany Greek forces on operations.

Today we're familiar with such slippery slopes, but in Greece the U.S. aid and military presence proved effective. America's first postwar counterinsurgency experience was also essentially painless against rebels who received no direct Russian support and whose Balkan patrons ended up at loggerheads. It would be cited in Washington as a model to follow in the utterly different circumstances of, first, Taiwan in early 1950, then Korea, and, by the 1960s, Vietnam.

British officials were pleased that the Americans were underwriting the Hellenic monarchy's expensive dictatorship. Nonetheless, it was Britain that had held primacy on and off in Greece at least since the 1850s, and in its diminished condition the Foreign Office was sensitive to any slights. To underscore the empire's stature, the license plate of His Majesty's ambassador had for decades been CD1, for *Corps Diplomatique*. Sinuous Greek courtiers wouldn't rescind the plate, but they also wanted to ingratiate themselves with the Americans. Thus, when Henry F. Grady arrived the following May as President Truman's new ambassador, he was issued plate CD100.[28]

DURING FEBRUARY 1947, THE AMERICANS RECOGNIZED THAT A RARE sort of ambassador would be needed in London to handle the British Empire and to deal with Bevin—especially as Congress was trying to figure out if Britain was a land of socialist slackers or of commercial predators, an empire of colonial exploiters or of global peacekeepers. The post had been vacant since October 1946. That's when Truman had asked the multimillionaire Averell Harriman—onetime Lend-Lease operations chief who had served as ambassador since April, after shifting over from Moscow—to be his secretary of commerce. In December, the Truman administration had appointed O. Max Gardner, a rich former North Carolina governor, but on the morning he was to sail for Southampton, Gardner died of a heart attack in his New York hotel, after much celebration the night before.

George Marshall hurriedly stepped in. Nearly by the day, this role in

London was becoming too important to hand to a political loyalist. Therefore, he brought Lewis Douglas, fifty-two, the president of the Mutual Life Insurance Company of New York, to Truman's attention. Similar to John Wesley Snyder, and to Marshall, Douglas soon became indispensable.

On February 12, six days after Gardner's demise, the White House switchboard found Douglas at the Pioneer hotel in Tucson, Arizona, about fifty miles north of his twenty-thousand-acre ranch near Sonoita. Truman and Marshall together offered him the ambassadorship. The New York insurance CEO was in fact an Arizonan through and through. Douglas's father, known as Rawhide Jimmy, had named the border town of Douglas after himself and his own father, James, once they'd both hit it big with the Copper Queen mine at Bisbee and the UVX copper mine at Jerome.

Thirteen-year-old "Lew," whose frontier childhood included being chased by renegade Apaches, was sent east to the Hackley School, in Tarrytown, New York, before entering Amherst, class of 1916, followed by a year at MIT to study metallurgy. He deployed to France as an army lieutenant and saw action at St.-Mihiel, the Meuse-Argonne, and Ypres-Lys. He returned to Amherst for spring semester 1920 as teaching assistant to the British Christian socialist R. H. Tawney and then headed home to make his name. In 1926, he was elected as Arizona's sole member of Congress. He was a conservative Democrat, and in 1933, at the start of his presidency, Roosevelt appointed him director of the Bureau of the Budget. Tall and lean, with a welcoming grin and candid brown eyes, he became known in Washington for a distinguished appearance that added a certain dignity to the mass of people arriving to staff FDR's New Deal. He lasted only eighteen months before condemning the administration as a "dictatorship" and resigning angrily. In Douglas's opinion, the president's devaluation of the dollar that year by 41 percent, in hopes of fixing the Depression, meant the end of Western civilization. FDR then observed that Douglas's mind ran "more to dollars than humanity," and the remark stuck.[29]

In fact, dollars weren't among Douglas's priorities, and from 1937 to 1939, as his family grew, he served as principal of McGill University in Montreal. Yet he became restless, went to Mutual Life, and, in parallel, got politically active to fight Roosevelt's tyranny. He campaigned hard in 1940 for FDR's Republican opponent, Wendell Willkie, the Wall Street utilities lawyer. Within months of Willkie's defeat, and with the Nazis dominating Europe, Douglas patriotically headed a petition drive to support the president's Lend-Lease initiative. That helped redeem him with the White House. Roosevelt, unlike Churchill, tended to bear grudges, and it was asking a lot for FDR to give Douglas another high appointment when America joined the war in December 1941, though the president did. Douglas became deputy administrator at the War Shipping Administration, where he cracked the cargo bottleneck, and the army chief of staff, George Marshall—a master of logistics himself—took notice. Not that Douglas would endorse FDR in 1944.

Quick confirmation of this pro-laissez-faire millionaire by the Republican-controlled Senate could be taken for granted. *The New Republic*, that era's leading progressive magazine, made a wry comparison: sending Lew Douglas to "the land of Keynes" was like "sending a Methodist missionary as ambassador to the Pope."[30] On March 15, he boarded the fourteen-hour flight to London, in those pre-jet days with refueling in Newfoundland, and his wife and daughter followed. The family settled into the ambassador's residence at 14 Princes Gate, opposite Hyde Park, which J. P. Morgan's son, Jack, a pivotal financier for Britain during World War I, had given to the U.S. government. They lived as simply as possible, under the circumstances, and the family voluntarily used food coupons to adhere to Britain's ration laws.

Soon after Douglas began work at the five-story, brick-and-columned embassy at 1 Grosvenor Square, he and Ernest Bevin were on a first-name basis, a unique development in those days for a British foreign secretary and an ambassador. Before long, it was easy to agree with *Time* magazine's judgment that Lewis Douglas was "the most important diplomat of the most powerful country in the world."[31]

DOUGLAS ARRIVED IN LONDON DURING BRITAIN'S BLEAKEST PEACE-time era since the "Hungry Forties" a century before, which had been another period of slumping trade, unemployment, and bad harvests. The coal industry had been nationalized on January 1, and Bevin reminded his countrymen that coal, from the island's 970 mines, was "the foundation of our prosperity."[32] The shortages that were being experienced, however, didn't result from nationalization. They had been decades in the making: no new pits had been dug for years; the infrastructure was crippled; there was no electrical grid for modern equipment; miners used outdated methods, among them blinded ponies to pull pit cars. Moreover, Britain's 692,000 miners composed a truly lumpen proletariat, of long and angry memory, that had been created by ham-fisted private ownership.

Now stocks of coal were piled up at snowbound railheads. Shipments faltered, then couldn't get through to power stations, which closed for lack of fuel. Industry ground to a halt. Radio broadcasts were curtailed, and newspapers had fewer and smaller pages. Women with bony faces and deep-set eyes lined up for potatoes, which were rationed at three pounds per week. In naval shipyards, submarines with their giant batteries were used to provide electricity. The Ministry of Fuel and Power saw fit to impose pathetic economies in its "Control of Fuel (Dog Racecourse) Order," which banned greyhound racing, a heavily working-class recreation.[33] In March came the floods from melting snow.

Americans nevertheless were hoping that the British Empire could play a supportive role. Compared with a year earlier, opinion polls showed that those who blamed the British for international trouble dropped from 19 to 9 percent, although, as a clever dispatch from the Washington embassy observed, Americans supposed this stemmed from "increased weakness rather than diminished wickedness."[34] Fears of Russia, on the other hand, were rising: Americans who believed the Kremlin sought to dominate the world jumped from 39 to 52 percent.

Another point in Britain's favor—which Washington insiders recognized—was Bevin's ability to gather some very tough anti-Communists around him as he drew in support from the Labour Party's fractious left wing. One of his backers in the cabinet, at least on these matters, was the equally fearsome Aneurin (Nye) Bevan, who described himself as "a projectile discharged from the Welsh valleys."[35] As minister of health, Bevan involved himself in everything, like demanding the extinction of the Tory Party. Churchill called him the "Minister of

Disease" and advised him to seek psychiatric care as one of the first patients in the new National Health Service.[36]

Nye Bevan, at late middle age, had short legs, a big head, eyes that smoldered with resentment, and a smooth pudgy face that made him look unthreatening—to people who didn't know him, until he spoke with a rapier tongue. Taking on Churchill at the height of his pride, as Bevan did routinely, was no weakling's work. He'd gone down into the pits at thirteen and was now set on changing Britain from top to bottom, but he didn't disagree at all with maintaining some form of national greatness. Like Churchill and the foreign secretary, Nye Bevan saw Nazism and Stalinism as essentially the same. But to him, oligopolistic America wasn't much better. It was not a responsible presence for stability and decency in the world. Yet it was clear where he would stand should worse come to worst. Today it's called "preventive war." If Soviet steel production ever exceeded twenty-five million tons annually, he concluded, Britain, perhaps in league with America, would have to consider attacking.[37] Otherwise the Soviet Union might become too strong to destroy. As Arthur Deakin, the onetime steelworker who'd taken over leadership of Ernest Bevin's union, the TGWU, said of the Kremlin's wolves, "We cannot get along with people like that."[38]

None of these men were from a school of moderation. Nor were they about to lead Britain to retreat from global power. They had no sense of the empire being lost and no intention to see tycoons from Chicago or Houston slice up the Asian subcontinent or the Middle East.[39] To Moscow, they represented a direct threat of unknown dimensions. Their country was now the standard-bearer of social democracy but remained the chief protagonist of colonial imperialism, despite the economic troubles and the imminent withdrawals from India and Palestine. For the Russians, this was a dangerously unprecedented combination.

AMERICANS IN 1947 WERE HYPOCHONDRIACS ABOUT THEIR OWN prospects. No matter that their workforce of nearly sixty million was surging upward with modern equipment and capable management and that consumer income was reaching new heights. They lived under the Depression's shadow, and few expected the immense productivity that would unfold. Even Keynes, preeminent lord of finance, hadn't foreseen the promise of grease-under-the-fingernails U.S. industry. He dealt with the partners at J. P. Morgan & Co., with corporate lawyers such as Dean Acheson and global traders like Will Clayton, not with the titans of Detroit and Pittsburgh. He had thought it unlikely America would run a big trading surplus, never anticipating the extent of the Republic's all-out industrial strength.

By the early spring, however, decision makers in Washington could see that it didn't make sense to keep doling out money for emergency after emergency in Europe. An efficient approach was needed—and fast, because recovery on the Continent was staggeringly slow. France and Italy, let alone Greece, appeared to be teetering on collapse.

Then on June 5, under the green elms at Harvard's 296th commencement, Secretary Marshall spoke of America assisting in Europe's rebirth, creating an initiative that Truman would name the "Marshall Plan." But it began unhappily. At State, the shrewd Will Clayton, serving as undersecretary for economic affairs, had been overseas until mid-May and wasn't involved in the preparatory staff work. Acheson was preoccupied with running the department. Marshall himself was spread thin, even spending early March to late April negotiating in Moscow. He had arrived from London just days before the speech. So other people were at the forefront of what transpired.

Today it's said that Marshall's "words had been crafted and recrafted by some of the most brilliant minds at the State Department and on its Policy Planning Staff." That would include George Kennan, who had returned to Washington the previous May from the embassy in Moscow, and who now directed the planning bureau. Kennan recalled that the substance of the Harvard speech "was largely my own."[40] However, those brilliant minds had barely consulted the Treasury Department on the matter of spending unprecedented billions of dollars in foreign aid. That was a very bad idea.

Today, John Wesley Snyder is unknown. There's a foolish Wikipedia post, two or three Federal Reserve monographs mention him, and he makes only cameo appearances in the better biographies of Truman. Like Marshall, he wrote no memoir and kept no diary. He dealt with the press at a courteous distance, and he, too, never cared to defend his decisions in public. Besides the fact that he worked largely with the hard details of finance, rather than in the state papers of diplomacy, there's another reason why he has been overlooked.

The dean of Washington newsmen during those years was *The New York Times'* distinguished Arthur Krock. Soon after Snyder was appointed Treasury secretary in June 1946, Krock observed that Snyder was "the object of one of the most implacable campaigns of detraction that has been conducted here since the intellectuals of the New Deal developed this technique to get rid of officials in conflict with their ideas."[41] Snyder, after all, not only had firm beliefs on government debt, but, it was said, he held a bias toward business. Some of those doctrinaire intellectuals, and many of their heirs, would write the histories.

By this time, Snyder had unique experience handling complex problems at the nexus of finance and politics. He was also Harry Truman's alter ego. They even looked similar despite Snyder being twelve years younger: small-city midwestern businessmen with the same wire-frame eyeglasses, Masonic rings, and gray double-breasted suits covering square builds of medium height. Each was just a high school graduate. They both possessed an easy laugh, were left-handed, and had one child—daughters who became friends. Snyder was the third of six children from hardscrabble Jonesboro, Arkansas. He quit Vanderbilt University after nine months for lack of money and soon joined the army when America went to war in 1917. He became a captain in the 57th Field Artillery Brigade, 32nd Division, and saw heavy action in France. In 1928, he met another artillery reserve officer, Lieutenant Colonel Harry S. Truman, at summer training camp. From the start of their friendship at Fort Riley, they would spend hours together talking of history, and, later in Washington, before Truman's presidency, they'd take day trips to walk the battlefields of Bull Run, Antietam, and Gettysburg.

By June 1947, as Treasury secretary, John Snyder chaired the National Advisory Council, a body newly created by Congress to be the "coordinating agency for United States international financial policy." This made him responsible for the terms of foreign assistance programs—that is, for the Marshall Plan, and much else. At Treasury, Snyder had started to build an elite cadre of civil servants on the model of Whitehall, the legacy of which can be seen today. One of his first steps in that direction was, in 1945, to get William McChesney Martin, then thirty-nine and known as the "boy wonder of Wall Street," discharged from the army and appointed chairman of the Export-Import Bank, the independent export credit agency that in fact reported to Snyder. Martin had the reputation of being a "hard banker," and, since early 1946, he had often opposed State on politically motivated loans. Nor had Martin heard much of anything about what State was planning, and he too sat on the National Advisory Council.

SECRETARY SNYDER HAD NO DISAGREEMENT WITH GEORGE MAR-shall over the Harvard speech. It's difficult to find any issue over which they disagreed. The trouble was in that "crafting" and "recrafting"—essentially in the expression of the Marshall statement. Marshall had unwittingly made an outright offer that the United States would pick up the entire relief and recovery tab for Europe. Or such was the impression, as ever more fantastic sums were day by day attached to his words. Suddenly a score, or maybe two, of billions of dollars was being bandied about in the press, on Capitol Hill, and in Europe.

Snyder had to counteract the astronomical estimates of how much the recovery tab would cost the United States. After all, foreign-aid programs on such an unheard-of scale had to exist within balanced budgets. To Snyder, the problem was a matter of emphasis, and a serious one. At the same time, he recognized that the confusion arose from a certain obliviousness at the middle rung of the State Department about how the country worked.

Three weeks after the Harvard speech, Snyder laid it down that this proposal shouldn't be construed as an offer of unlimited U.S. aid, nor as an invitation to European countries to compose wish lists of "what they need or want."[42] The United States was still burdened by war debt, and no one knew for certain whether the Depression had been licked. Even to suggest that Washington would meet open-ended outlays for goods and services, he argued, could endanger the U.S. economy. Not that he wasn't sympathetic, having personally examined conditions in Europe for Truman. But State couldn't run off half-cocked.

Truman had to intervene the next morning at a press conference, on

June 26. He said that he agreed with *both* his two most senior cabinet secretaries: rumors that the administration was in disarray were unfounded. Fine, but the confusion had three consequences. First, the Soviet news agency, Tass, had gotten the jump several hours before Truman spoke. In broadcasts and editorials, Moscow began a campaign to worsen the impression among stunned European observers that this dispute was 1919 all over again; for all their clamor, the Americans were unreliable and getting ready to pack up and retreat home, as after the last war. Second, there'd be little chance that the Marshall Plan would be run by the State Department, no matter what the Bureau of the Budget might recommend later that year.[43] And third, the Republican Congress—which held the purse strings—had been given reason to fear a spending spree despite Snyder's intervention.

In the Senate dwelled Robert Taft, fifty-eight, son of the twenty-seventh president and revered as "Mr. Republican" among conservatives of his day. Top of his class at Harvard Law, Taft could read a balance sheet. Not that he was inclined to write checks anyway, but the endless appropriations that had been implied that day at Harvard sounded like pouring dollars into an "Operation Rathole." Harsher voices echoed in the House, where sat the Nebraska isolationist Howard Buffett, who accused Truman of using "tricks of political terrorism" to extract taxpayer money. Other critics simply argued that the untold billions could better be spent at home as retail prices climbed.

Bevin was unfazed, however. He'd gotten to know Snyder well since 1945. Something would be resolved. So Bevin spearheaded a conference in Paris from July to mid-September that brought together the nations of Western Europe to present their needs coherently to Washington. He did this while ensuring that the Russians didn't attempt to join the Marshall initiative—Molotov thereafter preventing the nations of Eastern Europe, nearly all under Soviet domination, from taking part. Laying the groundwork, Bevin said, was "one of the impossible things that would be done as soon as it could be worked out."[44]

AMERICANS THESE MONTHS WERE ENGROSSED BY A RISING SENSE of danger. George Kennan aired his concerns in the July issue of *Foreign*

Affairs, a quarterly journal with 19,873 subscribers. His article, "The Sources of Soviet Conduct," was a version of the long telegram that he had sent in February 1946, which had described "the Kremlin's neurotic view of world affairs" (echoing the Freudian jargon).[45] Within a month, *Life* magazine, the Time Inc. picture chronicler of its era, which claimed to be read by 44.4 percent of college-educated males, published excerpts, as did the mass circulation *Reader's Digest* in October.[46] It all went viral.

"The Sources of Soviet Conduct" spoke to America's own anxieties. In the article, Kennan urged that Russia be contained by firm resistance. If America and its friends were patient and measured, a settlement with the Kremlin might eventually be possible, or the Soviet Union could even break up. Yet Kennan wound the essay down with a gloss that could have been signed by Pollyanna and the elder field marshal von Moltke. He hoped that his readers should "experience a certain gratitude to Providence which, by providing the American people with this implacable challenge, has made their entire security as a nation dependent upon their pulling together and accepting the responsibilities of moral and political leadership that history plainly intended them to bear."[47] This was silly. It suggested that war, even cold war, could not only build the health of the state but also improve the moral health of the people. The article did seem to get Stalinism right—even if few agreed on what Kennan meant by "containment"—and that's what stuck.

Today, the desperate improvisations of these fateful months—the Truman Doctrine, the Marshall Plan, and Kennan's articulation of containment—are described as the formation of a "strategy," or even of a "grand strategy."[48] But this view doesn't fit (even when adding in the North Atlantic Treaty two years later). Underpinnings of a strategy must have as few contradictions as possible. All the entities engaged need to be coordinated and aware of the others' necessities. Moving higher, a grand strategy entails unifying long-term ends with the most broad-based means. In a constitutional country, it involves conciliating and encouraging those who form the currents of national opinion and energy. Significantly, it takes time and knowledge to formulate a grand strategy, or at least it takes being aware of the many steps under way. In the spring of 1947 there wasn't an opportunity for all this, or so beleaguered U.S. decision makers had reason to believe.

Instead, the sequence of Truman Doctrine–Marshall Plan–Containment was just shy of winging it. The American public was up for little of this. Emergencies were being met with a mélange of tactics and with minimal long-term perspective. There was little interconnectedness; witness the difficulties between State and Treasury, or the incurious excitements over Greece. Not least, had these efforts been brought under any strategic direction, the U.S. armed forces wouldn't have been kept on a shoestring. It is rationalizing to say, well after the fact, that a grand strategy was even being imagined.

HEADLINES IN THE MIDSUMMER OF 1947 WERE DOMINATED NOT BY the Marshall Plan but by the Senate's spectacular investigation of Howard Hughes, the country's richest man and the president of Texas's Hughes Tool Company. Hughes had contracted to deliver reconnaissance and cargo planes to the Pentagon. Crashes, cancellations, and chicanery within the industry led a subcommittee to allege fraud. At the time, it was believed on both sides of the Atlantic that British aviation manufacturers had a decisive lead over the United States. During testimony, Hughes had to explain the context of his setbacks by insisting that he "did not agree about England's technical supremacy over us."[49] These were just routine screwups, he argued, and before long the case against him fizzled. As it did, the spotlight shifted once Britain plunged into financial disaster. Half the total credits from less than a year before had vanished. A further loan on any bearable terms wasn't in the picture.

Where had the money gone? In Washington, the new undersecretary of state Robert "Bob" Lovett was the right person to explain what had happened. He stepped into that office in July, when Dean Acheson left, saying he couldn't live on $10,000 a year. As a partner at Brown Brothers Harriman, the private bank at 61 Wall Street, Lovett had given scores of boardroom presentations to corporate chairmen whose hold on economics was slightly vague. He was also the firm's foreign-exchange expert. Now he offered a tutorial to President Truman and the cabinet. To start, U.S. inflation had slashed the loan's buying power by some $1 billion. In basic terms, even though Britain's productivity and exports were up, they weren't up enough to pay for imported goods in dollars. That left a gap in the balance of payments. Britain also served as banker to the sterling area, so it had to support not only its own deficit but the deficits of other sterling countries, which were running down their accounts in London. Britain was in the middle, with the terms of trade gnawing at it from both sides. It was not enough for Britain that markets existed for its goods. They had to be hard-currency markets whose yields could be traded worldwide. As Britain kept losing dollars, it risked having to depend for its survival on bilateral barter deals.

The best argument for taking the loan had been to obtain raw materials and specialized industrial equipment needed to get the country on sound footing. But 24 percent of the dollars were spent overseas to buy food, with more than expected being paid to the hard-currency countries like the United States, Canada, and beef-supplying Argentina. Additionally, 32 percent was said to be puffed away on American tobacco. (Smoking was deemed a point of public morale.) Then include spending on imported Hollywood movies, gasoline, and miscellaneous manufactured goods. This all added up to at least 80 percent of the loan just being devoted to living from hand to mouth. And there was some $60 million that had gone to feed the Germans. Looming over this sorry balance sheet, moreover, was overseas military and civil spending. To make matters worse, Britain, under the terms of the previous year's Financial Agreement, was obliged to make sterling convertible on July 15, 1947.

At the State Department, Kennan hired consultants to help produce a study. Together, they determined that Britain had become, regrettably, a socialist economy and, alas, one clogged with waste. But Kennan knew nothing of economics, nor much about Britain. He believed it to be no more sustainable than the northeastern United States might have been had it stood alone as a nation. Britain's five mail deliveries a day astounded Kennan, who didn't know that only some 12 percent of the population had phones and that cars were still a middle-class luxury, which made the Royal Mail essentially a public messenger service. He and his consultants calculated 440,000 people to be making a living from the football pools, while 75,000 accountants and clerks were doing the same in dog racing.[50] These findings were largely ridiculous. Much of Kennan's information was Tory propaganda, which he and his study group swallowed uncritically. Like soccer, for instance, greyhound racing was an activity disdained by Conservative Party toffs, in contrast, say, to racing at Ascot or Newmarket.[51]

For advice on this predicament, Truman turned to Snyder, who brought Kennan's findings to the president's attention during a cabinet meeting on August 29. "The crux of the whole matter is that men will only work for incentives," Snyder told his friend, "and the British are not producing the incentives, except in the form of dog races, soccer matches and horse racing."[52] For the moment, there was no reason for Snyder to recognize the report's shoddiness, though before long he had ample reason to distrust its author.

AT LEAST ONE THING WAS CERTAIN THAT SUMMER: IF BRITAIN MADE sterling convertible into U.S. dollars, as Attlee's government had pledged it would do a year earlier, calamity was in the offing. The many holders of sterling would be tempted to convert their pounds into dollars, thereby draining them from the Bank of England's reserves. After all, dollars were vital in buying raw materials, food, and products from outside the sterling area, meaning those nations such as the United States that would accept only dollars.

Yet Attlee's government had pledged in the Financial Agreement to adhere to convertibility, and it did so, as had been planned, on July 15. Ministers couldn't believe that anyone who owned British currency, once he or she had the choice, would suddenly exchange it all for dollars. But that's what happened. When the moment came, holders of sterling devoured Britain's solid international assets—its dollars, gold, and equities. "Safe as the Bank of England," people used to say. No longer.

Ambassador Lewis Douglas cabled Secretary Marshall about the "serious risk of losing most of Western Europe" once the dollar crisis worsened.[53] Trade flows would congeal, and who knew what might become of British military deployments in Germany, Austria, and Italy? Only European governments sympathetic to Moscow would survive the chaos. But there was worse. The more than two dozen countries that relied on sterling and that banked their overseas earnings in London could flounder as well, and those ranged from Iraq, Egypt, Jordan, Kuwait, and the Gulf sheikhdoms to India and Australia and Iceland. On Tuesday, August 12, the British confirmed those fears to Secretary Snyder firsthand. Sir Wilfred Eady, deputy governor of the Bank of England, and Sir Gordon Munro, the British Treasury representative in Washington, visited him in his corner office in the Treasury Department across from the East Wing of the White House. "There is a run on the bank," Eady said. Snyder had been one of the very few U.S. officials who had favored an outright grant to Britain the year before, rather than a loan. Now he learned that the Bank of England was hemorrhaging.[54]

Clearly the American loan had to be modified. Negotiations began on August 18 at the new State Department building—a boxy, soon-to-be-expanded, stripped-classical structure inherited from the War Department in the Foggy Bottom neighborhood. Secretary Snyder headed the talks for the Americans, though it would have been fitting for him to delegate this task to a senior U.S. Treasury expert. For across the table from him sat the redoubtable Sir Wilfred, who led Britain's mission team. Eady was a top-level career official from His Majesty's Treasury who had worked hand in glove with Keynes at Bretton Woods and in negotiating the original Anglo-American Financial Agreement. Within Whitehall, he was known for being more than shrewd, having behaved with impartial duplicity to both sides. But Snyder handled him well.

The temperature those days reached ninety-seven degrees, and at that time air-conditioning was spotty. Sweating diplomats spoke of a "blow-up in Parliament" and a "political explosion" in Congress.[55] London had one advantage, however. Snyder knew it would make little sense to pour hundreds of millions of dollars into Greece and Turkey, and more money into Iran and even South Korea, without also ensuring Britain's financial health—and, consequently, the political-military stability of Europe and the Middle East, among other places.

The Bank of England announced it would suspend sterling's convertibility the next day, on the nineteenth. U.S. negotiators balked. They claimed no time had been given to respond. A compromise was reached. Convertibility was halted on the twentieth, thereby preserving the pound's unreal value against the dollar—at least until the next time that there was a run on the bank. Snyder had little choice but to concur.

Britain essentially had defaulted on commitments barely a year old. But he also froze the remaining $400 million in accounts still left from the previous year's loan. It was a simple businesslike decision. In an editorial, *The Economist* charged the Americans with trying to ruin Britain—a libel considered so outrageous in Washington that it went straight to Truman's attention. An apology was demanded through the U.S. embassy and was given, abjectly, by the editor, Geoffrey Crowther.[56]

In late September, negotiations with Britain turned to examining the question of trade barriers, which had also been addressed in the previous year's Financial Agreement. "Imperial preference" still hadn't cracked. On the twenty-third, Bevin got double-teamed in his Foreign Office rooms by Will Clayton and Lew Douglas. Drop the tariff barriers, they told him, or get no help from the Marshall Plan. Bevin's aides documented the exchange as "blackmail."[57] But this time it was the Americans who were bluffing. In the weeks ahead, Bevin called them on it. Other than some compromises on tariffs, he made the sterling area *more* discriminatory in order to economize on the use of dollars.[58]

AMID THESE TENSIONS, AMBASSADOR DOUGLAS RETURNED HOME to help restore calm by testifying before the Senate Foreign Relations Committee in November—the first Senate hearings ever televised. Secretary of Commerce Averell Harriman joined him. The two of them had to dispel the prevailing impression on Capitol Hill that Britain's trading practices weren't much different from those of Hitler's Germany—a closed, centrally directed protectionist autarky and, in this case, one built around the empire and commonwealth.

On the twelfth, Douglas told the committee that it wasn't America's concern whether Britain produced its goods within a socialist or a capitalist system. He defended Labour's nationalization of the coal industry, considering its "squalid history" under indifferent private owners. Being scion to a mining fortune gave him authority. The white marble Caucus Room on the Senate Office Building's third floor was otherwise still. Douglas sounded like a Foreign Office mandarin when adding that "through lack of training" Americans were unable to assume defense burdens in distant lands unknown to them.[59] That's how it appeared even to such assertively internationalist men as he. Douglas and his friends might talk of U.S. "world leadership," but they were hesitant. The empire and commonwealth had to serve as an outer fortress.

Harriman's testimony followed. Fifty-six years old, six feet two, and faultlessly tailored, Harriman was a Gilded Age–type figure. In 1913, the year he graduated from Yale, he had inherited America's largest fortune, and in the years since he had become a film entrepreneur, financier, New Deal convert, discreet womanizer, and eight-goal polo player. He was a striking figure, and he worked relentlessly, yet he was also known to be cold and tight.[60] In public life, he played rough and was unapologetic about it. U.S. diplomats called him the "Crocodile," for the way he would maintain a quiet demeanor and then suddenly bite with deadly force. "The socialists are our best friends in Europe," he simply told the senators.[61] There was an awkward pause, this having been said by an imposing American plutocrat in high office. The committee chairman, Arthur Vandenberg, asked if there were any more questions. There weren't.

And then, toward the end of the year, Snyder unfroze the remaining $400 million of the loan—a necessary move, he explained to reporters, in order to help the British maintain their austerity program. Britain could hold on, assisted by legislation late in 1947 for interim aid to Europe. *The Economist* prudently kept to its original editorial opinion that Secretary Snyder was "the most understanding and helpful of the American officials with whom the British delegation had to deal."[62] In Parliament and Whitehall, the same men who'd been cornered and besieged seven years earlier, in the summer of 1940, were confident that U.S. backing in some acceptable form would again arrive.

II. A CHILLING WORLD

Diplomacy at the top, 1947: Secretary of State George C. Marshall, Foreign Secretary
Ernest Bevin, and, in the middle, U.S. ambassador Lewis Douglas—"the most
important diplomat of the most powerful country in the world."

5

WARFARE STATES

We're not going to blow it like the British.

—Colonel Albert G. Boyd, head of the flight test division, to Captain
Chuck Yeager, in the summer of 1947, before the World War II ace
broke the sound barrier that October

D URING THE HEIGHT OF THE FINANCIAL CRISIS, FROM AUGUST TO
October 1947, senior officials from His Majesty's Treasury and the
Foreign Office were negotiating with Secretary John Snyder and Undersecretary of State Will Clayton to gain enough solvency to feed York-
shire miners. Nearly at the same time, on the other side of the Potomac, an
equally senior Foreign Office delegation, backed by high-level military
advisers, was at the Pentagon laying down the terms by which Britain
might cooperate with the United States in the Middle East. No one seems
to have found this contrast odd. In neither meeting did the Americans
hear a word about imperial retreat from anywhere.

The latter negotiations, known today as the Pentagon Talks, occurred
from October 16 to November 6. They were top secret. But the financial
ones under way at State were covered in the press, and the outcomes were
apparent. Newspapers explained, for instance, that Attlee's government

was tightening gasoline rationing and limiting imports that had to be paid for in dollars. That included Hollywood films. They were suddenly taxed at 75 percent of gross earnings, despite one savvy negotiator who'd worked in Washington alongside Keynes having warned that the studios had "an extremely powerful lobby . . . capable of very considerable malice."[1]

An international incident followed within twenty-four hours of the tax being announced. The Motion Picture Association of America enacted a boycott against Britain's 4,709 cinemas. Exports of movies like *Nightmare Alley* with Tyrone Power were stopped immediately. The MPAA also sued Britain's government and retained Sullivan & Cromwell's senior partner, the Republican foreign policy adviser John Foster Dulles, for the job. The tax was a trade barrier anyone on Main Street could understand. So too was Britain's new "food before fags" levy on cigarette imports, which got R. J. Reynolds Co. and other tobacco behemoths to buttonhole the old bull committee chairmen in Congress, most of whom were southern Democrats. Both taxes were rescinded within months.

Americans still anticipated a robust near-term recovery for their former ally. From Capitol Hill, these movie and cigarette taxes looked like socialist claptrap rather than desperate measures by the Labour government to straighten out Britain's shaky finances. Americans still saw the empire and commonwealth as a grand, largely cohesive entity—one that could be an all-too-competitive trading rival, once it rebounded. Likewise, its supposed economic resilience meant that Washington regarded this colossus as a pretty substantial player when both sides tackled defense planning. That's seen at the Pentagon Talks.

On the first day, Undersecretary of State Bob Lovett heard Lieutenant General Sir Leslie Hollis, chief of staff to the British minister of defense, promise that Australia and New Zealand would be sending soldiers to the Middle East at the outbreak of a World War III to help secure imperial lifelines. That indeed showed impressive unity, although no one from either dominion was in the room to confirm this claim. Even India, which the British had ruled for nearly two hundred years, still looked to be securely within the empire's political, economic, and military sphere, to judge by what was and wasn't said between the two parties.

These three weeks of give-and-take churned out two dozen documents devoted to cooperation, and throughout this time British officials never addressed the fact that the peoples of the subcontinent—embracing two-thirds of the population recently under British rule—had been granted independence just two months before. Nor did Lovett or any other American make any observations about that epic development. Both sides merely discussed cooperation with "the Dominion of Pakistan" and the "Dominion of India," as if each of those states had existed independently forever within the British world system. While the talks were under way, furthermore, Hindu-majority India and Muslim-majority Pakistan were embroiled in a mutual religious genocide that accompanied the subcontinent's partition. This unfolding catastrophe—with between one and two million dead, and some fifteen million uprooted—also went unmentioned. U.S. government officials were deliberating with those of another huge united world power, the British Empire and Commonwealth, and neither side showed itself to be worrying about fissures within the other.

When Americans thought of the commonwealth, they generally accepted the picture offered by Whitehall—an evolving, multiracial, voluntary association that contained the familiar so-called white dominions (Canada, South Africa, Australia, and New Zealand) and the new dominions of India, Pakistan, and Ceylon (now Sri Lanka). But they didn't speak of it as such: "British Empire and Commonwealth" might be used by diplomats, but the usual term was "Britain" or the "British Empire." Functionally, it could be "the U.K." "England" was popular too and was used alike by Bevin and Churchill for its romantic ring.

As of August 1947, the commonwealth embraced the world's largest democracy, India, and the largest Muslim nation, Pakistan. There was no "abandonment of the Indian subcontinent," as is said today. Plausibly, the entire entity had become all the stronger. Nor did U.S. policy makers such as Lovett interpret independence as a "retreat" or a "surrender," let alone a result of Attlee's government having "appeased" the subcontinent's nationalists.[2] India had been advancing steadily to independence since the 1920s, and people at State, as well as savvy observers on Wall Street, knew it was merely a matter of time. The idea that the independence of Pakistan, India, Ceylon, and Burma (which didn't join the commonwealth) was synonymous with retreat and surrender is the interpretation of later years, and just echoes the last-ditch rhetoric of Churchill and other Tories who tried to stand in the way.

Of course, what had been the imperial Indian army—fielding over 2.5 million men by the end of World War II—no longer existed. But U.S. observers and Whitehall mandarins alike expected the armed forces of India and Pakistan to be British political-military assets within a tight alliance structure, replete with bagpipes, Sandhurst discipline, and expat advisers—just as those two dominions were expected to remain within the sterling area, as they did. Overall, Foreign Secretary Bevin claimed, the granting of independence displayed his country's "moral leadership of the world."[3]

INDUSTRY AND TECHNOLOGY ALSO MADE BRITAIN LOOK REDOUBTable because there was so much more to the economy in 1947 than dark satanic mills run by Old Etonians. Americans heard plenty about faltering coal mines, or about cotton mills with obsolescent spindles, or about shipyards dependent on worn-out machinery. But they likewise knew of Britain's military-industrial-science complex of war-related enterprise that's recognized today as the "British warfare state."[4] Washington saw it clearly: world aviation records were being broken in British aircraft, and British arms exports were booming in the decade after the war.

In many ways, Britain was running a war economy—one that included a huge financial commitment to military R&D and to arms production as well as deliberate overlaps between new military and civilian technologies such as atomic power, computing, and leading-edge chemical and biological research. The industries that supplied and supported Britain's military strength were maintained at a higher proportion of wartime output into the 1950s than that of similar U.S. industrial and scientific sectors that affected national security. Americans found this strength impressive and reassuring—which was important because, as one dispatch from the British embassy in Washington explained, they had grown "unalterably bored" by talk from London about the hardships Britain was enduring due to wartime sacrifices and the Luftwaffe's bombs.[5]

Jet aviation was Exhibit A of the "warfare state" complex in 1946–1947. Already in late 1944, the whine of gas turbine spools in fighter jets, along with the supersonic crack of Germany's V-2 long-range rockets, had signaled the arrival of a new age. The Royal Air Force's Gloster Meteor proved to be the first Allied jet fighter during World War II, and by 1946 Gloster's Meteor F.4 demonstrator G was the world's first civilian-registered jet aircraft. The latest military version entered service with the RAF in July, and then, on September 7, this version of the Meteor raised the world speed record to 616 miles per hour from 469 miles per hour—a record it had set earlier the same day. And the Gloster Aircraft Company was only one of Britain's manufacturers. Directors at Whitehall's Board of Trade asserted Britain's lead to be unassailable; nervous executives at Boeing, Lockheed, and the Glenn L. Martin Company feared they were right.

The ultimate contest in global aviation was to break the sound barrier, and only two nations could compete: Britain and the United States. Little was known about high-speed aerodynamics. Wind tunnels only measured to Mach 0.85. To go beyond that number to Mach 1, which is 760 miles per hour at sea level, test pilots encountered what they called the zone of the "Ugh-expected." Anything could happen. Many experts believed that the sonic wall couldn't be breached. A jet's controls would freeze, or buffeting would tear the plane apart.

If the sound barrier was to be broken, with the prospect of Britain dominating the frontiers of aviation for years to come, that would surely be achieved by the De Havilland Aircraft Company and by the De Havillands themselves. The business had been founded in 1920 by Geoffrey de Havilland, a mechanical engineer whose DH brand was first attached to creations of wood and cloth in World War I and then lived on to the threshold of the space age. De Havilland's youngest son, John, twenty-four, was killed in a midair collision in 1943 while flying a DH 98 Mosquito during a war training exercise. The eldest, Captain Geoffrey de Havilland Jr., became heir to this new dynasty as the company's chief test pilot. In the early evening of September 27, 1946, he was practicing for the breakthrough in his father's experimental, tailless, swept-wing DH 108 Swallow over the Thames estuary. He dove the jet down from ten thousand feet and got to the very edge of Mach 1, whether for practice or because, in fact, he decided to make history that day. The wings sheared off at seven thousand feet, when he reached Mach 0.9 (685 miles per hour). His body was found the following day with a broken neck in the mud of Egypt Bay.

This tragedy symbolized what Colonel Boyd meant, as shown in the epigraph at the start of this chapter, by "blow it." Surely his men could do better. That year—in the high elevations of California's Mojave Desert, at Muroc Air Base, among sagebrush and coyotes—some two dozen U.S. military pilots, civilian engineers, and mechanics were experimenting with supersonic flight. They followed every move of the British aviators, for whom they had no particularly warm feelings, and they also scrutinized what was being produced by Gloster, De Havilland, and other British firms such as English Electric and Hawker. These manufacturers, however, faced shortages of investment cash and skilled labor. They were also competing with a U.S. industry about five times as large and much more productive: its workforce was only twice the size of Britain's. Nonetheless, British corporations, such as De Havilland and also Rolls-Royce, which made the Nene jet engine, insisted that they possessed a qualitative edge. In their lights, that could trump America's advantages of scale.

U.S. companies were struggling too. Nearly two years after the war, defense spending had fallen from 40 percent of GDP to 6, and one result was that airplane sales plunged from $16 billion to $1 billion annually. The bankers who financed the onetime stunt flyer Glenn L. Martin wouldn't lend his pioneering enterprise—today's $45 billion Lockheed Martin—enough to fulfill orders. Republic Aviation, on Long Island, which was building the six-hundred-mile-per-hour F-84 Thunderjet, a single-seater capable of delivering an atomic bomb, kept losing money despite tax breaks.

The Russians, meanwhile, were ready to pay in gold for the world's most advanced engines and military planes. Doing business with the Americans was unlikely: U.S. export laws were tightening. Ohio's Goodyear Tire & Rubber Company, for example, couldn't even sell airplane tires to Russia. Besides, the Americans were also-rans. The Kremlin therefore turned to the British, who, as the Russians well knew, were desperate for hard-currency exports.[6]

It was in May 1946 that the British first agreed to sell top-performance jet engines, including Rolls-Royce's Nene, to Russia—a move agreed upon by Attlee and by Hugh Dalton, who was then Chancellor of the Exchequer, after having served, ironically, as minister of economic warfare under Churchill. Ernest Bevin signed on too, though he qualified his decision by saying he made it for the sake of thousands of British jobs. The chiefs of staff went along. Attlee's government hoped that in addition to helping the balance of payments, these military-oriented sales to Russia might, with a little patience, lead to vast opportunities for civil aviation, including routes across Eurasia for the British Overseas Airways Corporation (today's British Airways).

In February 1947, all of these officials approved additional sales, even after Moscow requested three De Havilland Vampire and three Gloster Meteor fighter jets. These were the latest RAF developments and hard for the government to approve, yet it did—while at least instructing the Ministry of Supply (whose work was overwhelmingly in defense) to tell the manufacturers to drag out their fifteen-month delivery time. Nevertheless, by March, fifty-five jet engines had been sold to Moscow with ninety-five still to come. Because the British believed their design and production skills would always lead the world, they also sold licenses to their technology, and Russian technicians were welcomed into British factories to learn how to manufacture these engines and fuselages.

Attlee's government was getting in deep by the time questions were raised in Parliament, during April, about selling Rolls-Royce Merlin *piston*—not jet—engines to Stalin. "The position is far worse than he dreams of," a Foreign Office trade specialist admitted to colleagues after one curious MP had expressed concerns about sales to Moscow. "We are selling the Russians up-to-date jets, let alone Merlins; we have sold or are on the point of selling 79 Derwents and Nenes. They regard Merlins as out of date, and are after actual jet aircraft too."[7] Pushback from the RAF began only when its chief, Marshal of the Royal Air Force Sir Arthur Tedder, suspected that British engines were heading straight into Russian frontline fighter planes.

The reckoning finally occurred on May 1, 1947, in Moscow. It was International Workers' Day, Marxism's annual rite of spring, and the weather was sunny and crisp in Red Square, which was filled with tanks, mobile artillery, and marching infantry. The Americans had known nothing of Britain's transactions, having been told that only obsolescent motors not on the secret list were being sent east. Standing on a reviewing stand in the square, U.S. and British military attachés shared Kodak film cassettes to photograph the flyover. They were equally shocked by what they saw: their practiced eyes recognized that the jets overhead were indistinguishable from the RAF's latest models. The Americans knew they had nothing that could compare, except for their most advanced fighter, North American Aviation's F-86—but that was still being tested and wouldn't be delivered to the air force until October. "We have felt very guilty about the whole business," scrawled one of those responsible at the Foreign Office on an internal memorandum.[8] They'd feel worse after trying to explain the situation to Washington.

The State Department threatened "far-reaching consequences." At the Pentagon, the forty-year-old major general Curtis LeMay, deputy chief of the air staff, said he'd never trust the British again.[9] They had to stop jet aviation sales to Moscow, he bristled, unless Washington specifically approved, and it might not be worth waiting.

In California, Captain Chuck Yeager, a twenty-four-year-old U.S. Army Air Forces ace, wasn't paying attention to politics. He'd never liked the British anyway, ever since he had arrived in England as an enlisted man during the war to fly P-51 Mustangs out of Suffolk. The laconic West Virginian looked remarkably like Sam Shepard, who played him in *The Right Stuff* (1983): tall, rangy, fearless.

That summer, Yeager was among the pilots in the windblown terrain of the high desert who were preparing to fly faster than sound. He did so on October 14, 1947, but the Pentagon immediately stamped everything top secret. Test pilots in England soon learned of it, however, and complaints arose that Yeager's orange Bell X-1, with its razor-thin wings and four rocket chambers, was a bullet-shaped British design anyway. And, besides, it didn't seem to be a real plane, because it had to be dropped from the belly of a B-29 Superfortress. So the competition continued. The next year, on September 9, John Derry, a De Havilland test pilot who'd be killed at the 1952 Farnborough Air Show, shattered the sound barrier conclusively in an actual military jet, a DH 108 Swallow. Success in the race for air superiority kept going back and forth across the Atlantic.

EACH OF THE THREE HAD DEMOBILIZED WITH THE PEACE. THE RED Army dropped troop levels from around 12 million to about 2,225,000 through 1948 (having mobilized more troops during the war and replacing far more casualties). The war had been devastating. James Forrestal's nineteen-year-old son, Michael—who served as a naval attaché and as a trained intelligence operative in Moscow during 1946–1947—shared personal assessments with his father via courier. For scores of miles outside Moscow, he reported, there was nothing to be seen except the burned remnants of villages and the circling flocks of ravens.[10] Stalin's tyrannical secretiveness ensured that the world knew little of the destruction within the Soviet Union, which is why military analysts in the West would talk for years about an unvarying number of 175 Red Army divisions poised to blitz to the English Channel.[11]

The Americans demobilized faster. By the summer of 1947, a military that was also 12 million strong had been reduced to 1,566,000 and not a single army division or air force group was rated ready for combat. The army even curtailed using expensive live-fire practice for training— a scrimping that Bevin wouldn't tolerate for Britain's armed forces. Three years later, on the cusp of the Korean War, the United States had only one division in western Germany, with but a single tank battalion in all the American forces in Europe. And within this battalion, there were only twelve tanks capable of fighting.

The slowest of the Three to demobilize was Britain. Of the 5.1 million soldiers, sailors, and airmen who had been on duty at war's end, 1.1 million were still under arms at the end of 1946, and Britain had about as many troops overseas as did the Americans. A million fighting men in a thousand garrisons and bases worldwide is how the American press would describe this force for years to come, and in this case the calculation wasn't far off.[12]

Britain's military budget in fiscal year 1947 was 25 percent of what it had been in 1945, at the height of the war. America's proportion was

16 percent. Defense spending alone accounted for Britain's entire dollar deficit during 1946, while its military manpower imposed labor shortages on industry. It retained conscription, whereas America abandoned it in 1946. Foreign Secretary Bevin kept promising his Treasury that he'd reduce forces overseas, but there were always reasons for delay: troops were needed in Germany until a formal peace treaty was reached (which didn't occur until 1990); twelve squadrons of bombers were required in the Mediterranean theater as a mobile strike force; the Royal Navy needed to patrol every ocean to defend sea communications; and so forth.

As a result, each had something to offer in the face of the gathering Russian threat. Collaboration wasn't easy, but it was managed best by the RAF and American airmen.

In the early summer of 1946, due to fears about how far Stalin would go against Turkey, the RAF's Arthur Tedder had prepared two airfields in England with pits and hoists to handle the Pentagon's ten-thousand-pound Mark 3 "Fat Man" implosion devices.[13] But to collaborate on deploying such weapons could be problematic. That August, Congress cut off all atomic R&D ties with Britain and Canada, whose scientists were no longer welcome in American laboratories and could not receive Q-level security clearances.[14] Should the British be uncooperative in turn—for example, by impeding U.S. access to uranium from Africa or from Canada's Port Radium, or thorium from India—the Americans were set to retaliate. They'd deny loans and aid. That's what Lovett meant several months later when he told the Senate Foreign Relations Committee that he was "keeping 'the big stick' in plain sight in the corner, even if we give no indication of an immediate disposition to use it."[15]

Cooperation between the two navies could be equally sensitive. America had built an enormous seagoing capability during the war, including fifteen battleships and seven aircraft carriers. Nearly half its ships, constituting the largest fleet in all history, dominated the Pacific. But the call of greatness couldn't be stilled at the Admiralty. In June 1946, the first sea lord insisted to Bevin that a strong fleet had to be kept on station in the Pacific to avoid appearing inferior to the Americans. To be sure, "the United States would be responsible for the Pacific area," said Admiral of the Fleet Sir John Cunningham, but he and his staff believed that the Royal Navy could—and should—command the Atlantic.[16] The idea wasn't far-fetched. Despite its size, the U.S. Navy by the summer didn't have enough sailors to take all its active fleet to sea and, in Europe, could only rustle up 170 combat-ready naval aviators.[17]

As 1946 ended, Bevin agreed to allow U.S. warships access to Malta, Gibraltar, and Britain's other Mediterranean ports. But only in emergencies. There was to be no formal arrangement with the U.S. Navy. All of this, Admiral Cunningham emphasized, was merely a favor to "a former ally."[18]

The Royal Navy was enduring its own upheavals: budget cuts arrived at the same time that the Admiralty began a high-tech modernization program, and it still had one foot in the past. Midshipmen entered the service at age thirteen, for example, and compulsory church attendance was required for enlisted men. Meanwhile, the biggest and fastest of the Royal Navy's battleships, HMS *Vanguard*, was commissioned in December—the world's last battleship ever to be launched, because aircraft carriers were about to rule the seas. In any event, the Admiralty kept reminding the Americans that naval mastery depended no longer on tonnage afloat but on innovations like angled carrier decks and naval fighter jets and on expertise in antisubmarine warfare. In such domains, the Royal Navy was unsurpassed.

U.S. admirals respected the Royal Navy. Vice Admiral Arthur Radford, who was then deputy chief of naval operations, recalled that he had not recognized until late in 1948 how seriously Britain had been hurt by the war. He'd been unaware until seeing for himself the food offered in the wardroom of HMS *Duke of York*, flagship of the Home Fleet, and the deteriorating scuppers on its teak quarterdeck, as well as the poor physical condition of its teenage seamen. The ship's medical officer told him they were of the "wartime generation" who had suffered from lack of vitamins while children.[19]

TRANSATLANTIC DEFENSE COOPERATION ALSO REQUIRED TIES OF A different sort. For more than a century, Britain's intelligence service had been feared in old-world ministries because of how its tentacles managed to snatch away jealously guarded secrets, and during the war the

Americans had set out to learn. Contrary to legend, wartime cooperation between MI6—also known as SIS, the Secret Intelligence Service—and America's Office of Strategic Services, which was the action-oriented forerunner of the CIA, had been abysmal. MI6 operatives scuttled much of what the OSS was trying to do, yet the Americans still had to depend on them (and on Britain's Strategic Operations Executive too) for bases as well as for special planes and submarines to infiltrate U.S. agents.[20] This had to change.

The first joint postwar intelligence arrangements were for "swapping" secrets. Washington expected access to British signals intelligence and code breaking, and the British complied. Experts from Australia, Canada, and New Zealand joined in the effort. From that evolved the inner circle of today's allied Five Eyes intelligence collaboration. But the Americans also wanted to see everything else they suspected Britain's Government Communications Headquarters to be scooping up—such as, they assumed, all the world's commercial cables, with insights that Whitehall certainly must be providing to British industries.[21] No such material existed, came the reply. The Americans were suspicious.

In September 1947, the CIA officially came into existence as part of the National Security Act, which codified the type of major government reorganization that tends to follow a convulsion. A unified Defense Department structure was formed, with the Navy Department moving to the Pentagon and Forrestal being chosen as the first defense secretary. An independent air force arrived, as did the National Security Council, to coordinate competing bureaucratic priorities, which Forrestal helped model on Britain's Committee of Imperial Defence. With the CIA, the Americans hoped to break once and for all their wartime dependence on British intelligence—an emphasis on self-sufficiency that the designers of the National Security Act knew would persuade Congress to open its wallet. Nevertheless, the Americans looked to MI6 for guidance, and there was enough working-level cooperation between the two organizations that the British strongly influenced the CIA's first generation of operatives.[22]

For several years after the war, MI6 outshone the Americans in the realm of intelligence gathering, which was intended to be the CIA's core mission. But from the start, the excitements of paramilitary adventures diverted the agency's "daring amateurs," as the historian David Fromkin calls these early enthusiasts, from the methodical tasks of stealing and studying secrets.[23]

In the organizational arrangements of that time, responsibility for managing what turned out to be a convergence of the military and the political-subversive came out of the State Department, and it's here, as one top CIA case officer recalled, that "the covert action that George Kennan had levied on the CIA" proved disastrous—in fact, more "stupid," as Howard Roman, an OSS veteran and early CIA operative with a Harvard Ph.D. in German, put it, than frequently recognized.[24] Kennan drafted instructions to inflict what he called "political warfare" on the Soviet Union. That entailed a peacetime resort to "economic warfare, preventive direct action, including sabotage, anti-sabotage, demolition and evacuation measures," which of course played into the hands of the better-practiced Soviet police state.[25]

As the CIA was being born in 1947, a key Russian spy had already embedded himself at the British embassy. Donald Maclean, thirty-four, tall, sandy-haired, considered handsome, had arrived in Washington in 1944 and risen to a pivotal role as counselor and head of Chancery. With conversational charm, Maclean enjoyed delivering what's known in British and U.S. embassies as the "security talk." He'd conduct somber one-on-one meetings in his office to warn newly arriving diplomats against sharing sensitive information with unauthorized persons. Moreover, he'd tell them that the embassy's phones were tapped by the U.S. government, which was trying to learn British trade secrets. Maclean oversaw the flow of all sensitive material between the two countries, including details about atomic weapons. He would work in Washington into 1948, when soon thereafter he became head of the American Department at the Foreign Office.

So it was a small blessing that summer of 1947 when, in Tokyo, the supreme commander of allied powers, General Douglas MacArthur, ignored the fact that MI6 had opened a station on his doorstep as part of Britain's liaison mission. MacArthur would have nothing to do with it, nor with the new CIA. He relied on intelligence from his own military staff and forbade any of the spy services to intrude in his vast area of responsibility. The head of the new MI6 station, however, was an astute

Canadian academic who had been born and reared in Japan. He reported something novel to London about the Americans he encountered. While they might be "amateurs on the European stage," when delving into political and military affairs, they had "studied the Pacific area very thoroughly" and could not "safely be regarded as clumsy amateurs in any part of the Far East where they operated in the past or are operating today."[26]

TWO WEEKS AFTER HE ARRIVED IN TOKYO ON AUGUST 30, 1945, Douglas MacArthur, a five-star general since December and, at sixty-five, the army's second-highest-ranking officer after George Marshall, established his headquarters in the squat, gray-stoned Dai-Ichi (Number One) insurance building that had survived the city's firebombing. MacArthur exercised complete control over the defeated enemy. He presented himself as a godlike figure to the Japanese, and to his devoted aides as well. He had the face of command, standing ramrod straight at a lithe five feet eleven and combining an imperial confidence with democratic symbolism—the khaki fatigues, open-necked shirt, crushed hat, and corncob pipe of legend.

The British Commonwealth Occupation Force—the BCOF, which comprised a quarter of the Allied troops in Japan that enforced unconditional surrender—was in place, but MacArthur gave them little to do. After nearly two years of his country being sidelined, the diplomat and historian of premodern Japan, Sir George Sansom, was exasperated. He had handled trade relations in Tokyo before the war and then returned in 1946 as part of the occupation. "Why didn't America just say it was going to make Japan a colony," he asked MacArthur's aides sarcastically, "and grant it dominion status in twenty-five years?" He was startled at the ingenuous reply: the idea sounded appealing but would never pass Congress.[27]

"If we had to consider narrow United Kingdom interests only," Attlee told his cabinet in June 1947, "there would be some military advantage and no disadvantage in the dissolution of the B.C.O.F."[28] But, as Attlee implied, a superpower must weigh many interests, and they're inevitably intertwined. Here they included supporting Australia, which feared not only Japan's revanchism but its peaceful rebirth as a fierce trading rival.

The British also had to look out for the crown colony of Malaya, the empire's chief dollar earner, which was uncomfortably near to Indochina, as the region was then called, where the Vietminh (League for the Independence of Vietnam) were fighting for independence from France. The defense of Hong Kong, which Bevin would soon be calling the "Berlin of the East," was another priority: Chiang Kai-shek's Nationalists and Mao Zedong's Communists were at war, but the British had no plans to hand over this colony to whichever side won the mandate of heaven. Altogether, to have an armed presence in occupied Japan and to show the flag were deemed essential to Britain's role throughout the Far East.

It wasn't only Japan where the Americans were suddenly holding sway. A year earlier, in June 1946, one senior British diplomat who visited China observed that "the Yanks have replaced us as the first power in the land."[29] Dollars had become standard currency in Shanghai, and U.S. companies were obtaining civil aviation routes. Driving rules throughout China had already changed overnight as of January 1, from the left-hand side of the road to the right.

Despite the heavy U.S. presence in both Japan and China, Bevin, in 1947, was questioning whether American political-military engagement with Asia might be other than temporary. He had reason to worry, and did so for several more years. In 1949, after all, a U.S. secretary of the army declared at a Tokyo press conference, and to General MacArthur's disgust, that America had no obligation even to defend Japan from Stalin.

Having strong commercial ties in the Far East didn't mean that Washington would open a military umbrella over these lands, except for its former colony, the Philippines. Maybe, people in London worried, the mercurial Republic would decide to rely solely on atomic retaliation across oceanic distances rather than on garrisoning faraway places or paying to maintain a thousand-ship navy. If the United States lost interest in the Far East, Bevin wrote to his ambassador in Washington in May 1947, there would be serious repercussions throughout Southeast Asia.

No one spoke yet about a line of falling dominoes, but—as when one examines the fate of Greece—sweeping consequences seemed certain if Communism advanced. Nationalist China was crumbling. Should Mao win, Communism might bolshevize Indochina's twenty-three million people in short order and then press down through the Thai peninsula, into Malaya and via the subcontinent to Suez. It sounds like paranoia, except that's what imperial Japan had apparently just attempted when attacking India.

By the summer of 1947, Bevin proposed that the State Department and the Pentagon place liaison staff within the empire's sprawling General Headquarters Far East, based in Singapore. That step, he believed, would help Washington to grasp the "British point of outlook."[30] In addition, Britain's military chiefs urged Washington to send a senior officer to attend meetings of their Defence Committee for South East Asia, also held in Singapore. But the Americans said no thanks to both. They wanted to stay aloof from shouldering more commitments, and decision makers of the era understood, because of a well-known exposition by Walter Lippmann, that a "commitment" entailed nothing less than an obligation that might have to be met by going to war.[31]

THE ISLAND COLONY OF SINGAPORE, WITH ABOUT A MILLION PEOPLE, was the heart of British power in Asia, and its General Headquarters Far East was the counterpart of General Headquarters Middle East in Egypt. Singapore sits at the mouth of the Strait of Malacca, through which one-third of the world's shipping passes today, and it has been a trading hub for centuries. In 1946, it was the world's largest naval facility, though roughly tied by Norfolk, Virginia. Authority over all British colonial possessions in Southeast Asia was exercised from here, and that included responsibility for neighboring Malaya—a peninsula about the size of Maine, whose southern tip lay right across Singapore's Johor Causeway.

Malaya from 1946 to 1948 was a colony (that is, under the direct control of London) but thereafter became, until independence in 1957, a protectorate—a federation of eleven states, of which nine semi-sovereign ones were ruled by Muslim sultans. Four-fifths of the federation was covered by jungle. In its north, the British operated tin mines and rubber plantations. Americans bought most of the output, which provided dollars essential to Britain's recovery.

In May 1946, Malcolm MacDonald arrived as governor-general of Malaya and Singapore. He was then forty-four, the son of Ramsay MacDonald, Labour Party prime minister during the interwar years, and had already won every glittering prize except becoming premier himself: colonial secretary ten years earlier; then secretary for dominion affairs; thereafter a role in Churchill's cabinet early in the war; followed by appointment as high commissioner to Canada, where the Americans had come to value him as an intermediary between FDR and Downing Street. To the British, and then to the Americans as well, he soon became known as one of the two "Macs" in Asia, the other being General MacArthur. MacDonald, however, was an ordinary, congenial-looking man of average height, having none of MacArthur's flair. Yet he had other formidable qualities, and in Whitehall he was said to be his country's most important figure east of Dover.

Two years later, in May 1948, MacDonald assumed the new overarching role of commissioner general for Southeast Asia, which regained him cabinet rank in London. He became responsible for the entire expanse of Malaya, Singapore, and the Borneo territories, and, in defense matters, for Hong Kong. He also chaired the British Defence Co-ordination Committee/Far East, which gave him "powers of direction" for overseeing the defense of Thailand, Burma, French Indochina, and what were still the Dutch East Indies. His remit covered some 150 million people plus a rich, vibrant terrain with its tin, rubber, timber, and rice, as well as the routes to India. In this role, he was a manifestation of both the Foreign Office and the Colonial Office, holding unique powers and reporting right to the top.

MacDonald encountered trouble in Malaya. Early in 1948, some twelve thousand ethnic Chinese guerrillas had launched what they called a liberation war, which had led to a spate of murders and abductions.[32] A month after he took over as commissioner general, MacDonald declared a state of emergency—a drastic measure in a polyglot society of 4.9 million subjects who were 38 percent unassimilated Chinese (with some half million as sympathizers) and a sizable Indian minority. Among other decrees, any unauthorized person caught carrying a firearm would be hanged. Nonetheless, Malaya's violence escalated fast, and this draining, low-level conflict would last nearly twelve years.

But the British were in Southeast Asia to stay, though not necessarily as colonialists, as they saw it. MacDonald recognized that Japan's quick and humiliating conquest of Malaya and Singapore in 1942 had wrecked British prestige. But he saw no reason why these lands couldn't be led firmly and peacefully to an independence that would keep them within the commonwealth. The whole would be greater than the sum of its parts, and the symbolism is telling. After arriving, MacDonald took the initiative to build Phoenix Park—an imposing, well-secured, fourteen-acre complex that dominated the heart of Singapore island around Government House, which U.S. visitors already described as resembling New York's Metropolitan Museum of Art in its size and architecture. Completed in 1949, Phoenix Park became Britain's inspiring center of political administration for this part of the world. It's named after the emblem of Southeast Asia Command, which featured the mythical bird, itself a representation of total revival after death.

In 1948, MacDonald began sending home dispatches about having to face "theatre-wide" Communist aggression that threatened all of Southeast Asia.[33] To him—and evermore to Whitehall, and then to the Americans—the fate of Malaya, with its lucrative tin and rubber exports, was inseparable from whatever befell Indochina. Bevin shifted three regiments of the Guards Brigades over from Germany, but that wasn't adequate for the type of jungle fighting at hand. The Australians, asked for help, declined at this point. MacDonald believed a U.S. commitment to Southeast Asia would be the strongest guarantee of all against Communist insurgency. Specifically, in his mind, the Americans needed to concentrate development dollars, diplomatic support, and military aid on Indochina, which he regarded as Malaya's first line of defense against Communism. He knew the Americans couldn't be rushed. So he sought them out carefully, telling, for instance, the U.S. ambassador in Thailand that unless political-military steps were pursued in tandem, the "U.S.-U.K. position" throughout Southeast Asia would fail.[34]

MacDonald was the only senior Western official who was on the scene in Southeast Asia for nearly ten critical years, from 1946 until 1955, and his influence on the Americans became profound. As we'll see, no French politician or general, no American congressman or admiral, comes close to having his impact on the U.S. decisions that led America step by step into Vietnam—as the Vietminh fought with increasing ferocity against French colonialism. Yet MacDonald is barely noticed by historians, though any examination of the making of America's own Vietnam war without him is incomplete.[35]

ALL OF THE BRITISH EMPIRE'S INTERESTS IN SOUTHEAST ASIA— political, military, and economic—were connected to those in the Middle East and in Continental Europe. That's how Bevin and Attlee, and of course the Foreign Office, understood the globe in 1947 and 1948. Senior U.S. policy makers—let alone Congress and Main Street— had a much narrower "mental map."[36] In these years, they looked at the world region by region. Interconnected worldwide alliances and aid programs were still unimaginable.

The insurgency in Greece had led to the Pentagon Talks of October 1947, and the result appeared to be that the Americans would support the British Empire from North Africa to central Asia. Until then, the Joint Chiefs had labeled the Middle East as "crucial" for the United States, but in early November, as the talks ended, Truman ordered that the designation be upgraded to "vital," which implies a threat to stability that would be a mortal danger to the state.[37] And that is how the British described their own stakes in the region. They were in a blaze of self-congratulation, in no small measure, as Sir Michael Wright, Bevin's top man for the Middle East, said, because officials in Washington seemed to acknowledge that "the United States would be quite unable to fill the vacuum which a withdrawal of British power would create."[38]

As a result of the Pentagon Talks, Britain's chiefs of staff, under Bevin's guidance, hoped the next step would be "to get a working agreement on Far East strategy with the Americans . . . in exactly the same way as we have in the Middle East."[39] The reason to cover so wide a landscape, Bevin explained to his government's defense minister, "is that there would be some counterbalance in our favor with the Americans, who tend to regard China, Korea and Japan, as well as the Pacific Ocean area, as practically their own preserve."[40] Indeed they did. As he prepared to cast his net over the Americans, Bevin was asserting the British Empire to be a global power second to none, while, at the same time, his country didn't even possess a stable currency. Whitehall officials weren't finding this strange, nor were their counterparts in Washington.

That fall of 1947, Bevin was pondering the ties between Malaya's population, which was about 60 percent Muslim, and the more than 100 million Muslims who were judged to live in the Middle East—if those lands were defined to include Pakistan's 75 million largely Muslim subjects. He envisioned a "connecting bridge" or "principal link" in a series of pacts that would form a defensive chain stretching from Europe to the Pacific. And Britain, he'd advise the Americans, could always provide the "best window" on this sweeping terrain.[41]

To start, Bevin envisioned the British Empire and the United States establishing some form of a common front, from Afghanistan to Indochina, that would serve as a dike against the spread of Soviet-sponsored Communism. It needn't be a military pact, he hastened to add in conversations with Ambassador Lewis Douglas, but rather an understanding between their two countries to emphasize political-economic development—"a world-wide system of regional arrangements," as he defined it. Let Australia and New Zealand be included too. In fact, the system he envisioned could spread through Arab lands. With defense of the Arab world ensured, new irrigation projects might channel the waters of the Nile, Lake Tana, the Tigris, and the Euphrates to transform agriculture. In this way, Iraq, for instance, could grow new types of crops and become one of that region's richest countries.

He elaborated on his vision: Markets would open for British and European exports, and rising standards of living would overcome the temptations of Communism among the dispossessed. Hopefully, in short order, a political-military pact could also be established in Western Europe—although, he admitted to his aides, that one might be the trickiest to craft, because it would involve countries so close to home.

THERE'D BE NO SUCH WORKING AGREEMENT ON ASIA FOR YEARS, and, anyway, within months of the Pentagon Talks' pledges of cooperation in the Middle East the Americans and British were again at odds over Palestine—a subject so volatile as to have been excluded from those planning discussions.

Together, they had been pushing a Palestine partition plan through the UN. It was adopted on November 29, 1947, creating two new states with Jerusalem as a separate unit and envisioning an economic union. "A few days later," reminisces Uri Avnery, the Israeli peace activist and self-described ex-terrorist, "the 'war of 1948' broke out." In parallel, tensions flared between the Americans and the British. Palestinian Arabs had their own specialists in terror tactics, but transatlantic abrasions became rawer due to U.S. arms smuggling. On January 7, 1948, Irgun detonated a car bomb at a bus stop in Jerusalem, killing seventeen Arabs and wounding over fifty. That same month, the American Export Lines' freighter *Exford* succeeded in slipping arms and ammunition through for the Haganah. British authorities weren't making distinctions and ordered all U.S. ships bound for Jewish Tel Aviv to instead dock at British-run Haifa, where they'd be searched for contraband.

The mandate was to end on May 14. As the year began, British authorities in Jerusalem anticipated an explosion once they relinquished final control, and Ambassador Douglas reported that all of Britain's interests in the Middle East needed to "be sandbagged to reduce to a minimum the damage from the blast."[42] The Americans feared that intensified violence would affect them directly. After all, according to the Joint Chiefs, U.S. and British strategic interests in the region were "so interrelated that they should be considered as a whole."[43]

In Washington, officials at the British embassy asked Undersecretary of State Bob Lovett for a meeting. Maybe an in-depth exchange of views with him and his top people, including select military men, could help gauge what lay ahead. Lovett demurred. He feared press leaks that might imply that the United States was inclined to support Britain in some direct attempt to uphold order.

As the clock ticked down to May 14, Washington policy makers shifted from favoring partition to weighing possibilities of a UN trusteeship as a way station to a Jewish-Arab binational state, as Bevin had originally envisioned. But that might require British troops to remain as peacekeepers. GIs or U.S. marines sure weren't going to be deployed. Ambassador Douglas, however, cabled Washington that overwhelming pressure existed in Britain "to get 'the boys' home from Palestine" in the face of terrorist attacks.[44] Churchill too, as opposition leader, wanted out. Today, it's bizarre to write that "the British cut and ran" or that Britain experienced a "loss of Palestine" in 1947–1948.[45] There wasn't much to hold on to, nor to lose.

The full Joint Chiefs of Staff, as well as Forrestal, opposed recognizing a state of Israel, as did Admiral Richard Conolly, who commanded U.S. Naval Forces/Eastern Atlantic and Mediterranean from his headquarters in London's Grosvenor Square. He warned that "to expel the Arabs from their territory was going to set up something that we were going to have to face for years to come."[46] The Joint Chiefs, for their part, anticipated getting into "a continuously widening series of operations" and agreed with British warnings that if "Moslem ideology" was "worked up along anti-western lines because of Palestine . . . it will constitute almost insuperable military problems."[47] There was also fear of jeopardizing access to oil, and that fear took hold just as Socal and the Texas Company discovered the biggest oil field that's ever been found, in Saudi Arabia's Eastern Province.

There were other reasons for caution, and one came from the newly established CIA: an Israeli state could set dangerous precedent for Russian demands to grant the Kurds a national homeland. Ultimately, Bevin and his military advisers told Douglas that they dreaded "a China situation."[48] The allusion mystified Douglas, and he asked for clarification. What they meant, came the weary reply, was Arab disenchantment with the West that could enable Russian penetration, as in China.

For his part, Secretary Marshall came to favor establishing a temporary trusteeship for Palestine and imposing some sort of peace until Jews and Arabs reached agreement. Along with Douglas, he deplored what he called "publicity campaigns" by Zionists in the United States, some of whom he believed were supporting terrorism. Each anticipated a lifetime to come of Arab-Israeli wars, riots, terror, and reprisals.[49] But debates over partition or trusteeship became moot.

The mandate ended as expected on May 14, 1948, hours before the last of the British forces left the port of Haifa. Israel declared independence the same day, and Truman extended de facto recognition. The Kremlin—seeing opportunities to disrupt the British Empire in the Middle East—one-upped the Americans on the seventeenth with formal de jure recognition. Then two wars blended into one: the war between the Arab and the Jewish populations that had been under way since December 1947, and the one that began in May when armies from Syria, Egypt, Iraq, Lebanon, and Jordan attacked the new state of Israel. In Washington, Bob Lovett predicted the outcome: the Israelis would win due to their superior weaponry and leadership and, as it turned out, due to outnumbering the Arab forces at every stage of the war as well.[50]

The Americans were caught in the cross fire—literally so, because, on May 22, Thomas C. Wasson, the U.S. consul general in Jerusalem, was struck by a sniper's bullet through his armpit beneath a bulletproof vest as Arabs and Jews fought for control of the Old City. He died from his wounds the next day. Each side blamed the other, while the identity of the assassin was never determined. The civil war between Arabs and Jews, which Forrestal had dreaded, continued into 1949, as Israel won.

During this turmoil, Undersecretary Lovett observed to his aides that the State Department was the easiest of targets for critics of all stripes. He anticipated wild denunciations, which, on the issue of Israel and Palestine, would arrive as charges of anti-Semitism, usually against Foreign Service "Arabists," regarded, then as now, as an "elite within an elite" or an "East Coast Establishment" unsympathetic to the Jewish state.[51] Forrestal was called anti-Semitic, and insinuations have besmirched Marshall. Similarly, Ernest Bevin—the Baptist trade union organizer whom British Zionists had seen as their ally in Churchill's War Cabinet—got smeared, as he does still by careless historians.[52] Bevin, of course, was loathed by Jews and Arabs alike, but the problem with Bevin was that he had lots of bile for people who opposed him, including Jewish opponents.

Lovett found himself being pulled into the refugee crisis as 726,000 people, about 70 percent of the population of Arab Palestine, left or fled the land captured by Israel.[53] This at least was one issue on which Washington could cooperate as Britain quickly offered humanitarian assistance. From the White House, Admiral Leahy pressed Lovett "to emulate" Britain.[54] At the Pentagon, Forrestal agreed with the urgency, except no government money could be found for the task. (Those were the days before enormous DOD contingency funds.) Therefore, U.S. aid to Palestinian refugees, which continues today, began ad hoc.

Estelle Manville, a well-known philanthropist and the American wife of Sweden's Count Folke Bernadotte, the UN peace negotiator, contributed. So did Stanton Griffis, the U.S. ambassador in Egypt and the former chairman of Paramount Pictures. He also took the unauthorized step of using his office to personally elicit emergency funds from the Arabian-American Oil Company and the engineering firm Bechtel. Lovett heard about that initiative and approved, though he advised that the entire Israeli-Palestinian question had become so heated that the effort be "handled by telephone and not by wire."

On September 17, Bernadotte, who had led rescue missions into Germany for the Red Cross during the *Untergang* of spring 1945, was murdered in an ambush by Yitzhak Shamir's Stern Gang terrorists.[55] Marshall and Bevin were in Paris that week attending UN General Assembly meetings. They stood next to each other at Orly four days later as the coffins of Bernadotte and his French aide, Andre Seraut, were carried off a white Red Cross Dakota C-47. All UN delegates attended the memorial ceremony at the airport before Bernadotte's remains were flown on to Stockholm.

Bevin and Marshall kept trying to coordinate "general principles of settlement" to this first Arab-Israeli war, but fighting continued and, in early December, Israeli forces conquered Gaza and entered the Sinai. For the two great-power democracies, enough was becoming enough.

By month's end, Harry Truman—his 1948 election safely over—sent a message to Israel's prime minister, David Ben-Gurion, so severe that Ben-Gurion remarked, "It might have been written by Bevin himself."[56] On the thirtieth, the Americans demanded unequivocal withdrawal from Egyptian territory. And then they took another step. Bob Lovett was serving as acting secretary that month in Marshall's absence, and he received a *note verbale* the same day from the British ambassador. What resulted was a coordinated, top secret ultimatum to Israel from Attlee's government.

On the afternoon of December 31, the U.S. ambassador in Tel Aviv, James McDonald, was handed an urgent cable from Washington, sent under Truman's name. Britain hadn't recognized Israel, which meant it had no ambassador of its own on the scene. So it was McDonald who got instructions to inform Ben-Gurion of a straightforward threat: Britain would enter the war against Israel "unless Israeli forces withdraw from Egyptian territory."[57] McDonald delivered this message to Ben-Gurion just before midnight, and the prime minister, as McDonald recalled, conceded furiously that "we really can't take on the British Empire."[58] Ben-Gurion promised that there'd be no Israeli feet on Egyptian soil inside of forty-eight hours, and his troops were gone in a week. The Americans filed away these details until 1957.

WHATEVER OCCURRED IN ISRAEL AND PALESTINE, THE U.S. NAVY wasn't going to allow sectarian upheavals to compromise its entry into Middle Eastern waters. In March 1948, the chief of naval operations extended Admiral Conolly's responsibilities to reach from the mid-Atlantic to the point where the Indo-Burmese frontier ran into the sea and met MacArthur's East Asian satrapy, given that MacArthur also served as commander in chief of the U.S. Far East Command. That move was made, as Conolly understood it, to parallel the Royal Navy's organizational structure for the region. By summer, the Americans were showing up in the Persian Gulf with new, comparatively large ships, among them the aircraft carrier USS *Siboney*.

They arrived with a specific purpose. The Gulf had been a British imperial preserve for more than a century, and the U.S. Navy now wanted to familiarize itself with the seas and shorelines in case Russia struck south into Iran's oil fields. Yet the rulers of Kuwait, Bahrain, and the coastal sheikhdoms—desert principalities all overseen by Britain—drew inferences. The Royal Navy visited them only with sloops, they whined, not with sizable vessels like these. When the USS *Greenwich Bay*, *Pocono*, and *Siboney* appeared off Kuwait, for instance, officials in the Foreign Office's Eastern Department, which administered British diplomacy in the Gulf, asked the Admiralty to increase Britain's presence. "The Americans," one of them wrote that summer, "do seem to be rather outdoing us in the way of visits by big ships."[59] Before long, Sir Michael Wright, who had much responsibility for Middle Eastern affairs, responded with an attempt to correct the impression. "Far from being an indication that the Royal Navy is prepared to take second place to the Americans," he wrote with nervous fluency, "these visits are a consequence of the very close cooperation built up between the armed services of the United Kingdom and the United States during the war."[60] Few of the locals were convinced.

Events in the Persian Gulf were delicate for Britain. In September, Admiral Conolly made a port call to the protectorate of Bahrain. That's the five-island archipelago slightly east of Dhahran, Saudi Arabia, and in Dhahran the Americans had renegotiated an airfield lease for what was their only military installation in western Asia. The navy had to consider establishing some presence too, and Conolly arrived on his flagship, the *Siboney*, in the company of vessels nearly as large. A visit to Bahrain's capital, Manama—the center of British naval and commercial activity in the Gulf—by the top American admiral was unprecedented.

In blazing afternoon sunlight, Conolly and a retinue of aides in dress whites were taken to see Salman bin Hamad Al Khalifa, Bahrain's ruler and a proud knight commander of the Order of the Indian Empire. In the grandest of his palaces, he waited atop the steps, just beyond an enormous wooden door. When the Americans entered, he eagerly introduced a young son who stood nearby. Towering alongside the ruler and his son, wearing a light double-breasted suit, was the six-foot-four Charles Dalrymple Belgrave, who for twenty-two years had served as Whitehall's personal adviser to the sheikh and who, of course, was fluent in the Gulf's dialects. The Americans, for their part, didn't know the language, comprehend the introduction, or know what to do with their caps. They assumed the son was a slave, treated him like a cloakroom attendant, and quickly buried him under their headgear—a series of gaffes that Belgrave duly reported home.[61] Maybe the empire wouldn't be taking second place to the Americans in these parts after all.

6

YEAR OF THE OFFENSIVE

1938 was overwhelmingly the year of the Fascist offensive.

—John Gunther, in his bestseller *Inside Europe* (1939), after Hitler
moved into Czechoslovakia and Austria. Ten years later, U.S.
and British leaders drew parallels with Stalin's offensive against
Czechoslovakia and thereafter against West Berlin.

ON THURSDAY, JANUARY 22, 1948, ERNEST BEVIN GAVE AN AD-
dress to the House of Commons that riveted Americans who saw a
giant step being taken toward a world remade. By now, there was no one
of comparable authority in Western Europe. The big, bruising foreign
secretary rose slowly from the green-leather front benches at 3:30 that
afternoon. He began by warning an unnamed police state—the Soviet
Union—not to play with fire; then he denounced old-fashioned balances
of power, and within minutes he was essentially saying that Britons are
Europeans. Above all, he claimed for Britain a "spiritual union" with
other "members of Western civilization" on the Continent, and he asserted
that "the time is ripe for a consolidation of Western Europe." Senator
Arthur Vandenberg called Bevin's speech "terrific." CBS News said it
was a "hard right swing from the floor" against Stalin's ambitions.[1] *The
Boston Globe* found it historic.

POSTWAR EUROPE AND THE RESCUE OF BERLIN

ICELAND

FINLAND

NORWAY

SWEDEN

North Sea

Baltic Sea

DENMARK

IRELAND

NETHERLANDS

BRITAIN

Berlin

POLAND

GERMANY

BELGIUM

CZECHOSLOVAKIA

LUXEMBOURG

FRANCE

AUSTRIA (occupied)

HUNGARY

SWITZERLAND

ROMANIA

Atlantic Ocean

YUGOSLAVIA

ITALY

BULGAR

PORTUGAL

SPAIN

ALBANIA

GREECE

SPANISH MOROCCO

Strait of Gibraltar

Mediterranean Sea

MOROCCO (Fr.)

TUNISIA (Fr.)

ALGERIA (Fr.)

0 Miles 400
0 Kilometers 400

Western bloc

Communist bloc/Soviet zone

Nonaligned nations

Iron Curtain

© 2018 Jeffrey L. Ward

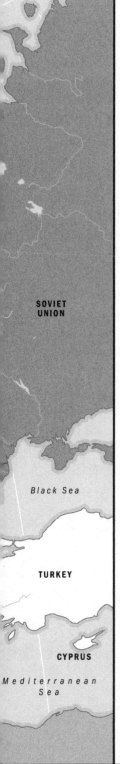

GERMANY, 1948

- - - - Berlin Airlift 1948–1949

North Sea

DENMARK

Hamburg

Hanover

BRITISH
ZONE

NETHERLANDS

GERMANY

BELGIUM

Berlin

POLAND

SOVIET
ZONE

Elbe R.

FRENCH
ZONE

Frankfurt

LUXEMBOURG

CZECHOSLOVAKIA

FRANCE

Rhine R.

AMERICAN
ZONE

Danube R.

FRENCH
ZONE

0 Miles   200

0 Kilometers 200

AUSTRIA

SWITZERLAND

DIVISIONS OF BERLIN, 1948

Havel R.

FRENCH

SOVIET

BRITISH

BERLIN

Spree R.

AMERICAN

0 Miles   10

0 Kilometers 10

Western Europe was still a vulnerable collection of separate nations barely able to cooperate. Merely taking the Étoile du Nord from Paris to Amsterdam required multiple inspections of passports, currency, and numbers of cigarettes. The result was a drag on U.S. interests, according to Undersecretary of State Bob Lovett. Like everyone else in Washington, Lovett wanted to see "a viable geographic unit"—that is, a unified Western Europe—"big enough and diverse enough to take the monkey off our backs."[2]

Bevin's initiative therefore looked vital: more than fear of Russia was needed to pass the Marshall Plan, which was still before Congress. Legislators demanded a unified Europe, and that was to include Britain, despite most of its inhabitants regarding themselves as distinct from a continent barely twenty-two miles away. It's a mind-set still in place, as the 2016 vote to leave the European Union shows; even the seasoned BBC political correspondent Rob Watson speaks reflexively about the primary cause of Brexit being "people coming from Europe."[3] At the time, Americans spoke that way too, as did John Foster Dulles, who described World War II's "non-continental victors—Soviet Russia, Great Britain, and the United States."[4]

Bevin, Churchill, and Anthony Eden used the same imagery when they had to counter the high-energy push for federation from across the Atlantic. Each spoke of three circles to demonstrate that Britain was a land apart, with distinct roles in the world. The first circle represented ties to the empire and commonwealth; the second represented the country's unique relationship with the United States; and the third represented its leadership of Europe. Like a Venn diagram, these circles intersected at a central point: London. Given this view of itself, in which the empire and commonwealth linked nations everywhere, how could Britain agree to being considered merely one state in a European community? According to Bevin and Churchill, it couldn't, although neither came right out and said that. Quite the contrary.

So not all was as it seemed when Bevin stood before the Commons. He wanted to protect Britain and the free nations on the Continent, and he'd say most anything that helped. He knew that no question of international life excited Capitol Hill and Main Street—in addition to planners at the Pentagon—as did that of a "United States of Europe." Every power player in Washington urged it, or something close, not merely "optimists like Eleanor Roosevelt," as is argued today.[5]

The concept of a "United States of Europe" had first arisen on both sides of the Atlantic after World War I. Following World War II, Bevin picked up on the term, as did Churchill. Bevin, however, spoke expansively of a unified Europe embracing lands in Southeast Asia, the Middle East, and Africa too, asserting that "Europe must be economically supported" by commodities from its overseas territories if it were to prosper.[6] This was getting rather far afield from Europe and from how the Americans imagined its federation. But they might as well have had their ears plugged when he offered those lines. They heard what they wanted to hear: the highly pragmatic yet magical words "United States," which made them hope that Britain, France, Italy, Benelux— and perhaps, eventually, Germany—might all flourish together, as had the United States of America.

Churchill scoffed at Bevin's speech. The foreign secretary had come rather late to the matter, he said. He himself had been heralding a "new kind of United States of Europe" since at least 1946 and described it as a "Union of Europe as a whole."[7] Americans loved hearing this, even if Churchill was as vague as Bevin about what "union" might entail for Britain.

Churchill had adopted the issue for different reasons, although with a touch of idealism. Because he intended to return to Downing Street, he had to tackle something big while in opposition, and if anyone knew the dangers of a divided Europe, it was he. It was also a subject that needed repeating to keep alive, requiring one high-profile address after another. Besides, there was only so far he could go in championing policy on Russia or the Middle East without running smack into an exceedingly turf-conscious Foreign Office dominated by Bevin. On the issue of unity, however, he was welcomed as the preeminent European, with much to offer. And a unified Europe appeared vital as history's greatest war was being replaced by history's least plausible peace.

IN 1948, A CLEAR PATH LOOKED TO BE OPENING TO WORLD WAR III. Tensions with Russia had been increasing since the previous September.

That's when Stalin's successor-in-waiting, the enforcer of cultural orthodoxy, Andrei Zhdanov, an alcoholic party boss known for his expressionless bloodshot eyes, had remarked that Czechoslovakia was the only country among Eastern Europe's 100 million people where "the power contest still remains undecided."[8] Stalin became the decider. On February 24, 1948, Communist apparatchiks seized control of its established parliamentary government, with the Red Army camped on the borders and ready to assist collaborators within.

Days later, Foreign Minister Molotov proclaimed that every state in Eastern Europe now enjoyed friendship treaties with Moscow. But more was to come. Sometime after midnight on March 10, unidentified killers entered the official apartment of Jan Masaryk, Czechoslovakia's popular foreign minister, who for the past two weeks had been virtually confined to his residence high in the Czech Foreign Ministry. Masaryk's mother was American, and his father had been Czechoslovakia's first president, from 1918 to 1935. Masaryk, who had previously been married to an American heiress, had served as his country's chargé d'affaires in Washington and then as ambassador to London for its wartime government in exile. By the time of the coup, he was living part-time with Marcia Davenport, Wellesley class of 1921, a *New Yorker* staff writer and bestselling novelist. Everyone knew him.

The killers dragged Masaryk clawing through his apartment bedroom and threw him out a bathroom window, where he fell to his death on the cobblestoned courtyard forty-seven feet below.[9] Davenport, who kept her own flat five minutes away from Czernin Palace, had gotten safely off to London three days earlier. The new authorities in Prague called Masaryk's death suicide. But this was a blood-soaked message anyone could understand, and it came on the heels of the coup, outraging influential circles in Washington, London, and New York. It is misremembering to say that "Marshall was unmoved" by the Communist putsch. Specifically, he declared that the murder evoked "the high-handed procedure of the Nazi regime," a statement that got attention coast-to-coast.[10] Nonetheless, all that could be done, said Marshall's deputy, Bob Lovett, was to encourage Bevin's push for European unity. "Unofficially," Lovett told the Senate Foreign Relations Committee, "we know there is a defensive alliance in the western union framework of Bevin's."[11]

Stalin was not finished. Having taken Prague, he focused on the large sectors of Berlin not in his hands: the three zones governed by the United States, Britain, and France. If he could oust his former allies from the city, he reasoned, the British and Americans would begin a general retreat from Germany. Once that happened, the Continent's fearful, demoralized democracies would succumb to Communist subversion, including labor strikes. The industrial heartland of Western Europe—the Ruhr valley, within Britain's occupation zone—would fall, and when that occurred, the factories and mines of France and the wealth of the Low Countries would follow. There'd be no need for the Red Army to invade. By controlling all of Germany, and then the rest of Europe, the Soviet Union would be the world's greatest economic power. And so, in the five months after the Czech coup, Stalin constricted the West's access to Berlin, placing 2.4 million citizens of its western districts under siege, plus 3,000 Americans, among whom were scores of women and children.

It was a chilling move. Herbert Morrison, another one of Attlee's hard-boiled ministers, and the son of a police constable, stated that the world was returning into "some sort of nightmare of aggression we thought we had buried by disposing of Hitler."[12]

Throughout 1948, no military alliance bound the Americans to Europe, nor was it clear to most of them why they should bear the risks and costs of shielding Western Europe's 200 million people—living in a score of quarrelsome nations—from outside aggression. In fact, General Lucius Clay, who served as the U.S. military governor for Germany, had been ordered the previous August not to retaliate should Russia strike into the British occupation zone, which covered more than a third of western Germany, north of the French and U.S. zones, and which bordered Holland and Belgium. Slicing through it would be Stalin's quickest route to the Channel. This order remained in effect until December 1948.

Truman, Marshall, and Forrestal weren't going to take their country to war without a direct attack on Americans. The Joint Chiefs' instructions to Clay were secret, but British commanders understood them perfectly, as did Foreign Secretary Bevin. So likely did Stalin, through his U.S. and British spy networks.

British diplomats in Washington, meanwhile, had their own perspective on events in central Europe. They were telling each other that the Czech coup and Russia's moves thereafter were perfectly timed. They expected the Americans to now ask them for deeper cooperation, and they were right. The Americans were compelled that spring and summer to reexamine the standoffishness of their political-military approach to Europe and to reconsider the value of the British Empire and Commonwealth. To be sure, Britain had been instrumental in organizing Europe's initial response right after Secretary Marshall's speech at Harvard the previous year, but it had still been one of sixteen nations in the queue hoping for Marshall Plan aid. Now U.S. officials concluded that Britain—as the world's second-strongest high-tech economy and oldest constitutional government—would be vital to every aspect of protecting and dynamizing the stricken Continent.

ONE OF THE MEN IN WASHINGTON WHO PLAYED A PIVOTAL ROLE that year in shaping the response to Moscow was Undersecretary Lovett. He was close, to the extent possible, with James Forrestal, and he was friends with Lewis Douglas, whom he'd known since their college days in New England. During the war, he had worked hand in glove with John Snyder on building up aviation. Lovett and Averell Harriman were friends, too, and had been since their teens, when Lovett's father had been general counsel to the Harrimans' Union Pacific Railroad.

In 1917, once the United States entered World War I, Lovett had left Yale during his junior year to fly for the navy. He did so in the kind of overgrown kites that a general in James Gould Cozzens's 1948 novel, *Guard of Honor* (in which Lovett appears), describes as "airplanes I'd have been scared to get in parked on the ground." He earned the Navy Cross for bombing raids against submarine bases at Ostend and Zeebrugge and for combat missions with the British Naval Air Service. He then returned to complete Yale and went on to Harvard Law. Thereafter he joined Brown Brothers, whose partners came from such dynasties as that of Peter Goelet Gerry, the Rhode Island senator who, when he opposed aid to Britain in 1940, said that his family still had bitter memories of the redcoats.[13] Like J. P. Morgan & Co., Brown Brothers was European in outlook, picking up loans to rehabilitate the Continent after World War I. Lovett guided his firm into a merger with the Harriman financial interests right before the crash shattered the world economy and left it a heap of sharp-edged national autarchies.

In March 1941, Lovett became "that charming man the Assistant Secretary of War for Air," as he's presented in *Guard of Honor*, which unfolds on a World War II U.S. Army Air Forces base. In that job, and in tandem with Snyder, he multiplied the nation's air fleets and factories. The war won in 1945, and the newly autonomous U.S. Air Force ready to emerge two years later, Lovett returned to Brown Brothers. He and his wife lived temporarily in the superintendent's cottage on his father's Locust Valley estate, and he took the early commuter train into Penn Station each weekday, complaining incessantly about his ailing stomach.

Then Truman appointed George Marshall, who asked Lovett to join him at State in a role Marshall described as his "co-pilot." "I was ripped out of a pleasant day-to-day life to go down as his Under Secretary," Lovett recalled.[14] (He had a wry humor and was also a gifted mimic.) To leave a firm like Brown Brothers, however, entailed having to extract himself from a co-partnership of unlimited liability in what was legally a New York State bank, and that was difficult in the days when men risked their own money on Wall Street. But suddenly Lovett found himself fit for the task, and even gave up his evening martinis. "Bob's only well when he's sleeping two hours a night and saving the world," said Forrestal's son with genuine affection.[15]

Lovett was key to implementing the Marshall Plan (formally called the European Recovery Program and executed by the Economic Recovery Administration), which Congress finally approved in April 1948. Washington would spend the equivalent of about 800 billion aid dollars in today's economy over four years. But Congress would tightly control the purse strings by requiring annual appropriations and careful accounting of how each recipient country had spent the previous year's money.

Britain received the lion's share, yet, from the start, failed to meet a key U.S. expectation—catalyzing a federation of Western Europe, of which it would be part.

By that April, sixteen recipient countries had assembled themselves into the Organisation for European Economic Co-operation, based in Paris. At U.S. urging, the OEEC intended to promote common European trade, labor, and payments policies as well as to coordinate requirements for aid dollars. Month by month, and then year by year, Washington came to recognize that the British were insincere about European unity: Whitehall officials gave lip service to the idea but dragged their feet about adopting common policies. Before long, Averell Harriman, who had left the Commerce Department to run the Marshall Plan in Europe, fumed that "the British had prevailed in setting the pattern of an organization whose impotency is now becoming alarming."[16] And he was being diplomatic: Sir Edmund Hall-Patch, who presided over the OEEC, would not allow Harriman to attend its meetings.

After the plan's first year of operation, Walter Lippmann was harsher about what had befallen the idea of a united Europe, "which Congress thought it was voting for." The British government, he wrote privately, had deliberately inflicted a "major defeat of a declared American purpose."[17]

Undoubtedly, Foreign Secretary Bevin had set in motion the forces that led to the European Union, today's twenty-eight-nation bloc that has helped provide stability on the Continent for more than sixty years. But he never intended that Britain would join in, as he had implied in the House of Commons. Bevin had another agenda: he soon admitted to his aides that his dramatic endorsement for European unity was "just a sprat to catch a mackerel"—the United States itself.[18]

AMID THE HOPES AND TENSIONS OF THE SPRING OF 1948, THE BRITish needed to have the right man as ambassador in Washington. For eighteen months, the post had been filled by a tweedy, elderly peer, Lord Inverchapel, whom reporters, when trying to find him, more than once had mistaken for the embassy's head gardener, due to his preference for tending the rosebushes rather than cultivating legislators on Capitol Hill. Bevin replaced him with the most formidable ambassador any nation has ever sent to the United States.

Sir Oliver Franks, forty-three, was admired in official circles for an unsurpassed intellect, startling analytical talents, and a sparkling clarity of speech. He'd brought these gifts to bear as the head of the high-profile delegation Bevin had sent to Paris to help prepare Europe's response to the Marshall Plan. Franks was a lean six feet four and austere. He had a clipped manner that made him appear emotionless. Even today, seeing his direct, unblinking straight-into-the-camera gaze on newsreels is unnerving. Franks served as ambassador from 1948 to 1952, years during which America would gradually eclipse the British Empire. That this occurred without harsher resentments has much to do with his genius.

The American public first got to know Franks from press accounts once he and his wife, Barbara, arrived in New York on May 13 after crossing the Atlantic on the *Queen Elizabeth*. Reports featured Lulu, the Frankses' cherished family cat, which had disappeared during the trip. The Cunard White Star Lines was conducting an exhaustive search from stem to stern. Lulu never resurfaced, but this incident helped to humanize the new ambassador, who was met with compassion as his work began.

Franks was the son of Britain's foremost Congregationalist minister and, in 1927, had graduated from Queens College, Oxford, apparently destined for renown as a philosopher. As a young don, he taught for a semester at the University of Chicago, a rare thing to do; the university was much more intellectually distant from Oxford than were the universities in Sydney or Bombay. He then joined the faculty of Glasgow University as Professor of Moral Philosophy, the position that had been held by Adam Smith, where Franks was a fitting contemporary for A. J. Ayer and J. L. Austin. Before he had a chance to transfix the world of learning with a summa on Meinong or Panaetius, however, Warsaw was in flames.

It wasn't unusual for truly capable British intellectuals to be recruited for unexpected pursuits. So it was with Franks. In the fall of 1939, the government brought him into the Ministry of Supply at the lowest-level civil service position. By the end of the war, he was its permanent secretary, making him one of the three or four most influential figures in the entire Allied war production effort. He left office in 1946 to return to Oxford as provost of Queens. By then, the political theorist Isaiah Berlin had also returned to the university from wartime duty in America. In his memoirs, Berlin recalls being summoned to see Franks about some administrative matter. Although Berlin was only four years younger, and already a famously intimidating character himself, he remembered feeling as though he had had an audience with God. "Franks is essentially a very simple man on whose shoulders a big, beautiful piece of mental machinery has been placed," said a friend of both.

Once in Washington, the boyish-looking professor quickly picked up on shifting opinions. "Americans, who at one time seemed to think every nationalist must be good," he reported, "now seem to see a Communist behind every nationalist bush."[19] It made no difference, Franks noted, whether those bushes were in Asia or the Middle East.

Many educated Americans held these views about Communism, and many of them had their ideas shaped by Walter Lippmann, who wrote during an era when newspaper columnists wielded an outsized influence in national politics. Lippmann was an inescapable presence in the fifty years of America's rise to international awareness, from helping to push the country into war in 1917 to retiring from his column in 1967 as a fierce opponent of the Vietnam cataclysm. He was the smartest and the most disciplined of the columnists of his day. His French and German were excellent. The British in Washington tracked him closely, which was easy: he lived a quarter mile away from the embassy, on Woodley Road, near the National Cathedral. They also knew he could usually be found at the right dinners and receptions, deep in conversation. He met annually in Europe's ministries and palaces with anyone he pleased, then shared his insights with readers in "Today and Tomorrow."

That spring, Lippmann was thinking hard about the British Empire, especially after Truman signed the Economic Recovery Act in April. Lippmann recognized "the extremely difficult question" of how Britain, with its imperial ties to most everywhere in the world, could possibly commit itself to joining a united Europe as Congress expected. Besides, he was trying to grasp the extent to which Britain's many alliances, client states, and imperial holdings could be valuable for America. He had worried for some time that this conglomeration was overextended militarily and economically and that London was working "to bring about a transfusion of American power," mainly by playing to U.S. fears of Communist expansion.[20] But was that a good or a bad thing? Was Britain pulling America into faraway vacuums or contributing some form of stability, or both? Even a man as shrewd as he couldn't figure that out.

"There ought to be a study made of the political consequences of the unexpected British weakness," he confided to friends. No one was tackling that issue, he said. Until recently, he reflected, Washington had supposed the British Empire would contain the Soviet Union all by itself.[21]

THE EVENTS OF THE SUMMER OF 1948 SHOW WHY THE TERM "COLD War" took hold. Life went on despite apocalyptic dangers. As the Olympic Games opened in London on July 29, the Red Army was staging a showdown across the Channel, in the middle of Germany.

The first Games since Hitler's 1936 extravaganza were another spectacle that made the empire appear strong and resilient. Britain's economic predicament had raised doubts about the wisdom of hosting them in London. Perhaps Baltimore or Lausanne made more sense. But George VI pressed the International Olympic Committee discreetly. In his way, the king understood power and presence, and, anyhow, youth activities were his principal public-spirited work. London had to be put back on the map as the world's largest city, an enormous high-energy metropolis of sturdy soot-blackened buildings alongside bustling new construction. Any impressions that its eight million people lived in a ruin—impressions held by many Americans—needed to be erased.

The Games were the first to be televised, and the only ones in which athletes had their food rationed. They got 5,467 calories a day, the same as for Britain's stevedores and miners. German POWs were put to work clearing rubble and hauling garbage, though the press worried that gangs of slave laborers might distress overseas visitors. So they toiled behind the scenes. (The last of some 400,000 were repatriated in late 1948.) Finally everything was set. On a brilliantly sunny day at the eighty-six-thousand-capacity Wembley Stadium, George VI, in naval uniform and speaking without a stammer, opened the spectacle from the royal box.

It all looked so reassuringly ordered and upbeat. But the British Empire was being challenged worldwide. Arabs and Israelis were at war. A no-holds-barred state of emergency existed in Malaya. Imperial possessions were being contested in Latin America. And there was worse to come.

BERLIN LAY 110 MILES WITHIN THE RUSSIAN OCCUPATION ZONE and was therefore essentially a huge island city, sitting on the sandy plain of what people still considered West Prussia: 344 square miles, an area 7 percent larger than the five boroughs of New York City. After Hitler's defeat, the Russians had assured the Allies that they would have free access to the city, although it was watched over by five Red Army divisions. Much of what remained was dead. Entrances to the burned hulk of the Reichstag were bricked up, and at night black marketeers, bony survivors, and child beggars all flitted like ghosts through the darkness. But a big part of Germany was starting to recover under U.S.-British-French occupation. Goods were even beginning to appear in shopwindows in the ruins of Berlin. Stalin realized that time was slipping. He had to stanch western Germany's recovery.

Marshall and Forrestal understood the perils should the Americans, as well as the British and French, be expelled from Berlin. So did Bevin. But as General Clay—a gaunt, laconic fifty-one-year-old West Pointer who had handled logistics for Eisenhower after D-day—pointed out, there were junior officials within the State Department who were causing headaches.

Clay was referring to noisy critics who wanted him to back the notion of a unified neutral Germany from which nearly all occupation troops would leave. That was to pave the way, their argument went, for Russian military withdrawal from Eastern Europe. Stalin surely wouldn't exploit neutrality, because a united Communist Germany was the last thing he wanted. It would become too dangerously strong.[22] Clay knew this reasoning was false. Neither Stalin nor the Red Army—which had just fought its way west with the cry "Blood for our blood"—would ever have allowed a unified, Soviet-backed Germany to threaten them. Besides, should Germany be neutralized, and all occupation forces be withdrawn, the Kremlin was ready to subvert it quickly by using an emerging indigenous army of military police, criminal police, armed railway forces, frontier guards, so-called alert police, and factory guards.

Meanwhile, the Soviet Military Administration curbed autobahn traffic in March, ostensibly in response to steps under way by the British and Americans to create a new West German democracy. It suspended train service from Berlin in April, restricted boats on the river Spree in May, and further tightened road, rail, and barge contact in or out of Berlin in June. For the first time, Russia claimed the entire city to be part of its occupation zone—a zone that extended within eighty miles of the Rhine at Mainz to Poland's frontier, itself recently redrawn.[23]

"Bevin had been sniffing around for a closer US association, getting nowhere," Franks recalled about the summer of 1948. "The Berlin blockade unloosed everything."[24] On June 24, the Russians turned the final screw: all roads and rails were obstructed, and they also closed routes by river and canal to the Baltic Sea. Both the Labour radical Nye Bevan and General Clay wanted the Americans, British, and French to jointly break through the blockade with an armored column that would force its way east along the autobahn. Such a move, however, would require Washington's approval, and would make sense only if taken immediately, no later than on the blockade's first day, to benefit from surprise. Otherwise an incursion along a single road could be waylaid without violence—by dynamiting bridges, for example. Sensibly, neither Washington nor London signed off. Stalin had what military planners call "escalation dominance." He could ratchet up (or down) whenever he wished, and Bevin knew it.

Bevin's moves at this point were shaped by memories of Neville Chamberlain's appeasement. He pressed top officials at State, Defense, and the White House for a public avowal against retreat. It didn't come. A turning point in the history of the twentieth century had arrived. The

West *had* to defend Berlin and thwart Stalin's policy of mass starvation, an approach in which he was well practiced, to recall the "hunger-extermination" he inflicted on Ukraine, then a Soviet republic, in 1932–1934, with 3.9 million dead. But official Washington vacillated.[25] Little was heard, and pessimism reigned, including among Marshall and Lovett. And with Forrestal too, whose endless work hours combined with a tightly coiled temperament to cause him ever more sleepless strain. Truman himself had reason to be cautious: the presidential election was four months away, and he had just signed the Selective Service Act on June 24, which authorized peacetime conscription. The Republicans were poised to exploit European "entanglements."

In the summer of 1948, as Lewis Douglas observed, Western policy was being made in London.

On June 25, the British were the first to deliver supplies by air into Berlin, doing so for their besieged garrison. The next day, General Clay made his own decision to follow suit. In Washington, the Joint Chiefs of Staff considered withdrawing from Berlin. But Bevin refused to permit General Sir Brian Robertson—who held a role in Germany similar to Clay's—even to set up a rear headquarters on the Rhine. That might indicate weakness. As an alternative, Robertson was told to prepare for more troops to arrive in the British zone. The JCS declined to issue a similar order to Clay.[26]

Bevin kept at it. On June 30, he gave a ringing speech in the House of Commons about what His Majesty's government would not tolerate. "The Russians intended the ruthless starvation of 2½ million people," he said, to produce "chaos and revolt," but that couldn't be allowed.[27] His perseverance proved effective. "It was Clay in Berlin and Bevin in London who rallied the Western cause," concludes Clay's biographer Jean Edward Smith, in one of the best analyses of this moment of decision, and Bevin did so by demanding that the Western allies stay put.[28]

That same day, the U.S. and British military chiefs convened at the Pentagon. Once they were all face-to-face, it was relatively easy to agree on a firm response to Stalin's blockade. The Truman administration made it official within twenty-four hours. "Had it not been for Bevin's resolute stand," concludes Smith, "Berlin could easily have been lost that fourth week of June 1948."[29]

Then Churchill openly compared the crisis to the aftermath of Munich in 1938, when Hitler had, in effect, been granted a free hand to absorb the Sudetenland and strangle Czechoslovakia's freedom. Hearing it from him, Americans were riveted. They understood that relations with Moscow had never been so perilous—and cooperation with Britain so important.

In a July 1 press conference, Truman signaled that the roughly six thousand U.S. troops would remain in Berlin even at the risk of war. The question, of course, was how to keep the West's occupation forces supplied with food, fuel, and medicines, along with more than two million West Berliners isolated by the blockade.

WITHIN THE PENTAGON, MILITARY PLANNERS DREW ON THEIR WORLD War II experience of flying 650,000 tons of food, weapons, and coal from India over the Himalayas into China to supply Chiang Kai-shek, at a cost of 1,314 lives. Now the challenge was to develop a 24/7 airlift that could enable the besieged city to survive.

Planners understood that the Red Army controlled the roads, rails, and canals but that the Russians might hesitate to shoot down U.S. Air Force or RAF aircraft within Berlin's three twenty-mile-wide flight corridors. That would have been a clear casus belli. Okay, but what if the Russians put up barrage balloons whose long-tethered cables caught propellers and wings? Bevin had no doubts about how to respond: Any anti-aircraft balloons would be destroyed immediately, he declared. Officials in Washington told General Clay, who maintained a command headquarters in Berlin, to do nothing of the kind, unless he first received clearance from the Department of the Army.

An endeavor as immense as supplying the city by air required that the Americans coordinate closely with the RAF. The British allowed the U.S. Air Force to base many of its aircraft at fields in their occupation zone, to shorten flight times to Berlin. The drama was bringing the two great powers closer. The Foreign Office, for example, decided it no longer had to rate every single contact with the U.S. military as top secret, which helped the flow of communications. But there was a hitch: working closer together juxtaposed the relative material contributions of each party, in a way that could only work to Britain's disadvantage. That said, the British Empire could draw on worldwide resources. There was a closing of civilized ranks as crews streamed in from the Royal Canadian Air Force, the Royal Australian Air Force, the Royal New Zealand Air Force, and the South African Air Force.

Once the effort got going, from eight outlying air bases, General Clay expected the RAF to be responsible for flying in 1,500 tons daily of food, fuel, and medicine. Why not? It was the RAF. Yet that was twice the maximum the British said they could deliver. At the start, they worked independently and, like the Americans, relied on dented, well-used twin-engine Douglas C-47 Skytrains. For three weeks in August, the RAF heroically met U.S. targets. But then its volume started to slip. Enough mechanics couldn't be found for flight checks and repairs. By October, the RAF and its far-flung coalition had fallen below even 950 tons, an amount Clay had begun insisting was the new minimum. Control of the RAF's efforts was then transferred to a joint organization, called the Combined Airlift Task Force—based at Wiesbaden, in the U.S. occupation zone, 280 miles southwest of Berlin. Meanwhile, the Americans began flying newer four-engined C-54 Skymaster transports that carried nearly five times the tonnage of the battered C-47 workhorses.

Attlee and Bevin were startled by warnings from their military chiefs. "The position of the Royal Air Force [is] extremely serious," one analysis concluded, while the army was "in a parlous condition in relation to its commitments."[30] Field Marshal Bernard Montgomery was then chief of the Imperial General Staff, the grand title used until the early 1960s for the professional head of the British army. He told them that none of this should be a surprise: British forces, after all, were spread through the Middle East and were now enmeshed in a Malayan guerrilla war. Montgomery warned that Berlin wouldn't survive its long gray months of winter.

Throughout this time in Berlin, the Red Army would periodically detain U.S. soldiers or civilians who entered the Soviet sector. The Americans generally accepted what Clay called "humiliation without retaliation" from the Russians. Ninety-three Americans, mostly soldiers, had been arrested arbitrarily just in the first half of 1948, often thrown in cells with German criminals and forced to scrub floors. Private John Sienkiewicz of Baltimore would be held for ten months in the borough of Pankow, where he was beaten and subject to "water treatment" by Soviet interrogators before escaping along with three British prisoners.[31] But no war cries were heard. These were primitive opponents, the Americans reasoned, and such cruelties could be expected.

There were acts of humiliation in the Western zones as well, amid nerve-rattling tensions. In early July, for example, one of General Clay's jeep patrols halted a speeding Russian motorcade in the U.S. sector. GIs hauled Marshal Vasily Sokolovsky, chief of the Red Army in Germany, out of his limousine. Sokolovsky's bodyguards raised their tommy guns, at which point an MP stuck a pistol into the pit of the marshal's stomach until the weapons were lowered.

In September, now Lieutenant General Curtis LeMay, who had led U.S. Air Forces in Europe for eleven months, was called to Washington to head the new Strategic Air Command. He then became the youngest four-star general since Ulysses S. Grant and would run SAC for nine crucial years. He took up a deadlier task than provisioning Berlin. Atomic bombers were being deployed to send a message to the Kremlin. These were Boeing B-29 Superfortresses with the internal configurations required to carry atomic bombs. It was no secret which USAF wings had these capabilities. Such planes were the subject of newsreels. Except for destroying Hiroshima and Nagasaki, however, they had never been sent overseas.

The only way for U.S. atomic bombers to strike the Soviet Union effectively, and perhaps to return safely via Egypt, was to take off from airfields in England. To this end, the British chiefs and Foreign Office experts knew the Americans had to consider the status of their basing rights and would be calling on London should worse come to worst.

The U.S. Air Force chief, Hoyt Vandenberg, the senator's nephew, had already caucused with his counterpart, Sir Arthur Tedder, marshal of the RAF, in May as the Russians were tightening the screws. That was also the month that the British government disclosed publicly it was building its own A-bomb. General Vandenberg and Tedder agreed that a visit by B-29 atomic-capable bomber groups to Britain could have "wholesome effects." Marshall had doubts but signed off. In June,

Pentagon officials nonetheless wanted to determine whether Bevin was merely consenting to their plan or was truly enthusiastic. So on the twenty-fifth, George Marshall's aides asked Ambassador Douglas to find out. Had Bevin "fully explored and considered the effect of the arrival of these two groups in Britain upon British public opinion"?[32] The reply the ambassador brought back to them was yes.

On July 18, the first two squadrons of B-29s arrived: sixty, with more to follow. (The 509th Bomber Group, the only formation actually to possess atomic bombs, remained in New Mexico.) The USS *Sicily* brought over the partly disassembled fighters, of which there were eighty-two. The only hitch with the plan was that an industrial strike on the rat-ridden Glasgow wharves delayed the unloading. Letters about how and where to base the bombers were exchanged between the U.S. Air Force commander in Britain and the Air Ministry. There was no formal agreement. This was not due to the "special intimacy of the Anglo-American connection," as Henry Kissinger—mythologizing the relationship—has claimed.[33] Instead, the administration preferred to keep matters on a flexible nondiplomatic basis, and Attlee hoped to avoid parliamentary debate.

American personnel began returning to Britain in force, starting with these airmen. The press in both countries featured nostalgic articles because many of the pilots were wartime fliers and ties remained strong.

Southampton was among the places in England that boasted inspiring wartime attachments, and they were renewed. The city had been the major port of transit between England and Normandy for centuries. Almost five months after D-day, on October 24, its mayor had stood on the docks to say farewell to Private Paul Shimer, 7th Army, 15th Infantry, a twenty-seven-year-old former assistant manager at J. C. Penney's from Chambersburg, Pennsylvania. He happened to be the one millionth GI embarking for France. Private Shimer stepped through the counting machine and talked quietly with the mayor. Shimer was promised that if he were to fall, his wife, Marian, and their three-year-old daughter would be cared for. Shimer saw much action in the months ahead, during which time he earned two Bronze Stars and two Purple Hearts and was promoted to sergeant, and on April 14, 1945, he was killed by a shell while leading his men against a fortified Bavarian hill. By 1947, Southampton had raised £1,000 for his daughter's education. Chambersburg in turn collected $3,000 to feed Southampton's children, and the fruit growers of Franklin County added in six hundred bushels of apples. The city itself, on the south coast, didn't provide a base when the U.S. airmen returned in 1948. But its townspeople embodied the "just like old times" spirit that welcomed them back.[34]

The B-29s were intended to stay only during the Berlin emergency. But Secretary of Defense Forrestal never imagined that the commitment would be that brief. He hoped that the planes would become an accepted fixture, as with U.S. warships in the Mediterranean. Even the Church of England accepted the use of the atom bomb, he said. But that claim could only surprise people unaware of the church's readiness to adapt to prevailing beliefs. The Americans, however, had yet to ask Prime Minister Attlee whether anyone minded, should the worst really occur, if the bombs to be used against Russia might be delivered from England.

As months passed, the airlift began going so well that Berliners' food rations were boosted by 15 percent. They received more sugar, fat, and cereal than before the blockade—and, for the first time since the war's end, cheese. Flights could continue indefinitely, said the Americans cheerfully. The airlift's entire cost, they added, was less than would be spent on forty-eight hours of war with Russia. The British struggled and kept flying. The overall tonnage was setting records. By midwinter, in February 1949, the totals were 5,437 tons per day, with 700,000 tons of supplies delivered overall, one-third of that now being flown in by the RAF and its commonwealth pilots and the remaining two-thirds by the Americans. This was about the same division of labor, by British calculations, as during the war.

THE BLOCKADE AND THE AIRLIFT WOULD LAST TEN MONTHS. AS today, when Russia's threats have produced the reinvigorated European alliance that Moscow claims to fear, Stalin's bullying was strengthening military ties in the West. France's dread of German revanchism was giving way to an immediate terror of the Kremlin. Western Germany, after all, was utterly tranquil.[35]

France's ambassador in Washington, Henri Bonnet, helped make the case for a formal U.S. defense guarantee. Without it, he argued, the Russians would occupy Western Europe, and "the entire economic and social elite of the nation [France] would be exterminated."[36] It would be worse than the Nazi occupation, he insisted. Like many other European public figures, Bonnet felt that the stakes for him were life or death, which is forgotten today. *The New York Times*' military correspondent Drew Middleton was among those who agreed. He was impatient with "the fools who delude themselves with the idea that a Russian occupation would be like the German occupation."[37] The Russians would be much crueler than the Nazis, he believed. The matter of more than seventy-five thousand French Jews deported to the death camps doesn't seem to have arisen. Instead, Bonnet, Middleton, and others argued that if Western Europe became a Soviet province, entire countries would experience the atrocities and deportations that Stalin had inflicted on Poland and the Baltic republics.

"Great Britain and the United States intend to fight side by side with France and Benelux on the Rhine," Field Marshal Montgomery asserted in Paris during an October 1948 planning meeting with General Jean Joseph de Lattre de Tassigny, a World War II hero of the Free French. Britain had become a member of the Western Union, a five-nation European precursor to NATO that functioned as a stopgap defense organization. De Lattre commanded its designated ground forces. U.S. officers were attending the meeting only as observers, and Montgomery was making some big assumptions about what the Americans would do if the Red Army invaded. Still no treaty of any sort existed with Washington. De Lattre asked Montgomery to repeat that statement slowly. "It is an indication of courage and an act of faith," de Lattre said, for anyone "to plan a defense for which they have not the means."[38]

The British, however, planned to withdraw to the Pyrenees after initially stalling the Red Army on the Rhine. There'd be no contest. De Lattre condemned this aspect of Montgomery's design. He warned that France's railway unions would block their retreat. And they'd block any U.S. withdrawal too, he said, should American occupation forces also try to pull back from Germany in the face of the Red Army. Later, Montgomery assured the Americans that such threats were "all nonsense."[39]

Bevin was meanwhile pushing hard to get a U.S. guarantee for a bigger, more established alliance. "He was living with the memory of America's fatal repudiation of Wilson in 1919," recalled Oliver Franks.[40] And so were all European leaders, one way or the other. Marshall was angered when Bevin told him Britain wouldn't again stand alone to buy time for civilization, as it had after Dunkirk. Did that mean it wouldn't fight? Marshall demanded. No, came the reply, but no one in Britain would tolerate another long wrangle on Capitol Hill while Congress waited "to be kicked into the war by some other power."[41] Everyone needed to resist hostilities with Russia from the start of a conflict. He urged Marshall to summon a conference and begin negotiating right away with would-be allies; a North Atlantic defense treaty that included the United States had to be drafted, signed, and ratified immediately. The Americans chose to proceed at their own pace.

TOWARD YEAR'S END, GENERAL CLAY STILL HAD NO AUTHORIZATION to help defend the British occupation zone. This wasn't some bungling Pentagon oversight. White House approval was required. The Joint Chiefs of Staff began to worry that Russia's war plans might be counting on such a "fatal delay" by the Americans.[42] Once elected in November 1948, and with the Republicans back in their accustomed role as the minority party in Congress, President Truman finally granted Clay his authorization. The JCS hoped this decision would give "notice to Russia and to the world that we are allied to Britain and will readily come to her defense if attacked," but the National Security Council insisted the authorization be kept secret.[43] Europe was still to be held at arm's length.

U.S. military attachés that fall were instructed not to let their views of Russia be affected by British opinions. Whatever they heard might be manipulative. As that alert was being circulated in October, another imposing ceremony of imperial splendor was under way in London. For the first time since 1939, the State Opening of Parliament involved red robes, ermine, royal heralds, and the Irish State Coach escorted by cavalry. The event was also attended by political and military dignitaries from throughout the empire and commonwealth, all of whom looked very much like allies.

Soon after, on November 12, three and a half years since President Roosevelt's death, a poignant and much quieter ceremony occurred in the Gothic grandeur of Westminster Abbey. Churchill and Attlee quietly drew back an American flag to uncover a simple stone tablet to Roosevelt's memory. It's on the west wall of the nave near the Tomb of the Unknown Warrior. They had jointly written the three-sentence inscription on the tablet, which called Roosevelt "a faithful friend of freedom and of Britain." Churchill, his voice shaking, spoke of brotherhood between the two nations; Attlee invoked friendship and gratitude.

7

DEFENDING THE WEST

I want to get Europe settled for a couple of hundred years.

—Foreign Secretary Ernest Bevin in Berlin, May 1949,
once the blockade had been defeated

B Y THE END OF 1948, THE AMERICANS HAD REALIZED THAT THE
British Empire and Commonwealth was vital to protecting the
half of Europe that hadn't yet fallen to Stalin. They believed the Continent's political and economic union depended on Britain and, by extension, so did Western Europe's military cohesion. The Kremlin held a similar view of Britain's pivotal role, and *Red Star*, the Russian army newspaper, denounced the "Marshallizing [of] Europe in the British manner."[1] Attlee's government and Churchill's opposition might be offering mixed signals about their views on a united Europe, but Washington was at least reassured by evidence of Britain's strength. In December, the Royal Navy and the RAF staged their largest naval and air exercises ever, from one side of the wintry Atlantic to the other. The weeklong war game included battleships, three carriers, eight destroyers, and other vessels, as well as submarines and RAF bombers labeled

as carrying atomic weapons. The Russians could show nothing like it, and even more dynamism was apparent as the new year began.

In January 1949, the largest passenger ship built since the war, the Cunard Line's luxurious RMS *Caronia*, sailed into New York on its maiden voyage. Painted in dramatic shades of green, it was instantly recognizable. The Attlee government's *Economic Survey for 1949* appeared in March, and that otherwise dry document was exuberant. The industrial machine was humming, it reported, as output kept increasing. There was even a slight trade surplus, which eased the chronic dollar shortage. And while Britain was receiving Marshall Plan money with one hand, its Treasury was giving huge amounts of aid (in sterling) to other Marshall Plan countries to cover their trading deficits with Britain. As for additional muscle, the Ministry of Supply—which provided military equipment to the three services and also handled atomic weapons research—let it be known that its reactors in Berkshire had made a batch of plutonium. Enough existed for bomb production.[2]

In May, the world's first jet bomber, the Canberra, built by English Electric, took its maiden flight. The Americans couldn't produce anything comparable on their own, and Baltimore's Glenn L. Martin Company paid for the rights to a license-built version, which would be the B-57. That summer, De Havilland Aviation unveiled a prototype of the world's first jet airliner, the secretly created Comet, which had four screaming turbojet engines buried in the wings able to zoom travelers to New York nonstop in six hours, claimed Fleet Street with some exaggeration. The military implications were obvious: Canberra- and Comet-like achievements could be combined with those of nuclear physics.

Even today, it's problematic for management consultants to assess the efficiencies and innovativeness of entire industrial sectors, which means that only in hindsight can writers assert that Britain's "decline in aerospace, automobiles, and information technology" was already fully apparent.[3] It wasn't. In fact, the biggest problem as 1949 began, observed Sir Edmund Hall-Patch, recent head of the Foreign Office's Economic Department, seemed to be his country's difficulty "to live up to the reputation we have been given" as America's partner in revitalizing the world.[4] Top U.S. officials such as Averell Harriman and Lewis

Douglas had worries too that year, but theirs were different. They were alarmed about Washington's "deep conviction that the U.S. needed Great Britain above everything else."[5]

Secretary Marshall, who turned sixty-eight on December 31, 1948, had a kidney removed that month and asked to retire. Harriman desperately wanted his job. But Truman selected Dean Acheson, who had been practicing law since leaving as undersecretary, eighteen months earlier. Acheson, after all, had previously been effective handling both sides of the aisle when he had spent eight months in 1945 as assistant secretary for congressional relations. Truman hoped he'd use similar tact to calm the turmoil on Capitol Hill, where Republicans and Democrats were fighting with their respective traditionalist wings (more so than with each other) over foreign policy. That belief proved spectacularly wrong.

Acheson took office as secretary of state on January 21, 1949. He would serve the four full years of Truman's elected term, and twenty years later he'd title his memoir *Present at the Creation: My Years in the State Department*. Although, as we'll see, this book must be handled very carefully, it's still the best account of government service ever written by a U.S. cabinet member, and this was indeed a time of "creation." The decisions that began being taken in 1949 proved irrevocable.

ACHESON WAS A FIGURE OF EXTREMES, WITH HIS REFINED MANners and volcanic furies. He was also one of the two most effective secretaries of state in his country's history.[6] It's long overdue to look at him anew.

Myth has it that Acheson was an "Anglophile" ("of the first order," according to the historian Fredrik Logevall) and a "WASP aristocrat" ("a caricature of the breed," says the cultural critic Jeffrey Hart).[7] He was completely the opposite of both stereotypes, and one can't understand the decisions he made at State—nor fully grasp the history of that era—without appreciating this.

Yes, he prepped at Groton and was Yale class of 1915, which was Nick Carraway's class. Yes, he went to Harvard Law, followed by brief service as a naval ensign. And in America to have attended such schools, along with being a naval officer, puts you in the patriciate, unlike in Britain, where the patriciate knows itself all too well.

Acheson also had an aristocratic bearing: he was a striking presence at six feet one, with piercing blue eyes and, from his early twenties, a neat mustache. A British journalist described him as a Velázquez grandee: tall, thin, elegant. The way he dressed infuriated his enemies and became an issue in itself. He looked "more like the British ambassador than the British ambassador" was one of many such observations by the press.[8] But even this matter is misunderstood. In writing of Acheson, Henry Kissinger wings it again by noting his "Bond Street tailoring," but there were no tailors on Bond Street in those days.[9] Acheson wore decent suits made by American shops: Farnsworth-Reed, in Washington; Brooks Brothers, in New York; J. Press, in New Haven. He wore them all with well-polished shoes and a slightly formal homburg. It seems to be the main reason for labeling him an Anglophile, other than his being an Episcopalian, which to some people means being part of a slavishly Anglophile elite.

Acheson's father, the Reverend Edward Campion Acheson, had humble origins indeed. He had emigrated alone at sixteen from Kent to seek opportunity in Canada. He was a veteran of the British imperial forces that had quelled a settler-Indian secessionist rebellion in Canada's Northwest Territories, and he'd worked his way through seminary as a warehouse hand, marrying the daughter of a prosperous Toronto distiller. In 1892, he accepted the call of the only parish he ever led, Holy Trinity in Middletown, Connecticut.[10] The town—just downriver from the bustling capital at Hartford—was one of the state's half a dozen largest, with 17,486 residents at the turn of the century. The self-confidence that would underpin his son's relentless independence in the years ahead arose from an infinitely nurturing childhood, and one in which he could thrive as a rebel. Acheson would reminisce that no rules existed for rambunctious boys in such towns except not to hang on the back of ice wagons—so he'd always hang on the back of ice wagons.

In 1921, Acheson joined the recently formed Washington law firm of Covington, Burling & Rublee. He became friends with Congressman Lewis Douglas in 1927 when he represented Arizona in a water-rights case before the Supreme Court. Like Douglas, he entered Franklin Roosevelt's first administration, as undersecretary of the Treasury in 1933, and also like Douglas he clashed with FDR over economic policy and resigned, albeit politely. He then returned to Covington, but the routines of corporate litigation in the firm's Union Trust Building offices paled beside the excitements he found at the heights of government. In 1940, during the run-up to America's entry into World War II, he began supporting the Committee to Defend America by Aiding the Allies and, in January 1941, rejoined the Roosevelt administration, shortly before Douglas began championing Lend-Lease. Acheson was one of the lawyers whose resourcefulness in creating postwar institutions so impressed Keynes, who hitherto had relegated the legal profession to clerkly obscurity.

Following the war, Acheson and Ambassador Douglas were the two in-house radicals of the Truman years. They were by no means ideologues but were always challenging authority, disputing accepted wisdoms, and showing contempt for all pomposity. Unlike Douglas, Acheson carried his radicalism into dealings with the British Empire.

After seeing Acheson engage Anthony Eden in a brutal argument over Iran, Evelyn Shuckburgh, who served as Eden's private secretary, described Acheson as "just another tough guy."[11] He was right about "tough guy" yet wrong about the "just." Acheson was tough like any good lawyer of the sort who likes to make an argument that's somewhat cleverer than the truth. But when it came to deriding Britain, he usually did so purposefully: describing to Senator Russell in 1946 its "decadence" over the loan; concluding in 1947, after Bevin stated there'd be no further aid for Greece, that Britain was "finished"; or threatening the Attlee government in 1950 over its delays in sending troops to Korea. Oliver Franks, who became a friend, recognized him as far from being an English or British type. To be sure, he was "pro-British"—and why not since Britain was a civilized country?[12] He was also pro-French. But there's no serious person of those years who was less of an Anglophile.

That Acheson regularly derided Britain isn't a surprise for the son of an Irish-Scots immigrant, from a people famous for disdaining English manners and prerogatives.[13] Tellingly, in his captivating account of his youth and early career, *Morning and Noon*, he avoids saying that his father was even born in England.[14] Who'd want to claim that? At the time, the empire still held much of America's establishment under its spell, and for that very reason Acheson enjoyed bucking it.

Republicans came to hate Acheson, and so did quite a few Democrats. Within eighteen months of his being in office, House Republicans tried to garnish his salary, a gesture that meant nothing under the Constitution but that offered another opportunity to denounce him for treason. He's also the only cabinet secretary to take a swing at a U.S. senator in full view of a sitting committee, his target being Nebraska's Kenneth Wherry, the Republican minority leader. Democrats could feel equally aggrieved. Leslie Fiedler, the wildly provocative anti-Communist literary critic, distilled mainstream Democratic Party opinion as well when he burned Acheson into a vitriolic cameo: Acheson, he wrote, "seemed the projection of all the hostilities of the Midwestern mind at bay; his waxed mustache, his mincing accent, his personal loyalty to a traitor [Alger Hiss] who also belonged to the Harvard Club."[15] Here indeed is one of FDR's effete "cookie pushers," as the president had called striped-pants diplomats at the State Department. But these are just caricatures, as if from some trash romance novel. Acheson was an original.

Acheson did see Britain and its empire as useful. He recognized that a special relationship existed, given a shared language and history, but to him the British were increasingly like Grenadier Guards wearing their bearskins in a splendid military tattoo. He wasn't disturbed that the British were "out of the business of world management," as one historian writes, because he was smart enough to know that they were never in it.[16] (The notion of "world management" is a recent American conceit and a core reason for today's foreign policy blundering.) Matters of social class, exemplified by Britain, also got on his wick. Acheson was repelled by dullards who'd obstruct the hopes of talented strivers rising up from nowhere, people such as his father. And another example of rising from nowhere in England, he understood, was Ernest Bevin.

Acheson and Bevin became close friends—even more so than Bevin and Lewis Douglas. In his memoir, Acheson writes of being in an elevator with Bevin, who began singing "The Red Flag," the revolutionary anthem of the world democratic Far Left and the old song of the Labour

Party. Acheson knew the tune and joined in: "The people's flag is deepest red. . . . Their hearts' blood dyed its every fold." Acheson was full of contradictions. His well-known hobby was woodworking, yet in time he would startle hypermodernist art collectors, such as Robert and Ethel Scull of the New York taxi fortune, with an informed admiration of their peculiar treasures, including Rauschenbergs, Warhols, and Jasper Johnses.[17]

Acheson also drank heavily, which wasn't unknown in the ante–*Mad Men* era. Drinking brought out both his self-regard and the angry streak that ran deep through his personality. "Dean Acheson's love affair with Dean Acheson was like what's-his-name's with Heloise," recalled the New York lawyer Thomas Finletter, who ran the Marshall Plan in Britain. "And you should've seen him drunk."[18] The Supreme Court justice Felix Frankfurter did: during Frankfurter's seventieth birthday party, at his house on Dumbarton Avenue in Georgetown, Acheson, despite adoring Frankfurter, nonetheless screamed drunken abuse at him.[19] Although he often displayed a remarkably cool temperament—which the chillingly cold Oliver Franks admired—public outbursts of anger were nothing new for Acheson. Right at the start of his career, during a 1923 shipping arbitration before the International Court of Justice in The Hague, he had leaped up and shouted at opposing counsel, "Are you calling my client, the king of Norway, a *liar?*"[20] The senior partner Edward Burling had to yank the young lawyer back into his chair by the belt loops. What nonetheless endures is Acheson's inherent moderation, which he above all used so effectively in navigating America's way from being an island superstate to a superpower.

AS LATE AS THE WINTER OF 1948-1949, WHEN THE TOPIC OF DE-fending Europe came up in international settings, the Americans tended to speak about opposing "an aggressor," unnamed. Ernest Bevin made it his driving purpose to get them to specify how, when, and under what terms they'd rise to the occasion of specifically opposing *Russia*. To that end, he inserted two paragraphs into a slowly emerging draft—soon to be the North Atlantic Treaty—that would commit all signees to respond together in case of attack, with retaliation to include the use of force. Those paragraphs would become the treaty's Article 5—then as today NATO's central principle—which has been triggered only once, after the 9/11 attacks.

Among those endorsing these paragraphs was a truly unsettling tough guy, the left-wing cabinet minister Nye Bevan, who still spoke, in his quietly melodious Welsh intonations, about the need for preventive war. Actually, his opinion had evolved since 1947: the Soviet police state should be invited to "make a mistake," by which he meant that London should provoke Stalin so that the British Empire could slam him hard in short ruthless combat.[21]

Stalin, at least, didn't see a need for war, nor a need to escalate over Berlin, because he still expected the two big capitalist powers to collapse, as his theoreticians at the Academy of Sciences' Institute of Economics in Moscow kept forecasting. But those experts were trembling, having by now given the *Vozhd* their erring predictions for several years.

By mid-March, Bevin was telling the Commons that the Cold War had been won. Dangers existed, of course, but West Germany had been saved, big Communist parties in France and Italy had been outmaneuvered, and Russia had not succeeded in dividing America and Britain. Now the Americans were about to step forward and promise to help defend Western Europe. Bevin described the treaty that was ready to be signed in Washington as "a most famous, historic undertaking." Two weeks later, he and his staff boarded the *Queen Mary* and set out for New York. The North Atlantic Treaty, he told these aides, would create "a well-organized nucleus" around which Britain would build wider security arrangements.[22] It had become central to his design for a series of interlocking regional pacts covering the globe.

The liner docked in New York during the mild breezy dawn of March 30. Churchill was already in Manhattan, having arrived a week earlier with Mrs. Churchill, and they were staying at Bernard Baruch's 4 East Sixty-Sixth Street apartment. The reason for Churchill's first visit to America in three years was to speak at a Massachusetts Institute of Technology symposium on scientific enterprise, and MIT had paid $1,000 for his appearance.[23] He had expected to see Truman at that gathering in Cambridge. When the president instead had to remain in Washington, Churchill went to the capital to be part of the mounting excitement that surrounded the Atlantic Treaty.

On the twenty-fourth, the Churchills and Baruch took a private train car to Washington. Police escorted them through cheering crowds at Union Station, where the former prime minister was officially greeted by Harry Vaughan (the White House official who'd brought Churchill to Fulton and who was about to be hauled before the Senate for influence peddling). Oliver Franks then whisked the small party some six miles straight up Massachusetts Avenue to the embassy. After a reception, Churchill left for Blair House on Lafayette Square for dinner with Truman, Snyder, Marshall, Acheson, and a dozen others. (The White House was undergoing complete reconstruction from 1949 to 1952, although West Wing offices kept being used.) He returned to New York the following day, and in Baruch's residence he met John Foster Dulles, the leading Republican foreign policy spokesman and future secretary of state.

Churchill had corresponded with Dulles after the 1948 presidential election, and now he showed Dulles a draft of the speech he'd be delivering four days later at MIT.[24] Dulles eagerly offered piercing criticisms, which is the last thing an author truly seeks when displaying an essentially completed work. Later, after the men had parted, Dulles recognized that he had gone too far and sent Churchill a letter confessing that he hadn't paid enough attention to the manuscript's "lofty thoughts and pungent expression."[25] There's no record of a reply.

As for Ernest Bevin, he headed directly to Washington by train after meeting in New York with the country's top labor union leaders and didn't see Churchill. Once in the capital, he moved into the same recently vacated suite at the British embassy. The following afternoon, Franks took him to Acheson's office, which was then a large two-story room, with a private elevator, on the department's fifth floor overlooking the main entrance on Twenty-First Street. It was their initial encounter and it went well.

Bevin spoke to the National Press Club on Friday. He bantered easily with American journalists. Big and burly, he talked in his rough way about the Atlantic Treaty and defending the West, telling them, "To would-be aggressors, it says: 'Think twice—think thrice.'" Reporters applauded.* He went on to confess to feeling more nationalistic when abroad. "Why, I don't even stand any criticism of Winston Churchill," he said, prompting laughs.[26]

Come Monday, April 4, the United States, Britain, and ten other nations—France, Canada, Italy, Norway, Iceland, Portugal, Denmark, and the Low Countries—signed the treaty near the National Mall, in what today is the Mellon Auditorium. Truman entered the building's blue-domed chamber, full of stone columns, and delivered a six-minute speech that echoed FDR's 1941 call for Lend-Lease. The nations of the West were coming together for self-protection, he said, like "a group of householders living in the same locality." But this was just the initial step, he added. Also needed was "a cooperative economic effort."[27] He didn't mention that the treaty still had to be ratified by the Senate, and not many people would have risked stating that, to be certain. In fact, its very name, the *North Atlantic* Treaty, was a concession to lingering isolationism. It was necessary to emphasize the security of the defending ocean, the Atlantic, and not of the sinful continent, Europe.

Meanwhile, on March 31, Churchill, with all the eagerness of a techno-enthusiast, had made headlines at MIT. The audience expected for his opening speech proved too large for the campus. Instead, thirteen thousand people were jammed across the Charles River into the Boston Garden, which was still cluttered from a hockey riot the night before. Baruch introduced his famous houseguest, the national anthem played, and Churchill stepped up to the podium. He wore a single decoration on his jacket—the insignia of America's Distinguished Service Medal, received from General John J. Pershing in 1919.

"We have suffered in Great Britain by the lack of colleges of University rank in which engineering and the allied subjects are taught," said Churchill. Then he spoke of the "terrible 20th Century" that had followed the glories of the Victorian era. By this point, neither he nor Bevin could give a speech without telling of Mongol hordes or Turks attacking Christian civilization. But like Bevin, Churchill preferred to speak opti-

---

*The "West" was a new geopolitical term coming to mean not just the United States and Western Europe but other areas of the world not part of the expanding Communist bloc, such as, eventually, Japan.

mistically. He closed with a line he had delivered at Fulton. "Do not suppose," he repeated, "that half a century from now you will not see seventy or eighty millions of Britons spread about the world and united in defense of our traditions, our way of life."[28] Three years earlier, many Americans had been repelled by his message of global cooperation with what he called British imperial forces. No longer, as the rousing applause showed.

Churchill stayed at the Ritz hotel on the Boston Common for another day and then returned with Baruch to New York. On Monday, April 4, the day of the Atlantic Treaty's signing, he sailed for Southampton.

That same day, Lewis Douglas was fly-fishing on the river Test, in the south of England, where this sport reaches its apogee in the local chalk streams. Fly-fishing was his passion, but he also used it for work. He'd given handcrafted Everett Garrison rods to fellow devotees of the art, including General Marshall and General Walter Bedell Smith, and he was fishing that day with a British aviation tycoon. Around noon, while he was casting against a strong wind, a sudden gust blew the line back and drove the hook of a heavy wet salmon fly deep into his left eye. His gillies cut the line close to his face and then raced him, in agony, fifteen miles on backroads to a surgeon at the Free Eye Hospital in Southampton. Excruciating operations ensued, but they were of little help. Douglas lost the use of his left eye and thereafter had to wear a black eye patch over it. Churchill heard the news aboard ship and wept. Bevin, for his part, rushed to see Douglas in the hospital as soon as he disembarked from the return voyage to America, on the fifteenth. Douglas had spoken after Truman's election about returning to Mutual Life, but the president now asked him, despite his injury, to remain on point. He agreed to stay in London, as Acheson and Franks tackled much of the policy work in Washington.

Following the treaty ceremonies, President Truman had told Bevin that he'd tried for years to reach an understanding with Moscow but had become convinced it was impossible "unless the Russians know they can't run over the rest of the world."[29] By now, Stalin had hit obstacles in Berlin. The airlift had rallied the West. When it started, General Clay had also imposed a counterblockade on eastern Germany, and it was biting hard. Perhaps, Truman began to feel, the Kremlin was ready for compromise. That was one benefit of having Andrei Vyshinsky appear in New York for meetings at the UN later that month.

Short, slim, and jittery, with a merciless glare, Vyshinsky had just replaced his boss, Molotov, as foreign minister. When he landed at Idlewild Airport, Vyshinsky startled reporters by casually speaking with them in English. The Americans and British had been following him for years, but they had no idea he was fluent, a telling indication of how little insight the West had on Stalin's court. Vyshinsky proved a useful conduit and helped the Russians find face-saving ways to cut their losses. Come May 12, they had ended restrictions on transport in and out of Berlin; the counterblockade was lifted soon after. By then, the British Empire's pilots had delivered 40 percent of the total tonnage—roughly as complete a division of labor, calculated Harold Macmillan, a future prime minister, as had occurred in the wartime partnership.[30] But the airlift itself didn't quite stop. The last tons of coal would be flown into the city on September 30. "I am a trade unionist," Bevin told the House of Commons, "and I never call off a strike until I am sure there is no victimization."[31]

Around two o'clock in the morning on May 22, ten days after the Berlin blockade ended—and a day before the three western occupation zones consolidated to form the Federal Republic of Germany—James Forrestal killed himself. He had suffered a nervous breakdown in early April and had left his room high up in Bethesda Naval Hospital. His last moments are too ghastly for fiction: the copying out of a passage from Sophocles (including the lines "better to die and sleep the never-waking sleep than linger on / And dare to live when the soul's life is gone"); a noose fumblingly made from pajama cord; pushing himself out of a small window; and then a jerk and brief strangling before a plunge through ten stories of air. He was one of the first Americans to understand the threat posed by Stalinism, yet Soviet apologists, among them the former vice president Henry Wallace, said his suicide was the fulfillment of a deep-seated psychoneurosis that manifested itself in hysterical and ungrounded alarms about Soviet Russia. They were wrong, but today writers who're similarly uninformed echo that claim.[32] Forrestal's legacy, however, was in place by the time his health broke: if the United States was to succeed as a world political-military power, it would have to work hand in glove with strong allies and do much to lift them up.

THERE WERE DIFFICULTIES OF A LESSER SORT WITH ANOTHER CABI-net member. A point about Acheson that hasn't been known—and that one would never learn from his own recounting—is that he had an uneasy relationship with Harry Truman during this first year in office. Unlike Marshall's decision to recruit Lovett as his undersecretary, for example, Acheson's second-in-command was selected by Truman and Snyder. That was James Webb, forty-two, whom they had come to trust completely during Webb's three years directing the Bureau of the Budget. Trying to be helpful, Webb summed up the problem for George Kennan later in 1949: "Mr. Acheson was a wonderful person," the president had told him earlier in the day. "But," continued Webb, who conveyed Truman's feelings, "he was austere and aloof and did not seem to establish a real personal contact with the President and his entourage."[33] And a blunter message was sent: "Do you still want to be a member of the team?" asked White House aide Admiral Sidney Souers, at Truman's behest, after Acheson caused a blowup with the CIA director.[34]

Truman's confidence was granted slowly, which made it important that Secretary Snyder approved of Acheson. At the same time, Acheson was coming under attack by Republicans in Congress in a way that they'd never have dared to attack General Marshall—and such vitriol also helped pull Acheson and Truman together. In fact, Truman and the men around him routinely felt besieged by an angry nation, or at least much of it, whether over foreign policy or the economy. Nearly twenty years later, Acheson and Snyder would coauthor an essay on party politics. They reflected wryly on themselves during this era. "All of us in the Cabinet knew who the whipping boys were," they wrote. "We were."[35]

CONGRESS THAT SPRING WAS SCHEDULED TO VOTE ON ITS SECOND annual appropriation for the Marshall Plan, a gigantic $5.5 billion piece of legislation. This meant it wasn't the best time for the administration to be submitting the North Atlantic Treaty for ratification. The treaty was certain to require additional expensive obligations, even though the White House and the State Department "absolutely repudiated" any idea of garrisoning a serious number of GIs across the Atlantic.[36] In any event, William Jenner, the Indiana Republican, wanted the United States completely out of Europe. Explaining why, he cited waste in socialist-governed Britain, where, he alleged, the National Health Service even supplied unfortunate men who'd lost their hair with "free toupees." Another Republican, William "Wild Bill" Langer, from North Dakota, attacked Churchill as a "cold-blooded foreign propagandist" who was pulling America "into one more big war."[37] Acheson disdained these sorts of legislators as "primitives," but it wasn't as easy for him to dismiss Ohio's senator Robert Taft, by now the most powerful member of Congress, with whom he sat on Yale's governing board. Taft yearned for an America free from world entanglements. The North Atlantic Treaty, he declared, was "more likely to produce war than peace."[38]

Moreover, the United States had slipped into recession the previous November, and that fact was undeniable by the spring of 1949. Eager observers in Moscow interpreted the U.S. downturn as a big promising step toward capitalist ruin.

The United States wasn't at all "at the zenith of its confidence," as is said today, again by Mr. Kissinger.[39] "In 1949," recalled Secretary of Commerce Charles Sawyer, a former lieutenant governor of Ohio, "many in and out of government were predicting a depression."[40] At issue was the first real test of the postwar economy's strength, and Main Street shopkeepers as well as Wall Street analysts, all of whom lived with painful memories of the 1930s, feared the worst. Stock issues were withdrawn. Detroit slashed prices for the first time in a decade. Department store sales fell 22 percent. Unemployment jumped. The Council of Economic Advisers warned Congress that a return of 1929's crack-up would gut $800 billion of value out of the country, and that meant a full, crippling three years of total production.[41]

From Europe, it looked as if the Americans still hadn't learned to master their cycles of boom and bust. British exports to the United States fell 38 percent in April as consumers stopped spending. The effects of a continued recession in the United States, Bevin said, "may drag us all down."[42]

In Washington, the bite of recession made a unified Western Europe imperative. Economists testified on Capitol Hill that a single currency and the falling trade barriers of a united Europe would reduce Congress's Marshall Plan costs by 66 percent. Business leaders said unity might double Europe's industrial output. America couldn't hold up the world alone: Marshall Plan aid was to end anyway in 1952, and maybe a full-blown 1930s depression was in the offing. All agreed that European unity couldn't be achieved without Britain's full participation.

As the North Atlantic Treaty waited ratification, U.S. officials were hearing ever more from the governments of France, Belgium, and the other new allies about London's obstruction of political-economic unity. "We should tell them straight, and as soon as possible," insisted Alec Cairncross about the Americans, "that we do not intend to enter a Western Union Federation and have no intention to concentrate our activities upon Europe." That sort of assertion, believed this outstanding economist who was advising Whitehall's Board of Trade, "would put an end to American hopes of a United Europe."[43] No matter that Congress, in its second appropriation, had just set Europe's unification as a key purpose of the Marshall Plan.

Impatient Americans were projecting their own "U.S." experience on a skeptical and weary Britain, and that was occurring as a worldwide economic catastrophe approached.

BEVIN'S CLOSEST AIDE IN "THE DIPLOMATIC" DURING THESE YEARS was Gladwyn Jebb, forty-nine, who had a wide-ranging remit that essentially enabled him to serve as a deputy. Jebb was an aristocrat, with a Tudor manor house, Bramfield Hall, in Suffolk. He'd entered diplomacy after Eton and Magdalen College, Oxford, and early in 1949 he had been knighted, having helped to organize the United Nations in the spring of 1945, when world leaders convened in San Francisco. Once Bevin arrived at the Foreign Office, in mid-1945, it was Jebb whom he had needled with "Must be kinda queer for a chap like you to see a chap like me sitting in a chair like this." Except, for Jebb, it wasn't queer.[44] He became a devotedly effective assistant to "Uncle Ernie," as he and his inner circle called the foreign secretary among themselves.

That May, Sir Gladwyn suggested to Bevin that they invite the State Department's planning director, George Kennan, to Britain. Discussing the problems of European unity might help clear the air. The honey-worded agenda that Jebb proposed seemed unremarkable at State. In fact, a closer look would have shown that it involved examining for the record the sum total of U.S. foreign policy—as when it asked, seemingly as an afterthought, if provisions for cooperation, as in the Atlantic Treaty, extended to the Middle East. Fully aware of this larger purpose, Bevin agreed that a visit by Kennan could be useful; it would also be an opportunity for the two sides to formally exchange position papers laying out their respective approaches. If handled well, the Foreign Office could, one way or another, use Kennan's remarks to buttress its own arguments in future dealings with the Americans.

Kennan's biographer describes Jebb as Kennan's "friend," but that is only Kennan talking.[45] In a 422-page memoir, Jebb lists Kennan's name once, among three other State Department officials, and he scoffs at the idea of indulging a "planning body" or "theoreticians" in the art of foreign policy.[46] To get such basics wrong today, and to see hands-across-the-sea friendship where none exists, is an example of why America's role in the world of that time is still little understood.

Kennan was from a modest Milwaukee background, but as his diaries show, he revered the social class that Jebb personified.[47] He was eager to accept the invitation, though he was warned not to go by the department's counselor, Charles "Chip" Bohlen, who like Kennan was forty-five and a Russia expert. Deputy Undersecretary Dean Rusk, forty, an army colonel during the war who was known as a master of procedure, advised caution. If a meeting really had to occur, Rusk said, it should be informal. But what harm could there be in open-ended Q&A with diplomats of America's key ally? W. Walton Butterworth, the assistant secretary for East Asian and Pacific affairs, offered his own caveat: convening with the British was never informal, because "they make elaborate records, and play for keeps."[48]

Undersecretary James Webb finally approved the trip. Kennan then accepted. But the Policy Planning office told Jebb—as Kennan had been advised within State—that its director would not be arriving with position papers. Additionally, Kennan himself told the awaiting British officials that nothing discussed in the meetings should "be thrown back at us later as an expression of the view of this Government."[49] Jebb and his colleagues were unfazed. They'd hand him position papers whether reciprocated or not.

While preparing for the trip, Kennan wondered how "England could hope to survive as an island off the coast of Europe." If its fate should indeed be grim, he told his staff with delicious defeatism, then "we ought to go into the discussions like the doctor who must face a patient whose disease is incurable."[50] He again brought in consultants. They included Frank Altschul, the chairman of General American Investors Company; Hans Morgenthau, of the University of Chicago; Reinhold Niebuhr, the eminent theologian; John J. McCloy, whom Secretary Snyder had elevated to president of the World Bank in early 1947; and General Walter Bedell Smith, who had been Eisenhower's wartime chief of staff and hatchet man. Also attending was Robert Woodruff, the chairman of the Coca-Cola Company, who knew something about cross-border integration, having built a soda business since 1920 that ran seamlessly throughout Europe.

Kennan's own views on a united Europe were eccentric, which included his thoughts on Germany. He had been one of those "junior officials" at State who, the previous year, had given General Lucius Clay headaches by advocating a conjoined, supposedly neutralized Germany. The Joint Chiefs thought his ongoing insistence preposterous. Why should the Allies give up West Germany without a struggle now that they had beaten the blockade? Kennan also claimed in these meetings that France had suffered little under the Nazis but that the French had since "been evil and uninhibited in their treatment of the Germans."[51] He expected the return of right-wing German nationalism. A unified Europe—without Britain—seemed to him the best way to direct those passions. After all, he insisted, a powerful nationalist Germany was going to dominate a European federation in any event; therefore, Britain should look elsewhere than the adjacent Continent for its regeneration. Otherwise, he continued, it would become little more than an educational and travel center. How financed, he failed to say. "You wouldn't eliminate the grouse shooting?" asked Woodruff, the genteel Atlanta mogul. "That's part of education," quipped the director of Policy Planning.*[52]

Late Sunday afternoon, on July 10, Kennan flew from New York to Paris, en route to London. He fretted about having to sit up for the fifteen-hour flight—which included two stops for refueling—because no one paid for a bed. He'd spend the week conferring with Jebb and other top diplomats, among them Sir Roger Makins, forty-five, an important deputy undersecretary who oversaw economics.[53] The talks started in the Foreign Office and then moved to a government-owned country house in Oxfordshire.

Ingratiatingly, Kennan in fact did show what his hosts regarded as State Department position papers. Those concerned Russia, as well as Europe. In line with earlier warnings at State, however, Kennan wouldn't admit disclosing anything to his colleagues at Foggy Bottom—though in his memoirs he acknowledges having shared "a personal paper" that, he says, hadn't been discussed within the government.[54]

Kennan then addressed Jebb and the others candidly. London, he told them, shouldn't go beyond a dangerous point of no return in its ties to Continental Europe. America was overextended, and its pledge to defend Europe, as promised in the North Atlantic Treaty, was really the extreme limit of what could be expected. He was close to contradicting U.S. policy, and then he went further. He added that it would be rash for Britain to count on even this commitment lasting for long. A dividing line had to be drawn, and that line must be the English Channel.

In sum, there was no need to take the urgings for European unity from Congress and the Truman administration seriously. Kennan went on to propose an Anglo-American union. That idea was so impractical, so invidious to every other U.S. ally, and so cloyingly sentimental that it would have been voted down even at the venerable New York Yacht Club.[55] According to Foreign Office records, he followed up by telling Jebb that "if the pace got too hot" for the British when being pushed by

---

*Sadly, that year's grouse season, which began the next month on the twelfth, is not remembered as among the best. Devoted beaters were being lured away by other callings, and shoots got canceled due to an absence of rich foreigners.

the Americans toward federation, they should then seek "other arrangements" with Washington.[56]

Despite Kennan's nay-saying about the North Atlantic Treaty (or the "Atlantic Pact," as it was known), the accord was finally ratified by the Senate 82 to 13 that July. It came into force the next month, and administration spokesmen again promised Congress that it would involve no U.S. troops. Instead, America would soon be backing a full, strong, politically and economically unified Western Europe. To help ensure that, Truman placed John Snyder as well as Dean Acheson on the NATO Council, the emerging organization's highest decision-making body.

Kennan nonetheless kept promoting his peculiar beliefs about some sort of Anglo-American federation when he returned to Washington. To him, as he'd told Jebb and company, a united Europe could then be "a balancing factor" between an Anglo-American entity and Russia. He also saw fit to tell the French ambassador that the British, just like the Americans, need not be part of a unified Europe. Henri Bonnet was a presence in Washington who had already served as France's ambassador for five years and would continue in that role for five more. He believed he was hearing the administration's truest intentions. In fact, Kennan was speaking for himself.

Weeks later, Kennan found himself put on the spot when Jebb and Makins appeared at the State Department. They asked for clarity on the U.S. position and referred to their records of earlier discussions in England—the ones in which he had minimized Washington's interest in Britain's unity with the Continent and had instead advised a federation with America. What, pray, might be the actual U.S. position? They also got him to confess to having placed stories in the press about this strange possibility, as shown in an account of September 2 by the prominent columnists Stewart and Joseph Alsop—though Kennan denied having done so to his friend Chip Bohlen. Then there had been disclosures in London's *Sunday Times*.[57] Kennan tried to be reassuring and insisted that others in Washington wanted to go even further than he in achieving union with comfortably Anglo-Saxon England. That was fantasy.

A curt yet generous man, Jebb concluded Kennan to be simply overwhelmed, rather than foolish. But Jebb still had to mollify Bevin about

Kennan's press leaks. Bevin had no interest in seeing his country absorbed into a federated Europe, but, equally, he'd never let it become a dependency of the United States. He also anticipated the damage that publicizing this idea of Anglo-American union would cause.

Writing in his study on Woodley Road, Walter Lippmann was appalled by such wishful notions of an exclusive Anglo-Saxon club. In his own widely discussed column of September 26, "Whither Britain?," he attributed this press campaign to George Kennan: two separate and unequal groupings, Lippmann feared, could open up dangerously in the Atlantic world. Lippmann, however, had inside information of his own about what had been broached in England. How so? "It is evident that much of George's thinking," Jebb explained to Foreign Secretary Bevin, who was then visiting the UN General Assembly in New York, "has come back to Mr. Walter Lippmann."[58] Bevin advised dispatching a letter back to the Foreign Office in which Jebb was to report that "Kennan or some people in his department have been talking much too much"— and he snapped about the fact "that so much should apparently be leaking out of Kennan's office."[59] Characteristically, Bevin also turned this situation to his advantage: he told Acheson that due to such confusion he couldn't interpret what the Americans truly meant by Britain's "uniting" with Western Europe.

Acheson also heard directly from a sharp Yale Law School professor, Eugene Rostow, who was working in Geneva on these issues. Rostow charged that this highly publicized foolishness from within State was "both ridiculously impractical and extraordinarily dangerous."[60] It was torpedoing the Continent's hope for unity, damaging U.S. influence, and helping to lay a smoke screen for further British delay. Without comment, Acheson forwarded Rostow's attack to Kennan, as well as to Rusk and Webb. Bohlen shared his opinion directly. "I was somewhat afraid," he wrote to Kennan as this mess continued, "that the British might try to utilize any informal long-range discussions with us as to the future of Europe for some such purpose."[61] As for the French, they saw bad faith in whatever it was that the Americans and British were concocting.

. . .

THE U.S. RECESSION PROVED TO BE A MILD ELEVEN-MONTH DOWN-turn that would be over in October, with a recovery into 1953 that was so strong it hasn't been equaled since. Yet a scary thing about recessions is that it's hard to know while living through them how they're going to turn out. By the time this one ended, it had still caused an unsettling $1.8 billion federal budget deficit that was 50 percent higher than Secretary Snyder had estimated in January. Britain, in turn, was sliding into far graver trouble, with consequences that appeared dire as well for America. "If Britain goes down, we'll go down in a matter of months," said the exceedingly influential senator Walter F. George, an honorable Georgian who chaired the Finance Committee and had previously chaired Foreign Relations.[62] No one had spoken like this during the 1947 financial crisis or, in fact, has done so since, and nearly every public figure in America weighed in, from Eleanor Roosevelt to New York's governor, Thomas Dewey.

A devil's brew had finally boiled over. No matter that Britain's industrial production was now 40 percent higher than before the war. It was ever harder to get dollars for such dutiful labor. Unlike in 1947, a buyers' market prevailed in world trade. Global supplies of manufactured goods and raw materials were rising, and thus becoming less expensive. Britain's exports to the United States and to other nations that paid in hard currency therefore had to be cheaper, of better quality, or both in order to be purchased. Such standards often weren't met. The Bank of England's gold and dollar reserves were again plunging to dangerous levels. Once those were gone, industry would sputter and unemployment would skyrocket. The causes of this crisis were like those of 1947, but repercussions looked far worse. The world was a more dangerous place in 1949, and there was more to lose. And unlike in 1947, the reserves of the entire sterling area were at risk of evaporating.

As in 1947, most of the monetary reserves of sterling area member countries were held by the Bank of England. In addition, when these depositors wanted to make purchases, as for domestic development, they found it far easier to do so from Britain or from other members of the sterling area than from the United States or from countries whose currencies (unlike those of the sterling area) were convertible into dollars.

Altogether, Britain had a protected market; that didn't enhance its ability to buy things from outside this enclosure.

Meanwhile, the costs of goods from America were rising unabated, and Britain had to pay off its sterling area depositors while committing its reserves to buying crucial American food and raw materials. This made sovereign bankruptcy—that is, the country not being able to pay its debts on any acceptable terms—an ongoing possibility. In sum, what Britain could earn from transactions within the sterling area couldn't pay off obligations to the United States, and Britain was importing much more than it had assumed it would from America and other countries (like Argentina, with its beef supplies) that demanded payment in dollars.

Financial calamity now threatened to pull apart the global political-economic-military structure that America had been struggling to build. If Britain's economy collapsed, all the money that had been invested in the Marshall Plan might as well be written off: Western Europe would return to the squalor of 1945–1946. The North Atlantic Treaty would be moot. Worse yet, given that the sterling area remained the world's largest multilateral trading zone, half the world's commerce might congeal. Even India could be hit hard, and at a moment when Washington expected that enormous democracy to succeed Chiang Kai-shek's Nationalist China (staggering under Mao Zedong's victories) as the West's closest Asian ally. Not only did U.S. hopes for global stability require a sound financial underpinning, but America's own prosperity might be infected permanently by such disorder.

Global investors call it "contagion": a shock of this magnitude to one major economy might reverberate hard through others. Because Britain's balance of payments was that of the whole sterling area rolled into one, Oliver Franks recalled, "a very, very grave and major operation" had to follow when the currency reserves of dozens of nations were threatened.[63] Could contagion and worldwide collapse really happen? Economically savvy critics like Walter Lippmann thought so, as did officials at State and Treasury, as well as in the Foreign Office, not least Bevin. Moscow believed it too. Looking back, we can see that some of this was conjecture. But the likelihood of unprecedented disaster looked all too real at the time.

Art was imitating life throughout these frenetic months. Orwell's *1984* was published in June and became an immediate hit. By that dystopian date, currency in the British Isles is shown to be the dollar, with Winston Smith paying $2.50 for his fateful diary.

Until then, however, Britain's government bonds, known as gilt-edged securities, were still denominated in sterling. During a single week in July, they lost a quarter-billion pounds of value, which was some 20 percent of total national holdings. Commenting on that development, *The New York Times* wrote of "the beginning of a long historic process" of transition between America and the British Empire.[64] The key words for us are "the beginning." The *Times* in September 1949 believed it was identifying something new—evidence that contradicts what is commonly written about this period, which is that the British Empire had closed shop in "the thousand days" after World War II.[65] That simply wasn't true.

By now, Dwight Eisenhower had left the army to head Columbia University, though he also presided temporarily over the Joint Chiefs at Truman's request. Looking at all this from Morningside Heights, he let the press know that he hoped the British would "regain their former position."[66] It's unclear what position he was imagining. That of 1914? 1939? 1945? *The New York Times* did run an article in September titled "Changes in British Empire," but it discussed "changes" only in terms of trade and finance—hardly of imperial retreat.[67]

ECONOMISTS, KEYNES HAD OBSERVED A GENERATION BEFORE, ARE the trustees not of civilization but of the possibilities of civilization. Such was the role in which the Treasury secretaries of each nation, neither of whom was an economist, found themselves. One, John Wesley Snyder, was a shrewd high-school-educated midwestern commercial banker. The other, Sir Stafford Cripps, was a patrician from the Labour Party's Far Left, who was reported to have been England's highest-paid barrister and whom Churchill described as the ablest brain in Attlee's cabinet. In the 1930s, the same cold logic that ensured Cripps won in court had made him his country's leading antifascist voice.

English gentry families who've held their land for six hundred years are often assumed to be hidebound beyond belief. But for a dynasty to have endured twenty generations of change can also be an indicator of startling flexibility. Such was the case with Cripps. He was a devout Anglo-Catholic, with no affiliation to a church, whom the Labour Party had expelled during 1937–1939 for having tried to get it into some Popular Front political arrangement with the Communists. Churchill had sent him to Moscow as ambassador for two years during the war (thinking he might get along with Stalin), then brought him home as minister of aircraft production in the coalition cabinet. A thin, scolding, vegetarian teetotaler who said he enjoyed cold-water baths, Cripps thereafter embodied austerity. By uniting legal ability with bone-deep religious trust, he was the nearest equivalent Britain had to John Foster Dulles. No one doubted his sincerity. As Chancellor of the Exchequer from 1947 to 1950, he controlled most everything in Britain's economic life.

In Washington, John Snyder was sympathetic to Cripps's difficulties. He understood the problem, as shown in his handling of the 1947 financial crisis. Starting with a visit to Britain in the fall of 1945, where he had conferred with Bevin and the rest of the leadership, much of Snyder's long tenure in the administration would be occupied by sterling's undulations. From start to finish during these years, he had to keep gauging if America in fact had a viable partner for revitalizing the world. Oliver Franks regarded him as "never in any sense unkindly to the United Kingdom."[68] He and Franks were friends, which was a high bar with Franks, who found Snyder courageous but cautious, fittingly for a secretary of the U.S. Treasury at this moment in history.

During February, Snyder had brought the Export-Import Bank chairman, William McChesney Martin—as he's remembered in twentieth-century history, and to elderly financiers—over to the Treasury Department as his assistant secretary. Bill Martin, as he preferred to be called, was then forty-two, a graduate of Yale in Latin and English, and had been the New York Stock Exchange's first paid president a decade earlier. He and Snyder were able to work even closer together, and all the more effectively.

The two of them spent July 2–24 overseas largely visiting Treasury Department representatives in U.S. embassies. Paris was their first stop. On Tuesday, the fifth, they met France's finance minister at his offices in the Louvre's Pavillon de Flore. While in Paris, Snyder received frantic calls from the U.S. embassy in London. On Wednesday afternoon, in the House of Commons, Cripps proposed a drastic solution to Britain's problems: halt new purchases of almost everything from the United States, in order to conserve dollars. That would include cotton, tobacco, paper, steel, and machinery. He wanted the other commonwealth countries to do the same (except for Canada, which was pegged to the U.S. dollar). The following day, July 7, Truman ordered an immediate analysis from State on crisis conditions in Britain.

Snyder and Martin flew over early on Friday morning, the eighth, joined by Averell Harriman, and at 11:00 a.m. they began four hours of talks at the Treasury, a baroque-inspired Whitehall pile near St. James's Park. On the British side sat Cripps, backed by his experts. On the American side were Snyder, Harriman, Lewis Douglas, and Bill Martin. Canada's finance minister, Douglas Abbott, placed himself somewhere in between. Snyder began by noting that Fleet Street was blaming the country's plight on America's recession. He dismissed that notion out of hand. Cripps then spoke, and he laid out a scene of the global disaster that he said would follow Britain's collapse.

Snyder made no proposals about how to address the dollar dilemma, though he was convinced that sterling's devaluation was inevitable. He just advised that the matter be examined when he and Cripps reconvened at the IMF and World Bank meetings scheduled for mid-September in Washington. (Snyder was U.S. governor of both institutions and therefore essentially chairman of the entire arrangement.) Snyder shared the same remarks with reporters on Saturday: he would not instruct Britain's government on which path it should take to solvency. On Sunday, he had lunch with Attlee at Chequers. There'd be no U.S.-prescribed solution, thank you.

Acheson would later claim theatrically that Snyder "flew back like a modern Paul Revere crying 'The British are coming!'" but he did no such thing.[69] Instead, on Monday, the eleventh, he and Assistant Secretary Martin journeyed on to Stockholm, as planned, where they examined Sweden's economic picture, then to Geneva for trade meetings, and finally to Cairo, where they visited American staffers in that city's U.S. Treasury Office. The same day that they left London, however, King George VI proclaimed a state of national emergency: he triggered the

Emergency Powers Act to respond to what Attlee's government charged were Communist-instigated strikes on the London docks. Before nightfall, contingents of soldiers, sailors, and marines were unloading freighters carrying foodstuffs. Snyder and Martin meanwhile continued with their business and only returned to sleepy summertime Washington two weeks later.

Stafford Cripps had implied he'd resign before devaluing the pound—in fact, that he'd prefer to die. One reason he said this was that in the days of fixed currencies devaluation was believed to make a nation look politically weak, even unstable. Attlee's cabinet shared this outlook: they desperately wanted to maintain the fixed exchange rate of $4.03 to the pound, established in 1940, and they hesitated to scare a public long accustomed to regard sterling as the world's currency standard. Another reason was that devaluation would raise prices for British consumers due to costlier imports, such as wheat. The working class would be squeezed hardest, no matter that sterling area exports to America would be cheaper, to the benefit of Britain's balance of payments. Yes, Britain had devalued in 1931, and America had followed two years later. But that was at the depths of the Great Depression. Now only the artificial device of officially fixed exchange rates maintained the pound's value.

Much of the task for responding to Truman's request on conditions in Britain fell to Paul Nitze, forty-two, a rich, largely self-made, and fast-rising protégé of the fallen James Forrestal who joined the Policy Planning Staff in early summer. Nitze began offering analyses in mid-July that wrote of "pessimism embracing fear," and he concluded that if Britain collapsed economically—or, nearly as bad, became estranged from the United States—the Americans would have "no acceptable foreign policy" open to them.[70]

The IMF and World Bank meetings were to convene on September 12. U.S. officials didn't know if Bevin himself was coming as part of the British delegation. Then his name, along with that of his wife, Florence, appeared on a list submitted for customs clearance, and they arrived two weeks later in New York aboard the RMS *Mauretania*. Now it was clear who'd be running the British side of the sterling-dollar talks that would precede the IMF and World Bank meetings. Ambassador

Douglas wrote Acheson a detailed, somewhat gratuitous letter counseling him to be careful and to show patience: Bevin, he warned, could be expected to knock the ball into America's court, and Acheson should be ready. Everyone was tense. When embarking at Southampton on August 31, Bevin had simply told the press that he was "probably on one of the most important missions in history."[71] By then, no one disagreed.

8

THE OUTER FORTRESS: PROTECTING THE MIDDLE EAST, AFRICA, AND ASIA

The British Empire is America's outer fortress and, without help, totalitarianism will have won an important victory.
—Senator Hubert Humphrey (D-Minn.), September 1949

IN THE FALL OF 1949, AMERICANS BEGAN USING THE WORD "BANK-ruptcy" again, but this time it applied to the entire British Empire and Commonwealth. Whatever Britain's predicament was called, anyone who had lived from 1919 on knew that financial catastrophe could eviscerate a nation, and in fact whole regions of the world. Ruination might spread to a recession-hampered America, as Walter George, chairman of the Senate Finance Committee, feared.

Britain's collapse would pull down fragile economies on the Continent before the North Atlantic allies had time to build themselves an "organization." But worse would follow. Policy makers expected that Stalin would then be able to take advantage of the disorder that a ruined Western Europe would cause in Asia, the Middle East, and Africa. He'd exacerbate instability and thus outflank the West. By cutting the European democracies off from vital commodities, he'd hammer another nail in their coffins. Stalin could then access those resources himself and, should all that occur, determined the deputy high commissioner to India, in a dispatch to the Foreign Office, Russia would "produce the economic and military strength which Great Britain could avail itself of in former years."[1]

The conventional wisdom of this era assumed that Western Europe couldn't survive without access to the raw materials and cheap labor of Asia, the Middle East, and Africa. "If France, the Netherlands and Belgium were suddenly restricted to their continental territory (or Britain to the United Kingdom and the Dominions)," wrote *The New York Times'* chief foreign correspondent, C. L. Sulzberger, "the Marshall Plan would swiftly end in failure."[2]

Acutely aware of this, Bevin argued that the North Atlantic Treaty couldn't just provide a demarcation line in Europe between East and West. It had to be the starting point of an alliance system that would stretch through to the Middle East and onward to Asia. Meanwhile, the treaty itself helped fill in a breach for imperial defense. It brought the Americans into Europe and made it easier for Bevin to support his country's fighting men elsewhere in the world. "Defending our overseas territories in the British Empire," he declared, remained the fundamental objective.[3]

One approach to protecting those lands, he believed, was to knit together big parts of the Middle East and Southeast Asia. Of course, most of this terrain had never been knit together in history. But doing so might strengthen the powers of resistance among 1.4 billion "dependent peoples" (a political term of the era) who were not, so far, under the Communist yoke. Thanks to its long experience in world affairs, Britain would do the knitting. Because this grand vision was being discussed in Whitehall at the same time that the pound sterling was crashing, it was implicit that the Americans would have to supply the yarn: aid dollars and expensive arms. Yet this was also the moment when Americans were learning the hard limits of what they could accomplish overseas. After all, China, with its 540 million people, was falling to Stalin in the autumn of 1949—or so it was said by Western observers who believed Mao Zedong would follow every Russian dictate.[4]

. . .

and other Foreign Office mandarins, George Kennan had opined that economics, over the long term, really wouldn't affect America's and Britain's ability to link themselves together. Dismissing concerns about money is a classic pseudo-patrician posture, and he was playing up to his hosts. Yet on August 18, within weeks of returning to Washington, he panicked. "The British structure outside the United Kingdom is going to have to be dismantled," he wrote.[5] By this time, more than half of U.S. voters knew of the sterling-dollar crisis. That was an extraordinary number in a country whose citizens have little interest in world affairs.

Kennan can't be blamed for panicking. Stakes were immense. That's why President Truman decided that his widely respected Treasury secretary, John Snyder, rather than Dean Acheson, would conduct the sterling-dollar talks—and would do so from within the State Department. Fortunately, Acheson and Snyder got on fine. "Well, it's always good to have the Secretary of the Treasury along to watch the financial side and not let us spend ourselves into poverty," Acheson enjoyed saying when they were together with Truman. The problem here is with Kennan.

In all his writings on the Cold War, Kennan's biographer John Lewis Gaddis only identifies Snyder once, and in just four words, as "a Missouri political crony" of Truman's—an odd way to present one of the most powerful Treasury secretaries in the nation's history.[6] Again, Gaddis is merely echoing Kennan. In his memoir, Kennan attributes Truman's decision to "obscure reasons of domestic politics," which Kennan knew at the time to be untrue.[7] There was nothing "obscure" about why Snyder was taking over. Undersecretary James Webb told Kennan the reason why, and did so after a meeting at State on August 23. Mr. Truman believed "there was no one in Washington who knew the British like Snyder," Webb explained.[8] Truman was right. It was Snyder who first developed personal ties with the new Labour Party government in the fall of 1945 and, of all members in its cabinet, Snyder's closest relation was with Bevin. Snyder's grasp of Britain's predicament was even helped by his loyal assistant, Bill Martin, being the brother-in-law of Sir Roger Makins, who headed economic policy at the Foreign Office.*

The purpose of that day's meeting, on the twenty-third, was for Snyder, Acheson, and Webb to examine the crisis, and Kennan joined in. In his memoir, Kennan would report being shocked to discover that the others intended "to meet the British with nothing other than the maximum reserve and unhelpfulness."[9] But State Department records don't show such hostility. Nonetheless, Kennan's version of the story is one that gets repeated. Kennan also wrote in his memoir that when Snyder noticed that some favorable references to the British had been inserted into a speech Truman was to deliver to the American Legion on the twenty-ninth, Snyder made "phone calls of protest" to the president. This is a line that his biographer and others parrot—except there's no record of such calls in the White House Telephone Office files.[10] Kennan concludes in his memoir that after immense effort on his part the United States followed his recommendations "with the greatest fidelity in all the practical aspects of the talks."[11] Snyder dismissed that claim when the book was published in 1967. But Kennan's biographer tells us that "Acheson was grateful to Kennan for having rescued the British negotiations from the Anglophobic Snyder."[12] The sole source for this remark, of course, is Kennan himself.

Snyder's role in chairing the high-level parley came as a relief to business, banking, and Congress. The New York Times' Arthur Krock wrote Snyder that he was "immensely pleased" to learn of it, saying that U.S. vital interests "will be better protected than otherwise."[13] Snyder set up the negotiations together with his peers in finance—Averell Harriman, Lewis Douglas, and, in an unpaid consulting role, Bob Lovett. He also received advice from his friend Bernard Baruch, who, throughout Snyder's years as Treasury secretary, served as his unofficial counselor. Bill Martin helped organize. At the State Department, Acheson followed Snyder's lead. That enabled Snyder to draw on top talents, including Paul Nitze, whose dealmaking abilities ensured astute staff

---

*Martin and Makins had married daughters of President Coolidge's secretary of war Dwight Davis, better remembered as founder of the Davis Cup in tennis.

work, and on George Perkins, the assistant secretary of state for European affairs, another solid subcabinet appointee to government who until April had served capably as executive vice president of his father-in-law's pharmaceutical enterprise, Merck and Co. No one had any interest in weakening the sterling area.

Allan Sproul, the president of the Federal Reserve Bank of New York, also weighed in. "Are we trying to re-establish the old system of international trade and currency relationships which worked with Britain at the economic and financial center of the world during the 19th Century?" he asked in a letter to Snyder, a man to whom he inevitably deferred. "Or," he continued, "must we contemplate a new and modified system which takes full account of the emergence of the United States as the world's economic and financial leader?"[14] Well, the latter. Sproul was one of the world's foremost central bankers, and yet a full five years after Bretton Woods he still had to pose the question. Even the best-informed Americans were slow to understand their country's rise into a new age.

The day before the talks started, Snyder and Acheson had to meet in executive session for ninety minutes with a nervous Senate Foreign Relations Committee. The hitch was that Marshall Plan aid, to the surprise of legislators, hadn't solved the basic problem: the British bought large amounts of U.S. goods but couldn't earn the dollars they needed to pay for these imports through the sale of their own products to hard-currency markets overseas. Side by side, Acheson and Snyder found themselves having to pledge that there'd be no new U.S. obligations of any kind. Snyder's approach was clear: as he had said in London, he wouldn't push the British toward taking what to him appeared the obvious way out, which was devaluation. They had to reach their own decision.

On Wednesday, September 7, Bevin arrived at the State Department flanked by Cripps and Franks. A crowd of photographers met them, and flashbulbs popped. "I never knew a man with an overdraft would get such a wonderful welcome," *The New York Times* quoted him as saying.[15] So far, he had evaded requests by Harriman and Douglas to outline how he and Cripps proposed to save Britain from bleeding out its gold and dollars. Snyder and Acheson, Cripps and Bevin, and their two Canadian counterparts—along with Paul Hoffman, the Marshall

Plan administrator, and a single aide for each party—then walked into room 5106, barely large enough for ten people and their documents, and shut the door behind them.

Snyder sat at the head of the table beneath a portrait of William Seward, with Bevin to his right and Acheson toward the middle. The Americans said not a word. They waited for the British to produce a solution, but didn't hear one. Instead, before long, as Acheson admiringly recalls, Bevin exploded. He denounced Congress's unceasing demands for free trade while its legislators imposed high tariffs and squawked about cheap foreign labor. He and Cripps then announced a secret: they planned to devalue their currency. Truman was informed, and the secret didn't leak.

Two days later, on Friday, Bevin and Cripps took a break to appear eight blocks away at the National Press Club. John Snyder joined them at the head table. The two visitors made clear—as Ambassador Franks had already been doing in Washington—that Britain felt a duty to keep all sterling area countries within its orbit. Otherwise, Soviet-induced struggles for power could devastate the Western world. Journalists applauded. Neither Bevin nor Cripps nor their advisers at any point considered dropping a single military involvement. Nor did journalists or U.S. negotiators even raise the possibility. Kennan, for his part, saw fit to tell contacts at the Foreign Office, several times, that Snyder was chairing the conference "for reasons of political expedience," but Kennan's intrigues changed nothing.[16]

On Monday, September 12, the negotiators released a twenty-five-hundred-word final communiqué, which declared, with sophisticated prolixity, that the United States had confidence in Britain. Canada's confidence was assumed. On the State Department steps that mild late summer day, Acheson stood nodding encouragement alongside Bevin. Demonstrating faith in one's counterpart, naturally, is an essential aspect of finance. Cripps later explained the details: there'd be further austerity in Britain; and the Americans had agreed to modify their tariffs and buy more sterling area goods such as rubber, tin, cocoa, wood, and diamonds. Disingenuously, he also assured the public that he'd not be tampering with the currency. By this time, however, speculators on the Swiss free market were betting against the pound, and even British textile salesmen in France advised customers to place orders conditioned on devaluation. "Their situation is terrible," Eisenhower said of the British. "But we must realize we are not a bottomless pit."[17]

Cripps flew back to London, arriving on Sunday afternoon, September 18. Three hours later, he announced sterling's devaluation with a huge quantum (the amount by which the pound was being devalued) of 30 percent, from $4.03 to $2.80. Devaluation shocked the world, including top officials in Attlee's government. "We have all been busy picking ourselves up off the floor," wrote Kenneth Younger, MP, who was minister of state at the Foreign Office, in his diary.[18] The British had revealed the size of the quantum to the Americans two days prior. The dominions (other than Canada) had only learned about the devaluation itself at the same time, and European leaders had been kept entirely in the dark. They were furious—all the more so due to ongoing rumors of an Anglo-American plan to seal themselves in a political-economic union separate from Continental Europe.

After Cripps's announcement, financial markets closed around the world, except for in the United States. Egypt had quit the sterling area in 1947 but shuttered its banks nonetheless. A chain reaction followed the news, and twenty-eight nations lowered their exchange rates. India announced a drop in the rupee. Israel devalued its pound by the same amount as Britain. The krone, franc, lira, and Dutch gilder all were pared. So too was Canada's dollar, by 10 percent. Snyder authorized John McCloy, who had just been appointed U.S. high commissioner for Germany, to devalue the deutsche mark.

The impact spread. In Idaho, six thousand miles away, the market for barley went out like a light, as the *Lewiston Tribune* reported, while merchants on Twenty-First Street worried about an influx of cut-rate English woolens.[19] The price in Manhattan of a Dunhill cigarette case, exported from Britain, fell 20 percent because of the cheaper pound; the price of Ovaltine in Delhi, imported from America and popular in India, jumped from 3½ to 5 rupees.

To be sure, devaluation would boost British exports by making them less expensive, thereby stanching the outflow of dollars. And the extent of the devaluation was so large because Britain's Treasury intended to solve its trade imbalance problem once and for all. But this decision caused a lot of pain, and not just to consumers at home. Fifty-odd governments were involved in this disruption. It was felt worldwide by the nations, businesses, and individuals who had assets in sterling and who experienced an overnight haircut of more than 30 percent against the dollar.

Acheson blamed himself for allowing the British to make their shocking move with America's apparent connivance. "Did they take advantage of us?" he asked his aides.[20] It sure seemed so. Had the Americans been informed of the size of the quantum earlier, or even been able to mention the imminent devaluation, they might have apprised France's smoothly run Ministry of Finance about the turmoil ahead. Instead, they had done nothing, and now were being blamed for at least half the chaos, and for cutting a secret deal with Britain. Still, under the circumstances, the U.S. players had made the best of the situation. First, they recognized that they were in a dangerous spot: the British could easily blame the Western world's financial ills on the United States for not buying enough from overseas, thereby having caused a world scarcity of dollars. Second, Snyder had helped guide Bevin and Cripps toward a tough decision that meant higher prices at home. As he and Truman had agreed, they wouldn't allow the United States to take "moral responsibility," nor risk a transatlantic split, by trying to force Britain into devaluation.[21]

World trade patterns improved, as did Britain's balance of payments, which benefited from fewer imports and greater U.S. demand. Britain would rebound in 1950, and sterling's new exchange rate endured for eighteen years. From the American perspective, Britain would remain what again was being called an "outer fortress," this time by Hubert Humphrey, the newly elected senator from Minnesota: U.S. interests in the Middle East, in Southeast Asia, and perhaps in Africa, too, could all be protected.[22] After all, as James Webb observed, "the idea of undertaking additionally the support of U.K. commitments on a global basis will be hard to support before Congress," which was putting it mildly.[23]

Five days after the devaluation, like a messenger stumbling in to raise tension in a Greek tragedy, news arrived of Russia's first atomic blast. "To the responsible men in government," recalled Walter Millis, a prominent military historian of the time, "the shock was extreme"—as it was to everyone else.[24] Stalin had been thwarted in Europe by the Atlantic Pact, the new allies concluded, but now he had neutralized the Americans' atomic advantage in a flash. Well-placed U.S. and British officials sensed he would be tempted to press south into Iran, Turkey, and the Arab lands.

BACK IN APRIL, WHEN HE WAS FIRST IN WASHINGTON THAT YEAR, Bevin had asked Acheson if a follow-on agreement to the North Atlantic Treaty might be crafted to "hold the outer crust," which he defined as "extending from Scandinavia to Turkey and including the Middle East."[25] Acheson dismissed the idea. Meanwhile, U.S. diplomats had kept trying to halt Arab-Israeli violence.

Earlier in 1949, the UN peace negotiator Ralph Bunche had been able to apply his skills, once Israel's prime minister, Ben-Gurion, had been compelled to leave the Sinai when handed Britain's ultimatum. Bunche was a rare being in those days: a diplomat who was an African American. He had succeeded the murdered Folke Bernadotte and then won a series of bilateral armistices between Israel and Egypt, Lebanon, Syria, and Jordan (Iraq's accession being covered by Jordan). In the process, Jordan received that part of Palestine west of the Jordan River, with 400,000 inhabitants. Unfortunately, the armistice didn't occur before Israel, in a deadly communications screwup on the afternoon of January 7, had shot down five Royal Air Force Spitfires conducting reconnaissance over the featureless Egyptian desert. Talk of war followed in Parliament. To heighten the drama, those Spitfires were flying out of Ismailia in the Canal Zone at a time when there were calls in Egypt to expel the British by force. Was it possible, went speculation in the press, that Israel wanted "to make common cause with Egypt against a resurgence of British 'imperialism' in the Middle East?"[26] No, it wasn't.

Cairo's venal regime had been weakened by its disastrous war with Israel, and King Farouk, twenty-nine, was the least inspiring of leaders. He was a plump and decadent Oriental monarch of the sort stereotyped in Hollywood who combined the worst available traits of East and West. But he knew he had to demonstrate a semblance of nationalist credibility. Squeezing Britain could help. That worried Bevin, who assumed, as many people do today, that Arabs in the street tend to detonate suddenly in mindlessly violent protest. So perhaps one way to calm Farouk's combustible subjects was for authorities in London to tell his government that Britain was once again a formal American ally. In Whitehall, a senior diplomat summarized this idea: "once Egypt was allied with us she was also automatically allied with the United States," or so Farouk could be assured.[27] And what better way to demonstrate this fact than to invite the hapless Egyptian military to participate in joint Anglo-American planning for the region, and at General Headquarters Middle East Land Forces, no less, in Fayid?

Whitehall mandarins envisioned killing two birds with one stone. By bringing together Egyptian and U.S. military officers, they could show Washington the unique influence of Britain's local relationships, and do so while the Americans in Fayid got to witness the dexterity and scale of combined operations among the Royal Navy, the RAF, and the army. Moreover, the Egyptians would be induced, with hopes of access to American largesse, to cooperate with Britain over the intractable problem of Suez. According to Britain's ambassador in Cairo, Sir Ronald Campbell, an Old Etonian himself, the king's "schoolboy propensities would be flattered to our advantage by a feeling that he was being let into the inner plans of the prefects' club for dealing with the bully."[28] For Egyptians, however, "the bully" wasn't Russia; it was Britain, which also still owed them some 300 million pounds from the war.

Admiral Richard Conolly was a major figure in the U.S. Navy of this era. Known as "Close-In" Conolly for taking his destroyers daringly near shore to support World War II amphibious assaults, he had been Forrestal's point man for the Middle East. His remit included command of the U.S. Navy's Mediterranean task force, of some twenty warships on patrol, recently designated the 6th Fleet, which linked the U.S. Navy's North European forces based in Plymouth with its recently created Persian Gulf Command. Conolly, who believed that the British could take the shirts off Americans in any negotiations, found himself at the center of this odd three-way arrangement.

In January 1949, Conolly and his staff had attended a planning meeting in the colony of Malta, home to Royal Navy Headquarters, Mediterranean Fleet, the war room of which lay within the twelve-foot-thick stone walls of Fort St. Angelo on the Vittoriosa peninsula. The British wanted a subsequent meeting to be at General Headquarters in Fayid because, they claimed, only there could they conduct detailed briefings on the full scope of military planning for the Middle East.

What followed when Conolly and eleven of his officers got themselves to Fayid in the late spring turned out to be a mess. First, the Egyptians wouldn't allow him to anchor his flagship, the heavy cruiser USS *Columbus*, in the Great Bitter Lake. (Anchoring a warship contravened Article 8 of the 1888 Convention, and only the British ignored that stipulation, as they did their 1936 pledge to keep no more than ten thousand troops in Suez.) So Conolly had been flown in by the RAF. Second, he hadn't expected the Egyptians to participate and had no authorization from the Pentagon to engage them in planning. And third, to make this contrivance more complicated still, the Joint Chiefs of Staff—well removed from Conolly's headquarters in London— were shifting fast to end any U.S. military commitment to defend the Middle East.

In late August 1949, Bevin had told the cabinet that the Middle East was "second only to the UK itself" in peace and war.[29] Yet in September, the JCS had come to conclude that no U.S. forces of any sort would be sent to the region in wartime, and began to so inform their British counterparts. America's fighting strength was spread too thin, the Joint Chiefs explained, because of both the new Atlantic Treaty obligations and, in Asia, the uncertainties that surrounded China's imminent fall. In a hypothetical World War III, therefore, the JCS could no longer allocate to the Middle East the three and a half army divisions, plus ships and some 350 tactical aircraft, that they had promised to deploy.[30]

In November, it was clear to Foreign Office decision makers that Britain was on its own, with "sole responsibility" for the Middle East.[31] Bevin sent his top man for the region, Sir Michael Wright, to Washington, but appeals to the State Department didn't help. No U.S. naval vessels would be assigned to control sea-lanes in the Mediterranean, nor would the JCS accept a plea from Britain's own chiefs of staff to designate a brigade of GIs to intervene in Israel at the outbreak of world war—something Whitehall officials believed necessary to ensure "Israel was for us and not against us" should the Red Army have to be met on its coastal plain.[32] U.S. air bases were by now in Libya and in Saudi Arabia. But they weren't part of a Middle East defense plan. As a result, no one—except perhaps for oilmen in Houston—wanted the British "jockeyed out" of the Middle East, as Field Marshal Montgomery, and others in London, imagined.[33] Quite the opposite. According to the Americans, the British Empire should stay, in some increasingly enlightened form, and surely it could handle defense requirements for the West. As for Cairo, from this point on there'd be ambitious colonels who could never sort out whether it was the British who were driving the Americans, or vice versa.

LIKE OTHER POWERFUL MEN IN LONDON, BEVIN DREAMED OF MAKing Africa the new center of imperial strength and believed that doing so could transform the nature of Britain's security and prosperity. Africa could replace the military manpower of India, it could backstop defensive lines in the Middle East, and it could help to boost Britain's economic recovery—all of which might additionally provide freedom of maneuver from the Americans.

Anybody who studied a map of sub-Saharan Africa could understand why these men saw the continent as an indispensable part of their country's future. At mid-century, the British controlled much of Central Africa, East Africa, and West Africa—territories that included Northern and Southern Rhodesia (today Zambia and Zimbabwe), Nyasaland (Malawi), Nigeria, Sierra Leone, the Gold Coast (Ghana), Kenya, Uganda, and Tanganyika and Zanzibar (which together became Tanzania). The white-ruled Union of South Africa was part of the commonwealth, and altogether this expanse from Cape Town to the Red Sea contained about sixty-five million people in a mostly fertile area as large as the United States itself. The only independent sub-Saharan nations then existing were Liberia and Abyssinia (Ethiopia).

To most Americans, including the Joint Chiefs, all of Africa—with a population almost equal to that of the United States—was still the Dark Continent, worthy of notice mostly for its cocoa, diamonds, and minerals. "Those people should be prepared for independence" was the official State Department view, though the Foreign Service officer Edward Mulcahy, principal officer in Mombasa, Kenya, conceded, "Maybe not in our lifetime, but eventually."[34] Anything sooner couldn't be imagined, and certainly not by the British, who had a wider, more complicated view of this continent.

Soon after the war, Attlee himself, like Bevin, was already examining how Britain might revamp its military planning, which placed the Middle East's defense as a top strategic objective. Attlee wasn't an imperial dreamer. He didn't necessarily object to the contraction of British power and was receptive to whatever looked practical—which needn't include hoary assumptions from Britain's chiefs of staff.

Even in 1949, the Royal Navy still identified Gibraltar, with its battle center buried within the Rock, as a "linchpin" of imperial defense for the Middle East and considered its bases in Malta and Cyprus and Aden to be critical guard posts.[35] This idea—of a supposed Mediterranean lifeline—was an old one. To Attlee, it looked thin. He therefore asked his military advisers to consider a protective girdle of sorts on the equator from Nigeria east to Kenya. Should deterrence fail, British forces could slam shut the gates of Suez against a Russian invader and strike the oil fields of a quickly occupied Iran with missiles launched in East Africa. Khartoum to Tehran was only seventeen hundred miles, and in 1949 British engineers were promising some rather accurate thirty-five-hundred-mile-range rockets—which meant it should soon be possible to produce missiles that could travel the four thousand miles from Kenya to Moscow.

Africa also held the promise of supplying soldiers. Churchill famously disdained "Hottentots" but had been a soldier himself, and he knew how impressive African fighting men could be. Half a million had fought for the British Empire in World War II. Since then, the Indian army had been broken apart, and its remnants were no longer under London's authority. Yet the colonial land forces that Britain maintained in Africa were larger than before the war, an advantage that visionaries in Whitehall felt they should exploit. At the least, wrote Viscount Hall, first lord of the Admiralty, "African soldiers should be employed in time of peace."[36] The number 400,000 was used. To explore all this military potential, Chief of the Imperial General Staff Bernard Montgomery visited his country's possessions in Africa during early 1949, including Nigeria, where much of the road construction under way was for military uses.

Moreover, swaths of Africa held barely exploited riches and at a time when the terms of trade favored commodities.* Yet the potential of some 4.5 million square miles of Africa couldn't be fully exploited because of trypanosomiasis, a parasitic disease carried by the tsetse fly that infected cattle, horses, and hogs, as well as people.[37]

Then, in 1949, scientists at Imperial Chemical Industries devised a synthetic compound called Antrycide. The Colonial Office ensured it was introduced to Africa. Americans named it the "empire building drug" because of what it could achieve for the British and their colonial subjects—among other things, better public health, higher prosperity, and, for Britain, more beef supplies than could be bought from costly hard-currency Argentina.[38] A British-initiated cure also looked imminent for schistosomiasis, a disease spread by water snails, which causes diarrhea and intestinal damage. It afflicted most of Egypt's fourteen million fellahin, or peasants, who composed 70 percent of the population, and infested much of sub-Saharan Africa too. If the British could eradicate it throughout Africa, they realized, they might not only transform the economies of their increasingly valuable colonial possessions but also win themselves goodwill among African subjects.

Helping to end disease might be its own reward, yet a series of failures soon narrowed British aspirations. The most publicized venture was the effort in Tanganyika to cultivate groundnuts, a legume that's part of the pea family. Here the idea was to produce a food that might add calories to stringent British diets. A project had been under way since 1946 to clear no less than thirteen million acres of wilderness that could produce a quarter-million annual tons of this product. Britain's big defense industry took part as Vickers-Armstrongs Ltd., for example, converted Sherman tanks into tractors. But crops failed because of too much rain, or not enough rain. Mismanagement, including accounting irregularities

---

*Oil wealth wouldn't arrive in Africa until the mid-1950s; meanwhile, the demand in industrialized countries for commodities was greater than the demand in underdeveloped parts of the world for manufactured products.

within Unilever, the British/Dutch consumer goods giant, added to the debacle. Also disappointing were British plans to open government-financed poultry farms in Gambia and to boost coal production by hoisting more tonnage from collieries in Southern Rhodesia.

Africans say that their continent looks like a ham bone. European carving knives were still slicing off its riches, but independence struggles were also emerging. Already in 1949, Nnamdi Azikiwe—who would become the first president of Nigeria, Africa's most populous country, when statehood arrived in 1963—was in London decrying the African blood that had been spilled for imperialism in two world wars. Why, he asked publicly, should his countrymen now "be ready to fight the Soviet Union"?[39] Western officials on both sides of the Atlantic assumed a very gradual path to self-rule for Africa's colonies—at least another generation, during which time Britain could use this part of the empire for its own recovery. Men such as Azikiwe knew differently. The fortress walls were cracking.

THE IMPERIAL PRESENCE IN AFRICA WAS NEARLY SELF-FINANCING until the Mau Mau rebellion hit Kenya in 1952, and Communism as a movement had little traction. It was British holdings in Asia that were threatened, and there the Americans were indeed getting involved.

During the winter and spring of 1949, in a series of rolling triumphs, Mao Zedong and his People's Liberation Army had brought swift disaster to America's client government, led by Chiang Kai-shek. The PLA occupied Beijing in January and then marched on to cross the Yangtze River in early April; on the twenty-fifth, they took Chiang's capital, Nanking. The PLA then descended on Shanghai, some 150 miles downriver, and a month later the city, choked with refugees, surrendered without a fight. Church bells tolled. For the first time, Americans watched as a well-equipped yet demoralized and poorly led army of a corrupt U.S.-backed ally crumbled before a determined foe.

In response to Chiang's defeats, Acheson infuriated many in Congress by testifying that the outcome of this civil war—so large as to finally account for at least eight million dead—"was beyond the control of the government of the United States."[40] Then as today, Americans couldn't believe that "managing" the rise of China might be beyond their grasp.[41] But it was true: by the midsummer, Chiang's armies were in pell-mell flight across the 115-mile Formosa Strait. On the mainland, the rule of his Nationalist Party dissolved. Suddenly the $3 billion in grants and credits that the United States had given China since World War II proved useless, and armories of U.S.-supplied weapons were in Mao's hands.

On September 13, right after the sterling-dollar talks had concluded at State, Acheson and Bevin had undertaken what Bevin called a "tower de horizon" (that is, *tour d'horizon*).[42] China was now their foremost priority. Chiang's government was clearly lost, yet there were Republicans on the Hill who demanded U.S. intervention pursuant to the Truman Doctrine. The British, on the contrary, had stayed neutral in the clash between the Communists and the Nationalists. Therefore, Acheson and Bevin had to coordinate their countries' next moves delicately. France's foreign minister attended part of their discussions that week, and Atlantic Pact ambassadors also convened for an afternoon. The British and Americans faced two big unresolved issues. First, if policies were to be synchronized, each side had to determine whether to recognize China's new regime. Second was the question of what to do about Taiwan, the big, rural, low-slung island—sitting between Okinawa and the Philippines—where Chiang sought refuge with 1.5 million Nationalist soldiers and civilians.

On October 1, atop Beijing's Tiananmen Gate, Mao stood before a giant portrait of himself to proclaim the People's Republic of China. A military procession followed. Suddenly—or so it seemed to Americans that fall—Asia's Pacific shores from the Bering Strait to the Tonkin Gulf had become part of a Sino-Soviet bloc. Malaya, Burma, and Indochina lay vulnerably beneath. Already a quarter of humanity had been lost to Communism, went the refrain, and most Americans saw the future of Europe, the Middle East, and Africa in light of that fact. "Stand Forever in Solidarity with Our Great Friend the Soviet Union of Socialist Republics," said the placards. Mao seemed set to follow Russia's example: carnage on a Stalinist scale in the name of Marxist-Leninist principles.

Britain had more investments than any other country in China, at least $850 million in coal mines, shipping, textiles, banking, and tobacco. Quite a few people in Washington suspected that this stake compelled Whitehall to appease the Communists and to keep a diplomatic foothold on the mainland after Mao's takeover. They also assumed that the British would compromise due to fear of losing Hong Kong. However, that colony wasn't going to be surrendered no matter what happened.

The Royal Navy had just abandoned its China Squadron's station at the mouth of the Yangtze River and redeployed its vessels nearly a thousand miles south to Hong Kong's Victoria Harbor, where they joined warships arriving from Singapore. A squadron of fighter planes zoomed around on maneuvers with the aircraft carrier HMS *Triumph* lying at anchor, flanked by two cruisers and screened by destroyers and frigates. Soldiers of the King's Shropshire Light Infantry and the King's Own Scottish Borderers, plus the Argyll and Sutherland Highlanders, waited as part of a well-prepared 40th Division on the Kowloon peninsula's seventeen-and-a-half-mile border with China. Altogether about forty thousand fighting men were dug in. The colony's governor and its regimental commanders said they knew the enemy. They were ready to fight and there'd be no surrender, as to Japan in 1941, which had come at a cost of nearly three thousand lives.

Privately, both Acheson and Bevin wrote off Chiang Kai-shek's stronghold on Taiwan, which China had ruled since the seventeenth century, until it was taken by Japan in the 1890s. Now Taiwan would surely fall to the PLA, probably by the following summer, depending on weather conditions during typhoon season. In public, Acheson kept being hammered by Congress: Republicans claimed China had been "lost" and blamed the State Department's "Oriental Munich" appeasement policies. Acheson was stunned by the vitriol, recalled Oliver Franks, and flailed when he attempted to respond. In November, for example, he called for U.S. and British warships to break Chiang's naval blockade of China's ports. It was a far-fetched attempt at placating the new regime in Beijing, and perhaps London as well. But Truman recognized that little would be accomplished by that move. The only result, he concluded, would be to throw gasoline on Acheson's fiery battles with Congress, and he overruled the plan.

Taiwan really was a fortress, and it could be held against PLA attack—if protected by outside naval and air power. Yet the administration wanted no part of this. One reason was the Joint Chiefs' belief that the United States didn't have the capabilities to oppose an invasion without a dangerous drawdown of forces elsewhere committed. Nevertheless, General MacArthur was insisting from his Tokyo headquarters that Taiwan was vital to America's future in the Pacific. It had to be saved. To this end, the Joint Chiefs spoke of at least sending an advisory mission, as had been deployed in Greece: Chiang's soldiers should somehow be trained to repel a PLA invasion. Additionally, the chiefs relayed to the White House a flurry of appeals from London. British commanders were saying that Taiwan's fall would undercut the empire's internal air and sea communications, although they, unfortunately, had no ships or soldiers available to help prevent the collapse.

Anxious officials at State and the Pentagon were scrambling for a solution. Perhaps there was a way that Taiwan and its 6.5 million original peasant inhabitants, who already hated the brutal new Nationalist overlords, could be saved from the havoc. Maybe an independence movement on Taiwan could keep the island out of both Nationalist and Communist hands. At the State Department, the Policy Planning Staff had been established to explore such blue-sky ideas.

During his July meetings near Oxford, Kennan had told Gladwyn Jebb and the others that he'd welcome a revolt by the ethnic Taiwanese against Chiang's Nationalist government, the vestiges of which claimed sole legitimate authority over all of China. Endless problems would likely arise for the United States if Chiang hung on. Trouble was, Chiang already had a brutal hold over the island—having two years earlier massacred some thirty-five thousand native Taiwanese rebels, according to figures available only in 2017. And he kept Taiwan under martial law.

Jebb and his colleagues knew that Kennan's scheme would, at this point, cause even worse butchery and be pointless: 300,000 cornered and armed-to-the-teeth Nationalist soldiers were then on the island, with more arriving. Kennan "refined" his idea when back in Washington a week later. U.S. forces, he argued, should themselves move with "speed, ruthlessness, and self-assurance . . . [in] the way Theodore Roosevelt might have done it" to evict Chiang's desperate troops.[43] This advice was equally foolish. He quickly retracted it, though the Foreign Office, of course, kept records of his original formulation. Years later, when U.S. archives were opened, and this nonsense exposed, Kennan tried attributing it to the Foreign Service officer John Paton Davies, a China hand and a friend, who in 1949 was already entrapped in McCarthyite loyalty investigations for having had insufficient faith in Chiang's Nationalist cause.

As for Hong Kong, Bevin was hoping by year's end that Mao and his new regime would see the advantage of avoiding a bloodbath and allowing continued imperial rule.

LATIN AMERICA WAS THE ONE PART OF THE WORLD IN WHICH WASHington didn't seek a British political-military role, yet events that occurred from 1948 into 1950 were a reminder, if such was needed, that imperial interests existed on every continent and that, when challenged, they'd be backed by force. These involvements also set the stage for one of Washington's uglier encounters with the British Empire, in 1954, and were a prelude to decisions that would reverberate for years in Guatemala and Argentina. Both those countries formally became U.S. allies in 1948, along with sixteen other Latin American nations, when the Inter-American Treaty of Reciprocal Assistance—or "Rio Pact"—came into effect, with its provision of an attack on one being an attack on all.

At the signing ceremonies in Rio de Janeiro, Argentina's delegate had reasserted his country's claim to the Falkland Islands, a British overseas territory (that is, internally self-governing), but had been brushed off by U.S. delegates. The Argentinians proclaimed sovereignty nonetheless, and in February 1948 Attlee declared to the House of Commons that His Majesty's government wouldn't be "checked or chivied out of British territory anywhere in the world."[44] The light cruiser HMS *Nigeria* sailed to the Falklands from South Africa's Simonstown Naval Base to clarify the point for Argentina's dictator, General Juan Domingo Perón. (Signals were also being sent to the government of Chile, which claimed islands south of Cape Horn that the British asserted were theirs.) Washington warned Perón that it would be neutral in quarrels over these moorlands, and Argentina backed down—until the ten-week Falklands War of 1982.

Eight thousand miles to the north, in the sparsely populated colony of British Honduras along the Caribbean, another showdown over value-less terrain was unfolding with far greater consequences for Washington. The small, impoverished, and adjacent country of Guatemala, with its cloud forests and glistening mountain lakes, was a fledgling democracy of 2.6 million. Like Argentina, it was now a Rio Pact ally of the United States. It too counted on Britain to be exhausted from the war, and declared the territory it called Belize—known elsewhere as British Honduras—to be its twenty-third provincial department. That was a long-standing claim which Washington had supported before the war. For the British, the colony was a money pit, but allowing it to be snatched by the likes of Guatemala, Bevin told the Commons in March 1948, would endanger the empire everywhere. In Guatemala City, demonstrators stomped around the British legation chanting "Death to John Bull," as if in Cairo or, before long, in Tehran.

Demonstrations were peaceful, but in the Commons, Bevin had to field questions about a "mob" and an "attack," which goaded him to say that Guatemala wouldn't get "a square inch of anybody else's soil."[45] Later that month, HMS *Sheffield*, flagship of the Royal Navy's Western Atlantic Squadron, arrived in the port of Belize (British Honduras) with the cruiser HMS *Devonshire*, which had left Jamaica carrying a detachment of the Gloucestershire Regiment. Soldiers and royal marines were put ashore to begin patrolling the pine forests and malarial swamps. The Guatemalans asked their new North American ally for help, and here too Washington had to choose between its pledges of good-neighbor hemispheric solidarity and its increasingly worldwide connections with Britain: U.S. officials ended up staring at the ceiling.

The U.S. ambassador in Guatemala, Richard Patterson, was an even-tempered businessman—a political appointee who never previously had a reason to learn Spanish. But he weighed in strong and urged the State Department to threaten Britain with cuts in aid unless it stopped intimidating Guatemala. In fact, Britain should hand over Belize, he said. London, for its part, was alleging that Communist exiles from Nicaragua and the Republic of Honduras, the former Spanish colony to Guatemala's east, were joining in a takeover attempt. That was preposterous, Patterson added. He ridiculed Britain's "itemized indications of alleged Communistic tendencies on the part of Guatemalan officials."[46] A local standoff ensued, and eventually tempers cooled. The warships withdrew, but the Colonial Office decided to garrison a company of soldiers permanently in the shantytown of Belize City, with its fifty thousand inhabitants.

This was another dispute that wouldn't go away. The British had used every opportunity to convince Washington that Guatemala's social-reforming government was plotting against U.S. interests, and before long they'd return to the charge. U.S. investors in Guatemala— notably the bondholders of Guatemala's International Railways of Central America, dominated by the Boston-based United Fruit Company— raised their own hue and cry about "pro-Communist elements in Guatemalan national life."[47] The din they caused, in tandem with the tocsin clanging from Westminster, drowned out the pleas from a democratically elected Guatemalan government that the best way to avert Communism was by supporting labor unions and land redistribution.

In March 1950, a highly dubious source would insert himself into the issue when George Kennan made his first visit to Latin America, a region he admitted knowing nothing about. He had become frantic about the "virus of Communism" that he believed to be infecting the 146 million largely impoverished people of Central and South America. In Guatemala City, he described Communism as stronger than anywhere else in Latin America, contrary to what the ambassador had been reporting.[48]

Once back at State, Kennan sent Acheson a ten-thousand-word essay describing Latin America as the most hopeless region on earth, due to its history, its geography, and its "human blood." Progress was unlikely because of the "unfortunate results . . . of extensive intermarriage . . . [with] Negro slave elements."[49] Then he went further: "Harsh governmental measures of oppression" might be the "only answer" to the Communist threat in Latin America.[50] In his memoirs, published in 1967, Kennan would write that his unadorned analysis was so shocking to "the operational echelons of the department" that Acheson had all copies locked up and kept out of official files, but this is untrue. His rant was circulated in the routine workflow, a fact that became clear nine years after he published his memoirs, when documents from the period were declassified. Death squad politics would arrive soon enough in Guatemala, following an anti-Communist coup in 1954, and twenty years thereafter in Argentina, backed in both cases by U.S. administrations.[51]

WITHIN WHITEHALL, GLADWYN JEBB SPOKE SHREWDLY OF "OUR various Colonial Empires." *Various* empires: that's the point.[52] Britain had a presence everywhere, and it was multifaceted. Colonies, dominions, protectorates, and overseas territories would all be defended, whether against Communists, Perón-like fascists, or dissolute monarchs. Despite the cracks, Americans tended to see rather sturdy fortress walls in the Middle East, Asia, Africa, and, problematically, even Latin America. The latest sterling-dollar crisis hadn't changed anything.

During that drama, in September 1949, Walter Lippmann had annoyed Bevin by predicting, in his "Whither Britain?" column, "the liquidation of the British imperial connections in Asia and the Middle East" and suggesting that it was time for the United States "to assume new responsibilities." However, Lippmann hadn't answered the question he posed in his title. Instead, he closed the essay by writing that "the British nation is not prepared to resign and to retire as a great power in the world."[53] That sure looked to be the case in all the regions examined above, including Latin America. So was there to be a "liquidation" or not? This became a pressing question in Washington against the backdrop of that year's financial emergency. Problems of "convertibility" and "currency reserves" had to be put into some context of military deployments and formal international obligations. Was an acceptable foreign policy really closed to the United States without the British Empire? And how strong were those fortress walls anyway?

III. CHIPS ON THE TABLE

Core of the Truman administration: the president with Treasury Secretary John
Wesley Snyder, 1949

9

AUDITING AN EMPIRE

Our biggest post-war difficulty is that there are many times when
we seem unable to say "No" to Great Britain.
—Averell Harriman, Paris, October 1949

D URING THE TEN MONTHS BETWEEN BEVIN'S ARRIVAL IN WASH-
ington on "one of the most important missions in history," at the
start of September 1949, and the first weeks of the Korean War, which
erupted early the following summer, Secretaries Acheson and Snyder
were scrambling to determine their country's place in the world. To do
so required a systematic understanding of the strengths and weaknesses
of the British Empire.

By now, talk of the empire's collapse, of the sun finally setting, and
of torches being plucked from chilling fingers, had effervesced for several
years in editorials, on Capitol Hill, and among those businessmen who
imagined an "American Century." Yet notions of imperial "retreat,"
"surrender," and "willy-nilly" handovers were as vague during that era as
they are when written about today. For instance, around this time, Dean
Acheson and Lewis Douglas (visiting from London) set out from the

State Department to have dinner with Oliver Franks. Before they left, one of Acheson's closest aides, Henry Byroade, a West Pointer who'd been the youngest American general during the war, remarked to him that the British had to "recognize that they had lost their old position of power and would have to face up to a changed status in the world."[1] Which meant what exactly?

Acheson needed answers. So did Snyder and President Truman. As a result, Acheson initiated a top secret National Security Council study for the president that stemmed from Truman's July 7 request for State to examine crisis conditions in Britain. The analyses produced by the study would document which "global commitments"—including treaties, other overseas agreements and obligations, and military deployments—might, in extremis, be abandoned by the British Empire. If such abandonments occurred, how might they affect America? Nothing like this had been attempted before.

Getting answers required deep-diving scrutiny by the CIA and the Defense Department, plus insights from diplomats and regional specialists at State, with the Treasury offering details about financial pressures. Rear Admiral Sidney Souers, executive secretary of the NSC's small staff within the White House, would have to coordinate. The NSC's key purpose, since being established two years earlier, was to integrate domestic, foreign, and military policies related to national security, on behalf of the president, and to ease cooperation among the departments for the sake of decision making at the top. In this case, Admiral Souers's role was to circulate the participants' highly classified drafts, calculations, and commentaries and then synthesize the results into a National Security Council report, to be delivered to Harry Truman. What emerged, in July 1950, would be NSC 75, *British Military Commitments*, which is an audit of the British Empire's military might. Historians have never seen this forty-page document, and few know of the CIA and Pentagon papers that went into it, which have gone unrecognized as part of a larger effort.[2]

During these ten months, events in Washington and London, and in Paris too, were, one way or another, shaping Washington's assessment of the empire's strengths. By the outbreak of the Korean War, at which point NSC 75 was nearly completed, high officials had developed a rough consensus about what lay ahead: the costs of "replacing" the British Empire's globe-girdling commitments would be "uncountable"; Americans weren't prepared to do so anyway; and, in fact, the empire and commonwealth really hadn't diminished since the defeat of the Axis— this enormous entity had instead *evolved*. Nor should any retreat be expected in coming years. As the second half of the twentieth century began, these beliefs changed surprisingly slowly.

NSC 75 BEGAN TAKING SHAPE AFTER SECRETARY SNYDER'S JULY 8 emergency meeting in London, where he, Lewis Douglas, Averell Harriman, and Bill Martin had heard the Treasury's Sir Stafford Cripps speak of global disaster. The Americans thereafter deliberated before Snyder and Martin flew to Stockholm on Monday, July 11, just as George VI declared a national emergency. They all agreed that the administration and Congress had, for years, been handling one of the era's gravest, most far-reaching issues ad hoc—that issue being the future of the British Empire and Commonwealth. The time had come for systematic scrutiny.

On the nineteenth, Douglas cabled Acheson about next steps. He and Snyder believed that a high-level investigation was required as to the consequences of possible retrenchment, but, Douglas added, "such a study as we have in mind has never been done in the past."[3] He knew it couldn't be limited to finance and trade. Questions about the sterling area had to be addressed in tandem with ones about the political-military stability of the Middle East, Southeast Asia, and anywhere else touched by British power.

Douglas's cable arrived at State as Paul Nitze—recently installed at Policy Planning—began to survey Britain's crisis-ridden political and economic predicament. Nitze had excellent contacts within Snyder's Treasury Department, where Bill Martin had come to suspect that Attlee's government might try to shift "global commitments" to America, should sterling indeed collapse while trade stagnated. Cooperation between the two departments was informal at the start, but this really was the type of analytical challenge for which the National Security Council process was created.

By the end of August, Pentagon experts had also begun to examine implications for the United States. To pull everything together, the NSC study was formally launched on September 1, ten years to the day since Hitler's invasion of Poland. The next morning, State's Policy Planning director, George Kennan, convened an interagency work group. It's at this point that government departments methodically embarked on the research, analyses, and informed speculations that led to an NSC report for the president.

Kennan began by trying to frame the problem, which proved difficult. It had to be broken down to the essentials. How and why were the British Empire's military deployments important to America? What if those dissolved as suddenly as everything else appeared to be dissolving, such as Nationalist China? Would Russia then exploit such worldwide collapses of authority? Could America take over? Or might it be possible to pressure or to subsidize Britain to stay in place? What about inducing its dominions to take bigger roles, as in Southeast Asia and maybe in Central Africa?

Kennan helped set the agenda, but he was skeptical about this work from the start. He hadn't had a role in initiating it, and research would have to delve into details of economics and military affairs—subjects of which he knew little. Moreover, he found the method of analysis abstract, so he offered an alternative to the big-picture global inquiry that Acheson had posed. "The best approach," he wrote, "would be to pick an area of repercussion, assume that the British have to cut their responsibilities 50 percent, and analyze what it would mean to us."[4] However, that idea made little sense. The British Empire and Commonwealth was too large and intertwined. No "area" could be plucked out for scrutiny without having to examine something else.

Even to define the task seemed overwhelming. Those British military commitments that were important to America had to be identified. Then the effect, should some dissolve, needed to be understood. All sorts of knots required untangling. Those included defense obligations within the commonwealth, the protection of scores of colonies, and the upholding of treaties with the Persian Gulf emirates. So too the amounts of financial and technical aid being dispensed from Guiana to Tanganyika to Sarawak.

Two other challenges existed. First, no British official was to learn of the NSC effort. That created difficulties because Pentagon analysts weren't even sure how many fighting men Britain possessed or where they were located, and Whitehall would be unlikely to cooperate if asked. Bevin had recently laid out for Douglas the domestic political reasons why it was awkward for him to even say publicly how much of his country's budget went to the military. And rarely were specifics offered when fielding broad inquiries from the Americans about troop deployments. Everything Washington didn't know about the British Empire's strength and cohesion, Whitehall mandarins seemed to believe, made the empire look the more formidable.

Second, extraordinary open-mindedness would be required for this study. The British Empire had covered the globe throughout the lifetimes of the men now examining it. As a result, they took Britain's imperial "responsibilities" for granted. Even trying to imagine the outcome of reducing them by 50 percent (and 50 percent of what?), as Kennan had suggested, would be tricky.

And there were other challenges as the NSC staff began to pull together a report. One was to agree on what "U.S. security objectives" might be in the first place. Another was to determine how Britain's immense commonwealth fit together and what significance this entity—with its so-called white dominions, and its three new members since 1947—had for U.S. defense. That question hit home in early October when America was transfixed by what the press acclaimed as "one of the century's most important visits of state."[5] The arrival of India's founding prime minister, Jawaharlal Nehru, offered an opportunity to grasp how unified, or not, the British colossus might be.

RIGHT AFTER THE STERLING-DOLLAR TALKS ENDED IN SEPTEM-ber 1949, Ernest Bevin had hosted the commonwealth ambassadors at the British embassy. The Foreign Office regarded these ambassadors, quite simply, as representatives of the king in Washington. Franks believed completely in this informal designation, while understanding that India's case was unique: its government merely acknowledged George VI as head of the commonwealth, rather than as a sovereign. Accordingly, every fortnight, except in summer, Franks met with all seven ambassadors in his study to coordinate, as much as possible, a joint approach to whatever the latest phase of U.S. policy might be. For him, as for Bevin, the commonwealth was the ticket that allowed Britain and its empire to play in the big league with the two continental powers. The difference with this meeting, however, was not only Bevin's attendance but that of Pakistan's foreign minister, Zafrullah Khan, who happened to be in Washington.

Bevin briefed them all on his recent "tower de horizon" with Acheson in hopes of getting their nations' support on China. He told the ambassadors, for instance, that he'd reached an understanding with Acheson about recognizing Mao's new regime in Beijing. That statement was false, though Bevin reported correctly that he had urged the Americans to assist France in Indochina because that "seemed to offer the only alternative to a Communist regime which would threaten the whole of South East Asia."[6] But he skirted details. He didn't trust partition-era India's ambassador, Vijaya Lakshmi Pandit, sister of Prime Minister Nehru, and she in turn was barely speaking to Pakistan's Zafrullah Khan.

The commonwealth was more divided than even well-informed Americans recognized. For instance, high Indian and Pakistani officials such as Pandit and Khan knew that Britain wasn't sharing its most sensitive military secrets with their governments, as it was with the white dominions, and they were furious. Yet the Americans accepted the picture of the commonwealth offered by Whitehall: It was a coherent, increasingly strong, evolving federation that served as a counterweight of democracy. Such an entity would be essential to winning the East-West clash of ideas, the argument went, and it provided a globally integrated military presence too. If one agreed with all that, then Britain rather looked like a superpower, and its future well-being would be inseparable from U.S. security at a time when Americans believed the Soviet Union intended to destroy them.

In truth, few Americans knew much about the commonwealth, which is why a Foreign Office economist could be asked, as the Bank of England's reserves dwindled in 1949, how come Britain didn't just take stocks of gold from South Africa, which produced over half the world's output?[7] Besides, most Americans would have been surprised to discover that the majority of people in the commonwealth didn't speak English, although they could have gotten some insight on the matter whenever Churchill extolled "Britain with her eighty million white English-Speaking people."[8]

Then Nehru arrived in Washington on October 11 for his first visit to America. He and his Oxford-educated daughter, Indira, had taken the president's plane, *Independence*, from London, where Nehru had been meeting with Attlee. At National Airport, Truman and a host of dignitaries greeted the visitors with a nineteen-gun salute before motorcading to Blair House. A roast turkey dinner awaited, and Nehru and his daughter spent the night.

Time magazine hailed him as "the Orient's greatest political and spiritual leader."[9] Everything to do with his stay focused on whether the democratic socialist premier of the biggest and most vibrant state in the commonwealth—with 353 million people—would side with America in opposing Communism. Politicians and editorialists spoke of India as the "new anchor in Asia." With China's apparent loss to Stalin, Nehru was "Asia's key man." That search for a "key man" in Asia, or, better yet, its "miracle man," has lasted ever since, as we'll see, despite the poor bet so recently placed on Chiang.[10]

The next morning, Nehru addressed the House of Representatives and then the Senate, as was the practice before World War II. Only slowly thereafter did it become customary for foreign dignitaries to appear at joint meetings of Congress. A twenty-three-day goodwill trip was to follow, or a "voyage of discovery," as Nehru called it. First he flew to New York for a week at the UN. Then he spent two freezing days in Chicago, followed by two in San Francisco, and he went on to see the University of Wisconsin and nuclear facilities in Tennessee.

The visit proved to be "a disaster."[11] Nehru shared the commonwealth ideals of democracy and rule of law, which had helped win him celebrity in America. But according to Loy Henderson, the Foreign Service officer who was ambassador to India, Nehru possessed "anti-American" attitudes that had been instilled in him by Bevin, Churchill, and an English elite determined to mediate U.S. dealings with the subcontinent. Henderson also pointed out that India had a contested 1,652-mile border with China, which might make Nehru hesitant to take sides against Mao's new regime.[12] The State Department's Bureau of Commonwealth Affairs weighed in with another warning: Nehru was eager, its director told Acheson, to chart a so-called third way between Russia and the West. Those insights were relayed to the president, and they weren't what Truman or anyone else wanted to hear.

Personal quirks helped cause the car wreck. Nehru was a Gandhian intellectual committed to industrialization and a strong centralized government—a specifically Indian modernity, in his eyes. Even before arriving in America, he agonized that a rapacious dollar juggernaut was poised to buy up India. Not only did boastful industrialists and civic boosters he met on his voyage confirm his fears, but suspicions of "socialism" were never far from their lips.

Another problem was Acheson. Nehru had attended Harrow and Cambridge before studying law at the Inner Temple, and he came from a family that had sent its shirts to Paris for proper ironing. He had spent thirteen of his sixty years in British jails in the struggle for independence, and his daughter had done her time behind bars too. Nonetheless, Nehru possessed a Brahmin cultural affinity for an aristocratic Britain that was likely to grate on the secretary, who found him "most difficult." Nehru, in turn, regarded Acheson as insouciant and "mediocre."[13] Ultimately, the administration didn't offer the expected flow of development aid to India, and by the end of 1949 the National Security Council was downplaying India's importance.

No matter: the British system of colonies and dominions looked impressive—as a trading bloc, a defense alliance, or both. Like most everyone in Washington, Senator Robert Taft didn't detect the fissures, and his views are the more striking given his reputed isolationist background. "The British Empire, because of its size," he observed, "has moved toward decentralization of government."[14] As he and many other informed Americans saw the situation, the independence of India in 1947 exemplified the empire's sensible adjustment. It was *decentralizing*; it wasn't retreating. Not fitting the caricature of an "isolationist," he deemed the whole entity vital to U.S. defense. "As long as the British are our allies," he wrote eighteen months after Nehru's visit, America could count on "control of the seas throughout the world." So too on control of the air, but that also required "an alliance with England."[15]

Taft was thinking large, as did everyone when speaking of the political and military role of "England" or "Britain." Americans weren't just sizing up isles in the North Sea. And that's how the analyses leading to NSC 75 were approaching the problem.

ON FRIDAY AND SATURDAY, OCTOBER 21 AND 22, ASSISTANT SECRE-tary of State George Perkins gathered eleven of his country's leading diplomats at the embassy in Paris to examine how Washington could do better in pushing Europe's democracies toward federation. Paris was coming to the end of an unseasonable twenty-day warm spell, and the embassy's tall windows, from which one has a diagonal view of the Place de la Concorde, were thrown wide open. Among Perkins's frustrations, he told his colleagues, was trying to assess Britain's role in Europe, which meant he had "the whole Commonwealth to think about."[16] The meeting also turned to exploring why U.S. officials seemed to defer so frequently to Whitehall.

Around the conference table were Lewis Douglas, who'd arrived on Thursday from London, and his brother-in-law, John McCloy, the new high commissioner to occupied Germany. Chip Bohlen was there, too. He had recently left Foggy Bottom to take the number two post of minister at the embassy, where his grandfather had been President Grover Cleveland's ambassador. Other attendees included the ambassadors in Moscow and Rome. Averell Harriman sat at the table as well; his Marshall Plan offices were just across the rue Saint-Florentin, in the Hôtel de Talleyrand.

The ambassador to France could have taken the presiding role, but he quietly gave Perkins the chair. That was David K. E. Bruce, fifty-one, who had worked for Harriman until five months before. In time, he'd serve with great skill as ambassador to Germany, Britain, South Vietnam, and finally China. President Eisenhower would call him "the best ambassador the United States had ever had."[17]

Bruce applied to his calling antebellum mannerisms that even his children found implausible in a man from Baltimore. He'd entered the Foreign Service after law school and served briefly in Rome. In 1926, he married the daughter of the Treasury secretary, Andrew Mellon, and he then pursued business, philanthropy, and farming in Virginia's Campbell County. An amicable divorce, a generous settlement, and another marriage followed. His calm dependability led to his running the OSS European theater of operations during World War II, before later joining the Marshall Plan. As a diplomat, recalled his son, a prominent sinologist, he was so smoothly calculating that when shooting with the *président de la République* at Rambouillet (a country residence for France's heads of state), he'd use his 12-gauge Purdeys to bag ninety-nine of the released pheasants, not one hundred, which would have been showy.[18]

After lunch that Friday, it was Harriman who cut to the chase, as shown in the transcripts. He had been conferring with Douglas off and on since they'd seen Snyder and Cripps in London in early July. "Our biggest post-war difficulty," Harriman said, "is that there are many times when we seem unable to say 'No' to Great Britain," at least to the same extent as to other nations. Nobody disagreed. Perkins then spoke up, calling attention to the "deep conviction that the U.S. needed Great Britain above everything else." That conviction was troubling, he explained—and he added that it prevailed in "the Pentagon Building and elsewhere when military questions were under consideration."[19] Agreed, but that missed the full picture. It wasn't just the Defense Department that believed the country needed this ally above everything else. After all, Paul Nitze at State had concluded in July that the United States couldn't have an acceptable foreign policy without Britain. Lewis Douglas now reminded his friends that being unable to say no also had serious economic consequences: since the war, he calculated, the Americans had handed over $7 billion in gifts, not loans.

High Commissioner McCloy identified a larger problem, and one that he believed was even more significant than the threat posed by Russia: that was "the collapse of the British Empire." It was a phenomenon that could suck the United States into wide-reaching power vacuums while the drums of world struggle beat ever louder in London and Washington.[20]

It's hard to imagine a more dangerous state of affairs: a collapsing empire to which one can't say no. And it's noteworthy that John J. McCloy offered this view. He could be relied on to warn of trouble, like a good family lawyer, and it was a role he otherwise performed at New York's Milbank, Tweed, and McCloy for the Rockefeller family office and its Chase Bank, which he'd be chairing in four years. When Mc-Cloy spoke, he was known to be speaking for some very substantial people besides himself.

There were two main reasons why it was difficult for the Americans to say no to the British. First, as Ernest Bevin confided to his staff, the Americans had to think of their self-interest: they couldn't risk relations being "blown up." Pressuring Britain on European unity, for instance, could lead to Whitehall doing even less for federation. Second, as savvy dealmakers like Harriman and Douglas knew, it would be foolish to break with the British over any single issue, and to this end the Americans often pulled their punches in disputes—just as in business, where you don't bankrupt or alienate a rival who might be useful in some future transaction. There were all sorts of global dramas to confront, such as a peace treaty with Japan and defense of the Middle East. Friends in London would be needed to offer insights, military clout, and the far-flung relationships of empire and commonwealth.

Ambassador Bruce agreed with McCloy. "The UK's collapse is one of the most dramatic events of recent history," he said.[21] "Collapse" might have sounded jarring, but Bruce was voicing how dire all had looked over the summer. Like McCloy, however, he didn't elaborate on "collapse" other than to note Britain's diminished influence in financial affairs on the Continent. That's how it was understood. Economic problems could be quantified, he knew, yet much else remained anecdotal.

Bruce reemphasized that a unified Europe was impossible without the British. Then he reported that since July loose talk within the State Department about encouraging Britain to disengage politically from the Continent had been causing "panic" in France. "We have been too tender with Britain since the war," he said. Moreover, he urged that the United States and Britain both needed to broaden their views to take in "the extension of Soviet control to Southeast Asia," which he said required their "immediate and searching attention." That meant confronting rebellion in Malaya and outright nationalist revolution in Indochina, which, he advised, would have to be faced jointly with the British. "Of course we [are] against colonialism," he said. "But [can] we afford to be purists and perfectionists? A more pragmatic approach [is] essential." And that approach, naturally, was to use French Indochina—the biggest part of which was the nation of Vietnam—as a breakwater against a Communist-dominated Southeast Asia. The United States, he concluded, had no other choice. Ho Chi Minh, the Vietminh revolutionary leader, was aligned with Stalinism, Bruce warned, "whatever he might think in his secret heart," and America could not break from France.[22]

Ambassador Bruce distilled what Bevin had been saying: the United States needed to uphold French efforts in Indochina for the sake of protecting Malaya. As for the British—at least on colonial matters—they never considered distancing themselves from France.

Lewis Douglas ended the Saturday meeting at 6:00 p.m. with a warning against "placing so much pressure on England that we lose her support."[23] To varying degrees, "pressure" was being exerted for European federation, for convertibility and free trade, and also for the resolution of geostrategic disputes such as those concerning China and Japan. None of the attendees seem to have noticed the irony. They had been lamenting their country's need for Britain "above everything else," and yet here they were, worrying about losing its support. Sooner or later all of them would have to calculate what that "support" might be worth in the decade to come, calculations that Douglas felt everybody was avoiding because the "conclusions will be unpleasant."[24] Six weeks later, on December 23, 1949, the CIA submitted the first paper in the departmental studies that would lead to NSC 75—a thirty-five-page, highly classified analysis titled *The Possibility of Britain's Abandonment of Overseas Commitments*.[25]

THE CIA'S PAPER ABOUT THIS DISTURBING POSSIBILITY WAS SENT to the White House and then circulated by the NSC staff. Its conclusions, however, don't jibe with its title: The British Empire, its authors wrote, had no intention of abandoning anything. Instead, the empire would keep evolving, they argued, as was the case with India. In time, more colonies would be guided to independence within the commonwealth. There was the chance that defense spending might be cut, because of Britain's uncertain economy, and this could one day compel some withdrawals. Should that happen, the paper predicted, Britain—ever sensitive to "power vacuums"—would negotiate with Washington for the

Americans to selectively step forward to fill whatever positions might in fact be "abandoned." One reason for such relative optimism, at this point, came from a rapid improvement in Britain's finances thanks to sterling's devaluation and a cutback in imports.

Kennan's Policy Planning Staff was contributing to the NSC study process, but he had let Acheson and Webb know in September that he wanted to leave as director. To believe, as his biographer does, that Kennan wasn't being eased out due to the quality of his performance shows some naïveté about how large organizations work.[26] As Kennan reflected, it had never occurred to him that Acheson and Nitze could "make foreign policy without having first consulted me."[27] But it turned out that they could, and he shouldn't have been surprised at their impatience. He always saw problems in the starkest and most despairing terms. Paul Nitze replaced him on January 1, 1950.

Nitze would be in and out of high government service from the year he arrived in Washington with Forrestal until the end of the Reagan administration, in 1989. The title of an excellent biography that addresses his later years, *The Master of the Game*, can apply to his entire career. He resembled Forrestal, who was fifteen years older: five feet nine, lean, tightly wound, with the same restlessly inquiring mind. His father had taught Romance languages at the University of Chicago, and he attended Harvard, where he was asked to join Porcellian, one of the college's final clubs whose brethren regard it as delivering a lifetime of access to anything in America they please. He graduated in the class of 1928 with a summa in economics, then joined Dillon, Read & Co., where he met Forrestal, made money, married well to become far richer still, and did his own venture deals. All of this gave him the wherewithal in 1937 to tour Hitler's Germany for six weeks and then to return to Harvard for a master's in sociology to absorb what he'd witnessed.

Basically, Nitze was a technologist with a quick mind for numbers and a passion for anticipating how societies can be molded by radical innovation. During the war, he worked on procurement issues, but toward the end he became vice chairman of the U.S. Strategic Bombing Survey, which—after he and his teams inspected the devastated enemy cities—produced impartial assessments of the effects of airpower against Germany and Japan. Thereafter he signed on with J. H. Whitney & Co.

in New York, which was the country's first venture capital firm. As he'd reflect when in his eighties, the best use of Porcellian during his career was that it kept opening talent pools of smart young graduates whose businesses he could appraise for funding.[28]

Within a year of joining Jock Whitney's firm, however, Nitze grew restless and entered the State Department, where he handled trade statistics, but also worked for Treasury Secretary Snyder in sorting out the 1947 sterling crisis. He combined a banker's focus with a technologist's disdain for imprecision, which by 1957 he'd demonstrate in a book review that shredded Professor Henry Kissinger's celebrated *Nuclear Weapons and Foreign Policy* for its basic errors of geography and math and then, fifteen years later, by skewering the technical details of the Nixon-Kissinger arms control orthodoxy with Moscow.[29]

It was this quality of rigorous analysis—combining youthful curiosity and an understanding of technology and finance, as well as of global affairs—that he brought to Policy Planning. And it served him well when Acheson tasked him in January 1950 with being the principal author of another, separate NSC study. This latest analysis was compelled by the shocking double tap of Russia's atomic detonation and the fall of China, as well as by leading scientists having agreed that America could likely achieve a hydrogen bomb within three years. Today the State Department considers the fifty-eight-page memorandum that resulted in April—National Security Council Report 68, *United States Objectives and Programs for National Security*—one of the most influential documents ever produced by the U.S. government.[30]

From the start, Nitze had to examine the core question of what the United States wanted to achieve in the world, and how to go about it. He focused on nuclear strategy, which included supporting Truman's decision to build a hydrogen bomb—based on the conviction that the Soviet Union was becoming ever more capable of executing its design to dominate Eurasia and destroy America.[31] Once war arrived two months after its completion, NSC 68 ended up creating a framework for expanding military power. Although he never saw it this way, Nitze was making the case for an increase in defense spending that, when costed out in full, could have swallowed 60 percent of GDP. That result makes large parts of NSC 68 polemical. Unsurprisingly, Treasury Secretary Snyder dismissed Nitze's request to participate in the study.

Nitze wrote in passing of "the decline of the British and French empires"; power had fully gravitated toward the United States and the Soviet Union, in this view. Yet only a fraction of Americans would have agreed that their country held the "responsibility of world leadership." There was also a big hole in Nitze's analysis about total warfare, as we'll see. Altogether, NSC 68's focus on the U.S.-Soviet nuclear face-off left a third global entity out of the picture. NSC 75 would redress the balance.

IN JANUARY 1950, AS NITZE TOOK CHARGE AT POLICY PLANNING, Stafford Cripps—the patrician ascetic—proposed tighter austerity measures to the House of Commons. Devaluation had alleviated Britain's finances, but few in London believed matters were stable. Cripps's talk of new stringencies suggested that Britain was again in store for carrots and cold-water baths. In Washington, his speech did more than spotlight the doubts surrounding his country's economy. Ironically, it also showed the grip that British officials seemed to have in America's capital.

This time Cripps recommended that the Labour government ban all imported fuel oil that had to be paid for in dollars. If his idea took hold, it meant that products being refined in Bahrain by U.S. giants such as the Texas Company, or pumped in Kuwait by Gulf Oil, could be shut out of British markets. Cripps wanted Britain to only use oil paid for in sterling, as from Iraq and Iran. That was because dollar-denominated oil imports were the cause of Britain's severest hard-currency drain.

Denying market access to the Americans was a desperate step, and Cripps provoked a controversy as bitter as the previous one with Hollywood: the oil giants were no less fierce in guarding their revenue streams. Events intensified even before any restrictions could be imposed, once a letter written by Arthur Creech Jones, the colonial secretary and a labor union protégé of Bevin's, mysteriously came to light. "The Americans," Creech Jones wrote to a subordinate about Cripps's latest plan to impede free trade, "have, as expected, not gone beyond expressing regret."[32]

The remark stung. It confirmed a prevailing belief among Americans—notably on Capitol Hill—about the passivity of their diplomats. *Of course* those "cookie pushers," to recall FDR's derision of the State Department's cozy inhabitants, weren't standing up to the imperious British to say no. It took Tom Connally, the chairman of the Senate Foreign Relations Committee, and a proud son of Eddy, population 150, in oil-rich Texas, to bury Cripps's initiative by threatening to cut off Marshall Plan aid.

In March, budget officials in Whitehall made another move. Since the summer of 1948, there'd been transatlantic quarrels over which country would pay about $32 million to upgrade the airfields in England being used by American bombers. U.S. negotiators insisted that the British bear the costs "since the bases were in the U.K."[33] Tempers rose in four separate clashes with Bevin, because the Pentagon refused to pay more than one-sixth of the cost. In the fall of 1949, Douglas had finally warned Washington to back off; everyone needed to calm down. But by midwinter, Britain's Treasury was asking if local vendors might at least be paid in advance for the services and supplies that they were providing to American airmen. No, replied Defense Department bureaucrats.

Pentagon analysts simply didn't regard the British Empire as economically desperate. That's apparent in their contribution to the NSC 75 process, *Effects of British Decline as a World Power on U.S. Security Interests*, which emerged on February 14, 1950. The title itself, referencing "decline," already seemed dated because Britain's economy had improved markedly. Fiscal hemorrhaging looked like history, and private consumption was back to prewar levels. Instead, the Pentagon's insights are categorical: it would be "highly improbable" for the British Empire to withdraw from places of interest to the United States.[34]

The colonies—as shown by Whitehall's expectations for Africa—still appeared to offer the likelihood of greater prosperity, and commonwealth ties looked strong. The Defense Department, furthermore, best understood the scope of Britain's high-tech military-scientific-industrial complex. Altogether, the picture of Britain's future was looking very different than it did in the depth of the sterling-dollar crisis when the NSC study had begun.

The NSC staff also circulated this document, as it had done with the CIA's. Titles of the evolving work began to change. In the Pentagon's case, *U.S. Security Interests* was dropped. (Nitze dominated the NSC 68 effort that had a monopoly on defining those.) As for the CIA's paper, no one was any longer talking abandonment, as during the previous summer. At most, the State Department's Bureau of Commonwealth Affairs injected, some British commitments might have to be curtailed, such as those that required big outlays of dollars—like keeping British occupation forces in Austria. Otherwise not, especially if Washington offered support. Any penny-pinching in Congress, warned the sympathetic director of this office, risked "our ability to utilize the British to help us protect our world position."[35]

The Pentagon's contribution, for instance, saw no evidence that Britain was going to leave Hong Kong, and certainly not Malaya. Gibraltar, as well as commitments in the Caribbean, involved no great dollar drain. Nor did those in Africa, which, with luck, could pay for themselves several times over. So there remained deployments in Europe, the Middle East, lots of air and naval bases, and scores of subsidies worldwide. All looked manageable given Britain's economic rebound. Moreover, the commonwealth seemed cohesive and the warfare state's industries could uphold a big, globally deployed fighting force, while also boosting exports. Britain had regained its lead in shipbuilding, and its achievements in jet aviation remained unsurpassed.

Diligent people at State, Defense, and the CIA were seeing no signs that justified the emergency-laden words "decline" and "abandonment," which is why the focus of the study came to be on British military commitments and capabilities. Policy makers expected the British to have enough resilience and worldly wisdom to stay in place. Dealing with "the complex political relations of the Near and Far East," the Pentagon's analysts wrote, "required generations of experience accumulated by the British civil service to deal with." Perhaps true, though it would have been fair to question the quality of work. Nonetheless, "the body of experience," they continued—yet sounding like Sir Gladwyn Jebb— "cannot be transferred to new hands without risking the possibilities of political upheaval in certain of these areas."[36]

ON JANUARY 11, 1950, FIVE WEEKS BEFORE POLLING DAY, ATTLEE dissolved Parliament, and one of the most bitterly fought contests in his country's recent history was under way. "I heard there was going to be a general election," Churchill quipped upon landing in Southampton via an Aquila Airways flying boat, having scooted home from the island of Madeira, where he had been writing and painting. "I thought I had better come back in case I was wanted."[37] As leader of the opposition, he was the Conservative Party's choice for the premiership. The Truman administration said it didn't care whether he or Attlee won. It just hoped for a decisive majority because "the time has come for fundamental decisions about the relations of the United States and Britain."[38]

The Conservative and Labour Parties agreed on a muscular foreign policy. That left their two leaders to dispute who could best improve an economy that still required rationing of bacon (5 ounces a week), fats (10 ounces), tea (2.5 ounces), and much else. Churchill found it demeaning for a British election to be based on expertise in delivering biscuits and bacon. Instead, he asked what nation could better address mankind's future in the atomic age. None. He then proposed a parley with Stalin and implied only he was qualified to lead it. Bevin dismissed this as "a stunt."

Attlee's Labour Party squeaked to victory with a 5-seat majority in a 649-member House of Commons. The margin was so unstable, Ambassador Douglas reported to State, that Churchill would soon get a rematch. It didn't make much difference to Acheson. He was vexed these months over London's intransigence on issues from finance to Europe to Asia. He questioned Douglas as to whether any British government intended to share U.S. objectives. If not, he added, "we would have to reexamine our whole foreign policy."[39] The French, for their part, remained convinced that an Anglo-American cabal was being formed at the expense of a united Europe.

At the Pentagon, however, the Joint Chiefs suspected that Bevin intended to limit his country's military ties on the Continent so that more British forces would be free to uphold distant imperial bastions. And they knew that half of France's army and 90 percent of its professional officers were stuck in Indochina fighting the Vietminh. It's at this point that the Americans, from behind their ocean moats, began to push the idea of rearming the terribly recent enemy—Germany—now that its Western occupation zones had coalesced into an independent state some fifty million strong.*

Concerning a united Europe, Attlee's government and the Conservative Party remained wary—despite determined men at State and on the Hill who expected federation. But perhaps there was a reason that went unsaid for Britain's detachment. Had Britain done otherwise, and embraced European unity, it would have faced a different kind of audit. The strength of its economic recovery would have stood in starkest contrast to the growth rates heating up in France and West Germany. If a recently half-desolate Continent was a challenge to one's world standing, then one's world standing was mighty thin.

ACHESON'S *PRESENT AT THE CREATION* CONTAINS FASCINATING IN-sights on Britain's evolving role, despite frequent sacrifices of authenticity for drama. For example, he describes a reception on Sunday evening, May 7, 1950, at David Bruce's official residence at No. 2, avenue d'Iéna. It was the fifth anniversary of the Nazi surrender, which goes unmentioned. Poignantly, it was also the day that France's foreign minister, Robert Schuman, quietly told Acheson of France's plan to link its coal and steel industries—the traditional sinews of war—with those of West Germany, making it impossible for either side to fight the other. Schuman's initiative would recast Europe. The Coal and Steel Community resulted two years later. That achievement led straight to today's European Union, and to the alignment between Germany and France that, to this day, is the heart of the European project. After flying to London on Tuesday, however, Acheson realized—once he disclosed the news to Bevin—that the British would have none of this.[40]

Acheson also addresses the notion of a "special relationship" between the United States and Britain, which has been said, largely by the British, to still exist today. Having just arrived in London, on the ninth,

_____

*Moscow, in turn, had created the German Democratic Republic the previous October out of its own occupation zone. It became known as East Germany.

he was handed a paper written by U.S. diplomats at the embassy in tandem with the Foreign Office—the subject being "the special nature of Anglo-American relations." Acheson reacted with disgust. In recalling the paper in his book, he rails against "the stupidity of writing about a special relationship" when America had to work as well with ten other North Atlantic Treaty allies. Of course, a special relationship did exist given the language and history that the two countries shared. But this relationship was not "affectionate," Acheson wrote, adding that Americans reserved that sentiment for their oldest ally, France.[41] In *Present at the Creation*, Acheson tells his readers that he ordered all copies of the paper burned. End of story, as far as he was concerned.

But one copy survived. The American coauthors at the embassy, it turns out, had proudly circulated their document to the Pentagon. The Joint Chiefs were furious when they saw it. Like Acheson, they didn't want Britain trumpeted as America's principal partner. "Important" was saying enough. Besides, the chiefs had other reasons to be angry. None of them welcomed the document's promises of endless bilateral conferencing and collaborating. Nor did they want to repeat the previous year's foolishness at State's Policy Planning bureau about an Anglo-American union. Moreover, "Essential Elements of U.S.-U.K. Relations," as this work is titled, was fulsome: it seems written by a foreign power, one that is confident it can dictate U.S. policy.

PRESIDENT TRUMAN RECEIVED NSC 75 ON JULY 15, AS DID ACHE-son. And so did John Snyder, who, as Treasury secretary, wasn't a statutory member of the NSC but whom Truman, eighteen months earlier, had asked to attend every NSC meeting. By now, *British Military Commitments* had itemized the empire's forces and obligations. Here was quantitative evidence and a crisp narrative elaborated by bullet points. Beyond all the "Whither Britain?" guesswork, the report indicated what help the Americans might expect in an East-West showdown, which looked imminent that summer. In light of all these conclusions, it would have been hard to find decision makers who, "by the end of the 1940s," believed Britain had neither "an empire nor an economy capable of competing with those of other major powers," as is claimed today.[42]

The report uses categories I through IV to rank the importance of British military commitments for U.S. defense and the British force levels that backed them. Arguments follow in each case to justify the grade. NSC 75 put Europe in Category I, meaning it was "considered of greatest importance." This was a region, the report declared, where the armed forces of both the United States and Britain could cooperate.[43] It deemed the Royal Navy's Home and Mediterranean Fleets, plus Britain's soldiers and air wings, indispensable to Europe's defense, and it measured a core of fifty-four thousand British troops designated, at this juncture, for the purpose.

The Middle East was placed in Category II and given slightly less importance than Europe. It was a region, the report asserts, that Britain would be responsible for defending largely alone. Looking at the Middle East, NSC 75 defines Britain's obligations as "a *major consideration* in the implementation of the present plans and policies of the United States."[44] As part of Britain's overall presence in the Middle East, the report recognizes an ongoing value to America of the RAF and the British army in the eastern Mediterranean—contrary to today's myth about "the British withdrawal from the eastern Mediterranean" having occurred in 1947.[45] To this end, their base on Cyprus—the strategically located island colony off the coasts of Turkey and Syria—is rated as Category II, like Britain's presence at Suez.

Classifying the Middle East itself as Category II reveals a key point as to how the Americans perceived the British Empire: that region was deemed vital for them, but Britain was believed capable of protecting it alone from Russia while keeping these lands generally stable enough day by day. "Insofar as the presence of British forces in the Middle East contribute to the assurance of Allied control of the Cairo-Suez area," NSC 75 stated, "the commitment is of extreme importance to us." That's the sole use of "extreme" in this effort.[46]

NSC 75 discloses a big wide-reaching apparatus held by reassuring hands. It concluded, with reasonable accuracy, that Britain had 718,000 of its own men and women in uniform, out of a population of 50 million. Total force levels in fact stood at 689,000 in 1950 and were about to rise to 872,000. In comparison, today's U.S. armed forces stand at 1.3 million in a world with three times the population of 1950. The RAF was identified as unsurpassed, which was in line with the British warfare state's high-tech profile. And this conglomeration didn't even include fighting men from the empire and commonwealth.

The Americans appreciated these capabilities. They lived under the shadows of the Depression and world war, and there were no certainties of their country's future prosperity as the 1950s began. The Dow Jones average was hovering at 200 during the months that NSC 75 was being prepared—somewhat less than twice what the stock market had been in 1940, although GDP had nearly tripled. Yet foreign aid stood at 3.21 percent of GDP. That's the highest amount ever, and it compares with about 0.2 percent today, a 93 percent reduction. Implications of further involvements were sobering for an America with less than half of today's citizens and about a third of our real income.

In an era of obsessive good economic housekeeping, with the war debt unpaid, all the analyses that went into NSC 75 concluded that the costs of trying to assume Britain's commitments were unmanageable. Attempting to carry them would be both a "tremendous financial burden and a grave political liability." Marshall Plan aid to Europe would have to be cut, including, ironically, aid to Britain. Garrisons of GIs on every continent would be required. Although there's reference in these NSC papers to the prospect of sending U.S. fighting men to Africa and the Middle East, should the British Empire ever retreat, that's done to show the possibility as far-fetched and repellent and to swat it away.

Ultimately, the message of NSC 75, and of all the work behind it, was this: The British Empire and Commonwealth would stay much as it had been, covering the globe with its nearly one million men under arms and who-knew-what in reserve. There had been no "retreat" that anyone could categorize, in contrast to "adjustment," and no need was expected for "replacement." Nor could American energy and goodwill substitute for the British Empire's experienced global presence. As for the need to vastly expand U.S. forces overseas, that wasn't necessary. Instead, the United States should support this formidable ally, which included backing its reserve currency. All this was an effective, efficient way to leverage U.S. strength and to achieve stability in parts of the world that had little to do with the American experience, places like Indochina, Malaya, and the rest of Southeast Asia.

10

PIVOTING TO ASIA AND INTO VIETNAM

It was crystal clear to me that the future and, indeed, the very
existence of America, were irrevocably entwined with Asia and
its island outposts.

—General Douglas MacArthur, in 1964, reflecting on his 1905–1906
  travels as a lieutenant through the Far East and India

I N LATE 1949, WHEN ERNEST BEVIN LEARNED THAT U.S. FORCES
were rescinding their commitments to the Middle East, the news
came as an embittering surprise. It dismayed Admiral Richard Conolly
too. He was still heading one of America's three largest military commands, and doing so from London, with responsibilities that reached
from the mid-Atlantic to the South China Sea, and he had to explain
the situation to the British chiefs of staff.

The reasons for retrenchment, Conolly told them, arose not only
from having to meet new Atlantic Pact obligations but also from the
need to reinforce Asia after the loss of China. U.S. interests in the
Middle East wouldn't change, he said: oil still had to be pumped, and
stability upheld in Turkey, Iran, and Egypt. He acknowledged that
Americans weren't going to reduce the presence of their diplomats, edu-
cators, and aid missions in the region, let alone that of their petroleum

companies. Nonetheless, in the event of World War III, the United States would leave the defense of the Middle East to the British. This new approach was in part attributable to Congress. There's "a definite limit to what we can do," concluded the Republican senator Robert Taft, who might as well have been speaking for the Democrats or for the Pentagon.[1]

Oliver Franks often discussed such sweeping issues with Secretary Acheson over drinks or dinner, either at the secretary's ivy-covered house in Georgetown or in the ambassador's study overlooking the embassy gardens. During the winter of 1949–1950, a lot of their conversation concerned "Red China," the colloquialism then used to designate that huge nation as part of the Communist bloc. In his dispatches to Bevin, Franks repeated much of what he heard—as when Acheson mulled that if Taiwan were ever taken by the People's Liberation Army, the "bad boys" among Chiang's generals would escape the island, only to resurface as troublemakers throughout Asia's overseas Chinese communities.[2] However, Acheson had more immediate worries.

THE PREVIOUS OCTOBER, IN 1949, FRANCE'S AMBASSADOR, HENRI Bonnet, had told Acheson of discovering that the British were set to open diplomatic relations with Mao Zedong. The Foreign Office, Bonnet helpfully related, had just delivered an accommodating note from Ernest Bevin to Chou En-lai, minister for foreign affairs, extending de facto recognition. This proved true, and Acheson felt deceived. Bevin had promised, during their mid-September "tower de horizon" in Washington, to coordinate any overture to Beijing with the Americans. Franks hastily called what had occurred an unfortunate oversight. Yet a legalistic note soon arrived from the Foreign Office that undermined Franks's claim. It explained that Secretary Bevin's earlier promise had only been to consult with the Americans over de jure recognition. That hadn't occurred (so far), and Britain had merely accepted the fact that Mao's regime was in charge.

More was to come from Bevin. The foreign secretary, Acheson was advised, might be persuaded to reconsider formally accepting Communist sovereignty, provided the Americans pledged to defend Hong Kong from the PLA. The Joint Chiefs turned this idea down flat.

Truman found the entire encounter souring, and he complained to Acheson that the British hadn't "played very squarely with us"—a remark Acheson relayed to Bevin, who, for once, apologized.[3] More or less, that is: he couldn't help observing that he had agreed on prior *consultation* concerning Beijing, not on prior agreement.

In London, Lewis Douglas anticipated what was coming. Using "every argument I had in my bag," as he later put it, he tried to dissuade Bevin from officially recognizing the People's Republic.[4] Bevin heard him out, but then asked, "Do you want us to go as slow on this as we have in the case of Israel?" Britain, as Douglas well knew, had delayed recognition for a full year after the founding of the Jewish state.

Nothing the Americans might have said would have persuaded Attlee's government to alter its decision. But Acheson dug in. During an early November meeting in Paris, he told Ernest Bevin and France's foreign minister, Robert Schuman, that the United States would not recognize China's Communist regime until it began to satisfy civilized conditions of behavior. Those did not include manhandling U.S. diplomats, nor welcoming Russian military advisers and fighter planes, nor encroaching on Tibet, which in November had appealed to Washington for weapons in hopes of remaining independent. The Americans wouldn't recognize China as a state for twenty-nine more years, during Jimmy Carter's presidency. Instead, for decades, they pretended China didn't exist, except for Chiang Kai-shek's clique on Taiwan.

On January 1, 1950, India became the first nation outside the Soviet bloc to offer full recognition to Beijing, what diplomats call "mutual benefit and mutual respect." Pakistan followed quickly, and then so did Britain, on January 5, withdrawing its ambassador to Chiang's government. Americans were stunned, except for some insiders at Foggy Bottom. Opinion polls showed that most were opposed to acknowledging Mao's rule, although a third didn't know Chiang's Nationalists had been beaten. There was little ambivalence on Capitol Hill. The Senate minority leader, Kenneth Wherry, a Nebraska Republican, said he now had "even more compelling reasons" to cut off aid for socialist Britain.[5]

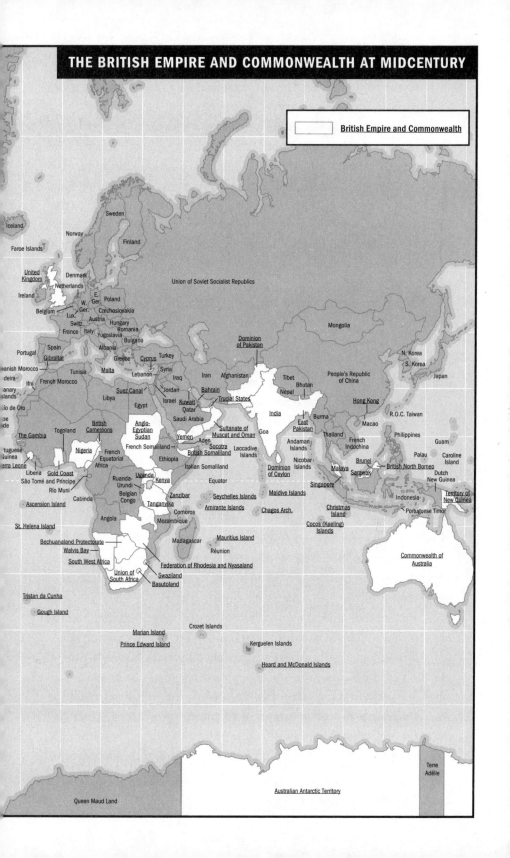

THE BRITISH EMPIRE AND COMMONWEALTH AT MIDCENTURY

British Empire and Commonwealth

Chief among them was appeasement, he insisted: America was merely enabling surrender to the Chinese Communists on the installment plan, just as Britain had done with the Nazis in Munich.

Bevin's overture to China reflected three priorities: to protect Hong Kong; to forestall trouble among the "vast Chinese communities in Southeast Asia" that were under British imperial rule; and to at least try to lure the new regime in Beijing away from Kremlin influence.[6] He cared little about protecting British investments on the mainland, as the Americans kept assuming he did, nor did he worry about how his decision might offend Congress. China's new leaders, for their part, didn't care what Bevin was doing. They ignored Britain's outreach and wouldn't reciprocate for years.

In any event, Bevin doubted that the Chinese Communists and the Russians would combine for long in a political-military bloc. They'd split in "a few years' time," he predicted, and he never saw the People's Republic as a Russian satellite.[7] Churchill shared that opinion, yet his deputy, Anthony Eden—who would have been jiggered to know that he was echoing anyone like Senator Wherry, who remained a licensed undertaker—also denounced Bevin's "policy of appeasement," claiming that it harmed "events outside China . . . in Indo-China and in Malaya, and throughout Southeast Asia."[8]

And it was in Southeast Asia that Washington detected further evidence of Communist expansion. On January 19, China—which supplied weapons to the Vietminh—bestowed diplomatic recognition on Ho Chi Minh's revolutionary movement, known as the Democratic Republic of Vietnam. Soviet recognition followed on the thirtieth. Then the Soviet Union and the People's Republic of China seemed to cement their own relationship on February 14 by signing a mutual defense treaty in Moscow. Acheson looked at all this activity and suspected that Stalin's next move would be to have his Chinese allies dispatch agents and saboteurs throughout Southeast Asia, probably disguised as merchants—a variation of the *maskirovka* model that had originally been applied in Iran. As a response, he learned from his staff that the Foreign Office was launching a full-scale campaign to encourage a strong American policy in Southeast Asia. He should expect to be pushed hard for dollars, weapons, diplomatic backing, and maybe more, he was advised, and not only for Britain's Malayan federation but also for the French in Vietnam.

At the Pentagon, the Plans and Operations unit was working during these months on its study *Effects of British Decline as a World Power.* The final NSC report would designate Malaya as Category II, meaning of high importance to U.S. defense. Should the British Empire ever falter in Malaya, the Pentagon's input concluded, "the U.S. may be forced to share military responsibilities with the U.K."[9] But no one was worrying. "It seems highly improbable," wrote the analysts, "that the United Kingdom would withdraw troops and training missions from *Southern Asia (to include Malaya and Singapore) and Central and South Africa.*"

One place not being mentioned by name in any of the NSC 75 papers, however, was Vietnam, which is where France's Indochina war was heavily being fought, to the increasing disadvantage of the French. And what if Vietnam were to fall? The British, at this point, were certain that the Communists would press outward from Indochina into Thailand, and then Malaya would fall, too. The Americans, who now placed Malaya among their uppermost defense interests, were coming to agree.

AS 1950 BEGAN, THOSE AMERICANS WHO SURVEYED THE ISSUE could be skeptical about France's requests for help in Indochina. Not only was France losing, but it appeared to be stifling political reform. However, a lot of opinion—among Washington policy makers and those citizens on Main Street who thought about Southeast Asia—was being shaped by the British. U.S. officials were quite simply following Britain's lead throughout the region, which meant they were adhering to Commissioner General Malcolm MacDonald's beliefs. From his headquarters in Singapore, over which flew a blue flag with the British crown and the legend "South East Asia," MacDonald began to make France's case far better than the French could possibly do themselves.

Prominent Americans sought MacDonald's counsel. Among them were Thomas Dewey, the governor of New York and the head of the Republican Party; Cardinal Francis Spellman, a popular Catholic leader and vehement anti-Communist, known as "the Powerhouse" for his influence on American politics; Congressman John F. Kennedy and his brother Robert; and Adlai Stevenson and Richard Nixon. The venture-some Supreme Court justice William O. Douglas named MacDonald "a top man in his thinking."[10] Editors at Henry Luce's Time Inc. declared MacDonald's abilities in Southeast Asia to be "the best any British possession has ever had," and newspaper publishers and columnists from around the country agreed.[11]

All traveled to Phoenix Park. MacDonald knew how to appeal to enlightened American sensibilities. He didn't visit colonial clubs that excluded Asians, and he invited what were then called brown and yellow people to official banquets—something that at the time was simply *not done*. He championed racial equality. He described himself as an "evolutionary socialist," and his pragmatic approach to the region—such as introducing power-sharing arrangements among the Federation of Malaya's antagonistic Malay and Chinese communities—made edified Americans regard him as a fair-minded progressive, which he was. He was also a trustee of the Rhodes Scholarship and a founder of the University of Malaya, in 1949, of which he was chancellor. His book *Bird Watching at Lossiemouth* (1934) is apparently a classic among ornithologists. MacDonald had a respectful fascination for the tribes of Borneo, and an enviable collection of Asian art. He repeatedly maintained that all Britain's colonies in Southeast Asia had to be led to freedom, eventually. He sympathized with the Vietminh's nationalism, he said, but, unfortunately, they had been pushed into Communism by French intransigence. Now that they were in thrall to Moscow, there was no alternative but to defeat them.

The only Westerner in Asia to compare with his standing was General Douglas MacArthur, but MacDonald was far more engaging. Modestly, he didn't carry the title "Sir," and he spurned the honors to which he was entitled as an official of distinction. In welcome contrast to the stuffiness of British society in Singapore, he embraced informality. He was fun. Momentously, one evening in 1952, he appeared at a concert in colonial Singapore without a dinner jacket, news that made *The Washington Post*'s society page. When he entertained in his towered, green-tiled granite palace, known as Istana, "Peaceful Hill," in nearby Johor, his guests used first names and dressed casually. His wife lived in Canada, but in Singapore he had a mistress: Elizabeth Marcos, whose brother Ferdinand would rule the Philippines from 1965 to 1986.

Basically, he bridged two worlds for the Americans: an older one that was supposedly steeped in colonial political-anthropological wisdoms, and a newer one of racial harmony. When it came to the Communists, his stance didn't vary. If Indochina fell, he'd quietly say, while pointing to a map, Thailand would follow automatically. Defending Malaya would then be so expensive as to outweigh its irreplaceable value to Britain. With its finances undercut, British trade and investment wouldn't be able to help strengthen Europe's recovering economies. That would end American hopes for having strong, unified, and self-reliant North Atlantic partners. This was his core position. He didn't disagree when British and French officials took the argument further, talking of how, if Indochina fell, the Communists would advance onward through India to the Middle East.

For MacDonald, only a deeper American commitment to Indochina stood in the way, because Vietnam was Malaya's first, and likely final, line of defense.

The Americans were becoming convinced—except they overlooked a critical element in MacDonald's perspective. Before World War II, he had been on a brilliant path to becoming prime minister but then had wrecked his chances by supporting Chamberlain's policy of trying to appease Nazi Germany. Churchill loathed him for that.[12] Finding himself once again confronting totalitarian appetites, MacDonald wasn't going to make the same mistake twice.

SINCE ARRIVING IN SINGAPORE IN 1946, MacDONALD HAD GARnered £750 million—nearly the equivalent of the original postwar U.S. loan—in British aid for southern Asia, including for India. During 1949, he kept making further strides toward what he regarded as uplifting this portion of the world. While fulfilling his duties, he landed in Tokyo at eleven o'clock on Saturday morning, September 3, aboard General MacArthur's personal plane, *Bataan*. The four-engine Lockheed Constellation had picked him up in Hong Kong, and MacDonald's purpose in Tokyo was to exchange information between what he described as Britain's part of the Far East, that being Southeast Asia, and the Americans' part, which he regarded as Northeast Asia.[13]

The "two Macs" had a private lunch at two o'clock. MacDonald reported on fifteen months of jungle fighting in Malaya, and he asked MacArthur to designate U.S. military liaison officers for Hong Kong and Singapore.[14] The supreme commander didn't promise anything. He just advised MacDonald to take the matter up in Washington, with officials at State and the Pentagon, who he was certain would say no, as they did.

MacDonald stayed in Tokyo for a week of briefings with U.S., British, and Japanese officials. He also held a press conference. The Kremlin had switched its emphasis from Europe to the Far East, he told reporters from some dozen nations. It was "the next stage of a plan to make a Communist conquest of the whole world." All was synchronized, he insisted: Communist victory in China, civil war in Burma, "terrorism and murder" in Malaya, and labor troubles in India.[15] (Nehru agreed with none of this.) U.S. and British interests were therefore inseparable.

MacDonald left Tokyo on a Pan Am Clipper for Indochina. He saw French administrators in Hanoi and Saigon, whom he knew well and spoke with fluently. He also met with Bao Dai, the plump, Paris-educated thirty-five-year-old who had been the thirteenth and final emperor of the Nguyễn dynasty, which, until not long before, had ruled over most of what we know as Vietnam. Bao Dai had been a Japanese puppet during World War II and then abdicated in 1945, after Japan's surrender. That was when the Japanese had passed civil authority directly over to the Vietminh. As revolution erupted, with France's reappearance, he fled to the Riviera. The French persuaded him to return in July 1949 as chief of state of the Associated State of Vietnam—that is, as the face of a nationalist government that could rival the Vietminh's Democratic Republic. He accepted the role, but his heart wasn't in it. He had a greater loyalty to Cannes and Monte Carlo, according to MacDonald, than to his homeland and, like Egypt's King Farouk, he favored the gambling tables of the Carlton hotel.

The British, like the French, realized that they needed to make Bao Dai look heroic for the Americans—a former monarch who represented his nation in a just cause and who was thus a good and proper man to back. Doing so was becoming urgent: In 1946, Paris had pushed the nations of Vietnam, Laos, and Cambodia into a quasi-colonial entity called the French Union, and the mashup was now being promoted as akin to the British Commonwealth. At this juncture, that raised vexing questions of U.S. diplomatic recognition.

Mid-level British diplomats in Washington supplied the State Department with excerpts from Commissioner General MacDonald's dispatches to London attesting to Bao Dai's courage, openness, and charm. MacDonald regarded him as the only chance to save Indochina from Communism, it seemed. But that wasn't quite true.

During this period, Washington was urging all colonial powers to guide their colonies to independence, and—as MacDonald saw it—the Americans had to be convinced that Bao Dai was up for the job in Vietnam. However, word leaked out to U.S. officials in London that MacDonald had been more candid in his full report to Whitehall. He barely disputed the general impression at the Foreign Office that the former emperor was "a dull dog" in thrall to France.[16]

That attempt at deception occurred as Acheson had to decide if America should recognize Bao Dai's State of Vietnam, thereby opening the possibility of direct military and diplomatic backing. The Americans knew essentially nothing about the place. Few visited (after getting the required smallpox and cholera shots), and only a dozen or so Americans could handle the language, most of them being Jesuits.

In November 1949, the State Department and the Foreign Office exchanged position papers on Southeast Asia. These reflected conventional wisdom, which at the time was whatever MacDonald was saying about the region. Truman initialed his approval on the U.S. document. One analyst at Policy Planning nonetheless suggested America "throw up its hands in despair over Indo-China." It would be better, he continued, to wait for the British themselves to "take the lead and suggest ways and means for staving off collapse."[17] Whitehall had other ideas. It wanted the Americans to walk out front.

As 1950 began, Malcolm MacDonald knew that Britain alone couldn't fulfill his visions of nation building in Malaya, in Indochina, and in the rest of a very widely defined Southeast Asia. There wasn't the money. Yet something had to be done to demonstrate unswerving U.S. as well as British commitment. Otherwise, as he wrote in one of his dispatches to London, "we shall find that we are too late to prevent Indo-China from falling to the Communists," adding that "the problem lies distinctively in persuading the Americans to play the part which they can now play."[18] This entailed getting Washington to do more to uphold Britain's priorities—defending Malaya, as he put it, "by defending Indo-China."[19]

Would the Red tide really wash down to Malaya's shores? Why not? Japan's armies had reached the fringes of India just a few years before. And so it appeared to Sir William Strang, the Foreign Office's top mandarin, the permanent undersecretary. Dikes would have to be built with British expertise and American money. One of Strang's aides, who went a bit further than MacDonald in pushing this argument, concluded that Washington's "military neglect" of the region could prove catastrophic: Communism, he argued, would spread throughout Asia and swiftly flood Japan too. The best approach would be to persuade the Americans to enter some form of collective defense arrangement—and that, of course, would have to embrace Indochina.

THE BRITISH WERE THINKING BIG IN THESE MONTHS BEFORE THE Korean War. In January 1950, for example, Malcolm MacDonald choreographed the six-day Commonwealth Conference on Foreign Affairs. It was held in Colombo, Ceylon, the first such gathering outside Britain. Nehru attended, as did the ailing Ernest Bevin, in one of his last odysseys abroad. MacDonald made the case for the stakes they all had in Indochina. He asserted that Bao Dai embodied Vietnam's future. No U.S. representative, to be sure, was sitting among these dignitaries in Colombo's white-domed Town Hall. But that didn't prevent an ambitious $5 billion Asian development plan from being crafted—costing roughly a third of the entire Marshall Plan—to which the Americans were expected to contribute most of the funding.

Paul Nitze's Policy Planning Staff viewed these British overtures with suspicion, and Nitze advised Acheson not to "forget that the majority of Asians are infinitely alien to us."[20] He was also using his ties to

Acheson to urge him to create a dramatic success of any type some-where in Asia or at least to inflict a Communist defeat. That was essen-tial to retaining the confidence of friends and allies, he advised. The vagueness wasn't rash or ill-informed. The East Asian borderlands, he felt, were bulging and swaying like a curtain with a tiger behind it. Surely the beast would incautiously stick out a paw, which an alert defender must be ready to stab.

Perhaps one way for the United States to show resolve, senior officials at Foggy Bottom came to conclude, was to recognize the sovereignty of Bao Dai and the three "Associated States," which the Americans did on February 3, to MacDonald's satisfaction. Within four days, Acheson's indispensable troubleshooter, Ambassador at Large Philip Jessup, was in Phoenix Park to examine next steps with the commissioner general. He heard that Washington needed to take even "quicker action" toward backing the new State of Vietnam.[21]

Republicans in Congress then promptly designated their own man to head a high-profile fact-finding mission to Southeast Asia. They chose R. Allen Griffin, who directed the Economic Cooperation Administra-tion's Far East program. He appeared in Phoenix Park four weeks later and thereafter gushed that MacDonald and his staff "were the only good advisors I had."[22] The result of that visit was the first big step in granting unrestricted civil and military dollars to the ruling authorities in Vietnam and Malaya.[23]

THE SEAT OF THE BAO DAI GOVERNMENT WAS SAIGON, WHICH ALSO contained French military headquarters for all of Indochina. After the Americans announced recognition, and elevated their consulate in the city to a legation, Britain and Australia extended recognition too. *The New York Times* announced that these initiatives placed "the United States and Britain squarely in opposition to the Soviet Union in this area," but that's not quite right.[24] Whitehall chose to delay the formalities of recog-nition, hoping that France might first give a more palatable appearance to the "independence" of not only Vietnam but also Cambodia and Laos.

By early spring, however, it was the fate of Malaya that dominated State Department cable flow from the region. Guerrillas were by then killing more than one hundred civilians a month, and colonial authorities could do little to stop them. They insisted that Malaya—any mention of which was followed by "Britain's source of hard currency"—would soon find itself as besieged as Vietnam. That could be catastrophic because this small, lucrative federation produced about one-seventh of the exports of all the United States.

"The frontiers of Malaya are on the Mekong," said one of MacDonald's high-ranking subordinates—the ambassador in Thailand—who was referencing Asia's longest river, which flows through Laos, Cambodia, and Vietnam before draining into the sea. MacDonald himself kept emphasizing to the Americans that he "would naturally prefer to defend Malaya by defending Indo-China."[25] Washington got deeper into the business of reinforcing the British and French as dollars began flowing directly to Southeast Asia. No longer would they need to be a by-product of Marshall Plan aid to London and Paris.

In May, MacDonald flew to Canberra to warn of "a general southeasterly movement of Communist activities in Asia."[26] Australia, he said, was gravely threatened. Partly for this reason, there was some talk in Britain of deploying its soldiers in Vietnam, though that notion was quickly dismissed by Downing Street.[27] In Australia, MacDonald instead requested bombers and fighter planes for the effort in Malaya, but all that the dominion's Liberal coalition government was willing to offer was a Royal Australian Air Force transport squadron. The Australians needed to know more about U.S. intentions before going out on a limb. British officials "complained bitterly about the slow evolution of U.S. policy," writes the historian Mark Lawrence.[28] MacDonald proved to be one of those officials, and he took steps to speed up progress.

On June 29, Donald R. Heath, fifty-five, landed in Saigon, as the first ministerial envoy, and then the first U.S. ambassador, to the new, supposedly independent nations of Indochina: Vietnam, Cambodia, and Laos. He was a graduate of Topeka's Washburn University and had been a United Press reporter before joining the Foreign Service, from where he rose to handling political affairs in Germany for General Lucius Clay, who valued his writing. He then got posted in 1947 as minister to Bulgaria, where Sofia's secret police implicated him in a purge trial. Declared persona non grata, he ended up in Saigon, a part of the world about which he knew nothing.

MacDonald was waiting in Saigon the day he arrived. Heath duly presented his credentials to Bao Dai's government, and from the start he began parroting MacDonald. The only difference in their views was that Heath came to loathe the Vietnamese and feared being poisoned or shot. When MacDonald was confident that France would crush the Vietminh, Heath was confident. When MacDonald had some doubts of victory, so did Heath. But Heath was no more compromised than the U.S. consul general in Singapore, whose own staff, recalled one of them, the political officer Joseph Greene, found him "under the sway" of MacDonald.[29] "Nationalism," Heath insisted, was a policy catchword the Communists were using falsely throughout Southeast Asia. They were threatening Australia too, he began to squawk, doing a poor imitation of MacDonald. The Philippines and Indonesia, he went on to claim, would be next.[30]

THE OTHER "MAC" IN ASIA—GENERAL DOUGLAS MacARTHUR, SUpreme commander of allied powers—had even stronger feelings than MacDonald about the importance of the Far East. The great events of the next thousand years, he predicted, would take place in Asia.

MacArthur had been first in his class at West Point, in 1903, and first captain of cadets. No one had equaled his scholastic record for a quarter century. As a lieutenant in the Corps of Engineers, he had served in the Philippines and was aide-de-camp to his father, Lieutenant General Arthur MacArthur Jr., and together, during 1905–1906, they visited Tokyo, Shanghai, Hong Kong, Batavia (today's Jakarta), Singapore, and Calcutta during a nine-month tour for the army. In 1917, MacArthur was the second-youngest general in the expeditionary force that the United States sent to France and during his World War I service earned two Distinguished Service Crosses and seven Silver Stars. He proved himself nearly invulnerable. Like Churchill, he was personally reckless under fire. After the war, he continued his glittering rise and in 1930 was named army chief of staff, a post he would hold until his retirement from the army, in 1935. Then he moved to the Philippines, where, with FDR's approval, he oversaw the creation of the Philippine army and granted himself a rank of "field marshal." He adopted a uniform of black sharkskin trousers and a white coat covered with gold braid, and received a gold baton. Four months before Pearl Harbor, as tensions worsened with Japan, President Roosevelt recalled MacArthur to duty and gave him the Far East Command.

Time and place mean everything for the destiny of a commander. The start of war in the Pacific became MacArthur's moment, and he brought to the fight a stronger intellect than any of the era's generals or admirals. He envisioned the ocean as a highway from Australia to Okinawa that American fighting men could master and, in doing so, head straight on into Tokyo Bay. After Pearl Harbor, MacArthur led an astonishing sequence of fifty-six amphibious attacks—superbly combining the arms of land, sea, and air against imperial Japan—until on September 2, 1945, aboard the USS *Missouri*, he formally accepted the Japanese surrender.

MacArthur remains the greatest synthesizing field commander of modern times, and attempts to diminish his achievements are weak.[31] He led with a high sense of drama. While General Eisenhower might go up to a gaping GI, in the presence, naturally, of reporters, and put out his hand—"My name's Eisenhower"—Douglas MacArthur would leap up as some favored figure was admitted from the battlefield: "Comrade in arms!" To be sure, he was a pathological egotist, and a whiff of Napoleonic sulfur still clings to his memory for having notoriously defied civilian authority, in 1951. But he was not employed for his lovability.

In January 1950, he was seventy years old—mentally sharp, but suffering from poor eyesight and Parkinson's syndrome. In his office atop Tokyo headquarters, he was isolated: no telephone, shielded by his worshipful aides, and reading intelligence reports exclusively from staff. He had only twice left Tokyo since 1945. At his residence, the prewar U.S. embassy, he'd soon come to pace the halls at night with insomnia. As one of his biographers has documented, he had reasons to worry about enemies in Washington eager to remove him on the grounds of emotional instability.[32]

. . .

FROM THE MOMENT HE HAD ENTERED TOKYO, EIGHTY-FIVE HUNDRED miles from Washington, MacArthur operated with near autonomy. There was no alternative, he claimed: waiting for the Pentagon to make decisions at such a remove was too risky. Nonetheless, the Washington bureaucracy ground on, and in 1948 George Kennan, then serving as Policy Planning director, had paid him a visit. Kennan held strong opinions about the Far East, though he says in his first book, *American Diplomacy* (1951), that he possessed no "personal familiarity" with that part of the world. But this fact didn't stand in the way of his certitudes, which he expressed gingerly in Washington. For instance, Japan required "some sort of empire toward the South." That might include Indochina, because Kennan feared Communist control of "the rice bowl of Asia." As for Korea, which had endured world-class massacres at the hands of the Japanese during World War II, he believed the peninsula would now be better off under Tokyo's rule as well.[33] In any event, Korea had no strategic significance, as he advised Acheson the following year. MacArthur meanwhile was teaching democracy to the Japanese and disassembling their war-making industrial combines, the *zaibatsu*.

In his office overlooking the grounds of the Imperial Palace, the general offered Kennan two congenial meetings—though MacArthur didn't bother to make transcripts or write a memorandum of what was discussed. But Kennan formed his own opinions of MacArthur's efforts, and they were harsh. When he returned to Washington, Kennan told the upper reaches of the State Department that MacArthur, whether through ignorance or duplicity, was pushing a "vicious" scheme to open Japan to Communist influence by his forced "socialization" of big business.[34]

Today, journalists and scholars alike believe that "the extraordinary brilliance of Kennan the strategist" provided "balance and restraint" during these years, along with "penetrating analysis."[35] It's said that he was a "giant of diplomacy" at State, even "sensitive and farsighted" while, again, showing "analytical brilliance"[36] In fact, he came to define many of his country's worst habits of policy making. He was emotional, often careless and impulsive, and frequently amateurish. He repeatedly acted from ignorance, as is apparent with Japan. Moreover, like many people in our own era who're accepted as foreign policy savants, he was indifferent to economics.[37]

In 1946, Kennan had usefully raised alarms about Stalinism. But by 1950, he had become an alarmist. He dove into all sorts of projects he knew nothing about: global finance, covert action, Middle East force deployments, Latin America, Japan. He even cooked up ideas for military operations, such as when he urged the bemused Joint Chiefs to establish two "mobile divisions" to fight British-style frontier wars.* Along the way, he casually shared his bitter views on black Americans—whose calls for civil rights he believed were manufactured in Moscow—with startled British leaders such as Richard Crossman, a Labour MP and future cabinet minister.[38] Nothing like his indecency on race is found in writings by Acheson or Snyder, Clayton or Nitze, let alone Forrestal.

On January 1, 1950, Kennan left Policy Planning. In noting his departure, *Time* magazine wrote of his frustrations in the job: how "he hated to see abandonment of Formosa" (as Taiwan was then called) and how "he had urged closest collaboration with Britain but the policy had been watered down."[39] There's only one place on the planet from which both those tales could have originated: Kennan himself. In that era, it was by no means routine for people in government to leak to the press, and leaking was regarded in official circles as abhorrent. Yet he did so repeatedly while causing other problems at State: he was also a bureaucratic intriguer, as well as terribly conscious of being a gentleman, which could be hard to square.

The leaks at Policy Planning stopped when he left, and Paul Nitze achieved a better working relationship with Acheson, Snyder, and other intelligent, informed wielders of power. Ten-thousand-word essays from the director, as on Latin America, were replaced with concise recommendations.

For several months thereafter, Kennan was the State Department's counselor. It's a senior yet solitary staff function with no line responsibility, and he made plans to take a sabbatical at Princeton. By June 1950,

---

*Kennan's useful thoughts on his country's lack of self-control kept conflicting with his oddball ones on strategy, like urging America's NATO allies to confront Soviet invasion by passive resistance. That's among his later pronouncements, as explained in my *Fifty-Year Wound*, which includes a discussion of the Soviet-staged encounter I had with him on these issues in Moscow.

the question arose at State as to where his talents might fit upon return-ing. The quietly authoritative undersecretary, James Webb, handled that one for Acheson. In Webb's office on June 14, Kennan proposed himself as ambassador to Great Britain, wanting—sooner or later—to "follow" Lewis Douglas.[40] Everyone knew Acheson was bending over backward to keep Douglas in London for as long as possible. Webb finessed the rejection. He replied that an appointment to the Court of St. James's usually requires substantial private assets. A master of detail, Webb surely knew Kennan was badly in debt.

THAT JUNE, WASHINGTON ENJOYED COMPLETELY BLUE SKIES AND A view from atop the Washington Monument that's recorded as having been astonishing. When Acheson and Ambassador Franks met during their late evenings in Northwest D.C., they were looking out at a world apparently in perpetual crisis. With China lost to the West, the Rus-sians seemed poised to dominate much of Eurasia's mineral resources, agriculture, manpower, and industrial potential. Moreover, Stalin might still be able to absorb the free nations of Europe. The North Atlantic Treaty had been signed, but little "organization" existed behind it. Nor was there a credible military deterrent, other than retaliating against a Red Army invasion by launching atomic strikes from England—ones that would likely incinerate allies as well.

Acheson had spoken during the spring of the world's "situations of weakness," which, to a careful listener like Ambassador Franks, implied a question. Would the United States repair such situations and, if so, on what terms? Not for nothing was Franks both a former moral philoso-pher and an armaments administrator. Did the weaknesses thus singled out include Taiwan and South Korea, if those were even considered "positions" at all? What about Southeast Asia, which everyone believed essential to Europe's recovery? And how might "situations of weak-ness" be buttressed if the Kremlin ignored Acheson's full-throated diplomacy?[41]

Over one of their dinners together, three weeks before the Korean War began, Acheson confided that still "the State Department was rack-ing its brains" to see whether Taiwan could be saved, short of America taking over its defense.[42] Franks's Foreign Office colleagues had meanwhile been telling him from London that U.S. behavior in Asia was "a gift to the Russians."[43] That included everything the Americans were and weren't doing. They were hesitating in Southeast Asia; they had yet to conclude a peace treaty with Japan or to recognize the new government in Beijing; they were antagonizing Nehru; and, for good measure, they were disrupting London's relations with Australia and New Zealand.

Korea itself wasn't in this inventory. A 525-mile-long peninsula, it had been part of Japan's empire for forty years, until the 1945 surrender. A U.S. initiative had then divided Korea at the 38th parallel, using a map from *National Geographic*. Below that line emerged an American-backed Republic of South Korea, with a population of twenty-one million, that had Seoul as its capital. Above the parallel arose a Russian-created Democratic People's Republic, with a population of nine million. And it named Seoul as its capital too. MacArthur, Acheson, and Senator Tom Connally of Texas, who chaired the Foreign Relations Committee, all said, in one way or another, that South Korea lay outside the U.S. security perimeter. A Communist takeover appeared likely anyway because the North was the more heavily armed and bordered by the Sino-Soviet juggernaut. So the best to hope for was a face-saving amount of time following America's departure—a posture in later years known as "a decent interval."[44] Something like the Czech coup in 1948 seems to have been expected. Few anticipated sudden outright invasion.

The Joint Chiefs, like policy makers at State and on Capitol Hill, were instead emphasizing the importance of Asia's "island outposts." That's what General MacArthur called Japan, Okinawa, Taiwan, the Philippines, Indonesia, and Australia and New Zealand, which can be imagined as a vertical picket line in the far Pacific for defending America's continent. The U.S. Navy would protect these outposts, the theory went, thereby upholding the nation's interests in Asia. After all, U.S. warships dominated the Pacific to such an extent that the Royal Navy's significance in this part of the globe had, very unfairly, fallen to a mere Category III in the NSC 75 assessments—akin to the value being placed on the Anglo-Burmese Defense Agreement.

The United States at the start of the summer of 1950 was still an island superstate, not a superpower, and as such it felt little obligation to lead. Even MacArthur's Far East Command wasn't as formidable as it sounded. The 8th Army mustered at tops 108,000 poorly trained men, their four divisions each being more than a thousand rifles short of what the U.S. Army required. The understrength 5th Air Force was also in Japan, but it had no jet fighters. Only five hundred U.S. military advisers were left in South Korea. But then, on June 25, at four o'clock on a drizzly Sunday morning, the North Koreans suddenly struck south across the parallel.

11

WAR ON THE RIM

It was the Korean War and not World War II that made us a world political-military power.

—Charles "Chip" Bohlen, minister, U.S. embassy, France, 1948–1953; ambassador to the USSR, 1953–1957

LATE THURSDAY EVENING, ON JUNE 1, 1950, OXFORD UNIVERsity's debating society passed a motion regretting "the influence exercised by the U.S. as the dominant power among the democratic nations." Journalists on both sides of the Atlantic compared the debate to the notorious 1933 resolution not to fight "for King and Country." That one had rocked the empire, according to Churchill, and swayed calculations in Hitler's Germany. Churchill's hot-tempered son, Randolph, attended the 1950 event as a graduate member, and what he saw made him shout that the Oxford Union was polluting relations with the United States. Proponents of the motion said Americans had a genius for entering wars late and, like ancient Rome, for using mercenaries, meaning the North Atlantic allies, with Britain having been given "the role of an atomic cushion."[1] That last detail referred to the U.S. Strategic

Air Command's four atomic bomber bases, which were by then dispersed in England.

Unlike in 1933, however, Oxford wasn't influencing enemy intentions. Stalin was already set to unify Korea, and to do so quickly and brutally. He had been preparing the attack since March 1949, and by that fall was sending tens of thousands of tons of weapons and matériel rolling east over the Trans-Siberian Railroad, to be transshipped at the Manchurian border for Korea. This included the world's best tanks and artillery, as well as vital supplies of petroleum, oil, and lubricants. In 1949 as well, the Soviet General Staff wrote the first Preemptive Strike Plan, updated and given to the North Koreans in the spring of 1950. As the Russians helped finalize preparations, an inspection mission from the Red Army's Far East Command scrutinized the forces of the dictator Kim Il Sung—grandfather of the current despot—down to battalion level and reported back to Moscow that all was ready.[2] Then seven disciplined, modern North Korean infantry divisions, led by young officers who'd served in the Red Army or fought with Mao, smashed across the border, backed by air wings and spearheaded by an armored unit with ninety Russian-made T-34 tanks.

Most historians, however, still describe Stalin as having been reluctantly persuaded to support an invasion devised by Kim Il Sung, or argue that Stalin just authorized Kim's aggression, only enabling a buildup that began in April—or even that the war arose from border clashes between the two Koreas, which were sparked that month. But the scale, timing, and sophistication of the attack make those suppositions impossible. The truth is simpler. "We started the Korean War," Nikita Khrushchev would avow.[3]

The Americans called South Korea's military a "constabulary," and as a constabulary it had neither tanks nor antitank guns, so the Korean People's Army overran it. Congress hardly balked at Truman's decision to fight: he didn't ask for a declaration of war, but used his authority under the United Nations Participation Act of 1945. He set precedent on Tuesday morning, June 27, by a unilateral announcement that U.S. air and sea forces would intervene. (By this theory, observed Senator Taft, a president could launch any adventure without the voice of

Congress—like trying to "establish a vast Garden of Eden in the Kingdom of Iraq."[4]) In the afternoon, the American delegation at the UN drafted a resolution that called on member countries to help repel the attack and "restore peace in the area." Surprisingly, it passed. Stalin's ambassador was boycotting the Security Council and, for reasons still debated, was unavailable to cast a veto.[5] Yet the quick U.S. reaction barely helped.

Seoul fell on the twenty-eighth. That was the day Britain's chiefs of staff advised Attlee's cabinet to place the Royal Navy's carrier, two cruisers, and destroyers in Japanese waters at General MacArthur's disposal. Attlee did so immediately, a move Churchill called "an inescapable duty," but still the Americans had too few ships to impose a blockade on North Korea. Planes from the RAF would have strengthened the force that MacArthur was assembling, but the chiefs determined they couldn't offer any, considering their worldwide obligations. MacArthur meanwhile asked the Australian occupation contingent in Japan for its air unit. This time, Britain's chiefs pressed Canberra to agree for the sake of commonwealth solidarity, and it did—though the Australians were warned that "we should be sorry to see you undertake any commitment to Korea that might hamper your preparations to send forces to the Middle East in a real emergency."[6]

As South Korea's forces collapsed, President Truman and Secretary Acheson saw Korea as "real emergency" enough. On the twenty-seventh, Truman ordered General MacArthur to rush the GIs based in Japan across the 120-mile-wide Korea Strait and into combat. There was no alternative but to fight. In short order, Japan was recognized as the strategic prize. Just to begin, it's unlikely Japan would have stayed lightly armed and quietly prosperous in the years ahead had the invasion brought about a united, aggressive Communist Korea right across the strait.

That afternoon, the Security Council, which met at Lake Success, the temporary home of the United Nations on Long Island, urged that "UN forces" be placed under American command. Events were spinning fast, and Americans expected their strongest, best-positioned ally to join them at the front. Moreover, high quarters at State and the Pentagon knew exactly what divisions and regiments they should expect from Britain, due to the research behind NSC 75.

By summer, Ernest Bevin was a shadow of his former self, "only 'alf alive," he admitted to his staff. He was plagued by heart trouble, high blood pressure, and digestive problems that regularly put him in the hospital. Attlee took a more active role and tried to attend all his cabinet's Defence Committee meetings. He deferred to the advice of his commanders, and they declared it "militarily unsound" to send troops to Korea. They acknowledged "extremely strong political and psychological reasons" for doing so, but the defense of Hong Kong, Malaya, and Suez had priority, and they said that they couldn't be everywhere at once.[7] So on July 5, when the invading Korean People's Army met its first Western resistance, it was only from a force of ill-prepared and poorly conditioned American GIs whose bazooka antitank rockets bounced ineffectually off the T-34s' heavy armor.

On July 7, Truman ordered MacArthur to lead the new UN Command, and by now the Netherlands, Canada, Australia, and New Zealand had also offered warships. At the same time, Russia's deputy foreign minister, Andrei Gromyko, hinted to Britain's ambassador in Moscow that a diplomatic solution might be possible in hopes of stopping this unfortunate violence. U.S. officials believed Gromyko was trying to divide the allies or to lure the British into mediating the conflict themselves. On the same day that MacArthur took over the UN command, Acheson's staff told the Foreign Office that there'd be no compromising over Korea.

On the eighth, U.S. and Royal Navy warships began their first combined actions: a two-day series of carrier strikes against airfields, trains, and bridges near Pyongyang, which was North Korea's de facto capital, eighty miles north of the 38th parallel. Shore batteries fired a shell that hit the cruiser HMS *Jamaica* dead center and instantly killed six men, who were buried at sea. A sacrifice like this was indeed noble, but hardly enough: Washington demanded that the British dispatch soldiers to the Korean battlefront.

Come mid-July, the U.S. Army's 24th Infantry Division was getting mauled, and GIs were being pushed into the peninsula's southeastern tip. They not only faced a better-equipped invader but were burdened with a retreating South Korean ally, no matter how stubbornly its soldiers fought. MacArthur ran the war from his Dai-Ichi Building headquarters, with his generals on the front lines, but their soldiers were outnumbered. He called for the free world to just send him men with rifles who could hold the shrinking bridgehead around the port city of Pusan. Meanwhile, American newspapers began to publish lengthening lists of the dead and missing, and the Pentagon issued an emergency call for nurses.

THERE WAS STILL NO SIGN IN MID-JULY THAT BRITISH SOLDIERS would appear. An RAF air vice-marshal who was serving in Tokyo as a military liaison to Supreme Headquarters told MacArthur that an infantry brigade might be committed, but it would be impossible to do so until December, at the earliest. By this point, the Americans—notably Acheson—began to assert seriously threatening pressure. He wasn't going to wait and he wasn't going to bargain: British soldiers were needed immediately under MacArthur's command. Attlee's cabinet concluded that Acheson was putting the entire Anglo-American relationship at stake if they didn't come through at Pusan. In Whitehall, officials said that his demands possessed "obscurely worded menace."[8]

Ambassador Franks dealt closely with Acheson and reported back. "Despite the power and position of the United States," he wrote, "the American people are not happy if they feel alone."[9] Resentments were also accumulating in Congress, where legislators were furious that the Royal Navy's Far Eastern Fleet had remained neutral in Chinese waters, even as Truman had interposed U.S. warships in the Taiwan Strait to block the PLA's invasion-ready divisions in Fujian province. "Britain is willing to share in our generosity but not in our risks," the New York senator Robert Wagner, a Democrat, fumed.[10] The British had also continued trading with Mao's regime, whereas the Truman administration restricted U.S. commerce. British exports ranged from oil to soybeans, and remittances still flowed from long-established enterprises like Jardine, Matheson & Co.—dealings that the Illinois congressman Noah Mason, a Republican, described as "utterly devoid of morality."[11]

The Americans, Franks noted, felt that they were unjustly carrying the burdens of others. Led by men whom he described as "avenging angels" (Harriman, Dulles, Acheson, Snyder), they were anxiously looking around for British support as they shouldered the "unparalleled undertaking," for them, of acting as "a policeman in the world," he reported.[12] British reluctance to send troops was hardening the Americans into an alarming mood: "Either you're with us or against us."

The Labour MP Kenneth Younger, forty-one, wasn't sympathetic. This suave and intellectual upper-class barrister, who held the Foreign Office's number two role as minister of state, served as acting secretary when Bevin was ill. "This is clearly a most unpalatable proposition," Younger wrote after reviewing the demand for troops, "and it would be right to consider it only if it were felt that it was our only way of influencing American foreign policy"—which, evidently, the British did not.[13] But this issue had gone far beyond the question of influencing anyone's foreign policy.

Younger just believed the Americans to be acting like Americans: they were exaggerating the dangers and not thinking globally. If they lost in Korea, he and others in Whitehall suspected, either they'd overreact and spark a global conflagration, or they'd retreat behind their oceans. Attlee tended to agree, and on July 6 he had cabled Truman with reminders of what else was at stake. Should the British send troops to Korea, he explained, this would leave Suez or Hong Kong or Malaya or Iran unguarded, and the Russians might exploit one or more of those trouble spots. They might even "relight the fire in Greece," he added.[14]

Truman was partially convinced. He agreed with Attlee that Iran was likely the Kremlin's next target, and a Communist victory in Korea, he acknowledged, might invite Stalin to "take over the whole Middle East."[15] In fact, Soviet military plans show that the next attack was to be against Yugoslavia, the only independent Communist state in Europe during these years.

Attlee, in turn, came to believe that it might finally be possible to work together with the Americans to develop a tight new political-military relationship. Together, the Americans and the British could address the global threat, but France, of course, would have to be left out, as he wrote to Truman when raising these possibilities; France need only be informed about plans and actions "as and when the situation demands."[16] Perhaps. Everything was moving fast. But the Americans were still demanding soldiers, both to join the fight in Korea and to serve as an example that was expected to compel the other Atlantic allies to give their full military support. Patience on Capitol Hill was just about gone.

The Korean conflict had to be confined to Korea, Oliver Franks told Acheson's trusted aide Ambassador Philip Jessup, among other senior officials at State. He offered the same advice to the five-star general Omar Bradley—the quiet, bespectacled "GI general" who had commanded the 12th Army Group under Eisenhower during World War II and had become the first chairman of the Joint Chiefs of Staff in August 1949. Franks hoped that "a possible gradual drift of the Chinese communist regime away from Moscow might not be interrupted."[17] That was a perspective found mostly in London, where observers assumed that China's defiant nationalism would inevitably distance Mao's regime from Stalin's grasp. General Bradley agreed with Franks up to a point, but the British, he said, believed Chinese intervention in Korea unlikely because they assumed Beijing wouldn't act at Moscow's whim, and about that he wasn't so sure.

In any case, Bradley and his chiefs wanted boots on the ground, and he stressed that "a platoon today is worth more than a company tomorrow."[18] Franks reported that Washington no longer cared in what condition allied units arrived. The Pentagon would supply heavy weapons, rations, and transport, but it would be Britain's problem to figure out where its soldiers came from. No one gave a damn about the geopolitical reasons why infantry couldn't be drawn from Fayid, Kowloon, Pahang, or some other godforsaken place.

AS LEADER OF THE OPPOSITION, CHURCHILL SEIZED THE MOMENT. The Labour government was purblind, he told a sharply divided House of Commons on July 27, in its vacillating response to North Korea's invasion. The chance of global war was very real, he continued, and Attlee had made things worse than even in 1938, at the time of Munich, just a dozen years before. In fact, Britain was more vulnerable to attack than ever in its history, he'd say. Red Army tank divisions could blitz to the Channel, and then seize airfields on the French coast to outnumber the RAF "more than Hitler ever could."[19] Churchill said something else that month: He reminded his countrymen that Labour had allowed the Americans to establish bases for atomic bombers in England. This might be reckless, he implied. It was the first indication that he wouldn't hesitate to play politics over the presence of the U.S. Strategic Air Command.

Anyone hearing this tirade in England would have been chilled to the bone. And, as he laid into Attlee, Churchill was spotlighting the extremely sensitive issue of those bases in East Anglia, Oxfordshire, and elsewhere which officials rarely discussed publicly. After all, no agreement existed with Washington as to whether, on their own volition, the Americans could use them to attack Russia.

In Washington, the possibility of a World War III had already placed the question of basing rights on the president's desk. The Wall Street lawyer Thomas Finletter had moved up from running the Marshall Plan in Britain to become secretary of the air force. He reminded Truman and Acheson that these airfields were still the only ones within reach of Moscow that could "be relied on at all" to penetrate deep into the Soviet Union.[20] Using the RAF's Abu Sueir airfield near Port Said, in Egypt, as planned, turned out to be a nonstarter. That was because the Pentagon had refused to fund the lengthening of the runways to make strategic bombing missions possible. Nor were U.S. bases in the Azores, Morocco, or Iceland suitable in the summer of 1950. As for ones in West Germany, those could be struck from the East before planes got off the ground. The Strategic Air Command's B-36s could operate intercontinentally, perhaps from Alaska in a pinch, and the runways in Dhahran could accommodate them as well. But those bombers represented only one-tenth of U.S. striking power. The rest of the punch would have to be delivered by B-50s and B-29s. The latter were the air force delivery system for atomic bombs but had only a two-thousand-mile range, and aerial refueling had yet to be developed. Failing to document these shortcomings turned out to have been the hole in Paul Nitze's NSC 68.

"We would for the moment have to play very closely indeed with the British in the formulation of our policy," Finletter elaborated.[21] That sort of intimacy didn't exist. The air bases themselves had been enmeshed in controversy since 1948. Number crunchers in the Pentagon and the Foreign Office still hadn't agreed on who would pay for them. On the one hand, they were in England; on the other, they were being used by the Americans.

Then, in July, the Joint Chiefs ordered General Curtis LeMay's Strategic Air Command to send two additional bomber groups to England. Unlike 1948, during the Berlin blockade, SAC would explicitly be bringing in atomic bombs, or what LeMay called his "hardware." The chiefs assured their counterparts in London that the bombs would sit on British soil "without the nuclear component" in place, by which they meant the plutonium core.[22] Those were to be flown over once the order to attack had been given.

Attlee's cabinet approved the plan. But Attlee himself told Washington that the B-29s' arrival couldn't be used as a show of strength. Their fly-in had to be treated as a normal rotation. He didn't want to scare his countrymen further, nor provoke the Kremlin.

The British tried to extract assurances that they had the right to veto an atomic offensive. Various ambiguities, evasions, and pledges came from the Pentagon. Okay, the Joint Chiefs agreed among themselves, it was reasonable for the prime minister to be consulted before they used the atomic bomb. It cost nothing for them to agree. But they would still reserve the freedom, as they put it, "to act with respect to the use of atomic bombs as circumstances may dictate."[23] With the air force relying on those bases in England for a nuclear Armageddon, no one in the U.S. chain of command intended to cool his heels while, as the chiefs asserted, "the British Cabinet is debating about things."[24] The Americans had had enough of waiting while their ally vacillated about committing soldiers to Korea.

Alliance obligations, like laws, have a way of being overlooked once the shooting starts. If necessary, the Americans decided, their bombers were going to fly against Russia without waiting for sign-off from Downing Street.[25] No one in Britain knew about that, but merely the presence of the bases made people joke uneasily of living on "Airstrip One," as Orwell calls his North Sea isles in *1984*, the "chief city" of which is London.

In the Commons, Nye Bevan wasn't amused. He disdained the

United States, but nonetheless he remained steadfastly committed to supporting the Americans if a shoot-out with Stalin were to occur. "When you are in a world-wide alliance," he chided Minister of State Kenneth Younger, "you can't retreat from it on a single issue."[26]

DURING THE SPRING, GLADWYN JEBB HAD BEEN EXPECTING TO leave Bevin's side at the Foreign Office and assume duties in New York as Britain's permanent representative to the United Nations. Friends told him the posting was a backwater, but he flew into Idlewild Airport two days after the war began. Immediately, he was on center stage. At fifty, a finely tailored six feet two and graying, he was perfectly cast for the role he was about to play. He had been known to U.S. officials since attending the Yalta Conference in 1945, yet his grand manner was hard even for Tory politicians to take. "You're a deb, Sir Gladwyn Jebb," went an epigram heard in London.

By summer's end, the new, respectability-conscious American TV networks were broadcasting live the Security Council debates about Korea to an estimated twenty-five million viewers. Radio stations beamed the debates to millions more. And the prime attraction was the sparring matches between Jebb and the Russian delegate, Yakov Malik—a man stuffed with vulgarities who moved around the UN surrounded by thugs and who seemed to have returned from his boycott as if to infuriate the West. Jebb, for his part, projected an aura of strength and refinement and seemed to speak for the entire British Empire and Commonwealth. Besides, he truly filled a vacuum: his American counterpart, Warren Austin, seventy-two, was an old-school former senator from Vermont who'd spent four years at the UN and was already befuddled by sacks of mail that demanded he expel Malik from the world body.

Gladwyn Jebb danced through the debates with Malik like a skilled boxer against a neighborhood bully. Even those Americans with no interest in global affairs loved this bloodlessly effective hurly-burly. Jebb ridiculed Russian charges of Anglo-American imperialism, and when Malik charged that America had started the Korean War, Jebb dismissed his argument as "so obviously absurd that it is hard to think it can be swallowed even by the automata who listen to the Moscow radio."[27] Malik and the Russians, he said, while echoing Bevin, were using Hitler's tactic: the Big Lie, a lie so colossal that no one would believe that somebody might distort the truth that brazenly.

Jebb received thousands of fan letters after his debates, including some, he informed George VI, "from Irishmen and Jews and other surprising people."[28] The British knew a lot about places like Uttar Pradesh, but they still did not comprehend the American melting pot. Anyway, cabbies insisted on driving him for free. He was called on to run for president, and Americans applauded his "King's English," as he told his sovereign. Standing shoulder to shoulder with them in the UN arena made him the most famous man in America, except possibly for the Yankees' Joe DiMaggio.[29] Jebb was even the subject of a *New Yorker* cartoon, which showed a plump citizen glued to his TV, enraptured by what he sees, and shouting to his dowdy wife in the kitchen that he's busy watching Sir Gladwyn. Bevin was delighted with Jebb's success, wishing that the Americans could give a few million television sets to the Russians.

But Jebb didn't quite reciprocate these affections. The Americans, he told the king, were too emotional, and they were letting the crisis of the day, Korea, blind them to other global concerns. Only the British, he believed, could think dispassionately and strategically at the level necessary to defend Western interests. To help the Americans at the UN, therefore, he handed them a numbered, itemized list of everything they were doing wrong.

"TOKEN BRITISH UNIT FOR KOREA LIKELY," *THE NEW YORK TIMES* headlined on Saturday, July 22. Despite the adjective, Americans were riveted. At last, it seemed, the British were going to send troops. But the article went on to explain that the deployment was being made purely for "psychological reasons" to show the Americans that England was doing its part. Four days later, Attlee made it official, announcing that "land reinforcement" would be sent as soon as possible.[30] Moreover, he said, he'd be lengthening conscription from eighteen months to two years and would be adding £100 million to the defense budget (though that required a U.S. subsidy). In a further attempt to placate the Americans, the Royal Navy disclosed that it had ten thousand commonwealth seamen and officers in the Far East—with seven thousand positioned near Korea. This news astonished the Americans.

Moreover, the British informed Washington of their Imperial Strategic Reserve, a capability overlooked in the NSC 75 audit. This was Britain's emergency instrument, ready to be deployed anywhere in the world within ten days. Also known as the "Fire Brigade," it offered the same rapid response capacity with worldwide reach found in today's Global Response Force of the U.S. Army 82nd Airborne (that is, the division's 1st Brigade) or the Marine Fleet Amphibious Forces. It was smaller than those units, of course, but this was a small world of only 2.5 billion people, compared with 7 billion today. Elements of the Imperial Strategic Reserve were based in Hong Kong, just thirteen hundred miles from Pusan.

Increasingly tense weeks of silence followed as the Pusan perimeter eroded. On August 21, the State Department finally declared itself "gratified" to know that the British had troops ready to go. Now the American press began to chart the actual movement of those soldiers— "from MacDonald to MacArthur," journalists wrote.[31] Heading to war were the 1st Battalion, Middlesex Regiment, and the 1st Battalion, Argyll and Sutherland Highlanders, who were mostly from Scotland. Together they were called the 27th Brigade, and they had a week to prepare. An advance group flew to Tokyo for planning. This "brigade" was much smaller than standard in the British army, and in total it would end up consisting of fifteen hundred soldiers.

Intelligence people from MacArthur's staff arrived in Hong Kong to deliver briefings and offer thanks. It looked unlikely, they confided to the brigade's officers, that any of them would return alive from Pusan. Days later, the men heard purposeful words of farewell from General Sir John Harding, the commander in chief, Far East Land Forces, who flew in from Singapore. Commissioner General Malcolm MacDonald also arrived to speak directly to his fellow Scots. Under a merciless sun on Friday, August 25, he gave a dockside speech to the Argyll and Sutherland Highlanders. They were embarking to save the world from "enslavement" by Soviet Communism, he told them.[32] That evening, as bagpipes skirled, the brigade boarded HMS *Ceylon*, a light cruiser, and

HMS *Unicorn*, an aircraft support ship. Joined by two Australian destroyers, the vessels then sailed for Pusan. And the British Far East Fleet was put on what the Admiralty called a "fullscale war footing."[33]

Besides the Americans, these were the first soldiers to arrive in Korea. News stories in the United States explained that the Argylls would change their kilts for green uniforms before battle and that the Middlesex were mostly Londoners, colorfully known as the Duke of Cambridge's Own. A squadron of fighter planes from the Royal Australian Air Force was already in-country, and one from the South Africa Air Force soon followed—the allies' only non-U.S. combat airpower in Korea.

On Tuesday, the twenty-ninth, the warships from Hong Kong docked at Pusan, and the advance party that had earlier gone to Tokyo was flown in by U.S. transport. The Argylls came ashore first, to the anthem "God Save the King," played by a U.S. Army band of "colored" soldiers, as black Americans were still called. GIs provided each British soldier with one cardboard box per day of C rations, plus a form of coffee that the Londoners and Scots found undrinkable. But there were plenty of cigarettes, and plans were made for urgent supplies of tea. Even before their vehicles or heavy weaponry could be unloaded, the soldiers boarded a train for the front. At the same time, railway cars, painted with enormous red crosses, were arriving in Pusan filled with mangled GIs. The trip was only twenty miles.

Once the British appeared in the battle line, they kept being asked, "Where are the rest of you?" But the Americans appreciated their field experience. The soldiers from the Fire Brigade, some of whom were conscripts, had been training for sixteen months on similar terrain in Hong Kong's New Territories, opposite the People's Liberation Army, which they expected would attack. Others were professionals who'd served in Palestine. Working together with the Americans, they got down to business, laying minefields precisely and lacing their Bren machine guns into tight fire patterns.

MacARTHUR'S GREATEST BATTLEFIELD TRIUMPH OF ALL CAME TWO weeks later, at Inchon, the well-defended Yellow Sea harbor near Seoul that lay about two hundred miles behind enemy lines up the Korean

Peninsula's western coast. Victory required perfect timing and perfect luck. On September 15, at 6:30 a.m., MacArthur launched a surprise attack at high tide. Supported by 261 warships from seven nations, he placed two marine regiments ashore, followed by the U.S. Army's 7th Infantry Division, and soon seventy thousand American fighting men were moving inland. North Korea's forces to the south were cut off. They crumbled and fled, allowing the Americans and their South Korean allies to break out of the Pusan perimeter and begin to advance north through scrubby hills rising to two thousand feet.

But tragedy followed. As part of the advance, the Argylls were five miles west of the Naktong River, heading toward Songju. They accompanied the U.S. Army's 24th Infantry Division and were assigned to seize the high ground and open a main road. They secured one hill the Americans called "282," after the military practice of naming a battleground for its height in meters. Then, on September 23, they pushed on toward an adjacent hill held by entrenched North Koreans. Before trying to take it, they called for backup from the U.S. Air Force's 18th Fighter Bomber Wing.

Napalm had been invented at the end of World War II but came fully into use during the Korean War. This form of jellied gasoline was delivered in hundred-gallon plastic canisters, or "eggs," that ignited on impact, letting the two-thousand-degree mixture seep into dugouts and stick to whatever it touched. The U.S. Air Force in Korea used it for close air support.

Several minutes after noon, the Argylls heard a loudening buzz of F-51 Mustangs, though they couldn't establish radio contact. The skies were clear, however, and they cheered as the fighter-bombers swooped in to destroy the nearby North Korean redoubt. But the Argylls weren't displaying their white air-recognition panels in the way the Americans expected, and at 12:14 the Mustangs struck the wrong hill, dropping their napalm eggs directly on the Argylls and raking them with .50-caliber machine guns. Flames detonated the battalion's ammunition. This part of the incident lasted two minutes, leaving seventeen dead and seventy-eight scalded and shot. And then, as they tried to evacuate the injured, the Argylls were hit by North Korean artillery. Some of their dead were brought back by moonlight; others were left on the field.[34]

The appalled U.S. 5th Air Force Command in Tokyo investigated immediately. In London, Julius Holmes, the minister counselor, or number two, at the embassy, delivered a letter of sorrow and regret to Attlee. The American bomber wing, for its part, quickly donated an $882.85 check for the families of the dead and maimed. Lieutenant General Sir Gordon MacMillan, the Argyll and Sutherland's regimental colonel, had the last word. "No hard feelings have arisen as the result of this accident," he said. "The Regiment's friendship with the United States Air Force can never be impaired by having suffered on one occasion from the risks which are inseparable from operations in modern war."[35]

Replacements arrived for the lost Highlanders. In late September, the 3rd Battalion, Royal Australian Regiment, entered the war zone. The Australians became the second nation to join the Americans on the ground. They were followed by Canadian light infantry, then by more British soldiers, New Zealand artillery, and an Indian medical unit. By the following summer, they would number upwards of twenty thousand men to form the 1st Commonwealth Division. A contingent of the British 41 Commando, which was part of the Royal Marines, also made its way into the theater, after flying surreptitiously via BOAC to Japan in ill-fitting civilian suits issued by the Admiralty. Turkey, Thailand, Brazil, Greece, Ethiopia, the Philippines, and Colombia sent soldiers as well. A Belgian volunteer battalion arrived, as did one from the Netherlands, and Luxembourg contributed a rifle platoon. The French sent a volunteer battalion, too, which fought gallantly until withdrawn for Indochina at the war's end. Yet the Americans concluded that all this was little more than token support. Alongside a still-feeble South Korean army, they were fighting mostly alone on the edge of the world.

ON SEPTEMBER 13, ERNEST BEVIN, WEAK BUT STILL INTIMIDATING, arrived on his final journey to the United States. He met in New York with Acheson and Robert Schuman, France's foreign minister. He stayed for the opening of the Fifth Session of the UN General Assembly on September 19, which by then had fifty-nine members. A week later, he pushed forth a British-written resolution that authorized MacArthur to ensure "stability throughout Korea."[36] The allied objective included nationwide, UN-supervised elections that would have turned Korea into a big international trusteeship on the border of Communist China. The resolution was adopted on October 7, formally instructing MacArthur's Unified Command to cross the 38th parallel, as South Korea's army had done a week earlier. Snyder explained the situation to James Webb: Truman believed he had little choice but to proceed northward.

The next day, MacArthur ordered his U.S., British, and Australian fighting men to march toward the Yalu River, beyond which lay Manchuria, today known as Northeast China, heartland of heavy industries and mines.

The few British officials who met with MacArthur during this period in Tokyo headquarters sensed disaster in the making. They also anticipated trouble for themselves. "He will be likely to become more of a dictator than ever," reported Sir Alvary Gascoigne, the British political adviser to MacArthur's Allied Command. "He is flushed with success not only about military matters but also about the tangled skein of international relations which we now have to unravel in the Far East." Gascoigne concluded that MacArthur would, at best, submit to the president's direct orders but would obey no one else. "He must be ridden by Truman," this former cavalry officer told the Foreign Office, "on a very severe curb."[37]

Perhaps, but Truman had to worry about midterm elections, and on November 7 the Democratic Senate majority leader and the majority whip went down in defeat. Commentators blamed the party's losses on outrage over Truman's policy in Korea: lots of voters now said that just being there was a mistake. And the worst was yet to come: Beijing was no more eager than today to see a unified, American-leaning Korean Peninsula.

It was nearly "Mission Accomplished" for MacArthur's advance into the north. All of Korea was to be united, after mopping up the Korean People's Army. MacArthur had released several ships and a British commando detachment from the theater, and his staff was planning a victory parade for Tokyo. Nobody at his headquarters realized that China was slipping 300,000 battled-hardened PLA veterans—concealed by night and fog—into North Korea's seventy-five-hundred-foot mountains, with more soldiers to come. They briefly revealed themselves on October 25 and 26, with heavier attacks a week later, and then disappeared.

MacArthur was uncertain what the encounter meant. Perhaps China was offering covert assistance or helping to conduct reconnaissance across its 850-mile border. He continued to advance, with approximately 245,000 fighting men, as winds swept down from Siberia, and the first light snows of the season fell on November 12. "You could almost see it coming," an American officer later recalled, "those young men moving into that awful goddamn trap."[38] It would be history's biggest ambush.

On the night of November 25, the jaws snapped shut. Seemingly endless numbers of blue-quilted, terrifyingly courageous PLA divisions rose up as if out of the frozen ground, heralding their attacks with bugle calls. They closed in on MacArthur's forces from every direction, and within hours he despaired of his army's "complete destruction." People at the Foreign Office hurriedly tried to calm the European allies by saying they'd all along been restraining Washington and that now they'd absolutely insist on being consulted about any directives to MacArthur from the Pentagon. If "the United States were so foolish as to cross the Manchurian frontier," Bevin said, "it would mean war."[39]

INSTEAD, A NIGHTMARE RETREAT—THE LONGEST IN U.S. HISTORY— began from the freezing north. As heavy snows arrived, the Americans blew up their stores of equipment, food, clothing, and ammunition. They dug up the battlefield graves of their comrades and stacked the rock-solid corpses of GIs and marines for transport out. High in the mountains, at the Chosin Reservoir, 235 warriors in their green berets from Britain's 41 Commando were among some 30,000 UN troops surrounded by four times that many PLA soldiers. GIs and marines were hacking out an airstrip from the frozen ground for supplies and evacuation of the wounded and the dead. U.S. Air Force C-119 Flying Boxcars and C-54s were arriving back-to-back straight from March Field, near Riverside, California, via Japan—techniques of aerial refueling had been innovated fast.

At a November 30 press conference, Truman addressed what his administration was calling the UN's "forced withdrawal." Then he answered a reporter's question by saying America would use "every weapon that we have" to prevent defeat.[40] The world heard that remark as "atom bomb." *Pravda* insinuated, with a combination of sorrow and satisfaction, that the British were finally seeing the abyss toward which the United States was dragging them.

In *Present at the Creation*, Acheson portrays Clement Attlee, whom he always found depressing, as suddenly "scurrying across the ocean," nearly quivering with fear of nuclear war. But that's absurd. First, Attlee was following through on a long-planned meeting with Truman that they had both expected to occur after November's midterm elections. And second, when Attlee arrived in Washington, late Monday morning, December 4—for what is correctly known as the Anglo-American Economic Defense Conference—he did so with a firm sense of purpose. He and Bevin, who was too ill to travel, agreed it was time for a "higher direction of the cold war," by which they meant that the West's two great powers, the British Empire and the United States, needed to ensure "properly co-ordinated, firm, and rapid control in all areas of the world."[41] Attlee also intended to buck up the Americans who, like Acheson and Marshall, were talking of "being licked" and of "a Dunkirk type of evacuation" from Korea.[42]

This is where Attlee came into his own as a world statesman. Unemotional, a politician who said he didn't like conversations, he was prime minister because of the hard-hitting way he ran the Labour Party, which earned him the fierce loyalty of Ernest Bevin, who sat opposite him in cabinet. He would murmur the same kinds of things when faced with planetary decisions as he said in regular life. On the composition of NATO: "In 1915, served at Gallipoli. Fought the Turks. Rather have them on my side than against me." If there's a U.S. president with a demeanor to compare, it would be James K. Polk—dusty, hard, without presence, yet steady while facing the great geostrategic issues of his day, which for him included national expansion while avoiding war with Britain. For Attlee, the immense questions that he handled astutely were India and now Korea.

Acheson met the prime minister at National Airport in a bitter pummeling wind. Attlee had brought along Kenneth Younger and Field Marshal William Slim, chief of the Imperial General Staff. His party also included Roger Makins, the deputy undersecretary who handled economics at the Foreign Office; Sir Edwin Plowden, the government's chief economic planning officer; Robert Hall, chief economic adviser to the government; and Sir Leslie Rowan, the Treasury attaché. They all convened with Truman at four o'clock that afternoon in the White House, which was still undergoing renovations, to be briefed by General Omar Bradley on the latest details of MacArthur's retreat. There'd be five more meetings between the president and the prime minister through December 8. Acheson, Snyder, Harriman, General Bradley, and Assistant Secretary of State Perkins were in nearly all of them. So too was George Marshall, who had returned to government in September as secretary of defense.

At the first meeting, around the twenty-foot table in the Cabinet Room, the British presented a paper which argued that "owing to the global responsibilities of both countries," a "structured relationship" should now exist between the two powers. The Americans had a different emphasis. When comparing the transcripts of each side, we see Truman remaining calm as he acknowledged Europe's defense to be paramount while also showing a willingness to fight to the finish in Korea. He wouldn't order MacArthur's forces to evacuate. "If we abandoned Korea," he said, "the South Koreans would all be murdered."[43] And after defeat in Korea, he insisted to the British, "it would be Indochina, then Hong Kong, then Malaya."[44]

Attlee had less to say. Anyone other than Clement Attlee would have reminded everyone in the room that it was only he who had experienced an amphibious evacuation, during December 1915 at Gallipoli. Instead, while peering through gold-rimmed spectacles, he just claimed to be soberly optimistic about Korea. There was no need to talk of Dunkirk, he said. He did add, however, that General MacArthur's politically charged statements, such as a recent one urging that Chiang Kai-shek's Nationalist army be pulled into the war, were improper for a UN commander.

There was plenty of time that week for other conversations, and several of them reveal how each side thought of the other and of itself. In one, late that first evening, Oliver Franks offered Acheson and other U.S. officials his assurances about Britain's intentions. Franks might as well have been sitting in the old State, War, and Navy Building circa 1910. Yes, his country had its differences with the Americans, he allowed, such as over China. But His Majesty's government really wasn't disputing the fact that the Americans had "prime responsibility in the Pacific." They shouldn't worry that Britain intended to weaken their position on the ocean's "western side." It did not. Nor did the government "wish to weaken" the U.S. approach of having a "two-ocean view" of the world, which included defending the Atlantic.[45] These American priorities were understood in London, and they were acceptable.

Another telling discussion occurred the following morning at Acheson's regular 9:30 staff meeting. Dean Rusk, ploddingly solid, was now the assistant secretary for East Asian affairs, and he tried to lift the gloom over an impending defeat in Korea. He harked back ten years to the summer of 1940. Hadn't the British soldiered on during their darkest hour? Didn't they fight two world wars from beginning to end against overwhelming odds with do-or-die determination? Well, Americans could do it too.

In any event, the world seemed on a knife's edge. "It looks like World War III is here," President Truman wrote three days later in his sporadically kept diary.[46]

As the talks continued, twenty-four Republican senators demanded that Congress examine any agreements that might be reached. California's William F. Knowland, the newspaper scion who was on his way to becoming majority leader in 1953, denounced the meetings as "the making of a Far Eastern Munich."[47] Yet the senators' ultimatum conveniently absolved the administration from tabling the sort of specific written promises that the British always hoped would be binding.

Attlee still expected a tight partnership, as he had since the Korean War began, due to America's dire predicament for most of this time. For instance, he regarded the U.S. atomic bomb—and the British one that he knew to be close—as making the two powers "trustees for the future of the world."[48] Truman agreed to "consult" should the bomb need to be used. In these meetings, Truman also made his intentions clear when it came to China: The Americans wouldn't bargain with Mao's regime, as Attlee had hoped they might do. The likely price of such negotiations, Truman lectured, would be the unconditional recognition of Red

China, the ensuing loss of Chiang Kai-shek's Nationalist seat on the UN Security Council, and, not least, the bloody assimilation of Taiwan.

There was one horror in these discussions. Attlee and his delegation were working out of the British embassy, which meant cheek by jowl with the Secret Intelligence Service's thirty-eight-year-old station commander, Harold "Kim" Philby, OBE. This seductive Cantabrigian was moving his way up to the role of chief of the service, and in 1949 he became responsible for all Anglo-American intelligence relations, including code breaking. Philby had arrived in Washington with the diplomatic title of first secretary, but above all he was a Russian double agent. Also in the embassy was Guy Burgess, thirty-nine, a second secretary who was part of the same spy ring. Donald Maclean, by this time, was back at the Foreign Office in Whitehall, where he was overseeing the workflow from Washington. It's fair to assume that everything significant the British and Americans did this December, including discussing their war plans, was conveyed to the Kremlin and then shared with Beijing.[49]

ATTLEE RETURNED TO LONDON ON DECEMBER 12, HIS DELEGATION having concluded that the U.S. approach to Asia was "half-baked and disastrous."[50] Within two hours of landing, he reported to the king and summoned the cabinet. In the House of Commons, he had to calm fears of itchy American fingers on the nuclear trigger. But his very statements opened him to an attack by Churchill that the Labour government had inexplicably failed to keep pace with U.S. progress on developing the atomic bomb. Possessing the bomb, Churchill claimed, was the only way to have influence in the world.

Meanwhile, American warships lay off the Korean coast to rescue MacArthur's forces, which turned out not to be needed. The U.S. Navy, however, had already just lifted out—through the northeast Korean port of Hungnam—41 Commando and those U.S. marines who were able to escape from Chosin.[51] That month, the U.S. Army alone had 2,065 men taken prisoner, mostly at Chosin. Few survived the winter.[52] Some 270,000 U.S. and allied troops and around 235,000 South Korean soldiers remained on the peninsula but were outnumbered at the front.

Then, on December 17, things got worse: U.S. F-86 Sabrejets and Russian MiG-15s met in the skies of northwestern Korea for the first time. These were history's first jet-versus-jet dogfights. The Sabrejet was the best American plane, but it couldn't match the red-nosed MiG-15s, which were lighter, faster, more maneuverable, heavily armed, and built with Rolls-Royce engines and from British designs. This was a direct, deadly consequence of the sales that Attlee's government had made to Moscow in 1946–1947. As infantrymen stared up from the battlefield, they saw U.S. pilots shot down routinely. MiGs with Chinese or North Korean markings were being flown by the best Russian pilots of World War II, including Sergei Kramarenko, who arrived in Korea with his entire air division. His own combat tour is credited with thirteen kills, and those Russian aces were just the tip of the lance.[53]

Stalin had sent some seventy-five thousand Russian fliers, technicians, trainers, and military advisers into the war zone. It would only take a spark for the United States and Russia to be directly at war, though at the time the extent of Russia's involvement was unknown. Nonetheless, MacArthur secretly requested what the army calls "commander's discretion." In this case, it entailed using atomic bombs as he saw fit, which would have been against air bases in Manchuria.[54]

Gladwyn Jebb wasn't privy to the details, but he sensed what MacArthur wanted, and found it chilling. MacArthur, he advised the Foreign Office, was so out of touch that "he must be conscious only of public opinion in the Philippines, some of the banana nations, and the lunatic fringe of the Republican Party."[55] Such views were rife in Whitehall, but Jebb shared his judgment of MacArthur right in New York, at one point openly calling him "this mad satrap." Jebb's office immediately used the familiar excuse of politicians to say that he'd been misquoted, but Jebb's personal papers, of course, show him quoted perfectly.

AS THE YEAR ENDED, SEVERAL OF THE ORIGINAL PLAYERS IN THE early postwar drama were leaving the stage. Right before Christmas, the tired and injured Lewis Douglas finally departed as U.S. ambassador—to then buy a bank in Tucson, back Eisenhower for president in 1952, and, as the striking former ambassador with his dashing black eye patch, be immortalized in popular culture as "The Man in the Hathaway Shirt," Ogilvy & Mather's iconic advertisement of the *Mad Men* era.[56] Douglas was followed in London by Walter Gifford, a genial major Democratic Party donor who'd spent years at the phone company. He was AT&T's chairman and hadn't visited Britain since an early 1930s motoring trip through Scotland.

Also gone was Stafford Cripps, who'd left the Treasury in October and was slowly dying, at a sanitarium in Switzerland, of bone cancer. As for Bevin, he had only months to live. He was so ill that Younger described him as "a mortally broken man."[57] He'd pause to take pills while struggling to speak in the Commons, and then he'd collapse afterward on an office sofa, holding his chest.

Without Bevin at his side—the foreign secretary having pneumonia that January of 1951—Attlee was struggling to resist U.S. demands. He tried but failed to prevent an American resolution at the United Nations that not only condemned Mao's regime as the latest aggressor in Korea but also identified the Chinese as joint conspirators with Russia in the original invasion. Which would prove true. Like Attlee, however, Gladwyn Jebb felt this denunciation to be spurious, and he reported that Washington's rhetoric was just indulging "the fire-eating section of its own public."[58] The Americans, for their part, believed, as always, that morality and national interest are interchangeable. Evil had to be named and denounced. And so it was, in a vote joined by Britain and forty-two other nations.

As MacArthur's forces continued to retreat, Stalin explained his purpose to Foreign Minister Vyshinsky, to the Moscow party boss Nikita Khrushchev, and to the rest of the Kremlin court: the war was to be dragged out against what Stalin called "the Anglo-American troops."[59]

From here on, fighting concentrated around the 38th parallel and would last another two and a half years. Defense spending almost tripled as a percentage of America's GDP between 1950 and 1953 (from 5 to 14.2 percent), and the draft call-ups that accompanied the state of emergency, which Truman declared in December 1950, became a national fixture. The outcome, however, was stalemate, and China reinstalled the Great Leader Kim Il Sung in Pyongyang. In July 1953—after a war that killed three to four million people—the United States, China, and North Korea agreed to an armistice. It would reestablish the boundaries that had existed at the war's start, which remain in place today. Before long, however, the Americans began to concoct the tragically misleading myth that they had won the war. But they had not. The best that can be said is that South Korea was rescued at a cost of 5,394 American dead. Yet the counterinvasion into North Korea failed terribly, leading to the deaths of 28,345 more Americans. In that light, the war was a bloody defeat.

12

ASIA'S THREE FIGHTING FRONTS

We cannot scatter our shots all over the world. We just haven't
got enough shots to do that.
—Secretary of State Dean Acheson, 1951

THE KOREAN WAR PROPELLED THE UNITED STATES TOWARD
world political-military power, but the Fortress America era really
wasn't over. Pentagon spending surged during the war's first year, and
then Congress began to cut the administration's budget requests. At the
same time, labor strikes hit twenty-one major defense plants, which delayed the U.S. buildup by a year, said the air force chief of staff.[1] As
winter wore on, Acheson got over his fears about a "Dunkirk type of
evacuation." Prospects of outright defeat yielded to stalemate, yet Americans still felt cornered.

Acheson sensibly spoke that winter of not having enough shots. The
country wasn't just straining under wartime demands; it was also placing army divisions in Europe to back the North Atlantic Treaty. How
long they'd stay was another question. In December 1950, President
Truman had recalled Dwight Eisenhower to duty as European supreme

commander of allied powers. However, as Eisenhower joshed with Secretary of Defense Marshall, who had been running the Pentagon since September, that title quickly had to be changed: "ESCAP" was but one letter shy of what the allies suspected of the Americans—that is, preferring to retaliate with atomic airpower rather than to stay on the Continent to face an overwhelmingly superior Red Army.[2] In any case, General Eisenhower, the new supreme allied commander in Europe, would recall that no one in Washington "ever believed for an instant" that the U.S. deployment would be other than temporary.[3] It was to be only a stopgap as the allies built up their own defenses.

Prime Minister Attlee knew that the Americans felt spread thin. Therefore, during his December 1950 White House talks, he had argued that the world was becoming so dangerous that it might be time for a new World War II–type partnership. This initiative made sense in Whitehall. Britain was rebounding economically, and to observers on Capitol Hill and in the administration its evolving empire and commonwealth looked pretty cohesive. Yet America's strength was growing faster, and an increasing disparity of power meant that ever more decisions would be made in Washington, no matter what notions of partnership existed, or how badly stretched the Americans might feel.

That said, the British Empire appeared necessary and imposing in the months after Attlee's visit. U.S. rearmament and strategic stockpiling ensured that gold and dollars poured into the Bank of England. Already at the end of 1950, Britain announced that it would stop accepting Marshall Plan aid, although Attlee's government welcomed military assistance dollars, which were regarded as different: that money arrived as part of a mutual defense effort, not as charity. By early 1951, the sterling area overall enjoyed nearly twice the working dollar reserves as before devaluation in 1949.[4] Singapore and Malaya, among other commodity-producing colonies, boomed. Furthermore, Britain's intense focus on exports was paying off. Even well-connected U.S. diplomats couldn't buy Scotch whiskey in London; every drop of alcohol from Scotland was being shipped abroad for hard currency. (The diplomats survived by couriering in Kentucky bourbon.) This also meant that Britain was exporting a sizable fraction of its arms production, such as Centurion tanks and jet fighters, to earn foreign exchange.

Mainstreet Americans were being impressed by courage in the field. Beginning on the night of April 22, and fighting nonstop until mid-afternoon of April 25, four thousand soldiers of the Gloucestershire Regiment made their epic stand on the high ground just south of the Imjin River, twenty-five miles northwest of Seoul. China had launched its spring offensive and the "Glosters" blunted an attacking force of some sixty thousand, thereby disrupting the PLA's timetable all across the front. Furthermore, Britain was defending Malaya and offering guidance on Indochina. In the end, wrote *The New York Times*, the Korean War wasn't "being fought in a vacuum." There were "three fighting fronts" in Asia, it explained, and Korea was but "part of the struggle against Communist imperialism taking orders from the Kremlin."[5] In addition to Britain being on the front lines in Asia, U.S. policy makers had to consider that it was also the major power in the Middle East. Besides, it was placing more troops and tanks on the European continent, in line with pledges to turn the North Atlantic Treaty's paper plans into actual military strength.

The industries of war appeared resilient too. Britain was building the world's fastest fighter jets and its only heavy jet bombers, which prompted U.S. aviation manufacturers to complain to Washington that they were still far behind. Britain had also reclaimed its lead as a shipbuilder and was about to commission HMS *Eagle* and the *Ark Royal* as the Royal Navy's largest aircraft carriers. This came as upbeat news to U.S. admirals who also felt stretched thin by having "to 'show the flag' in all of the seven seas simultaneously," as Chief of Naval Operations Forrest Sherman put it. The British seemed to have a key role even when it entailed atomic capabilities, although they were still cut off from America's R&D. To be sure, they didn't possess an A-bomb, but they were getting close, and rumor had it that they were developing a more technically advanced version than the Americans'. Not only that, they were well ahead in civil nuclear power, unquestionably the industry of the future. Given all this, the British seemed well positioned to influence policy makers in Washington.

But they weren't doing it, at least not to the extent that Walter Lippmann hoped in this situation. After Kim Il Sung's invasion in June 1950, Lippmann had proposed to John Foster Dulles that Britain use the weight of its diplomacy with Moscow to "bail us out of the consequences of the decision to land an army."[6] He had opposed sending troops to Korea because he anticipated China's intervention. By the spring of 1951, after China had indeed intervened, he told Harold Nicolson, the diplomat and author who'd been in Churchill's government, that he hoped Britain would give "firm advice" to officials at State and in the White House about the need to compromise with Beijing. Maybe that would enable America to finally get out. Instead, Lippmann saw London as hesitant to exercise its apparently decisive weight. "The effect of British appeasement of American opinion has created a fantastic state of mind in this country," he wrote to Nicolson—"the assumption that no one has a right to disagree with us and that if any one doesn't follow us instantly he has a bad motive."[7]

Lippmann's surprise is telling. He's assuming not only that British diplomacy could sway the Kremlin, and save America from its misadventures, but also that "firm advice" from Whitehall, if given, would redirect U.S. decisions in the middle of a war.

AT LEAST ON THE HOME FRONT, TRUMAN HAD REASON FOR CONFIdence. As the Korean War intensified, Treasury Secretary Snyder insisted that the burden be met by pay-as-you-go—and he made it clear to Capitol Hill that taxes had to be increased to avoid taking on endless debt.[8] It was he who urged the state of emergency in December 1950, which gave Truman nearly unlimited authority to coordinate the nation's defense programs. Such a prerogative hadn't existed since World War II. Inevitably, the Korean War incurred deficit spending. But after arriving at Treasury in 1946, Snyder had helped reduce the national debt while producing budget surpluses for three of those tumultuous years (the only balanced budgets since 1930). In fact, he was laying the groundwork for the booming economy of the 1950s. One way was by ensuring the appointment of his devoted second-in-command, Bill Martin, in April 1951, to be chairman of the Federal Reserve Board—a crucial role that Martin held for nineteen years. In sum, Snyder kept guiding his country through the financial complexity of this era, thereby enabling the United States to accomplish so much of what lay ahead.

International matters, however, looked grim in the late winter. Peace overtures had started in Korea, then floundered. Thankfully, Mac-Arthur retook Seoul on March 15, but nine days later he issued a personal ultimatum to Beijing that implied an atomic attack. At the same time, he challenged the president's authority by giving political support to Truman's opponents in Congress, such as the House minority leader, Massachusetts's Joseph Martin, who urged expanding the war to China.

From his office in the Empire State Building, Gladwyn Jebb quietly involved himself in the controversies swirling around MacArthur. He encouraged Oliver Franks and Arthur Tedder, marshal of the RAF, who was now working at the Washington embassy, to approach four well-known influencers: Assistant Secretary of State Dean Rusk, Chairman of the Joint Chiefs Omar Bradley, Chief of Naval Operations Admiral Forrest Sherman, and Paul Nitze. He requested that his colleagues inquire not only about MacArthur's trustworthiness but also about his state of mind. By taking this indirect approach, Jebb could avoid confronting Secretary of Defense Marshall and an unpredictable Dean Acheson. Better to raise questions about MacArthur's sanity via their trusted advisers and to do so at the right moment, as opinions in the capital wavered over how to face MacArthur's affronts to civil authority. Otherwise it was no secret: the British wanted him out.*[9]

By the spring, however, there was one development in Asia that helped lower the transatlantic heat. After five years of delay, the Americans were finally making headway on a peace treaty with Japan. They no longer saw Japan as a special place in need of redemption. Instead, they'd come to accept Whitehall's view that Japan's future was inseparable from the destinies of Southeast Asia, Australia, New Zealand, and, most of all, Korea. Responsibility for composing a draft fell to John Foster Dulles, who tackled it in his role as a U.S. delegate to the United Nations, to which Truman had appointed him the previous fall. Dulles did much of the writing in his four-story town house on East Ninety-

---

*In Tokyo, MacArthur was monitoring his clippings in the British press and receiving daily excerpts of everything from the august *Times* to the scurrilous *Daily Mirror*. He hoped that Whitehall could somehow "offset" such bad press, a request that the Foreign Office found "politically inexpedient," and Sir Alvary Gascoigne, its representative on the scene, was so informed.

First Street, to which he invited representatives from France, the Philippines, and Russia as well as those from Britain and its Asian-Pacific dominions. By March, he had readied thirteen concise pages that distilled all the key points—as the Americans saw them. But these ignored British appeals to earmark Japan's gold reserves for reparations and not to grant Japan most-favored-nation trading status.

Britain had a hundred-person mission in Tokyo and many proud diplomats with special knowledge of Japan. Critics in the Foreign Office said they found Dulles's effort lacking in detail, but their complaints really stemmed from a disagreement over substance and from the fact that they'd prepared a draft of their own, which the Americans ignored. Washington wasn't going to brook interference over Japan. Then, on April 6, Truman made Dulles an adviser to Secretary of State Acheson, with the rank of ambassador, in hope of building bipartisan support for policy toward Asia. It was the same day Truman met at Blair House with Acheson, Marshall, and Harriman, as well as with Generals Bradley and Bedell Smith, about how to handle MacArthur. Nothing was resolved, and Acheson, Marshall, and Harriman agreed to reconvene early the following morning, Saturday, the seventh, at which time Acheson proposed delaying a decision until Monday.

In fact, Truman had pretty much made up his mind that he'd have to strip MacArthur of all commands. John Snyder wasn't part of these meetings. Truman preferred to converse with him alone, especially on so significant an issue. They did so for much of Sunday morning at Blair House, where the two friends seem to have nailed down the decision. Acheson appeared briefly in the afternoon, and heard that they had caucused. Truman would confirm the decision on Monday once Acheson's group returned to Blair House—JCS chairman Bradley having over the weekend polled the three chiefs of staff, who all agreed.

At 1:00 a.m. on Wednesday, April 11, the White House pressroom announced MacArthur's firing. That brought havoc. "The President is appeasing the philosophy of Attlee," insisted Michigan's Homer Ferguson, who reflected Republican opinion in the Senate.[10] At the State Department, one top official, who was likely Paul Nitze, warned Jebb and Franks neither to gloat at MacArthur's dismissal nor to regard it as "appeasement toward the British point of view."[11] If U.S. policy changed at all, he said, it would be by becoming tougher on Red China. In London, Churchill tried to have it both ways, suggesting that Truman had every right to fire MacArthur but that Attlee was wrong for having reproached the great general.

No one knew MacArthur's intentions in the days after his dismissal. Perhaps he'd stay in Japan or go to the Philippines or come home to run for president. To assure the Japanese government that there'd be no significant changes in U.S. policy, Truman sent Dulles to Tokyo. He flew out from Idlewild on April 12, but rerouting over the Pacific delayed the journey. MacArthur, meanwhile, had decided to return promptly to the United States, which he hadn't seen for fifteen and a half years.

At a few minutes before 7:30 on a perfect Monday morning, April 16, and after the nineteen-gun salute due a departing five-star general, MacArthur and his wife and son boarded his new Constellation, again christened *Bataan*, at Haneda Airport for San Francisco. His plane and Dulles's passed each other on the leg between Tokyo and Honolulu. That allowed the two men to hold an air-to-air radio conference. MacArthur offered assurances of support. Right after landing in Japan, several hours later, Dulles was therefore able to deliver a riveting message to the Japanese people from the tarmac: General MacArthur, with whom he had just spoken in the sky, fully endorsed a peace treaty and wanted one signed promptly, as did President Truman.

Back in London, Ernest Bevin was fighting for his life. In a rare act of sentiment, Attlee had allowed him to stay in place at the Foreign Office, but that situation couldn't last. Attlee eased him out on his seventieth birthday, March 9, and Bevin felt he'd been sacked. He would live only five weeks longer.

This valiant spirit, who could have had the premiership but instead remained loyal to Attlee, died on April 14. Churchill eulogized Ernest Bevin as one of the greatest men who'd ever held the office. At the U.S. embassy, First Secretary Joseph Palmer disagreed: surely Bevin was Britain's greatest foreign minister of all, despite everything, and not least for what he'd done for America. Bevin was so familiar to Americans that reports of his death appeared throughout the United States. *The Tuscaloosa News*'s headline didn't even need to identify him when telling its central Alabama readers "Ernest Bevin's Funeral Is Set for Wednesday," with his ashes to be placed in Westminster Abbey.[12]

MALAYA WAS SHINING EVER BRIGHTER AS AN IMPERIAL JEWEL DURing these months of early 1951, despite the insurgency. Prices of rubber and tin were rising with the U.S. buying spree, and America was consuming 35 and 60 percent of the output, respectively. Malaya's rubber was still cheaper than synthetic products. Its strategic importance was so well-known that Orwell, in *1984*, made the superstate of Eastasia wage its endless "warfare of limited aims" in order to secure it. In the second half of 1950, Malaya had a favorable U.S. trade balance of $200 million, and in the first half of 1951 it handled trade worth twice as much as Hong Kong's.

The rubber that Malaya produced, Singapore processed, as anyone could tell by that colony's sulfurous smell, amid stifling heat and electricity blackouts. It was a profitable business. If these two interlocked possessions were lost, came arguments from Whitehall, the result would be "crippling to the United Kingdom and probably to the Commonwealth." The British made the implications clear to Washington: they might then be compelled to reassess global military commitments. On the other hand, they pointed out, if Britain held on to its lands, and if the struggle with Russia came down to a protracted World War III, Malaya's commercial ties to Detroit and Pittsburgh could prove crucial for the United States.

Today we know each of the so-called three fronts—Korea, Indochina, and Malaya—to have been distinct. The forces fighting in each of these places weren't "directed against the same enemy," as well-informed observers believed.[13] In Korea, the Americans were fighting a Russian-backed invader in a war that had pulled in the People's Liberation Army. In Indochina, the French faced Vietnam's struggle for independence, with the revolutionaries being supplied by Beijing. And in Malaya, the British were trying to defeat some seven to twelve thousand ethnic Chinese insurgents who were equipped by neither Moscow nor Beijing but instead used rifles, pistols, and light machine guns left over from World War II.

Nonetheless, British and French colonial administrators argued that one giant battle line existed from the Andaman Sea, south of Burma, to the Sea of Japan. The British justified their modest presence in Korea by insisting that they were upholding an equally vital part of the front in Malaya. The French said the same about Vietnam. Lots of Americans accepted this argument. But the three allies weren't making equal sacrifices. Between the summer of 1948 and the spring of 1951, British forces in Malaya suffered 891 fatalities (228 being soldiers and 663 police) and 4,683 overall casualties, while in Korea, since July 1950, the British contingent of the UN command had so far endured 892 killed, wounded, or missing. By that same time, in the spring of 1951, the U.S. Army alone had suffered 10,377 dead—with 31,719 wounded and 5,216 taken prisoner—yet Attlee's government was insisting that Britain was doing the world a favor by defending its own narrowest interests in Malaya.[14] It's a point that all great powers tend to make.

The British were deploying their full range of weaponry. They dispatched a virtual air armada to Malaya: bomber squadrons, jets, Spitfires, transports, and patrol planes. They sent over so much airpower, in fact, that the RAF told the Americans that these assets could be the nucleus of a bigger international air force should an all-out war occur in Asia against Russia or China. Fighting men of every kind were also being committed: Nepalese Gurkhas, local Malay battalions, Dayak trackers from Borneo, and storied regiments such as the Coldstream and the Royal West Kent. By the spring of 1951, Washington counted some 32,000 imperial and commonwealth troops in Malaya, including South Africans and Fiji Islanders, plus 100,000 local auxiliary police, which included militia, and what authorities called the Home Guard.

Among these combatants were increasingly effective commandos. Britain, the United States, and Russia had all disbanded such outfits after World War II, but now the British were re-creating theirs in the form of hundreds of small, increasingly professionalized patrols of Special Air Service operators who were being deployed beneath the jungle's triple canopy. (The 41 Commando, of the Royal Marines, was reconstituted during the Korean War at MacArthur's request mostly for amphibious raids.) A former British army welterweight boxing champion, Colonel "Mad Mike" Calvert, designed his SAS squadrons to win in the bush. He trained his men in unconventional warfare, made clear that their first battle had to be for the "hearts and minds" of local people, and taught them that torture is operationally stupid.[15] He set the tone on that by giving an exemplary pummeling to one trooper who boasted of manhandling a prisoner.

When the U.S. Army created its Special Forces in 1951, it looked to the British for lessons on counterinsurgency—another realm of global wisdom from which Americans set out to learn. The Special Forces adopted the Royal Marine Commandos' green beret, and in the years to come, the U.S. Army's Delta Force would be built precisely on the SAS model, right down to calling its units and soldiers "squadrons" and "troopers." But U.S. special operations in Korea were mostly disastrous, due largely to CIA amateurism: none of the agency's nearly two hundred personnel in Korea spoke the language; there were ceaseless turf fights with the U.S. Army and Air Force; and covert CIA missions into China proved to be as suicidal (mostly for local agents) as were its ongoing insertions of would-be guerrillas into Ukraine.

One pocket of brilliance did develop, however, under the ruthless direction of Donald Nichols, twenty-eight, a hefty former motor pool sergeant from Hackensack, New Jersey, with a sixth-grade education. Nichols made himself fluent in Korean, and he gained the confidence of South Korea's own brutal strongman, Syngman Rhee—a reassuring Presbyterian with an American Catholic wife. Nichols would be on-site to observe that holding diplomas from Harvard and Princeton didn't impede Rhee's habit of massacre making.

British commanders referred to Nichols, with real respect, as "Lawrence of Korea." He had Royal Navy warships at his disposal as well as whatever personnel, weapons, and money he required from the U.S. Air Force. Nichols and his men functioned with near autonomy out of a mountain valley compound, and his successes—such as stripping parts from a downed MiG-15, one hundred miles into enemy territory—led to the Communists placing a bounty on his head, said to be in the scores of thousands of dollars. He became known as "Mister Nichols," because the rank of sergeant didn't carry enough pull, and unlike Calvert, Mister Nichols used torture routinely: his commandos applied electric shock, blowtorches, and waterboarding to their captives. But Nichols had his regrets: he reminisced that these techniques were usually unhelpful because "many times false information would be given."[16]

Fortunately, in Malaya, the Americans didn't deploy troops of any kind, but instead conveyed modest amounts of equipment to the federation's government, such as ten Sikorsky helicopters. It was here, in Malaya, that choppers started getting a woefully mistaken aura as the secret to success in counterinsurgency. The Pentagon also sent one thousand carbines, to arm local planters against the ragtag Malayan Races Liberation Army, and private American mining interests, such as Pacific Tin Consolidated, quietly supplied weapons to friendly Malays. The British nonetheless asked for more: minesweepers, for example, were on their shopping list for Malaya. And why not? MacDonald was successfully convincing the Americans that this part of the common Far Eastern front was vital to the West, and the only reasons Malaya didn't receive more dollars and matériel was that the conflict was relatively small and, as anyone in Washington knew, Malaya was rich.

"The common belief in those days," recalled Hendrik van Oss, the U.S. consul in Kuala Lumpur, Malaya's capital, "was that the Soviet Comintern had orchestrated all these conflicts and that the Malayan conflict was part of the communist master plan to conquer the world. We were there to support the British."[17]

DURING THE FALL OF 1950, UNITS OF VIETMINH SOLDIERS RETURNED well equipped from training in China, and French generals were forced to relinquish northern mountain outposts. Even military positions in the south, which had been adequate against guerrilla tactics, were now endangered. By January 1951, the commander of the U.S. Navy's Pacific Fleet was preparing plans to evacuate French forces and American civilians from Haiphong. The navy also accepted responsibility for lifting Americans out of Malaya and Thailand and was ready to assist in the evacuation of Hong Kong. Later that winter, there was talk in the Foreign Office's South East Asia Department as to whether Malaya, Vietnam, or any part of that region could be saved without American help "in the shape of troops." Malcolm MacDonald was too sensible to say anything like that publicly, but he kept arguing for as much U.S. military aid as possible because a Vietminh victory, he was certain, guaranteed that Malaya would be next.

MacDonald kept advocating for France, and he laid out for the Americans the extent of France's sacrifices for the cause—no matter that France was becoming completely dependent on U.S. financial, diplomatic, and military support in Indochina. France had 659,000 men under arms, he told them, about 225,000 of whom were in the Asian theater. France had committed 51,000 of its regular professional soldiers there, as well as 18,000 Foreign Legionnaires and scores of thousands of colonial troops and auxiliaries. In six years of fighting, this force had incurred 28,929 dead, of whom 9,925 were from France itself (which included Algeria as part of the metropole). And that, he insisted, made the French sacrifice roughly equivalent to the American sacrifice in Korea. Moreover, France had been fighting the common enemy for six years, and Britain for at least three. The Americans had been in Korea for barely a year. So no need for U.S. resentments. Everyone was doing their part.

The tide seemed to turn for the French on December 17, 1950, when the resolute, meticulous World War II hero General Jean Joseph de Lattre de Tassigny landed in Saigon. He stepped from his plane in full-dress uniform, tailored by Lanvin, and made a point of putting on white gloves to show he'd clean up the failing "dirty war." Within a month, the sixty-one-year-old aristocrat took personal command and defeated what the Vietminh called their "General Counteroffensive" in the Red River delta around Hanoi and Haiphong. Yet his victory depended on U.S.-supplied aircraft, artillery, and ammunition and on U.S.-supplied napalm, used for the first time in Vietnam with devastating effect.

In Saigon, Donald Heath kept echoing MacDonald that the Vietminh were merely advance troops for Moscow. To this end, he urged the State Department to ensure that still more weapons and matériel be sent, and to do so "with the same rapidity as [they] would be moved to a US force engaged in the Pacific area."[18] Any delay would strengthen Ho Chi Minh while weakening the three-way front against Communism. Moreover, he questioned Washington's still "inadequate appreciation" of Indochina's importance to *all* of Southeast Asia.[19] By that he meant

Malaya, and the well-argued dispatches he sent might as well have been composed in Phoenix Park.

THE GRINDING STRUGGLE IN KOREA MADE THE AMERICANS DETER-mined to see Attlee's government meet its pledges to rearm. They expected Britain to double production of planes and tanks, add two and a half new divisions to its army, and boost spending by at least 25 percent. Surely, said Pentagon analysts, Britain could spend another $1 billion doing so, "with minor adjustments in the tax structure."[20] Such increased sacrifice didn't seem to be asking much, given America's own Pentagon budget, which was rocketing past 14 percent of GDP. (Today it is 3.5.)

Nye Bevan had objections. He was now minister of labor and national service. Yielding to U.S. pressure would damage the economy, he argued. It would corrode Britain's prestige and make the country increasingly dependent on America. Besides, there remained one big symbol of an aberrant working relationship. He doubted his government had any veto power at all should General LeMay's Strategic Air Command decide to launch its atomic bombers against Russia.

In Nye Bevan's protests, Churchill saw a heaven-sent opportunity to split the Labour Party. So he started his own draining guerrilla war in the House of Commons by forcing recurring late-night votes. In sibilant speeches delivered in the Commons during February 12–15, he demanded that Attlee's government be censured for ineffectively conducting the nation's defense. He again accused Attlee of failing to push hard for the development of an atomic bomb, which had caused Britain to "have been outstripped by the Soviet[s] in this field."[21] And then Churchill returned to another issue. It was one he'd raised months earlier, except now he was more explicit. He implied—without going so far as to make a formal accusation—that Attlee was endangering Britain by having no say at all concerning the U.S. atomic bomber bases in England.

Being in opposition, Churchill didn't have all the facts. He didn't know, for instance, of the government's progress in developing an independent nuclear deterrent, but on this matter of what the Pentagon today calls "permissive action," he was guessing just about right. That got White

House attention within hours. It was one thing for a fiery radical like Nye Bevan to spotlight the absence of a veto. For Winston Churchill to make the point was an entirely different matter.

President Truman sent Churchill a handwritten letter on February 16 in response to one received four days earlier in which Churchill said he had "little doubt" that Parliament would oppose America's use of SAC's atomic bombers without British consent. Truman warned him against pressing this controversy further, saying it could "ruin my whole defense program here and abroad."[22] The question of requiring mutual consent to use an atomic bomb went back to the days of joint R&D during World War II. Now Truman cautioned that opening this matter could spark a transatlantic row in which the Republican Right, which doubted any ally's reliability, and Nye Bevan's radical Left would be aligned.

Churchill backed off, but it was Bevan who led the Labour government's response to his accusation that the Attlee government was unable to defend Britain. Bevan mocked Churchill for aimlessly going from "generalization to generalization"—so aimlessly, he said with a smile, that bothering to answer him was like "trying to climb up a smooth, flat surface; I can get no hold." Unwilling to say anything more about these bases—for the moment—Churchill was left squirming.[23]

In early April, Attlee presented a large rearmament budget to Parliament, but it wasn't of the magnitude that the Americans were demanding, nor that Churchill was urging. Nye Bevan had been warning for months that Chancellor of the Exchequer Hugh Gaitskell, a former economics professor who had replaced the ailing Cripps, was being unrealistic about the price of the military burden. More military spending, Bevan said, would undercut nationalized health care, distort the economy, and worsen social inequality. The obsession with arms production, he continued, would be accompanied by "hatred and witch-hunting"—a reference to McCarthyism in the United States. He also denounced "the lurchings of the American economy," referring to the massive U.S. arms buildup, which, he charged, was playing into Russian hands by sucking up global resources.[24] Two weeks later, on the afternoon of April 23, frustrated that his government nonetheless gave priority to defense, Bevan resigned in protest from his post as minister of labor and national service. Churchill crowed that his departure was itself "a national service."

Nye Bevan, however, was about to be proved right. Britain's economy was far shakier than it seemed. But it was even harder for the Americans than for the British themselves to detect the underlying vulnerabilities. Among the reasons are these: First, the men who had shaped U.S. economic policy since 1945, and dealt officially with Britain, were mostly southern free traders, New York financiers, and corporate lawyers—all people inclined to rate Britain by past achievements. Had Detroit or Pittsburgh added a louder voice, such judgments might have been qualified earlier. Second, Washington's misjudgments about Britain's economic condition were shaped to some extent by the big and expensive national spectacles that kept being staged, among them the lavish Festival of Britain, starting on May 4 at the twenty-seven-acre South Bank Exhibition site reclaimed from the Blitz.[25]

The festival was an elaborately planned repeat of 1851's Great Exhibition, which had celebrated the British Empire as the heart of world enterprise. The 1951 adaptation began with a service in St. Paul's Cathedral. In his opening broadcast from the cathedral steps, George VI contrasted the relative serenity of Victorian days with present hard experience. Military parades, industrial displays, and tributes to empire and commonwealth followed. Eight and a half million visitors came over five months. There was even an amusement park, and spin-off exhibitions were held in ten other cities as well. Above all, the festival featured atomic research, jet propulsion, life sciences, and advanced manufacturing. When seen on newsreels in New York or Chicago, as around the world, it looked as if Britain alone were bringing the future to life.

A grimmer past was also being relived that spring when the first of four U.S. Army divisions to arrive in France that year began debarking at Bordeaux and La Pallice.[26] Their purpose was to help strengthen the Western European front. The GIs moved to an advance base in Verdun, where, thirty-five years after the great World War I battle that had killed 300,000 French and German soldiers, bones were still being plowed up daily by farmers, who placed them in the Douaumont ossuary.

. . .

THE TASK OF BUILDING AN ACTUAL NORTH ATLANTIC TREATY "ORGA-nization" couldn't be separated from the worsening violence in Southeast Asia. Britain needed its hard-currency profits from Malaya to boost its armaments, and it also had big deployments of soldiers and aircraft stuck in Malaya. France's foreign minister, in turn, said that his nation's combatants in Indochina couldn't be repatriated to Europe until they had defeated the Vietminh. On the other hand, France threatened to abandon its Southeast Asia battlefront unless the Americans provided sufficient dollars, planes, and weaponry for its soldiers to keep up the fight.

Everything was on the table when, in May, Malcolm MacDonald and Britain's military chiefs met for a strategy conference with General de Lattre and his large staff in Singapore's heavily guarded Phoenix Park. Commanders from Australia and New Zealand joined as observers and, for the first time, so did a U.S. vice admiral along with his aides. MacDonald dominated the four-day gathering and proposed a trilateral defense arrangement for Southeast Asia that could be adopted through the North Atlantic Treaty. For the Americans' benefit, he confirmed de Lattre's assurances that the Vietminh would be defeated in 1952, although his reports to London were more cautious. *The New York Times* wrote that the Singapore talks "represent an important further commitment by the United States toward joint military action by the three Western nations."[27] Not quite yet. When Omar Bradley, the chairman of the Joint Chiefs, heard of MacDonald's plan, he snorted with contempt.

France, however, was losing in Vietnam. And in the early morning of May 30, de Lattre's only son, Bernard, a twenty-three-year-old armored-cavalry lieutenant, was killed in action, some twenty miles south of Hanoi. Two days later, his body was flown home to France, but on July 4 he was honored in a sweltering Victorian memorial service in Hanoi's St. Joseph's Cathedral. All foreign representatives were summoned to attend. British and American officials flew up together from Saigon. MacDonald himself arrived from Singapore, having encountered Bernard during one of the many inspections that MacDonald and General de Lattre made together by scout planes throughout northern Vietnam.

Spurred on by the death of his son, the general delivered a stirring appeal from the pulpit to Vietnamese youth: they should fight against Communism for the sake of the independence they had been granted by France. In the traditions of *levée en masse*, oratory was soon followed by conscription decrees.

MacDonald's time, amiability, and acute efforts were paying off. He met tirelessly in Singapore with American opinion leaders who spread the word that the freedom of Southeast Asia depended on upholding Vietnam. By now, many Americans called him "the wise man of Asia."[28]

That July, he took Governor Dewey in a small RAF plane over the Malayan jungle battlefront, though who could tell what was happening below? He hosted the owlish syndicated newspaper columnist Joseph Alsop, who relished any crisis and who'd be a shrieking hawk during America's own Vietnam war. Barry Bingham, the owner of the Louisville *Courier-Journal*, had his audience too and celebrated MacDonald in print while tying Malaya's fate to defeating the Vietminh. When *Time* magazine did a glowing cover story on General de Lattre, who made a publicity tour of America later that year, it explained that he was defending not only Japan's rice bowl but "the Indochina rampart against the Communist surge toward Singapore."[29] Americans were being shown how, in the big picture, all of these strange places, including Korea, were connected. Meanwhile, Britain's Treasury was shoveling a million pounds a month into Malaya's "Emergency."

THAT SUMMER, JOHN FOSTER DULLES WAS COMPLETING HIS WORK on the Japanese peace treaty, though he still had to come up with "agreements" that might calm Australia and New Zealand. Each dominion had a visceral fear not of Russia but of Japanese revanchism. Less than ten years before, it had been MacArthur and the U.S. Navy—not Britain—that had checked imperial Japan, and just barely, on Australia's doorstep. Now each dominion wanted a guarantee of American protection. Yet even at this juncture Washington found it hard to say "defense pacts." So Dulles and the prime ministers of Australia and New Zealand explored entering some form of mutual understanding that would be separate from his draft concerning Japan.

Another impediment arose to a peace treaty: How would China be represented? It had also been a World War II belligerent, and Britain now had diplomatic relations with Beijing, whereas the Americans still recognized Chiang Kai-shek's Nationalists. Dulles insisted that the British agree not to have Beijing represent China among the signatories. They complied, but demanded a price: the Americans had to concede that Chiang wouldn't be included either. By July, Dulles could offer Japan a treaty that avoided the humiliations of past diktats and the treacherous myths that give rise to vengeance.

On the same day that the treaty was made public, the United States initialed an agreement with Australia and New Zealand. What resulted was the ANZUS pact. The two dominions regarded it as a shade against another dawn of the Rising Sun, rather than as a bulwark against Communism. In any case, the new alliance wasn't an example of the Americans thrusting outward to accept new "obligations in the southwestern Pacific," as commonly believed.[30] The Joint Chiefs wanted little to do with it, scoffed at the antipodeans' "grandiose ambitions . . . to have some forum of their own," and tried to discourage participation by drowning the new ANZUS Council in data. America had enough "obligations."[31] The British, for their part, were furious: no one in London had imagined being excluded from defense arrangements that involved Australia and New Zealand, which even Dulles called Britain's "two children."

Canberra's foreign minister didn't care about London's reaction. He was betting his country's future on America's staying power in Asia. After all, as he wrote to Dulles, "We live in the Pacific," and so, increasingly, did the Americans.[32] Fissures in the commonwealth were widening.

On September 8, 1951, at San Francisco's War Memorial Opera House, site of the UN's founding, forty-eight nations signed the treaty with Japan. India's prime minister, Nehru, refused even to send delegates. He professed neutrality between East and West and didn't want to offend Beijing—which, like Chiang Kai-shek's Nationalists—had been excluded. Recently converted Americans rebuked Nehru's naive isolationism.

The ceremony was brought live into American homes by the new transcontinental television network that President Truman inaugurated with his opening address. Dulles gave a speech as well but omitted any reference to British experts who had contributed to the treaty. The Foreign Office immediately detected a slight. Dean Acheson, who never set foot in East Asia during his years as secretary of state, was also in San Francisco. Unfortunately, the gathering had no sergeant at arms, though one might ask why a sergeant at arms would be needed at a peace conference. The reason became clear when a delegate from the Polish People's Republic refused to stop speaking and sit down. Watching on live television, viewers from coast to coast gasped as Acheson strode to the podium in San Francisco, ready to clobber the man. However, the Communist delegate quickly crumbled back into his seat. There'd be no fighting in the War Memorial that day.

ON SEPTEMBER 17, A HEADLINE SCREAMED FROM *THE ADVERTISER*, a large Australian newspaper: "Yet Another Financial Crisis in Britain."[33]

The third bust in five years had struck that summer, and now it was getting worse. The total cost of imports had soared, due in part to the voracious U.S. demand for industrial goods let loose by the Korean War. With the gap in Britain's balance of payments reopening, the pound sterling again plummeted on the Swiss free market. It was a new twist on a familiar problem. Britain couldn't get materials to keep its own factories fully at work, to produce exports, and to pay for the more expensive imports.[34] The crisis also overlapped, as we'll see, with some severely expensive turmoil for Britain in Iran. Altogether, this meant that the Bank of England's gold and dollar reserves were again hemorrhaging. The currency imbalance between the sterling area and that big part of the rest of the world that used dollars was therefore imperiling Britain's ability to carry on a life-sustaining volume of trade.

More bad news arrived. Britain faced another coal shortage for the winter ahead. Italian work hands had been recruited to boost production. In the Valleys, as the mining areas of Nye Bevan's Wales were called—where 230 pits provided the livelihood for 250,000 miners—the locals refused to work alongside foreigners, and this early example of labor mobility in Europe fizzled. Coal imports from America would be required to cushion the shock, and throughout Britain wartime controls were resumed on steel. There was a milk shortage, too, the worst ever experienced. Additionally—among butchers, restaurants, and farmers—the black market in horse meat thrived.[35]

Chancellor of the Exchequer Hugh Gaitskell, with his stern demeanor, promised higher taxes and a higher cost of living. Nye Bevan implied that Gaitskell was a "desiccated calculating machine," though Gaitskell was no more heartless than Cripps. In fact, at forty-five, he was a born upper-level civil servant—a child of the Edwardian administrative class, whose father had been consul general in Shanghai. Gaitskell was repelled by social injustice. He knew that severe measures were required and lamented that workingmen would be hit hardest. At least everyone still carried the same brown coupon books.

As the country again felt besieged, Fleet Street papers told of a West German couple who had visited London that September. They had entered a shop to buy tea and sweets and were surprised to be asked for ration coupons, which of course they didn't have. Even after losing two world wars, nothing in Germany was rationed, and cities like Frankfurt, Stuttgart, and Nuremberg were far ahead of England's in repairing war damage. This gave the couple pause. "If there's a third war," they were reported as saying, "we would be afraid of winning it."[36] Newspapers around the world picked up the tale.

Attlee's government nonetheless stuck to its targets of doubling arms manufacturing and commissioning new warships. Further strain ensued, but the defense minister argued that Britain wouldn't have to carry the burden alone: Canada, for example, might be a great industrial reservoir for arms production. Maybe, but that depended on whether Britain had the necessary dollars to *pay* Canada. Another reason to keep rearming, Attlee tried explaining to the Commons, was to maintain "our own special relationship" with America. At the same time, his ministers and the mandarins in Whitehall alike tried to convince the Americans that perhaps all this was enough.

On the night of September 4, Gaitskell flew to New York. He had lunch the next day with Gladwyn Jebb at Wave Hill, the twenty-eight-acre country residence in Riverdale, looking west over the wide Hudson River, that Jebb was renting. Gaitskell then headed from Penn

Station to Washington, where he'd spend ten days seeing everyone, except for the president. Acheson had nixed that request. Ostensibly, Gaitskell was arriving for the biannual IMF and World Bank meetings held in Washington, but his real aim was to see Secretary of the Treasury Snyder privately. He liked Snyder, whom he had met the previous year. They had cruised the Potomac together, sipping bourbon, and he felt they'd come to know each other well. Within the State Department, Acheson had already conceded that these issues involving Britain would again be "in Mr. Snyder's area."[37]

Gaitskell nonetheless began by visiting State, where he was warned by Willard Thorp, the gifted assistant secretary for economic affairs and a longtime professor at Amherst, that he'd find little sympathy over "the same old dollar problem."[38] (Thorp recalled that Gaitskell ended up having "to repeat his economic story a half dozen or more times" around Washington.[39]) Gaitskell then had two meetings with Snyder. The first went well as Gaitskell spoke about the strain of rearmament. At the second, several days later, Snyder had reached his limit. "The Americans [are] always the milch cow," he snapped, and had to "pay for everything." Moreover, he continued, in a perfect summation of recent experience—which reflected his two and a half years on the NATO Council—the British had an upside-down view on "who is helping who" in defense.[40]

Gaitskell fared no better when he returned to State, on the eleventh, to try making his case to Acheson. The Americans projected British military spending to increase 50 percent in coming years, which Gaitskell said was "moonshine."[41] He explained that even the existing military buildup was imposing crippling domestic political costs, with U.S. pressure causing "confusion and unpleasantness."[42] Acheson said he'd see what could be done.

During early autumn, the balance of payments worsened. Attlee was compelled to admit that the only way to restore the world's confidence in Britain's economy, and in sterling, was to declare the rearmament burden too heavy and to cut it. Churchill, who was still leader of the opposition, roared about incompetence and the further mishandling of imperial defense. By now he was circling in for the kill on Attlee and the tiring Labour government.

AMERICANS WERE PERPLEXED BY THIS LATEST REVERSAL OF FORtune. Britain was still an empire, and it presided over a huge commonwealth, yet sinews were snapping. *Time* wrote of the "hard knocks and humiliations forced upon the British Empire" since World War II. Such trials, it stated, had even "dealt deadly blows to Britain's Foreign Secretary," the fallen Ernest Bevin.[43]

Hugh Gaitskell knew that Britain was struggling—not just in absolute terms, but increasingly in relation to the United States. "We do not like to admit our relative weakness, because we should then look too much like a satellite," he reflected about living up to a military standard his Treasury couldn't afford. But to him, this seemed like a family problem: "A poor relation who is driven to live beyond his means by his rich cousins will not feel well disposed to them."[44] Few Americans were thinking of kinship. During these months, George VI welcomed the possibility that President Truman would reciprocate his own 1939 state visit to Hyde Park, New York City, and Washington. So the Foreign Office tried to re-create that famous hands-across-the-sea encounter. Acheson's staff replied that the international situation was too precarious for the president to leave his capital.

Whitehall mandarins told each other that they didn't intend "to make scenes" with the Americans, as one Foreign Office diplomat minuted, although it could be argued that Britain "might from time to time make use of appeals of an emotional or sentimental character."[45] But this was an admission that the mother country had few diplomatic arrows left in its quiver. "Might it sometimes be worth our while to turn awkward and prickly?" another senior official asked. Probably not. Playing hard to get might work for Chiang Kai-shek, or even for France. Men in Washington had come to know Britain a bit too well.

Americans themselves, however, didn't believe they were awash in prosperity. Corporate chieftains of the time urged tax increases to pay for Korea. The economy was growing, but meeting the demands of combat and an expanding world presence seemed overwhelming. Eighteen months after North Korea's invasion, America was producing 15 percent fewer military aircraft than planners had expected when rearmament began. The delays caused by labor strikes were worsened by shortages of machine tools—an alarming deficiency because such tools are the heart of any industrial process as they drill, bore, turn steel, or slice iron. Technical difficulties also arose. For instance, Boeing's B-47 Stratojet bombers had faulty landing gear, and the F-86 Sabrejets needed to be upgraded after losing dogfights to Russia's MiG-15s. Americans had been fed since World War II on a diet of "victory through airpower," yet they were now facing near defeat in Korea and shortfalls in aviation. That ate away at confidence.

Before Korea, Americans had never thought about the concept of "limited war." From now on, in the nuclear era, they faced the question not of whether to fight a limited war but of how to avoid fighting any other kind. Soldiers, air bases, and warships were needed worldwide for the West's defense, and the Joint Chiefs dreaded what they called "military vacua." To this end, the British Empire and Commonwealth was still expected—as in NSC 75—not only to defend lands that stretched from North Africa to Afghanistan, among other places, but to keep them stable. This obligation didn't appear unrealistic when seen from the Pentagon or State. Nor, necessarily, when seen from Whitehall, where determined men told themselves that there are many sources of national strength. The British possessed experience and diplomatic skill, and their top people, like Franks, knew it. They also knew that such attributes can combine with focus and global ties to raise mere influence into far-reaching power. To this extent, it was they, more often than not, who showed an enviable sense of assurance.

IV. THE GROUND CHANGES

Smooth operators: Secretary of State Dean Acheson
and Foreign Secretary Anthony Eden, 1952

13

"HOLDING THE RING"
IN IRAN AND EGYPT

The traditional British attitude is that in such a situation the United
States should follow British policy blindly and lend our strength to
the achievement of British aims.

—Henry Grady, U.S. ambassador to India, to Greece, and then to Iran
(1950–1951), about America's approach to nationalist passions in
the Middle East

D URING THE BLOODY, SEESAWING FIRST YEAR AND A HALF IN
Korea, the United States suffered casualties as high as in its first
twenty months of combat in World War II—without the consolations
of a Midway or Sicily. Come the late fall of 1951, U.S. armed forces had
expanded by 1.2 million fighting men, but military commitments elsewhere in the world were also increasing. America was sending weapons
and dollars to Southeast Asia, and by this time nearly 100,000 more
GIs had already been deployed in Europe.

At least the economy was booming that fall. Production was 9 percent
greater than when the war had started, and 83 percent higher than at
the beginning of our story in 1944. Yet Tom Connally, the Democratic
chair of the Senate Foreign Relations Committee, was demanding cuts
in overseas spending. So was Wisconsin's Alexander Wiley, a Republican
lawyer from Chippewa Falls who would replace Connally as chairman

THE BRITISH EMPIRE'S SOUTHEAST ASIAN HOLDINGS: REIGN OF THE PHOENIX

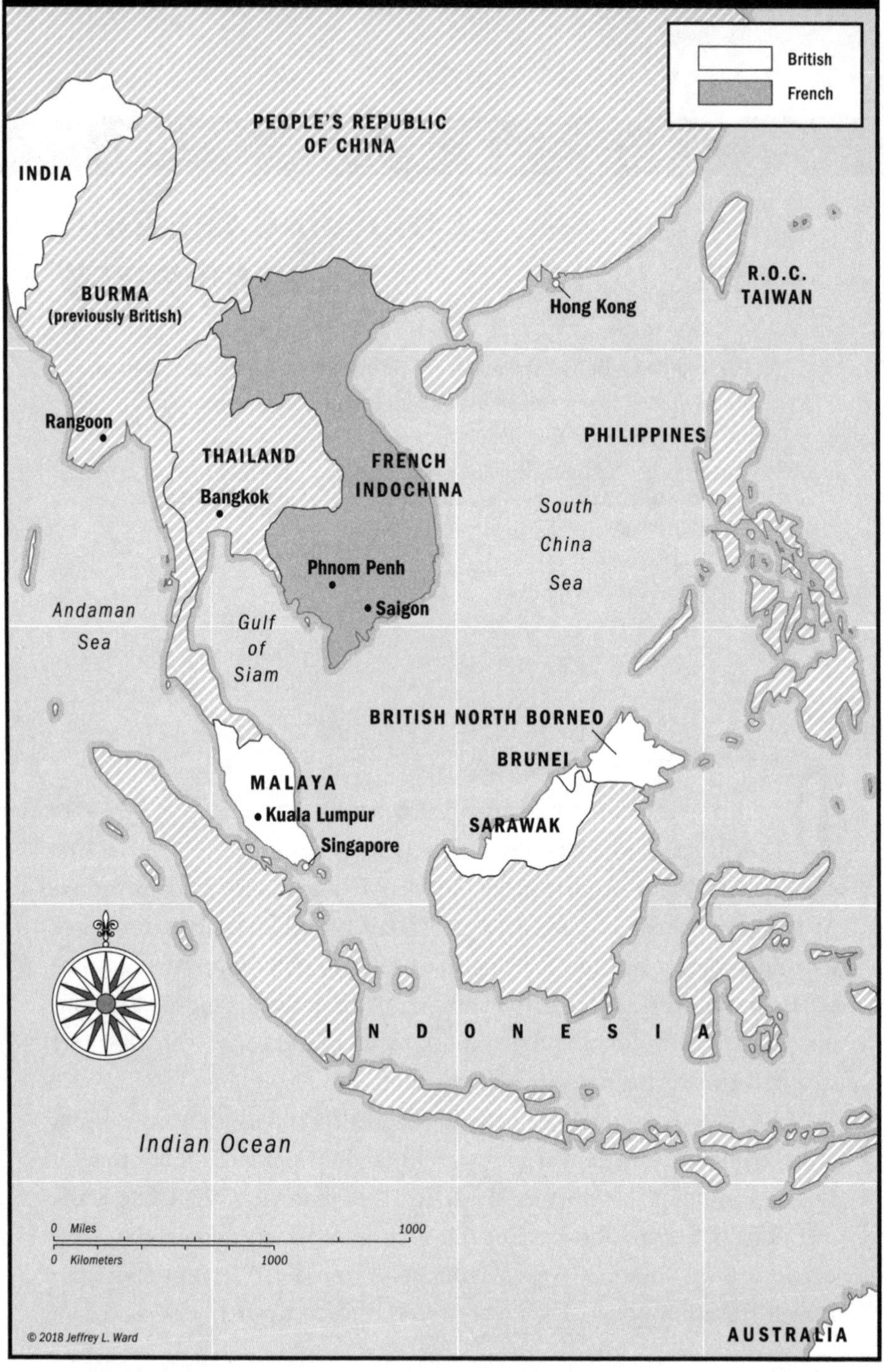

British
French

PEOPLE'S REPUBLIC OF CHINA

INDIA

BURMA
(previously British)

Hong Kong

R.O.C. TAIWAN

Rangoon

THAILAND

Bangkok

FRENCH INDOCHINA

PHILIPPINES

South China Sea

Phnom Penh

Saigon

Andaman Sea

Gulf of Siam

BRITISH NORTH BORNEO

BRUNEI

MALAYA

Kuala Lumpur

Singapore

SARAWAK

INDONESIA

Indian Ocean

| 0 | Miles | | 1000 |
| 0 | Kilometers | 1000 | |

© 2018 Jeffrey L. Ward

AUSTRALIA

after the 1952 elections. It didn't matter that the United States understood itself to be engaged in a worldwide battle against Communism. Connally and Wiley focused on what they considered an even scarier prospect: with this war, the national debt stood at $259 billion, or 79 percent of the GDP. Higher Pentagon spending, they felt—as did Snyder—risked torpedoing the economy. Thus, in the last quarter of 1951, defense outlays fell from $6 billion to $2 billion.[1]

Since the start of the war, and through 1951, attentive people in the U.S. government were again trying to determine what to expect of the British Empire and Commonwealth. Toward year's end, some useful insights came from Julius Holmes, the minister counselor in London. He was a stellar Foreign Service officer, from Pleasanton, Kansas, and a 1922 graduate of the University of Kansas, who, after Lewis Douglas's departure, essentially ran the embassy, absent a strong ambassador. The British, he reported to State, were trying "to maintain their position as a first-class power, seat of empire, head of Commonwealth and center of [the] sterling area," but they were having difficulty handling the job. Might some "junior partnership" role, in which they ceded responsibilities to the United States, be acceptable to any of their key people? he wondered. So far, he hadn't found anyone in Parliament or Whitehall who entertained the idea.[2]

The way the U.S. embassy in London was organized shows the extent to which the Americans were still dealing with a stern global entity. No other U.S. embassy was structured like it or has been since. It resembled a small State Department, with sections devoted to South Asia/Far East, to the Near East, to Europe, and to Latin America. This was deemed necessary for good working-level ties with the ministries of a busy worldwide empire. The embassy was unique in another way. American military officers stationed within the British Empire—in Singapore or Hong Kong, for example—had to be accredited by the Foreign Office and placed on the diplomatic list of the U.S. embassy in London. And those procedures were well policed.

Holmes described Whitehall as highly sensitive about U.S. policies that diverged from British ones in areas of Britain's "primary responsibility," which, obviously, were huge.[3] At the time, it was said quietly to distinguished Americans like Holmes, whether in St. James's clubs or on weekend shoots in Kent, that Britain was the only nation in the West, of course, that would fight to defend its interests without needing America to come to its aid. On the one hand, Holmes's superiors in Washington found such resolve reassuring. On the other, it raised problems because the Americans believed that in a postwar world the use of force—when, say, confronting difficulties in Iran or in Egypt—had to be approved by the United Nations. They were proud of themselves for having sought and received UN authorization to intervene in Korea.

Not that Whitehall paid attention to what the State Department or Holmes's embassy might say on these matters. When it came to Egypt, the British believed that any U.S. role should be limited: "a sort of passive collaboration with the British," which is how one American commentary summed up the situation.[4] The same held true for Iran. The Foreign Office assumed that its decisions would always take precedence over State's. In Iran, however, Washington was a bit more assertive, at least to the extent of asking the British not to "revert to their traditional tactics" of using or threatening violence.

By 1951, the National Security Council had concluded that unrest in Egypt and Iran arose from nationalist aspirations, and specifically the desire to stop British exploitation. But other passions were also at work. The imam of Cairo's As-Sayyida Zeinab Mosque, which contains the tomb of the Prophet's granddaughter, assured the faithful that taking up holy war against Britain's occupation conformed to Islam's acceptance of self-defense. In Tehran, Ayatollah Kashani, the charismatic nationalist cleric who led Iran's Fighters for Islam, proclaimed an "unprecedented liberation movement" in Islamic countries under foreign domination.[5] A foreigner is a foreigner, he averred, whether from the East or the West, whether appearing in Iran or in Egypt, and he wanted the British out.

Those few Americans who recognized the nature of that sort of strife were ambivalent. When the imams opposed Communism, the most rabid Islamic movement acquired an almost Rotarian tinge in Washington. But it was a different story when these guard dogs seemed to have ambitions to own the estate, as looked to be the case in Egypt and Iran. Not even the best-informed U.S. observers knew where that might lead, nor did the authentically expert Orientalists in Whitehall.

The British and Americans agreed on one basic idea: that the entire Middle East would be lost if Iran fell to Communism. Not only that, Western Europe's economies would be ruined without Middle Eastern oil—with 33 percent of Europe's oil imports coming from Iran, including 85 percent of the fuel used by the Royal Navy. Iran's "lift," as the oilmen say, represented 6 percent of total world production. This made the Anglo-Iranian Oil Company—a rapacious business detested by all Iranian patriots—the planet's largest oil-producing enterprise.

Iran's government and the AIOC had been debating the terms of their relationship at least since 1947 as feelings soured. Getting higher royalties wasn't even Tehran's top priority; the Iranians wanted the AIOC's tentacles to be cut. The AIOC had become a state within a state—a corporation on which 90 percent of Iran's government budget depended. It had its own intelligence and propaganda bureaus, and 52.2 percent of the business was owned by the British government. Its output not only made Iran a huge source of oil for Britain but could be paid for in sterling—in contrast, say, to acquiring oil from Venezuela, which required dollars. Much about the company was opaque. Tehran's ministries, for instance, weren't allowed to audit the AIOC's books, which were kept securely in London, and that was just one reason among many that the company was low-hanging fruit for nationalization.

At the Foreign Office, Kenneth Younger, MP, was still second-in-command during 1951. He saw a benefit to the Americans getting enmeshed in Tehran's politics. Clearly their backseat driving was annoying, but they couldn't keep evading responsibility. "Whatever we may think of the wisdom of the United States policy in this Persian dispute," he wrote that summer, "they are now up to the neck in it."[6] Soon he'd say the same about the U.S. predicament in Egypt, which was similar: the Americans couldn't just criticize; they had to take responsibility, which, to Younger, as it did to much of Whitehall, meant the responsibility of supporting Britain. That was the perspective of their military people as well. "We are in fact holding the ring for the Americans in this area," concluded Britain's chiefs of staff, "as we have been doing in South-East Asia."

. . .

REZA PAHLAVI, THE SHAH OF IRAN AND THE SECOND POTENTATE of the recently discovered Pahlavi dynasty, had first visited America when he was thirty years old, during a five-week tour in November–December 1949. President Truman addressed Pahlavi as "Your Imperial Majesty," which is how he'd be known to six more presidents until his subjects overthrew him in 1979. The Americans found him agreeable: although he was a Shia Muslim, he had acquired decent Christian European values at Le Rosey, a Swiss boarding school. King Farouk of Egypt was also a distinguished alumnus, and Pahlavi had been married to Farouk's sister Queen Fawzia until a year earlier.

Pahlavi's sole direct source of power in Iran's emerging democracy was the military, but it was merely a tatterdemalion collection of 115,000 men dressed as GIs who carried World War I–era Enfield bolt-action rifles. So during his visit to the United States, on a coast-to-coast trip that included the Air Materiel Command in Dayton, Ohio, and thereafter the Armor School in Fort Knox, Kentucky, the shah was on the lookout for weaponry and military aid. The Americans hoped to discuss problems of agriculture and irrigation with him, but he showed less interest. Congress, however, wasn't up to writing checks for anything on his shopping list. At the State Department, the Office of Greek, Turkish, and Iranian Affairs hoped Britain might instead satisfy his wants. "We've got much bigger things to do," said one official at State, which included having to help organize the defense of Western Europe.[7]

Nevertheless, the shah was promised a $25 million Export-Import Bank loan intended mostly for agricultural machinery. The administration hoped the money could jump-start a civilian farm-aid program and help address what State was already calling "The Iranian Crisis"—a combination of economic depression and political instability.[8] The Americans had a successful aid model up and running in Greece, and it made sense to redeploy their ambassador in Athens, Henry Grady, to Tehran so he could steer Iran's effort. But there was no rush. Only in May 1950, well after the shah's visit to America, did Acheson recommend Grady's new appointment. By the time the Senate voted on this nomination, at ten o'clock on Monday morning, June 26, 1950, the world was a different place. It was the day after North Korea's invasion, and Grady's name passed through the Senate in a flash. Within hours of Grady's being confirmed, Truman—standing next to a globe in the Oval Office—placed his index finger on Iran and said, "Here is where they will start trouble if we aren't careful."[9]

Iran looked more exposed than ever to Russian appetites. Its economy was even shakier than during the 1946 Azerbaijan crisis, when the Kremlin appeared ready to divide the country. Pahlavi's regime was also more unstable: nationalists, Islamists, and Communists were all agitating against it. The terrain seemed perfect for a new and bigger *maskirovka* hybrid conflict of Russian subversion, if not for outright invasion.

Grady's was the type of inspired appointment that—in a U.S. foreign-policy-making system that relies on political appointees for most senior positions—can, at times, inject freshness and creativity. Born in San Francisco sixty-eight years earlier, he had been trained as a statistician, worked at the Commerce Department, and, at thirty-seven, after World War I, had become the U.S. trade commissioner to London and Continental Europe. He returned to Commerce to work for that star entrepreneur, Secretary Herbert Hoover, and earned a Ph.D. in economics at Columbia University. Back in California during the 1930s, he served as dean of Berkeley's business school. From 1941 to 1947, he ran the giant shipping company American President Lines (today known as the Singapore-based APL). Truman used him right after World War II to negotiate with the British on Palestine. In 1947 he appointed him the first U.S. ambassador to India, and in 1948 he sent him to Athens.

All of which made British authorities uncomfortable. Grady was hard to buffalo. He knew big business, and he had seen the British at work, guided by their "imperial view," close-up in Palestine, India, and Greece. For these reasons, he was about the last person the Foreign Office wanted to appear in Iran, though Washington knew nothing of this concern.

On July 1, 1950, Grady landed in Tehran, only to discover that no one on his small staff of Foreign Service officers spoke Farsi, nor did the one person in place from the CIA. They were being quartered in the old ramshackle German delegation building, which compared poorly with the British embassy next door.[10] Grady chose to spend most working hours at his official residence, half a mile away, which troubled one of the men responsible for diplomatic security, but Grady assured him that his two standard poodles would handle any intruders.

Then as now, the British embassy in Tehran—set within a twelve-acre walled compound—is a place apart. (Britain has diplomatic relations with the Islamic Republic of Iran, unlike the United States.) The embassy itself was designed in the nineteenth century, based on what is today London's Victoria and Albert Museum, and it's surrounded by gardens, fountains, wisteria, privets, and walking paths. When Grady arrived, it was a hive of activity, full of not only diplomats but also military attachés, seasoned Oriental counselors, spies, and Indian servants.

Once in-country, Grady quickly became skeptical of the AIOC's commercial practices and grew alarmed about its grip on Iran's government. He began to document these facts for Washington and let British authorities know it. Looking back, Grady could see that the British viewed him as "poaching," which was a dangerous spot to be in.[11]

Grady believed his purpose was to encourage Iran's political and economic independence, but his staff warned him otherwise. Britain was protecting Western interests, they cautioned, and the Americans were there to help. "It was not part of our responsibility to buck the British," Grady's consular/political officer, John Stutesman, recalled.[12]

Grady gradually won over his people, but he also became convinced that London was driving U.S. policy. For instance, even though Truman desperately wanted to stabilize Iran's economy and had approved that small but urgently needed Export-Import Bank loan promised to the shah in 1949, the money wasn't released until October 1950—a delay Grady blamed on the British, who he believed had lobbied against the loan in Washington.

Oliver Franks and his aides intimated as much. They had let it be known at State and on Capitol Hill that such aid would be counterproductive to the West's defense and that the timing was poor. The Anglo-Iranian Oil Company, they explained, was vital to Iran's well-being. For many months, they continued, this important company had been struggling to renegotiate its concession while being hampered by irresponsible elements in Tehran. Failure to achieve a contract would cause terrible uncertainties beneficial only to Russia. Regrettably, the Americans—

good-hearted, to be sure, but unaware of the complexities—would only be encouraging Iran's foolishness if they provided that troubled country with dollars.

Even if the Russians didn't exploit the situation to invade, the argument went, they could foment subversion, and that might be worse. The giant refinery at Abadan, the island-city at the head of the Persian Gulf in southwestern Iran, near the Iraqi border, was the largest such facility in the world. It could slip into Stalin's hands intact, before the Royal Air Force had the opportunity to blow it up with air strikes, as was the plan in case of invasion. The entire prize was immense.

THE AIOC'S VALUE HAD BOOMED BY NEARLY 60 PERCENT IN FIVE years, and oil from Iran was vital to Britain's balance of payments. If lost, concluded Philip Noel-Baker, the minister of fuel and power, in July 1950, "We should no longer be on equal terms with the Americans in the sphere of international oil affairs."[13]

But if Iranian production was lost, equality with the Americans would be the least of concerns. Oil would likely have to be imported from the United States, because the AIOC wasn't expected to fill the gap from what was being pumped in Iraq and Kuwait. And those imports from America might have to be so large as to risk curtailing U.S. domestic consumption. That was sure to cause trouble. Furthermore, if the British had to pay hard currency to buy oil from the United States—or from Venezuela and companies like Shell, which largely sold oil denominated in dollars—Britain's Treasury could be drained of some 350 million more dollars annually. It was already paying vast amounts of dollars to buy U.S. coal. All that outflow of hard currency would risk another devaluation.

The AIOC, however, was blundering, and Grady and his staff recognized it. Out in the field, its expat employees proved themselves unable to gauge the local temper and did their part to court nationalization by refusing to alleviate living conditions for Iranian workers or to budge from nineteenth-century labor practices. Some 200,000 people lived on Abadan. At the center of the island was the refinery, which served as a metallic barrier to segregate the nonwhite population, jammed into some of the world's nastiest slums, otherwise known as AIOC company housing, from the British neighborhoods. That's where the oil giant maintained polo grounds, cricket pitches, gardens, and a golf course for a community of about 4,500 whites. AIOC headquarters were in London, and the Scottish entrepreneur Sir William Fraser, the chairman, ran his enterprise with all the contempt of a Glasgow accountant for anything that couldn't be shown on a balance sheet.

Sir William and his board of directors spurned any compromise—such as allowing Iranian officials to see the books—and the British embassy went along with his obstinacy while ignoring threats of nationalization from the Majlis, Iran's parliament. AIOC management, as well as Whitehall officials, knew that Iran didn't have the technicians or tankers to run oil operations alone, and they also assumed that Iranians feared the Russians more than they hated the AIOC. So why hurry to cooperate, especially if U.S. aid to Tehran could be impeded? Grady described this tactic to Acheson as the British being "bent on sabotaging our efforts to strengthen Iran."[14]

U.S. diplomats in Tehran also concluded that the AIOC had the British embassy under its thumb. Oriental counselors, among the select cadres of the elite Foreign Office, who spoke perfect Farsi, were said to demur to the wishes of the AIOC. In Washington, the assistant secretary of state for the Near East, George McGhee, a thirty-eight-year-old Texas oil millionaire and former Rhodes scholar, heard from Foreign Office spokesmen that no one in London was interfering in Iran's politics and that, anyway, Whitehall didn't have authority to control the activities of a private British corporation. Grady insisted both claims were ridiculous.

By the close of 1950, the Americans had moved into a big, bland, suburban-high-school-like embassy building, which was filling up fast with advisers and attachés. All of them were astonished to see that their British counterparts expected the AIOC's heavy hand to last, as one Foreign Service officer concluded, "forever." The British refused to believe that the Majlis was prepared to nationalize the company. Yet Grady and his observant team found it unlikely that "the British could remain in control for the next hundred years or even 20 years or even two years."[15]

U.S. embassy staff meetings were usually held at Grady's residence, joined by the large poodles. At these gatherings, recalled one of his staff, Foreign Service officer Lewis Hoffacker, the ambassador "would groan at the obduracy of the British, the blankness of their minds when it came to dealing with Iranians."[16] Yet Washington at this point was consumed by defeat in Korea and had neither the time nor the interest to act on Grady's despairing reports.

MONTH BY MONTH, EVENTS IN IRAN AND IN EGYPT WERE BECOMING intertwined, though officials in London sensed that in Egypt, unlike in Iran, time was not on their side.

In 1950, half of Egypt's children were dying of disease and hunger by the age of five. Social and political unrest was increasing: calls arose from Egypt's souks and officers' clubs alike for a reborn purposeful Arab state. Meanwhile, King Farouk I was haunting the Riviera's casinos, racking up notoriously high losses at chemin de fer, as well as enormous bills for himself and his entourage at the Carlton hotel in Cannes, only to return home on his 478-foot yacht, the *Mahrousa*, and loll around in his palaces, which were full of baroque-style furniture that British officials mocked as "Louis-Farouk."

That created difficulty for British policy in the Middle East, and specifically for London's grip on the enormous military preserves of the Suez Canal Zone along the waterway, though they were not "the size of Wales," which is how Anthony Eden came to exaggerate this stronghold. That would have made the Canal Zone twice as large.[17] Habitually being overlooked, as in our own time, was the fact of Egypt's ownership of the canal, with the Suez Canal Company being an Egyptian business listed on the Cairo stock exchange.[18] The distinction is essential, as we'll see several years hence.

One way that Cairo exercised sovereignty over the canal was by denying access to Israeli shipping, despite a provision in the 1888 Suez Canal convention, signed by the European powers of an earlier day, that guaranteed passage to all ships during peace and war. Yet the British had denied the canal to enemy shipping during both world wars, and Egypt was now doing the same to Israel because, its government argued, no actual peace treaty existed. In 1951, the UN passed a resolution telling

Egypt to adhere to the convention, and it was ignored. Moreover, Farouk's government had blocked the Straits of Tiran, thereby cutting off the port city of Eilat on Israel's southern tip from the Red Sea.

Cairo was also pressing its sovereignty by increasingly shrill demands for British troops to "quit Egypt," but negotiations had stalled, as did those that addressed the future of the Sudan. Top U.S. decision makers knew the scale of Britain's ongoing presence in Egypt because it had been assessed in NSC 75. At this juncture, it included twenty-one thousand British troops and nine thousand colonial ones, along with five fighter squadrons. There were at least thirteen thousand more soldiers nearby in Libya (which became independent in 1951), where the British still occupied two provinces taken from the Italians during World War II. According to the military chiefs in London, all these forces were positioned to defend the canal—and the rest of the Middle East—should Korea prove to be the opening gun of another world war. That was okay with the Americans, for the time being. They barely involved themselves in Egyptian defense matters, nor did they burden themselves with problems of Israeli navigation.[19]

Farouk's army had been defeated in the 1948 Israeli war, but its restless, demoralized officers readily adopted the familiar great-power idiom: they'd take "responsibility" for defending the canal. The British, for their part, told the U.S. ambassador in Cairo, Jefferson Caffery, America's most senior professional diplomat, that the Egyptians couldn't run something so complex, let alone protect it. Egypt's posture, they claimed, was inhospitable and ungrateful. "Britain does not think it an infringement of her sovereignty to have US forces in Britain," someone as sharp as Kenneth Younger could say when visiting Harvard, "and we don't see why that sort of issue need arise in the Middle East."[20] But the Yanks and the shopkeepers on the high streets of Southampton or Mildenhall, among other places, got along a lot better than did the occupying Tommies and the local "Gyppos."

BY EARLY 1951, IRAN WAS IN TURMOIL. THERE HAD BEEN MONTHS of street protests and assassinations, including of Prime Minister Razmara in March, a supporter of the shah, who was shot point-blank in

Tehran's Sepahsalar Mosque by a Shiite fundamentalist. The British now worried about what had seemed far-fetched: their oil holdings might be seized. Attlee's government was getting cornered. Should the AIOC be nationalized, Britain might indeed have to use force. "If Persia is allowed to get away with it," Attlee's defense minister stormed, "Egypt and other Middle Eastern countries will be encouraged to think that they can try things on; the next thing may be an attempt to nationalize the Suez Canal."[21] He meant the Suez Canal *Company*, but at least that possibility remained fanciful within Whitehall.

The Americans tried to keep their distance from upheavals in Tehran and Cairo. Yet Oliver Franks, for one, recognized that if Britain couldn't prevent chaos in these areas of "primary responsibility," then "the consequent deterioration in United States/United Kingdom cooperation will be serious." Not only that, he added in a dispatch to London, the Americans might think it time "to draw away from us and 'go it alone' in the Middle East."[22] To stave off that danger, the British manipulated American fears of Communist inroads. "When we knew what the . . . prejudices were, we played all the more on those prejudices," remembered a shrewd MI6 operative in Tehran about his dealings with U.S. officials.[23] Surely it was best to face these dangers with British expertise, though unobtrusive backing from Washington was expected.

On April 28, 1951, a majority vote of the Majlis compelled the shah to make Mohammad Mosaddeq the new prime minister of Iran. At sixty-eight, Mosaddeq was the de facto secular leader of a National Front coalition that comprised a spectrum of parties and associations, including supporters of Ayatollah Kashani, speaker of the Majlis. Writing about the appointment, *Time* magazine called him "right wing," which, for many Americans, came as a reassuring endorsement from an unimpeachable source on these matters.

In fact, Mosaddeq was an upper-class radical of the type not unknown in Britain's House of Commons. This bald, birdlike, and brainy figure with an enormous beak had studied law in Paris and had earned an engineering doctorate in Switzerland. He didn't mind keeping the Pahlavis as a constitutional monarchy, like the House of Windsor. He nonetheless enjoyed baiting the arrogant young shah, urging him to stand above politics and not soil his royal hands while offering to deal with that dirty business himself. But Mosaddeq saved his most infuriating behavior for the British. For instance, he'd grant an audience to the British ambassador but make sure that a junior American diplomat happened to be in the room: he'd then only speak to His Excellency the ambassador through this surprised U.S. intermediary.[24]

That spring of 1951, the AIOC was becoming ever riper for nationalization. It had recently offered a fifty-fifty split of operating profits to Iran—similar to the Arabian American Oil Company's terms with Saudi Arabia the previous December—but all faith had been lost with the Iranians, who'd still be excluded from managerial roles. The AIOC's offer was refused. While the Majlis debated nationalization during March, moreover, the British had sent the cruiser HMS *Mauritius* (redeployed from Korea) to the Gulf, where it showed itself off, with its six-inch guns, in the waters near Abadan. This "whiff of grapeshot" provocation had its limits. A rather large perimeter would be required to guard the AIOC's facilities and oil fields, which included 1,718 miles of pipeline.

Rioting followed in Abadan during April when the AIOC cut a hardship allowance for Iranian workers. Three British oilmen were killed. Events culminated on May 1 once Mosaddeq moved to nationalize the AIOC. He did so by implementing a law that compelled Pahlavi to confiscate its assets and end the company's concession. What had been AIOC property was renamed the National Iranian Oil Company, as it is today. Mosaddeq declared he would compensate the AIOC and its London financiers, and he was likely sincere. But he mistakenly assumed that the Americans—one big possible source of revenue—would be on Iran's side as his country sought sovereignty and raced to bring its own oil to market.

By July 31, the British had completely shut down Abadan, which produced all sorts of petroleum products, from gasoline to lubricants. The storage tanks were full, but Sir William, the AIOC chairman, proved able to block all shipments. He threatened to sue any competitor that dared buy oil from Mosaddeq's government. U.S. businesses, including the Texas Company and Standard Oil, weren't alarmed. Even though London kept a tight grip on the industry in the Middle East, and had resisted a U.S. political presence in the Persian Gulf, the Americans were making headway. A consul had been sent for the first time to Kuwait that spring, and Kuwait Oil, which Whitehall insisted had to be incorporated as a British company, was nonetheless half owned by Gulf Oil, America's eighth-largest industrial enterprise. Gulf Oil, in turn, cooperated with the AIOC to expand Kuwait's refinery production to meet European demand. And the Bahrain Petroleum Company was 100 percent U.S. owned, even though it had to be registered as a Canadian corporation. So the Americans already had plenty of business. With Abadan shut, moreover, the U.S. majors like Caltex realized they could enter India's marketplace with their own petroleum products.

By August—Abadan still being closed—Attlee's government used its full diplomatic influence to ensure that no Western nation could supplant British personnel. In Washington, Oliver Franks's embassy convinced the House Foreign Affairs Committee that U.S. technicians should be forbidden to work in Iran's oil sector, for reasons of fairness and stability. That wasn't too difficult because officials at State and the Pentagon, as Franks reported to London on July 15, recognized that they "can not and will not be ready to take over any position such as that we enjoy with the Middle East." Plus, he continued, Americans were getting worried by the "narrow, heady nationalism" springing up in Iran and Egypt.[25]

The British combined such persuasiveness in Washington with PR from Downing Street. This time it was a spokesman for Prime Minister Attlee who stated that neither the government nor the AIOC ever intruded into Iran's domestic affairs. The same day as that announcement, Grady recounts in his memoirs, the British ambassador appeared in his office to suggest removing Mosaddeq, the "fanatic nationalist," as prime minister.[26] Did this mean backing a coup? Oh no, came the embarrassed reply, but surely the British and the Americans could together help someone into the premiership who'd be more "reasonable" about oil.[27]

ACCORDING TO FOREIGN OFFICE RECORDS, ATTLEE'S GOVERNMENT during 1951 had no "machinery" in Iran able to gauge popular dissent or, if necessary, to oust Mosaddeq.[28] That meant operatives of MI6, also known as the Secret Intelligence Service. But this began to change by the summer. In July, U.S. diplomats on the scene witnessed strange comings and goings at the British embassy. "They began to send in some very, very powerful intelligence officers, men of great experience and real ability," recalled the consular/political officer John Stutesman, adding, "They had absolutely ace personnel in there working on the subversive side, the clandestine side."[29]

Officials around Mosaddeq were aware of that, but they expected worse—an outright invasion. The British insisted that their property had been stolen, and Mosaddeq was under no illusion that they wouldn't resort to what State had called their "traditional methods of violence." In Abadan, bedraggled Iranian soldiers with their U.S. rifles marched through the dusty streets of the city's "native quarter" (as the British called it), and townspeople frantically placed every available barge and small craft along the jetties as a barrier against amphibious assault.

The British military chiefs and Whitehall mandarins alike were indeed contemplating an invasion. They had several plans, one of which entailed striking hard with a force of seventy thousand fighting men. The idea of invading Iran amazed the Americans, who knew that a Russo-Persian Treaty of Friendship still existed from 1921 that gave the Kremlin legal cover to intervene should Iran be attacked by a third party. Yet the Royal Navy also readied itself for action, as did the RAF.[30] No one in Washington seems to have been surprised by the size of what was being mustered in the region. They were just astounded that anyone would take the risk of attacking as the Russians waited on Iran's borders.

The British had lots of muscle to flex, which Attlee's government did with much visibility. In Cyprus, the 16th Independent Parachute Brigade Group of some thirty-five hundred men was put on standby, as were pilots and crews at the RAF Nicosia air base, a nine-hundred-mile leap away from Abadan.[31] The RAF also reinforced its bases near Baghdad, just a three-hundred-mile flight from Abadan, well within the combat radius for that era's fighter planes. Moreover, infantry was also being prepared for airlift from the Canal Zone to Basra, then, when needed, to be transported rapidly by truck or boat the forty miles to Abadan. If such combined operations occurred, the RAF planned to cover the beachhead using fighter squadrons that it would move from Jordan to fly out of Iraq. Shipborne commandos were ready to penetrate the crude defensive barriers erected at Abadan, and the Royal Navy's Persian Gulf squadron was reinforced to fourteen warships.

No other nation had the ability to deploy forces like this in the Middle East, and the Truman administration worried that Britain was about to cause a disaster of history-bending scale, maybe worse than the West's loss of China. Anxious Americans in Tehran joked about the heightening tensions. "The 38th Parallel runs right through Iran," observed one Texas oilman about a possible conflagration. "We wouldn't even have to learn a new name."[32] At this point, no one in Washington was going to keep sitting back.

Chairman of the JCS Omar Bradley observed that the warships, commandos, airmen, and soldiers that were all being marshaled "may lead to Lord knows what." He and his three service chiefs told their counterparts in London that the Pentagon needed to be informed of all decisions.[33] Senator Taft, still the most powerful figure in Congress, believed that if Britain attacked Abadan it was "almost certain" that Russia would intervene, with World War III to follow.[34] Secretary of State Acheson, to no one's surprise, let the Foreign Office know that if London decided to pull the trigger, he'd support Iran and condemn Britain at the UN Security Council.

Much of America was by now riveted. "Should the British pick this time to intervene with arms at Abadan," stated the *Cleveland Plain Dealer*, "the fat would be in the fire, and Washington would be faced with an international situation whose gravity could dwarf that of Korea."[35] Walter Lippmann, in his nationally syndicated column, urged responsible people in London to "recognize the new era in Iran."[36] But who knew if anyone was listening?

During these months, a warning from the White House was conveyed via the State Department to Herbert Morrison, who served unimpressively as foreign secretary after Bevin's death. He heard that the administration "had every confidence that British forces will continue to conduct themselves, even in the face of unreasonable action, with the restraint which is so necessary in order to retain the support of world opinion."[37] Policemen might give less polite orders, but not more pointed ones. Sensibly enough, Attlee already had doubts about using force. At a late July cabinet meeting, he vetoed plans for an invasion.

So, in mid-August, Attlee's cabinet took steps to starve Iran into submission. The government imposed sanctions on a range of British-exported products from sugar to steel, and it froze hard-currency accounts held by Iran in the Bank of England. But Britain was getting squeezed too. Not having access to Iranian oil imperiled its economy by worsening the balance of payments. Every department in Whitehall that year had to cut 15 percent of its spending and even restrict the use of official cars, and here was one of the causes. Nonetheless, from Grady's perspective, London had no interest in compromise. Peace feelers that he relayed from Mosaddeq were ignored. This was hardball.

At State, Assistant Secretary McGhee believed a second Export-Import Bank development loan made sense. Grady agreed: a loan could buy time for Iran's economy, he advised, while protecting Mosaddeq politically from Communist rivals. Buying time for Mosaddeq, however, was the last thing anyone in London wanted, and the Ex-Im Bank denied the loan that September. It claimed vague technical reasons for the decision, but Mosaddeq and Grady each knew the cause: "British pressure" in Washington.[38]

Grady by now had crossed the Foreign Office once too often. The wider context of what occurred is this: Whitehall had never expected that Americans would remain so involved in world political-military affairs after World War II. By now, except for the special situation of Palestine, U.S. pressure in Iran had become the first and most unambiguous case since 1945 of unwelcome U.S. interference in an area of British primacy.[39]

Grady was recalled the same month—at British insistence, he was certain. No fingerprints appear in U.S. or British archives, but Grady assumed that Franks made the request during one of his evenings alone with Acheson. He was replaced in Tehran by Loy Henderson, a State Department Soviet and Eastern European specialist whom the British preferred. Henderson was by no means subservient, as shown by his advice to Washington when Nehru had visited in 1949. Nonetheless, he understood, according to Anthony Eden, then his party's spokesman for foreign affairs (known informally as the shadow foreign secretary), that "the United States ought not to obtrude their views too much in a matter where large British interests were at stake."[40]

If Acheson received such a request from Franks and acted on it, which is the only convincing explanation, he had good reason: Acheson couldn't afford another quarrel with the British. He had enough on his desk to deal with, including news in September that the Russians had detonated a second atomic bomb, in Kazakhstan. By now, he also knew that Churchill had the premiership in his sights and that Iranian matters could get a lot worse with the old warrior's return.

Grady left his post on September 19 for retirement after a final visit to the silent facilities at Abadan. That same day in London, Attlee called for a general election. As is British practice, it would occur five weeks later, on Thursday, October 25. That meant the polling date was on everyone's mind for a full thirty-five days of domestic economic crisis and international upheaval. All British newspapers predicted a Conservative Party win, and most of them were decrying the country's "kicked spaniel diplomacy" in Egypt and Iran. Churchill was threatening dire consequences should Attlee decide to evacuate the last oil technicians from Abadan or pursue compromise in Egypt. And it was toward Egypt these weeks that Britain's invasion-ready forces began to turn.

IN MID-MAY 1951, ANTHONY EDEN, WHO WAS CERTAIN TO BE FOReign secretary should Churchill arrive in office, had what the State Department found to be an extremely troubling lunch with the U.S. ambassador, Walter Gifford. Eden was already a world figure, nearly as famous, in his own way, as Churchill, ever since he'd defied fascism in the 1930s. He was a tall, athletically slim, perfectly tailored model of discreet authority. With his penetrating blue eyes, his height, and his carefully trimmed gray mustache, he looked like Dean Acheson, who was four years older, and the two were often mistaken for each other. Professionals at the State Department, as in the Foreign Office, found Eden impressive.

Eden eschewed the chummy male clubbiness of St. James's, so they met quietly alone in the large paneled dining room of Gifford's Hyde Park residence. If the West's role in Egypt deteriorated, Eden told Gifford, then Western influence overall would surely decline elsewhere in the Middle East. No need to spell out the details about "elsewhere":

Eden was tying Britain's quandary in Egypt to the U.S. presence in Saudi Arabia. That included the world's largest overseas community of Americans—living in an ARAMCO township near Dhahran—which itself was adjacent to the expanding air base that was still the only U.S. military installation in western Asia. Eden didn't dwell on this fact. He just emphasized that U.S. and British interests throughout the Middle East were "completely interlocked," and then he got to the point.*[41]

Britain should assert its rights in Egypt, he told Gifford, by having Royal Navy destroyers accompany oil tankers through the Suez Canal—a bellicose act that violated a host of articles in the 1888 convention that governed the waterway. He appeared to be laying the groundwork for getting U.S. diplomatic and military support should all-out violence follow, which was likely. When Gifford reported the dialogue to State, George McGhee and Nitze, as well as Acheson, were shaken. Sending in the gunboats at this juncture would have been wildly provocative, and Eden knew it—so much so that he didn't include this feeler in the memorandum of conversation he dutifully submitted to the Foreign Office. It was "hard to believe that Eden seriously entertains such views," came the reply from Foggy Bottom, and Gifford was instructed to tell all concerned to show "great restraint" in Egypt as well as in Iran.[42]

Washington was increasingly worried about keeping the wrong company in contests between "nationalism" and "imperialism"—at least beyond its own sphere of interest in Latin America. That Egypt had highly colonialist views toward the Sudan mattered not a jot to opinion at State as its officials tried to persuade Britain to concede that vast terrain, and its nearly six million inhabitants, to Farouk.

By late summer, insurgent attacks against British troops in the Canal Zone were multiplying as "liberation guerrillas" began to supplement their stones and homemade bombs with gunfire. The volatile cities of Fayid and Ismailia were within the zone—which had no formal

---

*By now, the only British presence within the Saudi kingdom were people involved with locust eradication, as well as a handful of RAF instructors. The British ambassador implored Whitehall to send more high-level delegations to show the Saudis that they hadn't been forgotten by old friends. Yet the sudden advent of wealth had released an enthusiastic materialism of the sort that tends to find friends only among those who can ensure the acquisition of even greater wealth. Britain had little to offer.

boundaries, let alone well-guarded ones—and were only eighty-five and seventy-eight miles, respectively, from teeming Cairo. Churchill, who growled that none of this cheek would be occurring if he were prime minister, declared the attacks to be a "bastard child of the Iranian situation."[43] During its last weeks in office, Attlee's government wearily tried to cope with defiance from Farouk, from Mosaddeq, and from each country's "fanatic nationalists," a term by now commonplace in Whitehall for what in the West would be called "patriots."

On October 8, Farouk's government announced an end to all negotiations with the British and, a week later, rescinded the 1936 Anglo-Egyptian Treaty. At about 8:15 on the morning of the sixteenth, protesters brought in from Cairo appeared in Ismailia. Riots followed. Vehicles were burned in the streets; the British equivalent of the American PX (post exchange) was looted, with families trapped inside; two Egyptians were shot dead; and the city's Muslim Brotherhood declared a jihad. Within twenty-four hours, Farouk threatened the British with "another Mossadeq-Iran tragedy," by which he seems to have meant nationalization of the Suez Canal Company. His only concession to peace and quiet was to say that his army would absorb the guerrillas, which had come to include suicide attackers, or fedayeen. And he now made himself king of the Sudan as well. Angry men in Whitehall, and others at General Headquarters Middle East in Fayid, accused Farouk of preparing the ground for Communism, while in the same breath they blamed the fiercely anti-Communist Muslim Brotherhood for providing recruits to the "liberation guerrillas."

Egypt's disorder became part of the ever-bleaker setting of Britain's elections. Churchill was nearly seventy-seven, hard of hearing, and remote. Tories in the Commons whispered that he dealt regularly with no more than twenty of them. But he was the leader, and he said this vote would be a historic choice. He faulted Labour for stripping the country's defenses. Attlee had caused the worst drop in stature, he blustered, since Britain had lost the American colonies. Nye Bevan replied to this invective by remarking that the idea of Churchill handling "peacetime problems" was as fantastic to him as seeing a dinosaur at an electrical engineering exhibition.

Three weeks before the election, Attlee evacuated all remaining

British personnel from Abadan. The Iranians would be left alone to twist in the wind. But toward Egypt, there'd be no restraint. Seeing little hope for negotiation, General Headquarters Middle East Land Forces prepared to occupy Cairo and Alexandria, Egypt's two largest cities. Clearly, there would be a grave cost in British lives, but there'd also be an upside. "A riotous mob would not distinguish between Englishmen and other Europeans," army planners concluded.[44] Vulnerable U.S. citizens would conveniently fall under "other Europeans" during the violence. Therefore, it was thought, warships from the 6th Fleet would accompany the Royal Navy to Port Said to evacuate whatever Americans survived— hence drawing in Washington to help "restore order."

Given the buildup of recent months against Iran, more than sixty thousand British fighting men were in Egypt. Meanwhile, General Sir Brian Robertson, now serving as commander in chief of the Middle East Land Forces, had been in London earlier that month. He spoke to reporters before returning to his troops. "I am taking back with me two dozen new polo sticks and have every intention of using them," he said.[45] Robertson had a four-goal handicap, and he saw no reason why regimental matches at General Headquarters shouldn't continue three times a week for years to come, provided the weather was cool.

Meanwhile, the largest airlift of troops anywhere since World War II got under way in mid-October. Six thousand more British soldiers swooped into Egypt, landing along the west bank of the Suez Canal. Docks and ordnance depots were secured by paratroop battalions flown in from Cyprus. Outside Paris, at Supreme Headquarters Allied Powers in Rocquencourt, Dwight Eisenhower, the West's foremost general on active service, was observing all this Middle Eastern turmoil. On October 20, he wrote to Averell Harriman, who was now serving in the White House as Truman's foreign policy adviser. "Our side deals primarily with the classes that have been exploiting their own people since time immemorial," he warned.[46]

As expected, Churchill and the Conservative Party won the election on October 25, and Dean Acheson, for his part, began to worry about whom the new prime minister would be bringing with him to power. Acheson likened them to "people who have been asleep for five years."[47] (Or longer, considering Eden's readiness for gunboat diplomacy.) The problem went deeper, however, than Acheson recognized. Churchill, Eden, and the war-hardened men around them had been out of office since the summer of 1945. They hadn't directly been responsible for any of the arduous dealings with Washington thereafter. Nor had they been on the front lines of global conflict since defeating the Reich. The notion of serving as anyone's junior partner was not in their experience.

14

CHURCHILL IS BACK

Sometimes there is a choice between being and well-being for a nation.

—Winston Churchill quoting Oliver Cromwell to Harry Truman, 1952

Eʀʟʏ on ꜰʀɪᴅᴀʏ ᴇᴠᴇɴɪɴɢ, ᴏᴄᴛᴏʙᴇʀ 26, 1951, ᴋɪɴɢ ɢᴇᴏʀɢᴇ ᴠɪ received Churchill at Buckingham Palace and invited him to form a government. Churchill spent the following week doing just that, assembling his cabinet from home, 28 Hyde Park Gate, near Kensington Gardens. Reporters stood outside the cream-colored house and chronicled the comings and goings of well-known political figures such as Anthony Eden and the former minister of war transport Lord Leathers. *Tailor and Cutter*, the London trade journal, observed these men to be properly dressed, most in their sixties, favoring stiff white collars and bowler hats in the Edwardian manner. Churchill conducted late-morning meetings, working in bed, smoking a cigar, wearing a quilted jacket, and gesturing languidly with his small, well-cared-for hands. He told each prospective cabinet member that the country's financial position looked dire and that the war years might have been easier. Then, within two weeks, he assured supporters that he'd seen worse. In the Commons, he saluted the memory of Ernest Bevin and stated that Britain's place in the world would be restored no matter what.[1]

The men who joined him in government were intelligent, experienced, and equally confident. Anthony Eden, who became foreign secretary for the third time, expected to be molding U.S. power and foreign policy to British ends. Another incoming minister, Harold Macmillan—who'd rise to head Defence, the Foreign Office, and then Treasury, finally to become prime minister in 1957—believed that the empire could approximate American wealth and power.[2] The new secretary of state for the colonies, the aristocrat-industrialist Oliver Lyttelton, anticipated that Britain would regain its pre–World War II global sway by maintaining a grip on world shipping. Another cabinet member, the science adviser Lord Cherwell, simply declared that the empire and commonwealth "in the end should dominate America."[3]

On the other side of the Atlantic, having tracked opinions in Congress and the administration, Oliver Franks also felt optimistic that Britain could have a global role second to none. He wrote to the Foreign Office of "our joint leadership of the world." Lots of Americans assumed Britain already had such a position. That's apparent in *This World of Ours: London*, a popular 1951 travel documentary. In one scene the camera shows the ministries along Whitehall, and the narrator points to a solid neo-baroque building identified as the War Office—from which, he explains, England is right now "governing the lives of millions of the world's people."[4] Yet the only way to ensure such joint leadership, Franks warned, was for Britain's economy to be free from U.S. aid. Then his government could project great influence "out of all proportion to our power."[5] Churchill couldn't have said it better.

Nye Bevan, of course, had his own twist on the subject. He didn't "believe the American nation has the experience, sagacity, or self-restraint necessary for world leadership," though he generously added "at this time."[6] As for the Russians, whom he'd recently wanted to attack, they remained what today the Pentagon calls the "most stressing competitor." For the moment, however, there were no outright clashes with the Kremlin at a time when the West faced an array of other, indirect dangers.

Churchill made himself defense minister, as he had during World War II. He insisted the duties were inseparable from being premier in hazardous times, and he and his cabinet believed the times to be hazardous indeed. Despite Churchill's pronouncement that the British Empire would be as strong as ever, it faced a series of emergencies: a faltering economy, an intensified guerrilla war in Malaya, rising violence in Egypt, humiliation and loss of oil revenues in Iran. One way or another, tackling each of these problems would involve Washington. But the Americans had their own challenges, which included stalemate in Korea and budget battles in Congress—those two being connected. Bob Lovett, who had replaced Marshall as defense secretary in September, had to plead on the Hill for what he called the "minimum safety level" of Pentagon spending. Unhelpfully, from the British perspective, the Americans kept demanding that Britain boost its own defense budget and stop "sabotaging" the hopes for European unity, to cite the Connecticut senator Brien McMahon, who chaired the Joint Atomic Energy Committee.[7]

"I wonder whether you would like me to come to see you," Churchill cabled President Truman ten days after the election. "There are many things I need to talk over with you."[8] Churchill had last been to America when he'd accepted MIT's invitation two and a half years earlier. Now he wanted to go as soon as possible. But there was much to arrange before he could leave, as well as bargaining chips to put on the table. Before writing to Truman, he had sent greetings to Joseph Stalin, with whom he had not communicated since the July 1945 Potsdam Conference. He received a "Thank You" in reply and then duly reported to Truman that he had been in touch with "U.J." (Uncle Joe). The remark dated him. No one had used that nickname since the war.

THREE WEEKS BEFORE CHURCHILL'S ELECTION, THE BRITISH SUFfered a blow in Malaya. Sir Henry Gurney—the high commissioner for the Federation of Malaya, aged fifty-three, and formerly the unshakable second-in-command of the Palestine mandate—was being driven to Fraser's Hill, a mountain resort sixty miles north of Kuala Lumpur that the British used as a weekend home for its cool air and golf. Gurney, traveling in a black Rolls-Royce that flew the Federation flag, was accompanied by an armored scout car as well as a Land Rover carrying five policemen. The last several miles of the road are cut into the side of steep, densely forested slopes and wind up to three thousand feet in a series of hairpin turns. At one of them, on the afternoon of October 6, 1951, at 1:15, the lumbering Rolls—led by the Land Rover, with the armored car trailing far behind—drove slowly into the killing box. A thirty-eight-man guerrilla platoon was waiting for a target of opportunity. The platoon first machine-gunned the Land Rover, shooting the police, then turned on the official car, killing Gurney's Malay driver. At that point, Gurney, wearing a light-colored tropical suit and stretching to his full height of six feet two inches, opened the right-hand door of the Rolls, stepped into the road, and walked into the fire, which killed him and sent his body spiraling into a drainage ditch.[9] The guerrillas then dashed back into the jungle. Gurney's wife and his private secretary both survived.

Immediately after winning the election, Churchill dispatched his new colonial secretary, Oliver Lyttelton, to Singapore. Malcolm MacDonald greeted him at the tightly secured airport, and the two made their way to the Phoenix Park headquarters, where, with MacDonald at his side, Lyttelton gave a speech promising law and order. Before long, the authorities had put a high bounty on the heads of the twenty-six top guerrillas, dead or alive. The biggest sum was equivalent to $83,500, which was as much as the first prize in the Malayan Chinese Association Lottery.

Meanwhile, in Egypt, a bounty was also to be had, though in this case it came from extremists who published an offer equaling $2,880 to anyone killing General Brian Robertson, the tough, polo-playing member of the Royal Engineers who commanded British forces in Egypt. But Egypt, as Churchill had kept repeating during his campaign, was only part of a wider disorder that included Iran.

When Churchill returned to Downing Street, Prime Minister Mosaddeq was at the midpoint of a six-week visit to the United States, which included stops in New York, Philadelphia, and Washington. The trip spanned the period from October 6 to November 18 and reaped hugely favorable publicity. Mosaddeq used his visit to explain both to

Washington officials and to the American public why the Anglo-Iranian Oil Company had been nationalized and why British invasion forces in the Gulf still posed a threat to his country. He met with Truman and Acheson. He addressed the UN. At the National Press Club, he spoke of the ideals of 1776 and of independence from the British Empire and received rousing applause. Thereafter, the Truman administration promised "careful consideration" for a $120 million loan. In the background, however, the State Department's Bureau of British Commonwealth and Northern European Affairs kept updating the Foreign Office on every step of Mosaddeq's journey.

Mosaddeq returned home via Cairo. At the city's King Farouk I Airport, he received a hero's welcome. According to Egypt's well-controlled press, two million people lined the streets to greet him as he was driven to Shepheard's Hotel, a longtime center of British social life. It was a time of growing insurrection against the foreign presence. In the cities of Fayid and Ismailia, and elsewhere in the Canal Zone, guerrillas were attacking British troops and planting improvised explosives. Mosaddeq spent three days in Cairo, during which he signed a treaty with Farouk's ministers pledging to end British imperialism. He then concluded his forty-seven-day journey before thousands of supporters in Tehran's Fawzia Square who cheered "the heroic Egyptian nation" and chanted, "Death to England."

In London, Churchill faced economic turmoil. As winter approached, stocks of household coal were lower than at any point since the war. In fact, this was the first time since the general strike of 1926 that domestic supply wouldn't meet demand, and hundreds of thousands of tons of coal now had to be imported from the United States and from India. Supplies of wheat, sugar, and fats were sparser than during the stark days before Lend-Lease in 1941. The black market in horse meat was reviving.

Britain was once again buying more than it could pay for out of current earnings, and it was also sliding ever more into debt with the rest of the sterling area, which was an acute difference from 1949. Besides, the entire sterling area was out of balance not just with the dollar but with Continental Europe and the rest of the world. On Tuesday afternoon, November 6, Churchill told the Commons that the country had to stop spending more than it earned or face "national bankruptcy."[10]

Meanwhile, the Americans were calling for Churchill's new government to boost defense spending, catalyze a united Europe, and compromise in Egypt and Iran, among other minor requests. So Churchill began playing rough. In the late afternoon of December 6, he spoke in the Commons about the "great and ever growing U.S. atomic bomber base in East Anglia" (in fact, there were now five bases equipped to service strategic bombers).[11] While acknowledging that Britain had agreed to the stationing of U.S. air wings, and saying arrangements would continue as long as needed, he also began to argue that His Majesty's government have the final say in all decisions to conduct an atomic offensive from any of these bases.

Truman and Acheson were concerned. So were Lovett and the Joint Chiefs. They had heard such demands from Churchill the previous February, but they thought he'd been stilled on this controversy. No one could figure out if he was serious, but he kept raising the stakes through December. Russian paratroopers might descend in a surprise attack, he said, and put the U.S. air bases out of action. To defend them, he argued, he therefore needed to mobilize 125,000 sharp-eyed volunteers, at some expense, and to revive the Home Guard, the local defense cadres who, armed with American M1917 rifles, had stood alert in their towns and villages during World War II to defend against German invasion. Parliament approved. The message was clear: Britain was taking grave and costly risks for the Americans, and those critically important U.S. bomber bases existed only by British consent.

It wasn't just the British who dreaded having to rely on the U.S. Strategic Air Command to counter a Red Army invasion of Western Europe; so did NATO allies on the Continent who feared SAC's bombs would be falling on them, once they were occupied. But maybe there was an alternative.

If there had to be a war, perhaps it could be fought only with conventional weapons, and—provided NATO's armies were strong enough—the Russian attackers might be brought to a standstill in central Europe. No one wanted the only option to be atomic bombs. As a result, the allies had promised General Eisenhower early in 1951 that they'd devote more of their GDP to building up their armies. The eventual target would be ninety divisions, a huge number considering that in World War II the United States had sixty divisions in Europe. Washington, in turn, created the Mutual Security Program—successor organization to the Marshall Plan—to offer the allies billions of dollars in military, economic, and technical aid. A strong conventional defense against the Red Army was intended to follow, and this design sounded promising. But it began to crumble in November, a month after Churchill's election, at a NATO Council meeting in Rome.

As today, Europe's social democracies really had little desire for high military spending, let alone at these levels, and they'd welcome any excuse to avoid such a buildup. Not least, the prospect of fighting another *conventional* war in Europe sounded nearly as ghastly to them as fighting a nuclear one.

All the alliance's military chiefs and ministers were in Rome, including General Eisenhower and his aides from Supreme Headquarters. The glamorous and popular foreign secretary Eden attended, though in paralyzing pain from stomach spasms, which he bravely tried to conceal. Acheson came too, having flown in from Paris with Ambassador David Bruce and Averell Harriman after attending the Sixth Session of the UN General Assembly, as well as Harriman's sixtieth birthday party, which was a black-tie dinner dance at the Ritz. They had been joined at Harriman's bash by Secretary of the Treasury Snyder, who, because he was traveling with his wife, Evelyn, chose the scenic route and went to Rome by train.

The conference extended from November 24 to 30 in the Foro Italico. Before his much-anticipated address on the twenty-seventh, Snyder therefore had three full days of listening to speeches ever more detached from economic and political reality. What occurred doesn't appear in Acheson's State Department memoirs, but as Lewis Douglas said when they were published in 1969, volumes could be written about what Acheson didn't include.

On November 27, Snyder presented a different view to all the busy alliance-builders. The United States, he explained, wouldn't provide unlimited financial support for a NATO defense force on the scale that everyone had been discussing. Moreover, Snyder said, he'd have to impose limits on the amount of machine tools and raw materials that the United States could deliver to Europe. The U.S. Treasury had not been budgeting for the "dreams" of munificent military aid that would be required to achieve such force levels in Europe, so "dreams" they'd have to remain.[12]

As a member of the NATO Council, Snyder conceded that Washington remained open to helping its allies. But he emphasized that everyone had to pay their fair share—as NATO's critics still demand today. The way Snyder saw it, he had jarred the delegates—including his friends—from their false hopes of open-ended U.S. largesse, and not for the first time.

From there, however, enduring quarrels arose within NATO. Of course, the allies never got close to the fanciful goal of ninety divisions. With some exception for Britain, as well as for France, which was fighting in Indochina, NATO members had little interest in higher defense spending. For decades, promises were made, and went unfulfilled. Despite Snyder's démarche, the allies began to insist that the best deterrent to Soviet inroads in Western Europe was to instead build up their generous social welfare states.

Within two weeks, Churchill's government was the first to backtrack. Churchill had devoted much of his previous year in opposition to tormenting Attlee for inadequate defense spending, yet in early December, just weeks after being elected, he declared that the military budget had to be cut. Arms production needed to shrink by 20 percent, Churchill said, and the $13.1 billion that Attlee had pledged for defense would have to be stretched into additional years. Fleet Street howled that the election's real winner was Nye Bevan, who had easily been returned to Parliament, as had his wife, Jennie Lee. After all, Churchill was now adhering to Bevan's position on bomber bases (have veto power) and defense budgets (cut them). Labour MPs gloated at Churchill's having been proved spectacularly wrong about spending. All he could say in response was that Nye, "by accident, perhaps not from the best of motives, happened to be right."[13]

. . .

TODAY IT'S SAID THAT "HISTORIANS TEND TO AVERT THEIR EYES" from Churchill's second time as premier because of his age and failing health. If so, they'd be myopic. The best prose heard or read was yet to come, as Harold Macmillan chronicled, adding that "Churchill's mastery of the House of Commons remained as great as ever."[14] These are also the years of Churchill's most forceful handling of the Americans by far. Altogether, they are an intensely dramatic part of his long life, as they are of the British Empire's modern history. Nothing is more riveting than to see how people, as well as nations, react when there is no way out.

On the evening of Saturday, December 22, a week before he was to set sail, Churchill spent twenty minutes delivering what he called a "State of the Nation" broadcast to his fellow subjects. He told them Britain faced peril of a different kind from in 1940. Financial disaster was approaching, and emergency measures were now being taken that required still deeper cuts in consumption, from food to Frigidaires. He warned against having illusions that any other nation would help solve these problems: no one, he said, was "going to keep the British lion as a pet."[15] The stage was set for Churchill to show himself all too effective in confronting the Americans.

Churchill also let it be known, before leaving for New York, that he wasn't coming to seek dollars. But, said Senator McMahon to Truman, this was, "of course, nonsense."[16] The Foreign Office didn't send over an agenda for the meetings. State Department officials nonetheless anticipated that Churchill wanted to explore "spheres of influence." It was a concept the Americans viewed with almost Wilsonian moral disdain, and the position papers being prepared at State abjured such ideas.

Yet tact was needed, the president told a rare assembly of the Joint Chiefs, the service secretaries, and the State Department's top echelon. He wanted to ensure that the British "would go all out for us in Asia rather than follow the policy of dragging their feet as in the past."[17] Privately, he told Acheson that he felt somewhat depressed that there was little he could do to make the trip worthwhile for Churchill, so the two of them devised an approach: Truman would concentrate on being friendly and noncommittal to the great man, and Acheson, casting himself as the blamable medieval minister, would handle the expected difficulties.

Churchill and his party boarded the *Queen Mary* in Southampton on December 29. There were thirty-four of these Argonauts, to recall the name he had given his fellow adventurers at Yalta. They included Eden, of course, and once more General Pug Ismay, now 1st Baron Ismay, the new secretary of commonwealth relations, who had been Churchill's indispensable military assistant during World War II. Also aboard were Frederick Lindemann, a.k.a. Lord Cherwell, currently handling atomic issues; the chief of the Imperial General Staff and the first sea lord; Oliver Franks and the U.S. ambassador Walter Gifford. Two detectives provided security.

Churchill was joined by his physician, Lord Moran—one of the original Argonauts—who, in his memoirs, recounts his patient's racing pulse and an anxiety so severe aboard ship that it was "a canker in his mind."[18] The trip was an enormous gamble. There was no telling how the Americans would react. Churchill lamented that on previous visits he had come as an equal, but probably not now. "They have become so great and we are now so small," he reflected to Moran the night before reaching New York.[19] Yes, these men had confidence in their abilities and in the empire's potential, but they also knew their nation's predicament. Moran reports a general feeling that they were all about to be thrown to the wolves.

The *Queen Mary* entered the choppy Hudson River Narrows early on the rainy Saturday morning of January 5, 1952, then stopped for these intrepid travelers to board a U.S. Coast Guard cutter that took them to the Brooklyn Army Terminal. When Churchill disembarked, into a crowd of thirteen hundred military police, soldiers, and city patrolmen, he cut a familiar figure, wearing a gray homburg and a gray storm coat with fur collar, smoking a cigar, and carrying a cane. He gave a brief press conference, fielded a question about also finding time to meet with Stalin, and tried to ignore some two hundred Irish American protesters in the distance shouting, "What's the next stop—Fort Knox?"[20] That meant the U.S. gold supply. The visitors were then driven to Municipal Airport, where the president's plane waited for the one-hour flight to Washington.

Ominously, during his last day at sea, Churchill had received via secure radiophone the Treasury's top secret, year-end figures, which disclosed Britain's plummeting gold and dollar reserves. Those numbers showed his country to be facing its third and worst economic crisis since the war—nearly a billion dollars of the sterling area's central reserves had been lost in just the previous quarter, which was far worse than analysts in Whitehall had expected. The Treasury was to release the latest numbers in London on Monday night.

Churchill had four objectives: to buttress Britain's waning prestige by demonstrating a special intimacy with the Americans; to obtain greater U.S. support in Malaya and in the festering Middle East; to gain a larger voice in NATO decisions, certainly on any atomic offensive; and to remind the Americans that British goodwill remained vital to their future. President Truman's sole objective, in contrast, was to indulge the prime minister in nonbinding discussion about current events. There was zero enthusiasm in Washington for taking on more international obligations. The Americans felt themselves "spread all over from hell to breakfast," as Secretary of Defense Bob Lovett had put it, and there were reasons.[21] In Korea, for example, the army compelled GIs to recover, whenever possible, every shell casing used in the heat of battle from rifles and artillery to be recycled as scrap metal, due to production and distribution failures at home.[22]

At 12:30 that Saturday afternoon, in thirty-degree winter weather, Truman was on the tarmac at National Airport's military terminal flanked by the entire cabinet, the Joint Chiefs, all the ambassadors of the British Commonwealth, and the 3rd Infantry Honor Guard. After welcoming words, the president, Churchill, Eden, and others were then whisked across Memorial Bridge to Blair House for a lunch of steak and strawberry shortcake. Everyone gathered that early evening on the 243-foot presidential yacht, *Williamsburg*, where serious talks began. It's been assumed ever since, including by Randolph Churchill and most of the press at the time, that the president and his guests cruised the Potomac. In fact, wind gusts were forbidding, and the boat didn't leave its berth at the Washington Navy Yard on the Anacostia River.[23]

The conversation aboard the *Williamsburg* amounted to four hours of often strained debate. Truman relayed a charge from the U.S. Navy:

that the British were, in effect, trading with the enemy, because their vessels made up half of all non-Communist shipping into Chinese ports. Churchill claimed to know nothing about the issue, which was odd; it had been raised in Parliament. (These were some 160 British-flagged vessels that had mostly ferried Malayan rubber and tin to China during 1951.) He in turn broached the possibility of America's sending "token forces" to Suez to help defend the canal in the face of intensifying violence. That was a nonstarter with the Americans. Their response was simple, as it had been to the Labour government: they'd give full diplomatic support to protecting the canal so long as Britain did "not go beyond what is necessary."[24] Yet Churchill wouldn't drop the subject.

A telling moment occurred when General Ismay expressed puzzlement that Washington dealt with the dominions—including Canada, Australia, and India—directly and not by going through the Commonwealth Office in London. Acheson in his memoirs writes that Ismay was "utterly dumbfounded" to hear this.[25] If Acheson's account is true, it's damning. For a soldier-diplomat-minister of Ismay's stature and competence to believe that London still managed the most sensitive international issues of these vast independent nations is evidence of self-deception at the highest levels.

Churchill professed himself pleased at how the evening unfolded. "We talked as equals," he told his physician before swallowing a sleeping pill and going to bed at the embassy.[26] The ability to cause excitement can, in the short term, translate into power, and—once again prime minister—Churchill availed himself of that. The anxiety that Moran had noticed in Churchill when crossing the Atlantic was gone. Moran would never mention such queasiness again in describing Churchill's dealings with the Americans.

The following afternoon, Churchill occupied himself with a visit to the Pentagon, where he met with Bob Lovett. Records are sparse about what they discussed and what Churchill might have seen. If full details of U.S. plans for nuclear war were revealed—as hadn't been done before—Churchill would have gotten an eyeful. All was set for the Strategic Air Command to attack 123 cities in the East, killing millions—with bombers launched mainly from bases in England. Whatever he saw,

Churchill said that he hoped the Russians themselves understood what might be ignited.

Then two days of White House talks began on Monday morning, January 7, in the West Wing's green-carpeted Cabinet Room (the mansion itself still undergoing renovations). Churchill had been dreading this moment. Given the five-hour time difference, the disastrous economic figures from the British Treasury would arrive in Washington at midday. Yet while Secretaries Snyder, Acheson, and Lovett looked on, he offered the president what he called a "declaration of independence," pledging to meet British needs with British resources. England's economic shortcomings were pitched as a measure of its virtues: it had paid dearly to rearm; it was sacrificing to ensure worldwide military deployments on behalf of the West; and half the world's trade depended on sterling. Anyway, this wasn't supposed to be an economics conference, was it? With that vexing issue pushed aside, all relevant military, diplomatic, and regional questions between the two nations then passed under review.

Churchill's listeners didn't grasp the severity of Britain's desperate finances, for two reasons: they'd seen the predicament before, and Churchill was trying to minimize the danger. Afterward, and privately with Snyder and Acheson, Truman would compare Britain's plight to routine U.S. budget decisions. If only it had been. But no one spoke about the cracking foundation of an outer fortress. Instead, the Americans asked for whatever surplus copper, aluminum, nickel, and tin the British might possess, saying they needed it all for defense production.

On this first day of the White House talks, Truman explained that the United States could only do so much for Britain, after which he felt compelled to tell Churchill and Eden that he hoped they would not think America was being "an ungrateful child."[27] (He is surely the last president even to have considered such an idea.)

Due to the year's approaching presidential campaign, Truman continued, there were political issues to consider. The Republicans were certain to cast Mr. Churchill as the embodiment of a grasping, mendicant ally. Any missteps at this point between their two nations, the president warned, and the British might soon be facing coldly unsympathetic Republicans in the White House. Churchill replied that his government intended "to do its duty," whether popular or not in America. It was a soldierly yet unhelpful sentiment.

The Eighty-Second Congress convened at noon on Tuesday, January 8, during the second day of the Truman-Churchill talks. Among other business, Republicans and Democrats alike charged that the United States had lost world leadership in aircraft production. With the prime minister in town—and an American Airlines lobbying campaign under way that claimed London was using aid dollars to manufacture jets—the Senate Armed Services Committee found it timely to explore why. Additionally, this week was becoming the costliest to date in the Korean War for U.S. planes lost to ground fire and dogfights. Therefore, Senator Taft and the Republicans, who already had General Omar Bradley in their sights for "appeasing" the Kremlin, hauled him out of the meetings to explain.[28]

Churchill ignored the politicking. In the Cabinet Room, he wanted to talk technology—about combining U.S. and British defense manufacturing, as he had proposed at Fulton in 1946, and even to discuss individual weapons.[29] For instance, he spent as much time comparing the innovative British .276-caliber rifle to the standard U.S. .30-caliber M1 as he did on other policy matters. It's not in the transcripts, but Churchill also put a bigger tech issue on the table: he informed the Americans that Britain was ready to test an atom bomb.

Other military issues were addressed, among them the question of where to locate NATO's permanent headquarters, and in the end the Americans made the decision, choosing France rather than Britain. Throughout these two days, one big problem went unmentioned: it was whether—within the NATO command structure—a U.S. or a British admiral would be responsible for commanding the Atlantic. The Americans had thought the issue settled in their favor a year earlier, but it had kept ringing like a cracked bell through British politics ever since, with Churchill voicing strong opposition in the Commons.[30] Each side now agreed to delay discussing the matter until later in the visit.

On Wednesday, January 9, the two parties released a closing statement: they intended to stand together in Europe, the Middle East, and Asia. The message was clear. The British Empire and Commonwealth was America's strongest ally in the world struggle, and close ties were vital. Although it was too early to announce, U.S. support for this stance would even be expressed materially at month's end by a grant of $300 million in military aid.

That same week, news arrived that reinforced a heightening U.S. appreciation of closer political-military cooperation, certainly in Southeast Asia. General de Lattre, who for fifty-five incandescent weeks had personified all hopes for victory in Indochina, had died in a Paris clinic, having been rapidly consumed by cancer. Should French forces in Vietnam now fail to halt the Vietminh, as again seemed possible, a strong British presence in the region would be more important than ever.

Truman gave his State of the Union address that Wednesday afternoon. Churchill received far more enthusiastic applause when entering the House of Representatives' gallery than did the president. The spirited ovation showed how Americans admired him as a friend, if not as the present director of British policy. Toward evening, he and a party of eight boarded a private car, attached to the regular Penn Central train, from nearby Union Station for New York. He visited Bernard Baruch for two days and received journalists in the Sixty-Sixth Street apartment, where he once more raised the need for "a token" U.S. Army brigade in Suez, or maybe just a battalion of marines. On Saturday, January 12, Churchill, Moran, and several aides took the night train to Ottawa to brief Canada's government on the week's accomplishments. Prime Minister Louis St. Laurent lost no time in reporting back to Truman and Acheson that he had heard a Churchillian tirade against even the idea of the U.S. Navy assuming command of the Atlantic.

Churchill returned to Washington on Wednesday morning, January 16, to address a joint meeting of Congress and to resume talks with Truman. Mrs. Truman attended on Capitol Hill, as did the president's cabinet, while the president himself watched on TV from the White House. Churchill was again wildly applauded. In a firm, strong voice, he once more used the same reassuring yet invidious line he'd spun out at Fulton and MIT: half a century from now, he told the legislators, they'd still be seeing eighty million Britons spread about the world and united in defense of Anglo-Saxon traditions. He also offered a word for Secretary of State Acheson's hard work in arranging the recent meetings. That brought silence. Parts of his thirty-seven-minute speech had an edge. He asserted there was no prospect of his country joining any federation of states—meaning a united Europe—nor, he said, would Britain accept any rebukes for failing to do so. And he asked Congress for "token forces" to be placed in Suez, which again brought silence. Within hours, Truman forbade any official response to that request.

On Friday morning, a British delegation led by the science adviser Lord Cherwell trooped to the Pentagon to get their own insights on U.S. war planning. Acheson reported that they were "shaken" when he encountered them later that afternoon.[31] Lovett gave his visitors lunch, his military men delivered a briefing, and thereafter the Pentagon allowed a public statement saying that use of atomic weapons would be "a matter of joint decision" between the two governments "in an emergency." Once Churchill read the communiqué, he tore it up and threw the pieces into the air.[32] No Americans involved with this issue ever thought those vague words gave Churchill or his successors a veto, which he understood perfectly.

At 3:00, Churchill, Ambassador Franks, Cherwell, and three other top advisers met with Truman in what was considered a "courtesy call" by the departing prime minister. It was anything but. Churchill insisted it was "incredible" to have a U.S. admiral in the role of supreme allied commander for the Atlantic, emphasizing that "it was possible not very long ago for one country to sink 525 German U-boats compared to 174 by the United States." (These unhelpful World War II comparisons always set the Americans' teeth on edge.) In *Present at the Creation*, Acheson describes what followed. The Royal Navy, Churchill told the Americans, had protected the young United States from European aggression in the days of its weakness; so now, in the plenitude of its power, bearing as it did the awful burden of atomic command and responsibility for the final word of peace and war, the United States should make room for Britain "upon that western sea whose floor is white with the bones of Englishmen."[33]

The silence thereafter was equally a tribute to the difficulty of answering such oratory and a sign that no answer would be made.[34]

Churchill had closed his speech to Congress by declaring that "the interests and ideals which unite our two peoples far outweigh those which divide them," and that remark had appeared harmless—a deft rhetorical move that allowed him at once to acknowledge a problem and wave it away.[35] But it didn't stop *Pravda* from reporting, in a well-informed jab at the end of his visit, that the White House talks had highlighted "contradictions" between the United States and what it referred to as the "junior" (*mladshiy*) capitalist partner.

CHURCHILL LEFT NEW YORK ON THE TWENTY-FOURTH ABOARD THE *Queen Mary.* Eden had flown back earlier after speaking at Columbia University about the strength of a united commonwealth and receiving an honorary degree. Returning to London swiftly meant that he served as acting head of the government while Churchill steamed across the Atlantic, with the two staying in touch via ship-to-shore encrypted radiophone. Eden, therefore, held responsibility on January 26, when Egypt exploded.

General George "Bobbie" Erskine, the short, brisk Royal Rifle Corps officer who commanded troops in the Canal Zone, had lit the match in Ismailia a day earlier. Erskine and local British authorities believed that Egyptian auxiliary police were arming nationalist guerrillas. So at 8:50 on the morning of January 25, he surrounded the city's police headquarters in French Square with Centurion tanks and fifteen hundred troops. He demanded surrender within the hour. The Egyptians refused, so Erskine ordered his men to take the building. The outgunned, outnumbered police fought with desperate bravery for two hours before surrendering. Forty-six of them lay dead and fifty-eight wounded. Survivors were taken prisoner on what, in 2009, Egypt's government began to commemorate as National Police Day. The British suffered three fatalities.

Cairo erupted the next morning, which Egyptians call Black Saturday. There'd be fifty-six dead, including eleven British residents burned alive, as was the Canadian trade representative, with hundreds injured. The famous Shepheard's Hotel was torched (today's government-owned Shepheard's is a replica), so too the Turf Club, the BOAC office, and the Ford dealership, which was believed to be British, as were scores of other buildings identified with the empire. Eden asked for U.S. support should British forces try to suppress the violence, but got nothing. The

Americans wouldn't agree to mediate, and British soldiers didn't dare to intervene further. The Russians, for their part, released incendiary propaganda aimed to madden Egypt's nationalists, with some special tailoring for the Muslim Brotherhood.

Rioters then turned on the king. "Go to your mother in America, Farouk!" cried the mobs. (His mother lived in Beverly Hills.) Within a month, London was weighing all sorts of contingency plans: for cooperating with the Israeli army, for transferring Middle East Headquarters to Gaza, for internationalizing the Suez Canal's operations, and for just letting Egypt stew in its own juice. The U.S. embassy received lucidly written reports from nameless sources that Communists had instigated the violence. For the sake of stability, Washington didn't use the opportunity to push the British to evacuate Suez. Instead, the State Department acquired police equipment to sell to Farouk's government, including a thousand submachine guns.

Churchill was back in the House of Commons on January 28. He praised imperial forces in the Middle East for keeping the Suez Canal open and defending civilization. He also praised the fighting men who were opposing Communist-inspired disorder in Malaya, Hong Kong, and elsewhere in the world. Encouragingly, news finally arrived that various U.S. bureaucracies had approved the $300 million of military aid that had been discussed during Churchill's visit, though no one in London would have realized that the Joint Chiefs had opposed giving the money. "From a cold-blooded military priority standpoint," the chiefs concluded, it didn't make sense "to furnish any military assistance to the U.K. in connection with its non-NATO missions."[36] Their judgment didn't mean that those missions in Asia, as in the Middle East, weren't critical for America. They were. But the British Empire was judged capable of handling them on its own.

Meanwhile, the Bank of England's gold and dollar reserves were evaporating so fast that it looked as if they'd be gone by summer. Should that occur, untold repercussions for world trade would follow, as Churchill knew. The Chancellor of the Exchequer, Richard Austen "Rab" Butler, had to announce a virtual ban on steel for rebuilding the country's blitzed cities—a glaringly visible phasedown. Churchill and his cabinet, with their thin parliamentary majority, looked hapless against these back-to-back emergencies. But then, as Nye Bevan said, they were saved in the nick of time, when, on February 6, George VI succumbed to lung cancer and died in his sleep, at the age of fifty-six. Parliament adjourned, and all political activity in Britain came to a halt. "The King walked with Death as if Death were a companion, an acquaintance whom he recognized and did not fear. In the end, Death came as a friend." Which is part of Churchill's enthralling broadcast.

The U.S. Senate went into recess. That night in Washington, the National Symphony opened its program at Constitution Hall with an unscheduled playing of Bach's "Come, Sweet Death," and, in tribute to the new queen, Clarke's "Trumpet Voluntary."

Three days after her father's death, Queen Elizabeth spoke to the world about "a new generation tempered by war and bred in adversity." That generation would now take leadership. Memorial services were held on February 15. In Tehran, Prime Minister Mosaddeq and three hundred dignitaries attended Anglican worship at the American Church on Stalin Avenue. Egypt's premier and others of the elite attended a memorial too, at Cairo's All Saints' Cathedral. In New Delhi, Prime Minister Nehru knelt in prayer with his sister and daughter at a requiem Mass in the Church of the Redemption. Truman and his wife and daughter attended service at the vast Cathedral Church of Saint Peter and Saint Paul, or National Cathedral, which dominates the Washington skyline. The Episcopal prayer "For the President of the United States and All in Civil Authority" was amended to say "and Queen Elizabeth."

CHURCHILL FOLLOWED UP HIS U.S. VISIT AGGRESSIVELY BY RESIST-ing American pressure on defense spending, on European unity, and, seemingly, on everything else. By March, Truman and Acheson were fed up. Churchill's tone was unacceptable. Acheson complained about the "ill-considered and ill-timed mortar shots from 10 Downing Street to 1600 Pennsylvania Avenue" and expressed a hope to Truman that Anthony Eden could be a restraining influence.[37] Yet it was unclear to Acheson how Eden might intervene without making matters worse. It couldn't be accomplished "through Oliver in Washington," Acheson wrote to Ambassador Gifford at the London embassy. "All sorts of trouble," he knew, would arise should a complaint of this sort get into the hands of the Foreign Office. Even Acheson thought twice about provoking its mandarins. He therefore chose to act obliquely by writing a "draft" dispatch to Eden that would be handed to Gifford, who'd let the foreign secretary read it in front of him at the embassy on the q.t. Gifford would then take the paper back. The point was to make Eden believe he was getting a secret glimpse of State's dismay. Gifford did so, and Eden soon responded amicably enough with a letter of his own to Acheson, not letting on that he had seen the State Department's censorious "draft."

The message was received. But it took a charade like this to ensure that the Americans weren't addressed as ungrateful children.

JOHN COLVILLE WAS A FOREIGN OFFICE MAN. HE HAD SERVED AS A private secretary to Churchill during the war, and then to Attlee, whom he held in contempt, and thereafter to Princess Elizabeth. He'd married one of her ladies-in-waiting, and by the time he returned on assignment to Churchill, he had developed serious Boswellian aspirations. He wrote in his diary for May 23, 1952, of Churchill's "advancing senility."[38] Indeed, Churchill's attention could drift, but it snapped back sharply when he heard a provocative word such as "defense" or "Egypt" or "Russia" or, for that matter, "Nye Bevan." Plus, he was showing himself sturdy enough to rebuff the Americans, and hard.

Plenty of defense questions occupied Churchill's time between the Washington visit and the U.S. presidential elections in November. To no one's surprise, he involved himself in every detail. For example, he remained furious that the Americans would get authority over all NATO forces in the Atlantic, yet there was nothing he could do about it. In April, a U.S. admiral based in Norfolk, Virginia, formally took over. But more was to come from Downing Street.

America was building mighty new aircraft carriers of the Forrestal class, destined to be the largest warships in the world. Meanwhile, the Royal Navy conceded that the Soviet Military Maritime Fleet had by now surpassed it in numbers of battleships, cruisers, and destroyers. That helped explain the heartfelt dispute over NATO's Atlantic Command.

The first lord of the Admiralty—equivalent to the U.S. Navy secretary—tried to put the Royal Navy's standing in perspective. First, he told the House of Commons, Russia's strength was still concentrated in northern waters and in the Baltic. Second, if the Royal Navy was no longer the biggest in the world, it remained the best. High-tech innovations, for instance, were being deployed nonstop, and those ranged from anti-submarine listening devices to angled decks and steam catapults for its own carriers. Therefore, no need to think of being junior, or taking second place, let alone third, to anyone.

Having held that position himself from 1911 to 1915, Churchill wasn't ready to cede his navy's most prestigious roles to the Pentagon, even if the Atlantic Command had been wrested away. So when it came time for a final decision as to who'd serve as NATO's supreme allied naval commander for the Mediterranean, he waded into battle.

Then as today, the U.S. 6th Fleet was the navy's operational arm for Europe. At home, it received so much publicity (as in *Newsweek*'s article "Sixth Fleet: Guardian of the Inner Sea") that even the Pentagon could forget that Britain's Mediterranean Fleet was equal in numbers.[39] This was a reason why the Royal Navy wouldn't put its fleet commander under the authority of an American admiral even for the sake of cohesive NATO arrangements. The Pentagon might argue that the 6th Fleet had greater tonnage and superior offensive combat power, but the British responded by claiming that such bulk was less significant in the Mediterranean's littoral actions and, anyway, that the Royal Navy routinely had more ships in the Red Sea and the Persian Gulf, whereas the U.S. Navy didn't have enough vessels to keep any on station.

Churchill had tackled this question within a week of returning to Downing Street, the previous October, which had caused an immediate argument between his military people and the chief of U.S. naval operations, who happened to have been in London. Not until more than a year later, in December 1952—and well after his visit to Washington—did Churchill allow the Admiralty to agree that the 6th Fleet might not, after all, have to come under British command in the Mediterranean during a World War III. A Solomonic decision was made: one U.S. admiral and one Royal Navy admiral, Churchill agreed at last, would share a joint command of equal standing and together would "co-ordinate" in time of war.

There was a reason he compromised. One of the West's most imposing military figures was already in place as commander in chief of the Mediterranean Fleet. That was the fifty-two-year-old Admiral Louis Mountbatten, now 1st Lord Mountbatten of Burma. Nine years earlier, as supreme allied commander in Southeast Asia, he had already been equal in rank to no one less than General Douglas MacArthur. Thereafter, he became the last viceroy to colonial India and oversaw the transfer of power. Churchill, for the moment, was giving up less than it seemed in the new structure. He knew that this elegantly handsome former commando officer, destroyer flotilla captain, and five-goal polo player—whose nephew Philip had married Princess Elizabeth and who himself was married to one of the richest English heiresses—would overshadow any admiral anywhere.[40] Moreover, Mountbatten was a genuinely skilled sailor and radioman who dazzled the Americans with his glamour. They were oblivious to his disdain for nearly all of them—an anti-American attitude so severe that a year before, just after entering office, Churchill had to tell him to tone it down.

Churchill proved less effective when he turned to the alliance that Washington had formed in September 1951 with Australia and New Zealand and that Congress ratified the following April. It was "a serious event in history," he stormed, when those two dominions could imagine defending the Pacific with the Americans alone. "What impudence," he wrote to Eden that June, and his foreign secretary was likewise amazed that either dominion could see the Pacific as an exclusive "U.S. responsibility."[41] Moreover, Churchill kept insisting, ANZUS was a bribe that the Americans had doled out to get Australia and New Zealand to sign the Japan Peace Treaty. He was right, and he dreaded that Washington would now use ANZUS to drag its two new allies along whatever disastrous course it was following against China.

To calm the waters, Australia's prime minister, Sir Robert Menzies, sent a conciliatory cable to London in the hopes of at least mollifying Eden. It ended up in the hands of Churchill, who then called Menzies to deliver, as Menzies jovially told the Americans, a blistering for being "an apostate of empire."[42]

Another reason the United States had entered the ANZUS pact, and had pledged to protect the Southwest Pacific, said the U.S. Army's chief of staff, was "to get some Australian and New Zealand troops into the Middle East" to fight alongside Britain in case of war with Russia.[43] For at least five years, the Americans had been hearing from Whitehall that such reinforcements underlay Britain's war planning. So, as seen from the Pentagon, this was at least one benefit that America got from an otherwise unwelcomed new alliance obligation.

During a 1951 strategy conference in London, however, Australian commanders had told Britain's chiefs that they could commit to designating only a single division for wider commonwealth needs, and they couldn't guarantee it would be going to the Middle East. Once that was aired, the entire meeting broke down. British defense officials asked why the Australians had bothered to come if they were "prepared to do nothing."[44]

The Americans heard of this encounter too, direct from Canberra, along with an admission that Australia really wouldn't have even one army division to place at Britain's disposal. Additionally, they learned that Australia wouldn't be sending troops to the Middle East at all, even if, as Vice Admiral Sir John Collins, Australia's chief of navy, put it, the U.S. presence in the Pacific "would be sufficiently strong to deal with a sea-borne threat."[45] This stance by the Anzacs (Australian and New Zealand Army Corps), as they'd been known when fighting gallantly in the Middle East during both world wars, ended the illusion in London, and in Washington as well, that they'd ever be returning to the theater. This would leave British forces alone to face any thrust south by the Red Army.

OLIVER FRANKS HAD BEEN BAD-TEMPERED DURING THE TRUMAN-Churchill talks at the start of the year. He had chided his superior, Foreign Secretary Anthony Eden, for having allowed Churchill to speak on every item of global policy, and he'd told other British diplomats of how keenly he felt the humiliation of their country's financial mess.[46] They needed to understand, he said, that Britain could never hope to deal as an equal with the Americans until these embarrassments ended. Thereafter, government securities fell to an all-time low, while the Treasury reached the bare minimum of gold and dollar reserves needed to finance trade with the sterling area. By the summer of 1952, however, a policy of severe austerity was beginning to show results. Britain achieved a favorable balance of trade in the first half of the year, though it couldn't be measured for several more months.

If the economy really could rebound—conclusively—maybe the country's influence might in fact be out of all proportion to its actual power, as Franks expected. But it was Britain's authentic hard power that was about to increase dramatically. At the White House during the previous January, Churchill had detected a change in the American attitude toward him and his delegation once he confided that R&D for an atomic bomb was essentially complete. Then, on February 26, he told the Commons, when making the news about the breakthrough public, that a "new atmosphere" prevailed in Washington following his disclosure.[47]

It's not difficult to see why. The Americans were more anxious than ever about Russia; they wanted the British Empire and Commonwealth firmly in their corner. Half of the U.S. Army was locked up in a remote peninsula on the other side of the world. To make matters worse, Asian opinion seemed to be swinging against them, and Mao's regime looked completely in thrall to Stalin. In Europe, the dividing line between East and West might have become inviolable, thanks to NATO, and despite the alliance's military muscle being in doubt. But much else was at stake in the world. Churchill, who might know what he was talking about, had also said during his visit to North America that he estimated a five-to-four chance of war with Russia that year.[48] This meant a 44 percent likelihood it would break out, and U.S. officials didn't disagree.

15

STEMMING THE TIDE

Personally, I am always ready to learn, although I do not always like being taught.

—Winston Churchill, November 1952

I N 1952, WASHINGTON DIDN'T HAVE A STRATEGY, SHORT OF OUT-right war, for countering Russia. It certainly didn't have "an American grand strategy," as believed today.[1] The wise Oliver Franks understood this well. Americans, he told Sir Roger Makins, deputy undersecretary at the Foreign Office who had asked where to find the hidden subtleties of U.S. foreign policy, never have grand strategies. What passes for considered policy, he maintained, is instead a twisting sequence of ad hoc decisions hammered out under the stresses of domestic politics.

As today, this approach to dealing with the world can be perilous, especially when confronting Russia. It was even riskier at a time when the rational side of Stalin's mind was giving way to lunatic imputations of conspiracies past and present, involving Trotskyites . . . doctors . . . Jews . . . the Vatican. Above all the Vatican, the obsolete dogmas of which Stalin, a former Orthodox seminarian, believed were a dire threat to his rule. The Roman Catholic Church, he told Pietro Nenni, a one-time Italian foreign minister who visited the Kremlin in July 1952, was conspiring with anti-Soviet cliques in Washington. Hadn't New York's Cardinal Spellman attended the Yalta Conference in disguise, the better to harden Roosevelt's opinion against Stalin?[2] Given these utterances, it was difficult to count on Stalin's remaining sane, at least in the operational sense of not launching another war.

Churchill, for his part, hoped to engineer some sort of dramatic détente with the Kremlin from the moment he returned to office. He couldn't reasonably wait for Stalin, five years his junior, to die, and since at least early 1950 he had been calling for a parley "upon the highest level."[3] From the moment he had left Washington in January 1952, as Harold Macmillan observed, "his eyes [had been] on Russia," and he had told the House of Commons in February about the need for "a high-level meeting" to examine world problems with Stalin, no preconditions required.[4] The word "enemy" was as temporary to Churchill as it is to any statesman. He was much less of a crusader than he had led Americans to believe at Fulton.

The timing here is important. In March, Truman announced that he wouldn't seek reelection. This curtailed his influence through the rest of the year. Churchill sensed opportunity. With Truman as a lame duck, he could assert Britain's primacy in all matters of global diplomacy: the Middle East, Southeast Asia, and maybe Russia too. He already had a useful platform because London, not Washington, was still the heart of the world's diplomatic activity, and he could call on an impressive second-in-command, that being Foreign Secretary Eden.[5] Should Britain's economy rebound, Churchill's case for doing so would be strong. Standing up to the United States became a key objective of his government.[6]

NOT THAT ANYONE KNEW WHAT WAS HAPPENING WITHIN THE TOTAL-itarian Soviet state. These were the days before satellite reconnaissance and sophisticated electronic intercepts. The CIA was unable to recruit agents within, and the agency's station chief in Moscow fulfilled his reporting requirements only by personally counting the number of trains that would pass through a provincial town, and then estimating the number of boxcars, to get an idea of the economy's vitality. Neither the U.S. nor the British intelligence services could answer the core question, "How strong is Russia?"[7] Moreover, the "bureaucratization of intelligence work" had already taken hold at agency headquarters on E Street.[8] Of course, the severest criticism of CIA performance originated from people within MI6 who concluded that when it came to clandestine tasks, "the US is not that clever, or patient, or hardnosed." But these judgments soon counted for little.

MI6, after all, had been compromised by a searing spy scandal—what James Jesus Angleton, a high CIA official in clandestine services, called the "dreadful penetrations."[9] It included Donald Maclean and Guy Burgess, who had vanished from London in May 1951, presumably for the East, as the mole hunters closed in. Maclean particularly had roles that made him privy to most every secret between Britain and the United States. Before arriving in Washington, Burgess, a colorful Etonian and genial alcoholic, had served as private secretary to Hector McNeil, MP, who was Ernest Bevin's minister of state from 1946 to 1950. Such details quickly became known in Washington, although the Kremlin said nothing about the disappearances, nor would anything be heard from the two diplomats until they surfaced publicly in Moscow five years later.

Even before Burgess and Maclean escaped, the CIA and the FBI were nervous about loose security within Britain's intelligence services. The Americans knew that the gravest of secrets were entrusted to officials who weren't even required to attest to details of their personal background under oath. But anxieties intensified because Burgess and Maclean had managed their getaway so easily as to indicate that at least one even better-placed friend still lurked within MI6. He did: Kim Philby, the original Janus-faced genius who by then had befriended both Allen Dulles, a senior official at the agency who would become director in 1953, and Angleton himself, who the year thereafter would take over CIA counterintelligence, which he'd run for twenty years. Philby's supreme talent was intimacy, not the "golden charm" of spy stories.[10] Charm wouldn't have worked on the cold, cerebral Angleton, who fell completely under his influence.

After the disappearances, General Walter Bedell Smith, the CIA's second director since 1947, came to suspect Philby and forced him to return to London under a cloud. Besides, the general was livid that the British weren't being straight about the defections. As one Foreign Office source initially told U.S. inquirers, Burgess and Maclean "merely went off on a prolonged toot" to Paris.[11]

Paradoxically, an intelligence service that suspects it has been penetrated can become startlingly uncurious. It doesn't want to discover the worst.[12] Should a mole be uncovered, after all, troubling questions arise for the people who have trusted him. How badly has the spy service been compromised, and what's the price of the damage done? How did he get embedded in the first place? Who oversaw his work and promoted him? Not least, other government departments start to pry into the organization and the dirtiest of laundry becomes embarrassingly public. So perhaps, murmured the British officials responsible, there were other reasons for perplexing failures within MI6—rather than the terrible fact that yet another traitor might be among them. It's a condition from which Philby benefited, and he wouldn't have to defect until 1963—never having taken the role of "C."

We hear this from Philby himself in an hour-long lecture, which the BBC discovered only in 2016. He's speaking to an audience from East Germany's spy service, the Stasi, in 1981. "Every evening I left the office with a big briefcase full of reports," he explains, looking aging and puffy, but sharing a sense of amusement. "I was to hand them to my Soviet contact in the evening" to be photographed, and they would be returned in the morning.[13] How was this possible? It was easy, he relates, because he lived in the cosseted world of public school chums, Oxbridge friends, and St. James's clubs that was the British establishment. He was above suspicion—just the sort of nightmare security lapse the Americans had feared.

BY 1951, AND AT LEAST UNTIL STALIN'S DEATH IN MARCH 1953, IT was difficult for U.S. and British diplomats in Moscow to have any sort of useful dealings with the Soviet government. Their embassies were sealed off in a freezing ideological quarantine, and the Kremlin essentially ignored them. Diplomats have experienced nothing like it in Moscow except during the early 1980s following a boycott Washington imposed after the Red Army invaded Afghanistan. The sense of isolation can be profound.

In early October 1951, the U.S. ambassador, a former admiral, had become fed up with the inactivity and returned home. The following month, a news leak in *The New York Times*, in contrast to the customary announcement from Foggy Bottom or the White House, disclosed that George Kennan would be his successor. Otherwise the nomination during this period of lockdown received little attention within State, and there was no rush in getting Kennan to Moscow, while the Soviet bureaucracy dragged its feet as well.[14] Kennan wouldn't arrive until May 1952, and, once there, he felt so cut off from Russia's ministries that he doubted the value of even keeping an embassy in Moscow. That's what he told his British counterpart, Alvary Gascoigne, formerly of Tokyo, who transcribed Kennan's musings over the next months and, of course, sent them to the Foreign Office. Stalin, for his part, believed Kennan's appointment came at the bidding of the Roman Catholic Church. He never received the new ambassador.[15]

Before leaving the United States, according to Harry Rositzke, another OSS veteran and the first chief of the CIA's Soviet division, Kennan had asked for and obtained cyanide capsules, which he planned to take if he was arrested while in Moscow. That's confirmed by Rositzke's subordinate Peer de Silva, who was responsible for clandestine operations. It's a bizarrely unique occurrence in U.S. diplomacy. Kennan expected his presence in the Russian capital to be so important that the authorities might bundle him off to the Lubyanka for torture. At CIA headquarters, in its E Street complex near the Lincoln Memorial, the decision to give him the capsules—and, in effect, to allow him to commit suicide—was made by the agency's top leadership and in a spirit that he was welcome to swallow them all.[16]

Ambassador Gascoigne's missives to the Foreign Office are a rich source on Kennan in Moscow. Kennan was angry, Gascoigne reported, that America was riding around like Don Quixote, trying to rescue damsels such as Poland and Tibet but only making matters worse. Given that the Russians were shunning him, Gascoigne wrote, Kennan was wondering whether it was "dignified and right to treat the Kremlin as a normal Government."[17] Not only that, as Gascoigne reported it, Kennan condemned prominent Americans for "the stupid utterances against Russia which they were continually making."[18] The sternest mandarins in Whitehall might have shared Kennan's views, but they were startled to hear them from a U.S. ambassador speaking within their own embassy. There was another point Gascoigne reported: Kennan re-emphasized, as he'd done since 1946, that the Kremlin wasn't thinking in terms of world war; it was instead preoccupied with creating disunity within the West and subverting the democracies. To illustrate his point, Kennan insisted that Russia was fomenting tensions between "blacks and whites in America."[19]

Kennan was prone to emotional outbursts and could turn purple in policy debates. After five months as ambassador, he was declared persona non grata for a public remark that compared life in Moscow to that under the Nazis, a widely publicized observation he saw fit to make during a stop in Berlin. As for Churchill's ongoing infatuation with détente, the prime minister spoke privately during these months about summoning a modern Congress of Vienna or of reopening the Potsdam Conference with Stalin. During his first full year in office, however, Churchill was otherwise consumed by trying to restore Britain to its rightful place in the world: summitry, as a top priority, would have to wait for the following year.

BY THE MIDSUMMER OF 1952, THE UNITED STATES WAS ENTERING what one caustic observer at Oliver Franks's embassy called its "pre-election purdah."[20] Dwight D. Eisenhower, the revered soldier of democracy, and the thirty-nine-year-old California senator Richard Nixon, challenged the Democrats for the presidency. Eisenhower kicked off his campaign in August at Madison Square Garden, where he told thousands of American Legionnaires that the worldwide Communist threat placed their country in greater peril than at any moment of its history. Nor, Eisenhower continued to thunderous cheers, would he be making overtures to the Kremlin "until the tidal mud of Communism has receded within its own borders."[21] As a campaign theme, however, that message was overshadowed by domestic issues, as is usual in a presidential race. Even though the economy and middle-class incomes were booming, with factory workers able to earn upwards of $3,000 a year, voters stewed over taxes and inflation.

America might be imperiled by Communism, but its citizens would only do so much to counter its manifestations overseas. Nothing, for instance, was certain about U.S. defense spending. And fears of entanglements ensured that Churchill's call in January for Congress to approve "token" forces for Suez went nowhere.[22]

It was just as well that the Americans didn't allow themselves to get lured into Egypt. State Department specialists were expecting King Farouk to be overthrown, and who knew what would follow? Even Farouk was anticipating his ouster, as he'd write later in the British weekly *Empire News*. The revolution came on July 23, in the form of a bloodless coup d'état led by young army and air force officers. Once they'd cornered Farouk at a summer residence (Alexandria's Montazah Palace), the U.S. ambassador, Jefferson Caffery, persuaded him to abdicate in return for his life. Caffery ensured the royal family's safety until Farouk could flee, and he advised the British not to interfere. But he also told Farouk that no U.S. plane or warship would be coming to evacuate him. That might get America entangled. So Farouk bolted on the *Mahrousa*, along with his queen, retainers, and a six-month-old son, now King Fuad II, who would also soon be deposed.

Once Farouk was bundled off to France, Caffery discovered that Egypt's new rulers hoped to align themselves with the United States— "to the exclusion of the UK," he reported.[23] They recognized the need for a strong friend and saw the Americans as a counterweight to the British.

Churchill's government had doubts about Farouk's successors but hoped negotiations over Suez and the Sudan could begin anew. Eden guessed the Americans wanted to "stand well" with the Free Officers Movement, as the junta was calling itself, and with its apparent leader, the fifty-one-year-old pipe-smoking, well-educated General Muhammad Naguib, who came from a long line of army officers. He was someone Whitehall could understand. Yet British diplomats in Cairo already suspected Naguib was merely a dignified figurehead for implacable young troublemakers in the background, whom Foreign Secretary Eden reliably called "fanatic nationalists." Eden believed that his firm handling of the Egyptians would be undermined if Washington got "out of step" with him, let alone began dealing with those extremists.[24]

In the same month as Farouk's ouster, demonstrators in Tehran took to the streets in support of Mosaddeq—who had resigned, temporarily, while wresting constitutional prerogatives from the shah. Twenty-nine people died. "The only thing to stop Persia falling into Communist hands is a coup d'etat," Britain's chargé d'affaires cabled the Foreign Office.[25] To that end, British agents were already sowing bribes and hiding weapons they'd carted off from the RAF's Habbaniya air base west of Baghdad. George Kennan was still in Moscow and could always be counted on to support the least progressive themes. "We must recognize and fight the elements of blackmail in the Iranian position," he cabled to State.

Iran's economy was being crippled by the Anglo-Iranian Oil Company lockdown of the nation's oil exports. This enabled the British to pay less heed to Mosaddeq, who, month after month over Radio Tehran, varied between threatening the British and trying to cajole world opinion. From retirement in San Francisco, Henry Grady, the former ambassador, was keeping an eye on this slow-moving disaster. After it became clear that Iran would not receive a U.S. loan, he went public. The entire mess, he said, was a result of his embassy's recommendations having been "ignored or flatly turned down by our Government, under British influence and direction."[26] He blamed Acheson. The British indeed were calling the shots, and it was getting late in the day for the United States to side with Iranian democracy.

Egypt's turmoil continued into the fall. By October 1952, the strongman in Cairo's junta looked to be Colonel Gamal Abdel Nasser, a rough-hewn thirty-four-year-old who had appointed himself interior minister. That month, he announced through an interview over Cairo radio that foreign soldiers would have to leave Egypt within six months. If they did not, he promised, to much celebration, guerrilla resistance would make it "far too expensive for the British to maintain their citizens in occupation of our country."[27] Egypt, Nasser was asserting, had become the property of the Suez Canal Company. The good news, Caffery reported, was that the new military regime seemed to think well of the Americans, although this, Caffery added, left the British "a little unhappy."[28]

The Americans weren't attempting to fine-tune the Middle East quite yet. They held back on alliances, troop deployments, and military sales. But they nonetheless were beginning to emulate the secret nips and tucks that British colonial officers had learned over decades—not yet in Egypt, but in Iraq, a country that was close to being a British fiefdom.

Iraq's population stood at around 5 million, with about 550,000 living in Baghdad, much of which contained festering slums. The country had a seventeen-year-old king and a depressed economy that was being mishandled by a prime ministerial regent. Political tweaking might be needed for the sake of stability, American diplomats concluded, and in 1952 the embassy began to explore ways of influencing elections. Officials in Washington approved, although they knew little more about the place than what might have been gleaned from that year's hit movie *Babes in Bagdad*, with Paulette Goddard. Then as today, U.S. attempts at implementing geopolitical adjustments are rarely as clever as their practitioners believe. On November 23, Iraqi mobs, screaming, "Down with forged elections!" firebombed the U.S. Information Service offices on Rashid Street and stoned the British embassy.[29]

With similar dexterity, the Americans were also trying to adjust politics in the Gulf, as when the U.S. consulate in Dhahran asked the State Department to help deliver a "friendly display of force" to assist Bahrain's ruling Al Khalifa family to stifle reformist political opponents who dared to oppose a British colonial presence.[30]

No matter who was in the White House, the would-be global architects—who increasingly inhabited the CIA—were at play with their Middle East intrigues. Blowback could overwhelm the genuinely valuable work that more seriously accomplished people were pursuing. For instance, U.S. pilots and technicians were doing more to eradicate locusts than anyone had thought possible. Plagues of desert locusts had swarmed across borders for millennia, and during the spring of 1952 Iran faced its worst infestation in eighty years. The Americans introduced aerial spraying for the first time in the Middle East, using their new insecticide Aldrin, an organochlorine. They then expanded their efforts to Iraq and ten more countries, including Pakistan and Lebanon. Nothing like this had been seen. Washington spent a total of $445,000 while saving scores of millions in crop damage. In darker corners of the region, however, other Americans were getting into the habit of trifling with Arab and Iranian politics, and often as apprentices to London.

NO WESTERN STATESMAN SEEMED TO KNOW MORE ABOUT THE MIDdle East than Anthony Eden. He was a politician so highly trained in global affairs that he could just as easily have headed the Foreign Office's career service, as permanent undersecretary, without missing a beat. He exemplified the worldly expertise that awed so many Americans after World War II, and he also embodied, even at age fifty-four, the "new generation tempered by war and bred in adversity" that Elizabeth II had extolled.

Eden's father, Sir William, had been known to throw stuck barometers into the rain "for the bloody fools to see for themselves," a kind of behavior that extended even beyond country-squire eccentric. His mother, the toast of Edwardian London for her beauty, had been born in India, where her father was governor of Bengal. Eden himself had something of both parents in him, said his most feline colleague, Chancellor of the Exchequer Rab Butler—"half society beauty, half mad baronet."

Eden had survived the western front with the King's Royal Rifle Corps long enough to become, by 1916, one of the youngest adjutants in the British army, and he received the Military Cross after the Battle of the Somme. He was a brigade major at war's end, having lost his two brothers in the inferno and a third of his classmates from Eton.[31] Following the war, he graduated from Christ Church, Oxford, with a first in Oriental languages. That gave him a rare grasp of Iran's literary qualities, though little sense of its present. His knowledge of Arabic as well as of Farsi would startle Middle Eastern potentates. In 1935, he became his country's youngest foreign secretary in more than half a century, and within months he met with Stalin in the Kremlin. He'd recall how Stalin, apparently puzzled, had pointed to Britain on a map and said, "It is strange that so much should depend upon one small island."[32]

Eden had ties of his own to America. During his first trip, in 1938, he had found the grave of his great-great-grandfather, the last royal governor of the Maryland Colony, in St. Anne's churchyard in Annapolis. The Maryland Club in Baltimore made Eden a member, and today a photograph of his visit hangs near the library. He'd mention his American experiences often, the lesson being that Britain had a timeless world presence. But he was of the last generation that construed this as a powerful world role.

Churchill writes that his only sleepless night in the long descent to World War II came at the moment in 1938 when Eden quit Neville Chamberlain's cabinet over the appeasement of Mussolini's fascism. With the war, Eden became the second man in what was essentially Churchill's one-man government, and Churchill nominated him as his successor should he be killed. The high-strung Eden suffered a breakdown but rebounded in the coalition, and he became a loyal friend of Ernest Bevin's. And then it was Bevin who would replace him in July 1945, not long after Eden had received a "Strictly Personal" cable from the Allied air commander, Southeast Asia, saying his son's supply-dropping Dakota transport was missing over Burma.

Sixteen months before Eden returned once again to the Foreign Office, his unhappy marriage finally collapsed. Then, in August 1952, amid murmurs in society over age differences and concern in the *Church Times* about the divorce itself, he wed Churchill's thirty-two-year-old niece, the beautiful and bewildering orphan Clarissa Spencer-Churchill. Churchill insisted on being the principal witness at the Registry Office, and the reception was held at Number 10.

People always remarked that Eden was young enough to be Churchill's son. But the tastes and dispositions of these two men were very different, except that they both liked children and small animals. Churchill reveled in the hurly-burly of politics, while Eden enjoyed possessing exquisite eighteenth-century furniture, translating Persian poetry, and viewing his art collection, which included paintings and drawings by Augustus John, Duncan Grant, Dunlop, and Constable. Churchill could burst into epic explosions of anger; Eden was prone to tantrums and sulks. Not least, Eden was a well-practiced seducer of married upper-class women—utterly different behavior from Churchill's. Eden also did not share Churchill's extraordinary physical endurance.

Time was beginning to tell on him. By 1952, the boyishly handsome foreign secretary looked like a gaunt young rifleman just pulled from the line. He was suffering jaundice, taking a mélange of painkillers from a black tin box, and using injections of morphine to relieve searing internal spasms. In town, Eden lived with Clarissa at the foreign secretary's official residence, 1 Carlton Gardens, and waited grimly for Churchill to step aside. Most everyone in Parliament expected the same: having made good his triumphant return to office, the aging savior of his country could now leave the premiership with his pride intact.

CHURCHILL KEPT BRUSHING ASIDE HIS CABINET'S INTIMATIONS that he might retire. He had plans. He wanted a summit with Moscow, and then there were those disturbances to be sorted out in the Middle East, Southeast Asia, and wherever a dog might bark within the empire. Perhaps he'd eventually hand the reins to Eden, he implied, but only "if Anthony is kind."[33]

That wasn't going to be easy. Months and years passed by. Eden meanwhile had to juggle the costs of Britain's big draining overseas commitments. They wouldn't be shed, but maybe some of them could be shared.

In Southeast Asia, the answer for doing so, he decided, lay in establishing some form of united defense pact akin to NATO that might bind the Americans, Australians, and New Zealanders to protecting Malaya and Indochina. "The more gradually and inconspicuously we can transfer the real burdens from our own to American shoulders," he advised the cabinet in June, "the less damage we shall do to our position and influence in the world."[34] That meant not retreating but instead using other people's money to advance British interests. Maybe that would work.

The Americans already feared Indochina's loss, though they also dreaded getting ensnared: in March 1952, Acheson had to assure the Senate Foreign Relations Committee that no U.S. troops would go to Vietnam.[35] It was the same week that one top official in Whitehall cabled his anxiety about "defeatism in Vietnam" to Malcolm MacDonald and reminded the commissioner general that "every month gained [in Vietnam] is valuable time for Southeast Asia and the Empire."[36]

As the year wore on, Eden had reason to be confident at least about Malaya. At the start, in January 1952, Churchill had decided to retain MacDonald as commissioner general for Southeast Asia, though he relegated him to a diplomatic role. That same month, Churchill picked a successor to the assassinated Henry Gurney: he selected General Sir Gerald Templer and gave him sweeping new powers as high commissioner for Malaya. MacDonald was therefore overshadowed—temporarily—on military affairs, but it didn't dim his influence. He conducted business as usual, calling on the emperor Hirohito in Tokyo that July to discuss Southeast Asia, for example, and he now had more time to diplomatize with the Americans about Vietnam.

Templer, for his part, was a skilled, resolute Irish Fusilier who had been wounded in World War II commanding an armored division and had then risen via intelligence duties on the Imperial General Staff. Once in Malaya, he used an armored car, not a Rolls-Royce, and he refused, like MacDonald, to heed the color barrier. Templer also employed MacDonald's strategy—political reform combined with overwhelming force—against the guerrillas, who'd been surviving through extortion and by tapping about 20 percent of the rubber trees on Malaya's plantations.

Templer additionally made progress on the Malayan "front" by mixing special operations with deadly science. Food-growing areas abutting the bamboo forests were sprayed with Trioxone, precursor to the more than twenty million gallons of Agent Orange–type herbicides that the Americans would later shower upon Vietnam, Cambodia, and Laos. The British gradually got the upper hand, and the guerrillas became ever more isolated in the deep jungle.

By the end of October 1952, Templer announced relative calm on his battlefront: attacks were down; the enemy had been reduced to fewer than seven thousand; and his forces had killed thirty-five guerrillas just in the past month. Clearly, this was good news. But these numbers show Britain's fight in Malaya to have been on a scale far different from

America's ordeal in Korea. In Malaya, for example, between 1948 and the end of 1952, British security forces lost 1,275 men (mostly local militia). In Korea, over eighteen months, upwards of 20,000 Americans had been killed.[37]

THAT OCTOBER, WHEN TEMPLER MADE HIS REASSURING ASSESS-ment, the Colonial Office faced another conflict that its officials believed could become as serious as Malaya. That was Kenya, a land of 5.3 million blacks and 100,000 Indians ruled by 35,000 whites, who controlled 212,000 square miles of the fertile agricultural highlands. Fifty-two thousand square miles of scrub were left for everyone else.

Marauding gangs known as Mau Mau, from the million-strong Kikuyu tribe, had begun launching sensational attacks from the fringes of the forests, mostly against blacks but including some whites, which made for garish international headlines. Press accounts circulated in the United States of ritual midnight disembowelings and blood drinking. White Americans, with their visceral fears of violent Negroes, were transfixed. Hollywood fan magazines wrote of British farmers having their throats slit while sleeping and fretted over the safety of Clark Gable and Ava Gardner, who were filming the brainless *Mogambo* in Kenya's Rift Valley.

In response to the attacks, the colonial governor declared a state of emergency that October. For the Americans' benefit, the Foreign Office's Information Research Department worked hard to spin the rebels as Communist terrorists, despite no evidence of Russian meddling. The rebels, who called themselves the Land Freedom Army, were in fact a breakaway wing of the pro-independence Kenya African Union political party, and their goal, as the name suggests, was land reform, not race war. That didn't prevent authorities from a brutal crackdown. They claimed the Mau Mau "infection" could spread to lucrative colonies like the Gold Coast and Nigeria that were being prepared for self-rule.

Kenya was one of four British East African dependencies, and it was a moneymaker. Nairobi was also headquarters for Britain's East Africa High Command, which had responsibilities stretching two thousand miles, from the borders of South Africa to Ethiopia. And Mombasa, which today contains support facilities for U.S. Africa Command, was East Africa's key commercial port. It had been an important British naval base in World War II, and the Pentagon was expecting it to serve so again should there be a World War III. The British also intended Kenya to provide a flanking position for a defense of the Middle East.

Given these stakes, the Americans got involved, doing so in the form of a nationally ranked tennis player with a Harvard political science Ph.D., Jack H. Mower, thirty-one, from Depression-era Oakland, California.

In 1953, the CIA dispatched this recently recruited officer to Kenya under the deep cover of writing a book on African politics. His agency ties were unknown to the British as he and his wife, Barbara, herself a spy, took up residence near Nairobi on the farm of Karen Blixen, the Danish author who, under the pen name Isak Dinesen, wrote *Out of Africa*. Combined with Jack's tennis, the connection to Baroness Blixen gave them complete access to the colonial political and military elite, which, he'd reminisce, looked upon Americans as "rubes."[38] Mower knew that colonialism was dying, and he wanted his country to be on the right side of history as he worked among the Kikuyu and reported on British operations. After two years, he was reclassified as a cultural affairs officer for the U.S. Information Service (a job that by then might as well have screamed "CIA"). Other officers quietly joined him, and three years later Mower was assigned to South Africa, Tanganyika, and Nigeria—secretly keeping tabs on British activities throughout.

The same year that Mower arrived in Kenya, General Bobbie Erskine showed up as commander in chief for East Africa. He was accompanied that summer by fifty-five hundred infantrymen as well as RAF bombers. London thought his experience with civil-military relations in the Suez Canal Zone to be germane. Erskine's role underscores a point about Britain's counterinsurgency wars that hasn't been understood: Palestine, Greece, Malaya, Kenya, and soon Cyprus were regarded in London not as distinct conflicts but as interconnected challenges that required similar tactics and many of the same people such as Erskine, Gurney, and, at this point, General Sir John Harding, who, after overseeing special operations in Malaya, was advising Churchill's government on how to respond to the Mau Mau uprising once he rose to chief of the Imperial General Staff on November 1.

Before long, Erskine launched a bombing campaign against the rebels who were concealing themselves in dense equatorial forests, and this helped drive them into the open. Even though the enemy was armed with little more than stolen firearms and long, machete-like knives, Erskine soon recognized that bullets alone wouldn't be enough to win against what *The New York Times* excitedly called "the anti-white Mau Mau terrorist organization."[39] Having first encountered guerrilla war against the Irish Republican Army in 1919–1922, he also understood the stupidity of using torture and ordered his soldiers to do nothing that they would be "ashamed to see used against their own people."[40]

Here, at least, was a similarity to Malaya. After fourteen months of bloodshed, colonial officials undertook belated agricultural reforms, and the savvy local political leaders of Kenya's African Union sought development aid from the Ford and Rockefeller Foundations, which they knew had assisted projects in India. That got them sophisticated attention in New York. But Erskine's sensible words didn't go far, as Mower documented.

The Mau Mau rebellion would last more than four years and involve some twenty thousand imperial forces. By the time most of it was crushed, not long after 1956—with the help of detentions, torture, and killings that the historian Caroline Elkins has described as "Britain's Gulag in Kenya"—colonial authorities listed 32 white settlers and 1,819 African civilians as murdered by terrorism. At least 20,000 Kikuyu ended up dead, including 1,090 who were hanged—usually in public, frequently at crossroads, and on a mobile gallows that traveled around the colony.[41] After that, as we'll see, the Americans began to involve themselves directly in Africa.

CHURCHILL'S GOVERNMENT HAD TO UNDERSCORE BRITAIN'S MILI-tary strength even as he cut and delayed additional defense spending. By no coincidence, military commanders and Whitehall officials alike began to speak openly about the nation's military capacity in ways never done before. For instance, Field Marshal William Slim, who preceded

Harding as CIGS, specified in an interview in June 1952 that the British army had a full ten divisions deployed overseas, which was a number nearly equal to U.S. deployments abroad, and America was fighting the Korean War.[42] This impressive news was cited widely in the press. These troops constituted the Army of the Rhine, which now included two armored divisions equipped with fifty-two-ton Centurions, rated by U.S. tankers in Korea's hard terrain as better than their own Shermans or Pershings; three divisions in Egypt; two in the Far East; and assorted soldiers elsewhere. Moreover, said the field marshal, his officers were cooperating seamlessly with the RAF and the Royal Navy. That meant an overall force of nearly 900,000, without counting fighting men from the empire and commonwealth.[43]

During the quiet days of August 1952, there was a creepier disclosure. The chief scientist at the Ministry of Supply, which also held responsibility for atomic energy, let it be known via an article in *The Lancet* that Britain had developed a form of nerve gas. U.S. officials were puzzled by the revelation. Why, for crying out loud, was this being discussed? To deter Moscow? To warn Britain's public? Details weren't offered, but the news was true: Imperial Chemical Industries had created one of the world's most lethal toxins, "Venomous Agent X." It's a tasteless and odorless liquid that catalyzes the breakdown of neurotransmitters, thereby shutting off the lung muscles. The Americans would eventually put it into production mode, but today it's banned (North Korea being the one place known to have stockpiles). Because VX is easily weaponized and scaled, the British seemed to be showing Washington and Moscow that there were horrific and effective means of mass destruction other than the atomic bomb.

Whitehall was also publicizing Britain's successful aviation industry, which, unlike nerve gas, brought in hard currency from exports. De Havilland's Comet seemed to ensure supremacy in civil aviation. British Overseas Airways Corporation soon began flying the world's first passenger jets on three weekly flights between London and Johannesburg. Schedules for Ceylon, Singapore, and Tokyo followed. Business was overwhelming, and BOAC announced an annual net profit. The press on both sides of the Atlantic doubted America's ability to catch up, and everyone knew these technological achievements had military implications. For example, De Havilland was building a cutting-edge, all-black, night-fighter prototype to be known as the Sea Vixen. It was intended for the Royal Navy, which, for its part, began rebuilding HMS *Victorious* that year. Plans were to make it the most modern aircraft carrier in the world, designed to carry atomic bombers.[44]

Then Britain's long-awaited detonation occurred on October 3, 1952.[45] It was an improved version of the bomb the Americans had dropped on Nagasaki, and it exploded with roughly double the force, at thirty kilotons. U.S. Atomic Energy Commission experts had been asking since January for the test to be conducted in Nevada, but British authorities chose a lagoon in Australia's Monte Bello Islands in the northwestern seas. After years of being cut off from U.S. research, officials at the Ministry of Supply had no interest in sharing all their data. Moreover, a test in Australia would underline Britain's independence in R&D and show that it was not, as one critic in the Foreign Office's American Department put it, "merely a satellite of the United States."

Churchill was a guest of the queen's, at Balmoral in Scotland, from October 1 to 3, and he received the news by phone early in the morning of the last day. He was ecstatic. The ministry soon announced it would produce two hundred bombs by 1957. But the Americans shrugged. Britain's achievement was "a Model T," according to *The New York Times'* military correspondent, Hanson Baldwin. *Time* magazine—which was read by vast numbers of Americans—ran a bland article with a smart-alecky title, "A Bomb of One's Own."[46] The physicist Robert Oppenheimer, known as the father of the atomic bomb, merely said from Princeton that it was a pity for so talented and poor a country to be doing this at all.[47]

A month later, on November 1, the United States detonated the world's first hydrogen bomb. The test occurred on Eniwetok, an atoll in the Pacific Ocean. The blast was so immense that Washington had to use a new measurement of power to explain it: megatons, meaning millions of tons of TNT, instead of kilotons, which were merely thousands. The bomb exploded with a force of ten megatons, dwarfing what the British had set off a month before. That said, there were still aspects of atomic weaponry in which Britain claimed a lead. They included theories of producing atomic artillery and developing guided missiles that one day might hurl a nuclear warhead across oceans. But mass-producing nuclear weapons—and soon jet bombers and every variation of military hardware—was a task just made for industrial America.

BY LATE 1952, THE RELATIONSHIP BETWEEN BRITISH AND U.S. IN-telligence was swinging in America's favor. The U.S. services, which that year came to include the National Security Agency, had already become the world's largest (leaving aside the organs of the Soviet police state), as they are today. The CIA presence in London was about ten times that of MI6's in Washington, and collaboration between the two organizations at headquarters, though not necessarily in the field, had grown so close that "any officer earmarked for high position in SIS would need intimate knowledge of the Washington scene."[48] So wrote Kim Philby.

However, what was occurring in the intelligence world was akin to the shifts in diplomacy and military capacity between the two nations. The Americans were by no means as dominant as has been thought. For example, Philby's memoir, *My Silent War* (written from Moscow in 1967), contains a passage worth rereading. It "is beyond doubt," Philby concludes, "that the decision in favour of co-operation doomed the British services, in the long run, to junior status."[49] The intriguing words here—always unnoticed—are "in the long run." How long was that? Longer than commonly believed, to judge from observations made by the OSS veterans and founding fathers James Jesus Angleton and William Colby, an astute operative in Western Europe who'd rise to director. Among the evidence for an extended length of time is an analysis from our own day in the CIA's peer-reviewed quarterly journal, *Studies in Intelligence*. MI6's "experience and sophistication far exceeded that of the CIA," writes the author about problems of strategic deception in 1956.[50]

The 1950s were no "golden age" for the CIA, as is commonly believed. There's never been one.[51] Through much of that decade, the CIA was a decidedly amateur outfit. Few "ace personnel" existed on the clandestine side, such as those whom U.S. diplomats had observed in Tehran. MI6 meanwhile played up its own quality, its singular expertise, and a global presence. Given such an allure, it wasn't unusual for the agency's enthusiasts to try to imitate British operatives.

Among those who did, in their styles and attitudes, were Frank Wisner, the rich and personable head of clandestine operations, who in fact did get his suits made in London, and also Ernie Cuneo, who had handled OSS and White House ties with MI6 during World War II and who maintained his involvement in the 1950s through the North American Newspaper Alliance, a syndicate with CIA connections (and with Ian Fleming, previously of British naval intelligence, as its European vice president). Cuneo never ceased to admire the *arcana imperii* of the Great Game. In unguarded moments, he'd parrot to friends what he believed to be a British colonial aphorism: "Always have 'em rubbed out by a plausible enemy, best if it's religious, but you can always find somebody, the trick lies in concealment."[52] There was a mix of initiative, cockiness, and a spirit close to play within the agency that by this time was affecting the lives of millions.

Around 1952–1953, a high British intelligence official, who was left unnamed in the records, visited Washington. (The document describing his visit is also undated.) He explained the situation between the two spy services to the U.S. Intelligence Advisory Committee, an early coordinating body that included the FBI director, J. Edgar Hoover. MI6 might have less money and manpower, he said, but it also had unique strengths. "We are so widely dispersed and can maintain a world-wide intelligence organization," the argument went, and "we intend to remain deployed in this fashion." Brilliance, secret "special facilities," deep experience, and presence to some degree everywhere, he concluded, enabled British intelligence to "compensate to a great degree for our comparatively smaller organization."[53]

The Americans were inclined to agree. They knew they needed these assets as well. Size didn't mean quality, as General Walter Bedell Smith, who'd leave the CIA for the State Department in 1953, understood. Moreover, he acknowledged it would take "a few years" to develop a corps of CIA officers that might be the best in the world.[54] Unfortunately, nearly every director who has followed Smith has made similar claims—after one disaster or another—and usually promising to develop top-quality personnel "in five years," pledges heard in our own day.[55]

. . .

BY THE END OF THE CENTURY, AN ODD MYTH WOULD ARISE ABOUT
Britain's despairing postwar years of empire. It's one in which the establishment got soft and complacent, like that of a refined civilization that
considers itself brotherly toward the world, characterized by high-strata
people, such as the former prime minister Tony Blair, who're known for
their malleability rather than cold-bloodedness.[56] But the myth is hard
to square when we meet some of the alarmingly harsh characters who
wielded power in the imperial activities of those earlier times.

One is George Kennedy Young, who was forty-one in 1952 and
working his way up in MI6. "G.K.," as insiders knew him, was the son
of a poor Scottish grocer, and G.K. liked to emphasize his proletarian
origins. He looked the part of a tough self-made Scot—square-jawed
with a chilling stare. On a fellowship, he'd pulled himself out of Dum-
friesshire to earn an M.A. in politics from Yale just before the war, then
used that exotic credential to move into intelligence, where he ended up
running MI6's Economics Requirements section, and, in 1947, to become head of station in Vienna. In 1961, after rising to the heights as
vice-chief, he would leave MI6 to be a hugely successful merchant
banker at Kleinwort Benson.

Much of the work underlying world order, Young believed, involved
killing. He operated at the edge of acknowledgment, and for him there'd
be no knighthoods. "I am unaware," he writes in one of his books, *Masters
of Indecision*, in which he heaps disdain on his superiors for their pallid
approach to global affairs, "that secret plans are classified as 'Moral' and
'Top Moral.'"[57] "You want to win, don't you?" he'd demand of them,
ignoring—as did others like him on the front lines of empire—the price
at which victory might be won.

In 1952, Young headed the Middle East Desk at MI6. He was among
the operatives who moved in and out of Tehran that year and who impressed the U.S. diplomats there with "great experience and real ability."
He also understood the Americans well, and he knew the arguments
that worked in Washington, especially with the sorts of men who would
be arriving with a new Republican administration, once Dwight Eisenhower won the presidency on November 4. The Americans didn't want

to be involved in every nook and cranny of the globe, as he saw it. That was true. No matter how strong they might be, they were struggling. During those months in Korea, for instance, they couldn't supply enough artillery shells, mortar rounds, and grenades to the battlefront; emergency stocks had to be diverted from U.S. forces in Europe. They'd likely be eager to collaborate, especially in the Middle East, where they had the least experience. To that end, he was busy preparing plans for counter-revolution in Iran.

16

CORONATIONS AND CRISES

By leadership we mean the art of getting someone else to do
something that you want done because he wants to do it, not
because your position of power can compel him to do it, or your
position of authority.
—Dwight D. Eisenhower

T WO WEEKS AFTER WINNING THE PRESIDENCY, DWIGHT EISEN-
hower designated John Foster Dulles to be secretary of state. That
caused annoyance in London. Some months earlier, in May, there had
been a white-tie dinner at 10 Downing Street for Eisenhower, on the
eve of the general's departure from Supreme Headquarters to seek
office. At the dinner, Anthony Eden, who'd known Eisenhower since
the war, urged him, should he win, not to appoint Dulles, and Eden had
returned to the subject after the election, letting it be known that he
preferred New York's governor, Thomas Dewey, in the role. This was an
era when a president-elect might not consider such nerve from London
outrageous and could end up being "almost apologetic," as one distinguished historian concludes, when nonetheless deciding to proceed with
his original choice.[1]

Churchill was eager to see Eisenhower and the men around him as soon as possible, including Dulles, whom he hadn't encountered since their troubled introduction at Bernard Baruch's apartment, in March 1949, when Dulles had offered unwelcome criticism of Churchill's speech for MIT. So he made plans late that fall to pay a visit to America, adding this stop in to a conveniently scheduled family holiday in Jamaica. As it turned out, Churchill arrived in New York on the same day, January 5, and on the same ship, the *Queen Mary*, as he had a year earlier. This time he came with his wife and one of his daughters and her MP husband, as well as a maid, a valet, and the same two detectives. He was heavier and more hunched over than a year earlier, and because this was ostensibly a personal visit Eden stayed behind, though also aboard were the new ambassador to Washington, Sir Roger Makins, and his young family.

Among the dignitaries waiting in the snow flurries that Monday morning were Churchill's friend Baruch and the famous Gladwyn Jebb. Churchill highlighted the visit's informality by arriving at the West Fiftieth Street pier in black nautical garb and carrying the peaked cap of Cowes, his country's oldest yacht club. During an impromptu shipboard press conference, a reporter asked if Britain's atomic program might now be scientifically more advanced than America's. The prime minister dodged.[2] Once the police had cleared the way through Irish American pickets, he was driven to Baruch's residence, where he'd stay for three days.

The president-elect was shaping his administration from a blocked-off, well-guarded sixth-floor suite at the Commodore Hotel, adjacent to Grand Central Station. But because he still led Columbia University, he was again living in the president's house on Morningside Heights—a grand six-story mansion designed by McKim, Mead, and White. Eisenhower looked nearly unchanged from his famous World War II photographs. He was a lean, broad-shouldered five foot ten with soft gray-blue eyes that could turn icy in a second. He had a decisive manner, walked like a young man, and, now at sixty-two, had developed nearly complete self-control, having spent a lifetime trying to stifle an appalling temper. His suits were custom-tailored, and he wore a gold Rolex Datejust, but his demeanor said "Kansas," not "New York." He came to Baruch's building that afternoon at five, on his way home, stepping out of his car before it fully stopped. Secret Service agents hurriedly secured the corner of Fifth Avenue and Sixty-Sixth Street and flanked him into the lobby, where he went up to the apartment alone.

Baruch and Churchill, joined by Jock Colville, the private secretary, were waiting for him there. They had drinks in the living room, and then the two leaders withdrew to talk alone for an hour as they overlooked Central Park. Eisenhower had to dash up to Columbia, but they all regrouped at eight o'clock for dinner and more discussion, which included questions concerning Asia, access to U.S. nuclear secrets, and how to deal with Moscow. Eisenhower remarked that he expected to meet Stalin sometime soon (having said the opposite in his campaign) and added that he intended to do so alone. Churchill, he said, was "quite welcome" to see Stalin by himself, should he like.[3] For the moment, Eisenhower had blocked any maneuvering for a summit of the Three.

Churchill met Dulles separately the next day and laid out his requirements: a U.S. commitment to a defense pact for Southeast Asia that could resemble NATO; Britain's entry into the invidious ANZUS treaty arrangements from which the mother country had been excluded; and an understanding of U.S. intentions for Taiwan. He ended up thinking even less of Dulles than before. He found him to be a dogmatic moralist and told Colville that he didn't want to see him again—a wish made unlikely when the Senate unanimously confirmed Dulles as secretary of state, on January 21.

Dulles, for his part, had doubts about Churchill, who, he scribbled in his notes, had no mastery of the facts. Dulles also recorded, with some concern, that "Mr. Churchill expressed a very low view of the French."[4] Eisenhower too found Churchill to be vague. He had heard nothing worth reporting to his other cabinet nominees and wrote in his diary that Churchill's idea of re-creating an FDR-type personal relationship was fatuous. The press revealed days later that Eisenhower, who was sixteen years younger, had asked Churchill if it might be time to retire.

Churchill saw these encounters differently, as did Colville, who had reminded Baruch at their dinner of Britain's "unrivalled technical ability." He implied it was several steps ahead of America's.[5] Colville wrote in his own diary that Churchill felt he had come out "on top" in his meetings with Eisenhower and that Eisenhower had deferred to his age and experience.

A little after noon on Thursday, January 8, Churchill flew with a small staff on the president's plane to Washington. Harriman, Acheson, and Ambassador Makins greeted him at National. "I'm looking forward to seeing Mr. Truman," Churchill told Harriman, who was heading the Mutual Security Agency, and he reminded Harriman that he'd gone to Fulton with Truman. "You remember Fulton," Churchill teased, before adding, "I got in trouble for being a little in front of the weather."[6]

Following lunch and Churchill's nap at the embassy, Makins took the prime minister to the White House, where, at 4:00 p.m., they saw the president, who was joined by Snyder and Acheson, as well as by Lovett and Harriman. Churchill again recalled Fulton and how his speech had been attacked. "There is not much point in being a prophet unless one is premature," he said. His emphasis on Fulton wasn't mere reminiscing. He was underscoring to Truman, as he had to Eisenhower and the powerful men who surrounded them both, that it was *he* who had the most experience in handling Stalin.

Weighing on Truman's mind, during these reflections, were Hiroshima and Nagasaki. "I know we did the right thing," he said.[7] Truman and Churchill agreed that the horrifying detonations had given Japan reason to surrender, and that the bomb had prevented Russia from lunging for the English Channel soon after the war. But the most difficult decision, Truman admitted, had been to intervene in Korea. Churchill replied that the rescue of South Korea was far less important than had been America's mobilization, practically overnight, into a worldwide military presence.

The Republicans had won paper-thin majorities in the House and the Senate on Eisenhower's coattails, and the Eighty-Third Congress had already been sworn in on January 3. Now the House Committee on Armed Services wasn't as buoyant about America's strengths. Earlier that day, its members had publicly grilled Secretary of Defense Bob Lovett about shortages of weapons and ammunition on the Korean battlefront. The Pentagon was beginning to reach its stride, Lovett testified, and factories were producing $2 billion to $3 billion of armaments a month—but that didn't divert the congressmen from focusing on screwups in logistics. Churchill had been well briefed by Makins on this exchange by the time he saw the president in the late afternoon. So he raised similar questions to those of the committee. Surely the British Empire could help, suggested Churchill—with jet engine production, for example. But this was no longer the concern of a departing president. They also discussed Iran and Egypt.

Churchill then returned to the embassy, where, at the unconvincing hour of 6:00 p.m., reporters were told that he was having "a late cup of tea" with Senators Lyndon Johnson and Robert Taft, joined by Vice President Alben Barkley and Speaker of the House Joe Martin.[8]

Churchill hosted a dinner that Thursday night at the embassy. Attending were President Truman, JCS chairman Bradley, George Marshall (retired once more), CIA director Bedell Smith, Snyder, and Acheson, as well as Harriman, Lovett, and others. Snyder was amicable. He had an easygoing rapport with Churchill. Before long, however, Acheson began to cause trouble. He declared that Britain would finally have to show more leadership in Europe because the incoming Republican administration was certain to stumble. Furthermore, Acheson said, he had been reading up on the Stamp Act of 1765 and America's War for Independence: Britain's rigidity in the Middle East could prove just as unfortunate as had been its handling of the American colonies. Churchill didn't respond to Acheson's latest jabs. Instead, he launched into a diatribe against Egypt, and he praised Israel—"to the disagreement of practically all the Americans present," Colville recounts, "though they admitted that the large Jewish vote would prevent them from disagreeing publicly."[9]

The next morning, Churchill flew to Jamaica to rejoin his family, but he was in for a surprise. The embassy discussions had been private, yet Bedell Smith shared much of what was discussed with *The New York Times'* James Reston. On Monday, the *Times* published the hardest-hitting points, such as Acheson's concern that the British were overestimating their strength in the Middle East. Ambassador Makins had this exposé sent to Churchill in Montego Bay.

. . .

"IT RATHER LOOKS AS THOUGH THOSE WHO WANTED A CHANGE ARE going to get it," remarked Edward R. Murrow, the renowned CBS broadcaster, on Inauguration Day, January 20, 1953. That seemed likely, but voters believed they already knew Eisenhower, the general who'd led the crusade in Europe. Journalists wrote of his "Tom Sawyer grin," though it helps to remember that Tom Sawyer is the supreme American trickster. Eisenhower offered a face to the world that masked a political operator whom it took another generation to understand: the shrewd master of deadly practicalities with the bumbling syntax of a local politician; a reader of westerns who studied the financial pages and had an expert grasp of statistics. Eisenhower was hard to figure out, and he liked the cloud of confusion that surrounded him. Clever people might believe themselves superior, but he was in charge.

Eisenhower was a figure out of the small-town, small-church past, environments that, just like the upper echelons of the old officer corps, can be more viciously competitive than larger impersonal ones. He had mastered organizational complexity, as he had demonstrated in World War II: colossal intellectual effort, after all, accompanies wartime supreme command, to consider just the preparations he undertook for D-day. He was a man of business, and his business was war. His diplomatic instincts were also acute, as they'd have to be after spending seven years as an aide for a vainglorious general, Douglas MacArthur, during the 1930s.

By the time he became president, Eisenhower had surrounded himself with new friends: this was a set of rich, shrewd, down-to-earth businessmen who all cheerfully called themselves "the gang." It included pals such as Ellis D. "Slats" Slater, the head of Frankfort Distillers, and W. Alton "Pete" Jones, the chairman of Cities Service Oil Company. Like Eisenhower, the members of the gang all shared his love of hard work as well as his pieties, among them balancing the budget and cutting taxes. His successor, John F. Kennedy, was fascinated by Eisenhower's newfound prosperity and friendships.[10] But the close-knit nature of the gang was comforting for Eisenhower. These men offered him financial support, to an extent that would raise eyebrows today; they also provided a useful sounding board on business and the economy, and they used golf as a common bond.

Churchill was ambivalent about Eisenhower. Right after the November election, for example, Colville notes Churchill's disappointment in Eisenhower's victory, though his regret had more to do with the GOP's inflammatory stance on Russia and China than with Eisenhower himself. Yet Colville wrote of Churchill's describing the president-elect as a "man of limited stature," a remark also recorded in the diary of Churchill's physician, Lord Moran.[11] Nonetheless, as Churchill had told reporters during his shipboard Q&A in New York, he and Eisenhower had met at least a hundred times over the years to resolve various sorts of business. The first was after Pearl Harbor, during the prime minister's twenty-four-day stay at the White House, when he and Roosevelt were forging the Grand Alliance against Nazism. Eisenhower had been a very new brigadier (that is, a one-star general) and was among several officers from the army's War Plans Division whom Roosevelt introduced. Churchill came to admire "Ike" as a commander but thought him naive on political issues—a view that hadn't changed by the time of the prime minister's 1953 visit.[12]

Much of America's greatness lay in its vaunted processes of mass production, and an assembly line might as well have stamped out the millionaire CEOs who filled Eisenhower's cabinet. They were solid, aging, stress-proven men—experienced, Protestant, humane, and distinctly children of an older America. John Foster Dulles, sixty-four, was one of them. Eisenhower described him as having been "raised to be Secretary of State since he was five," which he meant as praise but which implied a lot of useless preparation given how fast the world was changing.

With his wire-rim glasses and flat methodical voice, Foster Dulles, as people called him, also reminded one journalist of someone "out of Kansas," which is an odd description of Wall Street's highest-paid corporation lawyer. He, too, was different from what he seemed. Physically, at six feet, he came across as something of a bear: dour, lumbering, and ungainly, not a sophisticate. He wore rumpled Brooks Brothers suits and socks that slid down to his ankles. Churchill mocked his "great slab of a face." Another Foreign Office diarist said Dulles had chronic bad breath, which is untrue but has become a tidbit that writers keep using to fill out the picture of him as an oaf.[13] Yet Dulles could move with the sudden quickness of a superb rough-weather sailor, as he was, and he had both a powerful physique, conditioned by endless laps of swimming, and a brain that could slice through reams of data.

Foster Dulles was born in 1888 in Washington, D.C., the grandson and nephew of secretaries of state, though his father was the pastor of the First Presbyterian Church in remote upstate Watertown, New York. He graduated second in Princeton's class of 1908 and received a fellowship to study philosophy at the Sorbonne. "I remember," he once let slip, "when I was a student at the Sorbonne, I used to go and riot occasionally."[14] He had indeed, joining the fracas staged by Catholic true believers against Anatole France's scurrilous book *The Life of Joan of Arc* (1908), which was immediately placed on the Vatican's Prohibited Book Index. What other ambitious American Protestant, of the sort who'd end up in Eisenhower's cabinet, would have done such a thing? That outburst reflected his own lifelong romantic bent, which embarrassed his friends and set his enemies' teeth on edge.

At thirty-one, and working for his uncle Robert Lansing, he had attended the Paris Peace Conference, with all its hopes that a war had just been fought to end all war. He had the sense to argue against suffocating Germany in reparations, as occurred anyway in the treaty to be signed at Versailles. A generation later, right before being confirmed as secretary, he believed it appropriate to resign from the National Council of Churches' Department of Justice and Goodwill. Yet when the Senate Foreign Relations Committee chairman asked if he had any specific policy changes in mind, Dulles replied, "Well, I think the change that is most needed is a change of heart."

Eisenhower also appointed Foster's brother Allen, fifty-nine, as the new director of Central Intelligence. Allen had started out as a lawyer, rising to become a partner as well at Sullivan & Cromwell during the 1930s, and was nearly his brother's opposite: a pipe-smoking boulevardier who enjoyed Georgetown parties and discreet affairs and had the mind of "a bumble bee," recalled Richard Helms, CIA director from 1966 to 1973. Allen, he said, "would hop from issue to issue."[15] During the war, Allen headed the OSS office in Switzerland and by the time of Eisenhower's election had been a top official at the agency for two years. He became the first civilian director and remained for more than eight years, the longest duration ever.

Eisenhower had a specific reason for the appointment: he wanted close ties between CIA's intelligence gathering and the State Department. Foster's position as secretary made it easier for CIA officers to get diplomatic cover and logistical support. The brothers talked daily, with regular Saturday meetings in Foster's spacious stone house, on a wooded hillside along Thirty-Second Street Northwest, where they were often joined by James Angleton, of clandestine services, or other senior agency officers, and by occasional top people from State, such as Livingston Merchant, a Foreign Service professional who was the new assistant secretary for European Affairs.[16]

The president and the Dulles brothers held different views on the British Empire from their predecessors. During the war, Eisenhower had faced four bitter years of quarrels with the British over strategy and resources. Painful abrasions were nothing new. Foster had none of Acheson's inherent scorn for England, but as a Wall Street lawyer he had a keener sense for incipient bankruptcy, which he could at times detect. Moreover, he knew that Eden had tried blocking him from the cabinet role he'd coveted all his life, and a man as perceptive as he must have noticed the disdain Churchill harbored for him. As for Allen, he had personally felt the heavy hand of the Raj. Right out of Princeton, in 1914, he'd taught English for a year in a Presbyterian missionary school in Allahabad, where he'd been startled by the injustices of the colonial regime. He had attended secret meetings of India's independence movement and had met the young barrister Jawaharlal Nehru. He didn't forget the experience.

EISENHOWER HAD NEVER LIVED IN A BIG INDUSTRIAL CITY BEFORE becoming president of Columbia University. He didn't have the background, let alone the disposition, to anticipate the vitality of a wide-open consumer-driven democracy. To him, the economy was something fragile, and he was ever mindful of that as he strove to maintain high employment without the deficits and inflation of the Truman years. Big pork-filled Pentagon budgets didn't fit with his solid Republican fiscal priorities, which included paying off the public debt. Among other steps, he scrapped the sky-high spending implications of NSC 68 that had appeared two months before the Korean War. He felt duty-bound to impose prudent limits on what America could do overseas. The United States had no ambitions for world power, he asserted, decrying the very idea as alien to the spirit of the nation. He fondly remembered the thriftiness of the Coolidge years, when it would have been inconceivable to pay billions to the Europeans in hopes of maintaining their goodwill.

Given Eisenhower's outlook, Churchill had to devote himself, as one of his key ministers, Harold Macmillan, put it, to "keeping the Americans in the game."[17] The new administration's solid Republican bankers and businessmen were upset by a $256 billion national debt (with federal spending of $78.6 billion), and they knew military outlays to be a sinkhole. The U.S. Army divisions that were by then on the Continent were pledged to return home. In Asia, the Joint Chiefs expected GIs and marines to be withdrawn from Korea once the conflict ended, and from democratic Japan too as its economy strengthened. In April, Eisenhower proposed to cut $8.5 billion from the next military budget, even though Admiral Arthur Radford, who took over from the retiring General Bradley as JCS chairman in July, told anyone who asked that U.S. forces at existing levels were barely adequate for the times.

It might also be difficult for the United States to rely on friends and allies to help carry the burden. That's because Congress was getting weary of supplying economic and military aid, or what Idaho's isolationist Republican senator, Henry Dworshak, who sat on the Appropriations Committee, called offering "crutches and bribes."[18] Neither Churchill nor his government's sharpest civil servants could predict the outcome if the Americans chose to handle what defense commitments they had as cheaply and indirectly as possible.

The worst danger remained a miscalculation by Russia. With much drama in *Pravda* about "assassins in white coats," Stalin was preparing another purge during the winter of 1952–1953. And who could guess his next move? Arrests had begun of prominent Moscow doctors, mostly Jews, who were said to be conspiring with the "Anglo-American intelligence services" to kill Kremlin bosses. Even in that demented climate, Churchill kept angling for a summit of the Three, although he told the

Commons in February, to macabre howls of laughter, that if he went to Moscow, he'd be sure to bring his own physician.

Then Stalin died on March 5, 1953, from a cerebral hemorrhage. It was anyone's guess what might follow among the wolves of Stalin's court. Conceivably, the madness would wane. On the other hand, the new Republican chairman of the Senate Foreign Relations Committee, Wisconsin's Alexander Wiley, suggested that Stalin might have been a "restraining influence."[19] Kennan had predicted that a convulsion would occur within the Politburo, but that didn't happen, nor were State and the CIA quarreling over how to respond.[20] Along the Potomac, and within the fortress on the Moscow River, everyone watched and waited.

Just six days after the news about Stalin, Churchill called for "a high-level meeting" with the new Soviet leaders, whoever they were. In the two months that followed, Churchill wrote to Eisenhower thirteen times, pushing this idea of a summit. Eisenhower, who responded to Stalin's death calmly, was astonished by Churchill's urgency and dismayed by his readiness to trundle to Moscow, perhaps even alone, rather than to insist on seeing the Russians (including Molotov, who had returned as foreign minister) on neutral ground.

On Monday, May 11, Churchill issued another call for a meeting with the Russians "at the highest level." He did so late that afternoon in the House of Commons, and this time he added cuttingly that he saw no reason "why anyone should be frightened at having a try." The "anyone" he had in mind seemed to be Eisenhower, and *The New York Times* understood this remark as Churchill's bid for the diplomatic leadership of the West.[21]

IF CHURCHILL'S PRIORITY IN THE HALF YEAR AFTER THE PRESIDEN-tial inauguration was to keep the Americans engaged, Eisenhower's was to avoid appearances of collusion with the British Empire, and he had made that point to Churchill in New York. Being too close to Britain, Eisenhower reflected in his diary, would look like "a combination of forces to compel the adherence to the status quo."[22] He sought better ties with Muslim states, and he sympathized with the Egyptian officers' aspirations for sovereignty. Churchill feared the worst. "Surely you are not going to start your term," he wrote, "by supplying arms to Egypt which may be turned against the former comrades who fought under your command." Discreetly, he also conveyed two threats: the question of U.S. air bases in England might be revisited; and imperial forces, as he called British troops, were once more poised to reoccupy Cairo and Alexandria, if guerrilla assaults continued. The purpose, he said, was "to prevent a massacre of white people," which even then sounded a little selective.[23]

The attitude in Whitehall was equally harsh toward the Americans. "Those who are not with us are against us," wrote A.D.M. Ross, counselor at the Foreign Office.[24] But the seasoned Jefferson Caffery was still ambassador in Cairo, and he cautioned Secretary Dulles against "ganging up" with the British on the new Egyptian regime. Churchill made other threats. Perhaps he'd withdraw British troops from Korea, he told the administration, if he didn't receive support for Britain's rights in Egypt. Instead, the Export-Import Bank arranged a small $10 million grant for the Egyptians so they could buy midwestern wheat.

Churchill need not have worried. Eisenhower overcame his good instincts and didn't take the steps that might have developed a better relationship with the Free Officers. Anthony Nutting, the stylish MP known as "Eden's Eden," and the youngest member of Churchill's government, summed up what instead occurred: "The Americans tamely accepted Britain's veto on supplying arms to Egypt."[25] Nor, at Churchill's insistence, did they supply any more economic aid. John Foster Dulles explained why: at this point, he said, "we did not feel that we could afford an open break with the British."[26]

In London, Eden had been living on his nerves, constantly pacing, and suffering intestinal agonies. Only his charm and inherent decency helped him run the Foreign Office, as he suffered through workweeks of stomach pain. He needed a gallbladder operation, which, at the time, was a risky procedure. But Eden agreed to have it done nonetheless, on April 12, and as clinical records show, it didn't go well. A slip of the surgeon's knife cut into his biliary tract, which caused life-threatening complications and soon led to two more operations. Only after the third, on June 10, at the New England Baptist Hospital (twinned with Boston's adjacent Lahey Clinic), did his condition stabilize. The seventy-eight-year-old Churchill took over the Foreign Office for the first two months of Eden's ordeal, which meant he was very much in charge during May, when John Foster Dulles made the first trip of any U.S. secretary of state to the Middle East.[27]

ON MAY 9, FOSTER DULLES EXPLAINED AT A WASHINGTON NEWS CON-ference that he was about to embark on a Middle Eastern journey that might prevent these distant lands from falling to Communism, as had China. He left within hours on a twenty-day trip, the first stop being Cairo, where he arrived on the eleventh. Churchill managed to undercut this visit, starting with the speech he gave in the Commons that same day.

Churchill's speech of May 11 was one of his last great set pieces of oratory. It's the one in which he implied that Eisenhower feared a summit with the Russians. But that came after he'd done what the Americans feared most: he summarized his final confidential talk with Truman and claimed that the previous U.S. administration had agreed that the British and the Americans "should act together" in handling Egypt.[28] And he hinted that President Eisenhower felt the same way, but added coyly that he was not at liberty to disclose the details of how the two countries might now be cooperating. For good measure, he told the Commons, and the rest of the world, that Secretary Dulles was arriving that very moment in Cairo. This was all a gross breach of confidence and an exaggeration that made Dulles's motives in coming to Egypt suspect. It was no slip of the tongue. That's known because worse was to follow.

After arriving, Dulles called on Egypt's foreign minister, Mahmoud Fawzi, that same afternoon, at 4:00. Fawzi made two key points. Egyptians, he said, "would like to see the U.S. measure up to its role of leadership." He was also concerned that Dulles had plans to visit Jerusalem on this trip. Wouldn't that undercut America's position on the city— that it should be internationalized for all peoples, according to the 1949 UN General Assembly resolution? Dulles saw no political significance to his going. He explained that to him, as a Christian, Jerusalem was a sacred place. He didn't know whom he would see there; and, personally, he had always believed that its future would require a "large measure of internationalization."[29]

An hour later, Dulles, Ambassador Caffery, and the rest of the American party sat down with Prime Minister Naguib in his council room. Dulles handed the general an inscribed silver-plated pistol from the president. Israel for the moment wasn't among Naguib's priorities, though Dulles assured him "that the Republican Administration does not owe the same degree of political debt as did the Democrats to Jewish groups."[30] Naguib instead made a plea that the Americans "free us from British occupation," which at this point meant eighty thousand personnel in the Canal Zone. Dulles blandly replied that Egypt's military leaders had to appreciate how important Suez was for the West's defense, adding that "no one could afford to have a power vacuum in the Base." Naguib was hearing this while, at the same hour in London, Churchill was standing in the Commons wrapping up his speech about U.S. collusion.

Colonel Nasser, who was really the junta's strongman, met formally with Dulles the next afternoon, at 12:15, having already sparred with him over dinner at Caffery's Villa Mosseri residence the night before. Speaking quietly in English, Nasser presented himself as a sorely annoyed Egyptian patriot. No "vacuum" existed in Egypt, he explained: the Egyptians were living there. Dulles, for his part, suggested that Nasser enter a truce of sorts with the British who'd been attacked in their cities along the canal by guerrillas some thirty times in the preceding weeks. Might those fighters be restrained at least until he returned to Washington? They didn't discuss the Churchill speech, though by now it was common knowledge in Cairo. Whatever hopes or suspicions Nasser had didn't matter. Churchill's next move poisoned the dialogue.

On May 13, while Dulles and his party were still in Cairo, more news arrived from London: six hundred Royal Marine commandos were being sent from the island fortress of Malta to defend British interests in the Canal Zone. Neither State nor the Pentagon was forewarned. Dulles's attempt to calm the waters, not surprisingly, ended.

First with his speech, and then with the high-profile deployment of commandos to Egypt, Churchill was rapping the Americans' knuckles for "poaching," as Grady called it, in British terrain. Yet Dulles was undeterred. He continued with his larger mission to understand the region. He flew next to Tel Aviv, where he met with Prime Minister Ben-Gurion, and thereafter to Jordan, Syria, Lebanon, Iraq, Libya, and Saudi Arabia—twelve countries altogether, while avoiding crisis-ridden Iran.[31] He told reporters traveling with him that he hoped "we can now straighten things out" most everywhere in the Middle East.[32]

AFTER GEORGE VI'S DEATH, CHURCHILL, IN HIS ROLE AS PRIME MINister, was responsible for arranging Queen Elizabeth's coronation. He requested permission to delay the grand affair for a year, until the country was on firmer economic footing. As it turned out, the delay extended to late spring 1953. By that time, austerity had mostly disappeared. The pound sterling's free market price nearly hit its "official" or pegged value of $2.80, and for the first time in eleven years meat, milk, and white bread were all unrestricted.

The coronation finally occurred on June 2, 1953, in Westminster Abbey. It was not only a religious-cultural event but also one of the biggest political-military spectacles of the twentieth century. Eisenhower appointed General George Marshall to chair America's four-person delegation, which also included General Omar Bradley (who led the JCS until July), Governor Earl Warren of California, and the socialite-editor Fleur Cowles.

The three-hour service in Westminster Abbey began that morning at 11:15. Then came a two-mile-long procession. The weather was miserable, with dull skies, a chill wind, and squalls of rain. But every regiment in the empire and commonwealth was represented, including a Malay contingent in white uniforms and green sarongs, Canadian Mounties, Kenyan scouts, slouch-hatted Australians, and impressively modern warriors from Britain's Army of the Rhine. In the late afternoon, the queen appeared with her family on the balcony of Buckingham Palace. She waved to the cheering crowds as RAF jets streaked across the Mall in tight formation.

That evening, Elizabeth II thanked the public in a broadcast and promised to serve the nation. But she was really speaking to all her subjects "spread far and wide through every continent and ocean in the world." And she was doing so as the monarch of Pakistan and Canada, of South Africa and Australia, and of other lands big and small—all of them allies or possessions that had sent lofty delegations to see her crowned. That included India, whose republican constitution didn't regard the monarch as sovereign. But India was part of the commonwealth, which, Elizabeth made clear, resembled no previous empire in history. It was an ideal of equal partners of races and nations, of societies old and new. No need to add that this expanse—including the multifaceted empire itself—embraced some 600 million people: "every continent and ocean" still added up to one-fourth of the globe.

While Coronation Day services were being held at the National Cathedral in Washington, film of the ceremony was raced across the Atlantic to Labrador in an RAF Canberra bomber, which had set a new altitude record three weeks earlier. The canisters were then transferred to a Royal Canadian Air Force fighter jet to be sped to Montreal. Two more Canberras flew in with the latest batches of film, and the U.S. networks arranged for their own copies to be flown to New York. That same evening, ninety-five million people in North America watched a British monarch being crowned. Television feed was taken in France, West Germany, and the Netherlands for millions of more viewers.

Thirteen days later, with sun and a steady wind off the Hampshire coast, came the Coronation Naval Review. The Royal Navy was at its postwar peak. Aboard HMS *Surprise*, the queen surveyed over two hundred warships from the Royal Navy, Royal Canadian Navy, and Royal Australian Navy and vessels from the Indian, Pakistani, and New Zealand navies. Carriers, cruisers, destroyers, subs, and frigates all gathered in four parallel lines, in a procession that stretched seven nautical miles between the Isle of Wight and the mainland's shore. Nine British carriers then sailed in file behind the battleship *Vanguard* as, in a thunderous roar, every gun saluted twenty-one times beneath a three-hundred-plane flyby from the Fleet Air Arm. The sight and sound, as found on newsreels, is unforgettable. Among other ships on the scene were two visiting cruisers: officers aboard the USS *Baltimore* and Russia's *Sverdlov* observed every move.

As a display of might, it was impressive. And there was even more to the Royal Navy than could be seen. The press reported eight more carriers under construction.[33] The Americans may have possessed four times the naval manpower but still had plenty of reasons to believe that the Royal Navy, with its sixty young admirals overseeing three major high-tech fleets, was "indispensable" to U.S. defense.[34] In August, the RAF flexed some more muscle by conducting its biggest-ever exercise, one that drew in U.S. fighter squadrons and bombers stationed in England. After that was accomplished, the RAF let it be known that it planned to integrate the lessons learned with the R&D it had under way for supersonic rockets.

Russia could demonstrate nothing like this. If one didn't look too closely, Britain appeared to be a superpower at the height of its game.

Inevitably, there was carping on both sides of the Atlantic about the coronation's splendor. The big day alone cost more than twenty-five times what Americans had recently spent on Eisenhower's inauguration. On June 1, in an article that appeared on the front page of *The New York Times*, C. L. Sulzberger wrote that he believed the coronation to be a substitute for Britain's having "relinquished the position of superpower" (a rare use of the new term "superpower"). He wrote of the Royal Navy having fallen to third place and London no longer being the center of world finance. However, the Royal Navy itself wasn't resigned to being third, and, anyway, London hadn't been the world's financial center since 1914. Tellingly, Sulzberger had to acknowledge Britain's ongoing presence in "a high portion of the globe," as well as the belief that this might be the birth of a new era.[35]

That conclusion was more in line with how the actual *Times* (of London) saw Britain's stature. On June 4, it editorialized that America had little experience in world leadership and then extolled the virtues of an empire that was transforming itself into a global, multiracial commonwealth. Grumbling aside, Americans were riveted by this world-spanning display of ethnicities, cultures, and religions—along with plenty of heavy artillery.

The twenty-seven-year-old head of state offered her subjects the promise of half a century or so of predictable leadership. That said, her government was shaky. On the evening of June 23, nearly two weeks after Eden's intestinal operation in Boston, Churchill had a severe stroke at dinner in Number 10, and during the days ahead, his physician, Lord

Moran, felt he was likely to die. Amazingly, Churchill rebounded—to the extent possible for a man of seventy-eight who worked tirelessly, lived indulgently, and had taken little exercise since he'd stopped playing polo at fifty. Eden's recovery, however, was slow. After leaving the hospital, he recuperated in Newport, Rhode Island, nursed by Clarissa, then returned to London in late July. By October, he was working seven days a week at the Foreign Office, but he was not well.

IN 1953, WISCONSIN'S JOSEPH McCARTHY, FORTY-FOUR, WAS AT the height of his malevolence as chairman of the U.S. Senate Permanent Subcommittee on Investigations. By then, the phenomenon of "Mc-Carthyism" had married contempt for common law and decency with a midwestern detestation of foreign policy, and among the people he attacked in his wide-ranging campaign against Communists real and imagined was Clement Attlee, now opposition leader in the Commons. "Comrade Attlee," he told the Senate in his strange singsong voice, had saluted Communist troops in 1937 during the Spanish Civil War. That was a lie, but tensions rose when Attlee replied, with quiet sarcasm, that he and the Labour Party had been fighting Communism before Senator McCarthy was ever heard of. Matters escalated from there and swirled around the problem of China.

McCarthy's assistant counsel on the subcommittee was Robert Kennedy, twenty-seven, younger brother of the new Massachusetts senator, John F. Kennedy, and a son of the appeasement-oriented former ambassador to Britain, Joseph Kennedy Sr., who had become a pal of McCarthy's. Bobby got the job through his father and, as McCarthy's loyal aide, made the issue of Britain's trading with the enemy his very own.

Kennedy stoked the public's anger at the British, which reached an intensity that hadn't been seen since Britain had defaulted on its World War I debt in 1932. He claimed in May that an "absolute minimum" of a hundred British-registered vessels were trading with Communist China already that year and that twice the number had done so the year before—and who knew what strategic items their cargoes might contain?[36] Moreover, British ships were said to also be transporting Communist troops along China's coast. Kennedy claimed his sources to be naval intelligence, but much of the research he received came from the subcommittee's staff.

Other allied nations were also trading with China, among them Greece, which, like Turkey, had by then joined NATO. But under the hot glare of television lights, Kennedy and the McCarthy committee knew how to reap the most publicity. Two-thirds of all Western-flagged ships that arrived in China's ports, Kennedy claimed that summer, were British. McCarthy's publicity-hungry investigators were convinced that Britain could prevent Ceylon, for example, from conveying rubber to China. Ambassador Makins argued that Ceylon (today's Sri Lanka) was an independent nation, albeit in the British Commonwealth, and had a right to its own decisions, but few were convinced on Capitol Hill, or elsewhere in the country, and even Foster Dulles's Senate testimony in May on Britain's behalf hadn't helped. U.S. warships began to shadow British merchantmen near Chinese waters.

Eden responded. In one of his last statements before reentering the hospital, he asserted that the Royal Navy would protect British vessels from being harassed. Then McCarthy went further: "Let us sink any accursed ship which is carrying arms to the Communists killing American boys," he angrily told the Senate, referencing British merchantmen.[37] The inconclusive armistice reached in Korea that July—followed by a U.S. mutual defense treaty with Seoul in August—calmed matters slightly. By the winter, however, the Americans were placing armed guards on British ships that called at U.S. ports, such as Los Angeles, before sailing to the People's Republic.

ON AUGUST 8, RUSSIA SET OFF A HYDROGEN BOMB. IT WAS A SObering moment, but Churchill put a positive spin on it. His argument was simple, as it was after the U.S. detonation: Atomic bombs might make a small and crowded island terribly vulnerable, but the development of H-bombs, which were vastly more destructive, could destroy continental-sized powers too. Everybody was now equally exposed, and, by the way, it was only a matter of time before Britain entered the thermonuclear club.

Meanwhile, Churchill mended steadily at Chartwell and took satisfaction in how the U.S. approach to Iran was changing. Eisenhower and Dulles were more receptive than their predecessor to his outlook. They were convinced that Iran was about to plunge into chaos, and at best they saw Mosaddeq as the kind of well-meaning nationalist demagogue behind whose eccentric facade hard revolutionaries might move into place. The result, Christopher de Bellaigue concludes in *Patriot of Persia*, was that "the United States allowed itself to become Britain's accomplice and trigger-man."[38]

There had been a small CIA presence in the country since 1947, as the Iran Desk officer at State during 1953 would recall. It had been kept low-key, he said, because otherwise "the British would have squashed it."[39] Iran was British turf, and anything more substantial would have been regarded as meddling. Yet now there was collaboration. Mosaddeq's twenty-eight-month-old democratic government wouldn't last much longer.

No one at State or in the CIA was particularly hostile to Mosaddeq, recalled the counselor at the U.S. embassy in Tehran, but anxieties rose in Washington over the consequences of Mosaddeq's inability to reach agreement with the British.[40] And so Washington and London colluded in his ouster. In Tehran, government officials, reporters, businessmen, and local thugs were bribed to support the shah, and—after fits, starts, and violence in the streets—on August 19 a royalist army general consolidated the pieces to overthrow Mosaddeq. His life was spared, thanks to pressure from the U.S. embassy; his foreign minister executed. A new government, more attuned to Western interests, enabled an American consortium to break the British monopoly and work with the AIOC (renamed British Petroleum the next year) in operating Abadan and the oil fields, splitting profits with Tehran. As for G. K. Young, who was running British covert operations in the Middle East, this seemingly easy victory prompted him to set up MI6's Special Activities division the next year in hopes of routinizing such work.

In U.S. government circles, the CIA took credit for a successful coup, which was its initial attempt at third-world king making. The British implied that all the agency had done was to send the head of its

Near East section to pay off Iranian army officers and agents whom MI6 had already organized. The argument seems beside the point: the eminent Middle East scholar Ray Takeyh has shown that Mosaddeq had already lost his political base among constitutionalists, Islamists, merchants, and the civil service and was poised to fall anyway.[41] If events had taken such a turn, the outcome would likely have been the same, except for today's vilification of the United States.

ELSEWHERE IN THE MIDDLE EAST, ARABS AND ISRAELIS REMAINED in a state of war. Egypt was barring Israeli ships from the Suez Canal and still blocked the Straits of Tiran; the Israelis retained the bank accounts and safe-deposit boxes of all Palestinian refugees, and within Israel, Palestinians were subject to military rule—permits were required to leave their towns or villages.[42] Washington lawmakers, as *The New York Times* observed, were tempted to say "a plague on both your houses" and instead look to Turkey, Pakistan, and now Iran to create a defensive line—a so-called northern arc over the Middle East—to deter Russia.[43] This made sense to the chairman of the Senate Foreign Relations Committee, Alexander Wiley, who believed it disastrous for America to take either a "pro-Arab" or a "pro-Israel" approach.[44] But the Arab-Israeli truce was crumbling, which made it difficult to turn away. And the violence got worse.

On the night of October 14, in retaliation for the killing of three Israelis, 130 soldiers of the Israel Defense Forces struck the village of Qibya, twenty miles northwest of Jerusalem, on the Jordanian-occupied West Bank. "They shot every man, woman and child they could find," reported *Time* magazine, "then turned their fire on the cattle," dynamiting houses, a school, and a mosque.[45] The attack left sixty-nine Palestinians dead, with no IDF casualties. Churchill was appalled. He said he had not felt such shock since the killing of his friend Lord Moyne in 1944. In Washington, U.S. officials drew comparisons to a notorious massacre in the village of Deir Yassin during Israel's war of independence. Abba Eban, who served as Israeli ambassador to both Washington and the UN, declared he would "not say a single word" in justification.[46]

Qibya had three important consequences in the run-up to the Suez war in 1956. First, it undercut Britain's stabilizing role in Jordan: for many years, Britain financed, equipped, and commanded Jordan's army and security force—then about fifteen thousand volunteers known as the Arab Legion—and in 1948 it had pledged to protect Jordan if the kingdom were attacked. Second, Qibya generated international outrage and compelled Israel to instead focus its attacks and retaliations on military rather than on civilian targets. And, third, it further entangled America in the Arab-Israeli quarrel.

In Qibya's aftermath, Secretary Dulles publicly revealed that the Eisenhower administration had already withheld $26 million in construction funds from Israel due to charges of its diverting water from the Jordan River. Pressure from what the historian Benny Morris has called "the pro-Israel lobby" followed. Dulles detected the Israeli embassy's coordinating role and angrily told one group of Americans advocating for Israel that they'd do better "working with representatives of the Israeli Government."[47] Furthermore, on November 24, the Americans spearheaded the UN resolution that condemned Israel for Qibya and ensured that "the Palestine question" would be addressed for the first time since 1951.

CHURCHILL REBOUNDED FROM HIS STROKE, ALREADY OFFERING quips and epigrams to his cabinet in mid-August. On October 11, he made a rousing comeback speech at the Conservative Party conference in Margate, where he implied that the Americans stood in the way of a summit with Russia. For months, a discreet inner circle of the cabinet had expected him to resign. But he'd stay on for another year and a half, periodically clashing with Eden, whom he'd call ineffective and, in one blowup, "tired, sick and bound up in detail."[48] Eden himself was suffering the anxiety of a crown prince who sees his ascension in peril. John Foster Dulles didn't help. From time to time, when he'd see Eden, Dulles would ask, with seeming innocence, "Is it true they've made you Prime Minister?" and then chortle.[49] It's one of the few jokes anyone remembers from Dulles.

Not all Washington officials felt so jaunty that fall. The U.S. economy was sliding into a recession, and the predicament needed to be explained by Eisenhower's ambassador in London, Winthrop Aldrich, former board chairman of Chase National Bank. Aldrich was known at home as "Mr. Wall Street" for his decades of astute financial and legal work downtown. Now he had to convince the City that his country's economy was indeed sound, and one skeptic was Rab Butler, who ran Britain's Treasury. Butler, fifty, was a balding, pouch-eyed University of Cambridge historian and linguist who'd turned out to be a stunningly effective administrator, helped by connections that came from having married into one of the great Huguenot fortunes, the Courtaulds. He was number three in Churchill's cabinet and headed the government when both the prime minister and Eden were ill. Like Churchill, he relished pushing back against Washington. A taunting remark—that at least it wasn't the British economy that had just lost 9 percent of its productive capacity in a single quarter—rang across the ocean. At the end of the year, commonwealth finance ministers gathered in London, and all of them were rattled about what lay ahead for America's giant $370 billion GDP and for America's world role.

IN DECEMBER, EISENHOWER, DULLES, CHURCHILL, AND EDEN CON-vened for a three-day summit of their own—which, at Eisenhower's insistence, included the latest French premier, whom he compelled Churchill to invite personally. It occurred in Bermuda, a British overseas territory. Churchill arrived on the island in drenching rain on Thursday, the third, dressed somberly in a gray homburg hat and a gray tropical suit. Thousands of cheering spectators stood on the tarmac, and at a distance he appeared to be his usual self, but people who saw him close-up observed him to be stooped, with his right leg dragging. Eisenhower landed the next morning at the U.S. Naval Air Station, casually dressed and chain-smoking. His hand was bandaged: before leaving home, he had been showing off for his wife, Mamie, by trying to fan the hammer of a six-shooter, as in the westerns, with his palm. It can be a painful trick, and it rarely works.

This was President Eisenhower's first international conference. Despite the injury to his hand, more than one top official in Britain's delegation thought he looked "royal." He appeared ceremonial and withdrawn, as if he were aware of carrying an altogether different level of authority from any of the foreign leaders with whom he dealt. Once the talks got under way in an improvised hall at a Tucker's Town society resort, Churchill believed him to be acting like a king. Eisenhower seemed aloof from the conference's messy details as he sat impatiently, chewing on his heavy horn-rimmed glasses. At one point, he came down "like a ton of bricks" on Churchill for being too eager to hold a summit with the Russians.[50] The French leaked this scolding to journalists.

Eden, for his part, looked tanned and fit, but he showed his boredom at dinner, on the fourth, when trying to create a personal détente with Dulles. Peace was difficult, because Dulles (who called him "Antnee") used the gathering to warn Eden that he wouldn't withhold economic aid to Cairo forever. Dulles also said that Washington's patience was wearing thin as Britain's negotiations over Suez dragged on. This was tough talk, but Eden responded in kind. For Washington to give aid to Egypt, he told Dulles, would be "deadly to Anglo-American relations." In the end, Eden came out on top. Churchill persuaded Eisenhower to overrule Dulles. On December 20, after the conference was over, Churchill received a letter from the president stating that the administration wouldn't do anything "detrimental" in Egypt.[51]

Churchill left Bermuda as convinced as ever that a summit with the Kremlin was necessary. He intended to achieve one last crowning act on the world stage, and he expected to do so by initiating negotiations even if those didn't involve the Americans. Such proceedings were respectable, in his mind, no matter how abominable the Soviet regime. To him, compromising empire to empire with the Russians was fundamentally different from yielding to the ill-mannered demands of subject peoples, as in Iran or Egypt—an activity that partook of cowardice and Byzantine decadence. He had another motivation too: in Bermuda, he and Eden had both heard the Americans make no apparent distinctions between the use of high explosives and nuclear weapons.

V. A NEW SUPREMACY

FACING PAGE: **A crafty look: President Dwight Eisenhower observing Prime Minister Winston Churchill, Bermuda 1953** ABOVE: **Secretary of State John Foster Dulles: confident in himself and in his client, the United States, 1954**

17

THE BREAK POINTS OF 1954

The measure of success is not whether you have a tough problem
to deal with, but whether it is the same problem you had last year.
—John Foster Dulles, 1954

O N JANUARY 7, 1954, PRESIDENT EISENHOWER DELIVERED HIS
State of the Union address and reviewed the previous year's accomplishments. Communist aggression had been halted in Korea; military aid had enabled France and its associated states to get closer to winning in Indochina; U.S. policy still rested on building a united Europe, on which there seemed to be headway; a heartening political victory had been achieved in Iran; and elsewhere in the Middle East, America showed impartial friendship to all. Eisenhower believed that the nation held the strategic initiative and that its best chance to reduce the Communist threat was to keep strengthening those friends overseas with whom America's well-being was, as he put it, "interlocked."

The situation was more complicated than Eisenhower suggested, of course. GIs and air bases were in ever more places, and the U.S. Navy, as Admiral Bull Halsey said in 1947, sailed where it pleased, which included into the Black Sea, on Russia's doorstep. But European allies, an NSC analysis had determined the previous summer, showed little confidence in U.S. leadership.[1] America's ongoing political and military presence in the world appeared uncertain.

In October 1953, for instance, Secretary of Defense Charles E. Wilson, sixty-three, former president of General Motors, had spoken entirely at cross-purposes with Eisenhower. Wilson had promised that the 120,000 GIs sent to Germany over the two previous years would soon be shipped home, just as Congress had been promised. Eisenhower then had to insist publicly that he had "no plan for reduction of combat forces anywhere."[2] John Foster Dulles, for his part, urged the allies to quickly adopt a pan-European defense force—envisioned as being part of a European Defense Community—or they'd be risking an "agonizing reappraisal" of U.S. transatlantic ties. Churchill's government, of course, wanted no part of this, and two weeks later, in January 1954, Dulles told Anthony Eden that he thought their own two countries were approaching a parting of the ways.

Ever since entering office a year earlier, Eisenhower and Dulles had been trying to satisfy Republican demands for a steadier, more consistent foreign policy, and they derided the Truman-Acheson approach to world affairs as one of endless improvised "fire drills." The country couldn't keep dashing from emergency to emergency, in their view. Inevitably, their own policies kept being made on the basis of trial and error as well.

As part of this redefinition, however, the administration would take any measure to avoid another open-ended "limited" war as in Korea. Therefore, five days after the State of the Union, Dulles announced that America would henceforth rely on its "great capacity to retaliate, instantly, by means and at places of our own choosing."[3] Talk like this made allies worry even more, despite Eisenhower's measured words about "interlocked" freedoms. Might the Americans finally try to sidestep the political-military entanglements that necessarily come from backing one's partners? Did they mean a first use of nuclear weapons against Soviet aggression?

Sir Oliver Franks, after having served four and a half years in Washington, had returned home to accept a part-time role in the City as chairman of Lloyds Bank. He knew there was scoffing in Whitehall about Dulles, whose utterances were often dismissed as bluff. Yet Franks recognized that the secretary of state was in fact espousing a policy not too different from Truman's, at least before Korea: the Americans expected their allies to carry the weight of manning the front lines, beneath a U.S. nuclear umbrella.

Franks examined the problem. Talk of reappraising alliances and of retaliating instantly might have its place in Republican Party circles. But to him, it was irrelevant to the immediate challenges of confronting subversion, insurrection, and the grinding low-intensity conflicts in which Moscow seemed to specialize. The Americans would have to involve themselves directly if they expected to influence a wider world, as in Southeast Asia or the Middle East. That was trickier work than deterring an enemy along clear lines of demarcation, as in Europe, and it would require close collaboration with the British Empire and Commonwealth. He offered an epigram for the times: "It is much more of a business to make the use of force effective."[4]

In his State of the Union address, Eisenhower also said, right up front, that the nation had just completed the most prosperous year in its history. That was true, but he skipped over the fact that America's economy had been in a downturn since the fall and no one knew where it would bottom out. In early April, he appeared on television standing straight with his arms crossed and leaning slightly back against his White House desk. Looking right into the camera, he said that there was no reason to yield to "jitters."[5] America had enemies, of course, but we could all pull together. The country's economic fundamentals were strong. He didn't mention that America was by then well into a recession, but he did promise to do anything necessary to prevent an outright depression while helping the 3.7 million unemployed.[6] He also emphasized that fiscal responsibility was essential to the nation's defense. That meant belt-tightening. In July, Secretary Dulles told the Senate Appropriations Committee that the State Department was short of money. U.S. diplomatic missions, he testified, were handicapped when competing with freer-spending "foreign offices," none being named.[7]

The Americans still felt they couldn't do it all. They were adapting to an enhanced place in the world, but slowly. Eisenhower's vice president,

Richard Nixon, summed up the ethos when declaring that there would be no further retreat from Asia. The United States, he said that spring, had duties as "a leader of the free world."[8] Note the indefinite article. Neither he nor other top officials in the Eisenhower administration yet referred naturally to the United States as *the* leader of the free world, though that was about to change, and the new viewpoint was hastened by events in Vietnam and Guatemala.

IN OCTOBER 1953, EISENHOWER HAD SENT HIS VICE PRESIDENT ON a fact-finding mission to the Far East. He was giving Nixon ever more responsibility as his understudy, and everyone knew it, which made this mission significant. On Saturday, October 24, Nixon landed in Singapore, where a crowd of Malay and Chinese well-wishers at the airport offered a greeting by lifting him on their shoulders. Commissioner General MacDonald escorted him to Phoenix Park, and Nixon handed him a letter from the president that expressed America's gratitude to MacDonald for leading the fight against "Communist aggression."

The British by this time were close to getting Malaya's insurgency under control. In the spring of 1953, they had repealed their mass detention orders and were carrying out fewer hangings. (Total executions for this conflict exceeded two hundred, plus purposive massacres, as at Batang Kali, in 1948.) The SAS's counterinsurgency measures were proving effective, including the practice, borrowed from the Americans, of parachuting into treetops, like firefighters in the Pacific Northwest, and then fast roping to the forest floor below to stage ambushes. MacDonald's initiatives for self-government were another reason for success, and it helped to have negotiating partners such as the sultan of Selangor. These were Muslim gentlemen who, before making an appointment to discuss politics, would consult the racing calendar, whether at Epsom Downs or Singapore's Bukit Timah Turf Club.

With such slow but steady progress, MacDonald and Nixon chose to dwell on Indochina. MacDonald came to the meetings with a plan: his goal, he told Churchill in a cable, was to halt Communism's advance by cementing "Anglo-American resolve to take whatever action may be required."[9] He expected the Americans to keep providing weapons and dollars for the French, and also diplomatic support. This approach suited British interests, as the historian Mark Lawrence explains: "London could at last settle into the position to which it had aspired, that of benevolent but low-profile support for its close ally."[10] The ally was France.

Nixon, according to MacDonald's records, agreed with his perspective on Indochina and welcomed his experienced advice. To wit, France would continue to strengthen Bao Dai as a nationalist alternative to Ho Chi Minh, and the Vietminh would be crushed the following year. France's strategy was clear: the more that Bao Dai's Nationalist forces developed, the more French troops could be withdrawn from Indochina. So any negotiating with the Communists would therefore be a mistake. All of this would succeed, MacDonald concluded, provided Washington and London stayed united on Southeast Asia.

They also discussed China, which was a vital supplier of the Vietminh, and Nixon proved startlingly flexible. He acknowledged that Chiang Kai-shek's cabal on Taiwan was sordidly discredited. Speaking for the Eisenhower administration, he declared a willingness to bring Mao Zedong's regime into the United Nations. To be sure, that assumed a final peace agreement could be achieved in Korea, and a political blowup avoided with Chiang's China Lobby friends in Washington. However, an opening to the People's Republic might even help end bloodshed in Vietnam, Nixon said. Improving trade with Beijing could be a start. Eisenhower himself was "personally keen" on this matter, he added.[11] Not that any of this would be easy. These were the months, after all, when voices in Congress demanded that British merchantmen heading to Shanghai be sunk.

At 11:00 a.m. on October 26, Nixon's U.S. Air Force Constellation landed at the wooden-shack, two-strip airport in Kuala Lumpur. MacDonald had arranged for him to tour Malaya's tin and rubber estates and to consult with General Templer in his official residence—a grand structure, known as King's House, built in British colonial tropical style. Security was provided by the Eleventh Hussars' scout cars. Nixon, it had been decided, would not travel anywhere by helicopter, as had previous U.S. dignitaries. Back in April, Adlai Stevenson, the governor of Illinois and recent Democratic presidential candidate, had nearly been killed in a jungle crash following his own audience with MacDonald.

Nixon inspected troops returning from patrol and tested a machete with the Somerset Light Infantry. "The tide is turning in Southeast Asia," he told reporters.[12] He then flew to Cambodia, one of France's so-called associated states, where he got briefed by Donald Heath in Phnom Penh, as well as by French colonial authorities. All insisted that if the Vietminh won, Communism would wash through Malaya, into India, and beyond—which had become MacDonald's well-argued position too.

Eisenhower accepted this idea completely. By the time of his State of the Union address in January, he had already spoken publicly at least ten times about the immense stakes in Indochina, and in doing so he sounded ever more like those British officials who insisted that the defense of Malaya really had to be staged along Vietnam's Mekong River. America at this point was paying for 80 percent of France's war, and when asked in a February 1954 news conference if the Indochina situation was critical, Eisenhower replied that it had been critical for so long that the crisis was now almost normal. In fact, it was getting worse. The war was consuming France's officers and NCOs faster than they could be trained, which, of course, had consequences for NATO and for the need of having five-plus U.S. Army divisions on alert between the Rhine and the Thuringian ridges.

In late March, the president spoke to the press of Indochina's "transcendental importance" to the West's defense.[13] In this view, everything depended on the fate of Vietnam. If France lost to the Vietminh, Eisenhower had already stated in an NSC meeting, "the gateway to India, Burma and Thailand [would be] open to Communism"—as would America's line of island outposts that reached from Japan to Taiwan to the Philippines and then to Australia and New Zealand.[14]

Earlier in the year, at another NSC meeting, he explained that "he could not imagine the United States putting ground forces anywhere in Southeast Asia except possibly in Malaya."[15] But if he imagined dispatching GIs and marines to the jungles of colonial Malaya, it wasn't such a big step to imagine dispatching them to Indochina. And he did. On the one hand, he worried within the NSC that Vietnam "would absorb our troops by divisions." On the other, he began to make the case to Churchill and Eden that it was best for the United States and Britain to oppose Ho Chi Minh's forces together in Vietnam. If not, went this argument, France's 200,000-plus troops would be defeated and would leave. Then the United States and Britain would have to face an expanded Chinese-backed offensive in Thailand and in Malaya by themselves, without help from the French.

France's professional soldiers and Foreign Legionnaires fought alongside some 300,000 supposedly loyal soldiers of the Vietnamese National Army. But the enemy, whom the French deemed "terrorists," couldn't be beaten in forests and jungles. So French Union troops came to rely on fortified bases, such as the one established in the mist-shrouded valley of Dien Bien Phu, near the border of Laos, which sixty years earlier the British had already identified as a strategic crossroads. That's where Major General René Cogny, a Resistance veteran who had survived Buchenwald and now commanded the Tonkin delta, invited a set-piece battle with the Vietminh. He flew in his troops on American C-119s, supported by a U.S. Air Force detachment in Haiphong. All concerned thought this would do the trick, including Commissioner General MacDonald.

The fight began on March 13, when 40,000 superb Vietminh infantry and artillerymen, who occupied the high ground, opened a massive barrage against a garrison below of 16,200 troops of the French Union Forces—36 percent of whom were Vietnamese loyalists and 19 percent each of African and professional French metropolitan troops. Foreign Legionnaires composed the rest, and they included strapping blond warriors, speaking German, who passed themselves off as "Danes." By the end of March, France's Foreign Ministry was pleading for help at Dien Bien Phu. As a result, on Saturday morning, April 3, Secretary Dulles met secretly at State with eight top legislators, as well as with Chairman of the JCS Admiral Radford, to examine the entire issue of Indochina.

No one argued against acting unilaterally in Vietnam more persuasively than Texas's Lyndon Baines Johnson, forty-five, who was then the Senate minority leader but who, the following year, would come to rule the majority as "Master of the Senate" through the rest of the decade. An imposing six feet four, he was a sleeplessly ambitious, overbearing, shrewd idealist, with little interest in foreign affairs, despite serving on the Armed Services Committee. Now he asked Dulles which other nations would be joining the United States if it intervened on France's behalf. None, the secretary admitted. As a result, Johnson and his equally worried fellow legislators imposed a condition: Americans should intervene only as part of some form of "United Action" with the British Empire and Commonwealth; they shouldn't proceed alone. Only then, as Dulles and Radford told Eisenhower in a private meeting the next evening, would the congressional leadership "go along on some vigorous action."[16]

An editorial in that Sunday's *New York Times* emphasized U.S. responsibility to lead in Indochina. Scrambling to find precedent, the paper wrote of the Truman Doctrine and of the success in Greece. That same day, Eisenhower sent Churchill a letter stressing America's "efforts to save Indochina and the British Commonwealth position to the south."[17] He compared this moment to the one Churchill had described in chapter 2 of his second volume about the world war, *Their Finest Hour* (1949), which evokes the lost opportunities before Hitler struck the final blow against France in 1940. Eisenhower closed with a warning as well as a promise: "I have faith that by another act of fellowship in the face of peril we shall find a spiritual vigor which will prevent our slipping into the quagmire of distrust."

On the following Sunday, April 11, Secretary Dulles and his staff landed after dawn in a gray forty-degree chill at London Airport. He'd spend two days in and out of the Foreign Office discussing Indochina with Eden, and then they'd regroup in Paris, where their exchanges would grow sharp, and finally they'd meet in Geneva. To Dulles, it was beginning to appear that the long-held British position—as had been heard from MacDonald, from Attlee and Bevin, and from Eden himself—for a collective defense in Southeast Asia had suddenly flipped. Churchill's government now kept obstructing effective cooperation.

In London, Dulles doodled circles on yellow legal pads and urged Eden to agree to a defense pact that would cover Indochina and permit joint military steps, if necessary. That might be enough, he argued, to encourage France to keep fighting and to deter Ho Chi Minh from another offensive. In sum, he wanted Eden to declare a common front with America to prevent a Vietminh victory, which to Dulles was synonymous with Sino-Soviet conquest.[18] Not that Eden cared any less about the fate of Vietnam, but he hoped for a diplomatic answer—while, like Churchill, he was growing alarmed about a military adventure with the Americans. Not least, he was hearing from a shrewd, distinguished source that France's predicament was hopeless: Her Majesty's newly arrived ambassador in Paris, Sir Gladwyn Jebb, also observed that Bao Dai wanted to prevent elections and a cease-fire, because the former emperor feared his country would be partitioned.

Dulles still had a question for Eden. How could the Vietminh possibly be winning, he asked, when America was sending more than ten times the aid to its own side than China was sending to Ho Chi Minh? "Because," Eden replied wearily, "they had faith in what they were doing."[19]

During these meetings in London, Eden and his Foreign Office lieutenants played coyly at trade-offs and linkages with Dulles. They tried to obtain a U.S. commitment to defend Thailand, which bordered Malaya, in exchange for their unspecified support in Indochina. No dice. And they suggested that if Washington could pressure Egypt's military junta to reach an agreement on Suez, as Eden told Dulles, then perhaps Britain would at last have at its disposal some ground forces that could be deployed to other areas. Whether these "other areas" would include Indochina, he couldn't say. Might Royal Air Force mechanics at least join those from the U.S. Air Force who were servicing planes for the French in Haiphong? Eden said he would inquire.

Eden used the same tactic concerning Hong Kong. He reminded Dulles that a British infantry division provided the West's only bridge-head on the Chinese mainland. Perhaps if the Americans committed themselves to Hong Kong's defense, as London had often advised, then the British might be able to deploy some battalions elsewhere. After all, Her Majesty's forces were presently spread thin upholding fronts in Europe, Suez, Kenya, and Malaya, not to mention in Korea itself, where a commonwealth division remained, though being downsized. As matters now stood, alas, the British simply didn't have the manpower for Vietnam.

On April 13, the two sides issued a communiqué: "We are ready to take part, with the other countries principally concerned, in an examination of the possibility of establishing a collective defense" of Southeast

Asia. In this weaselly language, it wasn't difficult for Dulles to hear what sounded like a commitment to united action. Nye Bevan anticipated what would follow. He told the House of Commons that the statement was essentially an agreement in principle to jointly intervene, and, he said, the Americans regarded anything accepted "in principle" as a promise. As a result, he concluded, they'd now try to drag Britain into Indochina—something he'd never allow.[20]

On Friday, the sixteenth, in Washington, at a convention held by the American Society of Newspaper Editors, Vice President Nixon spoke of intervening in Vietnam. By now, people assumed he was talking for Eisenhower. "The Administration," he avowed, "must face up to the situation" and, if necessary, "dispatch forces."[21] Senator Wiley, who chaired the Foreign Relations Committee, responded that this would never happen.

As Nixon spoke, artillery shells rained down on the collapsing dugouts at Dien Bien Phu. At this moment, the stronghold had been reduced to a triangle of some thirteen hundred acres, and its defenses included three thousand tons of U.S.-supplied barbed wire, flamethrowers, and American infrared sniper scopes. On the brink of disaster, Commissioner General MacDonald expected to fly into the inferno from Hanoi. He was everywhere, as the Americans knew, which had long added to his authority. But in this case, the idea was scratched the night before; the dying garrison had no time for a visitor, even he.

Eisenhower gave "a soldier's appreciation" that "the odds are all in favor of the defender," but like Dulles he was puzzled.[22] The French and their Vietnamese loyalists seemed to have numerical superiority in the overall theater, so why couldn't they win?

The question is telling. Eisenhower had never fought guerrillas during his military career and underestimated what was required to oppose them. He'd do so again, during the 1960s, when counseling his successors, John F. Kennedy and then Lyndon Johnson, to use U.S. troops to swamp the enemy with overwhelming force, thereby cutting the Communist supply routes into South Vietnam.[23]

. . .

BY EARLY APRIL, DULLES'S PATIENCE WAS WEARING THIN. AS HE told Douglas Dillon, the forty-four-year-old ambassador to France and son of the founder of Dillon, Read & Co., the United States "cannot and will not be put in a position of alone salvaging British Commonwealth interests in Malaya, Australia, and New Zealand."[24] One of Dulles's aides, Walter Robertson, the assistant secretary for Far Eastern affairs, made a similar point to Ambassador Roger Makins in Washington: America would not defend these interests while the British "sat on their hands."

Admiral Radford was also in Europe that April and had been conferring with Dulles in Paris. Radford, at fifty-eight, was himself a presence, with, it was said, "the coldest blue eyes in the Pacific." Strong-willed and aggressive, he had been one of America's top guns before World War II, leading an aerial stunt team and later taking the carrier USS *Enterprise* into combat against imperial Japan. On Monday, April 26, he was in London for meetings at the Foreign Office and then, in the early afternoon, with Britain's military chiefs. He put a question to them that came directly from Eisenhower: How could the British possibly spurn a "united front"—which meant joining with the Americans against the Vietminh, to the extent of likely deploying troops—while French soldiers were still in place to uphold the fight? His counterparts stonewalled, and their memorandum of conversation says he wasn't sounding too intelligent, while records of the Foreign Office meetings insist he was "raring for a scrap."

Dulles by then was in Geneva for a gathering of the foreign ministers of all the major World War II allies—the United States, Britain, France, Russia, and China. It was their first conference since 1945 and was held in the Palais des Nations, the former headquarters of the ill-fated league. Britain and Russia were the cosponsors, and meetings began on April 26 to run through July 21. Eden played a major role throughout and had deep conversations with China's foreign minister, Chou En-lai, in fluent French. The conference had originally been called to address Korea, but the armistice along the 38th parallel seemed to be holding, whereas violence in Vietnam was intensifying. The Americans wanted an immediate decision out of London, and they expected Churchill's support as the defenses of Dien Bien Phu eroded. Waiting until *after* the conference to decide what to do, as Churchill and Eden argued, made no sense to them. By then, the game might be up for the French and their loyalists.

In London, early that Monday evening, a U.S. Navy car picked up Admiral Radford at Grosvenor Square for the forty-mile drive to Chequers, where Churchill was spending ever more time bloviating with friends such as Cherwell, the physicist, and Beaverbrook, most powerful of Tory publishers. It hadn't rained for days and the Bucks countryside was still awash in sunshine when Radford arrived, yet he felt uneasy in this damp, drafty country house. He found Churchill to be in excellent form; too good, in fact, for Radford to fulfill his design. Churchill gave a quick tour and pointed out his coat of arms inscribed in the windows of the seventeenth-century Long Gallery—relics from happier times, he said, when he'd held the office of prime minister during World War II. (Attlee hadn't followed suit with this short-lived prime ministerial tradition, saying he didn't think he had a coat of arms.)

Over dinner, Radford introduced trade-offs and linkages that suited the Americans. If Britain were to cooperate in Vietnam, he said, this would increase the likelihood that Washington would "revoke the present policy of aloofness" when it came to the "difficulties in Egypt." Churchill didn't bite. Snorting like an old warhorse, Radford recalled, he instead replied that everything could be resolved at a summit with the Kremlin's Georgy Malenkov, chairman of the Council of Ministers. Nor was Churchill inclined to have imperial forces fight anywhere in Indochina unless Malaya was in immediate danger, but he didn't think the crisis would come to that. Malaya was holding its own. Radford had heard similar words from Eden, whom he had seen in Paris, and, earlier in the day, from Britain's military chiefs.

Radford had a card up his sleeve, however. That afternoon, via top-priority cables sent through the U.S. embassy, he got permission from State to deliver an ultimatum. If the British remained unhelpful, he told Churchill, the administration would have no alternative but to lay out the entire problem before Congress, which would then be compelled to reexamine the Anglo-American relationship. U.S. negotiators always knew that the British dreaded Congress for its unpredictability. But Churchill was unfazed.

Radford sent an account of his meeting to Washington. Eisenhower was incensed, and in a fit of temper he spoke, uncharacteristically, of Churchill "promoting a second Munich."[25] Eisenhower rarely used historical analogies, let alone this one; he was too expert a military problem solver to be seduced by metaphor.

Eisenhower not only intended to intervene in Vietnam, he was poised to use nuclear weapons by, say, dropping two or three atomic bombs to save Dien Bien Phu. That came as no surprise to Churchill and Eden after what they'd heard in Bermuda.[26] "Engine Charlie" Wilson, the clearheaded defense secretary who had been president of General Motors, was shaken. He told Radford and Dulles that using nuclear weapons might endanger the status of U.S. bomber bases in Oxfordshire, East Anglia, and Berkshire, and cause a firestorm within NATO, "notably," he added, "in the UK."[27] That was superlative understatement.

"Make sure the British Government fully appreciates the gravity of the situation," Eisenhower instructed Dulles in Geneva. He didn't want them to "be able merely to shut their eyes and later plead blindness as an alibi."[28] In the halls of the Palais, Eden explained to Dulles from the start that he doubted his country would fight for Indochina. For the moment, the best way to proceed, as he had been saying since they'd spoken in Paris, would be to hold "prompt military consultations in Washington" about the bigger world picture.[29] Dulles stood firm. The president, he told Eden, was ready to seek congressional approval for intervention once Britain agreed to participate. Hadn't its backing— even its outright leadership on this vexing question of a united front toward Southeast Asia—long been ensured?

Churchill declared his position in the Commons on the day after he'd seen Radford. He wouldn't throw Britain's support behind the Americans, nor would he extend a military guarantee. During these years, Churchill would make a show of saying that he'd never heard about such places as Korea, Laos, and Guatemala, which isn't quite true: he knew of Guatemala all too well, as we'll see, and he knew of Vietnam, not just of "French Indochina." So he underscored his decision to Eden in Geneva by saying, "Great Britain will in no circumstances intervene in Vietnam."[30]

Churchill was baring the power of obstruction. When he said no, even at this increasingly frail stage of life, it was no—not that he ever cared about other people's colonies, unless they dangerously abutted on British terrain.

Eisenhower's famous temper was being tested. He knew Congress wouldn't permit any direct U.S. engagement without Britain. And he hesitated to get deeper into Vietnam without Congress's approval. If he did, his administration would have to face Lyndon Johnson, among other legislative titans, and "fight for it like dogs," as he said in an NSC meeting, "with very little hope of success."[31] To intervene unilaterally, he'd add, "amounted to an attempt to police the entire world."[32]

Dulles and Eden kept quarreling, and by now their differences were well established. At dinner in Paris, Eden had already accused Dulles of trying to "initiate World War Three," while Dulles had just about concluded, as he'd report to leaders on Capitol Hill, that "the US might be playing the wrong game if the UK was unwilling to give us moral and positive backing."[33] He also warned Eden that transatlantic ties would henceforth be "difficult vis-a-vis the Congress."

In Geneva, Dulles played a card of his own, coolly holding a meeting with the foreign ministers of Australia and New Zealand. Eden wasn't invited. This, after all, was the "ANZUS Council." Dulles's idea was to win the dominions' consent for united action, hoping that the British would then be compelled to follow behind them.[34] He sent a letter to Eden, who was staying with Clarissa down the lake at Le Reposoir, a villa lent to them by a friend; at least the Australians and New Zealanders understood the U.S. position, he implied. Understanding was one thing, however, and committing troops was another. Neither Australia nor New Zealand was willing to do that.

"They want to run the world," Eden said to his aides in a huff. "They want to replace us in Egypt too."[35] He might have been correct about U.S. impulsiveness in Vietnam, but here he was wrong. The Americans weren't that calculating; they didn't want to "replace" anyone, let alone "run" anything. They were still reacting crisis to crisis. And what they intended at this early date in Vietnam was another Truman-like emergency response to Communist aggression, implemented only with allies.

In Paris, an astute critic, writing in his weekly column for *Le Figaro*, drew conclusions. If permission from London was required before the Americans could act, said the political philosopher Raymond Aron, "then it would be clear that the U.S. was not yet ready to assume the obligations and risks of world leadership."[36]

Dulles and Eden had reached an impasse. In an ashen rage, Dulles headed to the airport on May 3, and only after intercessions from his staff did Eden extend Dulles the courtesy of seeing him off. It was an uncomfortable moment when they met on the tarmac. Dulles couldn't believe Eden had the gall to show up. Journalists were on hand, and the encounter was filmed. Newsreels of Dulles and Eden in all their fury doubled as a comic short in Swiss cinemas for weeks.

AMONG THEMSELVES, THE BRITISH ADMITTED THAT THEY HAD HAN-dled matters badly. Evelyn Shuckburgh, who was Eden's high-ranking private secretary, wrote in his diary that the Foreign Office was "getting very near to having cheated the Americans on this question of starting talks on SEA security."[37] Eden himself, who stayed on in Geneva until the conference's end, knew he hadn't been playing straight, or at best that he had flip-flopped with Dulles and helped cause a grave misunderstanding. "It is probably inevitable that the Americans should feel a little sore just now," he told Churchill, adding, "they will get over it."[38] They wouldn't.

Dulles had been back in Washington for barely a day when, at 5:30 in the afternoon of May 5, he met in the White House Cabinet Room with twenty-five of the nation's most powerful legislators. He delivered his case about Britain's faithlessness to the Senate majority leader, William Knowland, and to Minority Leader Lyndon Johnson as well as to Massachusetts's senator Leverett Saltonstall, the very model of an Atlantic-first Republican. And also to Georgia's Richard Russell, the undisputed leader of the Senate's inner club and an embodiment of southern patriotism. Among the dozen representatives attending was Speaker of the House Joe Martin, Democratic minority leader Sam Rayburn, and Congressman Carl Vinson, the once and future chairman of the House Armed Services Committee. They all heard of the duplicity, including the whole sequence leading to the rupture with Britain or, as Dulles called it, "the reversal of the British position."[39]

The assembled legislators weighed Dulles's evidence: months of meetings with Eden, who he claimed had "reneged" on a military coalition; letters and midnight dinners with Churchill; pleas from the French; and even a personal slight from Ambassador Makins, who had skipped a meeting at Foggy Bottom that had been intended to organize united action. "The British liked to use the carrot and stick," Dulles explained, and "they had a long tradition of holding the balance of power and in being the middle man in resolving disputes." That's what they were trying to do here, he continued. In sum, said Dulles, the United States was "obviously subject to U.K. veto." That, in turn, "was largely subject in Asian matters to Indian veto, which in turn was largely subject to Chinese Communist veto."[40]

Dulles had few peers as an advocate. In his closing arguments, he painted a picture of Britain as a perfidious ally trying to reassert its past dignity but unwilling to act forcefully. His arguments inspired righteous anger in his listeners, each of whom had memories of the summer of 1950, when, along with Acheson and the Truman administration, they had to threaten Britain into sending soldiers to Korea.

Two days later, on May 7, Dien Bien Phu was finally overrun after fifty-seven days and nights of ferocious combat. Churchill applauded the heroic defenders as an inspiration to the free world, and Dulles delivered another televised address that evening from his office at State. He spoke of the battle, telling the nation that the administration was taking steps for a "united defense effort" with its allies. A grave commitment might follow, he intoned.*[41]

As Dulles suggested in this forceful speech, Eisenhower remained set to intervene. Dulles still hoped to get the British to cooperate, but he wasn't entirely unsympathetic to their predicament. He knew they'd be risking the future of Hong Kong if they sided with him. After all, the Vietminh were believed to be a cat's-paw for Red China, which, in

---

*Speaking of France's National Army loyalists, Dulles also said Dien Bien Phu "showed that the Vietnamese can produce soldiers who have the qualities needed to enable them to defend their country." Of course, those qualities were really being displayed by the soldiers fighting with Ho Chi Minh, on the other side.

retaliation, could snatch Hong Kong at will. The colony had far fewer fighting men than four years earlier and, ultimately, was a hostage. Within Washington's decision-making circles, Dulles also would admit that America really didn't have a strategy in Asia. The reason it lacked one, in his mind, was due to Britain's refusal "to go along with us on any significant policies or objectives." This approach, along with British colonialism itself, was undermining U.S. objectives, Dulles told Eisenhower, and that was true "not only in Asia, but in Egypt, Iran, and elsewhere."[42]

Nixon's views had grown equally harsh. Everywhere he went overseas, he told Eisenhower in an NSC meeting that spring, he "was made aware of the millstone which British policy represented around the neck of the United States." The British were regarded as colonialists and imperialists, he added, "especially in Malaya."[43] It was odd that he emphasized Malaya, because he'd gotten along well with MacDonald less than a year before and had been impressed by the commissioner general's progressive political moves. But lots of informed Americans were getting fed up with the games they felt MacDonald was playing. From late March into May, for example, MacDonald had personally conducted an on-the-ground survey in Vietnam and had concluded that the French were close to achieving their goal of developing an effective National Vietnamese Army. All that was needed to beat the Vietminh, MacDonald said, were more dollars and weapons from Washington and a little more time. After Dien Bien Phu, anyone could see that the French had failed.

Come midsummer, large-scale fighting against the Vietminh had ended, and during the night of July 20–21, negotiators in Geneva worked out separate cease-fire agreements for Cambodia, Laos, and Vietnam. Eden's chief concern was to ensure an effective barrier as far to the north of Malaya as possible. One way to do so, he hoped, was to affirm the independence of Cambodia and Laos. For Vietnam, there would be a temporary partition along the 17th parallel, with nationwide elections to occur two years later, in July 1956, for the sake of reunification.

Rather than signing the Indochina accord, the Eisenhower administration, which wouldn't validate the fact that more territory had been lost to Communists, merely stated that it accepted the terms. As the smoke cleared, it became evident that if Churchill and Eden had offered even one battalion—and if Lyndon Johnson hadn't stood in the way—U.S. marines would by then be arriving in Vietnam.

ON FRIDAY, JUNE 25, WHILE THE GENEVA CONFERENCE WAS STILL in session, Churchill and Eden arrived in Washington. Churchill had basically invited himself, which made Eisenhower wonder if he "should be allowed to come or not." But disagreements with London were so intense, he told Dulles, that perhaps he and Churchill should have "one final talk"—even though he recognized that Churchill might publicly distort whatever they discussed, as he'd done before. "I've decided to let the old man come over for this visit," Eisenhower grumbled to his press secretary.[44] But when the United Press's Merriman Smith asked him for details, he replied that he hadn't "the slightest idea exactly what we will talk about."[45] Eisenhower made a freezingly cold response sound merely bewildered. In private, he complained to Dulles about being asked to change his habit of a light lunch just because Churchill expected a mid-day feast. They'd have a light lunch. Even Lady Churchill had sensed that Eisenhower's invitation—"Of course you are welcome"—wasn't encouraging. Churchill nonetheless received a rousing greeting, except from those who counted.

He and Eden deplaned from their chartered BOAC Stratocruiser in the early-morning heat at National. Churchill had spent the fourteen-hour flight napping in his sleeper berth, shuffling forward to gaze out the window at the clouds, eating well, including caviar and toast, and getting weary of Anthony Eden's bleating about what was wrong with the Americans. They were met by Nixon, Dulles, all the commonwealth ambassadors, and hundreds of well-wishers, to whom Churchill waved cheerily. President and Mrs. Eisenhower waited on the White House steps when the motorcade, with police sirens wailing, swung through the northwest gate. Here the prime minister would stay for the first time since World War II. But this visit was very different from Churchill's eleven earlier ones to America. Every mention of it in the press said he'd come in order to end misunderstandings.[46]

All was on the table for the three days of conferencing: a Southeast

Asian defense pact, Egypt and Suez, European security, a possible summit with Moscow, the potential sharing of nuclear secrets, and next steps in Korea, from which Eisenhower had just withdrawn four divisions. But the Americans had something more immediate on their minds: a coup was unfolding in Guatemala, engineered by the CIA, though in the context of a simmering dispute long influenced by the British.

The origins went back to the late 1940s and included ongoing British scuffling with Guatemala over its claims on the colony of Honduras. Britain retained troops in the colony, and by May 1953 men in Whitehall were again clamoring about Bolshevism. "Guatemala is in effect now a communist country," Minister of State for Foreign Affairs Selwyn Lloyd (serving under Eden) told Churchill.[47] Even U.S. assessments never went that far, and Churchill was more than inclined, as he put it, to use American support "to break the Communist teeth" in this part of the world.[48]

The events that followed do not match what's commonly believed. High quarters of the U.S. government didn't succumb to the influence of the United Fruit Company, a Boston-based corporate giant that was Guatemala's largest employer. UFCO, as it was known on Wall Street, or "the Octopus," as Guatemalans called it, had clashed with Colonel Jacobo Árbenz, forty, ever since he became Guatemala's second democratically elected president in March 1951. Árbenz was a thuggish, half-Swiss leftist who was nonetheless accomplishing some salutary reforms, such as land redistribution, and United Fruit had lobbying muscle in Washington to oppose these outrages. But as the coup began, it's apparent that the Dulles brothers had other motives. They weren't at all beholden to "friends" at UFCO, and no more evidence exists that Foster Dulles's "anticommunism was dictated by corporate interests" than there is that he was so robotic as to be "fun-hating."[49] (Dulles's idea of "fun" was navigating his small boat through the gales of Lake Ontario.)

At the time, the CIA was still finding its way around the covert tasks of regime change and, unlike in Tehran, received no guidance from London in how to stage a coup, with blunderings to follow. Through the winter of 1953–1954, senior CIA officials had been debating what to do about Árbenz. At the 9:30 a.m. staff meetings chaired by Allen Dulles, a paramilitary solution was assumed, recalled the operations officer at E Street headquarters who was responsible for the scheme. The only question was "how aggressive the Agency should be."[50] As relations with Washington deteriorated, Árbenz prudently abandoned his country's long-standing dispute with Britain over territorial claims to neighboring British Honduras. By early 1954, reported the U.S. ambassador in Guatemala City, the United States had replaced Britain in "the position of Public Enemy Number One."[51]

THAT SHIFT IN NOTORIETY DIDN'T DISTRACT THE COLONIAL GOVERnor of British Honduras, who was planning local elections for mid-April. As leftists surfaced on his own terrain, he charged that Communist propaganda and money were pouring across the border from Guatemala. That was untrue, but cries of Bolshevik subversion echoed in London. Churchill appointed a commission to investigate, which found Guatemala guilty on the flimsiest of evidence. In London, *The Times* thundered that "steps would have to be taken."[52]

The Americans were already taking them. Then they learned that on May 15 the *Alfhem*, a vessel flying the Swedish flag and sailing from Stettin in Poland, had docked at Puerto Barrios, Guatemala, with two thousand tons of Czech-supplied small arms and ammunition. In its voyage from the Eastern bloc, the *Alfhem* had been able to deceive both U.S. naval intelligence and the CIA by filing false papers with its insurance brokers at Lloyd's and sailing under blind orders on a cleverly misleading course. The *Alfhem*'s arrival confirmed the Eisenhower administration's suspicions of hands-on Kremlin subversion, and the CIA's leadership also felt humiliated.

Prensa Libre, Guatemala's largest newspaper, poked fun at Washington. The Americans needn't be hysterical, it said. It wasn't as if a Soviet satellite had given Guatemala an atomic bomb, the editors chided. Oh yes it was, and John Foster Dulles himself raised the nuclear specter. At an NSC meeting, he insisted that any ships suspected of carrying weapons had to be stopped on the high seas and searched. Legal justification was needed, however, and he discussed that matter with his brother Allen. Might suspicion of carrying atomic materials to Guatemala be apt justification to "stop and search" foreign ships? he asked him, three days after the *Alfhem* had slipped through. No one would believe that the Russians would send atomic anything to Guatemala, Allen, the CIA director, replied.[53] Okay, but Foster Dulles, with Eisenhower's approval, nonetheless imposed a quarantine. No need to explain.

The British had already embargoed arms to Guatemala in the course of their Belize dispute. Yet Secretary Dulles still worried what might be in the holds of their merchantmen steaming through the Caribbean. Hadn't British contraband gone to Red China? On May 25, Foster Dulles warned Ambassador Makins that the U.S. Navy would board any suspicious vessel approaching Guatemala, without exceptions. Makins sent a report to the Foreign Office. There's a scribbled annotation in the files that says Britain had "been to war with the Americans once over this general subject and very nearly a second time."[54] Then a formal State Department request to the Foreign Office sought agreement to stop and search British vessels. Eden was astounded at the effrontery, despite few British ships venturing to Guatemala anyway. Two days before the coup, he issued a rejection.

The CIA paramilitary plans involved two dozen agency personnel who trained and equipped a gang of 480 Guatemalan army dissidents at camps in Nicaragua and the Republic of Honduras, that independent nation which borders Guatemala to the east. The coup was launched on June 18 and dragged on bloodily for ten days, until the twenty-seventh—during which time, by coincidence, Attorney General Herbert Brownell was set to announce the U.S. government's prosecution of United Fruit Company.

The Department of Justice had several grievances. One stemmed from a $20 million suit against UFCO over price rigging, filed by fifty minority stockholders. That case had been under way for more than a year in Bronx Supreme Court. Another dispute was antitrust, with federal authorities charging that UFCO was monopolizing the banana trade. Given the other, more delicate events at hand, the attorney general checked with the Dulles brothers. "There would be no tears here," Secretary of State Dulles said when asked if the timing might be awkward to prosecute.[55] Allen, the CIA director, simply requested a few days' notice before the Justice Department dropped the hammer. United

Fruit was of no concern to them; the focus was on reversing what they saw as Soviet inroads just seven hundred miles south of Brownsville, Texas.

On the nineteenth, Árbenz's regime told the United Nations that unidentified forces were assaulting its territory and demanded to be heard before an emergency session of the Security Council. Churchill and Eden seem not to have known of the U.S. plot, but their diplomats in Guatemala City quickly recognized the coup as "an outside job," which is how Sir Pierson Dixon, who had replaced Gladwyn Jebb as Britain's UN representative in New York, put it to the Americans.[56]

Dixon's U.S. counterpart was Henry Cabot Lodge Jr., the former Massachusetts Republican senator who'd been defeated in 1952 by Congressman John F. Kennedy. Lodge denied any U.S. role in the rebellion and argued that the UN needn't concern itself with Árbenz's pleas. Violence in Guatemala, after all, was a civil matter for that independent nation. To Lodge's astonishment, the British delegation announced that it nonetheless supported Árbenz.

There was disagreement in London between the Foreign Office, with its generally disciplined habits and quiet effectiveness, and a heavier hand at the Colonial Office. Moreover, Árbenz seemed to have dropped his attempt to annex British Honduras, and Foreign Office decision makers weren't at all sure that a right-wing junta backed by Washington (which had previously supported Guatemala's territorial claims) was preferable for Britain's interests. Additionally, they worried that these widely suspected U.S. moves against Guatemala might set a precedent for China's designs against Hong Kong.

Because the CIA's paramilitary efforts turned out to be protracted and messy, it was difficult for Dixon not to take a stand at the UN. He had been Anthony Eden's principal private secretary during the war, and thereafter Bevin's. He shared Eden's high standards—famous since Eden had quit Neville Chamberlain's cabinet in 1938—and also possessed Bevin's proclivity for defiance. He now spoke of Britain's "moral position."

In the UN's new modernistic skyscraper along the East River, Dixon suggested to Lodge that Washington appeared to be supporting a flagrant act of aggression against a small state. This act, he regretted to say, didn't seem much different from what Russia had done four years earlier in South Korea. In fact, he continued, UN observers should be dispatched to Guatemala because such a cross-border attack was clearly a matter of international law.

Within hours of hearing this, Lodge responded with a message that, as he told Dixon, came from the president. And Lodge was the right person to deliver it. In 1944, this smooth Bostonian aristocrat had been the first senator since the Civil War to resign his seat and volunteer for combat, having previously, as an army reserve officer, observed U.S. and British forces go into action in North Africa. Firmly yet politely, he told Dixon that of course Britain was entitled to its own sovereign views. Because Lodge made his point orally, the best summary of what he conveyed is the cable Dixon sent to London. "If we took an independent line in an area of vital interest to the United States," Dixon reported being told, "they would feel entitled to take an independent line in areas vital to Great Britain such as Egypt."[57] No matter how gracefully Lodge might speak for the White House, this was intimidation—spawned by fury over Vietnam and by Eisenhower's vehemence that he was "being too damned nice to the British" and needed to "give them a lesson."[58]

IT WAS INTO THIS ATMOSPHERE THAT CHURCHILL AND EDEN HAD ARrived in Washington on June 25, which was also the day the UN Security Council was to vote on whether to accept the Árbenz government's emergency petition for help.

When they landed at National with eight principal advisers and eight aides, including the reliable two detectives, a five-car motorcade had been waiting on the tarmac as a distant thunderstorm approached. Vice President Nixon and Churchill took the first car, followed by Dulles and Eden, who, during the short drive into town, immediately quarreled over Guatemala as Ambassador Winthrop Aldrich sat awkwardly in between. Dulles believed Guatemala to be "the touchstone of the Anglo-American alliance," and Eden was primed for a fight.[59] All of which astounded Churchill, who, later that day, demanded that Eden have a sense of proportion. Churchill wasn't showing blind loyalty to the Americans, nor did he capitulate to Dulles. It was simply that Guatemala existed in the U.S. sphere of influence, for goodness' sake. He ordered Pierson Dixon to abstain at the UN. Accommodating the Americans was another shift in Britain's position—from originally decrying Árbenz, to sympathizing with him against the coup, to reluctantly abetting his ouster. As a result, the fate of Árbenz's duly elected government was handed to the Organization of American States, which predictably did nothing.

Churchill and Eden had a full policy agenda in Washington, but Guatemala shot back to the top on Sunday morning, the twenty-seventh, after a CIA officer involved in the coup authorized a U.S. pilot to sink a British freighter, the SS *Springfjord*, at anchor in the Guatemalan port of San José. Its cargo was believed to be gasoline; it was cotton. No one was killed, but Frank Wisner, the agency's head of operations, had to deliver a personal apology to the British embassy in Washington. The CIA also had to pay off—with a secrecy more adept than shown in its coup—the insurers at Lloyd's.

Árbenz fled into exile on the same weekend that Churchill and Eden were at the White House. After U.S.-backed reactionaries grabbed power, CIA headquarters sent a congratulatory telegram to its operatives in Central America. Secretary Dulles learned of this and was startled that anyone would put such a compromising communication on paper. His brother Allen replied that he had no idea how the message had been sent. Everyone involved was too flushed with success to care.[60]

NOT LONG AFTER THE COUP, EDEN AND HIS FOREIGN OFFICE STAFF began to rationalize their actions. They hadn't really buckled to U.S. pressure, they convinced themselves, nor had they yielded to Eisenhower and Dulles in a tacit exchange for past favors. Instead, they were going along with the Americans on a matter of great importance to this administration. They believed that they had acted strategically. Sooner or later, they expected accommodations in return. Guatemala came to be seen as a potential bargaining chip, according to one senior diplomat with much U.S. experience, when "we are about to solicit American help."[61] As in Egypt, perhaps.

After this visit, Churchill's perspective on the British Empire's stature seems to have changed. Until then, he hadn't been convinced that wealth and military muscle should grant the Americans an intrinsic leadership of the West. But he was reconsidering. "We do not realize her immeasurable power," Churchill quietly remarked to Lord Moran, his friend and physician, while sailing home aboard the *Queen Elizabeth*, and he said so as if he'd encountered something new.[62] He spoke to Moran of the Americans' possessing so much strength that they could conquer all of Russia, if they felt like it, maybe pinning down the Red Army within a month. They wouldn't even need allies, he said.

18

ORDERING CHAOS

For America to withdraw into isolation would condemn all Europe
to communist subjugation and our famous and beloved island to
death and ruin.
—Winston Churchill, October 1954

D URING THE EIGHTEEN MONTHS FROM JUNE 1954 TO THE BEGIN-
ning of 1956, America's wealth expanded on a far greater scale than
that of the British Empire, and with it came a heightened resolve. By
the end of 1954, the country had shrugged off recession and was racing
into the future: a swiftly expanding population of 164 million and a
roaring industrial machine sent consumer demand, employment, and
housing starts to record levels. A slew of companies, many of them part
of the newly designated Fortune 500, reported unprecedented earnings.
The Dow Jones average finally surmounted the 300 barrier, where the
stock market had stood a quarter century earlier before the Depression.
Military spending hovered at 13 percent of GDP, but much of that outlay
was essentially an industrial policy that spilled into the development of
infrastructure and technology.

Americans nonetheless remained leery of foreign entanglements, as they were of their flourishing prosperity. The Depression's shadow lingered, and in March 1955 the Senate Committee on Banking and Currency conducted hearings to see if the boom portended another 1929-like bust. Federal Reserve chairman William McChesney Martin thought this to be unlikely. So did former secretary Snyder, who was now advising the Treasury.

Churchill was sharp enough to detect these anxieties, and he worried about an American return to isolation. Many people in government were now reexamining what they could expect to accomplish overseas. There'd been recurring disappointments: trying to unite Europe, raise up China, win in Korea, and halt Communism in Vietnam. Voters might not tolerate more. For example, Dulles wrote to Eden in September 1954 that "the American people would never be brought to understand the need to make sacrifices in the Middle East."[1] Even Nye Bevan, a left-wing socialist, couldn't detect imperialist tendencies in Americans. They simply didn't have the "we're here, we're the boss, you can't get rid of us" attitude he felt was innate to the imperialist mind-set. That's why he dismissed them as "gadget monkeys" who were dashing hither and thither around the world and generally making things worse.[2]

Contrary to general opinion today, no U.S.-led international order had yet taken shape. America was reaching out across the globe. But thoughtful people recognized that its level of engagement was exceedingly tentative, and in a world still being formed. "The old system of international trade has broken down and no substitute has yet been built up to take its place," Oliver Franks explained in his 1954 Reith Lectures for the BBC.[3] Little sustained progress had been made on unimpeded multilateral trade and convertible currencies, as experts at the International Monetary Fund kept repeating. The following year, George Lichtheim, a German-born intellectual and first-rate political journalist, described any U.S.-protected world order as merely "emerging" and "vulnerable."[4] Meanwhile, the Korean War's lesson for lots of Americans, including top generals who fought it, was "Never Again" to a so-called limited war in Asia, or anywhere else.[5] Not least, 1945's visions of what the United Nations could accomplish were fizzling.

The Americans, it's true, were creating a network of alliances far beyond NATO—in Southeast Asia, the Pacific, and the Middle East—but they hoped that deeper political-military involvements would be temporary. That was the point of having allies and of building them up. Americans knew that theirs was the only nation with sufficient strength to offset the two Communist behemoths, but they didn't intend to do so alone or with mere token support. In particular, they still believed that Britain's bases, manpower, technologies, and geopolitical relationships were integral to the projection of U.S. power.[6] That's why delicate transatlantic diplomacy had to be part of all the political-military outreach that accompanied alliance building. A habit of give-and-take between Washington and London was the "tough reality," as Eden put it, of striving to achieve their shared objectives, such as stability in the Middle East and halting Sino-Soviet expansion in Asia.

Eisenhower and Dulles felt that the British had betrayed them over Vietnam, which created the worst breach between the two governments since before World War II. In the summer of 1954, Eisenhower even wondered if Britain, let alone France, should be treated as a sovereign power. "The happiest day in [my] life," Foster Dulles told him that fall, "will be when we don't have to modify our policies to keep up a facade of unity."[7] Nonetheless, they still had reason to cooperate.

In 1954, Britain, too, was enjoying a surge in economic growth. Records were being set in steel and automobile production, the Bank of England's gold and dollar reserves were on the rise, and at last the heart of Greater London—that mile-square financial district known as the City that had been laid waste by the Blitz—was being rebuilt. The volume of global trade was unprecedented. All this provided plenty of self-assurance for pushback against the Americans.

Churchill, for instance, was intent on dealing with the Kremlin no matter what the White House might think, and, he told Eisenhower, he'd keep his small island of fifty million people alive by exporting anything he pleased to Russia. But even his cabinet conceded that he was straining the U.S. relationship—to the extent that Eden found himself compelled to ask Foster Dulles to come to London to help him block Churchill's idea of making a solitary pilgrimage to see the party boss Malenkov in the Kremlin. (Before Dulles could check with Eisenhower, Eden rallied the rest of Churchill's cabinet to stymie that idea.)[8]

Rab Butler, Chancellor of the Exchequer and number three in the government, felt emboldened enough to threaten America with an "agonizing reappraisal" (imitating Dulles) of their trading ties if Congress didn't lower tariffs. Nye Bevan, for his part, warned that the United States would have to "go it alone" unless it changed its tune.[9] No decision maker was embracing a "junior partnership" with the United States, although, on the other hand, no one was voicing fantastical notions, as heard at the start of Churchill's government, about the British Empire's rivaling (or surpassing) the United States in wealth and power.

The Americans had nowhere else to turn for the kind of support that Britain could offer. France's military seemed demoralized after its Vietnam war. As for West Germany, it became a member of NATO only in May 1955 and was hardly the "core of the transatlantic alliance," as is believed today. Nor was anything like a "Pax Americana" in place (let alone since 1947).[10]

The British, by contrast, had many strengths that the Americans knew could be advantageous: a global presence; atomic bombs with the airpower to deliver them; and basic hard conventional power, including 813,000 active military personnel and by now four and two-thirds divisions in Germany. That included NATO's strongest formation—which were the Army of the Rhine's two armored divisions—and Britain's overall force was arguably the strongest military presence in Western Europe as well.[11] Moreover, international political influence came from being one of the two major Western arms suppliers. Most of the Arab militaries bought British, as did the Israelis. To be sure, part of this hardware was being subsidized by Pentagon dollars. But that assistance, of $155 million in 1954, was separate from Washington's own helpful purchases of British-made armaments, and it would be halved by Congress, which took note of its ally's robust economy.

There was another factor of power to consider during this year and a half. Minimal political friction existed within the American system of government. At least two-thirds of Republicans and Democrats generally agreed on the basic principles of foreign policy. The Republicans lost Congress in the 1954 midterm elections, but only by a whisker, and Eisenhower himself enjoyed a buoyant 62 percent approval rating at the time. He ran his government efficiently, by combining modern management techniques employed in business and the military. At the White

House, the lines of authority were direct, decisions were made with rigor, the vice president had a newly expanded authority, and the National Security Council did its job through a well-disciplined review process. Work got done in Washington, whereas, in London, infirmity and ferocious backbiting stood in the way.

ON WEDNESDAY, JULY 28, 1954, FOREIGN SECRETARY ANTHONY Eden announced in the Commons that a draft agreement had finally been reached to end Britain's seventy-two-year-long military presence in Egypt. "Those in Britain who see the agreement as a surrender to prestige and safety should consider soberly the alternatives," editorialized *The Times*.

Gamal Abdel Nasser, now thirty-six, initialed the document for Egypt. He looked just as Eisenhower would describe him six years later: "impressive, tall, straight, strong, positive."[12] But his regime had grown heavy-handed since winter. He had removed General Naguib as a figurehead, named himself prime minister, and begun collecting political prisoners, including leaders of the Muslim Brotherhood. These "nationalist-terrorists," he told Ambassador Jefferson Caffery, wanted to return to the eighth century and expel all foreigners. Less convincingly, he also accused them of colluding with the British.

The road to this deal—known as the Suez Canal Base Agreement—involved the Americans, but their influence wasn't as strong as they believed, nor as it's assumed to have been today. In March, Eisenhower instructed Caffery to help broker an agreement between the British and the Egyptians. Yet "far from acting as a junior partner," the Middle East scholar Ray Takeyh writes about the situation in Egypt, "Britain pursued its objectives tenaciously and obtained critical concessions from the United States."[13] The Eisenhower administration, for instance, withheld $25 million of economic aid in the face of Churchill and Eden's demands—no matter how desperate to release the money so that Washington could match a similar amount given to Israel in late 1953. The Americans still had to learn that styling themselves as honest brokers in the Middle East didn't mean that any of the antagonists would pay heed. What ended the deadlock over Suez was Churchill's conclusion that upholding an imperial monument costing £50 million a year, and beset by guerrillas, no longer made sense. Nor did it make sense, as Churchill told the Commons that spring, to keep eighty thousand fighting men in Egypt as a perfectly concentrated target for an H-bomb.

The terms of the base agreement were clear. All British and colonial troops would be out within twenty months; a maximum of twelve hundred civilian technicians could stay for maintenance in what was still the world's largest military depot; and the door was left open for a return of British forces should the Arab states, or Turkey, be attacked by an outside power. "Other than Israel," that is. Because no peace treaty existed between Egypt and Israel, the problem of allowing Israeli shipping to use the canal was unresolved.

Egyptians celebrated the agreement as a triumph, and it ended the random guerrilla violence that had taken forty-seven British lives and at least twice as many Egyptian ones. The Israelis, however, had valued Britain's presence as a protective buffer against Egypt's army. They viewed the agreement as a threat and resolved to destroy it.

Therefore a faction within Israeli Military Intelligence—aligned with the former prime minister, Ben-Gurion, and General Moshe Dayan, the IDF's chief of staff—activated what it called a "terror unit," secretly embedded in Cairo.[14] The purpose was to foment a bloody upheaval, which included planting evidence to incriminate the Muslim Brotherhood. Such violence, the Israelis hoped, might induce British forces to remain in Suez for the sake of (yet again) establishing order. Moreover, they anticipated, ties between Cairo and the United States would be ruined once Egypt spun out of control, with Nasser's leadership discredited. The plot became known as the Lavon Affair, after Pinhas Lavon, who was Israel's defense minister when it came to light.

On July 2, bombs hit Alexandria's post office; on the fourteenth, they hit U.S. consulate libraries in Alexandria and Cairo; on the twenty-third, two British-owned cinemas, Cairo's railway terminal, and the central post office were bombed. No fatalities occurred. The next attack was intercepted, and soon the Israeli saboteurs were arrested. They confessed and were imprisoned, with two condemned to hang.[15] Moshe Sharett, who served as Israel's prime minister and foreign minister between 1954 and 1956, had been kept in the dark about the campaign, initially. The Israelis denied any involvement and denounced the trials as a Nasserite pogrom.

Despite this clamor, the base agreement was formally signed on October 19, freeing the Americans to extend Egypt an enlarged $40 million economic aid package. But the long, British-imposed delay in delivering U.S. aid hardly made Washington look like an independent actor, and that impression took hold as the nationalism and neutralism of the restless Free Officers swelled.

NASSER'S TRIUMPH TORMENTED CHURCHILL BECAUSE IT ILLUMI-nated Britain's diminished place in the world. Consequently, he and his government needed a success elsewhere, and they turned to the East: Britain and its dominions could be instrumental to building a NATO-type defense apparatus for Southeast Asia. The idea was akin to the regional unified action for which Eisenhower and Dulles had struggled before France's defeat in Vietnam. In addition to reasserting the empire's clout, such a structure, Churchill's government expected, could wedge Britain into that discriminatory ANZUS defense triumvirate of Australia, New Zealand, and the United States. This led to what would be known as the Southeast Asia Treaty Organization.

From his Phoenix Park headquarters, Commissioner General Malcolm MacDonald began to rally support from within the commonwealth. Australia, New Zealand, India, and Pakistan were considered likely members. Meanwhile, John Foster Dulles was musing on the seemingly incredible fact of America's having become involved in Southeast Asia in the first place. The original sin, he concluded, was to have allowed the colonial powers to return to their holdings after World War II. But that was history, and now a bulwark was needed against further Communist expansion. Like the Joint Chiefs of Staff, he hoped that such an arrangement could off-load military obligations onto the states directly involved in that part of the world, states such as Britain. After all, that had been Washington's plan for Europe when crafting NATO.

Australia's prime minister, Robert Menzies, picked up on the Americans' ambivalence. By the end of August, he saw them having no "intention at all of stationing forces on the main-land of S. E. Asia in present cold war conditions."[16] Moreover, he found them increasingly wary of any treaty that might pull them into that part of the world. Whitehall officials relayed his concerns to Churchill and Eden.

Yet on September 8, after months of work, eight nations convened in Manila to sign the Southeast Asia Treaty. Its members pledged to defend Cambodia, Laos, and the newly created Republic of (South) Vietnam against unspecified "aggression."[17] Despite its name, only two Southeast Asian nations, Thailand and the Philippines, ended up signing. In the process, Dulles wouldn't let Hong Kong be part of this. Committing to Hong Kong's defense—beneath Mao Zedong's ominous gaze—was just too risky. The United States, Britain, France, and Britain's three dominions of Australia, New Zealand, and Pakistan were in. Nehru, who adhered to neutrality in the enlarging East-West divide, made sure that India stayed out.

Unlike NATO, however, this alliance ended up having no military structure. The Joint Chiefs of Staff insisted that allies merely "consult" in case of aggression, rather than act. That was fine with Dulles. Only reluctantly did he attend the ceremonies in Manila. He also understood the big so-far-unspoken question behind the Southeast Asia Treaty: What forces would the British Empire and Commonwealth contribute to enforce it?

The United States, of course, hadn't at all "played the role of regional policeman" since 1945, as said today, and it wasn't about to do so here.[18] Instead, it was Britain's role that the JCS chairman, Radford, called the "$64 Question," after a popular radio quiz show.

Once France repatriated the rest of its 207,000-man expeditionary corps from Indochina, after all, the primary Western military strength that could bear on the region would come from Britain. At that moment, its War Ministry allocated some 50,000 fighting men to Far Eastern Ground Forces alone, and this command had responsibilities from Singapore/Malaya to Hong Kong to South Korea/Japan. In Malaya, 17,000 British home troops, as they were called, were deployed, along with units of Gurkhas, whose Training Depot Brigade was in the Malayan state of Kedah. Eleven thousand more home troops were still guarding Hong Kong. There was the original commonwealth division of over

20,000 men in Korea, though shrinking into a Commonwealth Brigade Group, and about three hundred combat aircraft were at hand. Britain, Australia, and New Zealand were also in the process of creating the Far East Strategic Reserve, to be based in Malaya. In half a year, it would comprise an infantry brigade and a carrier group supported by air squadrons.

The Americans hoped to learn how these forces would be applied to the new Southeast Asian defense arrangements, and believed they had an opportunity to do so when Commissioner General MacDonald arrived in Washington, on October 9. He stayed for three days. There's no record of what they heard, though it's certain MacDonald offered no promises of troops, planes, or ships. He was nearly invisible on this trip, the dates of which overlap exactly with an ANZUS Council meeting at the State Department. Britain would never be a member of ANZUS, but it wasn't inclined to let U.S. dealings with Australia and New Zealand on these matters go unsupervised.

Less than three months had passed since the Geneva Agreements, yet the Americans already feared that the Republic of Vietnam, where Bao Dai remained head of state, was about to fall into Ho Chi Minh's waiting hands. And by now MacDonald's views had changed.

The type of war that Vietminh nationalists had been waging, he had come to believe, couldn't be won. Satisfying demands for liberty and prosperity was the only way to succeed, and that's what he believed he was doing elsewhere in Southeast Asia. Concerning Vietnam, he worried about the man who had been serving as Bao Dai's premier since June, Ngô Đình Diệm, a remote Catholic authoritarian—and recent resident in exile of New Jersey—who was ruling in a mostly Buddhist land. Having encountered Diệm in Saigon, MacDonald regarded him as "the worst prime minister I have ever seen."[19] Predictably, reports submitted by Ambassador Heath agreed. As for Secretary Dulles, he had doubts about the entire venture.

At this fateful moment, Dulles was open to writing off all of Vietnam. That's apparent from Eden's summary of a tripartite meeting held in Paris during December. Better to bolster Cambodia, Laos, and Thailand in cooperation with Nehru's India, Dulles believed. By now this was MacDonald's advice as well. Today, a detailed analysis from Hanoi's

National Economics University concludes that "Eden was pleased with signs of Dulles's malleability."[20]

And getting out at this point was the road not taken in Vietnam. Less than a year later, Diệm would replace Bao Dai to become South Vietnam's president, once the former emperor washed up permanently in Cannes. The year thereafter *Life* magazine labeled Diệm the "Miracle Man of Vietnam" under whom an independent nation could be preserved, as long as he was backed by America.

THREE DAYS BEFORE SECRETARY DULLES SIGNED THE SOUTHEAST Asia Treaty, China, with deliberate timing, began shelling the Nationalist-held island of Quemoy, two miles from the port of Amoy on the Taiwan Strait. Chiang Kai-shek had occupied several small coastal islands since fleeing to Taiwan, and he had heavily fortified them as his first line of defense. The shelling erupted after months of tension. That included Chiang's raids against the mainland and Beijing's assertions of sovereignty, along with its mistaken downing of a BOAC airliner near Hainan Island in July. Admiral Radford had dispatched two of his big carriers into Chinese waters to search for survivors, and the warships took their time doing so.

Chiang Kai-shek remained a deft manipulator of Washington politics, and Dulles stopped in Taiwan while returning from the SEATO conclave in Manila. He spent five hours assuring Chiang of U.S. backing. This emergency also spotlighted a recurring dispute between the United States and Britain that went back four years to Korea. Would the Americans really use atomic bombs against China?

At a special Sunday morning NSC meeting, held on September 12, 1954, within Lowry Air Force Base near Denver, where Eisenhower was on vacation, the answer was yes. Eisenhower and his JCS chairman seem to have been of one mind: there'd be no restraint should GIs and marines again tangle with the People's Liberation Army. But over Quemoy? Dulles was now cautious. "The British fear atomic war and would not consider the reasons for our action to be justified," he advised. Eisenhower answered that many Americans wouldn't see much justification either. Why should they fight over someplace like Quemoy anyway? he queried the fifteen others at this meeting. After all, he was constantly getting mail that asked, as he phrased it, "What do we care what happens to those yellow people out there?"[21]

Nonetheless, Eisenhower believed the use of atomic weapons might be necessary. He therefore ordered Admiral Radford to take "precautionary moves" that would put the United States in a posture of nuclear readiness for the area. During the weeks that followed, he assured his cabinet, as well as Congress's Republican leadership, with whom he met weekly, that this time his decisions wouldn't be subject to British veto. And he asked Dulles, who had plans to be in London later in the month for a NATO Council meeting, to confer with Churchill.

Dulles and Churchill met on September 30 at Downing Street. To begin, Dulles drew the prime minister a rough map on a piece of paper. He sketched what General MacArthur had called America's "island outposts" in the far Pacific. Churchill loved working with maps, as Dulles knew, and the secretary traced a line that stretched from the Aleutians down through Japan and Korea to the Philippines and Australia and New Zealand. Taiwan was somewhere in the middle. Dulles explained that it was the only one of these "outposts" that didn't have a defense treaty with the United States. Churchill was fascinated and, in his growling way, asked Dulles if he could keep the sketch, which he pocketed.[22]

Churchill regarded a nuclear showdown on Chiang Kai-shek's behalf as bizarre, and Britain's reluctance to back the Americans became more bitterly public than earlier disagreements over Vietnam. Churchill and Eden wanted the Eisenhower administration to demand that Chiang withdraw from Quemoy, and the island of Matsu, in return for Beijing's renouncing force against Taiwan—which opened them to charges of appeasement from the China Lobby, which reflexively backed Chiang. And there was another difference from the Vietnam experience. This time Australia and New Zealand, as well as Pakistan, supported Washington's hard line against "Red China." On December 2, the United States signed its second defense treaty that year, and it was with Chiang Kai-shek.* Then, the following month, Congress took a major step toward

---

*The same day, Ambassador Makins told Eden that the Americans, given their tendency to "divide the world into big and small powers and two 'superpowers,'" were unable to see the full

giving a president discretionary power to take the country to war: it granted Eisenhower advance authorization to use whatever force he needed to defend Taiwan.[23]

Beyond any reasonable doubt, as the historian David Watry observes, "Eisenhower never bluffed about atomic warfare."[24] Churchill knew this cold. By February 1955, as artillery duels and raids/counterraids intensified over the coastal islands, Churchill publicly had to urge the Americans not to use atomic weapons in response. Some compromise was made, and the U.S. 7th Fleet that month employed 132 ships and 400 aircraft to cover Chiang's evacuation of at least the highly vulnerable Tachen Islands (two hundred miles north of Taiwan, off the coast of the mainland city of Taizhou). On March 12, Dulles declared that the administration was nonetheless poised to escalate. Four days later, Eisenhower terrified the British, and every other U.S. ally, by remarking at a news conference that "A-bombs can be used . . . as you would use a bullet."[25] Nearly as alarming, he refuted Churchill's arguments about the offshore islands not being "a just cause of war" and, in another rare allusion, used "Munich" to explain America's resolve.

Hostilities eased, for the time being, and the PLA never invaded. Was that due to nuclear deterrence, or was it because new bosses in the Kremlin restrained Mao's regime? It's not clear, and there were other influences too, such as Beijing already having succeeded in showing the world that it would never accept a two-China outcome of the civil war. But the result was that the Nationalist government remained in Taiwan, holding on to a set of small fortified islands within sight of the mainland—as it still does today.[26]

THE JANUARY 3, 1955, ISSUE OF *TIME* MAGAZINE ACCLAIMED JOHN Foster Dulles "Man of the Year," but it barely mentioned one thing about Dulles's service as secretary of state that today seems extraordinary: he is the only person, other than a president, routinely to have delivered

---

complexity of foreign affairs. So the question was how to restrain them from "precipitate action" in any of these hot spots, and whether doing so required working closer together or just opposing them outright.

TV and radio addresses to the country on grave issues of national policy. He had already done so about eight times since February 1953, and he would deliver at least a dozen more before leaving State in April 1959— each time with an audience of more than ten million. No other government official has done that, or anything equivalent in the pre-electronic era, except for the president. In 1954 too, a White House cabinet meeting had been broadcast for the first and only time (until a brief, unctuous display in 2017), and it was conducted around Dulles.

That occurred on October 25. Viewers saw Eisenhower's cabinet seated at the long octagonal table as the president and his secretary of state enter the room. Dulles takes his place on the president's right, with their backs to the tall glass doors that open onto the garden. The customary silent prayer is forgone. And then for the next thirty minutes, Dulles, without notes, and in his well-known unmodulated voice, conducts a sweeping, crystal-clear exposition of the connections between America's alliances in Asia and in Europe. When Dulles is finished, the president calls the account "brilliant," as it is. Then the show ends. It was a testament not only to Dulles's mastery of policy but also to the unsurpassed trust that Eisenhower placed in him.

If one regards Eisenhower as a genial mediocrity, as many people used to do, then it's easy to assume, as Churchill did, that in foreign affairs he was little more than a "ventriloquist's doll" for Dulles.[27] But those who worked closely with Eisenhower knew he was in charge, even during moments like Dulles's star performance in the Cabinet Room. What was really on display in that meeting was a confident hands-on chief executive allowing the senior member of his team to take center stage.

Dulles's powers of concentration were intense, and he often ignored his surroundings. At Foggy Bottom, he preferred to lunch on an apple and cottage cheese alone in his map-lined office. He sharpened pencils with a pocketknife and doodled on yellow pads throughout the day, especially during meetings, which could prompt his staff, among others, to assume he'd forgotten their presence. Like Eisenhower, he combined self-command with surprising vitality, and a sense of purpose. "The ultimate weapon," he told the nation in one of his broadcasts, "is moral principle."[28]

Dulles believed that diplomacy divorced from morality was diplomacy divorced from the government and the people, and this belief guided his approach to the Kremlin. It's a conviction that sounds ever better in our own unmoored era.

Many historians dismiss him as a mindlessly rigid anti-Communist, but that's a misreading of the man. His anti-Communism stemmed from this devotion to principle—which included self-determination and racial equality—although in practice he could be all too flexible, as in Guatemala. And like "a Machiavellian prince of the Church," which is how another one of Eisenhower's trusted advisers viewed him, Dulles was adept with the stiletto, in bureaucratic infighting as well as in dealing with the likes of Nikita Khrushchev, the Politburo's fat and boisterously rude first secretary.[29] With the Communist bosses, he knew he was in the same room as mass murderers, and much of his difficulty with Churchill and Eden arose from this fact. If they weren't intentionally trying to appease the Russians, he figured, it was only because they had a narrower definition of what "appeasement" meant.

AT POTSDAM IN 1945, THE THREE HAD MET ON EQUAL TERMS. TEN years later, the United States and Russia overshadowed the British Empire and Commonwealth. But Britain's decision-making classes weren't reconciled to imperial decline, nor were the Americans lunging toward hegemony. This was a juncture full of contradictions.

The United States, in fact, remained politically insular. It was unsurprising, for instance, that the president's flinty chief of staff, the former New Hampshire governor Sherman Adams, fifty-five, had never left the country, although he seemed to recall a visit or two to Canada. Britain, in contrast, had no trouble asserting itself as a planetary superstate. Ambassador Makins made this clear to the Executives' Club of Chicago in February 1955, where he matter-of-factly explained that Britain, with its many possessions, its commonwealth, and other loyal allies, commanded as much power as it ever had when fully an empire.

Months earlier, Churchill had revealed to his own cabinet that he, Eden, and a small inner circle had decided that Britain would build a hydrogen bomb. In this sense, Britain remained a superpower beyond the imaginings of anyone in 1944, when the term was coined. Among the reasons for the H-bomb, Churchill explained, was to enable Britain to focus on its own military priorities should they diverge from America's in a World War III. "Continents are vulnerable as well as islands," he reminded the Commons in March 1955.[30] It was a cogent warning to Russia as well as an assertion to America of Britain's independent might.

Officials in Whitehall spoke candidly in early 1955 of establishing a global network of bomber bases in Cyprus, Jordan, Malaya, and elsewhere. Canberra jet bombers were already being deployed on constant monthlong rotations to the Middle East and Asia, and the RAF had been flying with atomic bombs since late 1953. Even newer planes, the V-bombers, were about to follow. When they did, promised Britain's chiefs of staff, the RAF's Bomber Command Main Force would possess superb long-range nuclear striking capacities. Its atomic stockpile was increasing, and its guided missile program was progressing rapidly.

Such words tended to be accompanied by reminders that British industry led the world in the glowing possibilities of civil atomic power. In August 1955, representatives of the sixteen U.S. companies in this sector, like General Dynamics, all attended the UN's International Conference on Peaceful Uses of Atomic Energy. It was essentially a twelve-day trade fair and engineering display in Geneva. Tech-savvy businessmen returned to Chicago and Pittsburgh to say that British claims of preeminence were true.

And yet these impressions told only part of the story. In the mid-1950s, the Americans were pulling away fast when it came to military high tech, and even Britain's proudest pioneering industry, jet aviation, was in trouble.

The most glaringly sudden deficiencies occurred among the airlines. The culprit was De Havilland's Comet, the world's only passenger jet. Relatively minor accidents in October 1952 and March 1953 had been attributed to pilot error. Then, in May 1953, forty-three passengers and crew aboard BOAC's Empire Service out of Calcutta's Dum Dum Airport were killed in a crash right after takeoff. By January 1954, a BOAC flight dropped from the sky off the Italian island of Elba, losing all thirty-five aboard. In April, a South African Airways jetliner fell into the

Mediterranean near Naples, with twenty-one fatalities. There was no explanation for those in-flight breakups. The Certificate of Airworthiness was pulled and the fleet grounded indefinitely. In October 1954, technicians had discovered that the Comet's fuselage life was far shorter than testing had revealed. That meant metal fatigue. Improved versions of the Comet eventually flew, but opportunities had been opened for Douglas, Lockheed, and Boeing. The larger problem went unstated: British designers weren't benefiting from the costly R&D and preflight testing that was routine in America, and this was a period when Britain, the *Financial Times* estimated, had only around a tenth the number of America's scientists and engineers.

Failures struck military aviation as well. The jet engines of Hawker Hunter fighter-bombers were known to stall, and the Supermarine Swift interceptor had to undergo five full redesigns before entering production, only to end up being used just for reconnaissance. Repeatedly, dazzling prototypes encountered manufacturing defects and delays. By summer, RAF Fighter Command was flying F-86 Sabrejets, built in California by North American Aviation, to protect the skies over London, the only city in Western Europe guarded by air defenses. Production runs had never equaled the Americans' anyway. That summer, Boeing's factories in Seattle and Wichita began rolling out one giant, eight-engine B-52 Stratofortress bomber a week.

THE FINAL LINK IN THE WEST'S DEFENSIVE CHAIN AROUND THE COMmunist world emerged from an agreement signed between Turkey and Iraq on February 24, 1955, in the Iraqi capital. What became known as the Baghdad Pact quickly turned into a wider mutual cooperation defense treaty that also embraced Britain, its Dominion of Pakistan (as that nation is styled on the treaty documents), and Iran. The United States was not yet included, but it had initiated the arrangement and supported it wholeheartedly. After his May 1953 tour of the Middle East, Dulles was eager to form a "northern arc" of allies—with a line of defense stretching from the Mediterranean to the Himalayas—to protect the region against Russia. Where Egypt might fit was uncertain.

Stories in the American press explained how the Baghdad Pact fit into the country's global alliance system. The U.S. ambassador in Iraq would participate as an "Observer," and the pact seemed to connect NATO to SEATO, and to America's arrangements in the Pacific, as with ANZUS, Taiwan, and Japan. In fact, Washington was prudently keeping its distance for several reasons: Soviet Russia might be provoked by formal U.S. defense ties with its neighbor Iran; and India could be alienated if America aligned itself formally with Pakistan. Additionally, the "pro-Israel lobby" was a reason for being aloof, at least according to what Britain's minister of defense said he heard from Dulles.[31] Whatever the specifics, Congress had had its fill of treaties.

Yet the Americans were slowly shedding their passivity in the Middle East. For example, they had inked a small military aid deal with Iraq the previous spring, to surprise in Whitehall, and they were also developing what sharp reporters called a "theory of Iraq's magnetism."[32] Pro-Western Iraq, by these lights, could serve as an alluring example for other Arab states. British diplomats were skeptical about all this, the new defense pact notwithstanding. Iraq's army, they said, had little potential, and Baghdadi politicians would never be able to mobilize their country into becoming a militarily effective alliance partner. Their preferred approach was just to prop up the monarchy and use Iraqi terrain as a base of operations, while pumping oil. Restive Iraqi nationalists, for their part, didn't think much of either idea: their corrupt government operated under Britain's thumb, they recognized, with the silent support of the United States.

CHURCHILL HAD TURNED EIGHTY ON NOVEMBER 30, 1954, SHOWING signs of his strokes (having also endured milder ones in 1949 and 1952), dreading the oblivion of old age, and disdaining a much-needed hearing aid. In the House of Commons that winter, Nye Bevan taunted him, saying he had nothing left to offer, except the desire to hang on to office. Churchill couldn't even meet directly with the Soviet leaders, Bevan would chide, because Britain was "now at the mercy of the U.S."[33] Meanwhile, Anthony Eden continued his long wait to succeed Churchill, with a controlled impatience that ate at his nerves, and he tortured himself further whenever rivals such as Harold Macmillan or Rab Butler appeared to be eyeing the prize.

Despite his failing strength, Churchill resolved to stay on as long as he could, even though, he admitted, "Anthony will mew a good deal."[34] But his cabinet finally pressed him to depart. When he reluctantly left Downing Street, on April 5, 1955, he did so amid the silence of a monthlong newspaper strike. "I don't believe that Anthony can do it," he reflected to Colville the night before resigning.[35] Cold-eyed Dwight Eisenhower agreed. He had a lifetime of appraising men under stress, and he had seen Eden a half-dozen times since becoming president. He had originally held Eden in high regard, but, he told Swede Hazlett, a friend from Abilene High with whom he corresponded, he had come to think less of Eden with each encounter.

Eden was no longer a young man, yet he saw visions of brokering peace between East and West and of realigning power in the Middle East and in Asia. The Americans were respectful. He called for a general election in May: the Conservatives won with three times the majority enjoyed by Churchill, and it seemed likely that Eden would remain in Downing Street into 1960. That same month, James Reston—*The New York Times*' acute reporter, bureau chief, and columnist—observed that Britain "has increasingly made its rising influence felt in Washington." The administration, he wrote, was being "forced to consider the power and influence of London."[36]

By now, however, those officials also had to consider the rising influence of West Germany and Japan, as well as of France, which was producing more cars, steel, and textiles that year than ever. Additionally, France was moving forward with West Germany (suddenly the world's third-largest steel producer) to build the European Economic Community. As for the Soviet satellites in the East, they were locked up that month by Russia in the Warsaw Pact military alliance, and it was anything but a "mirror image" of NATO, as described in our day.[37]

On June 13, Admiral Radford testified to Congress about the coming fiscal year's defense budget. After reviewing the numbers, he spoke of America's need for actual partners. He didn't name any country, but he wasn't talking of France. No sooner had France lost in Vietnam than half its armed forces were caught in Algeria's fight for independence— Algeria being an integral part of the French nation for more than a century. The number of soldiers France could offer to NATO remained about the same as were being supplied by Belgium, with a fifth the population. Britain's military chiefs, on the other hand, had just informed the Pentagon how they proposed to enforce the Baghdad Pact: they'd be placing an armored division northwest of Tehran within three weeks of any Russian incursion.

How could anyone in Whitehall seriously say that? After all, critics of the time described Britain's military backing of the pact as "flimsy," as they do today.[38] Maybe not. The British 10th Armored Division was headquartered in Libya and had detachments stationed at Aqaba and Ma'an (in southern Jordan), which could be supported from the huge air base at Mafraq, forty miles north of Amman. Those would be the designated forces, in addition to manpower drawn from Cyprus, the new headquarters base of Middle East Command. Was this real? No one disagreed in the Pentagon, and the Americans took the logistics on faith. Less than three years before, after all, they had seen what the British were set to drop into Iran.

On Monday, July 18, the East-West summit meeting, for which Churchill had yearned, finally occurred in Geneva, albeit without him. Georgy Malenkov, who had been the top party boss as chairman of the Council of Ministers, wasn't there either, having been demoted in February. Attending the conference instead was a new ruling triumvirate of First Secretary Khrushchev, Premier Nikolai Bulganin, and Defense Minister Georgi Zhukov, the foremost Red Army marshal of World War II. They convened with Eisenhower, Eden, and France's premier, Edgar Faure, at Geneva's Palais des Nations for five days.

Eisenhower crisply opened the conference that Monday morning. He had let it be known that he would not dine or be giving a dinner at the gathering. On the second day, he caused a traffic jam when out in the week's strange hazy heat to buy toys for his grandchildren. As he went about his business, he unconsciously confirmed the impression of an American president by now being something above other world leaders:

when asked, he matter-of-factly told reporters that he hadn't been in a shop in twenty years, nor did he carry money. Nothing significant came out of the conference, except a strong sense that on the West's side of the table, at least, Eisenhower and the Americans were in charge.

EISENHOWER USUALLY ASSEMBLED HIS NATIONAL SECURITY COUN- cil on Thursday mornings at 9:00 in the Cabinet Room. They were his favorite meetings. The NSC wasn't a decision-making body, and he enjoyed the informed, wide-ranging give-and-take. By law, the other NSC members at the time were the vice president, the secretaries of state and defense, and the director of the Office of Defense Mobilization. Usually a dozen or so additional people were invited as needed, including the JCS chairman, Radford, and the CIA director, Allen Dulles.

At the NSC meeting of March 3, 1955, the principals reviewed many of the issues, such as arms control, which they would raise that summer in Geneva with Khrushchev. But Director Dulles also made an upsetting presentation on the Middle East, which, he said, was "in a boil."[39]

Egypt's Prime Minister Nasser had become an increasing concern to the men around the table. They assumed Nasser would be reasonable, to judge by his article in the latest issue of *Foreign Affairs*, in which he emphasized land reform. Israeli policy, he'd written, might be "expansionist," but he acknowledged that his country's development would be undercut by a return to war, and the administration valued his apparently peaceful intentions.[40] So the CIA's report was worrying: Nasser deemed the Baghdad Pact a neocolonial threat and a means of splitting the Arab states, which, Nasser hoped, could be nonaligned between East and West. Moreover, he was said to regard the pact as strengthening Iraq, which he saw both as his rival for Arab leadership and, like Jordan, as a British fiefdom. He was therefore seeking to create a defense alliance of his own, with Syria and perhaps Saudi Arabia.

The Saudis were not fans of the pact either. They hated the Hashemite family monarchies of Iraq and of Jordan and resented U.S. moves to enhance Baghdad's stature. Besides, Riyadh saw the British as a threat.

In October, four squadrons of British-commanded Trucial Oman Levies expelled a Saudi police contingent from a disputed southeast Arabian backwater known as the Buraimi Oasis. Seven Saudis had been killed, and this completely obscure place then became yet another world issue. Lebanon, in turn, had various reasons of its own to oppose the pact and had furiously called home its ambassador from Washington. As for Syria—which, like Iraq, is a colonial creation—it was riven between pro- and anti-Iraqi elements. A coup in Damascus looked imminent, Allen Dulles explained, though he didn't bore his listeners by reminding them that Syrian generals had also launched coups in 1949, 1951, and just a year earlier in February.

Any sensible policy maker who heard this overview might have left the room screaming. Then as today, there was every reason for the Americans not to place themselves between these antagonists. Why jump into that briar patch? But what would happen if they didn't? The men around the table began to consider more fine-tuning. Perhaps, some participants suggested, they should take a more active role in the Baghdad Pact. And maybe a direct U.S. involvement in the pact could allay Israel's fears that the organization was going to be used against it, whether by the Muslim signatories or by Britain—the pact's linchpin—with which Israel's relations were delicate.

Tensions in the Middle East were also "in a boil" because of a surprise attack that occurred along the Egyptian-Israeli frontier on the night of February 28. A hundred and fifty IDF paratroopers struck a small army camp on the outskirts of Gaza city, killing thirty-eight Egyptian soldiers and losing five of their own. It was the bloodiest incident between the two states since 1948. "This action had been apparently precipitated by the Israelis," Allen Dulles told the NSC attendees that Thursday, "though the reasons for doing so at this particular time were difficult to fathom."[41]

No they weren't. By 1955, Israel and its four adjoining neighbors—Egypt, Jordan, Syria, and Lebanon—were entering the sixth year of intensifying border clashes. Sabotage and murder were followed by reprisals and revenge along a six-hundred-mile armistice line. For more than a year, there had been improvised sniping, infiltrations, and mine laying against Israel staged from Gaza, a six-by-thirty-mile sand strip overseen by Egypt. Then as today, Gaza was utterly remote from Egypt proper and inhabited by impoverished Palestinian refugees, who at the time numbered 219,000.

A few weeks before Israel's attack, on the morning of January 31, guards at Cairo's Bab-el-Khalk prison had raised a big black flag to announce the execution of the two Israeli saboteurs captured the previous summer. (A clemency plea from Eisenhower and repeated ones from the Foreign Office had been ignored.) Prime Minister Sharett declared these operatives to be martyrs, and IDF backers of the original terror unit plotted vengeance. "After the Gaza raid it was downhill all the way," concludes the historian Avi Shlaim, about the buildup to Israel's invasion of Egypt in 1956.[42]

Secret peace contacts that Nasser had initiated with Sharett in November were dropped; Egypt embarked on a policy of declared reprisals by using guerrillas to penetrate Israel; and Nasser sought modern weapons for his weak army, which he was also prompted to do by fears of what Britain might be concocting with the Baghdad Pact. His suspicion of the British ran so deep that he believed they were colluding with Tel Aviv; indeed, he even thought London had ordered the Israelis to kill his soldiers as payback for Egyptian opposition to the Baghdad Pact.

Unconvinced that the Gaza attack was self-defense, given the larger record of violence, the Americans moved quickly, along with Britain, to have Israel censured in the United Nations. That occurred on March 29. Egyptian-Palestinian commandos hit IDF patrols through the spring. Retaliations for these reprisals followed. A fedayeen campaign organized by the Egyptian army for cross-border special operations and terror then began in August. It was modeled on the one against the British in the Canal Zone during 1952–1954.

Late that August, Secretary of State Dulles proposed a security guarantee of Israel's borders. Maybe a sudden dramatic initiative could break open this prejudice-encrusted conflict, he hoped. Eden supported the move and arranged to help fund a U.S.-British loan to Israel that could be used to compensate Palestinian refugees. But the belligerents couldn't agree what those borders might be. Both statesmen were scrambling to tamp down the clashes that they believed were offering opportunity for Russia's intrusion, and then Nasser opened the door wide to Moscow.

On September 27, Nasser announced the signing of a massive arms deal with the Eastern bloc, brokered by Czechoslovakia.* Shipments of more than $250 million worth of modern Soviet weaponry began arriving in Alexandria within weeks: some 200 planes (MiG jet fighters and Ilyushin light bombers), 260 tanks, plus tank destroyers and hundreds of pieces of artillery, as well as 6 torpedo boats and 2 destroyers, and a promise of submarines.

This was the first arms sale between an Arab nation and, in effect, the Soviet Union. If the Egyptians also received adequate training and technical support, their ramshackle seventy-five-thousand-man military could be transformed into something serious. That prospect transfixed the Israelis, although U.S. experts judged the IDF to be "far superior" to all the Arab armies combined—in training, leadership, most categories of arms, and mobilized manpower too.[43] Before long, in early 1956, the Russians began signing similarly large arms deals with Syria. Washington and Whitehall, as well as the IDF's Intelligence Branch, dreaded the well-honed practice of *maskirovka*: Red Army operatives might gradually be inserted into the region, or, as in Korea, Soviet pilots would be deployed clandestinely to fly Egyptian or Syrian MiGs.[44]

Nasser was playing all sides—not only East versus West, but United States versus Britain, two countries that he described as the "coming and the going." At the same time, he also sought to develop Egypt's economy, especially with improved irrigation and agriculture, and dreamed of building a giant dam across the Nile, at Aswan in the south of Egypt.

ON SATURDAY, NOVEMBER 26, BRITAIN'S GOVERNMENT COMMUNICA-tions Headquarters intercepted a message from Moscow to Nasser offering far better terms to help build the dam than the West had considered. Eden was distraught, observed his wife, Clarissa. "If the Russians get the contract we have lost Africa," he said furiously.[45] From Whitehall, his government's colonial secretary tracked down Harold

---

*Nasser had concluded that a recent U.S. offer to grant him $27 million worth of weapons for free had too many strings attached, such as joining an anti-Communist alliance.

Macmillan, Chancellor of the Exchequer, who was on a weekend shoot in Kent. Macmillan scribbled out a telegram to Dulles, as did Eden to Eisenhower. They each proposed that Washington finance the dam. Foster Dulles agreed, to an extent. He warned President Eisenhower that the British "never forget the commercial and economic things" in their diplomacy.[46] Therefore, Macmillan first had to pledge that Britain would come up with 20 percent of the funding and that it wouldn't try to exclude U.S. engineering firms from the project.

Nasser was anxious. At home, he persecuted Communists relentlessly, but now he was taking not only money and arms from the East but also military training. He risked opening Egypt to Soviet influence. Moreover, he knew that arms buying from a Soviet satellite, just the previous year, had spurred the CIA's ouster of Guatemala's Jacobo Árbenz, another progressive young colonel who pursued neutrality. The Russians remained embarrassed by what had befallen Guatemala, and they implied to Nasser that they'd stand by him should Egypt be endangered. But he needn't have worried: Dulles concluded that it was "difficult to be critical" of the Egyptians for buying the arms, which "they sincerely need for defense."[47]

In early December, as the border clashes with Egypt worsened, Prime Minister Sharett told American friends that the optimism he saw emanating from London and Washington about Dulles's peace initiative was groundless. Neither he nor Ben-Gurion trusted Britain in a mediating role, given its military ties to Jordan and Iraq and its readiness, as Ben-Gurion charged, to "truncate" Israel.[48] At this point, Eisenhower blamed both Arabs and Israelis for the impasse. Dulles and Eden, meanwhile, spoke inconclusively about agreeing to jointly intervene against whatever side might start a war, while Syria and Israel, in turn, were filing hundreds of complaints with the UN over truce violations.

Then came another step toward all-out war. On the night of December 11, in response to what Israel claimed was Syrian provocation, the IDF launched a brigade-sized assault on Syrian positions along the northeastern shore of the Sea of Galilee, killing fifty-four and capturing thirty, while losing six of their own. The Americans were again unconvinced by Tel Aviv's justifications; *The New York Times* condemned the attack as "deplorable." The administration had been close to sealing an arms deal with Israel, and U.S. law, then as today, requires that parties to such a sale use American weaponry only for "defensive" purposes. Eisenhower and Dulles agreed they couldn't make that case to Congress, believing the Israelis had more than defense on their minds.

19

NO END OF A LESSON

I hope the day will never come when the American nation will be
the champion of the status quo. Once that happens, we shall have
forfeited, and rightly forfeited, the support of the unsatisfied, of
those who, . . . young in years or spirit, believe that they can make
a better world.

—John Foster Dulles

O N SATURDAY, DECEMBER 31, 1955, SECRETARY AND MRS. DULLES
arrived in New York from Washington aboard an air force Convair.
They stayed at the Waldorf Astoria and, on the first, attended the
11:00 a.m. service at Brick Presbyterian Church, where the secretary was
an elder. That afternoon, he issued a review of the previous year's accomplishments, including the Baghdad Pact, West Germany's entry into
NATO, and the summit with Russia. Journalists questioned him about
the president's health. Eisenhower had suffered a heart attack in late
September and had recently spent six weeks in a Denver hospital. "He's
fine," Dulles responded. "Fully recovered."[1]

The government ran smoothly during Eisenhower's convalescence—
a sure sign of his administration's quietly firm efficiency. He finally
returned to the Washington news arena on January 19, showing himself
at a press conference. He looked slightly thinner and spoke in a lower

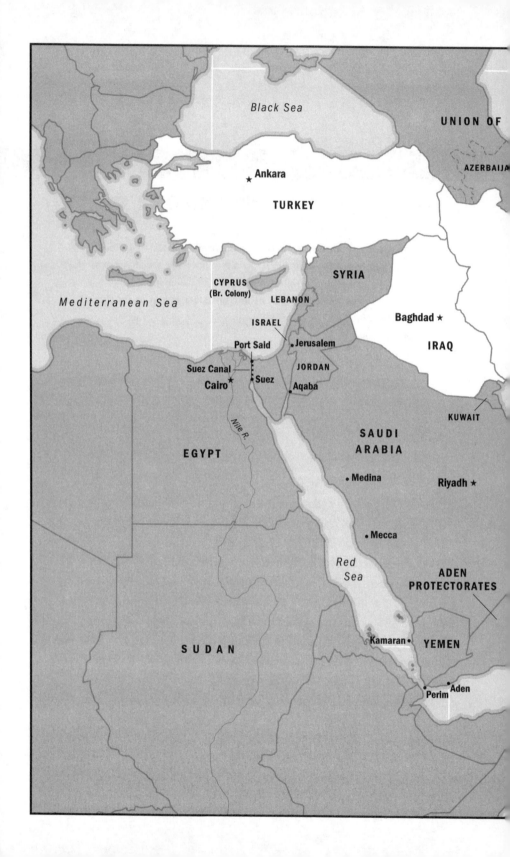

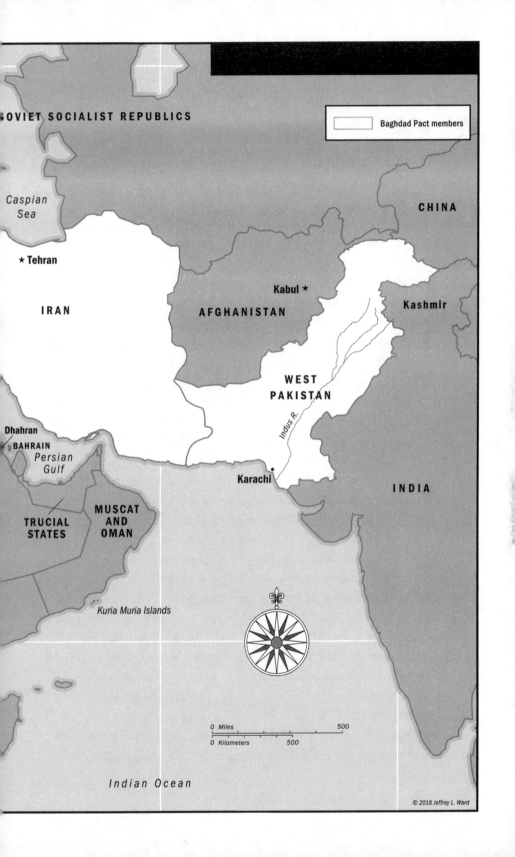

register, but he was clear-eyed and resilient and proved himself still to be in command of a global policy about which the two political parties were in basic agreement. And he had a remarkable secretary of state to execute it.

The American economy at this point was growing so fast that even the CEO of New York's First National City Bank said he hoped for a slowdown to avoid "a cycle of boom and bust."[2] The administration was able to achieve a balanced budget for the upcoming fiscal year, but everyone knew that it had been attained by defense cuts. A struggle continued between notions of fiscal order and the force levels that the hard-to-satisfy Pentagon considered barely adequate.

Nonetheless, the Strategic Air Command's intercontinental B-52s had entered service and were now flying "hot" (carrying nuclear bombs) from U.S. and overseas bases, though not from ones in England, where the "hardware" was to be kept stockpiled until truly needed. The second and third of the giant Forrestal-class supercarriers, which were launched in 1955 and 1956, added to this worldwide mobility of power. The country also had nearly three million men and women under arms. Admiral Radford, the JCS chairman, might at times question if this number was enough, but he assailed critics who alleged that the United States wasn't equal to the task of thwarting the Communist behemoths. Eisenhower offered his own assurances, telling the nation in March that Khrushchev's claim of Russia's military superiority was only bluster.

President Eisenhower also said he was spending most of his working hours on the Middle East.[3] He considered its importance second only to Europe's, and he believed the fates of these regions were intertwined. Two-thirds of Europe's oil passed through the Suez Canal. Much of the remaining third flowed by pipeline from Iraq's landlocked fields, near Kirkuk, to the Banias Oil Terminal in Syria, on the Mediterranean coast. The Americans used far less oil from the Middle East than did Europe, but everyone knew that Western Europe's industries would grind to a halt if those sources were disrupted, with an immediate effect on the United States.

Among the Western allies, Britain remained responsible for countering Russian penetration in the Middle East. The U.S. 6th Fleet, with its four hundred carrier-based aircraft, patrolled the Mediterranean, but

America's political-military presence was otherwise slim. There were no marines aboard those ships, as had been routine, and as practiced today. The eight-hundred-man detachment was dropped during the previous summer to save money. In the Persian Gulf and the Red Sea, only a single vessel was kept on station. It was usually a seaplane tender or a minesweeper, though it received occasional visits from U.S. destroyers. The air force had bases in Libya and Morocco, but long-term access to the big one in Dhahran wasn't quite guaranteed. As today, the Saudi ruling family was temperamental. For instance, the Saudis didn't allow U.S. military personnel to keep firearms in the country, though the Americans had managed to squirrel away a secret cache of rifles, pistols, and ammunition. As for political matters, Dulles said in April that he'd leave it up to the "traditional military suppliers" of the Middle East, meaning Britain and France, to determine the right balance of arms that should be exported to the Arabs and Israelis.[4] Hopefully, a prudent equilibrium would prevent one side or the other from launching a war.

The British, however, had increasingly less room for maneuver in their international dealings. By January 1956, the Bank of England's gold and dollar reserves had dropped lower than at any time since 1952. Three years of prosperity were buckling under an all-too-familiar balance-of-payments crisis. Exports were up 8 percent since the previous year, but imports soared by 15 percent. Productivity wasn't keeping pace with global competition, and inflation was skyrocketing. "Ultimately the Cabinet must choose between the demands of the domestic economy and of imperial responsibility," wrote *The New York Times*—an observation that, even at this date, it believed to be news.[5]

Prime Minister Eden had imposed cuts on the armed forces in October 1955. Yet at the same time he had vowed that Britain's role as a global power would be undiminished. Many of his fellow subjects agreed. By winter, a BBC survey showed that only 46 percent of adults "reckoned Britain had declined as a world power over the previous half-century."[6]

In December, he reshuffled his cabinet, hoping to quell charges of indecisiveness. Selwyn Lloyd, fifty-one, a fast-rising Tory star, became foreign secretary. He was a prosperous lawyer and had been a staff officer during World War II. Lloyd genially described himself as a "yes-man" for Eden, who, despite being prime minister, inserted himself into every detail of running the Foreign Office. That included handling the Americans.[7] *Punch*, the 115-year-old London humor magazine, still saw indecision. During that first week of January 1956, it featured a cartoon that depicted the British ship of state pilotless in stormy seas. "This country is not on its way down," Eden declared days later to cheering constituents. Newspapers in Texas and everywhere else in America picked up the quotation.[8]

Eden was scheduled to sail to New York on the twenty-fifth. The visit had been planned since the fall, and his cabinet hoped the trip might boost his standing at home. Before departing, Eden explained the purpose of the journey to the nation, announcing on television that he'd be working on all the difficult issues with Eisenhower, whom he referred to, in a terrible misreading of the man, as "your friend and mine."[9]

EDEN'S CROSSING ON THE *QUEEN MARY* PROVIDED A QUIET OPPOR-tunity to work with his staff, and he arrived in New York early Monday morning, January 30, then flew to Washington. Secretary Dulles, Ambassador Roger Makins, and their lieutenants awaited at noon in the airport's military transport terminal. The always-impeccable prime minister deplaned carrying a homburg and wearing a black-velvet-collared overcoat.

In his delegation were Selwyn Lloyd and Evelyn Shuckburgh, who had become the Foreign Office's head of Middle East policy. Eden thanked Dulles ("'Foster,' if I may call you that") for welcoming him. They motorcaded to the White House, where President Eisenhower greeted Eden on the North Portico with outstretched hand. "How have you been?" he asked. "First rate," came the chipper reply. Eden, Lloyd, Shuckburgh, and five other key officials chatted with the Americans about feeling at home beneath Washington's slate-gray, drizzly winter skies. Eden received a penknife with "DDE" engraved on the blade, and a lunch of steak and apple pie followed, as did discussion of the Middle East. The president excused himself for an hour after lunch, at which time, around 2:15, Dulles invited everyone into the Cabinet Room, including Ambassador Aldrich and top officials from State.

Watched over by the Gilbert Stuart portrait of George Washington, the parties got down to business. Dulles made two points: The Arab-Israeli conflict risked flaring up, and the tensions that resulted were intertwined with rivalries among Saudi Arabia, Iraq, Jordan, and Syria, let alone Egypt. But the American public wasn't accustomed to seeing the Middle East as a vital area, he told the visitors. It was assumed that London took responsibility for security matters in this part of the world. Israel and its many supporters were complicating matters, he continued, by seeking a U.S. treaty that would, they argued, supposedly prevent an Arab attack. But Dulles suspected nothing like this could pass the Senate. Hints of U.S. intervention if Arabs and Israelis again went for each other's throats, he suggested, were really a bluff.[10]

The administration, Dulles explained, had no constitutional foundation for military action. There was no treaty, no UN call for using force, no congressional resolution, not even a coherent understanding about the Middle East with leaders on Capitol Hill. Moreover, it would be difficult for Washington even to anticipate the type of intervention that might be needed to separate the belligerents. And merely to plan such a step would cause public suspicions of "Zionist efforts" to support Israel or, just as bad, of attempts "to protect investments of American oil companies," and the administration had been trying to downplay the influence of the oil companies since the day it entered office.[11]

Dulles's response didn't sound helpful. Eden and his colleagues found the administration to be vacillating, which wasn't unfair. "A policy that was good six months ago is not necessarily now of any validity," the president told reporters three months later about his approach to foreign relations. But that degree of flexibility couldn't reassure any U.S. ally, nor prove workable in the new terrain into which America was moving.[12] Dulles hadn't helped matters when, in a *Life* magazine interview on January 16, he had described the art of diplomacy as being able to take the country to the brink of war and then to pull back from the precipice. He admitted to Eisenhower that he'd misspoken dreadfully.

After listening to Dulles in the Cabinet Room, Eden replied that just a day earlier Nasser had denounced the Baghdad Pact as a new form of imperialism and had said that Iraq—serving as Britain's lackey—was fronting this effort to imprison all the Arab people. He didn't know how long Nasser could be tolerated, Eden confessed. Egypt's big arms deal with the Eastern bloc had occurred five months earlier. If Egypt became a Soviet satellite, as Eden believed was happening, then Britain's role in the Middle East would be finished. Dulles merely responded that America might have to change its generally supportive attitude toward Nasser.

Over three days, these statesmen debated European unity, a forthcoming visit to London by Khrushchev and Bulganin, and the prospect of civil atomic energy replacing the West's dependence on oil. Throughout, it appeared as if two superpowers were reviewing the world, and that's at least how Britain's ambassador, Sir Roger Makins, saw it. He attended all White House meetings and didn't fret about his country's comparative standing. In fact, Makins told a forum conducted by *The New York Times* that nothing occurred in the world from the North Pole to the South Pole that didn't equally concern both powers. By now, however, that was an exaggeration. Ten years earlier, in 1946, no one in Washington, wrote James Reston, would have imagined the extent of the British Empire's decline.[13]

AT HIS JANUARY 19 PRESS CONFERENCE, THE PRESIDENT HAD RE-emphasized U.S. evenhandedness in offering friendship to Arabs and Israelis alike. It was the same day that the eleven-nation UN Security Council convened to censure Israel over its attack on Syria in December. At the UN, Ambassador Lodge charged that "previous representations by the Council and the United States government had failed to halt the mass of Israeli attacks on its Arab neighbors and that the whole Palestine situation had deteriorated as a result."[14] Censure was approved unanimously with the help of the British representative, Sir Pierson Dixon. Recurrence, they warned, could lead to punitive measures.

Israel's ambassador, Abba Eban, argued that 880 Israelis had been killed or wounded by terrorists since 1951, but the Americans weren't persuaded by his comparison.[15] From the moment the resolution passed, Eban knew what this meant: the prospect of U.S.-backed sanctions.[16]

Throughout the spring, Britain, Egypt, France, and Israel laid out their grievances. Month by month, the Israelis saw Nasser putting his Russian-delivered armory into operational standing, as Syria benefited as well from its own Eastern bloc weaponry. Truly, the Israelis had reason to be "greatly alarmed," as Dulles's special assistant for intelligence concluded in a memorandum.[17] On the other hand, Selwyn Lloyd told the House of Commons that the Middle East military balance nonetheless favored Israel. David Ben-Gurion, who had returned as prime minister the previous November, responded furiously.[18]

Then there was the role of France, which reviled Nasser for supporting Algeria's fight for independence with money, small arms, and propaganda. Without Nasser, the French believed, Algeria's revolution would collapse. Besides, they found Israel useful in crushing the Algerian resistance. Unlike Arabs, who composed nine-tenths of Algeria's population, Jews were French citizens. The Israelis armed and trained Jewish-Algerian militias, shared intelligence with French authorities, and helped break codes between the rebels and the Committee for the Liberation of North Africa, based in Cairo. France had begun supplying Israel with jets, tanks, and radar in late 1955 and by April 1956 publicly announced the sale of twelve advanced Mystère IVA jet fighter-bombers. Between then and September, however, the French Defense Ministry secretly shipped an additional number of jets, and it wasn't until October 1956 that the Americans and British would fully grasp that Israel had received a total of seventy-two Mystère IVAs, along with much else.[19]

During March, Eden informed the Eisenhower administration that Britain intended to intervene within twenty-four hours if war erupted between the Israelis and the Arabs. Otherwise the violence would spread like an oil slick. But the chance of war, Eden told the Americans, would diminish vastly if they joined with him to impose order. His aides asked if the president might request standing authority from Congress to use force to help police the conflict. Recognizing the temper of Capitol Hill, State answered with an unambiguous no.

At a news conference on April 9, Eisenhower tried to offer clarity. He pledged that America would assist whatever Middle Eastern nation might be the victim of aggression. Although any intervention, he added, would require UN approval. Moreover, he'd never order American troops into anything that could be interpreted as a war—wherever in the world—without seeking Congress's authorization.

Nineteen fifty-six was a presidential election year, and decision makers in London saw their U.S. counterparts as being even more skittish than usual. The Americans wouldn't formally accede to the Baghdad Pact, as London kept asking. They wouldn't try to prevent the Saudis (who received a quarter-billion dollars annually in ARAMCO royalties) from using secret bank accounts to foment riots in Jordan and to bribe politicians, businessmen, and journalists throughout the Arab world. Nor, in April, would Eisenhower approve an Israeli arms list of some $63 million: that risked fueling an arms race. The Pentagon, at least, used its own initiative to return marines to the 6th Fleet. In late spring, eighteen hundred leathernecks were deployed among a dozen warships.

Meanwhile, Eisenhower, Secretary Dulles, and his brother Allen were wondering how to maneuver Nasser into the Western camp. Before the Russian arms deal, they had tried offering him $3 million in CIA cash if he'd sign a military aid pact with Washington. He proved incorruptible.

Eden's government, for its part, was demonizing Nasser. A CIA memorandum of April 1 reported that the British regarded him as an "out-and-out Soviet instrument."[20] By then, Eden had started comparing Nasser to Hitler and had already told Anthony Nutting, MP—the "Eden's Eden" who was now number two at the Foreign Office—that he wanted Nasser "murdered." Nutting recalled hearing the demand over an open phone line at the Savoy hotel, where he was having dinner.[21] Eden's apparently irrational behavior surely arose from the agonizing condition of his health, as later documented by the physicians Lord David Owen and John W. Braasch. Among the pills in his black tin box was the amphetamine Benzedrine, believed to help prevent the slow poisoning of his system after the three intestinal operations, and one side effect of Benzedrine in high doses is severe paranoia.

Unfortunately for Eden, his nemesis didn't exactly fit on the scale of hard-boiled dictators. The British would have loved to hang atrocities on Nasser, but they couldn't. Except for his rabble-rousing speeches, which championed anticolonialism and nonalignment, he was, according to the American embassy in Cairo, "rather restrained."[22] However, he was calling on Egypt to lead a unified Arab nation-state that would reach from North Africa to the Persian Gulf. For the British, this was about as ominous a prospect as massacre making. So they decided to poison him, although other plans included gas or just using a bullet.

The Foreign Office doesn't issue licenses to kill, however, so Eden got elements of MI6 into the act—notably G. K. Young, who, since ousting Mosaddeq in 1953, had held the usefully vague title of director of requirements. But when Young proposed to the CIA that Nasser be "terminated," he encountered objections. Key U.S. officials were friendly with Nasser. They included the CIA's Kermit Roosevelt Jr., forty-two, who headed the Middle East bureau, and the new ambassador in Cairo, Acheson's former aide Henry Byroade, forty-three, who, as a high-achieving young army officer, had also bonded with Nasser. Eisenhower, too, opposed the plotting. Once the CIA learned of British plans, its station chief in Cairo alerted Nasser. Soon afterward, the Kremlin dispatched two KGB officers to help professionalize Nasser's security detail—a sign of the strange new political alignments being formed.

EARLY IN THE MORNING OF APRIL 18, FIRST SECRETARY KHRU-shchev and the Soviet premier, Nikolai Bulganin, arrived at London's Victoria Station, having sailed into Portsmouth the night before on the cruiser *Ordzhonikidze*. Anthony Eden and his cabinet waited on the platform. That afternoon, the first of seven wide-ranging plenary sessions got under way at Downing Street. The Americans weren't involved and seemed indifferent to what looked more like tourism than summitry. Jokes circulated at State about the Communist bosses staying at Claridge's and being received at Windsor by the queen.

Eden showed his usual urbanity, but tempers flared when he got specific about protecting Middle Eastern oil, without which, he insisted, "we should slowly starve to death" or risk "being strangled to death."[23] For someone known to be reserved, and even shy, he spoke so heatedly that Khrushchev asked if he was issuing a threat. Five days later, while visiting an industrial fair in Birmingham, Khrushchev remarked that Russia was set to unveil a rocket able to carry a nuclear bomb to anywhere in the world. Listeners claimed that he had said it would be revealed "very soon" or "quickly," but no one could confirm the translation.[24]

Khrushchev's aside got the Americans' attention, fast. The next day, reporters excitedly asked Eisenhower about these rockets, which no nation yet possessed. The president spoke with the sureness of a deeply experienced commander in chief. There's a "very, very long distance" between laboratory research and "a really efficient, effective instrument of war," he explained.[25] Yet anxiety lingered.

The immediate danger to Britain, however, wasn't Russian warheads or lack of oil, at least so far. It was a worsening trade imbalance along with a lagging rate of productivity that one U.S. expert blamed on chronic "time-consuming inefficiency" in British factories.[26] That observation was, in fact, news. It's why his analysis got headlines on both sides of the Atlantic. At the same time, Eden spoke of Britain's being in mortal peril as it sank into poverty due to competition, as he phrased it, from "Europe," as well as from India and Japan. One result of the financial squeeze was that Britain could barely play in the heightening superpower competition of dispensing economic aid to third-world figures such as Nasser.

Yet tight finances didn't dissuade Eden's government from further boosting the nation's standing as a global power. In June, the Ministry of Supply announced that another "V-class" strategic bomber, Avro's Vulcan, was entering service as part of Bomber Command Main Force. And fighter-bombers were being adapted for what experts called "skip-bombing," in which A-bombs could be dropped from extremely low altitudes near the front lines of combat.

Why were these expensive apocalyptic capabilities being honed despite Britain's costly challenges in aviation? Among other reasons, Washington wasn't expected to be able to produce enough planes, pilots, and nuclear weaponry to cover every target in the Eastern bloc while also having to enhance North American air defenses against expanding fleets of Soviet bombers. As a result, the British believed they could fill a vital gap in protecting the West, with influence to be gained from doing so. They were wrong. The Americans built a deterrent so large that there'd be plenty of megatons left over, in a saying of this era, "to make the rubble bounce."[27]

The RAF's own plans for World War III included striking targets in the southern Soviet Union from air bases in Cyprus, which had become Middle East Command headquarters since the withdrawal from Suez in 1954. This sunny, arid "strategic colony," as it was called in Whitehall, had been ceded by Turkey in 1878 and lay 40 miles off its coast, some 250 miles north of Port Said, the top end of the Suez Canal. The entire island is only two-thirds the size of the stronghold that had just been lost in Egypt, but Cyprus seemed adequate as a springboard for launching mobile operations into the Middle East.

An island, however, is an awkward place from which to deploy tanks, especially an island without any port that can draw more than twenty-two feet. To accommodate the Royal Navy's Mediterranean Fleet, the British therefore had to spend heavily to build a massive base in the Bay of Episkopi. Moreover, Cyprus had been bled by terrorism since April 1955. Nationalist cells within a Greek-Cypriot population of 400,000 demanded union with Greece, no matter the hopes of 93,600 Turkish-Cypriots, who had their own anti-British resistance movement pushing for union with Turkey.

London wasn't going to hand over sovereignty to anyone. By 1956, the island had turned into an armed camp. Soldiers swept through the countryside and patrolled Nicosia's serpentine streets, placing coils of barbed wire at flying checkpoints to verify identity papers. Dusk-to-dawn curfews were imposed to prevent bomb-carrying motorcyclists from speeding through the dimly lit city. Colonial authorities insisted that Athens was behind the violence. By June, terror bombers were finding daily targets of opportunity among the 37,000 British troops spread out over Cyprus. Come late summer, colonial authorities had already hanged five Greek Cypriots in Nicosia Central Prison.

On July 22, Nye Bevan became the Labour Party's shadow foreign secretary. He asked the Commons whether the base on Cyprus might not have been more secure had Eden yielded sovereignty and just signed a long-term lease with the willing Greek locals. But he knew that possibility didn't square with the government's determination to "maintain the strength and influence of Britain and the British Empire."[28] The central fact about Nye was that his country was Wales, and his dislike of imperial great power started approximately on the Shropshire line. He took this opportunity to indict his fellow British subjects, whom he never considered fellow countrymen. Britain's obsession with retaining sovereignty over Cyprus, he charged, stemmed from the bitterness of having been evicted from Suez in the first place.

Just as he wouldn't take sides between Arabs and Israelis, Eisenhower let it be known that he wouldn't do so between Greece, Turkey, and Britain. London claimed Cyprus was a vital NATO stronghold, which it was using to defend the free world, but, as lots of Americans were startled to see, all three belligerents were NATO allies. Eisenhower also came close to saying that one man's "terrorists" might be another's "patriots," a point Bevan had said explicitly about Cyprus.[29] The American president didn't sound like the best person for Eden to count on when the chips were down.

EISENHOWER CONDUCTED LIVELY Q&A WITH THE PRESS CORPS about once a week, and he used his news conference on May 23 to dismiss the undue pessimism he said he was hearing about the nation's foreign affairs. *The New York Times*, for example, had recently editorialized that America had grievously compromised its prestige from Gibraltar to India—essentially from Europe through the Middle East—due to his administration's inconsistencies. When the Associated Press asked if there was reason, in particular, to worry about Nasser's Egypt, the president remarked that not every family spat goes to divorce court.

Secretary of State Dulles wasn't as blasé. He was coming to "hate" Nasser, according to his sister Eleanor, and to find him "devilish."[30] The passion was uncharacteristic, but Dulles was accustomed to the negotiating patterns of Wall Street and the industrial nations. Nasser was a supreme third-world rabble-rouser, a peasant boy made good, with lots of resentments, and there was no telling what he'd do. He thrived on drama. In part because he feared being killed by his own extremists, he refused to embrace the latest U.S. peace overture with Israel, which had Eisenhower's personal backing. Before long, Dulles slid into discussing Nasser's "Hitler-ite personality" with Eisenhower.

Nasser, however, had good cause to be difficult. He knew of the La-von Affair, Guatemala, MI6's assassination attempts, and Mosaddeq's ongoing solitary confinement in a Tehran military prison. He also knew that Eisenhower and Eden had agreed that spring to use diplomacy and covert measures to undermine his regime.

On the morning of June 13, the last detachment of eleven British officers and eighty men sailed out of Port Said for Cyprus, as half a dozen new Soviet-supplied MiG-15s from Egypt's air force streaked through the sky. The soldiers had lowered the Union Jack the night before, at the garrison's huge yellow stucco Navy House headquarters. For the first time in seventy-four years, it wouldn't be raised again in the morning. Instead, Egyptian troops hoisted their own country's flags, green with white crescent and three stars, over the Navy House build-ings, quay, and railyards. Anxious observers in London expected trouble.

In the House of Commons, Eden faced a crew of right-wing Tories known as the Suez Group, who opposed all this "scuttle." Two years earlier, they'd plagued Churchill's already burdened conscience as he presided miserably over concluding the base agreement. They'd since turned on Eden to demand that the empire (they disdained the term "commonwealth") stop retreating. A few of them were able politicians, but most were woolly intransigents. They counted among themselves the likes of Sir Walter Bromley-Davenport, whose cheer was likened to a hand grenade going off; the reactionary brigadier Otho Prior-Palmer; the crotchety admiral John Hughes-Hallett; and the group's maximum leader, Captain Charles Waterhouse, a presentable nullity with loud opin-ions about "niggers in the woodpile," which he might accompany with a stage whisper, "Too many of 'em about anyway." The ranks of these characters swelled that summer to over a hundred. As a faction, they seemed to come straight out of P. G. Wodehouse, but they were far from harmless: Julian Amery, their secretary, and several others, involved themselves in the secret attempts to murder Nasser.

In Washington, Eisenhower, as always, was in charge, despite hav-ing had emergency 2:00 a.m. surgery at Walter Reed Army Medical Center for ileitis on June 9. That hardly kept him out of action for five weeks, as many believe, nor did it allow Dulles to run off on his own.[31] When Dulles rescinded a seven-month-old U.S. offer to help finance the building of the Aswan Dam, on July 19, it was entirely consistent with the president's policy. Nor did Dulles act from anger at Nasser's nationalist stance, or in response to Nasser's having recognized Red China in May. (Israel, like Britain, had done so in early 1950.) Instead, that decision reflects how Americans were thinking about their own role in the world.

For months, Secretary Dulles, Vice President Nixon, and Admiral Radford had been battling with Congress over the foreign-aid budget. The administration had asked for an increase of 100 percent, but the House had slashed that request by a third. Nixon had declared in May that foreign aid was the "fourth service" of America's defense—akin to the importance of the armed forces—and both the secretary of state and the JCS chairman had testified to that effect.[32] But counterarguments on Capitol Hill were pointed: Why should the Americans be responsible for protecting and aiding everybody when, for instance, even the British were in the process of cutting their armed forces by seventy thousand? Dulles concluded it wasn't worth the candle to fight for a dam on behalf of a troublemaker like Nasser, nor to buck opposition from cotton-state Democrats who worried about competition from a newly fertile Nile valley.

Nasser, who'd been elected president on June 23 in a unanimous plebiscite, was shocked. So were the British, because they weren't consulted despite having agreed to put up their 20 percent of initial funding for the Aswan Dam. But they too pulled out the next day. For them, the administration's decision wasn't entirely bad news: Chancellor of the Exchequer Harold Macmillan confessed in his diary that Britain "never had the money" to follow through on its pledge anyway.[33]

A week after the funds were denied—and in an explicit quid pro quo on July 26—Nasser seized control of the Suez Canal Company, which for eighty-seven years had been operated under British and French supervision. Profits would now be used, he declared during a long speech in Alexandria that Sunday, to construct the High Dam. As he was speaking, a squad of black-uniformed police cordoned off the company's offices across the street from the U.S. embassy compound in the city's Garden City neighborhood, and the canal itself was placed under martial law.

. . .

NASSER'S TAKEOVER OF "THE SUEZ CANAL" WAS NOT JUST "ANother spectacular nationalization," as was commonly said.[34] The canal itself already belonged to Egypt, and this step wasn't like Mosaddeq seizing the AIOC. The Suez Canal Company was an Egyptian-registered corporation that ran an Egyptian-owned waterway, in Egypt. In fact, only the last twelve years of a long-term lease was being nationalized that July, because full ownership of the Suez Canal Company was to revert anyway to Egypt in November 1968. Fundamentally, the lease was being bought early. What had occurred should have been among the decade's nonevents. Instead, this incident became a defining moment of the twentieth century, and one that casts a shadow into the twenty-first.

Denouncements of "piracy" and "plundering" flew out of London, including from the Labour Party, now led by Hugh Gaitskell. Five days later, in Washington, CIA analysts laid out the possibilities ahead. Britain and France (which was a minority shareholder in the company) could simply acquiesce with as much grace as possible. They could try to join with the United States and the UN to use diplomacy in hopes that Nasser might backtrack. Or they could take military action. That was the move—hoped for by both the Israelis and the French—that Eden's government favored from the start. "They didn't want any peaceful solution," recalls Raymond A. Hare, the Foreign Service officer who would become U.S. ambassador to Egypt in September and who also came to respect Nasser. "What they wanted was a crack at Nasser."[35]

Eden never negotiated seriously with Cairo. The eagerness to fight reflected a rage against Afro-Asian nationalism and all the "fanatic nationalists" that had been plaguing the colonial powers at least since the war. By July 30, Eisenhower and Dulles recognized the eagerness in London to make a violent example of Egypt.

The next day, British and French officials ludicrously compared the Suez Canal Company's nationalization to North Korea's invasion five years before. That evening, Dulles flew to London. During a one-hour meeting the following afternoon in Downing Street, he handed Eden a letter from the president. It opposed force and had the effect of halting the momentum temporarily. But it didn't change minds. Harold Macmillan attended the meeting, and like Eden he saw Britain's survival to be at stake. "We *must* keep the Americans really frightened," he wrote a few hours later in his diary.[36]

The British had been willing to deal with General Naguib. He was the kind of Egyptian for whom you'd buy a drink at the club, of which he might even be a member. With a dark complexion and a scimitar nose, however, Nasser was something different. His informality reminded British officials that, despite his colonelcy, he came from the lower orders. Race was a motivator too. Arabs surely couldn't run Suez Canal Company operations or pilot the waterway without Western management. The Greek shipping magnate Aristotle Onassis scoffed at such concerns. It could be done by "an abominable snowman," he averred, and, indeed, the Egyptians kept the canal functioning smoothly.[37]

Eden railed about Munich. Appeasing the dictator would only increase his appetite. Suez, he felt, might even be a greater outrage than Munich, which at least involved defined geopolitical limits. The German state in 1938 was dismembering a neighbor, but what did the Egyptians and other Afro-Asian nationalists have in mind? There was no telling where their limits might be. The non-Caucasian world was turning on the West, or so it looked.

Eden spoke with the same vehemence he'd used with Khrushchev: Nasser had his "thumb on our windpipe."[38] Britain possessed only a six-week oil reserve; the Continent perhaps could last a month. Maybe so. But why would Nasser use control of the waterway as a political weapon against the West? If tankers were hindered, Egypt's economy would teeter; only the outlawed Communists within could benefit. And if Nasser really was a nationalist, why worry about his becoming a Soviet puppet? What sense would it make for him to free Egypt from the British, only to yoke it to the Soviet Union?

Had Eden done nothing in response to Nasser's takeover, he would have been denounced furiously in Parliament and the press. He'd have been reviled for several months and compelled to endure a fiery Conservative Party conference at Llandudno, Wales, in October, stoked by the Suez Group. But as an able diplomat, he could have rallied the support of his cabinet to withstand this onslaught. His party didn't have to face election until 1960, and the British public was unlikely to spend four years brooding over the canal.

Besides, if Eden didn't invade, France would have been bound to reconsider. It needed British logistical support; France had little standing in the Suez Canal Company; and 400,000 of its fighting men, plus divisions of mobile security police, were already bogged down in Algeria. As for Israel, Prime Minister Ben-Gurion was confident that no U.S. administration would dare criticize it in an election year. And Israel was by now receiving jets, tanks, artillery, ammunition, and napalm-drop equipment from France. To be sure, Ben-Gurion felt he had ample reason to invade. But for Israel to start a full-scale war alone was another story.

John Foster Dulles and lots of other people in Washington would have been happy to see Nasser cut down to size, but not at the price of war. He recognized from the start that the Suez Canal Company's nationalization needn't be a vital issue for anyone, despite what he was saying to assuage the British. He examined the problem as would a partner at Sullivan & Cromwell. The Suez Canal Company hadn't been harmed, and in effect nationalization meant that Nasser was buying the company earlier than planned. Additionally, international law allows a private company to be nationalized if "just and equitable" compensation is paid, which Nasser had vowed to do at the existing price on the Cairo stock exchange. That might involve raising tolls or risking another loan from Moscow, as had accompanied the 1955 weapons deal. But surely, Secretary Dulles believed, all this could be negotiated. In addition, he saw the world's nonwhite nations quickly lining up behind Cairo. That included Iran, Nasser's archenemy Iraq, and Nehru's India, which also had no diplomatic relations with Israel and fully supported nationalization.

Dulles explained the situation in lay terms to Eisenhower. It was like an easement. Someone owned the property, in this case Egypt, but many people had rights to cross the property. Dulles had returned to the State Department from London just after noon on August 3, and at seven o'clock that evening he gave one of his broadcasts to the nation—except this one was from the White House, with the president introducing him and sitting alongside. There'd of course be problems if access "to the world's greatest highway" were denied for "highly selfish purposes," Dulles warned, but so far he hoped for the best.[39] No mention that Israeli ships were still denied access.

Eisenhower backed his secretary of state, but officials in London, Paris, and Tel Aviv weren't persuaded. Earlier that same day, Eden had obtained emergency powers to requisition merchant shipping and call up military reserves. By August 31, planeloads of French soldiers and Foreign Legionnaires began arriving in Cyprus. More set sail from Algiers, seventeen hundred miles away. The troubled island became the principal base for the British and French to attack Port Said. Meanwhile, much of Britain was summoning up past glories: these two invaders called themselves the "Allied Command."

No one in Washington had been alerted to France's deployment. Once State Department officials learned about it, they again counseled patience and negotiation—with another rebuke from Eisenhower to Eden on September 4 warning against violence.

Eisenhower was still trying to find a way for the Egyptians to get money from the West to build the Aswan Dam, and he explored the possibilities with Dulles on the seventh. Their discussion offers three insights: they were keeping the Suez dispute in perspective; they remained willing to support Nasser; and Eisenhower was impervious to what his chief of staff, Sherman Adams, called "well-organized pro-Israeli lobbies" that had opposed the aid.[40] Maybe a restructured Suez Canal Company could sell equity, Eisenhower posited. Nothing came of this, however, as foreign ministers ebbed and flowed through London during August and September, trying to conceive ways of returning the canal to international control. Dulles was "looking as wizard-like as ever," wrote Eden's press secretary, William Clark, who described his own boss as showing "hysteria" while allowing his wife, Clarissa, to handle Downing Street's PR.[41]

Other global events kept shaping this drama. The Pentagon announced in July that its Far Eastern Command headquarters would move from Tokyo to Hawaii, and by August critics decried this decision as another sign of U.S. retreat, with a "psychological impact" on Asia.[42] A month later, West Germany called for a special meeting of NATO delegates. It was held in Paris, and the Germans spoke of their anxiety that the Eisenhower administration might reduce the number of GIs in Europe. Washington was "blowing now hot, now cold," editorialized

London's *Daily Telegraph*, and Americans—gearing up for their November 1956 presidential election—were said to be preoccupied by raucous political conventions in San Francisco and Chicago.[43]

In addition, Eastern Europe was convulsing. Polish workers had risen up during June and were able to extract some concessions from Moscow. By September, similar reformist hopes were surfacing in Hungary. Then, on September 27, in case anyone needed reminding, the British conducted their fourth series of atomic tests, at Maralinga Proving Ground, in South Australia.

IN EARLY OCTOBER, THE GOVERNMENTS OF BRITAIN AND FRANCE began conspiring with Ben-Gurion to back an invasion by Israel that would enable the two colonial powers to reoccupy the canal. The plan was for Israel to attack Egypt, then for Britain and France to intervene in order to "separate" the combatants. Their peacekeeping role was to commence by flattening Egypt's air force. Next their troops were to land in Port Said to commandeer the canal's major facilities, and then they'd thrust south toward Ismailia. Leaders of each of these conspiring nations swore to Washington that nothing was afoot, and both Dulles and Cabot Lodge took them at their word.[44]

The collusion should have been impossible to conceal. But—as an assessment in the CIA's quarterly journal, *Studies in Intelligence*, demonstrates—the plan worked, for two key reasons. First, the British and Israelis both conducted disinformation campaigns, which together fooled U.S. observers, including news media. Second, Washington assumed that the suspicions between Israel and Britain were deep enough to prevent collaboration. Eden and Ben-Gurion were known to detest each other, and a politician like Menachem Begin, who headed the extremist anti-Arab Herut Party, which the Americans regarded as "expansionist," couldn't even get a tourist visa from Whitehall's Passport Control authorities.[45] At this moment, furthermore, British forces looked set to pounce on Israel "which four times in the last month," wrote *Time* magazine on October 15, "has sent regular army units smashing into Jordan on bloody 'retaliatory raids' whose only logical purpose seemed to be to hasten Jordan's disintegration."[46]

Yet the conspiracy proceeded as the British and French prepared ineptly for what London called Operation Musketeer. By 1956, for instance, British military planners had been emphasizing nuclear capabilities at the expense of some basic conventional ones, including landing craft and transport planes. Additionally, the eighty-thousand-man invasion force, with close to half being French, was assembling on Cyprus, and Cyprus was nearly a war zone of its own. Paratroopers and royal marines stationed on the island were preoccupied with fighting guerrillas. They'd forgone up-to-date amphibious assault and jump training. Cyprus's governor, Field Marshal Sir John Harding—former chief of the Imperial General Staff during the Mau Mau uprising—was himself being hunted by Greek-Cypriot assassins. All personnel were endangered. This wasn't like the Allied Command of 1944 readying an invasion force in Hampshire for D-day, just a dozen years before.

There was another problem with the invasion, especially for the British: it lacked a strategic objective. The purpose wasn't only a military one of returning the Suez Canal to international control, but the broader political aim of eliminating Nasser. And then what? The war's promoters had an outsized faith in the shock and awe of Western military power. Arab governments were still presumed malleable, and Nasser's support among 22.5 million Egyptians was being grossly underestimated.

Within MI6, G. K. Young expected the invasion to reestablish British ascendency in the Middle East for another decade. A wiser participant, Admiral Louis Mountbatten, who had risen to first sea lord a year earlier, knew better. The hard-to-swallow earl Mountbatten of Burma was turning into a statesman and, three years hence, would fill the new role of chief of the Defence Staff. By September, he doubted an invasion could succeed and drafted a letter of resignation. An attempt to reconquer the canal, he understood, would spread chaos in the Middle East, undermine the authority of the UN, and split the commonwealth. Yet he kept his alarms private and dutifully prepared the Royal Navy for combat. The weeks dragged on from the emergency call-up of August 3 to the oft-postponed start of the attack.

In early October, with nothing having been resolved, Lieutenant Colonel Alexander Gregory-Hood of the Grenadier Guards, the most senior regiment of the elite Guards Division, found himself reading the army regulations governing mutiny to one of his battalions: guardsmen had been cooling their heels in Malta, a staging area for men and supplies, and were restive. At home on the docks of Liverpool, sullen infantry reservists loaded supply ships strictly adhering to rules—doing so at a snail's pace.[47] From top to bottom, an aura of failure surrounded Britain's run-up to war.

Washington's grasp of the situation worsened on October 23 as an epic rebellion exploded in Hungary. Attention at State and the White House was diverted: the Eastern bloc looked to be cracking. At the same time, top British and French officials stopped talking to the Americans. *Time*'s issue of October 29 then observed that "the Suez crisis disappeared from the headlines without having been solved." It sure hadn't. That was the day the joint invasion began.

ON MONDAY, THE TWENTY-NINTH, THE ISRAEL DEFENSE FORCE INvaded Egypt and quickly penetrated to the vicinity of the Suez Canal. Eisenhower returned to the White House that night from Florida, where he had been campaigning. "We are going to apply sanctions," he shouted to Dulles, adding that the Israelis had attacked to expand their territory.[48] Dulles, in turn, had been studying photographs from the CIA's high-altitude U-2 reconnaissance flights over Cyprus and the eastern Mediterranean. He already suspected that Britain and France were using Israel as a decoy. Tuesday, the thirtieth, proved frenetic. During back-to-back meetings in the White House, the president and his secretary of state learned around 11:00 a.m. that the second phase of the invasion scheme was unfolding. Britain and France played at being peacemakers by giving a twelve-hour ultimatum to Israel and Egypt: the warring parties had to stop fighting and withdraw ten miles from the canal or Anglo-French forces would "restore order." Nasser of course rejected the ultimatum. It was Egyptian territory from which he was expected to retreat.

Eisenhower regarded this violent upheaval as a slap in the face. His initial reaction, as he told Dulles, was to let them all "stew in their own juice for a while." On the other hand, the invaders had to understand, as he stated in a White House meeting on Tuesday morning, that "we are a government of honor and stick by what we say," and what the United States had said was that it promised to side with the victim of aggression, which was Egypt.[49]

Cabot Lodge, as people called him, was instructed to submit a cease-fire resolution to the UN Security Council. It contained a tougher condemnation of Israel than even Moscow was proposing, and was voted on that Tuesday night. Both Britain and France cast vetoes. Lodge reported to Washington that Pierson Dixon, the British representative whom he had handled so roughly over Guatemala two years earlier, had said, dismissively, that the U.S. resolution was "not appropriate to actual circumstances."[50] Then, on Wednesday, October 31, with Egypt's army nearly defeated by the Israelis, Eden put his cards on the table. He told the House of Commons that there was no reason to believe that "we must in all circumstances secure agreement from our American ally before we can act ourselves in what we know to be our vital interest."[51] Through diplomatic channels, Nasser asked Secretary Dulles for America itself to intervene; the means of doing so would have to be the 6th Fleet, which by now had mustered fifty ships and twenty-five thousand personnel.

Eisenhower gave a fifteen-minute address from the Oval Office on the evening of the thirty-first. Only a few hours before, he had learned that British and French bombers were striking Egyptian airfields. Speaking gravely, he first addressed the crisis in Eastern Europe: Hungary's struggle promised the dawning of a new day. Then he turned to the Middle East: The three attacking nations had violated the principles of the United Nations, he said, and he therefore planned to go to the UN General Assembly—where no veto operated—to end the bloodshed. America itself, he pledged, would not be involved in actual Middle Eastern hostilities.

Late the following morning, on November 1, Eisenhower tried his hand at writing a letter to Eden. He was too infuriated to complete it and at 12:25 p.m. called Dulles to come over to the White House and help. By day's end, the Americans had cut off their economic aid, and some small military shipments, to Israel. They were also preparing a General Assembly resolution against Britain and France to be submitted the next day. "No one could question the legal right of Egypt to nationalize the Canal Company," Eisenhower wrote that night to his friend Swede Hazlett, getting the terminology—and the situation—correct.[52]

Shortly after four o'clock in the morning of Friday, November 2, a historic break point occurred at United Nations headquarters in Manhattan. Canada, always so loyal to the motherland, abstained on the U.S.-backed Resolution 997 against Britain and its accomplices. Among the dominions, only Australia and New Zealand offered support. Nehru condemned colonialist aggression and encouraged Nasser, which made Eisenhower remark to his staff that by "colonialism" Nehru really meant any issue of "white over colored people."[53] There was some truth to that at Suez.

Eden rejected the General Assembly resolution, saying it would leave "a military vacuum."[54] Then events got trickier. Early Saturday morning, the sixty-eight-year-old John Foster Dulles was rushed to Walter Reed Army Medical Center for acute appendicitis: an hours-long operation discovered colon cancer, which would kill him within three years. Eisenhower essentially took the role of secretary of state in handling Suez. On Sunday, November 4, adding to the geopolitical stakes, Red Army tanks delivered a massive blow against Hungary's national uprising, or what the Kremlin called Hungary's "terrorists." Russia's brutality seemed to threaten Europe's balance of power: Who knew where the Red Army might stop?

That afternoon in London, Nye Bevan, performing at his best, gave a riveting "Law Not War" speech in Trafalgar Square. It was the largest street demonstration in Britain since before World War II. In Number 10, Anthony Eden had called a cabinet meeting the same afternoon, and he could hear the crowd roaring half a mile away. It all was becoming too much. "The PM is mad, literally mad," William Clark wrote in his diary, and he added that Eden had likely been so since October 5, when, afflicted by recurring fevers, his temperature had risen to 105 degrees.[55]

Eisenhower, in contrast, was the epitome of managerial calm. He separated the two emergencies in his mind and tackled the one where he could have an impact: Suez. He did so by turning against Britain, France, and Israel—provoked by knowing that the invasion was as much a challenge to the United States as it was to Egypt. He was correct: Eden, Macmillan, and other conspirators in London believed, in Macmillan's famous phrase, that the Americans would "lie doggo" no matter what; the French didn't much care about U.S. opinion anyway; and Prime Minister Ben-Gurion was counting on supporters in America to subdue the administration.

Unprecedented measures followed. For example, Eisenhower had elements of the 6th Fleet shadow and harass the more than two hundred warships sailing from Cyprus and Malta to Port Said. He took another step after the assault force landed on November 6, which was Election Day in America. At this point, Premier Bulganin laid into Britain, France, and Israel: the Red Army was set to intervene, he threatened, and Moscow's long-range "rocket weapons" were ready to fly. So on the sixth as well, Eisenhower warned the Israelis—as well as the French and British—that he'd not feel obligated to react to Russia's aggression and rally to their defense.

Meanwhile, the pound was plummeting under speculative pressure, and the U.S. Treasury, that same day, informed Harold Macmillan that it would block Britain's access to the International Monetary Fund. Without a cease-fire, there'd be no money to uphold the pound. No longer did the Americans equate sterling's collapse with global catastrophe.

Behind the scenes, Eisenhower ordered the top U.S. general in Europe, Supreme Allied Commander Alfred Gruenther, to tell the Kremlin that an attack on a NATO ally would trigger American atomic retaliation. For good measure, and not long after, he ordered the USS *Forrestal* to sea from Jacksonville, Florida, steaming at the head of a task force for the eastern Atlantic, to soon start its first deployment with the 6th Fleet.

Through his aides, Eisenhower refused Eden's plea to meet in Washington, though Eden still thought of "Ike" as a friend, never imagining such "vengeance," as he later described Eisenhower's response. But any friendliness was in short supply. "The British Embassy was treated like a leper colony," observed the Washington correspondent of London's *Sunday Times*.[56]

At 7:00 p.m. Eastern time, on the sixth, as early reports indicated an Eisenhower/Nixon electoral landslide, fighting halted in the Middle East.

But the crisis wasn't over. The United States still had to get the invaders to withdraw from Egypt. From his hospital room, Dulles advised the president that America held both the carrots and the sticks. And the need for oil offered another stick. The slow arrival of the Anglo-French invasion force had given Nasser—who remained more securely in power than ever—ample time to sink forty-seven barges, blocking the canal. To complicate matters, Arab saboteurs on November 4 had blasted the Iraq Petroleum Company's pumping stations in Syria, thereby stopping the flow of oil from Kirkuk to the Mediterranean. As winter approached, Eisenhower withheld U.S. supplies from Britain and France that could have offset those losses.

U.S. pressure for an unconditional cease-fire had forced the British to yield, which was a decision otherwise unacceptable for any great power. France then had to fold, because its troops were under British command.[57] But all three invaders had yet to leave Egyptian soil, and the canal remained blocked. Nor could Washington tell what the Russians might do next.

AS A PRIME MINISTER, EDEN PROVED TO BE A TRANSIENT EMBARrassment. He showed that he'd won his own election the year before on borrowed credit from Churchill. After the fighting stopped, his health collapsed, and on November 23 he flew with Clarissa to Jamaica to recuperate, leaving Rab Butler to run the government. In retirement, though still an MP, Churchill offered a postmortem. "If I had had a pain in my tummy," he told Butler, referring to Eden's long delay in assembling and launching the invasion, "I should not have put to sea for six weeks."[58]

Eden would reflect bitterly on what had occurred. Hadn't he stood aside, as foreign secretary, when the United States invaded Guatemala (without consulting Britain) so that Washington could rid itself of a Soviet-armed menace in its sphere of interest? Didn't he have reason to expect Eisenhower and Dulles to accord the same respect? Yet the Americans acted, he wrote in his memoirs, "in a precisely contrary manner towards us."[59] This wasn't all, as he told confidants. He suspected that Dulles had personally undercut him at Suez due to resentment for having refused to support united action in Vietnam two years earlier.

That said, Eisenhower in fact had saved the British from a far worse debacle. There was little thinking in London about what might follow an invasion—the perennial "And then what?" question of political-military affairs that often goes unanswered. Admiral Mountbatten understood this completely, as did Gladwyn Jebb in Paris, whom Eden had kept in the dark about the plotting. After it was all over, Jebb, in his way, mocked "the unfortunate effect that can be exercised on the mind of rulers by historical parallels," notably Munich.[60]

The chances were excellent that with Nasser dead or deposed, and Nasser's army humiliated, Egypt would have turned into an unholy mess, which is how Syria's condition was being described at that time. Or Egypt might have adopted an orthodox Muslim government, as the "Islamic Republic of Pakistan" had just done in March—except Cairo's version, courtesy of the Muslim Brotherhood, might not have been as mild. "Unless the occupying power was ready to employ the brutalities of dictatorship," Eisenhower wrote in his memoirs, "local unrest would soon grow into guerrilla resistance, then open revolt."[61] What he called "the area of jeopardy" would increase vastly. That's how the Pentagon saw it, thinking of U.S. air bases in Libya and Morocco, for starters. There might be no limit to the assassinations, urban warfare, and guerrilla insurgency certain to follow.

What's obvious is that no British viceroy or military trusteeship, and no Egyptian puppet, would have filled that biggest of "vacuums." There'd be no European reconquest of Suez, as Eisenhower recognized. The Middle East no longer worked that way. As a soldier, Eisenhower was renowned for not second-guessing his decisions, and at Suez his decisions were categorical. Which makes it unpersuasive to take his musings of later years seriously—to wit, that maybe the United States shouldn't have interfered.[62]

At 1:30 in the afternoon of December 3, Dulles, who seemed to be recuperating, phoned Eisenhower with breaking news. White House operators put him through to the Augusta National Golf Club, in Georgia, where the president was following events on the news ticker. Rab Butler and Foreign Secretary Lloyd, Dulles explained, had finally told the House of Commons that British forces would leave Egypt without delay. For the next two weeks, Eisenhower and Dulles tracked every step. Once convinced of evacuation, they offered carrots. U.S. oil supplies started flowing.

British finances, however, remained perilous. Sterling continued to plummet into mid-December, and Chancellor of the Exchequer Macmillan had to ask Washington to waive the annual interest payment on the original 1946 loan. Eisenhower approved. He also authorized a release of money from the IMF, and the fund thereby provided Britain and France with its largest amount of financial assistance to date. The Americans additionally opened a line of credit for the British government through the Export-Import Bank, but for that step they required collateral. As had occurred early in World War II, Macmillan had to arrange for his country to put up U.S. stocks, bonds, and other dollar securities that it owned.

Eisenhower still chose to keep his distance from London. There'd be no meetings to sort out difficulties. At the same time, he sent a signal to the world, and especially to the British Empire and Commonwealth. For the first time, he invited a foreign leader to his modest farm in Gettysburg, Pennsylvania. Just before 9:00 a.m. on Monday, December 17, the president and India's Jawaharlal Nehru drove up together from Washington for a day and a half of private talks. There was a light late-autumn rain by the time they arrived, yet they toured the battlefield and then walked about the farm. More conversation followed over supper in the small family dining room, and the next day they drove back together to Washington. In total, they talked one-on-one for fourteen hours. Eisenhower had never done anything like it.

Whitehall and Parliament got the message. The United States was going to be paying a lot more attention to the world beyond Europe from now on, and it would be doing so alone.

20

WHAT HAPPENED NEXT

There is going to be a great psychological advantage in world politics to putting the thing up. But that doesn't seem to be a reason . . . to grow hysterical about it.
—Dwight Eisenhower, October 1957

A MERICANS COULD SENSE THAT THEIR PLACE IN THE WORLD WAS shifting in the months after the Suez and Hungarian crises, more so than in the years immediately following World War II. In the late 1940s, the United States was still improvising its way into a North Atlantic alliance and finding it impossible to impose a liberal trading regime on even its closest ally. The Korean War then pushed the country toward becoming a global political-military power, but GIs were nonetheless expected to return from Asia once it ended, and from garrisoning Europe as well. Throughout, the American public was demanding that others be responsible for holding the front lines. Finally, in late 1956, a decade's worth of accumulated frustration overflowed.

On December 6, just weeks after the UN General Assembly had voted 65 to 5 against Britain and France, Vice President Nixon issued a "declaration of independence" from British authority. He had carefully worked the statement out with John Foster Dulles, and everyone knew Nixon was speaking for the White House.* He'd recall this moment as the point when the United States took over "the foreign policy leadership of the free world."[1] In fact, the president's own speeches were being hailed by the press as "Eisenhower's Declaration of Independence."[2] The whole country understood that great change was at hand. Even Canada was said to have issued its own declaration of independence when Prime Minister Louis St. Laurent snapped that "the era when the supermen of Europe could govern the whole world is coming pretty much to a close."[3]

Time magazine, ever the barometer of 1950s upper-middle-class opinion, concluded that "the U.S. now stands alone as the only major power in the free world."[4]

Suez was more than just a flash of lightning, revealing how extensively Britain's postwar greatness rested on memory and bluff. It illuminated a range of outdated notions: that Washington would routinely accept vetoes from Whitehall; that lesser breeds, such as the Arabs, couldn't manage something as complex as an international waterway; that sterling priced at nothing lower than $2.80 was the cornerstone of world exchanges; and that the Americans had neither the skills nor the resources to "replace" the British Empire, to recall NSC 75's conclusion of only six years before. From London, Geoffrey Crowther, longtime editor of *The Economist*, concluded that "Britain is no longer a super-Power," and the aftermath of Suez proved to be the deathwatch of his country's sense of itself as among the Three.[5]

Since World War II, the decline of Britain's imperial standing had been gradual, even "undramatic, almost painless," said *The New York Times*. But no longer. Margaret Thatcher, who entered Parliament in 1959, later observed that "a veritable 'Suez Syndrome'" came to burden her country's political class, which quickly suspected it could do nothing right.[6] This loss of belief upended nearly a dozen years of ferocious resolve during which the British Empire had indeed borne itself as one of

---

*Nixon suggested that the break applied to French influence as well, but France's government was so shaky, and so involved in its Algerian quagmire, that the inclusion of France was nearly gratuitous.

the Three, with its unique capabilities justifying this assertion. Now Britain's economy was again buckling, and the commonwealth was splitting.

Not least, in March 1957, Britain passed up the chance to lead a united, reinvigorated Europe. On the Continent, the Suez crisis had inspired a new rush toward federation, for an array of reasons, including the fact that France's waning Fourth Republic resented relying on the United States. As a result, more got accomplished for unity in two months than in the previous two years. West Germany and France—evermore the economic engines of Western Europe—joined Italy and the Low Countries in signing the Treaty of Rome, which created the Common Market. It is the predecessor to today's European Union of 510 million people, the world's biggest collective economy, although on a still fissiparous continent.

Britain instead looked to be pulling inward. In April 1957, Minister of Defence Duncan Sandys, Churchill's son-in-law, announced major cuts and consolidations in the army, the RAF, Royal Navy, and Royal Marines. At a press conference later that month, Eisenhower addressed the problems raised by a so recently mighty empire appearing to diminish itself. What's happening? asked *The Washington Post*. Were the British going too far and too fast in adjusting to a newer world, perhaps to the extent of undercutting the West's defense? Eisenhower replied by referring to what he called a country's "security position," which, he said, was determined not only by a people's armed forces but also by "their economic, their spiritual, their intellectual strength." (He could have also said something about the goodwill and global relationships they bring to the mix.) He further explained that Britain had tried heroically to sustain its economy following the end of World War II, despite having "been exhausted by two world wars." Britain had seen "all its foreign investments lost," he added, and had struggled valiantly to maintain its dollar balances to keep sterling "as a trading medium throughout the world."[7]

By delineating these factors, Eisenhower laid out why his administration, just like Truman's, had considered Britain to still rank among the Three. Its outstanding diplomacy and intelligence assets, its worldwide ports and air bases, and its unsurpassed high-tech innovations were among the features that gave this weary island its claim as a superpower. Not least, Britain's armed services by and large displayed a professionalism that, on their best days, made them all "a perfect thing apart."[8] By Eisenhower's formulation, a nation's military was only the tip of the lance, and the British Empire had, over the course of two centuries, developed a global mystique—perhaps the most impressive of intangibles. Ernest Bevin, by force of personality, and then Winston Churchill, by remembered triumph, spoke for England. And truly great powers are taken at their own proclaimed valuation: Britain had felt and behaved like a superpower since long before the term was coined. Presumption, said that great imperialist, Lord Curzon, is the secret of success.

Bevin, if not Churchill, knew in his bones the power of production. When he took over the Foreign Office in 1945, he wanted "them boys to think as much of sums as they do of treaties and protocols."[9] But it was tricky for Whitehall to align military strength with the country's relative economic decline. "Recovery"—which no one could quite define—always looked to be right around the corner. There were good reasons to be hopeful. They included the apparent dominance of futuristic industries such as jet aviation, atomic energy, and life sciences that promised new forms of primacy. And periods of economic buoyancy, such as those of 1948–1949 and 1953–1954, hid the consequences of being stretched thin.

Along the way, Britain had to maintain an unsurpassed political-military role, or so it was argued, because its prosperity relied so heavily on global trade. There was another reason why shrewd people in London were determined to uphold their country's military clout after World War II no matter the cost: the fate of the nation couldn't be left to the Americans, who, in the words of Nye Bevan, had "achieved material power without getting the necessary wisdom to use it." Both Bevin and Churchill agreed with this assessment, if less flamboyantly.

"Those British are still my right arm," Eisenhower had huffed to his speechwriter, Emmet John Hughes, as the Suez adventure got under way.[10] Ten years earlier, it would have been inconceivable to speak of the original "superpower" in such patronizing terms; ten years later, it would have been overblown to consider Britain anything so significant.

ON ELECTION DAY, NOVEMBER 6, 1956, THE DEMOCRATS HAD KEPT their majority in Congress, and Lyndon Johnson remained "Master of the Senate." On the thirteenth, he visited Secretary Dulles in Walter Reed, bringing books and a vase of roses and, as always, making time to speak with reporters. Johnson broached the idea of a UN police force for the Middle East, with the implication that GIs and marines would be among the cops. Headlines followed. Anything seemed plausible in those weeks—at first, even the possibility of the Eastern bloc collapsing. With Hungary in revolt, Dulles had gone so far as to let Khrushchev's regime know that he would not try to bring that Warsaw Pact nation into NATO. But a free Hungary was not to be. The Kremlin's post-Stalin moderation went only so far, and Eisenhower determined that aiding rebellion in Hungary would be a dangerously far-fetched enterprise. "Where do we go from here?" Johnson wondered aloud.

Dulles left the hospital to convalesce in Key West, where he drafted a paper about taking a new stance on the Middle East. He returned to State in early December, and on the eleventh he flew to Paris for a NATO meeting at the Palais de Chaillot. There he discussed how the organization could help create a lasting stability in that oil-rich region, while feeling compelled to emphasize America's determination to be a world presence over the long haul.

Under U.S. pressure, the last of the British and French invasion forces sailed out of Port Said's wreck-cluttered harbor on the twenty-third, ending their seven-week occupation. Authority was handed over to the first peacekeeping force to be established by the United Nations. Eden had returned from Jamaica on the fourteenth, lying to the Commons six days later about the absence of British "foreknowledge" of Israel's intentions. All these reversals had hollowed him out. On January 9, 1957, he resigned the premiership and was replaced by Harold Macmillan, the Chancellor of the Exchequer, who had been the strongest of voices for invasion, before throwing in the towel.

Macmillan, sixty-two, was a magnificent intriguer, a lonely, dour figure whom Thatcher would call a man of masks. His mother came from Spencer, Indiana, but there was little of the American about him. A foul marriage to an unfaithful wife, the Duke of Devonshire's daughter, pushed him to haunt such socially grand West End clubs as Buck's, the Turf, and the Athenaeum. He prided himself on being a man of business, having worked in the family firm, Macmillan Publishers. And, heaven knows, he was brave, having been wounded five times on the western front. His shuffle bore lifelong witness to a shattered pelvis. In World War II, he was equally courageous while serving as minister resident in the Mediterranean, where he also built a rapport with the then general Eisenhower—who, now as president, let it be known that he approved of Macmillan's appointment.

Just four days before Eden left office, Eisenhower delivered a "Special Message to Congress on the Middle East," having earlier briefed congressional leaders that "the existing vacuum in the Middle East must be filled by the United States before it is filled by the Russians."[11] On the afternoon of Saturday, January 5, he sought blanket authorization to use U.S. forces against Communist aggression, plus $200 million in military and economic assistance (considered a big amount from a $70 billion budget) for the Baghdad Pact nations and their neighbors. What became known as "the Eisenhower Doctrine" took another step toward routinizing a president's right to wage war at his discretion. It also ensured evermore CIA cloak-and-dagger activity in the Middle East—to the degree that one station chief worried that "we'd soon be out of key politicians for CIA personnel to recruit."[12]

The House and Senate committee debates that followed had countless references to the Truman Doctrine and, of course, to "power vacuums." Even hesitant legislators understood the need to insulate the rest of the world from the violence of the Middle East. Given Russia's recent nuclear threats, the cradle of civilization might very well become its grave. Everyone knew that the country was taking on immense new responsibilities in a region where, as *The New York Times* put it, "the reality bears little relationship to the common American fantasies."[13]

The immediate challenge was to pry Israel from Egyptian territory. That included the Gaza Strip (which nominally had its own All-Palestine Government) and Sharm el-Sheikh, which commanded the approaches to the Gulf of Aqaba. Israel insisted that holding these positions was essential to its freedom of navigation and to ending guerrilla insurgency. Being familiar with both sides of the record, however, the Eisenhower administration wasn't sympathetic. Earlier, in 1953, Dulles had complained that Israel regarded cooperation with Washington as "a one-way street."[14] And now Prime Minister Ben-Gurion wouldn't budge.

During a February 10 phone call from Cabot Lodge, the UN ambassador in New York, Dulles asked about the prospect of imposing sanctions on Israel, even though he anticipated trouble on the Hill.[15]

The administration had two approaches to skirting Congress's opposition to sanctions. First, Israel might not have to be singled out, Lodge advised the following afternoon. Egypt could be threatened with sanctions as well, should it resume belligerency once Israel withdrew. That would counterbalance "the idea of everybody picking on poor little Israel," he explained.[16] Eisenhower was quail hunting that week in Thomasville, Georgia. He was briefed by White House political operatives about the fierce pressure being exerted on Israel's behalf by way of mail and advertisements, but he also heard from Dulles that "we have a good case against Israel if they don't do as we propose." Therefore, as a second possibility, Eisenhower replied that any motion in Congress opposing sanctions initiated at the UN would have no legal effect. In either case—with Britain seemingly out of the picture—the United States was the only Western nation left with significant standing on the issue.[17]

All concerned knew the consequences. Dr. Ralph Bunche, who had received the Nobel Peace Prize in 1950 for bringing about the original armistices, had continued to work at the UN as a mediator for strife-torn regions. He concluded that "cutting [the Israelis] off would do the trick."[18] Sanctioning private business and financial dealings involving Israel, Dulles acknowledged, "would be fatal," whereas merely a slap on the wrist for Egypt. "Israel can't survive without proceeds of bonds," he informed Lodge, so "Israel's life [is] at stake."[19]

The Israeli ambassador, Abba Eban, scrambled to break the deadlock, first in off-the-record meetings at State, then back home for consultations. Dulles was also moving fast. "The Israeli Embassy is practically dictating to the Congress," he told the head of the World Council of Churches, while seeking support. Nonetheless, he got the Senate minority leader, William Knowland, an ardent supporter of Israel, to agree that "we could [not] have all our policies made in Jerusalem."[20] Everything short of sanctions had been tried, Dulles told Knowland on Saturday evening, February 16, and "he did not see how we could have any influence with the Arab countries if we could not get the Israelis out of Egypt."[21]

Unlike Acheson, who had a gift for infuriating legislators, Dulles handled Capitol Hill in masterly fashion. He coolly discussed the problem with the two weightiest leaders of the opposition, Senators Richard Russell and Lyndon Johnson, another strong advocate for Israel. Now Dulles played an unusual card. In late December 1948, the State Department had conveyed to Prime Minister Ben-Gurion the British threat to go to war against Israel if its forces didn't leave Egyptian territory. Details of the ultimatum—and of the U.S. role involving Ambassador MacDonald—were suddenly brought before the public, also on the sixteenth, in the form of released excerpts of closed hearings being conducted before the Senate Armed Services and Foreign Relations Committees. Coincidence seems unlikely. The message: this would not be the first time the United States was set to act hard indeed toward Israel.[22]

The following Wednesday, at 8:30 a.m. sharp, Eisenhower met with the congressional leaders of both parties in the Cabinet Room. There were few pleasantries, and his severe tone was adopted by Dulles and Lodge. Nixon attended but said little. Eisenhower explained why he favored placing sanctions on Israel. At 9:00 p.m., he broadcast his reasons to the country. "Should a nation," he asked, "which attacks and occupies foreign territory in the face of United Nations disapproval be allowed to impose conditions on its own withdrawal?"[23] If so, that would be a case for settling all international differences by force, and he therefore pledged to use "maximum U.S. influence" to remedy the problem. Dulles and Lodge returned to working the General Assembly, confident that "the Latinos would do what we ask."[24]

On March 1, Israel's foreign minister, Golda Meir, announced her country's readiness to withdraw from all Egyptian territory, with the UN Emergency Force left to supervise a supposed cessation of hostilities.[25]

The Americans had forced Israel back to the boundaries from which it had launched its assault. However, none of these steps—including a likely rescue by the Eisenhower administration—had kept Gamal Abdel Nasser from reverting to his tactic of playing off East against West.

(It was one to which Nehru reverted as well after leaving Gettysburg.) Two weeks after Israel retreated, moreover, Nasser announced that he wouldn't permit its ships to enter the newly reopened Suez Canal. A week after that, Allen and Foster Dulles were debating whether Nasser really sought the welfare of his people or merely his own self-interest. Eisenhower came down somewhere in the middle.[26] As for the castaway inhabitants of Gaza, whom Eisenhower estimated at 200,000 (and who today number 1.8 million), the president suggested that Israel be assured that these refugees wouldn't be a source of trouble because "we were now in there."[27]

A cold peace descended on these borders. For all the grinding of teeth in Washington, Israel at least was the region's most capable military power and also its most stable nation—except possibly for Iran, where the CIA that year began training an unusually vicious secret police for the shah, known as SAVAK.[28] Elsewhere was mayhem. Beirut had experienced a wave of bombings in retaliation against the government of Lebanon's refusal to break relations with Britain and France; Iraq suffered from pro-Nasser riots against the British-aligned monarchy and prime minister; and in March, King Hussein abrogated the 1948 Anglo-Jordanian Treaty. Even in Bahrain, Sir Charles Belgrave—who, since monitoring the first visit of a U.S. fleet in 1948, had become the island's "chief administrator"—was expelled in April after anti-British violence. Worst of all, Syria, which had already been described as a running sore, gave Russia opportunity to appear as its champion as both states combined to threaten Turkey, the country in between.

Against this backdrop, Macmillan and Eisenhower met at the Mid Ocean Club in Tucker's Town, Bermuda, over March 20–24. It's where Eisenhower and Churchill had convened in 1953, but now it was Eisenhower who encouraged the dialogue, saying he wasn't interested in mopping up spilled milk. Thrilled British officials talked archaically of a "Big Two" conference, and results looked promising. The Americans pledged to be more involved with the Baghdad Pact. They joined its military committee and, two years later, would become members of what they mellifluously renamed CENTO, the Central Treaty Organization. The British, in turn, muted their criticism of Washington. Their chief complaint in Bermuda was of America's overreliance on the UN. As for

Egypt, Macmillan conceded that the Americans were more than welcome to deal with it themselves. That view reflected some sound thinking at the Foreign Office. From his palatial embassy on the rue du Faubourg Saint-Honoré, Gladwyn Jebb advised that Britain should pursue only a "limited commitment" to the entire region.[29]

Stronger bilateral ties appeared likely once Eisenhower agreed to supply Britain with intermediate-range ballistic missiles (though their atomic warheads were to remain under U.S. control). Yet here too elements of American insularity can be seen. This arrangement would "give the United States a strategic wall of defense in the British Isles," said Eisenhower's chief of staff, Sherman Adams.[30] During the last day in Bermuda, a dispute arose. Macmillan's people wanted the communiqué to include a line attesting to Eisenhower's enthusiasm for reestablishing "intimate wartime cooperation, including joint intelligence and planning systems, to meet international problems." Secretary Dulles nixed that idea. Forty-eight hours later, those very words were leaked to *The New York Times* as Eisenhower's allegedly truest intentions.[31] Both Dulles and the president were livid; Dulles blamed a British source.

MALCOLM MacDONALD HAD LEFT SINGAPORE IN 1955 TO BECOME high commissioner to India. By then, he had triumphed in his long, patient task of ensuring an American military presence in Vietnam—while avoiding a British one. Under the auspices of SEATO, for example, British and commonwealth forces had conducted large-scale exercises in Southeast Asia with the Americans in 1956. These covered Thailand, the Gulf of Siam, and beyond. Regarding Vietnam itself, the British were exemplarily detached. Malaya, after all, was secure and would receive independence in July 1957. Meanwhile, the Americans were getting in deeper. A U.S. Military Assistance Advisory Group began training Saigon's army as the last French soldiers departed in 1956—and this was the fateful year of Washington's refusal to accept the Geneva Accords' stipulation for nationwide elections, from just two years before.

Then President Ngô Đình Diệm flew into Washington on May 8, 1957. Eisenhower showed the significance of this trip by greeting him personally at National Airport—the first time he did so for any foreign visitor, including Prime Minister Churchill. That night, Diệm received a state dinner whose guests included Senator and Mrs. Lyndon Johnson. The next day Diệm addressed Congress, and the National Press Club the day after. Everyone applauded his call for help in thwarting the Sino-Soviet plan of conquest: "terrorism" must be defied. Diệm's meeting with Foster Dulles, however, went poorly. As always, Diệm talked nonstop, leaving Dulles even more skeptical of his abilities. Nonetheless, Diệm was on his way to being extolled five years later as "the Winston Churchill of Southeast Asia" by Lyndon Johnson, when vice president. The star-obsessed Americans, unlike the world-weary British, were making it a lifetime habit to elevate beyond all reason a cluster of third-world supermen as heroes, or "miracle men," having started with Chiang Kai-shek. Most were required to fit the part: speaking English, dressing for success, perhaps being Christian, but in any event being a recent U.S. resident, or at least well-connected in Washington.[32]

The Eisenhower administration already acknowledged that its nation-building efforts in Vietnam were an unprecedented step. To Secretary Dulles, however, "the coming continent" was Africa. It was there that his country truly needed to do all it could, he asserted, to be "spokesman for those wanting independence."[33] And he was quick to denounce the colonial order.

During the Suez crisis, Dulles had underscored U.S. opposition to "colonialism," and his alleged hypocrisy had infuriated Fleet Street, Whitehall, and everyone else in Britain. After all, 1956 was the year of the Montgomery, Alabama, bus boycott, with violence to follow nine months later in Little Rock, Arkansas, as black children began to attend white schools. In fact, Foster Dulles had long recognized that the brutalities of Jim Crow were defiling America's would-be standing as "champion of freedom and democracy" in the nonwhite world. Within the administration, he had a unique means to help oppose segregation. He did so by ordering every U.S. ambassador to report the extent of damage being done to America's image in each accredited nation of the world.[34]

The trouble with Dulles was that thirty years of Wall Street practice had made him sound always the same, whether arguing in Foggy Bottom from a heart that had not forgotten the internationalist ideals of his chief, Woodrow Wilson, at Versailles or arguing at Sullivan & Cromwell on behalf of another ample corporate retainer. Meanwhile, the Gold Coast became the first black African colony to be granted independence, and Dulles pressed Vice President Nixon to attend the ceremonies in Accra in March 1957, at which the Union Jack was hauled down and replaced by the Black Star of the nation to be known henceforth as Ghana.[35]

In Kenya, which the British had turned into a police state during the insurgency, the Mau Mau rebellion was being forced to a close by 1956, due to a heightened ruthlessness, as the CIA's Jack Mower reported to headquarters. The following November, the colonial secretary, Alan Lennox-Boyd, declared that British rule would continue "for a very long time." Not quite. When Eisenhower had fruitlessly urged Churchill to turn his back on an imperial lifetime by invoking "*a right to self-government* for colonial peoples"—the president's emphasis—"callable in, say, twenty-five years," Churchill dismissed the idea. He believed that Britain's civilizing mission of "opening up the jungles" had to extend well beyond 1980.[36] But the will at the center was gone, as Macmillan would soon be muttering. Kenya gained independence in 1963—Malcolm MacDonald being its last colonial governor—along with most of British East Africa.

In central London, the proposed site of a huge new Colonial Office complex had already been cleared. It stood empty for years, until it was quietly built over. "Only a mob's demented howl, or a rabble-rouser's frown," observed *Punch*, consciously borrowing Kipling's meter, "and, almost apologetically, the flag comes fluttering down."

For their part, the Americans in 1957 were stumbling into the habit of pouring aid dollars into the developing world, and within two years Eisenhower would appear in Afghanistan. One of the grandest of U.S. aid projects, still known today as the "Eisenhower Highway," which links Kabul and Kandahar, has since been destroyed and reconstructed some half a dozen times. He described such nation-building efforts as a "means of defense against Communist conspiracy and encirclement."[37] Before long, however, the Americans showed that they weren't too selective about whose defense they were upholding with their development aid—usually offered in tandem with police equipment and military hardware. Odious clients who were called "friends"—not least in Africa and, as before, in Latin America—helped complete an imperial carica-ture of the United States that endures to this day.

IN THE WEEKS BEFORE THE TWIN CRISES OF NOVEMBER 1956 BROKE open, Eisenhower had told the country that Egypt and Hungary were among "the most distant points on earth," which was how well-informed Americans generally still thought of both places.[38] Yet the world was flattening, and 1957 became the first year in which more travelers were able to cross the Atlantic by plane than by ship. The year began with an astonishing example of superpower mobility. In January, three of SAC's Boeing B-52 Stratofortresses became the first aircraft to circle the globe nonstop, refueling in mid-flight and deliberately showing, according to mission plans, that American hydrogen bombs could strike any place on earth.

During much of the period since World War II, Britain had pro-vided the underlying service industries of American outreach: secret intelligence, select military innovations, often-useful diplomatic exper-tise, and, significantly, the "outposts" of empire. For all the noise it made—and despite such displays of reach—America had, for instance, no troops in the Middle East other than the personnel manning several airfields. Meanwhile, its ally kept offering ports and bases, as it did with its British Forces Arabian Peninsula Command. In the Middle East, as matters turned out, the Suez crisis was much less a watershed than has been believed. Although America thereafter increased its presence, Britain held on to remaining strongholds such as Aden and Cyprus, at least for a while, and maintained its outsized influence in the Gulf. Washington did nothing in the Middle East to undercut its ally. According to Sir Harold Caccia—who arrived as ambassador in Wash-ington during December 1956, in hopes of starting fresh—the Americans instead helped achieve "the partnership in the Middle East we have been seeking for years."[39]

Then there came a huge jump in Britain's military strength.

On May 15, 1957, a Vickers Valiant bomber dropped a hydrogen bomb over Malden Island, officially a British protectorate in the South

Pacific. (The irony was noted.) Macmillan implied that his country had thus elevated itself back into the ranks of the two continental-sized powers. Even today, a savvy news editor can title a look back at history "Britain Reclaims Superpower Status with First Successful H-Bomb Test," though at the time few in Whitehall went that far.[40] British officials valued their four mega-detonations that year as a means of being treated as an equal. They could finally seal the long-sought bilateral agreement to coordinate R&D, production, and control of nuclear weapons with the United States. But there was another motivation to getting the H-bomb, for Macmillan's government as for Churchill's: a thermonuclear capacity would provide a last, independent line of deterrence should the United States again slide into isolationism.

Plutonium for the May 15 blast came from Calder Hall—the world's first nuclear power station—on the shores of the Irish Sea. This facility had a dual military and commercial role. It also generated electricity on an industrial scale, and its reactor had been connected to the national grid the previous August, in 1956. Newsreels show Queen Elizabeth pulling a switch, thereby also illuminating Britain's lead in civil atomic energy. Inevitably, the Americans would surpass this achievement— opening their first nuclear power plant in Shippingport, Pennsylvania, in 1957—as did the Russians, and before long the French.

U.S. experts claimed to be unimpressed by May's three-hundred-kiloton detonation because it proved smaller than expected. Instead, what truly united the physicists and weaponeers on both sides of the Atlantic was the eruption of Soviet technology in the form of Sputnik, the first artificial earth satellite. No other event before or since has so stunned the American nation, including Pearl Harbor and 9/11. It was the sense of helplessness. "When will they hit us?" the Virginia senator Harry Byrd asked after listening to Director Allen Dulles's briefing several days later.[41] Suddenly, all of America appeared to lay open to thermonuclear incineration, and the haunting "ping, ping, ping" heard from orbit on radio coast-to-coast was a reminder 24/7.

Intercontinental ballistic missiles were already described as the "ultimate weapon," and everyone knew that the U.S. and Russian satellite programs were dress rehearsals for a missile race. America's lead was assumed to be unrivaled. Then came Moscow's multiple triumphs: in August 1957, the first successful test of an ICBM, followed by Sputnik on October 4, and then by another satellite in November—this one carrying a dog, Laika, to the fury of the British public. All occurred while U.S. rockets were blowing up on launchpads, as seen live on television.

Suppose America couldn't catch up? The era's bestselling novel, *Advise and Consent* (1959), captures how deep the blow went: Americans had seen their country "rise and rise and rise—and then . . . the golden legend crumbled, overnight the fall began. . . . Now the reaction was on." Time was running out, Americans believed, "with the winds of the world howling around their ears."

Allen Dulles's briefing preceded the long-scheduled arrival in Washington of Queen Elizabeth and Prince Philip on October 17. Eisenhower and Dulles met them shortly before noon at National Airport with a twenty-one-gun salute. This was the first royal visit since the darkening days of 1939, and it was also the second and last occasion Eisenhower would go out to the airport to meet anyone (except for an elderly, retired Churchill who visited in May 1959 as a personal guest). A private lunch at the White House followed, and the presence of this young couple turned into a breather for a temporarily demoralized nation. Over four days, they attended a state dinner and services at the National Cathedral. They ventured to a suburban shopping mall and watched the Maryland–North Carolina football game in nearby College Park. Yet behind the scenes, Dulles was agitating to get Prime Minister Macmillan and his advisers to Washington—reaching out to a Britain he had recently dismissed to a tertiary role.

Eisenhower and Dulles knew they had to avoid looking desperate by leaping into sudden consultations about imminent apocalypse, as augured by Sputnik. Macmillan, for his part, had to consider his queen's prerogatives. He couldn't arrive in America until after she had departed, he explained to the uneasy Americans, and indeed her approval would be required before he could leave London. The slower measures of an older world were colliding with the unfolding space age.

While waiting, Secretary Dulles told his staff that America was "in a psychological crisis" and that he felt as severe an anxiety about what lay ahead as when he had been visiting in Korea on the eve of invasion.[42] That's why caucusing with America's strongest partner was essential.

But he kept this event in perspective. Macmillan couldn't be allowed to play it up as an exclusive bilateral summit. To be sure, Britain was pivotal to NATO and SEATO, as well as to the Baghdad Pact, and Dulles knew all the alliances needed strengthening. Doing so, however, would involve other nations, too. Britain couldn't appear as a favored friend. Overall, Dulles believed that these weeks might be decisive for the next several centuries.

Macmillan finally came to Washington on the afternoon of Wednesday, October 23, a day after he had greeted the queen upon Her Majesty's return to London. His arrival in the capital was pitched as a follow-through on personal discussions begun in Bermuda, back in March. No matter how the visit was portrayed, the British, to their surprise, found themselves yielding to most every item on the U.S. agenda. Foreign Secretary Selwyn Lloyd's request that the two sides announce a "declaration of *inter*dependence" was ignored. In the Cabinet Room, Eisenhower brooked no complaints about the European Economic Community, or "Common Market," and gave the British a thinly veiled warning that they must not attempt to ruin it. Meanwhile, Macmillan pledged to oppose the entry of any more Communist states to the UN—which meant that he'd help to block China, a reversal of Britain's position toward Beijing. Then Dulles raised the eternal problem of Syria.

During August, the latest upheavals in Syria suggested suspicion that there had been a Communist takeover in Damascus. Turkey (a NATO ally) deployed thousands of troops to the border, and General Secretary Khrushchev, in turn, threatened to launch missiles against Turkey, which, under Article 5, would have brought U.S. retaliation against Russia. But perhaps Washington had a subtler alternative.

During this visit, Eisenhower approved what the CIA and MI6 called a "Preferred Plan" to topple Syria's militarist Ba'ath Party/Communist regime by, according to a joint working group, "mount[ing] minor sabotage and *coup de main* incidents." In fact, it entailed staging fake border clashes, arming paramilitary political factions within Syria, funding the "Free Syria Committee" as a false front, conducting a few assassinations, and provoking the Muslim Brotherhood in Damascus. The plan wasn't implemented, partly because Syria's Arab neighbors couldn't be co-opted. Nonetheless, it showed how much further the

United States had descended in trying to emulate long-established British manipulations in the Middle East.[43]

By 1957, the CIA's intrigues were developing a momentum of their own—starting at the incompetent and hurtling down from there, as was to be seen in Indonesia (1958), the Congo (1959), Cuba (1961–1963), and Vietnam. Come 1984, the CIA proposed inciting America's ally of the time, Iraq's Saddam Hussein, to attack Syria's dictator, Hafez al-Assad, whom global architects in Washington wanted ousted at the same time they backed Saddam in his war against Iran.[44] By then, MI6 had become a wing of the agency, a shift that reflected the overall change of authority between the two nations. "We bought ourselves a stay of execution for our vision of our colonial selves," says George Smiley, who embodies the admirable qualities of MI6 in John Le Carré's novels, reflecting on how Britain steadily subjected its national identity to U.S. foreign policy. "Worse still, we encouraged the Americans to behave in the same way. Not that they needed our encouragement, but they were pleased to have it, naturally."[45]

FOR WASHINGTON, THE SHEER MESSINESS OF THE MIDDLE EAST was combining with Sputnik into a single, ghastly Soviet-wrought emergency. But small wars in the Middle East and Southeast Asia weren't, for the moment, top priority, nor was the need for "outposts." Russia's ICBMs showed that America's Atlantic and Pacific moats could quickly be bridged in the sky. On the one hand, the shock of Sputnik compelled Americans to reassure themselves that they were not alone in the world. On the other, Sputnik worked to set the United States apart from its friends, foreclosing any willingness at State, the White House, or the Pentagon to keep up any "facade of unity" in their dealings with troublesome allies—Britain and its empire being the most consequential of these. From this point on, the faintest tremor in the world could be expected to bring direct U.S.-Russian confrontation, with every showdown having the potential to go nuclear. Any pretense of three superpowers existing on the planet was laid to rest: only the United States and Russia could compete indefinitely at this level.

At the same time, the size of Britain's economy was being surpassed by that of West Germany. Only two-thirds a country, West Germany enjoyed a level of productivity second only to America's. Japan's economy was surging too. It led the world in shipbuilding for export, and soon in cotton textiles, while moving to create its own "special relationship" with the United States, as ties were already being called.[46]

Another shock befell Britain's stature when France's aloof, regal World War II hero General Charles de Gaulle was called out of retirement in 1958, with heavy support from the armed forces and the 1.2 million settlers in Algeria, to head a new government. France's Fourth Republic was nearly finished as it limped from one unstable parliamentary coalition to another. Then de Gaulle midwifed a new constitutional system, the Fifth Republic, that gave France's presidency a potent role.

Foster Dulles, like Acheson, said that what sentiment he had for a country other than his own was reserved for France, but both statesmen had until then viewed France as a crippled veteran, holding out a cap. De Gaulle's bold decision to abandon the Algerian settlers, rather than have France be pulled into endless guerrilla war, reinforced his vision of a French-led European union, fueled by France's own hard-won economic dynamism. He ensured his country (and himself) primacy in democratic Europe.

For Britain, the handwriting was on the wall. In February 1958, a letter to *The Times* from William Clark, who had resigned as Eden's press secretary over Suez, caused a sensation by suggesting that the empire could not last another five years. The limits of British power were again thrown into relief in the early morning of July 14 when a Nasserite-nationalist Free Officers cabal—denouncing "imperialism"—slaughtered the old regime in Baghdad. The twenty-three-year-old Harrow-educated king, the crown prince, three princesses, other members of the dynasty, and their servants were shot in the palace courtyard. The prime minister would be discovered and lynched the next day. Mobs ransacked the British embassy, shot the defense attaché within, and tore to pieces three Americans.

Eisenhower urged Britain's riposte, which was to fly two thousand of its crack "Red Devil" paratroopers into Jordan to shore up King Hussein's own shaky throne. Because they came from Cyprus, this elicited a protest from Israel against the overflights. But it was about all Britain could do.

At the same time, Lebanon was facing its first civil war between Christians and Muslims: the former wanted to align Lebanon with the West and with the Baghdad Pact; the latter favored Nasser and notions of Pan-Arabism. Within hours of the upheaval in Iraq, the president of Lebanon, a Maronite Christian, cried "Communist" against his opponents and called in the Americans under the Eisenhower Doctrine. On July 15, two thousand U.S. marines from the 6th Fleet landed south of Beirut. An astonished crowd of beachgoers observed the excitement, and boys dashed to help the marines pull their equipment through the surf. Thirteen thousand more fighting men quickly followed. All departed after two quiet months. Arabs remember the drama as the "first American invasion of the Middle East."[47]

As for Iraq, the overthrow of its decades-old pro-British regime laid the ideological foundations of a vicious demagogic nationalism that would endure until March 2003.

Nearly five years after Clark's letter appeared in *The Times*, Dean Acheson, while addressing cadets at West Point in December 1962, cuttingly observed that "Great Britain has lost an empire and not yet found a role," adding that any role "based on a 'special relationship' with the United States . . . is about played out." And he continued with his insults: Britain's standing, he said, was "based on being head of a 'commonwealth' which has no political structure, or unity, or strength."[48] By then, all that remained of the empire was just the question of arranging its packing.

THE "STAY OF EXECUTION" ON WHICH THE FICTIONAL SMILEY WOULD later reflect was running out too. Warriors of Britain's "Finest Hour," with their medals and their memories, were being left to reminisce with elderly colonels eking out their pensions in Cheltenham, while senior diplomats tried to remember whether some insufferable third-world minister sounding off at the UN had been imprisoned for sedition back in 1929. Apart from a well-aimed kick at Nye Bevan's rump on the staircase at White's, not one act of right-wing violence in Britain marred the passing of an empire so much greater than Rome's. There would be no analogue to the tanks that would roll through Lisbon or de Gaulle's bullet-riddled car at Pont-à-Mousson, while the most dominant color on the map contracted into its home archipelago. Only a few islands and headlands would remain as geographic memorials of the triumphant sea power that had launched the Industrial Revolution.

Many of the British elite drew a parallel with France's collapse in 1940 in the face of German determination. They believed that Britain's retreat was the result of having fought two world wars from beginning to end and from having won them at terrible sacrifice—above all from having suffered the generation-winnowing horror of the western front. Something had cracked in the depths of their country, much as a spirited racehorse's heart may finally be broken by the whip. More than a few sympathetic U.S. observers believed that, too.

In Washington, the restraint that Eisenhower had voiced in his first term about not seeking "to police the world" was fading fast. Nonetheless, influential people insisted that the five-star general in the White House wasn't doing enough: there was now a "missile gap" with Russia; the country was unready to fight a conventional war; and defense spending was negligently insufficient for an economy that had grown more than 25 percent in nearly eight years. "I can't understand these United States being quite as panicky as they are," said the president—as he referred to his country in the plural, old-fashioned way.[49] And indeed the country was primed for the call of John F. Kennedy, the magnetic young senator from Massachusetts who ran for president by invoking "a struggle for supremacy" against Moscow's "ruthless, godless tyranny," fired by the immensity of "Soviet productivity."[50] He campaigned "on the Churchill ticket," observed Harold Macmillan, who'd be prime minister until October 1963.[51] Kennedy insisted that the nation was asleep, as Britain had been when failing in the 1930s to prepare against Hitler.

KENNEDY ROSE FROM AMONG THE JUNIOR OFFICERS WHO'D BEEN on World War II's front lines. When he took office in January 1961, he was forty-three, and he brought with him youthful and vigorous men ready to command the institutions and practices that had settled in place over the preceding fifteen years. "American frontiers are on the Rhine and the Mekong and the Tigris and the Euphrates," he declared.[52] This was an immense change in disposition from the era when policy was shaped by Snyder, Marshall, Acheson, and Foster Dulles, and by Truman and Eisenhower. Tasks that Eisenhower had regarded as grim obligations, such as ousting Mosaddeq in Iran and Árbenz in Guatemala, were now embraced as the true art of world management.

Never had such power fallen so suddenly on a nation as in the years after World War II. The sense of possibility that this generated included a confidence that swelled into commitments wise and also foolish, as when SEATO was invoked to provide an appearance of legality for the United States to intervene in Southeast Asia. Kennedy made explicit what Eisenhower had started in quiet drips, and by November 1963 some sixteen thousand fighting men had been sent to Vietnam, although he insisted to anxious legislators that these were not "combat troops in the generally accepted sense of the word"; they were Green Berets, Navy SEALs, CIA operatives, and other helpful personnel.[53]

During the canonical "Thousand Days" of the Kennedy administration, the British mystique, which so nearly had been shattered by Suez, retained its power over ambitious young Americans seeking a mystique of their own. One of Kennedy's favorite books, for instance, was Lord David Cecil's *Melbourne*, which depicts the kind of skeptical, enlightened patriciate worth emulating. Even Ian Fleming's James Bond fantasies, which came wrapped around the superagent's "license to kill," were discussed by the president with Allen Dulles (one of Kennedy's first two reappointments), who admitted that he found the novels professionally useful.

Indeed, Britain's authentic expertise abroad still seemed unsurpassed. The widely syndicated columnists Joseph and Stewart Alsop observed that any serious correspondent wanting to understand events in a foreign country should start with the British embassy.[54] In Washington, Britain's ambassador, David Ormsby-Gore, was essentially part of the Kennedy administration. Lots of Americans saw an enduring stature. As the Senate majority leader says to Her Majesty's ambassador, Lord Claude Maudulayne, in *Advise and Consent*, of course the Republic doesn't share Britain's gifts for world leadership. It's a mystique, at least about British diplomacy, still to be found in Washington today.

Meanwhile, the Kennedy entourage saw opportunity. Henry Fairlie, a former editorialist of the London *Times*, wrote ten years later in *The Kennedy Promise* about how much these new leaders had reveled in crisis. They seemed to thrive off adrenaline. During the campaign, Kennedy had warned Americans that they would "live on the edge of danger" in the decade ahead, in a cold war of infinite duration.[55] A level of excitement and incaution followed that, with few interruptions, has characterized U.S. foreign policy making ever since.

In part, this habit is due to another shift that occurred in the executive branch: professors and think tankers who, at best, had been consultants to the departments handling defense issues became practitioners overnight. The press portrayed these often unworldly men, who moved into roles like the president's national security adviser, as "action intellectuals," or "defense intellectuals," the latter being a label they keep to this day. But no matter where they originated, the door was being opened to that type of enthusiast who has come to be known as "emergency man." These are the clever, energetic, self-assured, well-schooled men, and now women, who seize on the opportunities intrinsic to the American system of political appointments to juggle enormous risk and are drawn to national security policy by its atmosphere of secrecy, decisiveness, and apocalyptic stakes.

During the Kennedy years, men with these enthusiasms made their way into decisive foreign policy roles with an ease rarely possible in other advanced nations. That was due, then as today, to the more than four thousand patronage slots that every U.S. administration can use to bend the government to its own taste—not just cabinet secretaries and ambassadors, but eventually office directors and deputy assistant secretaries at the Pentagon and Foggy Bottom. The expertly professional U.S. Foreign Service became marginalized as bureaucracies grew. The National Security Council staff, for example, expanded from fewer than 12 under Truman, to around 36 in the Eisenhower years, followed by Kennedy-imposed cutbacks; then it grew again under Johnson, and onward to a bloated 143 with Nixon/Kissinger. Today, it's more than 400 personnel (still heavily being political appointees at the top). This is an utterly different situation from that found in Whitehall or in the foreign policy apparatuses of any serious nation, such as China or Russia or

France or Japan, in which professional diplomats and elite civil servants hold sway.

Looking back, we see that the State Department possessed three strong secretaries in a row from George Marshall's arrival in January 1947 to Foster Dulles's death in May 1959 (to be succeeded by the capable Christian Herter, Paul Nitze's brother-in-law, for the remainder of Eisenhower's term). It was inconceivable that Marshall, Acheson, or Dulles would be crossed by a secretary of defense, let alone an adviser on the White House staff, or that State would routinely be contradicted on any relevant matter of global affairs. The Kennedy administration turned that pyramid upside down, with pride of place going to the Pentagon and the national security adviser, who at that time was McGeorge Bundy, forty-two, down from Cambridge, where he'd been dean of arts and sciences at Harvard. The result ever since the 1960s—with few exceptions—has been an increasingly excitable, short-term, ad hoc, and all-around amateurish approach to the nation's defense and foreign policies.*

The Vietnam War was the first large-scale manifestation of the Kennedy era's "valor of ignorance," and the United States ended up playing into enemy hands.[56] Unstable juntas in Saigon followed the U.S.-enabled overthrow of Ngô Đình Diệm on November 1, 1963, and his murder, along with that of his sinister younger brother, the next day. After Lyndon Johnson became president following John F. Kennedy's assassination on the twenty-second, he spoke of having "sat down with Eisenhower in '54" at an earlier decision point about Vietnam. Sadly, Johnson retained JFK's entire defense policy cohort, which ensured that the United States took over the war from the faltering South Vietnamese army. "I *want* them to send more troops," Ho Chi Minh told the astonished Soviet deputy chairman, who was visiting from Moscow. The aging revolutionary recognized that an industrial democracy would

---

*Popular distrust of the State Department arises from a republican antipathy to ceremony, braid, and social elites and from having had few vital interests abroad for most of the country's history. A professional, merit-based U.S. Foreign Service was established only in 1924, and—except for the extraordinary double generation that made the 1778 alliance with France and the treaties of 1814—the people involved in foreign affairs were a random lot, such as the minister to London who was recalled in 1874 for peddling worthless mining stocks.

eventually sicken of such an ill-conceived war, as Americans did, with their 58,220 dead.[57]

The British, however, were not to be found in Vietnam, contrary to their own myth, as heard today, about having always been at "the front of the line" in America's fights since 1945.[58] Dean Rusk was the weak secretary of state from 1961 to 1969, in both the Kennedy and the Johnson administrations. He seethed over Britain's refusal to send even a token battalion to Vietnam while conducting a brisk seaborne commerce with Hanoi. The next time, he said, America would leave this supposedly special ally to defend the White Cliffs of Dover alone.

By then, the East-West struggle appeared endless, which prompted such bile from an otherwise sober figure as Rusk. Hot wars have horizons: roughly speaking, the closer the horizon, the further a war will be waged *à outrance*. But a more or less cold war that continues over decades will harden the worst habits and self-deceptions. It corrodes alliances and drains the morale of whole nations, as began to be seen in the 1960s and as we experience today in yet another conflict with no end in sight.

President Eisenhower and President-Elect John F. Kennedy, 1960: living on the edge of danger

CONCLUSION

THE FINAL THREE DECADES OF THE "COLD WAR" HAVE BEEN AS little understood as the first dozen years. In this book, I have avoided using the term, except when quoting others. In fact, each continent, each decade, perhaps each nation drawn into the struggle experienced its own cold war, and those two weighty words are now loaded with fables and errors. Consider the difficulties we have in construing how the conflict came to an end. Time was by no means on the side of the West, as general opinion has it. And, contrary to standard accounts, the ideological/geostrategic offensive that America undertook in the last, most dangerous decade proved decisive to Soviet Communism's fall in December 1991.[1]

Thereafter, lots of fantasies arose, including a triumphant "end of history," beliefs in the transformation of Russia, and arguments that America had caused the East-West antagonism in the first place. The

CIA—whose deficiencies Eisenhower was already growing alarmed about in 1957—spent the following decade devoting enormous effort to rationalizing its embarrassments about failing to detect Soviet economic disintegration and to plastering fig leaves over a new generation of operational disasters.[2] It all proved a terrible backdrop to September 11, 2001.

Never have so many people seen so many others die—and in real time—than when the twin towers fell. NATO's North Atlantic Council, the alliance's highest decision-making body, swiftly invoked Article 5, which provides that an attack against any member will be deemed an attack against all. Within six weeks, U.S. commandos and elements of the SAS had reached deep into Afghanistan, and the alliance's first campaign outside Europe was under way. But what began as a convincingly targeted response soon turned into another horizonless struggle—largely because of delusions that had become embedded in U.S. foreign policy establishment doctrine since the late 1950s. One was the belief that the hearts and minds of distant peoples yearn to be magicked into something akin to our own. Another was that any resolute action, usually against the backdrop of "Munich," is superior to restraint. Soon enough these failings lured America into Iraq, trailed by a partner that would never have so uncritically obliged during the years of our story.

With the Defense Department saying that the war in Afghanistan had been won, a joint U.S. and British invasion of Iraq followed in March 2003 against America's former ally Saddam Hussein. The Labour government was by then in a "frenzy of aggression," according to one senior diplomat who worked on Middle East issues for Britain's UN delegation.[3] And, as before, a prime minister said that he had to cooperate in order to "exert influence on American policy making."[4] So observed Sir John Chilcot, the eminent former civil servant who conducted his country's official postmortem. Despite flimsy U.S. intelligence—no surprise to those familiar with CIA analyses of the Soviet Union—the Americans charged in with 138,000 warriors; the British with 28,000; and the Australians, who were among a motley coalition of thirty-six other nations, with 2,000.

An overarching U.S. motive was the desire to "realign" the pattern of Middle Eastern politics—a purpose that Eisenhower, when formulating his doctrine, might have approved.[5] But this time the method was "to lay a Big Bang on the Middle East's calcified political landscape," said one player at the Pentagon, and to "begin a transformation of the Middle East," crowed another, by inflicting a blow that would shock Muslim states.[6] A liberal democracy was supposed to follow a clean, quick victory.

Another delusion had penetrated Washington decision making: that sheer effort will be rewarded with easy and wondrous returns, despite taking intellectual shortcuts. Two weeks before an adventure in Iraq that the secretary of defense promised the nation would last five days (or five weeks—maybe at worst five months), his deputy secretary, a political scientist and academic dean, was insisting that any distinctions between Sunni and Shia were surely "exaggerated."[7]

Americans are hardly alone in their ignorance, although the self-deceptions of a superpower entail larger consequences. On the cusp of invasion, the ghost of an earlier Western disaster was conjured up. Andrew Roberts, a prominent historian at the University of Cambridge, drew positive lessons from Suez as he urged the Americans into what he insisted was a necessary war: "Eden was quite right to want to punish Egypt for her piracy, which—had it come off successfully—would have proved 'no end of a lesson' to the Middle East in its dealings with the West."[8] A big "if." But an approach at the start of the twenty-first century that harked back to what were called "small wars of the empire" in the 1930s fared even worse in a networked world that embraced 24/7 CNN and Al Jazeera.[9]

Oliver Franks's quip from 1953 remains apt: Americans don't do "grand strategy." What passes for considered policy is instead a twisting sequence of ad hoc decisions hammered out under the stresses of sudden foreign urgencies and heavily politicized responses. Why would it be otherwise, whether in Asia or the Middle East? Added to the mix are dreams about what unrivaled political-military strength can accomplish.

By now, the United States has failed at four wars in a row. After Korea, we've gone stumbling from Vietnam to Afghanistan to Iraq, and back to Afghanistan, while using the same sound bites and justifications. (If the Gulf War of 1990 against Iraq's third-tier army—which had vastly extended itself into Kuwait—couldn't have been won in a hundred hours, the Pentagon might as well be shuttered.) More than fifteen years since invading Iraq itself in 2003, America is still throwing its energies to the desert winds as each day uncovers further limits to its unparalleled military capacities, including limits to special operations.[10] Tactical successes tend to be meaningless without strategy.

Military policies, after all, are repeated over and over too. That includes "Vietnamization"—which is the hope of successfully expanding local forces in order to draw down U.S. combat troops—as applied in Iraq and Afghanistan. At the same time, the basics keep having to be learned and relearned. Counterinsurgency is an example. Fascination with the subject vanished after failure in Vietnam, and the techniques of protracted war against indistinct enemies had to be learned anew in Iraq and Afghanistan. Each of these wars, like the fight against ISIS, leaves uncounted civilian dead, and evermore we feel the aftershocks of our blunders as the world becomes an increasingly tighter place.

When outcomes do not match expectations, emergency men (and women) assume that it was the particulars that were gotten wrong, not that the overall objective was misconceived. For instance, it's heard today from one defense intellectual that "our ideals" will work in the Middle East only "if we first restore order" to the region—"restoring order," of course, having already been a cliché at Suez, as it is wherever a great power sees fit to discipline the natives.[11] Another writes, when discussing Korea, that "had Americans been willing to resume the offensive" during 1950–1953 by *again* storming into the North, then U.S. forces "would probably have pushed the Chinese all the way back to the Yalu."[12] It's a view that contradicts judgments of the time by the Joint Chiefs as well as by the Senate Armed Services and Foreign Relations Committees. Nor can Vietnam be left out: the war was unwinnable on any terms acceptable to Americans, yet we learn from a Pentagon adviser that "far fewer than 58,000 Americans would have died there" if only the magics of counterinsurgency had truly been applied.[13]

The outcome would have been the same. So Americans grow skeptical as they evaluate this record of failure, along with such opinions. The nation's gravest decisions appear not to have been thought through.

MEANWHILE, CHINA'S GOVERNMENT DEVOTES INTENSE EFFORT TO examining the rise and fall of empires, while it expands and hones an excellent diplomatic corps—doing so with the same intensity devoted to boosting its military. Western books concerning empire are translated and critiqued, with hopes of learning from two stellar examples: the Soviet Union's downfall, and how the conveniently named American "empire" is said to have "replaced" the very real British one after World War II.[14] In Beijing, the case of imperial Britain is being found ever more worthy of scrutiny. That's because planners at the Ministry of National Defense, as well as concerned scholars at Fudan University and elsewhere who advise their government, expect the United States to follow a similar downward path as Britain's, though faster.

Like their peers in the West, Chinese experts continue to get much of the record wrong about America's rise to supremacy. The United States no more ended up "replacing" the British Empire than Britain, say, "replaced" imperial Spain in the seventeenth and eighteenth centuries.[15] In both instances, it's a story of apples and oranges. The adventures of proselytizing, gold-seeking Spain can't be compared to those of Protestant, mercantile Britain. The upheavals following World War II marked the latest passage into another technological and political epoch. Yet the origins of what had occurred even up to that point remain clouded by myths.

Henry Kissinger, for example, repeats one of the most persistent. "Between Lincoln and [Theodore] Roosevelt's time," he writes, "America was protected by huge oceans and, in practice, by the British navy."[16] This endearing tale about the Royal Navy, which originated decades earlier, was heard often in the dozen years after World War II, but the truth is that the United States was never protected by British fleets. Quite the contrary, although the fiction that Britain basically enforced the Monroe Doctrine frames nineteenth-century American history as durably as the ones that we've addressed have framed the twentieth.[17] Nonchalantly dipping into history, however, is another characteristic of emergency men.[18] It arises, in part, from the United States being relatively unburdened by its past, at least on foreign policy. The country of endless tomorrows is intent "to look forward, not back," no matter how many failed wars it endures.[19]

In recent administrations, for instance, the upper ranks assume—as do most writers on foreign affairs—that an international order snapped into place right after World War II, enabled by a handful of luminaries popularly called the "Wise Men." Americans rallied behind Churchill's Iron Curtain speech, the Truman Doctrine, and then the Marshall Plan: "and so a grand strategy was born," it's said today.[20] What really occurred, we can now see, was much closer to the peppy Harry Truman's "being an unnerved riverboat gambler improvising his way through the biggest crap game in Western history," as John Updike wrote soon after Truman left office.[21] Not that Eisenhower and Dulles weren't improvising, too.

The trouble is that America's successes after 1945 look easy if we believe that a "national security strategy" suddenly appeared. All we need now is some bipartisanship and Wise Men.[22] Then we're surprised when GIs and marines get bloodily entangled in jungles or deserts, and when a new generation of Wise Men (and women) are revealed as winging it too. "I didn't think it would be *this* tough," conceded the secretary of state in 2008 about Iraq and her administration's attempt to "realign" the Middle East.[23]

Instead, after World War II, the Americans struggled mightily to build upon remnants of liberal international arrangements that were a bequest of the latter nineteenth century. "World order" became a loose term for constitutionalism, free trade, resistance to aggression, and, at the top, as much international cooperation as possible. The order that was achieved really didn't arrive until the end of the 1950s. It developed in fits and starts from a confluence of factors: America asserting itself to take over "the foreign policy leadership of the free world," as Nixon averred; the launch of the first earth satellite, which signaled the beginning of a connected planet; developing NATO, SEATO, and CENTO into actual "organizations"; and, by 1958, a big shift in global finance.

It was in 1958 that eleven European countries finally declared their currencies to be convertible, with others soon to follow, and it was also the time when the United States faced its own balance-of-payments deficit. The U.S. economy faltered that year, costing five million Americans their jobs and once more spreading fear of outright depression. The Eisenhower administration was shaken to see dollars and gold draining from the Treasury. However, this reversal of fortune showed that the dynamized industries of Western Europe and Japan were finally competing vigorously.

Americans didn't single-handedly create this framework, just to recall Ernest Bevin's stand against the Berlin blockade or the writing of NATO's Article 5. Over the years of our story, the Truman and Eisenhower administrations found it difficult to raise the money to maintain America's unrehearsed but, as it would prove, remarkably steady alliance system. When Washington finally moved forward on the scale required to "lead the free world," it did so choppily—and hardly as an "empire."

The trope buzzing around Whitehall after World War II was that America embodied a greater rebirth of Rome—muscular, coarse, and, to be sure, in need of guidance. A crude version of this notion was taken up by the Far Left in the 1950s to depict America as bully and occupier. Then the notion of "a new Rome" got revived among U.S. opinion makers in the early twenty-first century.[24] For many of them, this idea was part of a mashup that urged America to adopt the great liberal ideals of an always mythical "Pax Britannica."[25] Yet primacy, which entails being able to speak the loudest in asserting one's interests, is hardly "empire."

Like "bankruptcy," the word "empire" doesn't lend itself to ambiguity, and has a specific meaning. It asserts some final authority of command, as has been seen since Athens designed to be supreme in Hellas. Aneurin Bevan, the sharpest and most free-ranging intellect of the postwar British Left, was closer to the mark when he mocked the Americans as "gadget monkeys"—with their faith in the silver bullet of airpower, incessantly frantic over the *crise du jour* while rushing to pursue fixes (however temporary) and eagerly confronting each new drama with hopes that their country's latest know-how might pay off. (As sometimes it did.)

An empire would not permit its ever-richer allies to pay so little for the common defense over decades or tolerate defiant clients like Chiang Kai-shek or, in Iran, its spineless installee, the shah, who initiated an oil boycott that would cripple the U.S. economy during the 1970s. The merest squeak from Washington that a friendly dictator might do well to moderate his rule is still routinely brushed away—whether by the dictatorships of Egypt and Saudi Arabia or by that of Bahrain, which today is home to the U.S. Navy's 5th Fleet, with its fifteen thousand sailors, marines, and airmen. Meanwhile, both Israelis and Palestinians venerate their pantheons of terrorists and martyrs and shuffle unhappily toward a de facto binational state, which both antagonists had rejected at the start. No matter that Washington wrings its hands over an imagined "peace process."

Worst of all, to believe that we're an empire now inures the country to the horrors of war. It opens the door to high-risk adventuring, like choosing to invade Iraq, or arguing that the Middle Eastern entanglements of our current forever wars should be fought by American contractors (sensitive about being called mercenaries) rather than by GIs and marines.[26] Ultimately, a mighty roadblock to America becoming an empire has been that the nation would then have to immerse itself in the sordid politics of all these foreigners.

Nor has America ever gotten around to building an effective administrative class, or an elite cadre, which would have been necessary for formulating the long relationships demanded of empire. Over the years of this story, the country did okay when following its familiar habits of filling high offices: to every victorious administration belong the legitimate spoils of government. This approach has merits. Energy and fresh perspective can be injected into the system; the talent that arrives may be random but can be impressive.

Consider James Webb, the quietly capable lawyer and former U.S. Marine Corps pilot who served as Truman's undersecretary of state from 1949 to 1952, as Acheson gave him increasingly difficult operational problems to solve. G. K. Young, a tough piece of work who reviled his own country's mandarin class, concluded that "the Americans have not been badly served by political appointees."[27] But he wrote that in 1961. That's when "national security" became the trellis up which professors, think tankers, journalists, executives from foundations and defense industries alike, and Hill staffers—indeed, almost anyone in addition to the usual lawyers and bankers—could build a career that let them flow in and out of the administrations. At the same time, the superb professional Foreign Service sank deeper into the background. Near-constant sensations of "crisis" arrived, along with short attention spans and the taking of all-around shortcuts.

BEVIN AND CHURCHILL GRASPED THE EXTENT OF AMERICA'S UNDERlying insularity and spent their last years of power seeking to dispel it.

They could see how precarious was the engagement of this greatest of island powers and how easily it could return home or be distracted into costly disappointments. Nearly two decades through the twenty-first century, there's no assurance that the United States will remain the world's sole superpower, or even that it will long continue to be one at all.

Instead, China appears to be rising as an authentic "superpower," combining great power and an ever-greater mobility of power. It's doing so in ways never imagined when the United States finally recognized the People's Republic in 1979, a dozen years before the Soviet Union's end. China plays to its strengths as nearly the largest economy in a globalized world by presenting itself as a champion of free trade and by investing strategically in Africa, Latin America, and Eastern Europe while pledging to dispense foreign aid in amounts greater than the Marshall Plan. It backs a new international financial regime, changes the rules of the game from within existing institutions (such as the World Trade Organization), and, naturally, races for the commanding heights of technology.

Aspects of China's ascent are akin to those of Britain, and thereafter of the United States, in bygone years. History courses in China teach that the United States became a great power in part by, early on, stealing technology like steam-powered looms from Britain. What's clear is that economic penetration and China's vision of global integration will also be followed, soon enough, by military power. A lament by a Chinese strategist is revealing, and it was offered ingenuously to an American friend during one of the periodic confrontations between the U.S. Navy and his government over China's spectacular land grab in the South China Sea (that is, the building of militarized artificial islands in contested waters). "It's too soon for us to be doing this," he said.[28]

During the later years of our story, *Scientific American* popularized the phrase "acceleration of history." That meant more things were happening faster, with more twists and connections. I had this phenomenon in mind while writing and, toward the story's end, began wondering who among the major figures of those years, when the United States rapidly came to overshadow history's greatest empire, will be remembered five centuries from now. Probably Churchill and Franklin Roosevelt, for what they did to avert the Thousand-Year Reich. Maybe Truman and Eisenhower will catch the attention of 2520's brainier students for having drawn a line against Stalinist barbarity. And Mao Zedong and Nehru will likely be known. But so many men who once stood against the sky—Marshall and Acheson, and Ernest Bevin—are already pretty much forgotten except by historians, while such titans as John Wesley Snyder and Lewis Douglas and Malcolm MacDonald are unknown even to them. For most travelers scurrying in and out of the U.S. capital, "Dulles" now means only Washington's international airport.

But I suspect that one person whose name will resonate, perhaps even a millennium hence, is James Webb, who left Washington in 1952, at the age of forty-five, for an adventurous oil firm in Oklahoma City. This North Carolinian, son of the school superintendent in the hamlet of Tally Ho, returned to Washington in February 1961, along with a rush of younger men. They were "the best and brightest" of their generation, and all of them were eager to prove their valor and vigor. John F. Kennedy acclaimed "the burden and the glory" of the hour at which America had arrived. Webb focused on his task of running the National Aeronautics and Space Administration—which Eisenhower had set up only three years before—and on figuring out how to get a man to the moon "before the decade is out." That's what JFK promised soon after his inauguration, while showing a justified American confidence that no other country could match.

And that's what Webb did, as he simultaneously used NASA's clout to thwart Jim Crow. He imposed new rules to desegregate NASA's workforce in Houston, at the Manned Spacecraft Center; in Hampton, Virginia, at the Langley Research Center; and in Huntsville, Alabama, at the George C. Marshall Space Flight Center. Moreover, Webb "broke the lock," as he described it, that the Ivy League, as well as Caltech and MIT, had on the nation's brightest graduate students.[29] He did so by enabling Oklahoma and Ohio and Louisiana, and the University of Michigan too, among other graduate schools, to hire top professors and by distributing NASA's predoctoral fellowships in physics and astronomy throughout the country. Webb knew, as Eisenhower had said after Sputnik, that America's future, and perhaps its survival, lay in drawing on all its talents, irrespective of color and faith, of wealth and national origin.

Ultimately, America's rise sprang from the sheer power of production, a culture of discovery and technology breakthroughs, and Hollywood's idealization of middle-class living, not from any expansionist yearnings in Washington. For us, the fate of "the country of tomorrow" now lies in extending those qualities: an incandescently free intellectual life, the bringing together of genius and hope from everywhere, the spurring of research and forceful enterprise. Which is just why Webb has his chance of a thousand years' remembrance.

In March 2022, America will take another giant leap as NASA launches the James Webb Space Telescope (the Webb), which will serve as the world's premier space observatory into the 2030s. It's a time machine, the astronomers tell us, that will peer back 13.5 billion years "to see the first stars and galaxies forming out of the darkness of the early universe."[30] This acknowledgment of Webb's dutiful work reminds us how, ultimately, it's the men and women of science, and those who sustain them, who are spiriting us into an accelerating future—more so than the politicians, diplomats, and soldiers. Behind the headlines of summits and showdowns, and beyond the destinies of empires, it's such a breadth of achievement that has given the United States its historic advantage, in the past as today.

INTRODUCTION

1. The historian Andrew Roberts writes that "an exhausted Great Britain handed on the baton to the United States" circa 1947–1948, in "Book Review: *Mapping the End of Empire*," *Wall Street Journal*, April 18, 2014. "Liquidation" is what another historian, Peter Clarke, believes occurred—and, moreover, within a thousand days of the end of World War II. See *The Last Thousand Days of the British Empire: Churchill, Roosevelt, and the Birth of the Pax Americana* (New York: Bloomsbury, 2008), xxiv. Others conclude "that the game was up" and, by 1945, "British power had quietly vanished." See, respectively, Niall Ferguson, *Empire: The Rise and Demise of the British World Order and the Lessons for Global Power* (New York: Basic Books, 2004), 295, and Joseph S. Nye, *Bound to Lead: The Changing Nature of American Power* (New York: Basic Books, 1990), 59, referencing the historian Correlli Barnett. The economist Benn Steil argues "collapse of the British empire" during 1947, as well as "liquidation," in *The Marshall Plan: Dawn of the Cold War* (New York: Simon & Schuster, 2018), 51, 200. Geoffrey Wheatcroft reflects all this conventional wisdom by arguing in *The New York Times Book Review* that Britain after World War II was "in no condition, or mood, to play the part of great power or imperial ruler anymore" ("Imperial Son," August 17, 2014).

2. The columnist Bret Stephens believes that Britain "wanted out," in *America in Retreat: The New Isolationism and the Coming Global Disorder* (New York: Random House, 2014), 26, while Clarke writes that World War II "made the United States, willy-nilly, into the dominant power," not distinguishing between preeminence and primacy. *Last Thousand Days of the British Empire*, xiv. The historian Fredrik Logevall sees the United States, in September 1945, as "the only real superpower, and therefore uniquely able to affect the course of events in the developing world." *Embers of War: The Fall of an Empire and the Making of America's Vietnam* (New York: Random House, 2013), 98.

3. The absence of a "world order," as we'll discover early in chapter 18, was being addressed in 1954 and 1955 by—among others—both the philosopher/ambassador/armaments administrator Sir Oliver Franks and the political journalist/intellectual George Lichtheim. In contrast, today's conventional wisdom from academia and the U.S. government alike is that a "U.S.-led world order" snapped into place "immediately after 1945." That's seen, for example, in *"Building Situations of Strength": A National Strategy for the United States* (Washington, D.C.: Brookings Institution, 2017), and *U.S. Role in the World: Background and Issues for Congress*, Congressional Research Service, Washington, D.C., July 2017.

1. THE THREE IN 1945

1. http://news.bbc.co.uk/onthisday/hi/dates/stories/may/1/newsid_3571000/357 1497.stm?first=1.

2. "Bloodlands" is the description immortalized by Timothy Snyder in his heartrending *Bloodlands: Europe Between Hitler and Stalin* (New York: Basic Books, 2010).

3. Duff Hart-Davis, ed., *King's Counsellor: Abdication and War: The Diaries of Sir Alan Lascelles* (London: Weidenfeld & Nicolson, 2006), 297, Ismay quoted on February 23, 1945; "dentures" is diary entry for March 14, 1945, 303.

4. Ibid., 294.

5. CAB 65/50, WM (45) 39, April 3, 1945 (Cabinet Minutes and Papers, National Archives, U.K.).

6. "Very weak" is John Colville, diary entry for February 19, 1945, in *The Fringes of Power: 10 Downing Street Diaries, 1939–1955* (New York: Norton, 1985), 560; Hart-Davis, diary entry for February 12, 1945, in *King's Counsellor*, 294. In Kori Schake's *Safe Passage: The Transition from British to American Hegemony* (Cambridge, Mass.: Harvard University Press, 2017), 15, the Colville diary entry for February 24 concerning Churchill's views at Yalta on the changed dimensions of power is incomplete. Schake drops the essential clause. It reads in full: "The P.M. said that a small lion was talking between a huge Russian bear and a great American elephant, *but perhaps it would prove to be the lion which knew the way*" (564). In 1945, London expected such loyal support—and for about a dozen years hence. Moreover, Churchill was being melodramatic. He knew there was nothing "small" about the British Empire.

7. Another of FDR's digs, when speaking to Stalin, was to say that the British "had never sold anything without commercial interest." See the definitive S. M. Plokhy, *Yalta: The Price of Peace* (New York: Penguin, 2011), 226.

8. Robert Rhodes James, *Anthony Eden: A Biography* (New York: McGraw-Hill, 1987), 306, referencing Eden's diary; diary entry for September 6, 1945, in *Churchill: Taken from the Diaries of Lord Moran* (Boston: Houghton Mifflin, 1966), 322.

9. Colville, diary entry for February 28, 1945, in *Fringes of Power*, 566.

10. Hart-Davis, diary entry for March 9, 1945, in *King's Counsellor*, 300, referencing Churchill's telegram to FDR describing Russia's handling of Poland as a "test case"; and March 8, in which Churchill is disturbed over the Soviet foreign minister Molotov's attitude concerning Poland and Romania, "so inconsistent with the Yalta agreements."

11. H. G. Nicholas, ed., *Washington Despatches: Weekly Political Reports from the British Embassy* (Chicago: University of Chicago Press, 1981). "Brand new 100 per cent" is p. 473; "eager to convert" is May 20, 1942, p. 39.

12. See their discussion in Derek Leebaert, *The Fifty-Year Wound: How America's Cold War Victory Shapes Our World* (New York: Little, Brown, 2002), 5.

13. Christopher Thorne, *Allies of a Kind: The United States, Britain, and the War Against Japan, 1941–1945* (Oxford: Oxford University Press, 1978), 78.

14. Vice Admiral J. Victor Smith, oral history, U.S. Naval Institute. (Smith was a senior aide to Admiral Leahy.)

15. Nicholas, *Washington Despatches*, 571.

16. McKellar to Harry S. Truman, Official File, OF 48, Harry S. Truman Library (hereafter cited as HSTL).

17. Bernard M. Baruch, Report to President Truman, April 20, 1945, box 35, folder 1, "UK Dollar Crisis," John W. Snyder Papers, HSTL. The same month that Baruch visited London, John Maynard Keynes was also optimistic about what lay ahead, even on balance-of-payments issues and sterling indebtedness. He shared these opinions with U.S. officials. See Report by Mr. Lauchlin Currie on Conversations with British Officials, March 1945, April 24, 1945, in *Foreign Relations of the United States: Diplomatic Papers, 1945: The British Commonwealth: The Far East, Volume VI. (Foreign Relations of the United States* is hereafter cited as *FRUS.)*

18. Jon Meacham, *Franklin and Winston: An Intimate Portrait of an Epic Friendship* (New York: Random House, 2003), 340. It is difficult to see the "friendship" of which the author writes.

19. Nor did FDR look forward to Churchill's White House visits, according to the U.S. Army chief of staff, George Marshall, in entry for July 3, 1958, in *Diaries of Lord Moran*, citing Ambassador Lord Halifax, 791.

20. Churchill chose the title *Triumph and Tragedy* for the final volume of his war history (1953). Here's the drama that has been overlooked: if that title didn't come directly from the essayist Max Beerbohm's line about "Lord Randolph's career of triumph and tragedy," it surely was somewhere in the mind of Lord Randolph's son. Churchill adored his father, and Beerbohm had regarded his fellow Mertonian Lord Randolph as the great parliamentarian of the 1880s.

21. FDR's biographers overlook key aspects of his ancestral affinity with the Netherlands, including his ability to speak some Dutch, which would not have have been difficult due to his fluency in German and French. He kept childhood books written in Dutch in the Oval Office and in 1941 had whisked the first escapee to arrive in America from Nazi-occupied Holland into the White House to deliver a

personal account of conditions in the homeland. At Yalta, FDR proposed letting the Netherlands annex German territory. The sprawling Dutch Empire, largely in the East Indies, was the only one FDR didn't condemn. (Virginia Lewick, archivist of the Franklin D. Roosevelt Presidential Library, helpfully confirmed Roosevelt's fluency.)

22. Isaiah Berlin, *Personal Impressions* (New York: Viking, 1981), 17.

23. Harold Macmillan, *Tides of Fortune 1945–1955* (New York: Harper & Row, 1969), 507.

24. John Raymond, *England's on the Anvil, and Other Essays* (London: Collins, 1957), 123. John Raymond was the *New Stateman*'s sparkling literary editor, and here he is quoting Hilaire Belloc on Churchill.

25. Diary entry for September 27, 1952, in Peter Caterall, ed., *The Macmillan Diaries: The Cabinet Years 1950–1957* (London: Macmillan, 2003), 187; also see Nicholas, *Washington Despatches*, 602.

26. Diary entry for July 19, 1945, in *Diaries of Lord Moran*, 295.

27. Diary entry for July 23, 1945, in ibid., 301.

28. Diary entry for August 8, 1945, in ibid., 310–11.

29. John Bew, "Clement Attlee: An Unromantic Hero," *New Statesman*, September 26, 2013.

30. John Wheeler-Bennet, *King George VI: His Life and Reign* (London: Macmillan, 1958), 636.

31. September 8, 1948, DEFE 4/16 COS (48) 124 (Ministry of Defense, National Archives, U.K.).

32. Lord Gladwyn, *Memoirs of Lord Gladwyn* (London: Weidenfeld and Nicholson, 1972), 175.

33. William Roger Louis, *The British Empire in the Middle East 1945–1951: Arab Nationalism, the United States, and Postwar Imperialism* (Oxford: Clarendon Press, 1984), 4. Louis's classic work remains an indispensable analysis of U.S. foreign policy for these years, and not just on the Middle East.

34. "Great Britain: Break-Up," *Time*, June 3, 1946.

35. Alan Bullock, *Ernest Bevin: Foreign Secretary, 1945–1951* (Oxford: Oxford University Press, 1983), 90.

36. John Foster Dulles, Digest of Meeting, October 30, 1945, Council on Foreign Relations (hereafter cited as CFR) archives.

37. "World Affairs, 1945," in *Junior: Articles, Stories, and Pictures*, as referenced in Bernard Crick, *George Orwell: A Life* (London: Penguin, 1980), 494. In *1984*, however, one of those superstates isn't Britain per se, because it has been absorbed into Oceania, the currency of which is the dollar.

38. *Hansard*, HC Deb., August 20, 1945, vol. 413, cols. 283–400.

39. H. V. Hodson, *Twentieth-Century Empire* (London: Faber and Faber, 1948), 49.

40. I write of "Russia" when referring to the ongoing geopolitical fact and of "Soviet" when meaning the regime. People spoke of "the Russians" throughout these years, as in "the Russians are coming," and the Soviet Union was a Great Russian empire.

41. "Speech to the 20th Party Congress," *New York Times*, March 18, 1956, 2 (section 4).

42. Oleg V. Khlevniuk, *Stalin: New Biography of a Dictator*, trans. Nora Seligman (New Haven, Conn.: Yale University Press, 2015).

43. Gabriel Almond, *The American People and Foreign Policy* (New York: Harcourt, 1950), 73.

44. FO 371/60996 AN 193, January 27, 1947 (Foreign Office Papers, National Archives, U.K.).

45. "Excess deaths" is V. F. Zima, *Golod v SSSR 1946–1947 godov: Proiskhozdenie i posledstviia*, as referenced in the superb study that is Robert Gellately, *Stalin's Curse: Battling for Communism in War and Cold War* (New York: Knopf, 2013), 15. I'm grateful to Professor Gellately for the opportunity to correspond about these issues.

2. KEYNES & CO.

1. The mistaken argument that Americans were "confident in their power" has become conventional wisdom, as can be found in Daniel J. Sargent, *A Superpower Transformed: The Remaking of American Foreign Relations in the 1970s* (New York: Oxford University Press, 2015), 1. The belief that Americans were "eating handsomely" is Max Hastings, "Our Battle with Britain," *New York Review of Books*, August 27, 2007.

2. Any informed observer of age sixty would have grown up seeing a roller coaster of U.S. financial excesses: the gold crisis of 1893 and alarms of demonetization thereafter; frantic capital raids on world markets during its pre–World War I panics; the demented tariff walls preventing the settlement of European debts in the 1920s; the fevered boom and the 1930s bust.

3. William Clark, *From Three Worlds: Memoirs* (London: Sidgwick & Jackson, 1986), 30.

4. *Chicago Daily Tribune*, August 25, 1945, 8. The British, thundered this editorial, expected America to accept "the permanent post of grand almoner to the rest of the world."

5. Hastings, "Our Battle with Britain." That "Britain was bankrupt" is also Anne Deighton in her overview, "Britain and the Cold War, 1945–1955," in *The Cambridge History of the Cold War*, ed. Melvyn Leffler and Odd Arne Westad (Cambridge, U.K.: Cambridge University Press, 2010), 1:117. Some writers go further to imagine an entire "bankrupt empire," as in Niall Ferguson, *Colossus: The Rise and Fall of the American Empire* (New York: Penguin, 2005), 68. However, a nation goes bankrupt by being unable to pay its debts on any terms. That never happened, nor is it what Keynes feared might occur.

6. Keynes applied metaphors carefully, as in his *General Theory* when he compared beauty contests and asset markets or when he equated marginally useful projects with burying banknotes in disused coal mines.

7. Clark, *From Three Worlds*, 34, xi.

8. Robert Skidelsky, *John Maynard Keynes: Fighting for Freedom, 1937–1946* (New York: Penguin, 2001), 381, 386. Keynes used the phrase "time being" several times, as when he wrote that a Dunkirk-like disaster could mean "the acceptance of the position for the time being of the position of second-class Power, rather like the present position of France." See BBC British History in Depth, "The Wasting of Britain's Marshall Aid," www.bbc.co.uk/history/british.

9. Richard Davenport-Hines, *Universal Man: The Seven Lives of John Maynard Keynes* (London: William Collins, 2015), 333.

10. FO 371/68013 B AN0669, March 14, 1948, Hall-Patch.

11. Clark, *From Three Worlds*, 34.

12. Ibid., 39.

13. Hugh Dalton, *High Tide and After: Memoirs, 1945–1960* (London: Frederick Muller, 1962), 77.

14. Today it seems odd that the $3.75 billion loan to Britain was considered enormous. Even when multiplying for inflation, it would only be $48.3 billion—still a drop in today's $3.9 trillion federal budget. Instead, that $3.75 billion, or the Marshall Plan's $13 billion in grants and loans, is better understood by comparing those sums with average annual income in the United States ($2,850) or with percentage of GDP ($230 billion) in 1946. To add to perspective, all the gold within Fort Knox didn't quite equal $21 billion.

15. Skidelsky, *Keynes*, 128.

16. *The Collected Writings of John Maynard Keynes*, ed. Donald Moggridge (Cambridge, U.K.: Cambridge University Press, 1979), 23:21.

17. Skidelsky, *Keynes*, 418. One result of feeling outsmarted, concludes the Oxford historian John Darwin, was an "era of American deference." See John Darwin, *The End of the British Empire: The Historical Debate* (Oxford: Blackwell, 1991), 74.

18. William P. N. Edwards, oral history, HSTL.

19. Vaughan to Sir Leslie Rowan, August 29, 1945, Official File, HSTL. In 1948, the *Washington Star* accused Vaughan of enabling a friend to buy perfumes in France and ship them back on a military plane, which required bumping a wounded soldier from the flight. Vaughan rebounded from that scandal, only to be reprimanded in 1950 by a Senate committee for accepting seven home freezers as gifts for himself and various friends. His public service continued until Eisenhower's inaugural in January 1953.

20. The speech can be heard clearly at https://www.youtube.com/watch?v =PJxUAcADV70.

21. Walter Lippmann, oral history, Columbia University.

22. Editorial, *Times*, March 7, 1946.

23. Nicholas Henderson, *Inside the Private Office: Memoirs of the Secretary to British Foreign Ministers* (Chicago: Chicago Academy Publishers, 1987), 27.

24. FO 371/66279, N2227/38 G, May 28, 1946. This would have been the new British ambassador, Sir Maurice Peterson, who had presented his credentials to the Kremlin on May 26. Stalin had kept his predecessor dawdling.

25. The Americans loved to cite Keynes's description of "Foreign Office frivolities," as in "The British Crisis," *Life*, February 24, 1947, 34. "Slop money out" can be found in Correlli Barnett, *The Lost Victory: British Dreams, British Realities, 1945–1950* (London: Macmillan, 1995), 3.

26. Roy Harrod, *The Life of John Maynard Keynes* (New York: Norton, 1983), 640–41.

27. "Conferences: Night Shift," *Time*, October 14, 1946.

28. Theodore G. Bilbo, *Take Your Choice: Separation or Mongrelization* (Poplarville, Miss.: Dream House, 1947).

29. Congressional Record, 92nd Congress, Senate, April 26, 1946.

30. Godfrey Hodgson, *The Colonel: The Life and Wars of Henry Stimson, 1867–1950* (New York: Knopf, 1990), 267.

31. Acheson, Memcon with Manafee and Bunn, April 27, 1946, President's Secretary's File (hereafter cited as PSF), HSTL.

32. Nicholas, *Washington Despatches*, 576.

33. Tom Connally, *My Name Is Tom Connally* (New York: Thomas Y. Crowell, 1954), 322.

34. *Times*, June 1, 1946. The editors' use of "billions" is puzzling, unless it was being used ironically, in the American sense of "billions." All the world's annual product was much less than half of how the English calculated a billion pounds, meaning a million millions.

35. Darwin, *End of the British Empire*, 46, regarding "second colonial revolution." The author of this excellent study documents a 45 percent increase in Colonial Office staff from 1945 to 1954.

36. Bernard Baruch, *Baruch: The Public Years* (New York: Holt, Rinehart, 1960), 271.

37. Editorial, *Times*, May 4, 1946.

38. The myth of "trappings" is from Tony Judt, *Postwar: A History of Europe Since 1945* (New York: Penguin, 2005), 111; "superpower was a facade" is from Sargent, *Superpower Transformed*, 1; "illusions of Great Power status" is from Paul M. Kennedy, *The Rise and Fall of the Great Powers: Economic Change and Military Conflict from 1500 to 2000* (New York: Random House, 1987), 368.

3. ENTERING THE MIDDLE EAST

1. January 16, 1948, COS (48) 3, DEFE 4/10. During these years, Chief of the Air Staff Tedder, among others, kept defining the strategic priorities as "Defending the United Kingdom; Sea Communications; and the Middle East."

2. Daily Summary, October 16, 1947, 5559, from London, Executive Secretariat, Department of State.

3. October 16, 1946, CAB 131/1, DO (46) 27. Some academics, including Anne Deighton, claim that Bevin was essentially captive to the mandarins—men such as Orme Sargent, Frank Roberts, and Pierson Dixon. This notion is refuted by memoirs of the key principals such as Jebb, by the U.S. and British archival records, by timelines of Bevin's decision making, and not least by the U.S. diplomats in London during those years, who finally concluded that Bevin was "the premier foreign secretary that Britain has had," to cite the embassy's first secretary, 1948–1951. One quality they admired was Bevin's complete independence.

4. Simon C. Smith, *Ending Empire in the Middle East: Britain, the United States, and Post-war Decolonization, 1945–1973* (London: Routledge, 2012), 2.

5. *Al-Ahram*, April 19, 1944, on "shares," and April 4, 1944, on "volcano."

6. RG 84, 88, ME, June 12, 1947 (London Post Files, U.S.).

7. Jamil Hasanli, *Stalin and the Turkish Crisis of the Cold War, 1945–1953* (Lanham, Md.: Lexington, 2011), x.

8. Numerous press interviews exist of Red Army veterans who participated in the 1983 Syrian operation. See, for example, "Russia May Aid 'Comrade Tourists' Who Were Really Soldiers," *New York Times*, December 19, 2015, and "Russian Military Mission in Syria Brings History Full Circle," Reuters World News, October 23, 2015. Also see CIA NIO/NESA, "Talking Points: Syrian and Soviet Options in Lebanon," SSG Mtg., August 29, 1983, Situation Room, Chaired by the Vice President.

9. Hasanli, *Stalin and the Turkish Crisis*, 209. Today the *CIA Factbook* estimates that close to 28 million Kurds live in Turkey, Iraq, Syria, Iran, and Armenia.

10. William Linn Westermann, "Kurdish Independence and Russian Expansion," *Foreign Affairs*, July 1946.

11. Charles E. Bohlen, *Witness to History, 1929–1969* (New York: Norton, 1973), 250.

12. Minute by F. B. A. Randall of the North American Department, January 11, 1947, FO 371/60153.

13. Order, in Stalin, *Sochineniia*, 15:218–21, as referenced in Gellately, *Stalin's Curse*, 151. Additionally, Stalin wanted to participate in what his Ministry of Foreign Affairs called the defense of the Turkish Narrows. That would require a fortified Russian naval base in the Dardanelles, and the MFA could produce evidence, including from Yalta, that Churchill had agreed to some such role.

14. In the first volume of his memoirs (1967), Kennan says that this was "a telegram of some eight thousand words"—unprecedented for State—and he offers "excerpts from" that telegram in his book's appendix C. But appendix C doesn't contain "excerpts": save for three introductory covering sentences to the department, the appendix is in fact the entire five-part, 5,327-word telegram—as became evident when the document was declassified on December 11, 1972. Why care about the discrepancy? In a helpful response to my inquiry, Frank Costigliola, the meticulous editor of *The Kennan Diaries*, explains the "8,000 words" as "just an estimate that Kennan somewhat carelessly made." However, Kennan had been claiming "8,000 words" well before 1967, as to Joseph Jones of Time Inc. and the State Department. Another view is that Kennan was inflating the significance of his role. Americans tend to believe that long or large is equivalent to quality—in contrast to short and concise, as the French value in their essayists. Moreover, the discrepancy shows how uncritically historians approach Kennan's work—repeatedly taking his assertions at face value. For example, his authorized biographer, John Lewis Gaddis, repeats the "eight thousand words" figure in two books: *The Cold War: A New History* (New York: Penguin Press, 2005), 29, and *Strategies of Containment: A Critical Appraisal of American National Security Strategy During the Cold War*, rev. ed. (Oxford: Oxford University Press, 2005), 29. In the echo chamber of writings on diplomatic history, and on national security, the error persists, as with Mark Mykleby, Patrick Doherty, and Joel Makower, *The New Grand Strategy: Restoring America's Prosperity, Security, and Sustainability in the 21st Century* (New York: St. Martin's Press, 2016), 30. It also penetrates textbooks, such as Howard Jones, *Crucible of Power: A History of American Foreign Relations from 1945* (New York: Rowman & Littlefield, 2008), 6.

15. Forrestal's wife, the former Josephine Ogden, was not suffering solely from alcoholism. Their son Michael spoke easily about his parents, by then deceased, with me in New York during the 1970s.

16. Today Secretary Knox still reflects the bonds of that era; he's remembered in Harvard's Knox Memorial Fellowships for scholarly exchanges between the United States, Britain, and its commonwealth.

17. Alexander Wooley, "The Fall of James Forrestal," *Washington Post*, May 23, 1999. Kennan's famous Long Telegram helped to crystallize opinions in Washington during 1946. But decision makers such as Forrestal were already alert to implacable

Russian hostility; otherwise these busy men wouldn't have read even a 5,327-word Foreign Service cable on the subject.

18. John O'Hara, *My Turn* (New York: Random House, 1966), 46. Concerning O'Hara: Michael Forrestal, told of this years later, replied, "All very fine as far as it goes, but Father no more let O'Hara alongside him than he allowed any other friends—men friends anyway." That said, investment banker and public servant Ferdinand Eberstadt was Forrestal's one true friend, ever since Princeton. As for Michael's mother, she apparently did make such allowances. She was O'Hara's lover, says the diary of Arthur Schlesinger Jr., the historian and inveterate gossip.

19. "U.S. Too Weak to Get Tough," *Chicago Daily Tribune*, March 7, 1946, 7. Citing Republican congressmen such as Michigan's Paul Shafer.

20. Walter Millis, ed., *The Forrestal Diaries* (New York: Viking, 1951), 184.

21. Stalin to Seyid Jafar Pishavari, from *Novaiia i noveishaiia istoriia*, as referenced in Gellately, *Stalin's Curse*, 155.

22. Louis, *British Empire in the Middle East*, 88.

23. *Wall Street Journal*, October 26, 1992, A12.

24. Louis, *British Empire in the Middle East*, 193, quoting Thomas Wikeley.

25. "Palestine: An Anglo-Jewish War?," *Time*, July 1, 1946.

26. Michael J. Cohen, *Palestine to Israel: From Mandate to Independence* (London: Routledge, 1988), 177.

27. Martin Gilbert, *Churchill and the Jews: A Lifelong Friendship* (New York: Henry Holt, 2007), 245.

28. Harold Beeley minute, July 10, 1945, FO 371/45378 E 4939.

29. Martin Gilbert, *Churchill: A Life* (New York: Henry Holt, 1991), 784.

30. "Yitzhak Shamir: Why We Killed Lord Moyne," *Times of Israel*, July 5, 2012, citing Joanna Saidel, October 26, 1993, interview with Shamir.

31. *Hansard*, HC Deb., November 17, 1944, vol. 404, cols. 2242–44; also see "Churchill Warns Jews Roust Gangs," *New York Times*, November 18, 1944. In 1975, the murderers of Walter Guinness were buried in Israel in a state funeral with full military honors, despite London's protest.

32. Paul Johnson, *Modern Times: The World from the Twenties to the Eighties* (New York: HarperCollins, 1991), 482.

33. "Historian on King David Hotel Bombing: 'It Was an Act of Terror,'" *Haaretz*, July 23, 2016.

34. Tim Jones, *Postwar Counterinsurgency and the SAS, 1945–1952: A Special Type of Warfare* (London: Routledge, 2001), 121. Also see Tim Jones, *SAS: The First Secret Wars: The Unknown Years of Combat & Counter-insurgency* (London: I. B. Tauris, 2005).

35. Dr. Watts received the George Medal for his "courage and devotion to duty of the highest order." It's announced in the official *London Gazette*, August 6, 1948.

36. Clark, *From Three Worlds*, 64.

37. The role of the New York–based Bergson Group, which supplied money to Irgun and directed some operations in Palestine, is examined in Benjamin Grob-Fitzgibbon, *Imperial Endgame: Britain's Dirty Wars and the End of Empire* (London: Palgrave, 2011), 19.

38. *Hansard*, HC Deb., March 3, 1947, vol. 434, cols. 33–37.

39. Millis, *Forrestal Diaries*, 344–45.

40. Ibid., 218, 322.

41. Daily Summary, October 16, 1947, 5559 from London, Executive Secretariat, Department of State.

42. Millis, *Forrestal Diaries*, 411.

43. The amount of compensation from Hitler was discovered by Professor Bruce Hoffman, Georgetown University, as discussed on April 3, 2015, Washington, D.C.

44. Liel Leibovitz, "The Jewish State's George Washington," *Wall Street Journal*, January 30, 1951. In the two years since August 1945, the death toll of British soldiers and civilians due to Zionist terror was 169. Jewish deaths were 88, the Arab dead being 85.

45. Bohlen, *Witness to History*, 255. During Bevin's visit to France, the Ministry of the Interior supplied him with forty police guards of its own, while casting a nationwide dragnet against purported Zionist terrorists at the request of Scotland Yard.

46. John Morton Blum, ed., *Public Philosopher: Selected Letters of Walter Lippmann* (New York: Ticknor & Fields, 1985), 505.

47. Ibid., 508.

48. Secretary of State Condoleezza Rice being determined to "realign" the Middle East. Press conference, January 11, 2007.

49. *The Diaries of Sir Alexander Cadogan, 1938–1945*, ed. David Dilks (London: Cassell, 1971), 633.

4. FALSE STARTS

1. Efforts to diminish Marshall, such as *George Marshall: A Biography* (2014), by Debi and Irwin Ungar, prove inept, as they dispute even whether he was a Virginian. See my review essay in *On Point: The Journal of Army History* (Spring 2015). Marshall was born in Uniontown, Pennsylvania. His father, George senior, had roots in Virginia, as well as in Kentucky, but raised his family in Pennsylvania coal country.

2. John Balfour to Nevile Butler, January 31, 1947, FO 371/61045.

3. Ibid.

4. General Hardy to Eisenhower, April 12, 1947, RG 165, U.S. Army Chief of Staff Decimal File, England, 1947.

5. Memorandum of Conversation with the British Ambassador, February 24, 1947, RG 59, Central Decimal File, 868.00/2-2447 (General Records of the Department of State).

6. The importance of the Suez Canal Zone in the origins of the Truman Doctrine is made by Peter L. Hahn in his enduring *The United States, Great Britain, and Egypt, 1945–1956* (Chapel Hill: University of North Carolina Press, 1991), 40. He criticizes historians of the time who then, as today, missed this critical point, including John Lewis Gaddis, Daniel Yergin, and Stephen Ambrose.

7. Gregory A. Fossedal, *Our Finest Hour: Will Clayton, the Marshall Plan, and the Triumph of Democracy* (Stanford, Calif.: Hoover Institution Press, 1993), 216. Churchill too spoke that winter of "the clattering down of the British Empire"—for example, on March 6, in his "Europe Unite" speech—but he was leader of the opposition and had to present the Attlee-Bevin policies as catastrophic.

8. "Foreign Relations: The Year of Decision," *Time*, January 5, 1948.

9. Joseph Jones, *The Fifteen Weeks: An Inside Account of the Genesis of the Marshall Plan* (New York: Viking, 1955), 7.

10. The foreign policy scholar Walter Russell Mead asserts "gave up" in his September 26, 2017, lecture at the Center for Strategic and International Affairs: "Presidential Role Models, FDR, Truman, and Reagan." (There was no mention that the Soviet empire, with vastly more "destruction at home," didn't give up.)

11. Minute by Sir Nevile Butler, March 5, 1947. Having served as minister at the British embassy in Washington right before the war, Butler at this point was an assistant undersecretary at the Foreign Office.

12. Synder's title was executive vice president of the Reconstruction Finance Corporation and director of the DPC—which mean hands-on leadership. To this end, see Carl Spaatz, commanding general, U.S. Army Air Forces, letter to John Snyder, May 19, 1947, box 92, folder "S," John W. Snyder Papers, HSTL.

13. "Steadfast" is from Robert Lovett's letter to John Snyder, January 8, 1949, box 92, folder "L," John W. Snyder Papers, HSTL. During my year as a Smithsonian Fellow, I assisted Forrest Pogue, George Marshall's official biographer. We spoke often of the notoriously aloof Marshall's views on friendship. Snyder was Marshall's peer, whereas Acheson, Lovett, Eisenhower, and nearly everyone else were subordinates. Marshall could have a deep-seated capacity for friendship that, in Snyder's case, included sending him birthday cakes, going on spontaneous fishing trips, and so on. This occurred with none of the others. In letters to Snyder, General Marshall refers to Mrs. Marshall as "Katherine," a familiarity otherwise unknown.

14. On "the first modern Treasury secretary," consider: twenty-five times the number of public debt securities were issued in 1946 than in 1940; tax returns had jumped from 19 to 81 million; and the Treasury was suddenly writing hundreds of millions of checks (all by hand). Then the numbers grew larger. At the same time, the Treasury's founding statutes remained in place, which preserved the autonomy of huge operating functions like tax collection (and deep-going political patronage at the IRS). All of that changed with Snyder. On "economic reins," see Cabell Phillips, "The Man Who Holds Our Economic Reins," *New York Times*, September 23, 1945, 13.

15. President Harry S. Truman's Address Before a Joint Session of Congress, March 12, 1947, Yale Law School, the Avalon Project: Documents in Law, History, Diplomacy.

16. Jones, *Fifteen Weeks*, 19.

17. Sir Maberly Esler Dening, March 26, 1947, FO 371/67582A UN 2001/1754/78.

18. On September 22, 1947, Andrei Zhdanov, third secretary of the Communist Party of the Soviet Union, attacked the United States during a key speech in Poland. See http://soviethistory.msu.edu/1947-2/cold-war/cold-war-texts/zhdanov-on-the-international-situation/.

19. "The Nations: Rustle of History," *Time*, March 10, 1947.

20. American Department, February 18, 1947, FO 371/61053.

21. Louis, *British Empire in the Middle East*, 100, as to whether Bevin was "sincere" about leaving Greece. Careful historians who specialize in postwar Britain and the Middle East, such as Professor Louis, have posed the question in contrast to taking this episode at face value.

22. Britain's defense budget even rose in 1947, following cuts in 1946 because of demobilization.

23. British training of the Greek National Army in irregular warfare went uninterrupted during 1947, as Bevin escalated the British presence with more "commando deep patrolling," offensive operations, and maximum use of airpower. Additional evidence for what actually occurred in Greece between Bevin and the Americans, with an emphasis on intensified British counterinsurgency until the end of the civil war period, can be found in Eleftheria Delaporta, *The Role of Britain in Greek Politics and Military Operations, 1947–1952* (University of Glasgow, Department of History, Ph.D. thesis, 2003).

24. Undated memo, August 1947, RG 218 Leahy Files, No. 36, box 7 (Records of the Joint Chiefs of Staff).

25. Stephen Dorril, *MI6: Inside the Covert World of Her Majesty's Secret Intelligence Service* (New York: Simon & Schuster, 2000), 325.

26. FO 371/70194 WL 157/457/50G, January 15, 1948.

27. "Terminate" is from Hal Brands, *What Good Is Grand Strategy?: Power and Purpose in American Statecraft from Harry S. Truman to George W. Bush* (Ithaca: Cornell University Press, 2014), 23; "withdraw from the eastern Mediterranean" is Melvyn Leffler, *For the Soul of Mankind: The United States, the Soviet Union, and the Cold War* (New York: Hill & Wang, 2008), 61. In Bret Stephens, *America in Retreat*, 24, 26, America, as "world policeman," would "fill the vacuum" of a world that Stephens thinks had been policed by Britain. But that had never occurred either. See my Conclusion below, note 25.

28. The license plate story was told to me by Sir Michael Palliser, at Harvard University in October 1982. He led the Diplomatic Service as permanent undersecretary (1975–1982), and Greece was his first post when he joined the FO in 1947. Then he added, "I've spent my whole career turning things over to the Americans."

29. Robert Paul Browder and Thomas G. Smith, *Independent: A Biography of Lewis W. Douglas* (New York: Knopf, 1986), 152.

30. "Vacuum to Fill," *New Republic*, March 10, 1947, 11.

31. Cover story, *Time*, December 1, 1948.

32. NUM annual conference, July 7, 1947, FO 371/68944.

33. *Hansard*, HC Deb., March 13, 1947, vol. 434, col. 482, Dog Racing restrictions.

34. FO 371/61046, March 28, 1947.

35. "Bevan's Memory Lives in Home Town," http://news.bbc.co.uk/2/hi/uk_news/wales/south_east/7471740.stm.

36. "Great Britain: Deep in the Heart," *Time*, July 19, 1948. Nye Bevan's full position was minister of health and housing.

37. Joseph Alsop and Stewart Alsop, *The Reporter's Trade* (New York: Reynal, 1958), 85.

38. Daily Summary, September 13, 1947, Executive Secretariat, Department of State.

39. Strong evidence for these dispositions can be found in the John Osborne Papers, Library of Congress, given his extensive reporting from throughout Britain during these years. Also see Clark, *From Three Worlds*, 54.

40. Paul M. Kennedy writes of those "brilliant minds" in "Plotting a New Course for the West," *Wall Street Journal*, Books, February 10–11, 2018, C5. Crafting of the Marshall Plan is addressed in George F. Kennan, *Memoirs, 1925–1950* (Boston: Atlantic Monthly Press, 1967), 335. In chapter 14, Kennan writes of his planning paper that went into Marshall's speech, and of the accolades he reaped. There is no mention of the U.S. Treasury Department, even though Treasury had already become more involved in international affairs than ever before in the nation's history.

41. Arthur Krock, "New Truman Nominees Classed as 'Sound' Men," *New York Times*, June 9, 1946, 3.

42. "Snyder Says U.S. Didn't Ask Aid Bids," *New York Times*, June 26, 1947, 2.

43. After much discussion, Secretary of State Marshall agreed with his friend Snyder, as well as with key members of Congress, that operating the European recovery program within State "would be inadvisable for very serious reasons." See Marshall to Lovett, cable, December 21, 1947, in *The Papers of George Catlett Marshall*, vol. 6, *"The Whole World Hangs in the Balance,"* ed. Larry I. Bland et al. (Baltimore: Johns Hopkins University Press, 2013), 278.

44. Hall-Patch, oral history interview, June 8, 1963, HSTL.

45. RG 59, 861.00/2-2246: Telegram. See part 2, paragraph 5.

46. In 1946, the 44.4 percent of college-educated males who read *Life* would have been about 4 percent of the nation's population.

47. George Kennan, "The Sources of Soviet Conduct," *Foreign Affairs*, July 1947.

48. See Gaddis, *Strategies of Containment*, ix; and Tim Kaine, "A New Truman Doctrine: Grand Strategy in a Hyperconnected World," *Foreign Affairs*, July/August 2017, 38–39.

49. *Hearings Before a Special Committee Investigating the National Defense Program*, U.S. Senate, 80th Congress, pt. 40, Aircraft Contracts (Washington, D.C.: U.S. GPO, 1947), 24114.

50. Staff meeting, June 1947, RG 59, Policy Planning Staff (SP).

51. In mid-1947, some ten million people were filling in their football pools coupons each week, but no evidence exists for nearly half a million "making a living" from this. Kennan's figure about accountants and clerks in dog racing is equally implausible. The historian David Kynaston, author of *Austerity Britain, 1945–1951*, is a definitive source on these questions, and he shared his skepticism with me.

52. Browder and Smith, *Independent*, 257.

53. Memorandum for the President, August 1, 1947, "Reported Impending Dollar Crisis," PSF, HSTL.

54. U.K. Alphabetical File, August 18, 1947, British Financial Delegation with the National Advisory Council, Snyder Papers, HSTL. During the previous month, the Bank of England had lost almost a billion dollars from its dwindling reserves.

55. First Meeting of the British Delegation with the National Advisory Council, U.K. Alphabetical File, Snyder Papers, HSTL.

56. Crowther's pen often outran his thoughts. Harriman, Lovett, and Forrestal, as well as President Truman, were all incensed by this editorial and read it as essentially an official statement from Whitehall. When called to account in Grosvenor Square, Crowther explained to Ambassador Douglas that his editorial had been written one morning between midnight and three when he had been suffering a bilious attack. See RG 59 from Douglas, September 16, 1947, 711.41/9–1347.

57. Bullock, *Ernest Bevin*, citing Pierson Dixon, 462.

58. Britain at month's end signed the General Agreement on Trade and Tariffs with twenty-three nations in Geneva, but face-saving provisions left generous room for continued protectionism.

59. Congressional Record, November 12, 1947, Hearing, Interim Aid for Europe, November 10–14, 110; Averell Harriman, oral history, HSTL. In contrast to Douglas's testimony, and to all other evidence, today's conventional wisdom is that "the Truman team" was busily ensuring that "American power and diplomacy would replace the British" and would "manage the global economy and the emerging post-colonial world." See Walter Russell Mead, "What Truman Can Teach Trump," *Wall Street Journal*, July 21, 2017.

60. For example, Arthur Schlesinger Jr. interviewed Harriman for a profile in *Reader's Digest*. Harriman thought it only fair that the professor hand over half his writing fee from the *Digest*, because, said Harriman, he had been the one who had been interviewed. See Arthur Schlesinger Jr., *Journals, 1952–2000* (New York: Penguin, 2007), 518.

61. Congressional Record, November 12, 1947, Hearing, Interim Aid for Europe.

62. "Mr. Snyder in London," *Economist*, September 13, 1947. Smack before the financial crisis negotiations in Washington, Treasury Secretary Snyder and his friend Will Clayton of the State Department were in London on IMF/World Bank business. They directly got important insights on the crisis.

5. WARFARE STATES

1. The negotiator was Sir Wilfred Eady, who was then joint second secretary at the Treasury. See "British Import Duty, 1947–1948," http://www.terramedia.co.uk/reference/law.

2. Paul M. Kennedy asserts "abandonment" in *The Rise and Fall of British Naval Mastery* (Amherst, N.Y.: Humanity Books, 1998), 326. In *The Marshall Plan: Dawn of the Cold War*, Benn Steil writes that Palestine and India show "one pillar after another of Britain's imperial power came crashing down," 9. Many other historians write of "retreat" and "appeasement" in India, or of outright "surrender." However, anyone at the time who thought about India for more than ten seconds could realize that trying to keep its population subjugated—which meant, at best, using British troops to defend the ports—would have invited colossal violence. That came anyway, though directed within.

3. Henderson, *Inside the Private Office*, 28.

4. David Edgerton, *Warfare State: Britain, 1920–1970* (Cambridge, U.K.: Cambridge University Press, 2006), 101.

5. "Sentiments Toward Britain," September 5, 1947, FO 371/61050, AN 3124/28/45.

6. A fine study is Jeffrey A. Engel, *Cold War at 30,000 Feet: The Anglo-American Fight for Aviation Supremacy* (Cambridge, Mass.: Harvard University Press, 2007). But these details of gold, cabinet decision making, the May Day discovery, and other events are new.

7. FO 371/65658, May 22, 1947. This was said by Thomas Brimelow, a young Russia expert who'd spent three years in Moscow during the war and had dealt with Stalin. He became head of the Diplomatic Service in 1973.

8. Ibid.

9. Engel, *Cold War at 30,000 Feet*; "far-reaching" is on p. 83.

10. Michael Vincent Forrestal was on active duty from March 1946 to September 1947 with service as the assistant naval attaché in Moscow. He had learned basic Russian at the navy's language school in Boulder, Colorado, but was also trained at the new Naval Intelligence School in Anacostia, Washington, D.C., established by his father. The Kremlin knew America's *nomenclatura* as well as its own, and Michael received travel privileges outside the Russian capital offered to no one else on the embassy staff. I've accessed Michael Forrestal's military records via a FOIA request from the National Personnel Records Center. Additional details come from our conversations in the 1970s. Father and son otherwise had a difficult relationship.

11. General Eisenhower was astonished in 1945 to learn that Red Army divisions could have just eight thousand soldiers or fewer; his counterpart, Marshal Zhukov, was equally surprised that U.S. divisions were maintained at seventeen thousand. Divisional strength is usually around twenty thousand soldiers. But many Red Army divisions in this period were undermanned or merely shells.

12. Britain was spending 7 percent of the world's second-largest advanced GDP on defense, a greater share of national income proportionately than were the Americans.

13. RG 319, P&O 092 TS Section X Cases 151–167 (Records of the U.S. Army Staff). Also see Memorandum for General Spaatz, July 6, 1946, Office of the Military Attaché, American Embassy, London. It's been known that America's navy and air forces had begun war preparations to counter Stalin's threat to Turkey; what's new is discovering the extent of Britain's cooperation to take that U.S. effort nuclear.

14. British and Canadian scientists got booted from U.S. laboratories, and their security clearances were pulled. America by now had an advantage in R&D of about six years. Britain's mastery of the atom, as in the hands of the physicists William Penney, Henry Tizard, and J. D. Cockcroft, was no longer needed. I am grateful to the distinguished historian Graham Farmelo, author of *Churchill's Bomb: How the United States Overtook Britain in the First Nuclear Arms Race* (New York: Basic Books, 2013), for sharing documentation from Christopher Hinton, who from 1954 to 1957 was managing director in the industrial group of Britain's Atomic Energy Authority.

15. Minutes of the Meeting of the American Members of the Combined Policy Committee with the Chairman of the Joint Committee on Atomic Energy and the Chairman of the Senate Foreign Relations Committee, Washington, November 26, 1947, in *FRUS, 1947: General: The United Nations, Volume I*.

16. June 4, 1947, COS (47) 70 DEFE 4/4.

17. Millis, *Forrestal Diaries*, 196.

18. Admiral Richard Conolly, Oral History Research Office, Columbia University, 1960.

19. *From Pearl Harbor to Vietnam: The Memoirs of Admiral Arthur W. Radford*, ed. Stephen Jurika (Stanford, Calif.: Hoover Institution Press, 1980), 130.

20. Fisher Howe, Executive Officer, OSS London 1941–45, interviewed October 8, 1980, Kennedy Archive. Between 1978 and 1981, Victoria Kennedy, initially a RAND Corporation analyst and later with the U.S. Naval War College, conducted in-depth interviews of nearly every key figure among the CIA's founding generation. She also interviewed officials who had unusual insights on these men, such as Eleanor Lansing Dulles, Gordon Gray, and Andrew Goodpaster. Transcripts

are privately held and haven't previously been open. I'm grateful to Ms. Kennedy for allowing me complete access.

21. Vice Admiral William R. Smedberg III, 1944–1946, oral history, USNI, 317–18.

22. James Jesus Angleton, first interview, September 28, 1978, Kennedy Archive. Organizationally, the CIA's tie to the State Department, through its covert action Office of Policy Coordination, was intended to replicate what the Americans believed to be British practice. This approach would make it easier to use "diplomatic passports as cover," said Angleton, just as they assumed MI6 and the Foreign Office were doing.

23. David Fromkin, "Daring Amateurism," *Foreign Affairs*, January/February 1996, 171.

24. John Kenneth Knaus, *Orphans of the Cold War: America and the Tibetan Struggle for Survival* (New York: Public Affairs, 1999), 157, on Kennan; Howard Roman, interview, September 9, 1978, Kennedy Archive: "Many of the OPC early operations were stupid." Such operations included parachuting Ukrainian partisans into their homeland—only to be immediately captured and executed by the NKVD. The first mission occurred in September 1949, and by 1950 the CIA was coordinating them with the British. See Kevin Ruffner, "Cold War Allies: The Origins of CIA's Relationship with Ukrainian Nationalists," *Studies in Intelligence* (1998), declassified 2008. Also see my analysis of these missions in *To Dare and to Conquer: Special Operations and the Destiny of Nations, from Achilles to Al Qaeda* (New York: Little, Brown, 2006), 505–6.

25. "Emergence of the Intelligence Establishment," doc. 292, NSC 10/2, June 18, 1948, in *FRUS, 1945–50: Emergence of the Intelligence Establishment*, 714. Kennan's personal irresponsibility is well chronicled in Sara-Jane Corke, "George Kennan and the Inauguration of Political Warfare," *Journal of Conflict Studies* 26, no. 1 (2006).

26. Keith Jeffery, *The Secret History of MI6, 1909–1949* (New York: Penguin, 2010), 704.

27. Sir George Sansom, "American Policy in Japan," lecture, July 1947, Royal Institute of International Affairs (Chatham House).

28. September 13, 1947, CAB 131/4, OD (47) 67.

29. Killearn to Sargent, June 11, 1946, FO 371/3565 F 16334/25/10.

30. FO 371/67543 UN 1106/86/78G, February 18, 1947.

31. Walter Lippmann, *U.S. Foreign Policy: Shield of the Republic* (Boston: Little, Brown, 1943), 9. In his book, Lippmann places this definition in bold.

32. One of the best analyses of the Malayan conflict, including its casualties, remains R. W. Komer, *The Malayan Emergency in Retrospect: Organization of a Successful Counterinsurgency Effort* (Santa Monica, Calif.: Rand, 1972). I spoke with Komer extensively, when he was undersecretary of defense in the Carter administration, about what he saw as parallels between Malaya and Vietnam.

33. FO 371/76033 F 4545/1073/G1G, March 23, 1949, to Bevin.

34. Daily Summary, March 31, 1949, FE 281 from Bangkok, Executive Secretariat, Department of State.

35. For example, there's no mention at all of Malcolm MacDonald in Fredrik Logevall's 837-page *Embers of War: The Fall of an Empire and the Making of America's Vietnam*. Mark Atwood Lawrence's *Assuming the Burden: Europe and the American*

Commitment to Vietnam is a rare exception in weighing MacDonald's influence, but he ends the story in 1950, which is the point where MacDonald becomes decisive to the making of America's Vietnam.

36. What I'm showing is the opposite of the argument of "mental maps" posited by Aiyaz Husain in *Mapping the End of Empire* (Cambridge, Mass.: Harvard University Press, 2014). He contends that British policy makers, which would include Bevin, looked at issues narrowly as they "ended" the empire. Nor was there a "British Empire willingly in retreat" circa 1947–1948, 130.

37. *FRUS, 1947: The Near East and Africa, Volume V,* November 24, 1947, doc. 401, 575.

38. FO 371/68041 AN 70/45/G, December 29, 1947, Sir Michael Wright.

39. January 6, 1948, JP (48) 4, DEFE 4/10.

40. FO 371/68014 AN 517/45456, January 18, 1948.

41. Bullock, *Ernest Bevin*, 673.

42. RG 84, London Post Files, 800 Britain, January 20, 1948.

43. RG 330, to Forrestal, CD 27-1-12, August 10, 1948 (Office of the Secretary of Defense).

44. Browder and Smith, *Independent*, 306.

45. "Cut and ran" is from Ferguson, *Empire*, 297. (Just twenty pages of this book concern events after 1945.) "Loss of Palestine" is posited in John Charmley, *Churchill's Grand Alliance* (New York: Harcourt Brace, 1995), 311.

46. RG 218, to Forrest Sherman 57, Leahy File, May 31, 1948.

47. The Ambassador in the United Kingdom (Douglas) to the Secretary of State, May 25, 1948, in *FRUS, 1948: The Near East, South Asia, and Africa, Volume V, Part 2.*

48. Bullock, *Ernest Bevin*, 647.

49. Browder and Smith, *Independent*, 304. Marshall told Truman that recognizing Israel, in the way it occurred, was risking America's security for election-year votes.

50. Avi Shlaim, "Israel and the Arab Coalition in 1948," in Shlaim and Eugene Rogan, eds., *The War for Palestine: Rewriting the Israeli-Palestine Conflict of 1948* (Cambridge, U.K.: Cambridge University Press, 2001), 81.

51. Debates over these stereotypes of Arabic-speaking Foreign Service officers have long been disappointing. See William Quandt's *Foreign Affairs*, December 1993, review essay in which Quandt criticizes writers such as Robert D. Kaplan— author of *Arabists* (1993), which propagates the myth of a New England WASP elite—for not getting the names straight of such supposed "Arabists." The diplomat Richard Holbrooke claimed when writing of these events—without evidence and naming no one—that there was "real anti-Semitism on the part of some (but not all) policymakers of the time." *Washington Post*, May 7, 2008. That insinuates George Marshall, among others, who also has been called an anti-Semite for his policy disputes with Zionism. See Mark Perry, "Petraeus Wasn't the First," *Foreign Policy*, April 2, 2010.

52. Forrestal was smeared by the gossip commentator Walter Winchell, who had the country's top-rated radio show, and by the muckraking columnist Drew Pearson, among others. Pearson also claimed Truman to have said New York Jews were "disloyal" to the United States. See his column, *Washington Post*, March 12, 1948. As for Bevin, his biographer Lord Bullock shows the emptiness of such accusations, though

they continue—and the same discredited sources are repeated, such as charges by the U.S. ambassador to Israel James MacDonald, who, foolishly, also charged Bevin with being anti-American. The controversy gets sillier when the historian Andrew Roberts lauds a book on this era as "impeccably academic" and brilliantly researched, yet chides its author for not documenting Bevin's "personal anti-Semitism." It might have occurred to Roberts that there wasn't evidence to be documented. See Andrew Roberts, review of *Mapping the End of Empire*, by Aiyaz Husain, *Wall Street Journal*, April 18, 2014.

53. This number was according to the UN Conciliation Commission and is used by Louis in his definitive *British Empire in the Middle East*, 575.

54. Lovett to President, September [no day], 1948, White House Signals Detachment.

55. The decision to murder Bernadotte on September 17 was made by the Stern Gang's Central Committee, in which Yitzhak Shamir, the former commander and future Israeli prime minister, participated. It's a role never disavowed or prosecuted. See Kati Marton, *A Death in Jerusalem: The Assassination by Jewish Extremists of the First Arab/Israeli Peacemaker* (New York: Pantheon, 1994).

56. Bullock, *Ernest Bevin*, 649.

57. The Acting Secretary of State to the Special Representative of the United States in Israel (McDonald), December 30, 1948, in *FRUS, 1948: The Near East, South Asia, and Africa, Volume V, Part 2*. The Americans realized, as James Forrestal wrote in his diary on the thirty-first, that "the failure of the Israelis to withdraw promptly would automatically bring into operation the Anglo-Egyptian mutual defense pact."

58. McDonald is quoted in "Reveal 1948 British War Threat to Israel," *Chicago Sunday Tribune*, February 16, 1957, 7.

59. FO 371/68360 E 14869/11/91, September 11, 1948.

60. FO 371/38360 E 14291/12869/G, November 8, 1948.

61. Charles Dalrymple Belgrave, *Personal Column* (London: Hutchinson, 1960). My description of his "double-breasted suit" is known from the photographs of Belgrave during that era.

6. YEAR OF THE OFFENSIVE

1. Department of State, Daily Press Summary, January 23, 1948, citing the previous day's commentary by Richard C. Hottelett, CBS.

2. Robert A. Lovett, oral history interview, HSTL.

3. Rob Watson, interview, *Here and Now*, NPR, May 28, 2015.

4. "Dulles Urges German Pact," *New York Times*, January 18, 1947, 1. Dulles was speaking to the National Publishers Association.

5. Walter Russell Mead, "Europe Needs Its Realist Past," *Wall Street Journal*, September 30, 2016.

6. *Hansard*, HC Deb., January 22, 1948, vol. 446, cols. 383–517.

7. For example, see Churchill's speech of September 17, 1946, at the University of Zurich, http://www.cfr.org/europe/churchills-united-states-europe-speech-zurich /p32536.

8. Speech of September 22, 1947, "Report on the International Situation to the Cominform." See http://www.csun.edu/~twd61312/342%202014/Zhdanov.pdf.

9. The 1948 outrage was revisited during the Prague Spring of 1968. The best account in English followed, which is Claire Sterling's *Masaryk Case* (1969), with extensive interviews. Also see *Life* magazine's book review of her work by the British spy novelist Eric Ambler, "Investigating the Masaryk Mystery," January 23, 1970, 16. Finally, during 2009 in Prague, the police investigator Ilja Pravda "solved" the case by confirming the murder but was unable to identify the killers.

10. Believing "Marshall was unmoved" is Steil, *Marshall Plan*, 299. Instead, the nationwide reaction to Marshall's high-profile response can be seen, for example, in "Marshall Says Soviets Follow Methods of Nazis," *Hopkinsville Kentucky New Era*, March 19, 1948, 1.

11. Daily Log Sheet, March 4, 1948, to Henry Cabot Lodge Jr., Lovett Papers, New-York Historical Society.

12. Herbert Morrison speech, March 14, 1948, CFR archives.

13. "You see, you haven't got what I have—a memory of the red coats," Senator Gerry told Felix Frankfurter, a fervent supporter of Britain, in 1940 at a Norwegian embassy dinner. See Harlan Phillips, *Felix Frankfurter Reminisces* (New York: Reynal, 1960), 276.

14. Lovett, oral history, HSTL.

15. I recall this from one of my many conversations with Michael Forrestal during the 1970s. Lovett's only frailty, and it seemed a small one to his friends such as Michael, was hypochondria, the one neurosis Freud said might be forever incurable.

16. Doc. 271, October 21–22, 1949, in *FRUS, 1949: Western Europe, Volume IV*.

17. Lippmann to J. William Fulbright, March 11, 1949, in Blum, *Public Philosopher*, 534.

18. "The Papers of R. G. W. Mackay, Group 7, Til 2, Deposited at the London School of Economics and Political Science," as cited in Avi Shlaim, Peter Jones, and Keith Sainsbury, *British Foreign Secretaries Since 1945* (London: David & Charles, 1977), 48.

19. FO 371/69927 F 8227/6139/G, June 10, 1948.

20. Walter Lippmann, "Today and Tomorrow," *Washington Post*, February 11, 1947.

21. Blum, *Public Philosopher*, May 20, 1948, letter to Robert Strausz-Hupe, 512. In September 1948, Barbara Ward, foreign editor of *The Economist*, would publish *The West at Bay*, which discussed the United States as Britain's successor. But this is not a serious "study," as Lippmann envisioned, with Ward's key point being the need for a supreme European effort toward Western union.

22. It was George Kennan who, in Washington, was pressing hardest for a disarmed and neutralized united German state. See my analysis in *Fifty-Year Wound*, 36–38. For a book reviewer to still take seriously Stalin's proposal "that Germany be unified as long as it became a neutral state" is to place an astounding amount of faith in the better angels of Stalin's nature. Ditto to argue, as does Odd Arne Westad, that Stalin would have been mollified "if more attempts had been made by the stronger power [the U.S.] to entice Moscow toward forms of cooperation." See Jonathan Steele, "Who Started It?," a review of Westad's *The Cold War: A World History*, *London Review of Books*, January 25, 2018, 27. In fact, Bevin tried mollifying Stalin in 1946, and Bevin and Marshall tried it again in 1947.

23. Moscow, of course, had many excuses for the blockade. They ranged from serious ones, like opposing the formation of a West German government, to ridiculous effrontery, as in saying that roads and train tracks needed repair.

24. Oliver Franks, oral history, HSTL.

25. Jean Edward Smith, *Lucius D. Clay: An American Life* (New York: Henry Holt, 1992), 495.

26. Attlee and Bevin agreed, however, that in an emergency General Robertson could withdraw to the Rhine, and the RAF prepared two airfields in the Netherlands to provide cover. On the JCS refusal, see Memorandum for the Record, Berlin Airlift, July 8, 1948, RG 218.

27. *Hansard*, HC, 1802–2005, GERMANY, Ernest Bevin, June 30, 1948.

28. Smith, *Lucius D. Clay*, 495.

29. Ibid., 507.

30. July 29, 1948, DO (48) 49, and "State of the Armed Forces," DEFE 4/16.

31. "4 Western Soldiers in Berlin Flee Soviet Jail," *New York Times*, September 17, 1949, 1.

32. Millis, entry for July 2, 1948, in *Forrestal Diaries*, 455; and also see Memorandum from Symington to Forrestal, CD 6-2-9, June 25, 1948, RG 330. See Stephen Twigge and Len Scott, *Planning Armageddon: Britain, the United States, and the Command of Western Nuclear Forces* (Amsterdam: Harwood Academic, 2000), 31, for asking Bevin.

33. Henry Kissinger, "Reflections on a Partnership," *International Affairs*, Autumn 1982, 575.

34. I'm grateful to two excellent military historians for helping me to document the story of Sergeant Paul Shimer. They are Matt Seelinger, chief historian of the Army Historical Foundation, and Tim Stoy, historian of the army's 15th Infantry Division.

35. Germany's tranquillity at the time is contrary to tales in our own day when, in 2004–2006, the U.S. secretary of defense, Donald Rumsfeld, and his staff compared Iraq's insurgency to an entirely mythical guerrilla resistance that they claimed Nazi diehards had staged in Germany after World War II. See my analysis of their *Werwolfkommando* fantasies in *Magic and Mayhem* (New York: Simon & Schuster, 2010), 212–13, 313–14.

36. Irwin Wall, *The United States and the Making of Postwar France* (Cambridge, U.K.: Cambridge University Press, 1991), 139.

37. Drew Middleton, *The Defense of Western Europe* (New York: Appleton-Century-Crofts, 1952), 311.

38. Kilber to Wedemeyer, European WU July/October 1948, October 4, 1948, RG 218.

39. Forrestal meeting with Alexander and the COS, November 13, 1948, PSF, HSTL.

40. Oliver Franks, oral history, HSTL.

41. See both Lovett to Douglas, April 14, 1948, RG 59, 840.00/4-1348, and Bevin to Inverchapel, April 15, 1948, FO 371/68068A AN 1618/1195/G.

42. RG 319 Army Acting Director of Intelligence, P&O TS Section XIII, October 21, 1948.

43. RG 319 P&O 381 TS Section X, August 24, 1948. For the NSC decision, see NSC 39, Proposed Directive to CINCEUR, January 24, 1949.

7. DEFENDING THE WEST

1. The *Red Star* editorial was sent to the Foreign Office by the Moscow embassy. See FO 371/77678B N/32/167138, December 25, 1948.

2. "British Produce First Supply of Rare Plutonium," *Chicago Daily Tribune*, March 7, 1949, 18.

3. See Thomas E. Ricks, *Churchill and Orwell: The Fight for Freedom* (New York: Penguin, 2017), 197. Ricks argues that these industrial vulnerabilities were already apparent, as do others who've written on Britain's economic decline, such as Professor Correlli Barnett, whom he cites. But that's not the case, and Barnett is unreliable. See David Edgerton's review essay, "Declinism," in *The London Review of Books*, March 1996, and the subsequent exchange of letters with Barnett.

4. Sir Edmund Hall-Patch, February 28, 1949, FO 371/73005.

5. Summary Record of a Meeting of United States Ambassadors at Paris, October 21–22, 1949, in *FRUS, 1949: Western Europe, Volume IV.*

6. The judgment of "most effective" is due to Acheson's ability to maintain a record of continuous proactive achievement over four years—in which world affairs would otherwise have been much worse. Another possibility, as I'll demonstrate, is Secretary of State John Foster Dulles (1953–1959). Contenders might be Secretaries Adams and Seward, but there are surprisingly few effective secretaries of state in U.S. history. This rarity is due in part to a constitutional structure that spotlights the president when international affairs are forefront, as with Wilson, both Roosevelts, Kennedy, Nixon, and Reagan. Then there is the odd case of Henry Kissinger. Theodore Draper, the preeminent freelance social critic of the last fifty years, knew Kissinger since they were GIs together in World War II. He sensibly observed that Kissinger will likely belong to the history of publicity rather than to the history of diplomacy. For details, see Leebaert, *Magic and Mayhem*, 117–25.

7. Fredrik Logevall, on "Anglophile of the first order," in *Embers of War*, 218. He also believes that Acheson wore "Savile Row suits." Also see Jeffrey Hart, "The WASP Gentleman as Cultural Ideal," *New Criterion*, January 1989. In *The Wise Men: Six Friends and the World They Made* (1986), Evan Thomas and Walter Isaacson assume Acheson to be a "lifelong Anglophile" (51). There are many other examples. More careful discussions of Acheson are those by James Chace, *Acheson: The Secretary of State Who Created the American World* (New York: Simon & Schuster, 1998), and Robert L. Beisner, *Dean Acheson: Life in the Cold War* (New York: Oxford University Press, 2006). Beisner concludes that calling Acheson an "Anglophile [is] laughable" (162).

8. "Dean Acheson: An Antithesis to 'Common Man,'" *Montreal Gazette*, April 21, 1958, 23.

9. Henry Kissinger, "Cold Warrior," *New York Times Book Review*, October 15, 2006. Moreover, Acheson hadn't been to Britain for eleven years by the end of World War II, and he had no time for tailoring when he did appear in London.

10. The Reverend Edward Campion Acheson did not rise to suffragan bishop of the Episcopal Diocese of Connecticut until the year his son graduated from Yale.

11. Evelyn Shuckburgh, diary entry for November 22, 1952, in *Descent to Suez: Foreign Office Diaries, 1951–1956* (New York: Norton, 1986), 57.

12. Dean Acheson, *Present at the Creation: My Years in the State Department* (New York: Norton, 1969), 387.

13. As the son of an immigrant, Acheson behaved as would have been predicted by Marcus Hansen, the historian of immigration. Children of immigrants, it's argued, tend to turn their backs on the lands from which a parent has fled, in this case England. See my analysis of the theory in *Magic and Mayhem*, 152–53. Predictably, Acheson's disdain also included Canada, to which his father had immigrated and then had left. See Robert Fulford, "Explaining Dean Acheson," *National Post* (Toronto), November 25, 2006.

14. On pages 9–10 of his partial autobiography, Acheson bends over backward to avoid saying his father, whom he notes was a subject of the queen-empress before becoming a U.S. citizen, was in fact born in England; his "coming to Canada" seems to have been as if he had arrived from Mars. Dean Acheson, *Morning and Noon: A Memoir* (Boston: Houghton Mifflin, 1965).

15. Leslie A. Fiedler, *The Collected Essays of Leslie Fiedler* (New York: Stein & Day, 1971), 77.

16. Beisner, *Dean Acheson*, 43.

17. Tom Wolfe, *The Purple Decades: A Reader* (New York: Farrar, Straus and Giroux, 1982). See Dean Acheson's appearance in the first essay, "Bob & Spike." By this time, his curiosity in painting had expanded far beyond his wife Alice's landscapes.

18. Thomas Finletter conversation with *Harper's* magazine editor Timothy Dickinson, Down Town Association, New York City, 1976, as recalled to the author in 2016.

19. W. S. "Lefty" Lewis was a close friend of Acheson's and a colleague on the Yale Corporation. He told the story of Acheson's drunken abuse at Frankfurter's birthday party to Timothy Dickinson at Lewis's residence in Farmington, Connecticut, during 1975, as recalled to the author in 2016.

20. Edward Burling shared his recollection with the law student John Price in December 1962, emphasizing "by the belt loops." Price would be a White House domestic policy staffer and later CEO of the Federal Home Loan Bank of Pittsburgh. We've smiled about this story for years.

21. Arthur Schlesinger Jr., *A Life in the 20th Century: Innocent Beginnings, 1917–1950* (New York: Houghton Mifflin, 2000), 475. Schlesinger is recalling a conversation with Nye Bevan of late September 1948.

22. FO 371/79228 R 1843/1072/67G, February 14, 1949.

23. MIT's invitation was initiated through Baruch, who told the institute's president, the physicist Karl Compton, that Churchill was planning to visit New York in the early spring of 1949. Compton then wrote Churchill that MIT would cover his expenses. Additionally, $1,000 was transferred to Churchill's New York bank account, and further correspondence shows that MIT paid for larger accommodations than expected at the Ritz-Carlton hotel for Churchill's expanded party of family and staff. Records of John E. Burchard, AC.0020, box 2, folder 86, Office of the Dean, School of Humanities and Social Science, MIT.

24. Previously, Churchill had written to Dulles, whom all had expected to be Thomas Dewey's secretary of state, of his own experience with bipartisanship: "It is a great pity that His Majesty's present Government fall so far below American stan-

dards in this respect." Churchill to John Foster Dulles, December 12, 1948, General File, Churchill 1945–1950, HSTL.

25. Churchill Archives Centre, Cambridge University (CHUR 2/162/124).

26. "Bevin Says World Must Find Permanent Peace," *New York Times*, April 2, 1949, 1.

27. "Addresses by President and Foreign Ministers," *New York Times*, April 5, 1949, 6.

28. Winston Churchill Address, MIT Mid-century Convocation, March 31, 1949, https://libraries.mit.edu/archives/exhibits/midcentury/mid-cent-churchill.html.

29. Truman to Bevin, April 16, 1949, PSF, HSTL.

30. Macmillan, *Tides of Fortune*, 128.

31. "Big 4 Meet: Agenda Holds Problems," Associated Press, May 19, 1949.

32. An example of "uninformed writers" is Eric Bennett, a professor of English, who, in 2016, concluded Forrestal to be "as paranoid as the cold war he helps to start." See *New York Times Book Review*, April 29, 2016, 20.

33. George Kennan Diaries, August 23, 1949, describing a conversation that day with Webb, Seeley Mudd Library, Princeton University.

34. First interview with James J. Angleton, Kennedy Archive, September 28, 1978, 16. According to Angleton, Acheson didn't get along with CIA director Roscoe Hillenkoetter, another admiral, and Acheson tried to cut off Hillenkoetter from reporting directly to Truman. Acheson was then compelled to back down and apologize to Hillenkoetter, who had complained to Truman.

35. John Wesley Snyder and Dean Acheson, foreword to *Concerns of a Conservative Democrat*, by Charles Sawyer (Carbondale: Southern Illinois University Press, 1968), v. Sawyer, a former Ohio lieutenant governor, who succeeded Harriman as secretary of commerce.

36. Robert A. Taft, *A Foreign Policy for Americans* (New York: Cowles, 1951), 101.

37. Jenner is found in Congressional Record, Congress Session 81–1, March 28, 1949, and Langer is Congressional Record of March 1, 1949.

38. Speech on the North Atlantic Treaty, July 26, 1949, http://teachingamerican history.org/library/document/speech-on-the-north-atlantic-treaty/.

39. Henry Kissinger, "The Man Who Saved Europe Last Time," *Wall Street Journal*, April 29–30, 2017.

40. Sawyer, *Concerns of a Conservative Democrat*, 256.

41. "Truman Aides," *New York Times*, February 9, 1949, 1. This article concerns Leon Keyserling, vice chairman, Council of Economic Advisers, testifying to Congress.

42. Bevin to Acheson, June 22, 1949, FO 371 UE 4007/150/53G.

43. Alec Cairncross, memorandum, September 27, 1948, in Richard Clarke, *Anglo-American Economic Collaboration in War and Peace* (Oxford: Clarendon Press, 1982), 201.

44. Jebb politely disagreed when he got needled by Bevin at this early encounter. Some four hundred years earlier, he told the foreign secretary, a butcher's boy from Ipswich, one Tom Wolsey, had risen to become Henry VIII's right hand, and a cardinal too.

45. John Lewis Gaddis, *George F. Kennan: An American Life* (New York: Penguin, 2012). On "friend," see p. 360.

46. *Memoirs of Lord Gladwyn*, 227. The Foreign Office had no policy planning staff, as did the U.S. State Department. The FO's new Permanent Under Secretary's Committee was composed of line chiefs, not analysts.

47. *Kennan Diaries*, ed. Frank Costigliola (New York: Norton, 2014), 347. Kennan later considered becoming a British subject and moving his family to England, and he hoped to do so "without a backward glance" at the United States, as seen in his diary entry of January 3, 1955.

48. Department of State, Undersecretary's Meeting (UM), April 27, 1949, William Walton Butterworth. This astute forty-six-year-old professional diplomat had been a Rhodes scholar and knew the British well.

49. PPS Meeting, April 28, 1949, RG 59.

50. PPS Meeting, June 8, 1949, RG 59.

51. PPS, 101st Meeting, June 14, 1949, RG 59.

52. Ibid.

53. While in London, Kennan used the opportunity, given his intelligence role within OPC, to also meet with the Joint Intelligence Bureau in Whitehall.

54. Kennan, *Memoirs, 1925–1950*, 456.

55. Jebb had little faith in Kennan's reasoning. That's shown by his ensuing instructions to Foreign Office staff to dampen down "by the application of bromides" such interest as Kennan might have raised in an Anglo-American combination. See FO 371/76383 to Bevin, September 28, 1949.

56. Jebb, Record of Conversation, September 20, 1949, FO 371/76383.

57. Leaving aside Kennan's own press leaks, in this instance they occurred in the *Sunday Times* via Policy Planning's Dorothy Fosdick, who was romantically involved with the reporter Henry Brandon, as Jebb uncovered.

58. Jebb to Strang, September 27, 1949, FO 371/76383 W5339/G.

59. Ibid. On Bevin's anger, see FO 371/76383 W5460/G, October 1, 1949, to Hoyer-Miller.

60. Memorandum by the Secretary of State, October 19, 1949, in *FRUS, 1949: Western Europe, Volume IV*, 849; Rostow to Acheson, October 15, 1949, RG 59 841.10/10-1549.

61. Bohlen to Kennan, October 6, 1949, Bohlen Papers, Library of Congress.

62. "British Needs Tied to Trade," *New York Times*, September 8, 1949, 1.

63. Oliver Franks, oral history, HSTL.

64. "U.S., Britain, Canada Agree on Steps," *New York Times*, September 13, 1949, 1.

65. Peter Clarke's well-received and utterly incorrect *Last Thousand Days of the British Empire* has the sun setting in his last chapter, which takes us to August 1947.

66. American Opinion Report, September 5, 1949, Schuyler Foster Files, State Department.

67. "Changes in British Empire," *New York Times*, September 2, 1949, 3.

68. Oliver Franks, oral history, HSTL.

69. Acheson, *Present at the Creation*, 322.

70. Truman's request for this analysis was made on July 7, 1949, with an initial deliverable on July 21, 1949, as shown in PSF, HSTL. Citations are from "Points for the Secretary's Consideration," August 15, 1949, RG 59, Chronological File, SP.

71. "U.S. Will Sidestep Pound's Devaluing," *New York Times*, September 1, 1949, 1.

8. THE OUTER FORTRESS: PROTECTING THE MIDDLE EAST, AFRICA, AND ASIA

1. Frank Roberts, March 15, 1949, FO 371/76031 F 5517/1071/61.

2. C. L. Sulzberger, "U.S. Policy Makers Divide," *New York Times*, January 17, 1949, 2. Sulzberger's conclusions are identical to those of the CIA, as seen in ORE-2548 (Office of Reports and Estimates), "The Breakup of the Colonial Empires and Its Implications for US Security," September 3, 1948, 2, 12–13.

3. *Hansard*, HC Deb., March 18, 1949, vol. 462, cols. 2533–43.

4. Critics such as Senator Taft counted 180 million people having lived under the Kremlin's rule in 1941, when Russia seemed defeated by Hitler's Wehrmacht, and now, they said, Stalin "directed" more than 800 million subjects. See Taft, *Foreign Policy for Americans*, 8.

5. "Implications of the Sterling Area Crisis to the U.K. and the U.S.," August 18, 1949, RG 43. This emerged from a work group organized by Nitze.

6. Gaddis, *George F. Kennan*, 361. For a historian to ignore the secretary of the Treasury (which would otherwise require addressing economics and finance) also shows how stove-piped the writing of diplomatic history can be.

7. Kennan, *Memoirs, 1925–1950*, 459.

8. Kennan recorded Webb's statement in his diary for August 23, 1949. George F. Kennan Diaries, Seeley Mudd Library, Princeton University.

9. Kennan, *Memoirs, 1925–1950*, 458.

10. Otherwise, some record of "phone calls of protest" to the president from a key cabinet secretary should be found for these dates in box 9, Telephone Memoranda and Appointments List, April 1–September 30, 1949, Harry S. Truman Papers, Staff Member and Office Files, 1945–1953, HSTL.

11. Kennan, *Memoirs, 1925–1950*, 461.

12. Gaddis, *George F. Kennan*, 365.

13. Letter from Arthur Krock to John W. Snyder, August 19, 1949, John W. Snyder Papers, box 34, folder 2, "UK Dollar Crisis Meetings," September 3–11, 1949, HSTL.

14. Sproul to Snyder, August 24, 1949, Snyder Papers, Personal Correspondence, HSTL.

15. "British Needs Tied to Trade Pact," *New York Times*, September 8, 1949, 1.

16. Andrew J. Rotter, *The Path to Vietnam: Origins of the American Commitment to Southeast Asia* (Ithaca, N.Y.: Cornell University Press, 1987), 143. Rotter's deepgoing research cites Foreign Office correspondence of August 24 between Makins and Hoyar Miller on this matter.

17. General Dwight D. Eisenhower, Junior Chamber of Commerce Banquet, Topeka, Kansas, September 2, 1949, Pre-Presidential Speeches, Dwight D. Eisenhower Presidential Library (hereafter DDEPL).

18. Diary for October 2, 1949, Kenneth Younger Papers, University of Leicester. (I am grateful to his son, Sam Younger CBE, for encouraging me to explore these papers.) Cripps's purpose in devaluing was to erase the dollar deficit, get a fresh

start, and, ideally, exploit a big reserve of workforce capacity as was emerging in the steel industry.

19. "Lewiston Business Feels Impact of Britain's Pound Devaluation," *Lewiston Tribune*, September 20, 1949, 1. The City of Lewiston's Laura von Tersch helped me identify Twenty-First Street as "the place to be" for merchants in 1949, because it was essentially the commercial Main Street.

20. *FRUS, 1949: Western Europe, Volume IV*, 847.

21. The useful Policy Planning position paper, PPS 62, September 3, 1949, on devaluation, sterling balances, and deflationary measures was written by Paul Nitze to help prepare Snyder, Acheson, and the other U.S. principals. Kennan says in his memoirs that the U.S. Treasury handled matters poorly—for example, by not offering the British a way out; Snyder, he suggests, should have helped them to produce a solution from the start. But Kennan knew nothing of finance, nor, when examined closely, did he have much experience in high-level negotiations.

22. Hubert Humphrey, Congressional Record, September 8, 1949.

23. James Webb memorandum, September 5, 1949, RG 330.

24. Walter Millis, *Arms and the State: Civil-Military Relations in National Policy*, with Harvey Mansfield (New York: Twentieth Century Fund, 1958), 246.

25. Memorandum of Conversation, by the Secretary of State, April 4, 1949, *FRUS, 1949: The Near East, South Asia, and Africa, Volume VI*.

26. "Middle East: Peace in a Smoke-Filled Room," *Time*, March 7, 1949.

27. FO 371/73490 J 2776/19345/16G, March 31, 1949.

28. Campbell to FO, January 29, 1949, FO 371/73555 J 776/1199/16G.

29. A year earlier, the JCS had told the British that the Defense Department had designated significant U.S. forces for the Middle East, though essentially just to help protect the Cairo-Suez nexus. See RG 319, September 8, 1948, Review of Emergency Plans, 381 TS, Section VIII-A; and also see Bullock, *Ernest Bevin*, 113, citing C. P. (49) 188, August 25, 1949.

30. October 19, 1949, COS (49), DEFE 4/24. "If it were not for their appreciation of United Kingdom national policy," a naval attaché in Franks's embassy reported, "it seems likely they would not have included the Middle East as a priority at all."

31. RG 319, JSPC 757/63, October 11, 1949, P and O, 1949–50, 384 TS Case 7/22, box 255.

32. JP (49) 126 (Final, November 3, 1949), DEFE 4/26, as referenced in Michael J. Cohen, *Fighting World War Three from the Middle East: Allied Contingency Plans, 1945–1954* (London: Frank Cass, 1997), 199.

33. September 8, 1948, COS 124, DEFE 4/16.

34. Edward W. Mulcahy, Principal Officer Mombasa (1947–1949), interview, Association for Diplomatic Studies and Training (hereafter cited as ADST).

35. *Mediterranean Exercise: The Navy Shows the Flag* (British Pathé, 1949).

36. *Hansard*, HL Deb., December 16, 1948, vol. 159, cols. 1176–78WA.

37. F.H.S. Curd and D. G. Davey, "Antrycide—a New Trypanocidal Drug," *British Journal of Pharmacology* (March 1950).

38. "Science: Antrycide," *Time*, January 10, 1949.

39. Nnamdi Azikiwe, *Zik: A Selection from the Speeches of Nnamdi Azikiwe, Governor-General of the Federation of Nigeria Formerly President of the Nigerian Sen-*

ate, *Formerly Premier of the Eastern Region of Nigeria* (Cambridge, U.K.: Cambridge University Press, 1961), 93.

40. Statement by Secretary of State Dean Acheson, August 5, 1949, in *U.S. Relations with China with Special Reference to the Period 1944–1949*, Department of State Publication No. 3573 (Washington, D.C.: GPO, 1949), xiv–xvii.

41. See Leebaert, "The Mystique of American Management," in *Magic and Mayhem*, which explains why Americans believe they can "manage" China in the first place.

42. *The Art of the Possible: The Memoirs of Lord Butler* (Boston: Gambit, 1972), 257.

43. Gaddis, *George F. Kennan*, 357. Gaddis tells of Kennan's blame shifting but not that John Davies—whom he blamed—was being investigated by Congress.

44. *Hansard*, HC Deb., February 23, 1948, vol. 447, cols. 1600–1601, answering a question posed by Anthony Eden.

45. *Hansard*, HC Deb., March 10, 1948, vol. 448, cols. 1208–10, Guatemala (British Protest).

46. Patterson is referenced in Sharon Meers's superb article, "The British Connection: How the United States Covered Its Tracks in the 1954 Coup in Guatemala," *Diplomatic History* 16, no. 3 (1992): 409–28.

47. Ibid.

48. *Kennan Diaries*, 244.

49. Kennan's views on intermarriage and the deficiencies caused by impure (that is, Negro) "human blood" are from "Memorandum" by the Counsellor to the Secretary of State, in *FRUS, 1950: The United Nations/The Western Hemisphere, Volume II*, May 29, 1950, 601. Acheson would have found the language repellent, given what's known of his later strong stand on civil rights.

50. Ibid., 607.

51. See "America's Role in Argentina's Dirty War," *New York Times*, March 17, 2016. Also see Jon Lee Anderson, "Does Henry Kissinger Have a Conscience?," *New Yorker*, August 20, 2016. This article uses recently declassified materials concerning Argentina to conclude that Mr. Kissinger was "the ruthless cheerleader, if not the active co-conspirator, of Latin American military regimes engaged in war crimes."

52. Gladwyn Jebb, speech to Imperial Defence College, February 24, 1950.

53. Walter Lippmann, "Whither Britain?," *Washington Post*, September 26, 1949.

9. AUDITING AN EMPIRE

1. Memorandum of Conversation, by the Officer in Charge of United Kingdom and Ireland Affairs (Jackson), March 7, 1950, in *FRUS, 1950: Western Europe, Volume III*. Acheson and Douglas were seeing Franks that night, as we know from Browder and Smith, *Independent*, 334.

2. I submitted the original FOIA request to declassify NSC 75, and the document hasn't been digitized. A review of the literature shows no other references to it at all. As for the key CIA and Pentagon contributions, they exist in the President's Secretary's Files of the Harry S. Truman Papers, having been collected at the White House by the NSC's executive secretary.

3. *FRUS, 1949: Western Europe, Volume IV*, 841.5151/7–1949: Telegram, July 19, 1949, Douglas to Acheson.

4. PPS, 132nd meeting, September 2, 1949, RG 59.

5. "India: Anchor for Asia," *Time*, October 17, 1949.

6. FO 371/76024 F 14305/1024/61G, September 16, 1949.

7. Even today the State Department writes, "At the onset of the Second World War, both Australia and New Zealand were members of the British Empire." Except membership in a voluntary association of fully independent nations formed by mutual agreements—which would be the commonwealth—isn't the same as being within an *empire*. See https://history.state.gov/milestones/1945-1952/anzus.

8. The quotation here is from Churchill's April 5, 1953, letter to Eisenhower. The figure of eighty million is also used in his speeches at Fulton in 1946 and at MIT in 1949. *The Churchill-Eisenhower Correspondence, 1953–1955*, ed. Peter Boyle (Chapel Hill: University of North Carolina Press, 1990), 34.

9. *Nehru in USA 1949* (British Pathé), http://www.britishpathe.com/video /nehru-in-usa.

10. "India: Anchor," *Time*, October 17, 1949; "miracle man" as cited when describing Diệm, in Logevall, *Embers of War*, 199.

11. Meena Ahamed, interview, Washington, D.C., June 1, 2017.

12. John McNay, *Acheson and Empire: The British Accent in American Foreign Policy* (Columbia: University of Missouri Press, 2001), 114–15.

13. Beisner, *Dean Acheson*, 217.

14. Taft, *Foreign Policy for Americans*, 45.

15. Ibid., 75, 83.

16. Telegram, October 19, 1949, in *FRUS, 1949: Western Europe, Volume IV*, 840.00/10-1949.

17. Nelson D. Lankford, *The Last American Aristocrat: The Biography of Ambassador David K. E. Bruce* (New York: Little, Brown, 1996), 293, citing *New York Times*, December 7, 1977. I am grateful to Mr. Lankford for sharing his own experiences with the Bruce family.

18. This corrected version of a previously told anecdote was conveyed to me by Ambassador Bruce's son, the late sinologist David Bruce.

19. Summary Record of the United States Ambassadors at Paris, October 21–22.

20. Ibid.

21. Ibid.

22. Ibid.

23. Ibid.

24. Ibid.

25. December 23, 1949, ORE-1949, 90–100, PSF, HSTL. Ian McLaine references the CIA paper in his excellent *A Korean Conflict: The Tensions Between Britain and America* (London: I. B. Tauris, 2015). But the paper isn't understood as part of a larger work, and he makes the common mistake of presuming Acheson's "Anglophilia," as on p. 70.

26. Gaddis, *George F. Kennan*, 362. Acheson's biographer Robert Beisner also believes that Kennan's departure was "self-propelled." See *Dean Acheson*, 118. From the perspective of a management consultant, however, Kennan's departure is a clear

case of being discreetly removed by the senior executives to whom he reported, such as Acheson and Webb. Pink slips aren't handed out in such roles, and a dismissal can be hidden behind soothing words.

27. Paul Nitze, *From Hiroshima to Glasnost: At the Center of Decision* (New York: Grove Press, 1989), 86.

28. I worked with Nitze during the late 1970s and the 1980s on national security issues, and we also discussed common interests in high-tech entrepreneurship. For example, he was an early backer of the serial entrepreneur John Henry, now CEO of DryStone Capital.

29. See Nitze's "Limited Wars or Massive Retaliation," *Reporter*, September 5, 1957, 41. Later, he spotlighted SALT's technical failings, due largely to Kissinger's unhelpful involvement, such as confusing the words "dimensions" and "volume" in the final document, thereby permitting the Russians to increase the size of a missile silo by nearly a third. See Leebaert, *Fifty-Year Wound*, 387–93.

30. The State Department's Office of the Historian describes NSC 68 as "among the most influential documents composed by the U.S. Government during the Cold War." See https://history.state.gov/milestones/1945-1952/NSC68. On the literature of NSC 68, the best discussion remains two articles I commissioned for *International Security*: Samuel Wells, "Sounding the Tocsin: NSC 68 and the Soviet Threat" (Fall 1979), and John Lewis Gaddis and Paul Nitze, "NSC 68 and the Soviet Threat Reconsidered" (Spring 1980).

31. "A Report to the National Security Council-NSC 68," April 12, 1950, 31, PSF, HSTL. Nitze's effort specified that Britain would be important to achieving U.S. objectives in Southeast Asia, but in his description of the Soviet threat, and in pressing for a buildup of conventional and nuclear weaponry, he overlooked some key questions of leverage while writing that the United States "lacks tenable positions from which to employ its forces in the event of war."

32. The colonial secretary's opinion was read far and wide in the United States, as in "Restrictions Placed on Imports," *St. Louis Post-Dispatch*, February 1, 1950, 15.

33. Strang to Bevin, December 1, 1949, FO 371/75668 UE 7696/104/50G. The Pentagon was also refusing to pay to expand the RAF's Abu Sueir air base in Egypt, which meant it couldn't be accessed by long-range bombers, except in emergency.

34. *Effects of British Decline as a World Power on U.S. Security Interests*, February 14, 1950, P&O Plans Op., RG 330.

35. "Subjects Other Than Economic," Satterwaite to Perkins, August 9, 1949, 711.41/8–949, RG 59.

36. NSC 75: *A Report to the National Security Council by the Executive Secretary on British Military Commitments*, July 10, 1950.

37. *Southern Daily Echo* (Southampton, U.K.), as reported by the chief archivist Jez Gale, April 8, 2016. Churchill had been writing and painting at Reid's Palace, the cliff-top hotel, in Madeira.

38. "Washington Hopes Results in Britain Will Be Decisive," *New York Times*, February 24, 1950, 2.

39. Memorandum of Conversation with James Webb, Dean Rusk, George Perkins, Henry Byroade, Paul Nitze, Ambassador Lewis Douglas, John J. McCloy, and Wayne Jackson, March 7, 1950, Secretary of State File, Acheson Papers, HSTL.

40. After the 1949 financial crisis, Washington modulated its pressure on Britain to federate with Europe. Even Acheson had come to believe the arm-twisting had become counterproductive.

41. Acheson, *Present at the Creation*, 387.

42. Ricks, *Churchill and Orwell*, 204.

43. NSC 75, 13.

44. NSC 75 documented 20,700 British soldiers and 8,700 colonial ones in the Suez Canal Zone, along with RAF squadrons.

45. The myth of "withdrawal" from the eastern Mediterranean in 1947 is repeated by John Lewis Gaddis in *George F. Kennan*, 293, by Martin Rubin in "Losing Hope, Glory, and Assets," *Wall Street Journal*, June 20, 2008, and by many other writers.

46. NSC 75, 20.

10. PIVOTING TO ASIA AND INTO VIETNAM

1. Taft, *Foreign Policy for Americans*, 73.

2. FO 371/83320 FE 1034519, June 4, 1950, to Dening.

3. Summary, October 14, 1949, FE 3722 to London, Executive Secretariat, Department of State.

4. Browder and Smith, *Independent*, 332.

5. "Congress Divided on British Action," *New York Times*, January 7, 1950, 4.

6. Bevin to Acheson, December 16, 1949, *FRUS, 1949: The Far East: China. Policy of the United States with Respect to the Question of Recognition, Volume IX*, 225.

7. Bullock, *Ernest Bevin*, 803.

8. "Chancelleries: Disenchantment," *Time*, June 5, 1950.

9. *Effects of British Decline as a World Power on U.S. Security Interests*, 3.

10. "Douglas Sees Gain in Southeast Asia," *New York Times*, September 3, 1952, 5.

11. "War: The Jungle Terrorists," *Time*, January 8, 1951.

12. Churchill also never forgave MacDonald for returning the treaty ports to Ireland three years before the start of the Battle of the Atlantic, and, less so, for his strong Arab sympathies in Palestine during the 1930s.

13. MacDonald's description of the two parts of Asia is found in a subsequent letter to MacArthur from Singapore, September 17, 1949, RG 5: SCAP, OMS MacDonald, MacArthur Memorial Library and Archives.

14. "Meetings in Tokyo," *New York Times*, September 12, 1949, 1.

15. "U.S.-British Stand in Asia Held Vital," *New York Times*, September 6, 1949, 4.

16. MacDonald to Foreign Office, December 19, 1949, FO 371 F 19106/1055/86.

17. *FRUS, 1949: The Far East and Australasia, Volume VII, Part 2*, November 4, 1949, 1208.

18. MacDonald to Foreign Office, September 2, 1949, FO 371 F 13136/1024/61.

19. Memorandum of conversation, Singapore, August 21, 1950, FO 371 FZ 1198/8.

20. "East and South Asia," June 6, 1950, SP, RG 59.

21. Sir Percy Spender, *Exercises in Diplomacy: The ANZUS Treaty and the Colombo Plan* (New York: New York University Press, 1969), 195. Spender was Australia's ambassador to the United States from 1951 to 1958.

22. This was the Griffin mission, and R. Allen Griffin's quotation comes from an interview conducted by Andrew J. Rotter in *The Path to Vietnam*, 194. Professor Rotter is one of the few scholars who observe the influence of Malcolm MacDonald.

23. Griffin's deputy on this mission wrote of the sequences that led to economic and military assistance. See Samuel P. Hayes, ed., *The Beginning of American Aid to Southeast Asia: The Griffin Mission of 1950* (Lexington, Mass.: D. C. Heath, 1971).

24. "U.S. Recognizes Viet Nam," *New York Times*, February 8, 1950.

25. Rotter, *Path to Vietnam*, 207, citing a memorandum of conversation between U.S. and British officials in Singapore, August 8, 1950.

26. "Threat to Australia Seen," *New York Times*, May 18, 1950, 4.

27. Lawrence, *Assuming the Burden*, 265, regarding Bevin's instructions.

28. Ibid., 242. This fine work, however, only takes readers to 1950.

29. Joseph N. Greene Jr., oral history, March 12, 1993, ADST.

30. An example of the quality of Heath's analysis, and of his myopic dismissal of nationalism, is seen in "France Is Fighting the Good Fight," *Life*, September 21, 1953.

31. See Derek Leebaert, review of *15 Stars: Eisenhower, MacArthur, Marshall: Three Generals Who Saved the American Century*, by Stanley Weintraub, in *On Point: The Journal of Army History* (Winter 2007–2008).

32. D. Clayton James, *The Years of MacArthur II: Triumph and Disaster, 1945–1964* (New York: Houghton Mifflin, 1985), 370.

33. On "empire," see Lloyd Gardner, *A Covenant with Power: America and World Order from Wilson to Reagan* (New York: Oxford University Press, 1984), 112; on Korea and "control," see S. J. Ball, *The Cold War: An International History* (New York: Arnold, 1998), 55. See George Kennan, *American Diplomacy, 1900–1950* (Chicago: University of Chicago Press, 1951), in which Kennan admits to having no "personal familiarity" with Asia and to being no "expert on Far Eastern Affairs," 38.

34. Michael Schaller, *Altered States: The United States and Japan Since the Occupation* (New York: Oxford University Press, 1997), 14. In the meetings, Kennan properly had to listen. We know it was congenial, however, because otherwise Kennan, then forty-four, would have been thrown out. Thereafter, as one shrewd twenty-first-century editorialist observes, "he and his allies in Washington engineered a 180-degree turn in U.S. policy" that included the end of war crimes trials and "short-circuited economic and political reforms that could have made Japan a much more vibrant and dynamic society today." James Gibney, "Blame George Kennan for Abe's Bad History," *Bloomberg View*, April 29, 2015.

35. "Extraordinary brilliance of Kennan" is Fareed Zakaria, "A Guest of My Time," *New York Times Book Review*, February 21, 2014; others are Henry A. Kissinger, "The Age of Kennan," *New York Times Book Review*, November 10, 2011.

36. "Giant" is from Lawrence J. Goodrich, "Kennan: Giant of Diplomacy," *Christian Science Monitor*, May 3, 1989. "Sensitive" as well as "analytical" are each from Kissinger's review essay, "Age of Kennan." The "brilliance" that Kissinger describes is supposedly shown during Kennan's Foreign Service years before 1952; Kissinger is not discussing Kennan's later life as a historian and writer. In sum, Kennan's exaggerated reputation comes largely from literary men who're inflating the role of one of their brethren. Because he proved to be such a good historian and writer after leaving government, it's assumed that he must have excelled at his duties while in government.

37. The foremost example of a foreign policy academic and high U.S. government official dismissing the role of economics is Henry Kissinger himself. Of the

more than 140 National Security Study Memoranda prepared during the first three years of the Nixon administration, about 4 dealt with economic matters. An NSC staffer of the time contends that discussing economics with Kissinger was like discussing military strategy with the pope. See Schaller, *Altered States*, 212.

38. The indecency that Kennan displayed to such listeners as the fellows of All Souls, Oxford, included his belief that African Americans had to have a separate state of their own. See Richard Crossman, diary entry for January 31, 1969, in *The Diaries of a Cabinet Minister* (New York: Henry Holt, 1976), 3:352.

39. "Foreign Relations: Expert's Expert," *Time*, December 19, 1949.

40. *Kennan Diaries*, 248.

41. See "Acheson Tells What He Means by Total Diplomacy," *Life*, March 13, 1950, 55–56. He meant a complete focus by all branches of government, including Congress, plus essentially every institution in American life, such as business, labor, and the press, on the East-West struggle.

42. FO 371/83320 FE 1034519, June 4, 1950, to Dening.

43. FO 371/83108 FJ 1023/1G, May 6, 1950.

44. Kissinger first used "decent interval" in private talks during 1968 about leaving Vietnam, according to Daniel Ellsberg, and as the historian Jeffrey Kimball discovered. By August 1972, President Nixon was worried about South Vietnam's inevitable collapse. Kissinger offered guidance: "We've got to find some formula that holds the thing together a year or two. If we settle it, say, this October [right before the presidential election], by January '74 no one will give a damn." Saigon fell thirty-two months later. In Washington, when I use "decent interval" facetiously in think tank or U.S. government meetings that concern Afghanistan, the term, and the concept, are welcomed as cleverly novel.

11. WAR ON THE RIM

1. "Oxford Union Regrets 'Domination' by U.S. in Vote After Fiery Debate," *New York Times*, June 2, 1950, 3.

2. Amid useful work by Katherine Weathersby and other scholars on the origins of the Korean War, the definitive account is by William T. Lee, probably the foremost intelligence analyst from the late 1940s through 1991 of Soviet Russia. He was at the CIA when the war occurred. See his *Korean War Was Stalin's Show* (University of Virginia, Center for National Security Law, 1999). For the Korean War overall, I've distilled a correction of the conventional interpretations in my review essay "'Limited War' on the Edge of the World," *Army*, March 2008, 118–20.

3. The enduring belief is that "Stalin reluctantly agreed to support Kim's invasion plans," David Milne, *Worldmaking: The Art and Science of American Diplomacy* (New York: Farrar, Straus and Giroux, 2015), 283. Milne claims, as do many other writers, that such agreement was given "in April." But an invasion of this scope couldn't possibly occur under any conditions over two months, especially with the transport of oil and lubricants, and the time-consuming change of rail gauge at the Manchurian border. Other misleading writings say that Stalin gave North Korea "permission" to attack—all of which reflect a misunderstanding of military operations and logistics. See Evan Thomas, *Ike's Bluff: President Eisenhower's Secret Battle to Save the World* (New York: Little, Brown, 2013), 69. For Khrushchev's admission, see Lee, *The Korean War Was Stalin's Show*, 60, citing the Communist Party Plenum of 1955.

4. Taft, *Foreign Policy for Americans*, 33.

5. Why was Stalin's mouthpiece at the UN, Yakov Malik, not on the scene to cast a veto? One explanation is that Stalin didn't expect the strong U.S. response. Another is that Stalin was deliberately luring the United States into a quagmire, or into a war with China. That explanation arose as America got bogged down in 1951, as addressed in Taft's *Foreign Policy for Americans*.

6. FO 371/84159 FK 1202/2/G, July 25, 1950.

7. July 19, 1950, DO (50) 13 CAB 131/8.

8. Dixon minute, July 12, 1950, FO 371/84087 FK 1022/128/G.

9. FO 371/84159 FK 1202/2, July 25, 1950.

10. Wagner to Truman, July 27, 1950, Official File, HSTL.

11. Mason to Truman, July 25, 1950, Official File, HSTL. France was profiting too, having just closed a multimillion-dollar deal to supply strategically useful steel rails to Beijing. Washington was able to stop this sale of the militarily significant rails by blocking dollar deposits in New York.

12. "Avenging angels" is FO 371/83014, F 1022/24F, August 5, 1950; "policeman" is FO 371/84159 FK 1202/2, July 25, 1950.

13. Copy of letter of July 11, 1950, to Bevin, Younger Papers.

14. Attlee to Truman, July 6, 1950, PSF, HSTL.

15. William Steuck, *Rethinking the Korean War: A New Diplomatic and Strategic History* (Princeton: Princeton University Press, 2004), 101.

16. Attlee to Truman, July 6, 1950, PSF, HSTL.

17. RG 330 CD 092.3 NATO General, July 24, 1950.

18. Ibid.

19. A good distillation of that day's parliamentary debate, with all the excitement being brought home for Americans, is "British Defense Poorer Than in 1938: Churchill," *Chicago Daily Tribune*, July 28, 1950, 1.

20. Finletter to Defense Secretary Johnson, July 7, 1950, CD 092.2 UK.

21. Ibid.

22. Norstad to LeMay, July 9, 1950, JCS Files, USAF.

23. Strategic Plans, SPD Director to DCNO Ops re Air Chief Marshal correspondence with General Bradley.

24. Vandenberg to LeMay, August 9, 1950, JCS Files. UAAF.

25. A Permissive Action Link is the security device that enables an ally to exercise some control over locally based U.S. nuclear weapons, but this approach wouldn't arrive for another decade.

26. Diary, July 6, 1950, Younger Papers.

27. "Hitler Tactics Charged to Malik," *New York Times*, August 23, 1950, 1.

28. To George VI via Alan "Tommy" Lascelles, October 6, 1950, FO 371/88407 UP 1022/1.

29. Jebb reflected that his fame was "quite odd." See Gladwyn Jebb, June 21, 1983, United Nations Oral History Project, UN Dag Hammarskjöld Library. The measure of his celebrity comes from his Hooper Rating survey of that time.

30. "Token British Unit for Korea Likely," *New York Times*, July 22, 1950, 2.

31. "From MacDonald to MacArthur" is *Time* magazine's article title on the subject, September 4, 1950.

32. "1,500 British Troops Sail," *New York Times*, August 26, 1950, 3.

33. In August 1950, the fleet contained one light carrier, three cruisers, sixteen destroyers, and frigates. Two thirteen-thousand-ton aircraft carriers were then reactivated.

34. This tragedy equally horrified the Australians, who were set to deploy soldiers of their own in Korea. See "US Planes Bomb British Units by Mistake," *Canberra Times*, September 25, 1950, 1.

35. George Ian, *The Argylls in Korea* (London: Thomas Nelson and Sons, 1952), 93.

36. United Nations, General Assembly Resolutions 5th Session, 376V, "The Problem of the Independence of Korea," October 7, 1950.

37. FO 371/ 84498 F 1015/13G, October 16, 1950, from Gascoigne.

38. David Halberstam, *Coldest Winter: America and the Korean War* (New York: Hachette, 2008), 382. In chapter 2, "Emergency Men," in *Magic and Mayhem*, I show the reasons behind "the temptation to build on success" and the lure to invade the North. (The term "emergency men" is from Burckhardt.) See pp. 42–47. One of the few analogues in history to the triumph of Inchon is the shock of China's intervention nine weeks later.

39. Bevin with the Dutch foreign minister, Dirk Stikker, FO 371/83015 F 1022/50G.

40. President's News Conference, November 30, 1950, *Public Papers*, HSTL.

41. CAB 130/Gen 347/2, December 14, 1950. Ernest Bevin wasn't part of this visit to Washington, contrary to Michael Burleigh, *Small Wars, Faraway Places* (New York: Viking, 2013), 148. Attlee otherwise wouldn't have had reason to come, and Bevin would have conducted all meetings for the British side.

42. *FRUS, 1950: Korea, Volume VII*, 1313, on Marshall and Dunkirk.

43. Ibid., 1395.

44. Ibid., 1368.

45. Memorandum of Conversation with the Ambassador of Great Britain, Sir Oliver Franks, Sir Roger Makins, Robert Scott, Dean Rusk, and Philip C. Jessup, December 4, 1950, Secretary of State File, Acheson Papers, HSTL.

46. Diary entry of Harry S. Truman, December 9, 1950, PSF, HSTL.

47. Dean Acheson, *The Korean War* (New York: Norton, 1971), 91.

48. Memorandum for the Record by the Ambassador at Large (Jessup), December 7, 1950, in *FRUS, 1950: Korea, Volume VII*.

49. It's likely that MacArthur's plans at this juncture were flowing into enemy hands through the Foreign Office. Lieutenant General James Gavin, who was then on the army staff in the Pentagon, came to believe so. NKVD files, unlike those of the Ministry of Foreign Affairs and the Red Army, weren't opened to researchers after the collapse of the Soviet Union.

50. Diary entry for December 11, 1950, Younger Papers.

51. Offshore, the U.S. admirals complained that their worst problem was "command relations" with the British Commonwealth task force in the Yellow Sea. The decision in February/March 1951 to subordinate the aircraft carrier USS *Bataan* to the British chain of command when operating with the heavy cruiser HMS *Belfast* is not the example of cooperation some analysts think. The Royal Navy had a different ranking system, and the brass were quarreling. The Russian magnetic mines, which were sinking naval vessels in these bristling seas, got less high-level attention.

52. Thirty-eight percent of U.S. POWs (2,730 out of 7,190) died in captivity from death marches, ill-treatment, and lack of food and medicine.

53. The best source on all technical details remains Doug Dildy and Warren Thompson, *F-86 Sabre vs MiG-15: Korea 1950–53* (Oxford: Osprey Publishing, 2013), which includes a fascinating profile of Kramarenko, p. 47, who was promoted to lieutenant colonel.

54. "Commander's discretion" is from an excellent distillation of the Korean air war by the historian Bruce Cumings. See "Korea: Forgotten Nuclear Threats," *Le Monde Diplomatique* (English ed.), December 2004.

55. Forrest C. Pogue, *George C. Marshall*, vol. 4, *Statesman, 1945–1959* (New York: Random House, 1992), 479.

56. Ogilvy & Mather created the ad, inspired by a picture of Ambassador Douglas; alternatively, an executive of Hathaway shirts came up with the idea, having observed the ambassador with his eye patch during an Atlantic crossing, and had David Ogilvy execute the concept. The ad campaign was launched in 1951 using Baron George Wrangell, a Russian aristocrat, as the model for Lewis Douglas.

57. Diary entry for January 7, 1951, Younger Papers.

58. Graves to Livingston Merchant, January 30, 1951, RG 59 795.00/1-3051, citing Jebb. Jebb at least succeeded in toning down the U.S. draft of the condemnation, but only because of a full vote of the British cabinet against this U.S. maneuver.

59. Gellately, *Stalin's Curse*, 349.

12. ASIA'S THREE FIGHTING FRONTS

1. "Mobilization: Boiler Trouble," *Time*, November 19, 1951. Thirty-eight hundred planes rather than forty-five hundred were produced, according to General Hoyt Vandenberg, the air force chief of staff.

2. RG 319 Army Ops General File Section IV-A, December 20, 1950. Eisenhower joked that maybe the title should be "Colossal Supreme Commander."

3. Eisenhower to Gruenther, October 27, 1953, Ann Whitman File, Administrative Series, box 16. Dwight D. Eisenhower Library (DDEL).

4. Those reserves were at the highest level since before World War II, albeit at one-third the purchasing power of the prewar peak.

5. "Three Fighting Fronts," *New York Times*, May 21, 1951, 34.

6. Lippmann to John Foster Dulles, July 18, 1950, in Blum, *Public Philosopher*, 553.

7. Lippmann to Nicolson, May 2, 1951, in ibid., 564.

8. "Snyder Says Federal Levies Will Be Increased Substantially," *Wall Street Journal*, September 27, 1950, 3.

9. MacArthur's request was made to Gascoigne and communicated to London. FO 371/92721 FK 1001/1, January 11, 1951.

10. Homer S. Ferguson, Congressional Record, Senate, Session 82-1, April 13, 1951.

11. Daily Summary, April 18, 1951, Executive Secretariat, Department of State.

12. "Ernest Bevin's Funeral Is Set for Wednesday," *Tuscaloosa News*, April 16, 1951, 1.

13. "Three Fighting Fronts," 34.

14. The argument went as follows: If the empire and commonwealth had contributed some 26,000 troops in Korea, by May, it was only fair to add them into an overall presence of imperial forces on the "Far Eastern fighting front." That would total at least 58,000 combatants, and many times more if colonial Malayan forces were included.

15. I've examined the operational stupidity of torture in Derek Leebaert, "The CIA in Unknown Terrain: The Education of an Interrogator," *Intelligence and National Security*, August 2012, 582–91, and I speak often with one of the leading experts on the subject, Robert Coulam.

16. Nichols in old age self-published 250 copies of an autobiography, *How Many Times Can I Die?* The foreword to this disturbing volume is by one of the top four-star generals of the Korean War era, E. E. Partridge, USAF. More on Nichols, and on Calvert, each of whom was cashiered in disgrace, is in Leebaert, chapter 17, "Dawn Like Thunder," in *To Dare and to Conquer*.

17. Hendrik van Oss, February 8, 1991, Singapore, oral history, ADST.

18. Daily Summary, October 16, 1950, Executive Secretariat, Department of State.

19. RG 335 Secretary of the Army, Indochina, Heath to Rusk, October 15, 1950.

20. "Background Book for Attlee Talks," December 4, 1950, John Snyder Papers, HSTL.

21. *Hansard*, HC Deb., February 12, 1951, vol. 484, cols. 41–158; HC Deb., February 15, 1951, vol. 484, cols. 623–70.

22. David Reynolds, *In Command of History: Churchill Fighting and Writing the Second World War* (New York: Random House, 2005), 402–3. In this valuable book, Reynolds is addressing the original 1943 U.S.-British understanding, known as the Quebec Agreement, not the later impasse surrounding the atomic bombers and air bases.

23. *Hansard*, HC Deb., February 15, 1951, vol. 484, cols. 671–743. I describe Churchill as "squirming" because he had to apologize to the House for his contortions, saying that he was searching for a dropped sweet.

24. *Hansard*, HC Deb., April 23, 1951, vol. 487, cols. 34–43.

25. Construction costs alone were about $18 million in public funds, and Attlee's cabinet deemed this to be large.

26. Arriving in 1951 was the 4th Infantry Division in May, followed by the 2nd Armored Division and the 43rd and 28th Infantry Divisions during the summer and fall. Note that at the time a U.S. division had an authorized strength of about 18,500 men, but the 28th and the 43rd were both National Guard divisions and likely were not at full strength—hence calculating 70,000.

27. "U.S. Military Joins Talks in Singapore," *New York Times*, May 15, 1951, 8. In fact, the only agreement achieved in Singapore was to coordinate intelligence with the British.

28. Thomas E. Dewey, *Journey to the Far Pacific* (New York: Doubleday, 1952), 260. Dewey also wrote in his bestseller that he was "tremendously impressed" by the commissioner general: "calm, philosophical . . . completely informal and friendly."

29. "The Nations: The French MacArthur," *Time*, September 24, 1951. De Lattre's U.S. visit received enormous acclaim. On September 25, he flew from Washington to Paris, then to London to reconvene with Britain's top commanders before

returning to war. He told them he had been assured of more U.S. support. That was only partly correct: the Joint Chiefs, according to their records, had refused to even imply they'd ever "agree to the formation of an allied command" in Southeast Asia. At the time, the U.S. presence involved only some two hundred civilians in Saigon.

30. Kennedy, *Rise and Fall of the Great Powers*, 389, with "outward thrust" on p. 359.

31. State-JCS Staff Meeting, April 23, 1952, in *FRUS, 1952–1954: Korea, Volume I, Part 1*, 12:81–84.

32. Spender to Dulles, March 8, 1951, in *The 1951 ANZUS Treaty*, vol. 17, Historical Documents, Department of Foreign Affairs and Trade, Australian Government.

33. "Yet Another Financial Crisis in Britain," *Advertiser* (Adelaide), September 17, 1951, 1.

34. Half of Britain's exports came from metal-using industries. So when these exports rose, as they had been doing, less material was available for defense production. Moreover, the prices of imports were 40 percent higher than a year earlier, which entailed spending a billion pounds more for the same volume of goods.

35. It was illegal to slaughter horses under seven years old for food, and it was also illegal to serve horseflesh in restaurants if other meat was available. But a black market existed for horse meat of all kinds.

36. "Yet Another Financial Crisis in Britain." The tea shop story is from Trevor Smith, "London Diary."

37. Memorandum of Telephone Conversation with Secretary of the Treasury John Snyder, August 23, 1951, Secretary of State File, Acheson Papers, HSTL.

38. ECA mtg., September 6, 1951, RG 59, Washington FM, box 75. Also attending was Richard M. Bissell Jr., head of the Economic Cooperation Administration, who would segue to the CIA in 1954 and become deputy director of plans (that is, clandestine operations).

39. Memorandum of Conversation, by the Special Assistant to the Secretary of State for Economic Affairs (Schaetzel), December 7, 1951, in *FRUS, 1952–1954: Western Europe and Canada, Volume VI, Part 1*.

40. *The Diary of Hugh Gaitskell, 1945–1956*, ed. Philip Williams (London: Jonathan Cape, 1983), 281.

41. The 50 percent increase is in "Background Book for Attlee Talks," December 3, 1950, Snyder Papers, HSTL; "moonshine" is from Gaitskell/Bissell meeting, September 6, 1951, RG 59, Washington FM, box 75.

42. United States Delegation Minutes of the Second Meeting of the Foreign Ministers of the United States and United Kingdom Held at Washington, September 11, 1951, in *FRUS, 1951: European Security and the German Question, Volume III, Part 1*.

43. "Foreign News: The First Failure," *Time*, April 23, 1951.

44. *Diary of Hugh Gaitskell*, 317.

45. FO 371/90931 AU 1054/11, March 20, 1951, Sir Pierson Dixon et al.

13. "HOLDING THE RING" IN IRAN AND EGYPT

1. On the drop from $6 billion to $2 billion, see "The American Economy in 1951," *Economic Weekly*, May 24, 1952, 523.

2. The Ambassador in the United Kingdom (Gifford) to the Department of State, December 28, 1951, in *FRUS, 1952–1954: Western Europe and Canada, Volume VI, Part 1*. ADST oral histories indicate that this memorandum would have been written by Holmes and not Gifford.

3. Ibid. Contrary to what the historian Paul M. Kennedy has argued in *Rise and Fall of the Great Powers*—that Britain at this stage was "dependent upon the United States for security" (368)—such was not the perspective in London. Certainly, Holmes and other Americans did not see the relationship this way.

4. "Egypt: The Locomotive," *Time*, September 10, 1951.

5. "Iran Rally Backs 'Heroic' Egyptians," *New York Times*, November 7, 1951, 5.

6. Diary entry for April 6, 1951, Younger Papers.

7. John H. Stutesman, Consular/Political Officer, 1949–1954, oral history, Iran, ADST.

8. Memorandum by the Assistant Secretary of State for Near Eastern, South Asian, and African Affairs (McGhee) to the Secretary of State, April 25, 1950, in *FRUS, 1950: The Near East, South Asia, and Africa, Volume V*.

9. Stephen Kinzer, *All the Shah's Men: An American Coup and the Roots of Middle East Terror* (Hoboken, N.J.: Wiley, 2008), 85.

10. The U.S. Chancery itself was located on Roosevelt and Takhte Jamshid Avenues in Tehran and had been acquired in 1946.

11. *The Memoirs of Ambassador Henry F. Grady: From the Great War to the Cold War* (Columbia: University of Missouri Press, 2009), 169.

12. Stutesman, ADST oral history.

13. Ministry of Fuel and Power, July 24, 1950, DO (50) 60 CAB 131/9.

14. Grady to the Secretary of State, October 31, 1950, in *FRUS, 1950: The Near East, South Asia, and Africa, Volume V*, 613.

15. Stutesman, ADST oral history.

16. Lewis Hoffacker, Third Secretary/Rotation Officer, Tehran, 1951–1953, oral history, Iran, ADST.

17. *Full Circle: The Memoirs of Sir Anthony Eden* (London: Cassell, 1960), 260. "Size of Wales" is then echoed, for example, by Niall Ferguson in his overview, *Empire*, 295, and even by Robert Tombs in his erudite *The English and Their History* (New York: Knopf, 2015), 779.

18. Confusion that the actual canal was instead to be nationalized is unending, as, again, by Ferguson in *Empire*, 296, and even by James MacDonald, another serious student of finance and power, in *When Globalization Fails: The Rise and Fall of Pax Americana* (New York: Farrar, Straus and Giroux, 2016), 206.

19. One exception during the fall of 1950 was to accept three hundred Egyptian officers into the Pentagon's service schools, including the newly reopened Army War College at Fort Leavenworth. But that was to be a onetime event to offset any disarray caused by the Attlee government's decision to withdraw its military training mission from Egypt. Otherwise the Joint Chiefs didn't want to be tutoring Arabs or Israelis. That risked creeping entanglement.

20. Speech dated November 12, 1950, Younger Papers.

21. This was Emmanuel Shinwell, MP. DEFE 4/43 COS (51) 86, Confidential Annex, May 23, 1951.

22. FO 371/91185 E 1024/24.

23. Karl E. Meyer, *The Dust of Empire: The Race for Mastery in the Asian Heartland* (New York: Public Affairs, 2003), 73.

24. The prime minister talked in his perfect French to the American and then insisted that his words be translated into English for the ambassador, which wasted everybody's time. The ambassador of course was also fluent in French, as Mosaddeq knew.

25. Franks to Bowker, July 19, 1951, in George McGhee, *On the Frontlines of the Cold War* (Westport, Conn.: Praeger, 1997), 110.

26. The British ambassador, Sir Francis Shepherd, was at the same time writing that Iran had descended into "Asiatic decadence." It had never benefited, he concluded, from the instruction of authentic colonial rule. See Louis, *British Empire in the Middle East*, 639.

27. *Memoirs of Ambassador Henry F. Grady*, 186.

28. Memorandum, undated, "C" being the director of SIS (MI6), Younger Papers. A big source of failure in Iran, as Younger observed, was that "the Embassy concerns itself almost exclusively with a limited circle of political personalities in Tehran and that its appreciation does not go much deeper than that." Nearly word for word, this was the U.S. government assessment as well following the shock of the shah's ouster in 1979.

29. John H. Stutesman, oral history, Iran, ADST, http://adst.org/2015/07/the-coup-against-irans-mohammad-mossadegh.

30. The Admiralty was scrambling to find enough ships for such a big assault, given commitments in Korea, but those shortcomings weren't apparent to the Americans. See Lawrence James, *The Rise and Fall of the British Empire* (New York: St. Martin's Press, 1994), 565, citing Admiralty records.

31. Power projection from the RAF Nicosia air base had problems of its own. That would have meant overflying Syria, or Israel and Jordan, as well as Iraq. But the niceties of getting authorization weren't discussed.

32. "Iran: Dervish in Pin-Striped Suit," *Time*, June 4, 1951.

33. Bradley to Cook, September 26, 1951, RG 218, JCS 092.2 Bradley Files.

34. Taft, *Foreign Policy for Americans*, 112–13.

35. "Clouds Over Iran," *Cleveland Plain Dealer*, April 15, 1951, 22A.

36. "Today and Tomorrow," column of May 24, 1951, as syndicated in that day's *Washington Post* and elsewhere.

37. Daily Summary, October 18, 1951, to Morrison, Executive Secretariat, Department of State.

38. Christopher de Bellaigue, *Patriot of Persia: Muhammad Mossadegh and a Tragic Anglo-American Coup* (New York: HarperCollins, 2012), 170. Part of the pressure was British refusal to release Iranian funds in sterling accounts that would enable the loan to be paid back.

39. This point is made by Donald Logan, who had left the British embassy in Tehran earlier in 1951 to handle Iranian affairs in the Foreign Office's Eastern Department. See his unpublished memoir at Churchill College, Cambridge: https://www.chu.cam.ac.uk/media/uploads/files/Logan.pdf.

40. Eden, *Full Circle*, 203.

41. Eden's summary is found in his memorandum, Eden to Morrison and Strang, May 17, 1951, FO 371/91185 E 1024/22.

42. The State Department's alarmed response to Gifford is Daily Summary, May 24, 1951, Executive Secretariat, Department of State.

43. Beisner, *Dean Acheson*, 555.

44. Mohamed Heikal, *Cutting the Lion's Tail: Suez Through Egyptian Eyes* (London: Andre Deutsch, 1986), 21.

45. "Middle East: A Shaky Do," *Time*, October 29, 1951. The article doesn't identify General Robertson, just describing him as Commander in Chief Land Forces, but that's who the four-goaler was.

46. Piers Brendon, *Ike: His Life and Times* (New York: HarperCollins, 1986), 257.

47. Beisner, *Dean Acheson*, 463.

14. CHURCHILL IS BACK

1. "Great Britain: This Last Prize," *Time*, November 5, 1951, as told to a group of visitors in Abbey House the preceding week.

2. Entry for May 15, 1951, in *Macmillan Diaries*, 74. Colville, *Fringes of Power*, has Macmillan asserting this more categorically at the Turf on May 30. See Colville's diary entry on p. 649. Macmillan knew that such a feat would require some form of unity with Europe, of which he was a proponent.

3. Colville, diary entry for June 13, 1952, in *Fringes of Power*, 651. The Defence Ministry's chief science adviser, Sir Henry Tizard, might rail during these months, "We are not a Great Power," but he was doing so against prevailing wisdom. See Farmelo, *Churchill's Bomb*, 373.

4. *This World of Ours: London* (Dudley Pictures), January 1951.

5. FO 371/97593 AU 1051/31, January 27, 1951.

6. "The Matter of Leadership," *Miami News*, March 18, 1952, 37.

7. Memorandum by the Chairman of the Joint Committee on Atomic Energy (McMahon) to the President, December 5, 1951, in *FRUS, 1952–1954: Western Europe and Canada, Volume VI, Part 1.*

8. Churchill to Truman, November 5, 1951, in *Defending the West: The Truman-Churchill Correspondence, 1945–1960*, ed. G. W. Sand (London: Praeger, 2004), 186.

9. The firsthand account of the ambush is from the platoon commander known as Sui Mah, to be found in the memoir of Chin Peng, leader of Malaya's Communist Party and of the insurgency. See *My Side of History* (Singapore: Media Masters, 2003), 104.

10. *Hansard*, HC Deb., November 6, 1951, vol. 493, cols. 54–170. Britain was spending 40 percent more for imports of raw materials and food than before Korea; prices for exports were up only 25 percent amid an uneven global inflation. Moreover, a drop in global commodity prices was now affecting countries throughout the sterling area. Unlike in 1949, that meant the problem was not just a shortage of dollars but one of having to meet debts with the world as a whole.

11. *Hansard*, HC Deb., December 6, 1951, vol. 494, cols. 2591–688. By now the U.S. Air Force occupied thirteen fields with five of them in East Anglia equipped to handle the nuclear-capable B-29s.

12. "Snyder Dispels Allies' Hopes of More U.S. Help for Arms," *New York Times*, November 28, 1952, 1, regarding "dreams." Snyder maintained the pressure when he and Acheson attended the NATO gathering at Lisbon in February 1952,

where the allies pledged the forces necessary for a long-term defense plan. Despite these policy differences, Snyder had fine relations with Acheson.

13. *Hansard*, HC Deb., December 6, 1951, vol. 494, cols. 2591–688. Britain's defense spending, however, remained the second largest in NATO.

14. Ricks, *Churchill and Orwell*, 238. Historians have indeed averted their eyes from these years, from October 1951 to April 1955. Most accounts of Churchill's life wrap up around 1945, or soon after, as does Ricks's book. It's a reason why these events after World War II are poorly understood—as is Churchill's role. Macmillan's more persuasive observations about Churchill are found in *Tides of Fortune*, 493, as well as in his diary.

15. His description of "the British lion as a pet" struck a chord throughout the commonwealth, as it did in the United States. For instance, see "Churchill Warns British Nation," *West Australian*, December 24, 1951, 1, and "Churchill Tells Britons No One 'Will Keep British Lion as a Pet,'" *Ottawa Journal*, December 24, 1951, 24.

16. Memorandum by the Chairman of the Joint Committee on Atomic Energy (McMahon) to the President, December 5, 1951, in *FRUS, 1952–1954: Western Europe and Canada, Volume VI, Part 1*.

17. No. 318 Memorandum of Conversation, by the Under Secretary of State (Webb), December 10, 1951, in ibid.

18. Diary entry for January 7, 1952, in *Diaries of Lord Moran*, 381.

19. Ibid., 377.

20. "Churchill-Truman Begin Talks," *Chicago Daily Tribune*, January 6, 1952, 1.

21. Robert Lovett, oral history, HSTL.

22. The U.S. Army adopted such desperate measures for recycling both because it needed the metal and due to accusations of waste by Senator Lyndon B. Johnson's Preparedness Subcommittee to the army secretary, Frank Pace.

23. Randolph's miscue is in his edited *Churchill: His Life in Photographs* (New York: Rinehart, 1955). The impressive *Churchill Defiant: Fighting On, 1945–1955*, by Barbara Leaming, also has them taking a cruise. Acheson's biographer Robert Beisner writes of them being at "a large Potomac party" (rather than dockside on the Anacostia River), *Dean Acheson*, 462, and Graham Farmelo, like most historians, writes of their "cruising down the Potomac on the Presidential yacht." See *Churchill's Bomb*, 384. The *Chicago Daily Tribune*, which angrily scrutinized the Churchill visit, got this detail right, as did *The New York Times*.

24. "Egypt," Truman-Churchill Negotiating Paper, December 1951 (no day), HST Papers, HSTL.

25. Acheson, *Present at the Creation*, 598.

26. Diary entry for January 5, 1952, in *Diaries of Lord Moran*, 378. John H. Mather, MD CIP FACPE, has written an excellent, medically oriented critique of Moran's book for the International Churchill Society (March 2016).

27. Truman/Churchill Talks, 1st Session, January 7, 1952, PSF, HSTL.

28. Taft, *Foreign Policy for Americans*, 62.

29. We can see the "British warfare state" at work on this matter of military collaboration: If the Pentagon bought a certain number of Britain's Centurion tanks and radar sets, that acquisition could help finance Britain's annual output of 740 Canberra and Venom jets for the RAF. U.S. purchases would also boost London's

dollar reserves. But advantages existed for America too. The British could produce equivalent jets to the United States at half the price. Moreover, Britain's overall spending on R&D was impressively half that of America's, despite the big differential in population and GDP.

30. As recently as the November 1951 NATO Council meeting in Rome, all the members' military chiefs had agreed that a U.S. admiral would indeed oversee the Atlantic. The British chiefs of staff had approved as well. Responsibility for the North Sea and the Channel would be reserved for the Royal Navy; perhaps for the Mediterranean too. Yet four days later, on November 26—just as the Pentagon prepared to name the admiral it had selected to command in the Atlantic, and only hours after General Eisenhower had urged top NATO representatives to conclude their structuring of the treaty organization—the British delegation reversed itself, on "Churchill's orders." See Walter S. Poole, *The Joint Chiefs of Staff and National Policy, 1950–1952* (Washington, D.C.: Office of Joint History, Office of the Chairman of the Joint Chiefs of Staff, 1998), 120.

31. Acheson, *Present at the Creation*, 601.

32. The jointly written Pentagon statement that angered Churchill in effect ratified earlier NATO decisions, according to Acheson, which included the subjects both of nuclear weapons and of the Atlantic Command. Two solid analyses of the nuclear controversy are John Saville, "The Price of Alliance: American Bases in Britain," *Socialist Register* (1987): 32–60, and Ken Young, *The American Bomb in Britain: US Air Forces' Strategic Presence, 1946–64* (Manchester: Manchester University Press, 2016).

33. Acheson, *Present at the Creation*, 602.

34. The Atlantic Command drama went to the heart of Britain's worldview of occupying an intermediate place between global empire and the North Atlantic world. U.S. transcripts ploddingly sum this up as Churchill complaining that "the British had earned equality with British blood." Churchill's argument that the Royal Navy ever protected the young United States was dubious history, as I discuss in the conclusion, and anyway, present fleet strength was speaking louder than battles past. The only compromise offered Churchill was a small extension of the area designated the United Kingdom Home Waters Command. The U.S. Navy for the moment did not want to patrol there anyway, though it was generously prepared in wartime to dispatch a carrier task force to make "a Russian invasion of the British Isles impossible." See USN Plans, Strategic Plans & Operations, Lectures and Speeches, undated 1952, Admiral Forrest Sherman Papers.

35. Winston Churchill, *Speech to the Congress of the United States of America, January 17, 1952* (London: H.M. Stationery Office, 1952).

36. Ohly to Nash, December 8, 1951, RG 330, CD 091.3 UK 1952.

37. Draft of letter from Dean Acheson to Ambassador Walter S. Gifford, ca. March 1952, Secretary of State Files, Acheson Papers; letter from U.S. Ambassador to Great Britain Walter S. Gifford to Dean Acheson, with attached letter from Foreign Secretary Anthony Eden of Great Britain to Dean Acheson, April 19, 1952, Secretary of State Files, Acheson Papers, HSTL.

38. Colville, diary entry for May 23, 1952, in *Fringes of Power*, 649.

39. The size of the Royal Navy's Mediterranean Fleet is significant and had previously been gauged in NSC 75. At this point, given rotations, it was likely to consist

of the 2nd Aircraft Carrier Squadron; the 1st Cruiser Squadron; the 1st, 2nd, and 3rd Destroyer Flotillas; the 2nd and 3rd Escort Flotillas; the 1st Submarine Flotilla; and the 2nd Minesweeper Flotilla.

40. Mountbatten was also courageous, as shown in the sinking of his destroyer, HMS *Kelly*, off Crete in 1941. Years later, in the summer of 1979, he and I were working on a project concerning nuclear proliferation. He mentioned he'd be gone later in August for holiday in County Sligo, on Ireland's northwest coast. I was alarmed and told him of the IRA terrorist fund-raising then under way in Boston, where I lived. He said others had warned him too, but he couldn't concern himself with threats. On the twenty-seventh, an IRA bomb killed him at sea, along with his fourteen-year-old grandson and a fifteen-year-old deckhand.

41. Graham Freudenberg, *Churchill and Australia* (Sydney: Macmillan Australia, 2008), 524.

42. Memcon with Casey, October 13, 1952, in *FRUS, 1952–1954: East Asia and the Pacific, Volume XII, Part 1*, 229, 333.

43. State-JCS staff meeting, April 23, 1952, in ibid.

44. RG 330 CD 092.3 NATO General, July 16, 1951.

45. Director, Strategic Plans, to DCNO Ops, Strategic Plans, A16–12 War Plans, Navy, November 10, 1951.

46. Diary entry for January 8, 1952, in *Diaries of Lord Moran*, on "humiliation," 382.

47. *Hansard*, HC Deb., February 26, 1952, vol. 496, cols. 945–1066.

48. Churchill gave these odds during his interlude in Ottawa. See Woodward to State, January 14, 1952, in *FRUS, 1952–1954: Western Europe and Canada, Volume VI, Part 1*, 844.

15. STEMMING THE TIDE

1. Gaddis, *George F. Kennan*, 249. By this time, "containment" had come to mean anything to anyone.

2. An excellent overview of Stalin's ravings about Catholicism, with reference to Pietro Nenni's visit, is in an October 2, 1952, memorandum from J. W. Russell at the British embassy in Rome to Paul Mason, the assistant undersecretary, at the Foreign Office, found in FO 371/100826 N 1023/29.

3. *Hansard*, HC Deb., March 28, 1950, vol. 473, cols. 189–333, FOREIGN AFFAIRS. Churchill is debating Ernest Bevin.

4. *Hansard*, HC Deb., February 26, 1952, vol. 496, cols. 945–1066, FOREIGN AFFAIRS.

5. A sharp Associated Press reporter knew London to be the "center" when posted there, as he monitored Radio Moscow and relayed cables from other foreign bureaus. See Seymour Topping, *On the Front Lines of the Cold War: An American Correspondent's Journal* (Baton Rouge: Louisiana State University Press, 2010), 167.

6. Leon D. Epstein, *Britain: Uneasy Ally* (Chicago: University of Chicago Press, 1954), 35, which argues that "the desire to stand up to the United States became especially meaningful politically in 1952 and 1953." It was a deliberate reassertion of British initiative, stating that the worst years of recovery were now over.

7. Hanson Baldwin, "How Strong Is Russia? Intelligence Agency Under Fire on Method It Uses to Estimate Soviet's Armed Might," *New York Times*, January 29,

1953, 3. He writes that "the sole criterion by which our agencies should be judged is whether or not they can answer successfully the question—how strong is Russia?"

8. "A false notion of competence" was already apparent, recalled Howard Roman, an OSS veteran, a former Harvard faculty member, and a branch chief for James Angleton. Deficiencies included operations as well as analysis. Interview, May 16, 1980, Kennedy Archive. The Office of National Estimates, formed by the Yale history professor Sherman Kent in 1953 and headed by him for fifteen years, did bring disciplined analysis—but still could tell little about the Soviet Union's economy and military capacities. Material on Kent's intelligence career can be found in the Sherman Kent Papers at Yale, but after retiring from the CIA in 1967, he retained what seems to have been the most revealing of his letters and documents, keeping them at his residence in Washington, D.C. He died in 1986. When his wife, Elizabeth Gregory Kent, died ten years later, these papers were burned by the family, though I heard summaries of them, after the fact.

9. The Kennedy Archive contains multiple interviews of several individuals, among them Angleton. Referenced here is one from April 5, 1979, Kennedy Archive.

10. Ben Macintyre, *A Spy Among Friends: Kim Philby and the Great Betrayal* (London: Bloomsbury, 2010), 35.

11. "Missing Diplomats," *Washington Post*, June 8, 1951, 24.

12. The CIA would demonstrate this mole-hunting paradox thirty years later with its slow-motion, nine-year failure to catch its own traitor Aldrich Ames, who at the time was heading the counterintelligence branch of its Soviet/East European Division. See my account of Ames and CIA personnel in *Fifty-Year Wound*, 568–71.

13. The previously unseen footage of Kim Philby can be viewed at http://www.bbc.com/news/uk-35954685BBC, April 7, 2016. Also note "Kim Philby, Lecturing in East Berlin in '81," *New York Times*, April 4, 2016, 9.

14. Kennan's appointment as ambassador goes unmentioned in Undersecretary David Bruce's meticulous diaries that chronicle every important development in the State Department for this period. But then Bruce didn't pay much attention to Kennan, whose work he found long-winded. See David Bruce Papers, Virginia Historical Society, Richmond.

15. Kennan had grave illusions about Stalin, again contrary to myth. That's seen in Kennan's advocacy of a neutral Germany and in his apparent belief, at this point in 1952, that one might reason with Stalin.

16. Kennan's request for poison was reported by Walter Hixson, *George Kennan: Cold War Iconoclast* (New York: Columbia University Press, 1989), 125, citing the CIA's Peer de Silva. What's new are insights of the decision being made by top CIA officials.

17. Kennan "has the question of his own dignity very much in mind," reported Gascoigne to the Foreign Office, in light of his being ignored by the Kremlin, except for what would be a single audience granted by Foreign Minister Andrei Vyshinsky, on June 19. See Gascoigne to Strang, May 20, 1952, FO 371/100836 AS 10345.

18. Ibid.

19. Additional insights on Kennan in Moscow come from a memorandum that Gascoigne sent to Assistant Undersecretary Paul Mason at the Foreign Office. Having seen Vyshinsky, for example, Kennan is said to have been impressed by "the very kind way" Stalin's former chief prosecutor dealt with him. FO 371/100836, June 20, 1952.

20. The official who is quoted meant that the United States would henceforth be focusing inward. The term "purdah," as the head of Britain's Civil Service, Sir Jeremy Heywood, explained in 2015, is an unofficial one that the British use to describe the weeks before their own elections when restrictions are placed on the activity of civil servants (that is, the "preelection period").

21. "Eisenhower Urges Helping Nations Escape Red Yoke," *New York Times*, August 26, 1952, 1.

22. Poole, *Joint Chiefs of Staff and National Policy, 1950–1952*, 178. The Joint Chiefs made their opinions known on the idea of a "token" U.S. force in Egypt. If even small numbers of GIs or marines were deployed, especially into guerrilla shoot-outs adjacent to inflammable cities, then America better be ready to send in big reinforcements when needed. That ended discussion of Churchill's proposal.

23. H. W. Brands, *The Specter of Neutralism: The United States and the Emergence of the Third World, 1947–1960* (New York: Columbia University Press, 1989), 235.

24. Acheson to Caffery, September 8, 1952, in *FRUS, 1952–1954: The Near and Middle East, Volume IX*, 1956.

25. This was George H. Middleton, serving in an acting capacity. He is quoted in Parviz Daneshvar, *Revolution in Iran* (New York: St. Martin's Press, 1996), 29.

26. "Iran: Diplomacy by Blackmail," *Time*, October 27, 1952.

27. Hahn, *The United States, Great Britain, and Egypt*, 158.

28. Caffery to McGhee, September 19, 1952, box 1, George McGhee Papers, HSTL.

29. "Mechanics of Controlling an Election," July 18, 1952, RG 59, Records of the Department of State, Decimal Files, 1950–1954.

30. Max Bishop to Parker to Hart, Military Show of Strength, July 28, 1952, RG 59, Records of the Department of State, Decimal Files, 1950–1954.

31. Eden's account of his youth, *Another World, 1897–1917*, published a year before he died, is, like Acheson's equally evocative *Morning and Noon*, the most powerful material he ever wrote.

32. Eden, *Full Circle*, 50.

33. Shuckburgh, *Descent to Suez*, 128.

34. "British Overseas Obligations" of June 18, 1952, by foreign secretary, para. 30, CAB 129/53 Memorandum no. C(52)202.

35. Acheson emphasized throughout the year that the United States would not be sending troops to Vietnam, as he also did to Nitze at al. See Memorandum of Conversation, by the Director of the Policy Planning Staff (Nitze), May 12, 1952, in *FRUS, 1952–1954: Indochina, Volume XIII, Part 1*.

36. Graves to MacDonald, March 22, 1952, FO 371/101066.

37. By the close of 1952, 128,238 Americans would be killed, wounded, or missing in Korea.

38. Author interviews. Jack H. Mower died in his Washington, D.C., residence in 2016, aged ninety-four, and played in USTA matches until he was over eighty-five.

His daughter, Joan Mower, is writing what likely will be the definitive book on the early years of the CIA in Africa.

39. "British Troops Launch Drive on Mau Mau in Mountains," *New York Times*, February 23, 1955, 3.

40. *The Kenya Papers of General Sir George Erskine, 1953–1955*, ed. Huw Bennett and David French (Stroud, U.K.: History Press, 2013), 96. See "Message to Be Distributed to All Officers of the Army, Police, and Security Forces," November 30, 1953.

41. The figure of at least 20,000 killed is offered by David Anderson in *Histories of the Hanged: The Dirty War in Kenya and the End of Empire* (New York: Norton, 2005). Caroline Elkins makes the explicit comparison to the Soviet Gulag in *Imperial Reckoning: The Untold Story of Britain's Gulag in Kenya* (New York: Henry Holt, 2005).

42. In Korea and Japan, the U.S. Army had eight divisions: the 2nd, 3rd, 7th, 24th, 25th, 40th, and 45th Infantry Divisions and the 1st Cavalry Division. It also had two regimental combat teams, the 5th and 187th, in Korea. In addition, the 1st Marine Division was in Korea. In Europe, the army by now had five divisions: 1st, 4th, 28th, and 43rd Infantry and 2nd Armored. Finally, there were several separate armored cavalry regiments and infantry units.

43. This mobilization of around 900,000 men and women, including conscripts, for the armed forces was in a country with acute shortages of labor, including at least 50,000 more skilled workers being needed in aviation.

44. HMS *Victorious* might have been intended to be the most modern aircraft carrier in the world, but it wasn't launched until 1959, whereas the USS *Forrestal* arrived in 1954.

45. Progress had been delayed for perhaps a year: Canada had failed to supply certain research, though delivering the plutonium, and the Ministry of Supply couldn't afford the salaries of enough design engineers.

46. The article title in *Time* is unflattering because the most famous line in Woolf's extended essay, *A Room of One's Own*, may be "Give her a room of her own and five hundred a year, let her speak her mind and leave out half that she now puts in, and she will write a better book one of these days."

47. Robert Oppenheimer, Digest of Meeting, February 17, 1953, CFR archives.

48. Kim Philby, *My Silent War: The Autobiography of a Spy* (New York: Modern Library, 2002), 145.

49. Ibid., 120.

50. Ricky-Dale Calhoun, "The Art of Strategic Counterintelligence: The Musketeer's Cloak: Strategic Deception During the Suez Crisis of 1956," *Studies in Intelligence* 51, no. 2 (2007).

51. Descriptions of a CIA "golden age" have been prevalent among writers for at least two decades, despite overwhelming evidence of serial blundering. See, for example, Loch Johnson, "The Golden Age of the CIA," *Diplomatic History* 20, no. 4 (1996): 675–80, in which he reviews Peter Grose's book on Allen Dulles. More recently, the CIA itself keeps calling these years a "golden age," as can be seen at https://www.cia.gov/news-information/featured-story-archive/allen-dulles-becomes-dci.html.

52. Thomas Finletter conversation with Timothy Dickinson (of *Harper's* magazine), New York, November 1973, as told to me in 2016.

53. Melvin Goodman, "The Foundations of Anglo-American Intelligence Sharing," *Studies in Intelligence* 59, no. 2 (June 2015): 22.

54. "Soviet Espionage Best, Smith Says," *New York Times*, January 26, 1953, 4.

55. Personnel shortcomings within the CIA have been chronic, of course with exceptions. See Ishmael Jones, *The Human Factor: Inside the CIA's Dysfunctional Intelligence Culture* (New York: Encounter Books, 2010). "Jones" is a pseudonym for a widely respected operations officer. After 2001, the 9/11 Commission established that the agency lacked "the human capital to do the job," echoing conclusions of another commission right before the atrocity that Langley was suffering "personnel problems."

56. See Christopher Hitchens, *Blood, Class, and Empire: The Enduring Anglo-American Relationship* (New York: Nation Books, 2004), 316–17.

57. George K. Young, *Masters of Indecision: An Inquiry into the Political Process* (London: Methuen, 1962), 82.

16. CORONATIONS AND CRISES

1. Klaus Larres, *Churchill's Cold War: The Politics of Personal Diplomacy* (New Haven, Conn.: Yale University Press, 2002), 183.

2. It's an overstatement to say that the United States and Britain ever had a "nuclear arms race," as in the subtitle of Graham Farmelo's excellent *Churchill's Bomb: How the United States Overtook Britain in the First Nuclear Arms Race*, but politicians and the press were attuned to competition.

3. Barbara Leaming, *Churchill Defiant: Fighting On, 1945–1955* (New York: Harper, 2010), 189.

4. Memorandum of Conversation, by William J. McWilliams of the Executive Secretariat, conversation of January 8, 1953, in *FRUS, 1952–1954: Western Europe and Canada, Volume VI, Part 1*.

5. Colville, diary entry for January 6, 1953, in *Fringes of Power*, 660, 661.

6. Makins, January 10, 1953, FO 371 10357 AU 1051/9.

7. Snyder, oral history, HSTL.

8. "Churchill Wishes Truman 'Good-By,'" *New York Times*, January 9, 1953, 1.

9. Colville, diary entry for January 8, 1953, in *Fringes of Power*, 663.

10. Paul B. Fay, *The Pleasure of His Company* (New York: Harper and Row, 1966), 216, on Kennedy's fascination with Eisenhower and his prosperity. "Red" Fay was JFK's undersecretary of the navy and had served with him in the Pacific. As Eisenhower spent time among the newly rich, he adopted behaviors and accepted favors that would be troubling today: the gold stationery with the initials DDE he used while at SHAPE; a golf cottage built for him in Augusta, Georgia, by his friends; the 18-karat gold Rolex Datejust shown on a 1952 cover of *Life* magazine; and his bespoke suits. Getting wobbled like this is also an American military phenomenon— after a rising officer endures decades of poor housing and low pay and then ends up orbiting the rich when finally obtaining top rank. President Ulysses S. Grant is an example, though it's impossible to imagine General George C. Marshall with such a "gang," or accepting expensive gifts, or playing golf.

11. Colville, diary entry of January 12, 1953, in *Fringes of Power*, 665.

12. On "brigadier," see the entry of July 19, 1953, in *Diaries of Lord Moran*, 467.

13. Writers keep repeating the canard of Dulles's "bad breath," and it surfaces in Townsend Hoopes's *Devil and John Foster Dulles* (Boston: Little, Brown, 1973), 169, to be echoed in Thomas, *Ike's Bluff*, 51, and elsewhere. It seems to have originated with remarks by the Foreign Office permanent undersecretary who found Dulles to be uncouth. See diary entry for July 13, 1942, in *Diaries of Sir Alexander Cadogan, O.M., 1938–1945*, ed. David Dilks (New York: G. P. Putnam's Sons, 1972), 462.

14. "Thoughts on the Business of Life," *Forbes*, May 25, 1992, 316.

15. Richard Helms, interview, May 29, 1980, Kennedy Archive.

16. On "cover functions," see the former CIA director William E. Colby, interview, November 17, 1978, Kennedy Archive. The secretary of state had a secure phone in his office, but it was difficult to use. A secure call had to be scheduled thirty minutes in advance, and Foster hated it. President Eisenhower had a secure phone too, and it was slightly easier to use, but the contraption still had to be pulled over and plugged in. He avoided it as well. Lots of inappropriate telephone conversations were therefore in the clear. The transcripts provide rich source material.

17. Entry for February 18, 1952, in *Macmillan Diaries*, 144.

18. Committee on Appropriations, July 9, 1953, Henry C. Dworshak, R-Idaho, Records of the United States Senate, National Archives.

19. "New Soviet Regime Held Up as a Threat," *New York Times*, March 14, 1953, 3.

20. Eleanor Lansing Dulles, then working in State's Office of German Affairs, took issue with a reference in Kennan's memoirs that, she concluded, implies that Secretary Dulles was uninterested in Stalin's death; see *George F. Kennan: Memoirs, 1950–1963* (Boston: Little, Brown, 1972), 2:180. She asserted "there was no dispute between CIA and State on what to do after Stalin's death, propaganda or policy wise." Kennedy Archive, Interview of October 8, 1980. Also in 1953, Kennan would work as a consultant on Project Solarium, along with Admiral Richard Conolly, who led one of the other three work groups. Kennan writes, "I had my revenge by saddling him [Foster Dulles], inescapably, with my policy" (*Memoirs, 1950–1963*, 182). Unsurprisingly, Kennan is being deceptive, as declassified records would show. The historian Jeffrey Barlow concludes that the Solarium encounter was a clear victory for Dulles. See *From Hot War to Cold: The U.S. Navy and National Security Affairs, 1945–1955* (Stanford: Stanford University Press, 2009), 362–63.

21. *Hansard*, HC Deb., May 11, 1953, vol. 515, cols. 883–1004; Eisenhower and Dulles didn't show "indifference" over Churchill's mischief making; they were furious. But "indifference" is assumed in Burleigh's *Small Wars, Faraway Places*, 262.

22. Entry for January 6, 1953, in *The Eisenhower Diaries*, ed. Robert Ferrell (New York: W. W. Norton, 1981), 223.

23. Presidential Correspondence, lot 66 D 204, "Churchill Correspondence with Eisenhower, February 1953 thru March 1955," February 18, 1953, in *FRUS, 1952–1954: The Near and Middle East, Volume IX, Part 2*.

24. Ross to Burrows, June 5, 1952, FO 371/98828 ES 1051/5.

25. Anthony Nutting, *Nasser* (New York: Dutton, 1972), 50.

26. No. 41, Memorandum of Conversation, by the Secretary of State, May 22, 1953, in *FRUS, 1952–1954: The Near and Middle East, Volume IX, Part 1*.

27. John W. Braasch, "Anthony Eden's Biliary Tract Saga," *Annals of Surgery*, November 2002.

28. *Hansard*, HC Deb., May 11, 1953, vol. 515, cols. 883–1004.

29. No. 3, Memorandum of Conversation, Prepared in the Embassy in Cairo, May 11, 1953, in *FRUS, 1952–1954: The Near and Middle East, Volume IX, Part 1*.

30. No. 5, Memorandum of Conversation, Prepared in the Embassy in Cairo, May 12, 1953, ibid.

31. Eisenhower to Churchill, June 10, 1953, in *Churchill-Eisenhower Correspondence*, 69.

32. "Dulles Predicts Better U.S. Treatment for Middle East," *New York Times*, May 19, 1953, 1. Nasser also scoffed at the notion of British occupiers upholding "the security of the 'Free World.'"

33. Altogether, the commonwealth navies boasted twenty-seven carriers, in service, in reserve, or under construction. Although the Royal Navy had some of the largest warships afloat, such as the *Ark Royal* and the *Eagle*, comparing its fleet air arm with the Americans' is inapt because the U.S. Navy assigned its carriers a large role against land objectives whereas British ones were used chiefly for shipping protection and antisubmarine warfare.

34. "Britain Develops Offensive Navy," *New York Times*, February 19, 1954, 3. The Royal Navy's three major fleets are nonetheless seen as stretched "for the global-embracing peacetime role Britain must play."

35. "Birth of New Era Is Britain's Hope," *New York Times*, June 1, 1953, 2.

36. "100 British Vessels Cited in Red Trade," *New York Times*, May 21, 1953, 8.

37. Congressional Record, U.S. Senate, May 13, 1953, 83-1, 4912.

38. Bellaigue, *Patriot of Persia*, 6.

39. Stutesman, ADST oral history.

40. William M. Rountree, Iran, Counselor at the U.S. Embassy, 1953–1955, oral history interview, September 20, 1989, ADST.

41. Ray Takeyh and Steven Simon, *The Pragmatic Superpower: Winning the Cold War in the Middle East* (New York: Norton, 2016), 75–85.

42. Israel slowly began to release such Palestinian funds in 1953, via Barclays bank. The Israelis allowed a single pound sterling to be exchanged for each Israeli pound unfrozen, limited to fifty pounds per month. On Palestinians being subjected to military rule, see Odeh Bisharat, "November 8, 1966: Military Rule on Israeli Arabs Lifted," *Haaretz*, June 16, 2013.

43. Hanson Baldwin, "The Arab-Israel Gulf," *New York Times*, October 27, 1953, 4.

44. Ibid.

45. "Israel: Massacre at Kibya," *Time*, October 26, 1953. Another future Israeli prime minister, Ariel Sharon, the commander of "Unit 101," conducted the atrocity, which was launched while a highly publicized White House peace envoy, Eric Johnston, was due to arrive in the Middle East.

46. Benny Morris, *Israel's Border Wars, 1949–1956* (Oxford: Oxford University Press, 1993). See chap. 8, "Qibya" (240–76), and p. 263 on Washington and Eban.

47. Ibid., 265.

48. Shuckburgh, entry for January 23, 1953, in *Descent to Suez*, 75.

49. *Clarissa Eden: A Memoir: From Churchill to Eden*, ed. Cate Haste (London: Weidenfeld & Nicolson, 2008), 178.

50. Shuckburgh, entry for December 3, 1953, in *Descent to Suez*, 113.

51. Eisenhower to Churchill, December 20, 1953, in *Churchill-Eisenhower Correspondence*, 117.

17. THE BREAK POINTS OF 1954

1. Robert J. Watson, *The Joint Chiefs of Staff and National Policy, 1953–1954* (Washington, D.C.: Office of Joint History, Office of the Chairman of the Joint Chiefs of Staff, 1998), 40, referencing NSC 162/2, which concluded in 1953 that "allied opinion, especially in Europe, has been less willing to follow US leadership."

2. Dwight D. Eisenhower, President's News Conference, October 28, 1954, American Presidency Project.

3. Speech of Secretary of State John Foster Dulles before the Council on Foreign Relations, January 12, 1954, *Department of State Bulletin*.

4. Franks offered this epigram to James Bowker at the Foreign Office, who was head of department for the Middle East, 1950–1953. FO 371/91182 E 1022/10, July 19, 1951.

5. Dwight D. Eisenhower, Radio and Television Address to the American People on the State of the Nation, April 5, 1954, American Presidency Project.

6. The recession of 1953–1954 that followed the Korean armistice was relatively brief and mild, albeit with a cost of roughly $56 billion. But, as in 1949, no one knew it would be that unthreatening at the time.

7. So-called austerity budgets from the Republican Congress had cut State Department personnel by 20 percent, even compelling State to cable merely the excerpts of its important documents, rather than full copies, to its Moscow embassy.

8. "U.S.-British Relations," *New York Times*, June 24, 1954, 3.

9. MacDonald, June 30, 1953, to Foreign Office, FO 371/106768 FF 1071/128.

10. Lawrence, *Assuming the Burden*, 284–85.

11. Note on MacDonald's Talk with Vice President Nixon, October 1953, FO 371/105221.

12. Nixon's judgment on the turning tide was published everywhere in the United States, such as in the *Chicago Daily Tribune*, October 26, 1953.

13. "Eisenhower Calls Indo-China Vital," *New York Times*, March 25, 1954, 1.

14. Eisenhower NSC meeting, April 28, 1953, in *FRUS, 1952–1954: Indochina, Volume XIII, Part 1*.

15. Memorandum of Discussion at the 179th Meeting of the National Security Council, Friday, January 8, 1954, in *FRUS, 1952–1954: Indochina, Volume XIII, Part 1*.

16. Dulles to the President, April 3, 1954, JFD telephone transcripts, Seeley Mudd Library, Princeton.

17. The Secretary of State to the Embassy in the United Kingdom, April 4, 1954, in *FRUS, 1952–1954: Indochina, Volume XIII, Part 1*.

18. Secretary Dulles told his brother Allen this week that he wasn't "hooked on ground troops" and that he preferred to apply "his theory" of deterrence by massive retaliation to the problem of Indochina. Conversation with Allen Dulles, April 19, 1954, JFD telephone transcripts.

19. Why the Vietminh should be winning seems to have been a recurring question for Dulles. See Nong Van Dan, *Churchill, Eden, and Indo-China, 1951–1955* (New York: Anthem Press, 2011), 134, citing Tel. no. 7 of April 26, 1954, from Eden, Geneva, to FO.

20. "United States Parallel Efforts for 'United Action,'" referencing the joint statement of April 13, in *FRUS, 1952–1954: Indochina, Volume XIII, Part 2*. Bevan objects to "surrendering to U.S. pressure" in *Hansard*, HC Deb., April 13, 1954, vol. 526, cols. 969–75.

21. "High Aide Says Troops May Be Sent," *New York Times*, April 17, 1954, 1.

22. Dwight D. Eisenhower, President's News Conference, March 24, 1954, American Presidency Project.

23. *Taking Charge: The Johnson White House Tapes, 1963–1964*, ed. Michael Beschloss (New York: Simon & Schuster, 1997). See LBJ to John S. Knight, February 3, 1964, 214, and LBJ to McGeorge Bundy, March 4, 1964, 267. On Eisenhower's advice to escalate in Vietnam—the alternative being that the Communists would be "cutting the world in half"—see DCI John McCone, memorandum for the record, May 10, 1962, CIA/DCI files, Job No. 80BO1285A, box 2, folder 2.

24. Dulles to Dillon, April 5, 1954, in *FRUS, 1952–1954: Indochina, Volume XIII* (two parts).

25. Memorandum of Conversation, by the Secretary of State, May 19, 1954, in *FRUS, 1952–1954: Indochina, Volume XIII, Part 2*.

26. Two of the best scholars of the subject show irrefutably Eisenhower's readiness to use nuclear weapons. See David Watry, "Atomic Brinksmanship," in *Diplomacy at the Brink: Eisenhower, Churchill, and Eden in the Cold War* (Baton Rouge: Louisiana State University Press, 2014); and John Prados, *Vietnam: The History of an Unwinnable War, 1945–1975* (Lawrence: University Press of Kansas, 2009). Prados is an author and historian (and game maker) who has long been among the few consistently reliable analysts of U.S. national security policies.

27. Memorandum by the Counselor (MacArthur) to the Secretary of State, April 7, 1954, in *FRUS, 1952–1954: Indochina, Volume XIII, Part 1*.

28. Eisenhower to Dulles, April 23, 1954, Dulles-April (2), box 2, Dulles-Herter Series, Ann Whitman File, Papers of Dwight D. Eisenhower, 1953–1961, DDEL.

29. Dulles's telegram to Washington, April 23, 1954, as shown in Editorial Note, in *FRUS, 1952–1954: East Asia and the Pacific, Volume XII, Part 1*.

30. Watry, *Diplomacy at the Brink*, 70, referencing the Avon Papers, Churchill to Eden, telegram, June 13, 1954, FO 800/785 Far East.

31. Memorandum of Discussion at the 192d Meeting of the National Security Council, Tuesday, April 6, 1954, in *FRUS, 1952–1954: Indochina, Volume XIII, Part 1*.

32. Memorandum of Discussion at the 194th Meeting of the National Security Council, Thursday, April 29, 1954, in *FRUS, 1952–1954: Indochina, Volume XIII, Part 2*.

33. Memorandum of a Conference at the White House, Wednesday, May 5, 1954, in *FRUS, 1952–1954: Indochina, Volume XIII, Part 2*.

34. At first, Dulles's maneuvering with Australia and New Zealand looked as if it might work. "The tight little island must [always] be considered first," Canberra's long-serving foreign minister, Richard Casey, told the Americans, on May 3, about Britain's worldview.

35. Shuckburgh, diary entry for May 2, 1954, in *Descent to Suez*, 187.

36. Ambassador Dillon to State, April 26, 1954, in *FRUS, 1952–1954: Indochina, Volume XIII, Part 2*.

37. Shuckburgh, diary entry for May 3, 1954, in *Descent to Suez*, 189.

38. Watry, *Diplomacy at the Brink*, 31, referencing the Avon Papers, Eden to Churchill, April 28, 1954, FO 800/841.

39. Record of the Secretary of State's Briefing for Members of Congress, Held at the Department of State, May 5, 1954, in *FRUS, 1952–1954: Indochina, Volume XIII, Part 2*.

40. Ibid.

41. Radio and Television Address to the Nation by the Secretary of State, Delivered in Washington, May 7, 1954, in *FRUS, 1952–1954: The Geneva Conference, Volume XVI*.

42. Memorandum of Discussion at the 192d Meeting of the National Security Council, Tuesday, April 6, 1954, in *FRUS, 1952–1954: Indochina, Volume XIII, Part 1*.

43. Ibid.

44. No. 457 Hagerty Diary, Monday, June 14, 1954, in *FRUS, 1952–1954: Western Europe and Canada, Volume VI, Part 1*.

45. Dwight D. Eisenhower, Press Conference, June 16, 1954, American Presidency Project.

46. For example, see "Eisenhower and Churchill Confer," *New York Times*, June 26, 1954, 1.

47. Watry, *Diplomacy at the Brink*, 100, referencing the Avon Papers, Lloyd to Churchill, May 9, 1953, FO 800/802 Latin America 1952–1954.

48. Stephen Rabe, *U.S. Intervention in British Guiana: A Cold War Story* (Chapel Hill: University of North Carolina Press, 2005), 39.

49. On this mistaken notion of "friends," see Stephen Kinzer's conspiratorial *The Brothers: John Foster Dulles, Allen Dulles, and Their Secret World War* (New York: Times Books, 2013), chap. 6. "Dictated by corporate interests" is Ian Buruma, *Year Zero: A History of 1945* (New York: Penguin, 2013), 312. "Fun-hating" is again Kinzer, *Brothers*, 234. That fine historian Jean Edward Smith is more nuanced, for example in *Eisenhower in War and Peace* (New York: Random House, 2013). But he too implies a tie between the Dulles brothers' decisions and their legal work for UFCO at Sullivan & Cromwell. See p. 629.

50. Richard Bissell, first interview, in his office, May 26, 1978, Kennedy Archive.

51. Meers, "The British Connection," 413.

52. "Trouble in Store?," *Times* (London), March 11, 1954.

53. Telephone call to Allen Dulles, May 18, 1954, JFD telephone transcripts.

54. Meers, "British Connection," 413.

55. Conversation with Attorney General Herbert Brownell Jr., June 30, 1954, JFD telephone transcripts.

56. See a detailed discussion of the CIA's Operation Success, which included such serial blundering as encountered in Guatemala, including the CIA's lies to Eisenhower, in Leebaert, *Fifty-Year Wound*, 171–72.

57. Meers, "British Connection," 415.

58. John W. Young, "Great Britain's Latin American Dilemma: The Foreign Office and the Overthrow of 'Communist' Guatemala, June 1954," *International History Review* 8, no. 4 (1986): 583–84.

59. Description of the motorcade and the thrust of Dulles's conversation is from General File, 1954, Winthrop Aldrich Papers, Baker Library, Harvard University. Dulles described Guatemala as the "touchstone" to Ambassador Makins. See Meers, "British Connection," 413.

60. "Memorandum of Telephone Conversation with Allen Dulles," July 3, 1954, JFD telephone transcripts. The CIA routinely has parties after operations deemed successful. Kim Roosevelt had one in Tehran in 1953 after the shah returned from exile, and in 1989 there was a champagne celebration at Langley headquarters when the Russians were compelled to retreat from Afghanistan.

61. Minutes by J. G. Ward, July 20, 1954, FO 371/108742 A 1076/116.

62. Entry from July 5, 1954, in *Diaries of Lord Moran*, 614.

18. ORDERING CHAOS

1. Eden, *Full Circle*, 212.

2. "Cold War: The Weighing Room," *Time*, January 11, 1954.

3. Oliver S. Franks, *Britain and the Tide of World Affairs* (London: Oxford University Press, 1955).

4. George Lichtheim, *The Pattern of World Conflict* (New York: Dial Press, 1955), 17, 38.

5. See Major David Petraeus, "Korea, the Never-Again Club, and Indochina," *Parameters: Journal of the U.S. Army War College* (December 1987): 61–63, in which he attributes the "Never Again" slogan to General Mark Clark, who had been appointed head of the UN Command in Korea in May 1952.

6. That U.S. policy makers recognized America could not otherwise be "fully effective" is James Reston's conclusion in "U.S.-British Relations—III," *New York Times*, June 25, 1954, 1.

7. Kevin Ruane, "SEATO, MEDO, and the Baghdad Pact, 1952–1955," *Diplomacy and Statecraft* 16, issue 1 (2005).

8. Call from General Walter Bedell Smith, July 21, 1954, JFD telephone transcripts.

9. Entry for April 9, 1954, in *Diaries of Lord Moran*, 577, about "go it alone."

10. In "For the U.S.-European Alliance, Everything Has Changed," *Washington Post*, April 28, 2017, Anne Applebaum sees Germany as the "core of the transatlantic alliance for more than 70 years"—except no such alliance existed in 1947, and a disarmed western Germany was then under occupation. Elsewhere she argues that a "Pax Americana" of U.S.-backed rules has "governed transatlantic commerce and politics for 70 years." But there was nothing like this in 1947 either, nor in 1955. See Anne Applebaum, "Is Pax Americana Doomed?," *Washington Post*, February 9, 2017.

11. The Army Historical Foundation's chief historian, Matt Seelinger, discourages such comparisons as "strongest" and "best." That said, informed U.S. observers of the time understood how the two forces ranked side by side. America's six divisions were really five reinforced ones and didn't have comparable armor. However, their artillery was superior (for example, number of tubes, better quality, better

coordination). Moreover, the U.S. Army had deployed the M65 atomic cannon to Europe by 1954. Hence, I say "arguably."

12. Eisenhower and Nasser finally met in New York on September 26, 1960, at the annual meeting of the UN General Assembly. Dwight D. Eisenhower, *Waging Peace, 1956–1961* (Garden City, N.Y.: Doubleday, 1965), 584.

13. Ray Takeyh, "United States Diplomacy and the Anglo-Egyptian Treaty of 1954," *UCLA Historical Journal* 16, no. 0 (1996): 77.

14. On "terror unit," see "IDF Declassifies Docs," *Haaretz*, May 11, 2015, quoting documents from Nehemiah Argov, Ben-Gurion's military secretary.

15. A good overview, with emphasis on Tel Aviv's intention to ruin the Anglo-Egyptian peace talks, is Jerome Chanes, "The Lessons of the 'Lavon Affair,'" *Forward*, May 16, 2014; also see Leonard Weiss, "The Lavon Affair: How a False-Flag Operation Led to War and the Israeli Bomb," *Bulletin of the Atomic Scientists*, July 2013. In 2015, Israel saw fit to honor the two "heroes" of this affair, Marcelle Ninio and Robert Dassa. See www.haaretz.com/opinion/.premium-1.679075.

16. Tel. no. 645 of August 28, 1954, from the U.K. high commissioner in Australia. This is attached to a letter Churchill sent to Eden, August 29, 1954, Avon Papers 20/17/189A.

17. On "aggression," see "The S.E.A. Collective Defense Treaty," in *FRUS, 1954: East Asia and the Pacific, Volume XII, Part 1*.

18. Ian Buruma, "How Much of a Threat Is China?," *New Yorker*, June 19, 2017, 64.

19. Denis Warner, *The Last Confucian: Vietnam, South-East Asia, and the West* (London: Penguin Books, 1964), 101.

20. Nông Văn Dân, *Churchill, Eden and Indo-China, 1951–1955* (London: Anthem Press, 2011), 172, referencing "Indo China—Conversation Between the Secretary of State and Mr. Dulles at the British Embassy, Paris, on December 16, 1954 at 10 p.m.," FO 371/112042.

21. No. 293 Memorandum of Discussion at the 214th Meeting of the National Security Council, Denver, September 12, 1954, in *FRUS, 1952–1954: China and Japan, Volume XIV, Part 1*.

22. No. 351 Memorandum of Conversation, by the Assistant Secretary of State, October 18, 1954, in *FRUS, 1952–1954: China and Japan, Volume XIV, Part 1*; also see *Volume V, Part 2*, p. 1368.

23. Charmley, *Churchill's Grand Alliance*, 293, referencing Avon Papers, Makins to Eden, December 2, 1954.

24. Watry, *Diplomacy at the Brink*, 88.

25. Dwight D. Eisenhower, President's News Conference, March 16, 1954, American Presidency Project.

26. Steve Tsang, *The Cold War's Odd Couple: The Unintended Partnership Between the Republic of China and the UK, 1950–1958* (New York: I. B. Tauris, 2006), 136.

27. Entry for December 7, 1953, in *Diaries of Lord Moran*, 540.

28. John Foster Dulles, "The Ultimate Weapon Is Moral Principle," *Vital Speeches* 20, no. 11 (March 15, 1954): 325.

29. The trusted adviser was the distinguished economist Dr. Gabriel Hauge, who served as assistant to the president for economic affairs from 1953 to 1958. Hauge became chairman of Manufacturers Hanover Trust Company and shared his apt description of Dulles with the bank's secretary, John Price, whom I've interviewed.

30. *Hansard*, HC Deb., March 1, 1955, vol. 537, cols. 1893–2012.

31. Selwyn Lloyd, *Suez 1956: A Personal Account* (London: Jonathan Cape, 1978), 27.

32. Alsop and Alsop, entry for March 21, 1956, in *Reporter's Trade*, 295.

33. *Hansard*, HC Deb., March 2, 1955, vol. 537, cols. 2066–199.

34. Entry for July 15, 1953, in *Diaries of Lord Moran*, 464.

35. Colville, undated entry for early April, in *Fringes of Power*, 708.

36. James Reston, "A New World View," *New York Times*, May 2, 1955, 12.

37. President Bill Clinton made that clueless comparison between NATO and the Warsaw Pact, as have many others, at a press conference in Helsinki with Russia's president, Boris Yeltsin, March 21, 1997.

38. "Flimsy" is from Paul Johnson, *Journey into Chaos* (London: MacGibbon & Kee, 1958), 9.

39. Editorial Note, 239th Meeting of the NSC, March 3, 1955, in *FRUS, 1955–1957: Near East Region, Iran, Iraq, Volume XII*, 18.

40. Gamal Abdel Nasser, "The Egyptian Revolution," *Foreign Affairs*, January 1955.

41. Memorandum of Discussion at the 239th Meeting of the National Security Council, Washington, March 3, 1955, in *FRUS, 1955–1957: Regulation of Armaments, Atomic Energy, Volume XX*.

42. Morris, *Israel's Border Wars*, 287, where Morris argues "almost directly." Also see Avi Shlaim, "Israel's Dirty War," *London Review of Books*, August 8, 1994, which is a review essay of Morris's book.

43. Hanson Baldwin, "Mideast War Cloud," *New York Times*, November 7, 1955, 3. The Arabs' advantage was in population and space: 41.6 million people compared with 1.6 million Israelis. But only the quality of Jordan's relatively small Arab Legion (some 25,000 officers and men at this point) compared with the manpower that Israel could muster.

44. See Yair Even, *Syria's 1956 Request for Soviet Military Intervention*, CWIHP working paper 77, February 2016, for material on Soviet arms sales to Egypt and Syria and the accompanying political maneuvers.

45. *Clarissa Eden*, 224.

46. Tel. to the President, November 29, 1955, 4:23 p.m., JFD telephone transcripts.

47. Hoopes, *Devil and John Foster Dulles*, 328.

48. "Israelis Suspect Britain," *New York Times*, December 18, 1955, 4.

19. NO END OF A LESSON

1. "Dulles Sees Rise of Liberty in '56," *New York Times*, January 1, 1956, 1.

2. "State of Business: The Postcardiac Bulge," *Time*, November 28, 1955: "The boom cannot continue at the pace set this year," Howard C. Sheperd warned. "We have to accept some slowing down and prevent inflation."

3. Dwight D. Eisenhower, President's News Conference, March 14, 1956, American Presidency Project.

4. "Dulles Outlines Policy," *New York Times*, April 4, 1956, 1.

5. Drew Middleton, "British Rule Out Cuts in Defense," *New York Times*, September 8, 1955, 3. Nonetheless, cuts came a month later, but they still left Britain

shouldering a defense burden of 9 percent of GDP, which was nearly twice the average of other Western European NATO members.

6. David Kynaston, *Family Britain 1951–57* (London: Bloomsbury, 2009), 617. Kynaston's precise and engaging books are essential to understanding modern Britain.

7. Anthony Nutting, *No End of a Lesson: The Inside Story of the Suez Crisis* (New York: Clarkson Potter, 1967). "Yes-man" is on p. 99.

8. For Eden's declaration, and the wide-ranging U.S. reaction, see the reporting in "Eden Says Bombs Deterrent to War," *Corpus Christi Caller-Times*, January 19, 1956, 4; and "Fear of Atomic Reprisal Called Chief War Break," *Odessa American*, January 19, 1956, 1.

9. "Eden Expects New Hope from Washington Talks," *Canberra Times*, January 23, 1956, 1.

10. Memorandum of Conversation, White House, Washington, January 30, 1956, in *FRUS, 1955–1957: Arab-Israeli Dispute, January 1–July 26, 1956, Volume XV.*

11. Ibid.

12. Eisenhower to the American Society of Newspaper Editors, in Washington, reported in James Reston, "Administration Alters Tone of Its Foreign Policy Line," *New York Times*, April 27, 1956, 1.

13. James Reston, "Foreign Policy Criticisms Nettle Washington Officials," *New York Times*, April 15, 1956, 1. Reston makes this comparison to 1946 and notes what would have been astonishment about the British Empire's stature ten years later.

14. "50 Years Ago: 1956: Censure of Israel," *International Herald Tribune*, January 13, 2006. Oddly, there are books on this subject of Eisenhower/Britain/Nasser/Israel—such as Michael Doran's *Ike's Gamble: America's Rise to Dominance in the Middle East* (2016)—that make no mention at all of the Americans repeatedly spearheading censures of Israel in the UN.

15. In spring 1975, I enrolled in a small colloquium taught by the former Israeli diplomat Abba Eban, who was then a visiting professor at Columbia University. Each week during the spring, as well as in personal tutorials, he and I discussed these issues of Palestine, Israel, the United States, wars, and border clashes. In 1956, Cabot Lodge would also have known of the asymmetric record of destruction. Benny Morris concludes that "upward of 2,700 Arab infiltrators, and perhaps as many as 5,000, were killed by the IDF, police, and civilians along Israel's borders between 1949 and 1956. . . . [T]he vast majority of those killed were unarmed," and Morris describes these dead as shepherds, farmers, Bedouins, and refugees trying to return to their villages. *Israel's Border Wars*, 147.

16. My conversations with Eban, 1975.

17. Memorandum from the Secretary of State's Special Assistant for Intelligence (Armstrong) to the Secretary, December 5, 1956, in *FRUS, 1955–1957: Suez Crisis, July 26–December 31, 1956, Volume XVI.*

18. Ibid.; also see "Ben-Gurion Assails British over Arms," *New York Times*, July 4, 1956, 3.

19. Even in December 1956, Secretary Dulles's intelligence specialist, who wrote a long postmortem of the Suez conflict, is uncertain about how many jets France had supplied to Israel.

20. Calhoun, "Art of Strategic Counterintelligence." The article further explains that officials within Britain's spy service, MI6, claimed that their masters in Whitehall believed "western interests in the Middle East, particularly oil, must be preserved from the Egyptian-Soviet threat at all costs."

21. Nutting, *No End of a Lesson*, 34.

22. "The Suez Crisis—a Different Side of Nasser," Ambassador Raymond Hare, interviewed by James Howard, August 20, 1993, oral history, ADST.

23. "Visit to the United Kingdom of Bulganin and Khrushchev, 19–27 April 1956," FO 371/122836, History and Public Policy Program Digital Archive, International History Declassified, Woodrow Wilson International Center for Scholars.

24. "Khrushchev Says Soviet Will Make H-Bomb Missile," *New York Times*, April 24, 1956, 1.

25. Dwight D. Eisenhower, President's News Conference, April 25, 1956, American Presidency Project.

26. "Great Britain: Consumers, Arise!," *Time*, October 8, 1956. This shortcoming was announced by Francis Rogers, a New York businessman, who'd spent five full years on a U.S. aid mission observing British factories.

27. The saying has ever since been attributed—incorrectly—to Churchill, including by the National Churchill Museum, in Fulton, Missouri (on its website), and by authors such as Craig Nelson in his gripping *The Age of Radiance: The Epic Rise and Dramatic Fall of the Atomic Era* (2014). The Churchill Archives at the University of Cambridge can't verify the quotation and is suspicious. In fact, Churchill was never this breezy when discussing nuclear weapons, and the reference sounds American.

28. "British Reaffirm Policy of Force," *New York Times*, May 22, 1956, 1. By 1959, as Cyprus moved toward independence the following year, there would be 371 British dead.

29. "Harding Pledges Firm Cyprus Grip," *New York Times*, March 10, 1956, 1.

30. Third interview with Eleanor Dulles, October 8, 1980, Kennedy Archive.

31. The argument about Eisenhower being out of action is even made in the otherwise meticulous Smith, *Eisenhower in War and Peace*, 692.

32. "The Foreign Aid Battle," *New York Times*, May 29, 1956, 1.

33. Entry for July 25, 1956, in *Macmillan Diaries*, 578.

34. Ferguson, *Colossus*, 111.

35. Hare, oral history, "The Suez Crisis," ADST.

36. Entry for August 1, 1956, in *Macmillan Diaries*, 578.

37. Randolph Churchill, *The Rise and Fall of Sir Anthony Eden* (London: MacGibbon & Kee, 1959), 255.

38. For an example of how these events would be remembered fifty years later, see the reference to Eden's quotation in Paul Reynolds, "Suez: End of Empire," BBC News, http://news.bbc.co.uk/2/hi/middle_east/5199392.stm.

39. "Secretary Broadcasts from White House," *New York Times*, August 4, 1956, 1.

40. Smith, *Eisenhower in War and Peace*, 690.

41. Clark, *From Three Worlds*, 174.

42. James Reston, "The U.S. and Its Allies," *New York Times*, July 20, 1956, 5.

43. Editorial, *Daily Telegraph*, October 10, 1956.

44. Call of October 30, 1956, from Senator Knowland, JFD telephone transcripts. Dulles tells Knowland that he had received Ambassador Eban's "solemn assurances" in private that Israel would not attack.

45. In 1955, Herut was the second-largest party in the Knesset, and Begin, according to the Americans, was a "member of the extremist anti-Arab Herut Party." "Expansionist" is also in Memorandum from the Secretary of State's Special Assistant for Intelligence, December 5, 1956, in *FRUS, 1955–1957: Suez Crisis, July 26– December 31, 1956, Volume XVI*. Foreign Office and Passport Control documents are referenced by Marcus Dysch in *Jewish Chronicle*, June 23, 2011.

46. "The Three Vultures," *Time*, October 29, 1956, 27. Also see "Israel Is 'Alarmed' by British Warning," *New York Times*, October 15, 1956, 3. These attacks included the IDF's October 10 killing of forty-eight civilians in the village of Qalqilya, said to be in retaliation for the killing of two citrus workers the day before.

47. A.J.P. Taylor, *A Personal History* (London: Hamish Hamilton, 1983), 212. In his memoirs, this great historian tells of his son Giles's experience as a conscript during the months of Suez.

48. Isaac Alteras, *Eisenhower and Israel: U.S.-Israeli Relations, 1953–1960* (Gainesville: University of Florida Press, 1993), 224.

49. Memorandum of a Conference with the President, White House, Washington, October 30, 1956, 10:06–10:55 a.m., in *FRUS, 1955–1957: Suez Crisis, July 26– December 31, 1956, Volume XVI*.

50. "Rift in West Big 3 Emerging at U.N.," *New York Times*, October 31, 1956, 1.

51. *Hansard*, HC Deb., October 31, 1956, vol. 558, cols. 1446–572.

52. Eisenhower to Hazlett, November 2, 1956, cited in *FRUS, 1955–1957: Suez Crisis, July 26–December 31, 1956, Volume XVI*, 944.

53. Memorandum of a Conference with the President, White House, Washington, November 5, 1956, in *FRUS, 1955–1957: Eastern Europe, Volume XXV*.

54. Eden to Eisenhower, November 5, 1956, PREM 11/1147 (Prime Minister's Office).

55. Clark, *From Three Worlds*, 209.

56. Henry Brandon, *Special Relationships: A Foreign Correspondent's Memoirs from Roosevelt to Reagan* (New York: Macmillan, 1988), 134, 129.

57. France lost ten soldiers, and the British twenty-two. Nine hundred and twenty-one Egyptians had been killed, and the Israelis claimed two hundred fatalities.

58. Butler, *Art of the Possible*, 193.

59. Eden, *Full Circle*, 566.

60. *Memoires of Lord Gladwyn*, 284. As for Hugh Gaitskell, who was now head of the Labour Party, he both was married to a Zionist and detested Nasser—but he opposed the invasion out of sheer principle.

61. Eisenhower, *Waging Peace*, 40.

62. "Years later," Richard Nixon wrote in the 1980s, "I talked to Eisenhower about Suez; he told me it was his major foreign policy mistake." And, in 1965, Eisenhower would say, "I never should have pressured Israel to evacuate the Sinai." Eisenhower's oft-cited regrets need to be examined skeptically, however. First, Eisenhower was always a minimalist: a decade after the fact, he would have seen 1956–1957 with regret, as the dreadful moment when the United States got irrevocably entangled in the Middle East. Which accounts for his remarks to Nixon. Second, his words on evacuating Sinai

were made to a Republican Party stalwart who was also general chairman of the United Jewish Appeal. Musings by aging statesmen need to be put in perspective—like Dean Acheson's observation in 1970 that "the biggest mistake in post-war American foreign policy . . . isn't the war in Vietnam. It was the Truman Administration's decision to support the creation of the state of Israel." See Douglas Johnston, *Religion, Terror, and Error: U.S. Foreign Policy and the Challenge of Spiritual Engagement* (Westport, Conn.: Praeger, 2011), 32, citing the Harvard College senior thesis in which Acheson was interviewed by John Henry. Old men not only forget; they can also become embittered.

20. WHAT HAPPENED NEXT

1. Automobile Manufacturers Association–New York City—Speech, Pre-presidential Papers of Richard Nixon, 1964–1962, Series 207, Appearances, box 59, folder 12/6/56, Richard Nixon Presidential Library; *RN: The Memoirs of Richard Nixon* (New York: Grosset & Dunlap, 1978), 178. On coordination with Dulles, see Telephone Calls, box 5, Nixon to Dulles, October 31, 1956, JFD Papers, Princeton University.

2. "Eisenhower's Declaration of Independence on Foreign Policy," *Time*, November 12, 1956.

3. "Canada: Declaration of Independence," *Time*, December 10, 1956.

4. "Great Britain: Entering the Missile Age," *Time*, April 15, 1957, 2.

5. Geoffrey Crowther, "Reconstruction of an Alliance," *Foreign Affairs* (Winter 1956–1957). A generation after coining the term, William T. R. Fox published "The Super-Powers Then and Now" (*International Journal*, Summer 1980). He said it was a mistake to have described Britain as a "super-power" in 1944. But Fox's original designation had indeed been correct. By 1980 he was looking at Britain against the backdrop of the despairing 1970s. Nor would he have seen the U.S. and British documents presented here. Nearly all were still classified.

6. Margaret Thatcher, *The Path of Power* (New York: HarperCollins, 1995), 91.

7. Dwight D. Eisenhower, President's News Conference, April 10, 1956, American Presidency Project.

8. Sir Edward Spears, *Liaison 1914: A Narrative of the Great Retreat* (London: Eyre & Spottiswood, 1930), 127. Spears is quoting Germany's General Staff leading up to World War I, which acclaimed Britain's army as "a perfect thing apart" for its long service contracts and worldwide experience, among other qualities.

9. Butler, *Art of the Possible*, 252.

10. Emmet John Hughes, *The Ordeal of Power: A Political Memoir of the Eisenhower Years* (New York: Atheneum, 1963), 220.

11. Douglas Brinkley, *Dean Acheson: The Cold War Years, 1953–71* (New Haven, Conn.: Yale University Press, 1992), 50, citing Eisenhower's legislative meeting notes from January 1, 1957.

12. The former CIA station chief was Wilbur Crane Eveland, who presented a devastating account of U.S. incompetence in his *Ropes of Sand: America's Failure in the Middle East* (New York: Norton, 1980), his quotation being on p. 250.

13. "U.S. Mideast Bid Tied to War Peril," *New York Times*, December 30, 1956, 1.

14. Morris, *Israel's Border Wars*, 265.

15. Call from Ambassador Lodge, February 10, 1957, 3:45 p.m., JFD telephone transcripts.

16. Call from Ambassador Lodge, February 11, 1957, 4:30 p.m., JFD telephone transcripts.

17. Call to the President in Thomasville, Ga., February 12, 1957, 6:49 p.m., JFD telephone transcripts.

18. Call to Ambassador Lodge, February 12, 1957, 2:22 p.m., JFD telephone transcripts, in which Lodge tells of Bunche's conclusion.

19. Ibid.

20. Call from Senator Knowland, February 16, 1957, 6:40 p.m., JFD telephone transcripts.

21. Ibid.

22. "Reveal 1948 British War Threat to Israel," *Chicago Sunday Tribune*, February 17, 1957, 7. This is part of a front-page story titled "Dulles-Eban Talks Make No Progress," and the news was carried widely. The Senate committees had been reviewing what became known as the Eisenhower Doctrine. In his reminiscences, Ambassador James MacDonald had mentioned Britain's December 1948 U.S.-conveyed ultimatum but with minimal detail. See *My Mission in Israel, 1948–1951* (New York: Simon & Schuster, 1951), 116–21.

23. Dwight D. Eisenhower, "Radio and Television Address to the American People on the Situation in the Middle East," February 20, 1953, American Presidency Project.

24. Call from Ambassador Lodge, February 22, 1957, 5:40 p.m., JFD telephone transcripts.

25. The Israelis refused to permit the UNEF to be on their soil, which became an obstacle for Eisenhower and Dulles, as seen in JFD telephone transcripts; peacekeepers would have to be placed on Egyptian territory only. When Nasser dismissed the UNEF from his country in 1967, Israel claimed this step to be a prelude to war.

26. Whereas Foster Dulles had come to "hate" Nasser, his brother Allen disagreed and saw Nasser's leadership as generally positive. Interview with Eleanor Dulles, October 8, 1980, Kennedy Archive.

27. Eisenhower's estimate of the number of refugees is in Call to the President, February 24, 1957, 3:03 p.m., JFD telephone transcripts. Eisenhower wanting to assure the Israelis of U.S. involvement in Gaza is in a later call that day, at 6:45 p.m.

28. The former ambassador Henry Grady died in 1957, the same year that the CIA ramped up its police training in Iran; he passed on quietly as a passenger aboard one of his company's ships, the USS *President Wilson*, far in the Pacific. After being recalled from Tehran in 1951, he had blamed Acheson for much of the turmoil that followed in Iran.

29. Jebb to Deputy Under Secretary (Economic Affairs) Paul Gore-Booth, Kirkpatrick, et al., January 4, 1957, FO 371/127747/V1051/4G.

30. Sherman Adams, *First-Hand Report: The Story of the Eisenhower Administration* (New York: Harper & Brothers, 1961), 288.

31. See Editorial Note 284, in *FRUS, 1955–1957: Western Europe and Canada, Volume XXVII*.

32. For the bizarre degree of personalization that keeps undercutting U.S. foreign policy, see Derek Leebaert, "Our Envoys, Ourselves," *New York Times*, Decem-

ber 11, 2010. Recent examples of such heroes are the corrupt MIT-trained banker Ahmed Chalabi for Iraq and the stylish Hamid Karzai for Afghanistan.

33. Call from Congressman Judd, June 24, 1954, JFD telephone transcripts.

34. Memorandum for the White House from Brigadier General Andrew Goodpaster, "Treatment of Minorities in the United States," December 31, 1958, 811.411/12-458. See my discussion of civil rights and Dulles's role at State in *Fifty-Year Wound*, 211–12.

35. The Constituent Assembly in Khartoum—Sudan being a British dependency, not quite a colony—had simply declared independence, effective January 1, 1956; Middle Eastern crises meant that neither Britain nor Egypt tried to stop it.

36. DDE to WSC, July 22, 1954, in *FRUS, 1952–1954: Western Europe and Canada, Volume VI, Part 1*, 1047–48.

37. Dwight Eisenhower, "Radio and Television Address to the American People on the Need for Mutual Security in Waging Peace," May 21, 1957, American Presidency Project.

38. "Radio and Television Address Opening the Campaign for Reelection, September 19, 1956," in *Public Papers of the Presidents of the United States: Dwight D. Eisenhower* (Washington, D.C.: Government Printing Office, 1958), 210.

39. Hugh Wilford, *America's Great Game: The CIA's Secret Arabists and the Shaping of the Modern Middle East* (New York: Basic Books, 2013), 274.

40. See British Telecom news editor Andy Jackson's *BT News* article of May 15, 2016.

41. Joseph Alsop and Stewart Alsop, "The New Balance of Power," *Encounter*, May 1958, 4. The CIA, for its part, is tireless in trying to rewrite past failures, as shown in "Orbit of Sputnik Surprised Many, but American Spies Saw It Coming," *New York Times*, October 7, 2017, which is incorrect. The CIA report underlying the article perpetuates the myth that "data from the U-2 flights had told Eisenhower the Soviets were not that far ahead." See Amy Ryan and Gary Keeley, "Sputnik and US Intelligence: The Warning Record," *Studies in Intelligence* 61, no. 3 (Extracts, September 2017). I've tried to correct the record, as in the *New York Review of Books*, May 13, 2010, apparently without success.

42. Record of a Meeting, Secretary of State Dulles's Office, Department of State, Washington, October 17, 1957, 5 p.m., in *FRUS, 1955–1957: Western Europe and Canada, Volume XXVII*, 307.

43. "Macmillan Backed Syria Assassination Plot," *Guardian*, September 26, 2003.

44. On ousting Syria's Assad, see Graham Fuller, "Bringing Real Muscle to Bear Against Syria," September 14, 1983, Central Intelligence Agency, CIA library reading room, document CIA-RDP88B00443R001404090133-0. On Saddam as an "ally," and being embraced as an intelligence partner, see my *Fifty-Year Wound*, 555.

45. John Le Carré, *The Secret Pilgrim* (New York: Knopf, 1990), 206.

46. Memorandum from the Secretary of State to the President, Washington, June 12, 1957, in *FRUS, 1955–1957: Japan, Volume XXIII, Part 1*, 173, concerning the official visit to the United States of the prime minister of Japan, Mr. Nobusuke Kishi.

47. "Legacy of US 1958 Invasion," Feature/U.S. and Canada, Al Jazeera, July 15, 2013.

48. Douglas Brinkley, "Dean Acheson and the 'Special Relationship': The West Point Speech of December 1962," *Historical Journal* 33, no. 3 (September 1990): 599–608.

49. Rick Perlstein, *Before the Storm: Barry Goldwater and the Unmaking of the American Consensus* (New York: Nation Books, 2009), 77.

50. John F. Kennedy, Speech, Salt Lake City, Mormon Tabernacle, September 23, 1960, American Presidency Project.

51. Barbara Leaming, *Jack Kennedy: The Education of a Statesman* (New York: Norton, 2006), 231, citing the Macmillan Diary, Bodleian Library, Oxford.

52. John F. Kennedy, "Remarks of Senator John F. Kennedy, University of Kentucky, Lexington, KY, October 8, 1960," American Presidency Project.

53. President's News Conference, February 14, 1962, American Presidency Project.

54. Alsop and Alsop, *Reporter's Trade*, 46.

55. John F. Kennedy, Speech, Citizens for Kennedy, New York City, September 14, 1960, American Presidency Project.

56. I've taken the term "valor of ignorance" from the title of a little-known book that proved to have immense influence on the twentieth century: *The Valor of Ignorance* (1909) by the West Point dropout Homer Lea. The book addresses an "Inevitable Japanese-American War," and was derided in America but quickly sold eighty-four thousand copies in Japan, where it was studied by the officer class.

57. "I *want* them to send more troops," Ho Chi Minh insisted to the astonished Soviet premier Aleksei Kosygin, who conveyed details of this discussion to President Nasser and to Mohamed Heikal, *Al-Ahram*'s editor in chief and a Nasser intimate. See Heikal's *The Sphinx and the Commissar: The Rise and Fall of Soviet Influence in the Middle East* (New York: Harper and Row, 1978), 164.

58. See Andrew Roberts, "Britain and Obama's 'Back of the Queue,'" *Wall Street Journal*, June 18–19, 2016. This British historian, while believing that his country was in every war with America since 1945, also cites a transatlantic "special relationship" as a sound reason for divorcing the European Union that year.

CONCLUSION

1. The Soviet Union excelled at feeding off the West, and a strong case can be made as to how the economically weak yet powerfully armed regime could otherwise have continued—ever more dangerously—into the twenty-first century. Many Americans not only misgauged the extent of Moscow's economic vulnerability but also were (and are) unable to accept the possibility of a U.S.-assisted Soviet economic implosion. However, the numbers don't support that interpretation. Serious, standard works on the end of the Cold War range from Jack Matlock, *Reagan and Gorbachev: How the Cold War Ended* (2005), to Robert Service, *The End of the Cold War, 1985–1991* (2015), and include such scholarly articles as Archie Brown, "How Did the Cold War Really End?," *New York Review of Books*, March 23, 2017. Yet all have three faults in common: First, the longtime apparatchik Mikhail Gorbachev— who boosted military spending by a third while building an enormous arsenal of deadly pathogens and intensifying the war in Afghanistan—is assumed to have smacked his forehead one morning circa 1986 and realized his life's work to have been in vain. Presumably U.S. pressure hadn't already cut off his room for maneuver.

Second, these works give little or no attention to NSDD 75 ("U.S. Relations with the USSR," January 1983), the five-part White House strategy that—point by point—shows itself to have been instrumental to Soviet collapse. Third, they do nothing to quantify the cause and effect of Soviet collapse, for example by examining the flow of Moscow's minimal hard-currency income, the consequences of Moscow being unable to double dip in European syndicated loan markets or to access the New York bond markets, the price of no longer accessing U.S. high tech, and so on. Such analyses are offered in Leebaert, *Fifty-Year Wound*, chaps. 10 and 11. Further evidence can be found in my "Shaking Loose," a review essay of Matlock's book, in *Claremont Review*, June 2005, and in my concluding chapter for *The Grand Strategy That Won the Cold War*, ed. Douglas E. Streusand and Norman A. Bailey (New York: Lexington Books, 2016). Because of its emphasis on economics, finance, and politics—not just on military power—NSDD 75, and its associated efforts, became one of the few effective examples of grand strategy in U.S. foreign policy. In contrast, the Yale University historian John Lewis Gaddis—endorsed by no one less than the former president George W. Bush—claims that Gorbachev was "the most deserving recipient ever of the Nobel Peace Prize" (which is to leave aside Martin Luther King, Nelson Mandela, Lech Walesa, even George C. Marshall). See Books, *Financial Times*, November 15/16, 2015, 9.

2. The legendary intelligence analyst William T. Lee often spoke of "the pros" when discussing U.S.-Soviet espionage rivalries in the Cold War decades, and he wasn't referring to the Americans. On CIA embarrassments of 1991–2001, see Leebaert, *Fifty-Year Wound*, 563–66, 609, 618–20, 625–27. On plastering fig leaves, see Leebaert, *Magic and Mayhem*, 309–10, concerning the academic research and conferences the CIA was sponsoring during that decade. As today, had the CIA accomplished marvelous secret successes during any of these years to offset its dispiriting record of operations and analysis, such details would have been leaked or declassified with lightning speed.

3. Carne Ross is the British diplomat who served as Middle East expert on the UN delegation, as interviewed on *1A*, March 29, 2017, NPR.

4. "Sir John Chilcot Accuses Tony Blair of Not Being 'Straight with the Nation' over Iraq War," *Telegraph*, July 7, 2017. Chilcot, a retired civil servant, concluded that the former prime minister "Tony Blair made much of, at various points, the need to exert influence on American policy making." As Chilcot explained, "To do that he said in terms at one point, 'I have to accept their strategic objective, regime change, in order to exert influence.'"

5. Secretary of State Condoleezza Rice, Department of Defense press conference, with Secretary Gates, January 11, 2007.

6. "Big Bang" is argued by Thomas P. M. Barnett, who at the time of the invasion was the assistant for strategic futures, Office of Force Transformation, Office of the Secretary of Defense. See his *Great Powers: America and the World After Bush* (New York: G. P. Putnam's Sons, 2009), 62. "Transformation of the Middle East" is Eliot Cohen, also an academic, who in 2003 served on the Pentagon's Defense Policy Board Advisory Committee. See his "Iraq Can't Resist Us," *Wall Street Journal*, December 23, 2001, with his latest thoughts on "a blow that would shock" being found in his *Big Stick: The Limits of Soft Power and the Necessity of Military Force* (New York: Basic Books, 2016), 35.

7. "Deputy Secretary Paul Wolfowitz Interview with Nolan Finely of the *Detroit News*," Department of Defense news transcript, March 5, 2003. Wolfowitz also lost count of the American forces killed in Iraq, not knowing it was a searing 51 percent higher than he guessed in 2004, when asked for the number of dead by a House subcommittee in open testimony. See Leebaert, *Magic and Mayhem*, 87. Today Wolfowitz is a scholar at the American Enterprise Institute.

8. Andrew Roberts, "How Eden Was Sunk by Suez," *Telegraph*, March 16, 2003. He also repeats the mistake that Nasser "nationalized the Suez Canal," rather than merely the last twelve years of the Suez Canal Company's lease. Oblivious to much of contemporary history since World War II, Roberts thereafter made himself a mobilizing voice for the Iraq War, including in the ears of President George W. Bush.

9. See L. A. Bethell, ed., *Tales from the Outposts: II: Small Wars of the Empire* (Edinburgh: William Blackwood and Sons, 1932).

10. For a discussion of "limits" on the abilities of U.S. special operations forces—including problems of bureaucratization and of being dependent on technological superiority—see Derek Leebaert, "New Strengths, New Dangers," *Army*, January 2018, and my conclusion in *To Dare and to Conquer*.

11. Michael Doran, "A Trump Doctrine for the Middle East," *New York Times*, May 19, 2017.

12. Professor Cohen writes of resuming the offensive against China in his *Big Stick*, 118. A review essay of this influential yet historically uninformed book—including his views on Clausewitz—is Derek Leebaert, "No End of a Lesson on the Big Stick," *Bulletin of the Atomic Scientists*, March 2017.

13. Robert D. Kaplan, "Review: 'The Road Not Taken' in Vietnam," *Wall Street Journal*, January 5, 2018. The book being reviewed is a well-written biography of the eccentric operative Edward Lansdale. But how did Lansdale "get to know the indigenous people" or "befriend" various Vietnamese sects when he spoke nothing but English? Kipling would have snorted at this lack of sense about the dispassionate hardness of the third world and the romanticizing of counterinsurgency (e.g., dumping "his cargo of dirty weapons" on the desk of the obtuse defense secretary Robert McNamara).

14. For example, *The Fifty-Year Wound* appears in Chinese as a two-volume work from Shanghai People's Publishing (2009).

15. Even the most serious students of foreign policy, such as the Johns Hopkins SAIS professor Michael Mandelbaum, speak of "replace," as when observing that "the United States stepped in to replace" Britain. He's quoted in Thomas Friedman, "Superbroke, Superfrugal, Superpower?," *New York Times*, September 4, 2010. That said, an argument can be made, such as Hugh Wilford offers in *America's Great Game*, that America's feckless covert adventures and attempts at fine-tuning in the Arab world have indeed "replaced" the earlier imperial machinations of Britain.

16. Andrew Roberts, "Henry Kissinger Interview: I Don't See the Wisdom There Once Was," *Spectator*, September 20, 2014.

17. This myth arose in the early twentieth century amid that era's hands-across-the-sea sentimentality. But the Royal Navy never had such a protective role. A laboratory demonstration of that fact is 1861–1865. The only time that Europe's powers intruded—Spain, France, and Britain itself—was during the Civil War, when the

U.S. Navy was otherwise engaged. That interference in the Americas stopped pronto once the Union was restored, with Spain pulling out of the Dominican Republic eighteen days after the surrender of the last Confederate battle force. Britain was the only power to hold on to its winnings, as in British Honduras, and by 1895 the Cleveland administration was set to go to war with Britain during the Venezuelan crisis. In sum, the Lords of the Admiralty weren't warning away anyone from the Americas, let alone on the United States' behalf. Altogether, the idea of a nineteenth-century "cordon sanitaire" is unconvincing, and difficult to define physically. If it were a conscious condition, can we imagine the Americans saying, "Oh well, Britain will protect us"? And if there was such a cordon sanitaire, we might expect to have seen some U.S. participation. Yet the Royal Navy didn't even intercept the French army when it invaded Mexico.

18. President Nixon observed that Henry Kissinger was one of those people who foment crises "to earn attention for themselves"—which is a sound definition of an emergency man; Nixon added that Kissinger would have set one off over someplace like Ecuador had not Vietnam been in play. See Diane Kunz, *Butter and Guns: America's Cold War Economic Diplomacy* (New York: Free Press, 1997), 214.

19. Days before coming to office, for example, President Barack Obama intuited "a belief [in the nation] that we need to look forward as opposed to looking backwards." He was speaking to the problem of examining the CIA's use of torture, but he could just as easily have been addressing the likelihood of a British-type post-mortem on the Iraq War, which never occurred.

20. Kaine, "New Truman Doctrine," 38–39.

21. John Updike, *Assorted Prose* (New York: Knopf, 1965), 86.

22. Ibid.

23. Condoleezza Rice, former political science professor and Stanford provost, cited as "Quote of the Week," *Washington Post*, March 31, 2008.

24. Debating America as "empire" has been academic swordplay but leached into real-world policy decisions before and after the Iraq War. Notions of "a new Rome" can be found in Niall Ferguson's *Colossus*, with a more serious treatment being Vaclav Smil, *Why America Is Not a New Rome* (Cambridge, Mass.: MIT Press, 2010).

25. The myth is that a "Pax Britannica" kept the peace among great powers and their surrogates in the years between Bonaparte's overthrow in 1814 and the outbreak of war in 1914. Yes, the Royal Navy was the world's largest during an epoch of relative calm, and Britain was the most pervasive presence in the world, though not in a Europe crowded with land powers. Pervasive, however, doesn't mean preeminent. Britain controlled sea-lanes, put down pirates and slavers, and arrested cannibals in the Solomon Islands. But any wider tranquillity on the planet wasn't due to such clout. European powers had excellent reasons for refraining from war, such as fears of revolution, and the dogs of war were scratching their own troubles like the strictly local question of Schleswig-Holstein. Neither Britain nor its navy stood in the way of conflict, and fleets couldn't sail between Austria and Prussia. Bismarck would have scoffed at the idea of Britain having a unique leverage on the European political system, as do shrewd Europeans today. As the historian Barry Gough cautions at the start of his provocatively titled book, "Pax was an idea, even a state

of mind; it was never an actual state of affairs." See his *Pax Britannica: Ruling the Waves and Keeping the Peace Before Armageddon* (New York: Palgrave Macmillan, 2014), x.

26. My friend Erik Prince, who founded the company formerly known as Blackwater, nonetheless makes a lucid case for outsourcing the endless Afghanistan war and other problems to contractors. See "Contractors, Not Troops, Will Save Afghanistan," *New York Times*, August 30, 2017.

27. Young, *Masters of Indecision*, 41, 160.

28. The strategist is the distinguished academic Guo Xuetang, director of the Institute of International Strategy and Policy Analysis, Shanghai University of International Business and Economics, who also serves as a policy adviser to his government. He and I had this discussion in November 2016.

29. James Webb, interview, March 22, 1985, Webb No. 4, National Air and Space Museum Oral History Project. The best discussion of James Webb, Sputnik, and NASA is Walter A. McDougall's *The Heavens and the Earth: A Political History of the Space Age* (New York: Basic Books, 1985). On the foreign policy issues examined in this Conclusion, an equally indispensable book from McDougall is *The Tragedy of U.S. Foreign Policy: How America's Civil Religion Betrayed the National Interest* (New Haven, Conn.: Yale University Press, 2016).

30. NASA, http://jwst.nasa.gov/index.html.

ACKNOWLEDGMENTS

FOR MANY YEARS, MY FRIEND TIMOTHY DICKINSON HAS OFFERED guidance in writing, as in business. George Plimpton, who worked with him since the early days at *The Paris Review*, summed it up: "I always come away from Timothy keenly aware of the empty stretches in my brain." Tim's cheerful generosity keeps filling those voids for authors, editors, fund managers, and military officers alike.

Vital to every worthwhile effort of nonfiction are the unobserved experts, without whom the greatest libraries could not be drawn upon. For more than thirty-seven years at Oxford, Rosamond Campbell—an Oxonian herself—served as the librarian at St. Antony's College, where she advised historians, politicians, diplomats, and graduate students. Her kindness toward young Americans is memorable, and she elevated everyone's work. Her legacy embodies the goodwill and patience at the heart of the lasting transatlantic relationship.

I'm also grateful to the experts at the presidential libraries of Franklin D. Roosevelt, Harry S. Truman, Dwight D. Eisenhower, and Richard Nixon. One keen historian deems Richard Norton Smith—the eminent biographer who has directed several of the libraries—to be "incomparable." Absolutely, and Richard's wisdom has counseled his friends for decades.

Leon Aron continues to share his knowledge of Russia, as well as of literature and life. Other authentic foreign policy wise men who've shaped my thoughts on this story include Andrew Bacevitch, Christopher Coker, Christopher Gray, Walter MacDougall, and Michael Mandelbaum. I've additionally benefited from the insights of Sophie Jacobsen at Georgetown, Kirstyn Raitz at Durham University, Cullen Steffan at Fordham, and the soldier-scholar Gregor von Ledenbur, also at Durham. They are each stars of a successor generation. And anyone who discusses the twentieth-century British Empire, let alone who presumes to write on the subject, is indebted to Professor William Roger Louis for his lifetime of study and illumination.

The Army Historical Foundation's chief historian, Matthew Seelinger, has fielded countless "author's inquiries" about the post–World War II era. The foundation itself is a singular educational resource, and in addition to aiding researchers, its congressionally mandated task—to build the National Museum of the United States Army—is just about complete (2019). To this end, General William Hartzog and Brigadier General Creighton Abrams, plus Command Sergeant Major Jimmie Spencer, are teaching me and countless others about the army's role in American life—past, present, and future.

Helpful and creative friends with whom I've discussed this book include Liaquat Ahamed (who contributed the title *Grand Improvisation*), John Hauge, the sculptor Bobby Haft, and the playwright John Henry, whose latest work, *Republic Undone*—on Woodrow Wilson and British persuasiveness in the run-up to World War I—is germane to my story. It's fun to read history and politics with all of them. I've been fortunate to have done so as well with Susan Grimes, Shelby Coffey, Stacey Wagner, and Annie Day Thacher, previously of the Dumbarton Oaks and Harvard libraries. The journalist Meena Ahamed has shared her profound knowledge of U.S.-India relations. The entrepreneur, reformer, and author Jim Strock helped me to clarify many of the issues addressed in the book, as did the social tech innovator Maximilian Weiner, and Donna Carey, former head of the Scrum Alliance.

In management consulting, David Webster, John Park, Kurt Revling, the next-gen networking visionary Steve King, and Bob Coulam shared their insights on the functioning of complex organizations, as epitomized by the Pentagon, the Foreign Office, the State Department, and multinational high-tech enterprises, namely 1950s aviation. The leadership specialist Caroline von Ledebur and the historically savvy Stephan von Ledebur offered their uniquely peaceful library for studious reflection, and napping, while overlooking the Danube.

Recent U.S. Marine Corps officers Andrew Erlich, Michael Haft, and Harrison Suarez exemplify devotion to country, as do ambassadors Marc Wall and Eunice Reddick of the elite U.S. Foreign Service. So did the intelligence officer Tyler Drumheller, who began his unsurpassed career in clandestine services while still a grad student at Georgetown. The courage and kindness of each of them have been inspiring.

The Reverend Timothy A. R. Cole reminds us to be thankful for the tasks at which we've been set. Moreover, Tim knows much about the dramatic context of this story. Before being called as the rector to Christ Church Georgetown in 2016, he served with the Royal Army Chaplains' Department for twenty years, including as British senior force chaplain in Iraq and as theater and joint force senior chaplain in Afghanistan. In New York, the Reverend Canon Brian J. Grieves, director of Peace and Justice Ministries for the Episcopal Church, has offered perspective on the enduring conflicts of this era. As did Stephen Feinberg, the Holocaust educator and student of twentieth-century European history.

Mary Ann "Terry" Bradley, now ninety-seven, is deeply acknowledged for explaining the texture of American life in the 1940s and 1950s. Year after year, she has offered vivid oral histories, along with lunch and brownies. Mrs. Bradley is also a reminder of sacrifices made. As we talk, I often think of her brother, Lieutenant Gerald Michael Sullivan, USN, who disappeared over the South China Sea in early 1945 while flying off of the USS *Hancock* to search alone for two of his lost aviators.

In memory, too, are early mentors: Bob Bowie, Paul Doty, Forrest

Pogue, Ray Vernon, Sam Beer, and Vernon Walters. As for the future, much of that lies with Michelle Kingue, her daughter Angela, and other new Americans—many of them refugees, as was my father. With luck, as Dean Acheson used to say, our country can hope to endure and perchance to prosper.

Finally, I'm grateful to the publishing team: David Kuhn and Lauren Sharp at Aevitas; Alex Star, Dominique Lear, and Jeff Seroy at FSG; and, for additional editorial guidance, Jim Thompson and Toby Lester.

Washington, D.C., 2018

Page numbers in *italics* refer to illustrations.

Army of the Rhine, 7, 368, 388, 429
Arnold, Gen. Henry H. "Hap," 80
Aron, Raymond, 414–15
Asia, 7, 57, 129, 148, 188–89, 209, 230, 254, 307, 417, 427, 438, 470; *see also specific regions and countries*
Assad, Hafez al-, 496
As-Sayyida Zeinab Mosque (Cairo), 308
Associated Press, 464
Aswan Dam, 448, 466, 470
Atlantic, Battle of the, 546*n12*
Atlantic Pact, 179, 196, 203, 235; *see also* North Atlantic Treaty Organization
atomic bombs, 23, 28–29, 62, 82, 275–77, 293, 323; planes capable of carrying, 116, 155–56, 257, 263–64, 292–93, 440, 552*n22*
Atomic Energy Authority, British, 531*n14*
Atomic Energy Commission, U.S., 369
Attlee, Clement, 14, 24–25, 43, 46, 88, 129, 143, 154, 160, 161, 183, 200, 230–31, 335, 347, 526*n7*, 536*n26*, 552*n25*; American attitudes toward, 43, 62; armaments sales to Russia by, 117; atomic bomb project of, 82; BCOF dissolution opposed by, 124; and B-29 squadrons' arrival in England, 156–57; economic policies of, 34–36, 104, 111–12, 162, 185, 186, 194, 215, 281, 293; House of Commons speeches of, 30, 206, 276, 299, 391; and Indian independence, 113, 219; during Korean War, 258–64, 266, 270, 273–78, 285–86, 288, 292, 550*n41*; Middle East policy of, 134, 317, 319–23, 325–26, 554*n19*; at Potsdam, 22, 23, 27; Zionist threat to, 74
Auschwitz, 22, 71
Austin, J. L., 137
Austin, Warren, 165
Australia, 29, 30, 44*n*, 50, 105, 112, 122, 124, 128, 130, 247, 250, 254, 259, 284, 295–98, 339, 363, 369, 388, 389, 406, 411, 414, 432–34, 436, 471, 475, 506; armed forces of, 154, 248, 268, 270
Australia, New Zealand, United States (ANZUS) treaty, 297, 349–50, 376, 414, 432, 434, 442

Austria, 104, 229
Avnery, Uri, 131
Axis powers, 4, 29, 61, 89
Ayer, A. J., 147
Azerbaijan, 63–65, 68–69, 311
Azikiwe, Nnamdi, 202
Azores, 263

Ba'ath Party, 495
Baghdad Pact, 441–42, 444–47, 451, 457, 460, 485, 488, 495, 498
Bahrain, 135, 136, 227, 360, 488, 511
Bahrain Petroleum Company, 319
Baldwin, Hanson, 369
Balkans, 12, 84, 92
Baltic republics, 158
Bank of England, 24, 47, 61, 104–105, 181, 218, 281, 322, 345, 428, 455, 529*n54*
Bao Dai, 244–47, 249, 405, 409, 434–35
Barkley, Alben, 378
Barnett, Correlli, 517*n1*, 537*n2*
Baruch, Bernard, 18–19, 54, 75, 168, 169, 191, 342, 375, 376, 519*n17*, 538*n23*
BBC, 140, 355, 427, 455
Beaverbrook, Lord (Max Aitken), 52, 412
Bechtel, 134
Bedouins, 69, 572*n15*
Begin, Menachem, 73, 76, 471, 574*n45*
Beisner, Robert L., 537*n7*, 544*n26*
Belgium, 143, 175, 189, 270, 444
Belgrave, Charles Dalrymple, 136, 488
Belize, 207, 421
Bell, Gertrude, 69
Benelux, 141, 158
Ben-Gurion, David, 134, 135, 196, 388, 431, 449, 469, 471, 476, 485, 487
Bennett, Eric, 539*n32*
Bergen-Belsen, 22
Bergson Group, 525*n37*
Beria, Lavrenti, 12
Berlin, 23, 76, 143, 150–55, 157–59, 168, 171, 172, 264, 357, 511
Berlin, Isaiah, 16–18, 20, 148
Bermuda, 396–97, 413, 488–89, 495
Bernadotte, Count Folke, 134, 196, 534*n55*
Bethesda Naval Hospital, 172

Bevan, Aneurin (Nye), 47, 95, 151, 168, 292–94, 298, 299, 329, 335, 346, 347, 427, 429, 475, 483, 498, 511, 526n45, 528n36; House of Commons speeches of, 264–65, 325, 410, 442, 463–64

Bevin, Ernest, 25–27, 29–30, 37, 42, 47, 78, 92, 94–96, 109, 113, 156, 175–76, 189, 209, 228, 230, 270, 272, 354, 362, 422, 483, 512–14, 526n7, 533n36, 535n22, 550n41; Acheson and, 165–67, 203, 219; African policy of, 199–200; arms sales to Russia approved by, 117; during Berlin blockade and airlift, 150–52, 154, 159, 161, 511, 536n26; and British economic crises, 29, 30, 45, 52, 53, 81–82, 100, 106, 182, 184, 186–87, 192–93, 195; China policy of, 204, 206, 236–37, 240; commonwealth ambassadors' meeting with, 217–18; death of, 286–87, 301, 321, 329; demobilization concerns of, 119–21; European and American unity supported by, 142–44, 167–71, 196, 223; House of Commons speeches of, 29, 31–32, 63, 137, 140, 146, 152, 168, 172, 207, 278; illness of, 246, 259, 261, 273; independence of colonies advocated by, 63, 114; Jebb and, 175–76, 179–80, 265–66, 539n44; labor union background of, 26, 96, 133, 172, 227; Middle East policy of, 59–60, 62–63, 69–71, 131–34, 196–98, 200, 235–36, 533–34n52; at Paris Peace Conference, 76–77; Southeast Asia policy of, 126, 128–30, 224; Soviet threat response of, 31–32, 60, 67, 87–91, 95, 167, 527n21, 528n23; Zionist assassination targeting of, 74

Big Lie, 266
Bilbo, Theodore "The Man," 48
Bingham, Barry, 296
Bird Watching at Lossiemouth (MacDonald), 242
Bismarck, Otto von, 581n25
Bissell, Richard M., Jr., 553n38
Blair, Tony, 372, 579n4
Blixen, Karen (pseud. Isak Dinesen), 366
Bloodlands, 12
Board of Trade, British, 37, 42, 115, 175

Boeing Aircraft, 115, 441
Boer War, 18n
Bohlen, Charles "Chip," 176, 179, 180, 221, 256
Bolshevism, 15
Bonaparte, Napoleon, 59, 581n25
Bonnet, Henri, 158, 179, 236
Borneo, 127, 242, 288
Bowker, James, 566n4
Boyd, Col. Albert G., 111, 116
Braasch, John W., 460
Bradley, Gen. Omar, 80, 262, 274, 284, 295, 321, 341, 378, 383, 388
Brandon, Henry, 540n57
Brazil, 270
Bretton Woods Agreement, 37, 38, 47, 50, 105, 192
Brewster, Owen, 17
Brexit, 140
Brimelow, Thomas, 530n7
British Commonwealth Occupation Force (BCOF), 124
British Defence, 329; Co-ordination Committee/Far East, 127
British Forces Arabian Peninsula Command, 492
British Military Commitments (NSC 75), 214–15, 221, 224–28, 232–35, 241, 254, 258, 267, 302, 316, 481, 546n44, 558n39
British Overseas Airways Corporation (BOAC), 117, 368
British Petroleum, 393
British Purchasing Commission, 38
British War Production: 1939–1945: A Record (Times editorial staff), 54
Bromley-Davenport, Walter, 465
Brownell, Herbert, 421
Bruce, David K. E., 221–24, 231, 334, 560n14
Buchenwald, 22, 407
Buddhists, 434
Buffett, Howard, 100
Bulganin, Nikolai, 444, 458, 461, 476
Bulgaria, 76, 248
Bullock, Alan, 522n52
Bunche, Ralph, 196, 486
Bundy, McGeorge, 502
Bureau of the Budget, U.S., 93, 100, 173
Burgess, Guy, 276, 354, 355
Burling, Edward, 167, 538n20

Churchill, Winston (*cont.*)
558*n34*, 573*n27*; American
isolationism concern of, 393, 426–27,
512; anti-American attitudes of, 219,
346–49, 396, 429; ANZUS criticized
by, 349–50; at Bermuda summit,
396–97, *398*, 488; Bevan's verbal
attacks on, 95–96, 442; Bevin's
similarities to, 25–26, 37, 113;
Chinese policy of, 240, 436–37;
Congress addressed by, 44, 342–44;
détente with Soviets sought by, 353,
357, 363, 428, 444; Eden as heir
apparent of, 25, 362–63, 395, 442–43;
Eisenhower's relationship with, 19–20,
382–86, 430, 438–39, 491, 558*n30*,
564*n21*; Elizabeth's coronation
arranged by, 388; financial problems
during administrations of, 54, 332–33,
338, 340, 345–46, 350–51; in general
elections, 23, 230, 325–27, 328–31,
335; House of Commons speeches of,
11, 15, 262, 292, 325, 329, 333, 336,
341, 345, 351, 383–84, 386, 413, 431,
440, 526*n7*, 552*n23*; Iron Curtain
(Fulton) speech of, 43–44, 46–47, 52,
68, 169, 171, 341, 342, 353, 377, 510,
544*n8*; during Korean War, 258,
262–63, 276, 286; Labour Party split
manipulated by, 292–94, 300, 335;
MacDonald and, 243, 404, 546*n12*;
Middle East concerns of, 71, 331–32,
345, 358, 363, 394, 430–32, 561*n22*;
military budget cut by, 335, 367; MIT
speech of, 44, 168–70, 330, 342, 375,
538*n23*; nuclear weapons program of,
352, 369, 392, 440, 493, 558*n32*; at
Potsdam, 22–24, 31; racism of, 27,
200; Southeast Asia concerns of,
330–31, 363–64, 366, 367, 406, 409,
411–13, 415–16, 418, 433; State of the
Nation broadcast of, 336; strokes
suffered by, 390–91, 393, 395, 442;
U.S. visits of, 42–47, 168–71, 336–44,
346, 350, 374–80, 418–19, 423–25,
490, 494, 519*n19*, 557*n23*; during
World War II, 11–12, 16–20, 32, 35,
61, 84, 117, 127, 133, 184, 330, 347,
362; at Yalta, 12–17, 31, 518*n6*,
519*n10*, 524*n13*; Zionist terror attacks
denounced by, 75

Church of England, 157
Civilian Conservation Corps, 80
Civil Service, British, 561*n20*
Civil Service Union, 46
Civil War, U.S., 580–81*n17*
Clark, Gen. Mark, 80
Clark, William, 48, 74, 470, 475, 497, 498
Clarke, Col. Frank, 42
Clarke, Peter, 517*n1*, 518*n2*, 540*n65*
Clay, Gen. Lucius, 143–44, 150–55,
159, 171, 177, 248
Clayton, William Lockhart (Will),
38–40, 47, 49, 83, 85, 97, 106, 111,
252, 530*n62*
Cleveland, Grover, 221, 581*n17*
Clinton, Bill, 571*n37*
CNN, 507
Coal and Steel Community, 231
Coast Guard, U.S., 34, 337
Cockcroft, L. D., 531*n14*
Cogny, Gen. René, 407
Cohen, Eliot, 579*n6*
Colby, William, 370
Cold War, 25, 77, 101, 149, 168, 190,
273, 433, 501, 503, 505, 539*n32*,
545*n30*, 578*n1*, 579*n2*
Collins, Adm. John, 350
Colombia, 270
Colonial Office, British, 74, 127, 201,
208, 365, 422, 491
Columbia University, 6, 65, 182, 311,
344, 375–76, 382
Colville, John "Jock," 347, 376–78, 380,
443
Combined Airlift Task Force, 154
Commerce Department, U.S., 41, 146,
311
Committee to Defend America by
Aiding the Allies, 165
Common Market, 482, 495
Commonwealth Brigade Group, 434
Commonwealth Conference on Foreign
Affairs, 246
Commonwealth Office, 339
Communism, 26, 47, 55, 80, 90, 126,
150, 184, 189, 218, 251, 207–209,
357–59; *see also* anti-communism;
China, People's Republic of; Korean
War; Soviet Russia; Vietminh
Compton, Karl, 538*n23*
Conant, James, 17

concentration camps, 22, 71, 407
Congo, 496
Congress, U.S., 17, 34, 35, 89, 122, 124, 129, 159, 191, 215, 229, 321, 402, 442–44, 460, 548*n41*; Anglo-American Financial Agreement in, 41, 49, 68, 105; ANZUS ratified by, 349; atomic R&D ties canceled by, 120; Bevin's request for emergency appropriations from, 89, 91–92; China policy in, 202–204, 240, 405, 436; Churchill's speeches to, 44, 342–44; Democratic control of, 483; Douglas in, 93; foreign aid budget in, 466; during Korean War, 257–58, 260, 275, 280, 329–30; Marshall Plan in, 140, 145, 173–75, 529*n43*; Middle East policy of, 236, 321, 358, 485–87; National Advisory Council created by, 98; Republican control of, 84, 100, 566*n7*; Southeast Asia policy of, 247, 412, 490; Southern Democrats in, 112; trade and tariff policies of, 51, 193, 195, 429; Truman addresses, 87; united Europe advocates in, 146, 148, 178; *see also* House of Representatives, U.S.; Senate, U.S.
Congress of Vienna, 357
Connally, Tom, 49, 228, 254, 305, 307
Conolly, Adm. Richard, 132, 135–36, 197–98, 235, 564*n20*
Conservative (Tory) Party, British, 21, 22, 42, 95, 104, 230–31, 265, 323, 325, 326, 395, 412, 443, 455, 465, 468
Constitution, U.S., 166
containment, 67, 101–102, 559*n1*
Coolidge, Calvin, 191*n*, 383
Costigliola, Frank, 524*n14*
Council of Economic Advisors, 174
Covent Garden (London), 46
Cowles, Fleur, 388
Cozzens, James Gould, 144
Crimea, 12, 13
Cripps, Stafford, 183–86, 192–95, 215, 222, 227–28, 278, 293, 299, 541–42*n18*
Cromwell, Oliver, 328
Crossman, Richard, 252
Crowther, Geoffrey, 4, 106, 481, 529*n56*
Cuba, 496
Cunard Line, 14, 147, 162
Cuneo, Ernie, 371

Cunningham, Adm. John, 59, 120–21
Curzon, Lord, 483
Cyprus, 200, 233, 320, 326, 366, 440, 444, 463–65, 470, 472, 473, 476, 492, 497
Czechoslovakia, 142–44, 254, 420, 448, 535*n9*

Dachau, 22
Dalton, Hugh, 24, 117
Darwin, John, 522*n17*
Dassa, Robert, 570*n15*
Davenport, Marcia, 142
Davies, John Paton, 206
Davis, Dwight, 191*n*
Dayak, 288
Dayan, Gen. Moshe, 431
D-Day, 150, 156, 379, 472
Deakin, Arthur, 96
de Bellaigue, Christopher, 393
"Declaration on Liberated Europe," 15
Decline and Fall of the Roman Empire, The (Gibbon), 66
Defence Ministry, British, 556*n3*
Defense Committee for Southeast Asia, 126
Defense Department, U.S. (DOD), 122, 134, 151, 214, 222, 506, 542*n29*; *see also* Pentagon
Defense Plant Corporation (DPC), 85, 86, 527*n12*
de Gaulle, Charles, 497–99
De Havilland Aircraft Company, 54, 115–19, 162, 368, 369, 440
demobilization, 18, 119, 528*n22*
Democratic Party, U.S., 19, 48, 49, 71, 93, 112, 163, 166, 236, 260, 271, 278, 305, 341, 357, 387, 405, 415, 429, 466, 483
Democratic Republic of Germany, 231
Denmark, 32, 170
Derry, John, 118
Derwent jet engines, 117
de Silva, Peer, 356
deterrence, 200, 253, 292, 335, 437, 462–63, 493, 566*n18*
Detroit, 174, 287, 293
Detroit Club, 51
devaluation, 93, 185–86, 192–95, 225, 227, 281, 313, 542*n21*

Dewey, Thomas, 75, 181, 241, 296, 374, 538*n24*, 552*n28*
Dhahran, 263
Diệm, Ngô Đình, 434–35, 489–90, 502
Dien Bien Phu, Battle of, 407, 410, 411, 413, 416
Dillon, Douglas, 411
Dinesen, Isak, *see* Blixen, Karen
Diplomatic Service, British, 528*n28*, 530*n7*
Dixon, Pierson, 422–23, 458, 474
Dominican Republic, 581*n17*
Dominions Office, 14
Douglas, Lewis, 17, 93–94, *109*, 130–32, 144, 152, 156, 162–66, 171, 217, 221–24, 230, 237, 253, 277–78, 307, 514, 529*n56*, 551*n56*; Acheson and, 164, 165, 187, 213–15, 230, 253, 334, 543*n1*; and British economic crises, 104, 106, 191, 192, 215; in Congress, 93, 164–65; Senate Foreign Relations Committee testimony of, 106–107, 530*n59*
Douglas, William O., 242
Douglas Aircraft, 441
Dow Jones, 426
Draper, Theodore, 537*n6*
Dulles, Allen, 354, 381–82, 419–21, 424, 445–46, 460, 488, 493–94, 500, 566*n18*, 576*n26*
Dulles, John Foster, 60, 65, 140, 184, 261, 380–82, 385, 392, 402–403, 435–36, 411, 442, 480–81, 484–91, 494–95, 500, 510, 537*n6*, 538*n24*, 564*nn13, 16, 20, 21*, 567*n34*, 569*n59*, 570*n29*; antagonism between Eden and, 374, 382, 397, 402, 409, 413–16, 423, 424, 427–28, 439, 477–78, 497; appointed secretary of state, 374; at Bermuda summit, 396–97, *399*; during Churchill's U.S. visits, 374–76, 418–19; death of, 502; Indochina concerns of, 407–10, 416–17, 432–35, 490, 567*n19*; Japan peace treaty drafted by, 296–98; during Korean War, 282–86; Middle East policy of, 386–88, 393, 395, 447, 449–50, 455–59, 487–89; Nasser hated by, 464–66, 469–70, 576*n26*; nuclear weapons policies of, 420–21, 437, 566*n18*; as Republican Party foreign policy adviser, 59, 112, 169; during

Suez crisis, 466–67, 473–75, 477–79, 485, 490, 572*n19*, 574*n44*; TV and radio broadcasts of, 437–39
Dunkirk, 11, 36, 37, 159, 273, 274, 280, 521*n8*
Dutch East Indies, 77, 88, 127
Dutch Empire, 20
Dworshak, Henry, 383

Eady, Wilfred, 105, 530*n1*
East Africa High Command, British, 365–66
Eastern Europe, 16, 31–32, 100, 142, 150, 322, 513; *see also specific countries*
East Germany, 231
Eaton, Alfred, 67
Eban, Abba, 394, 458, 486, 572*n15*, 574*n44*
Eberstadt, Ferdinand, 525*n18*
Eccles, Marriner, 38
Economic Cooperation Administration, 247, 553*n38*
Economic Recovery Act (U.S., 1948), 148
Economic Recovery Administration, 145
Economic Survey for 1949, 162
Ecuador, 581*n18*
Eden, Anthony, 21, 140, 240, 315, 349, 350, 353, 362–63, 375, 409, 419, 428, 442–44, 455–65, 477–78, 561*n31*; Acheson and, 165, *303*, 326–37, 346–47; antagonism between Dulles and, 374, 382, 397, 402, 409, 413–16, 423, 424, 427–28, 439, 477–78, 497; background of, 361–62; at Bermuda conference, 396–97; boosting Britain's standing as global power attempted by, 462–64; as Churchill's heir apparent, 25, 362, 395, 442–43; and CIA action in Guatemala, 421–24, 477; at Geneva gathering of foreign ministers of World War II allies, 411–12; government formed by Churchill and, 328–29; House of Commons speeches of, 42, 72, 430, 465, 474; illnesses of, 385–86, 390–92, 396; Khrushchev and Bulganin meet with, 461–62; Middle East policies of, 57, 315, 322–24, 358–59; at Potsdam, 22–23; resignation of, 484, 485; at Rome

Fairlie, Henry, 500–501
Falklands War, 207
Far East, 229, 235, 249, 307, 368; *see also* China; Japan; Korea
Far East Strategic Reserve, 434
Farouk, King of Egypt, 58, 61, 62, 70, 82, 196–97, 310, 315, 316, 324, 325, 332, 345, 358–59
Faure, Edgar, 444
Fawzi, Mahmoud, 386
Fawzia, Queen, 310
Fay, Paul B. "Red," 563*n10*
Federal Bureau of Investigation (FBI), 354, 371
Federal Republic of Germany, *see* West Germany
Federal Reserve, 38, 86, 97, 192, 283, 427
Ferguson, Homer, 285
Festival of Britain, 294
Fiedler, Leslie, 166
Fifteen Weeks (Jones), 83
Fifty Year Wound, The (Leebaert), 252*n*
Fiji Islands, 288
Finletter, Thomas, 167, 263
Five Eyes intelligence collaboration, 122
Fleming, Ian, 371, 500
Ford Foundation, 367
Foreign Office, British, 25–26, 32, 37, 45, 56, 58, 65, 68, 69, 71, 78, 79, 84, 89, 91, 92, 106, 111, 117, 118, 127, 129, 141, 153, 155, 175–76, 178, 180, 182, 189, 190, 193, 194, 205–206, 217, 218, 232, 236, 240, 246, 254, 259, 264, 271, 272, 274, 276, 277, 284*n*, 285, 286, 298, 301, 307–309, 311, 314, 321–24, 329, 332, 336, 346, 352, 355, 356, 361, 362, 380, 385–86, 391, 409, 411, 415, 421, 422, 447, 456, 460, 483; American Department of, 123; Eastern Department of, 135; Economic Department, 162; Information Research Department, 365; Southeast Asia Department, 290
Foreign Service, U.S., 200, 206, 219, 221, 248, 307, 311, 315, 382, 467, 501, 502*n*, 512
Formosa, *see* Taiwan
Forrestal, James, 66–68, 70, 119, 122, 143–45, 150, 152, 197, 225, 252, 524*nn15, 17,* 525*n18,* 529*n56,* 531*n10,* 533*n52,* 539*n32*; Israel concerns of,

72–73, 75, 76, 132, 133, 534*n57*; suicide of, 172, 186
Forrestal, Michael, 119, 145, 157, 524*n15,* 515*n18,* 531*n10,* 535*n15*
Fortune 500, 426
Fosdick, Dorothy, 540*n57*
Fox, William T. R., 6, 575*n5*
France, 15, 18*n*, 57, 64, 97, 127, 151, 165, 194, 203, 222, 227, 232, 261, 285, 301, 376, 389, 428, 489, 502, 521*n8,* 522*n19,* 524*n14,* 526*n45,* 580–81*n17*; colonies of, 77, 218, 481*n,* 497 (*see also* French Indochina); Communist Party in, 55, 168; economic growth of, 231, 443, 549*n11*; Finance Ministry of, 184, 195, 237; Foreign Legionnaires, 291, 407, 470; German occupation zone governed by, 14, 143, 150; in Korean War, 270; Middle East concerns of, 455, 458, 488; and North Atlantic Treaty, 170, 175, 179, 180, 189; nuclear power industry in, 439; Paris Peace Conference in, 76; in SEATO, 433; Soviet threat to, 88, 157–58, 262–63; in Suez crisis, 62, 358, 397, 467, 469, 471–77, 480, 482, 484, 572*n19,* 574*n57*; in World War I, 93, 394; in World War II, 15, 60*n,* 83, 156, 499 (*see also* Allied powers)
France, Anatole, 381
Frankfurter, Felix, 74, 167, 535*n13,* 538*n19*
Franks, Oliver, 147–48, 151, 159, 169, 217–18, 253, 254, 262, 302, 329, 337, 343, 346–47, 350–52, 357, 402–403, 427, 518*n3,* 542*n30*; Acheson and, 165, 171, 204, 214, 236, 260, 322–23; in British-American sterling-dollar talks, 182, 184, 192, 193, 543*n1*; during Korean War, 260, 274–75, 284, 285; Middle East unrest addressed by, 312–13, 317, 319, 566*n4*
Fraser, William, 314, 318
Free French, 158
Free Officers Movement, 358
French Indochina, 22, 127, 223–24, 243, 247–49, 270, 335, 413; *see also* Vietnam War: French-Vietminh conflict in

Middle East, 56–78, 130, 141, 154, 176, 209, 223, 236, 252, 363, 443, 484, 496, 542*n29*, 573*n20*; Africa and, 366; Australia and New Zealand troops in, 112, 350; British dominance in, 5, 30, 96, 282, 353; Communist threat in, 148, 188–89, 203, 261; General Headquarters, Land Forces in, 58, 126, 197, 198; instability of, 4, 80, 215; Muslim population of, 130; U.S.-British cooperation in, 7, 45, 91, 111, 129, 338, 341, 428; U.S. involvement in, 195, 234, 403, 427, 542*n30*; *see also specific regions and countries*
Middleton, Drew, 158
Middleton, George H., 561*n25*
Military Assistance Advisory Group, U.S., 489
Miller, Hoyar, 541*n16*
Millis, Walter, 195–96
Milne, David, 548*n3*
Ministry of Fuel and Power, British, 95
Ministry of Supply, British, 117, 147–48, 162, 368, 369, 462, 562*n45*
Molotov, V. M., 12, 27, 31–32, 59, 63, 77, 100, 142, 172, 384, 519*n10*
Molotov-Ribbentrop nonaggression pact, 27
Moltke, Field Marshal Helmuth von, 101
Monroe Doctrine, 509
Montgomery, Field Marshal Bernard, 154, 158, 199–201
Moran, Lord, 23, 337, 339, 342, 380, 390–91, 425
Morgenthau, Hans, 177
Morning and Noon (Acheson), 165–66
Morocco, 263, 455, 478
Morris, Benny, 395, 572*n15*
Morris Motors, 51
Morrison, Herbert, 143, 321
Mosaddeq, Mohammad, 317–20, 322, 325, 332, 346, 359, 393–94, 465, 467, 500, 555*n24*
Moscow, 200, 502; intelligence operations in, 119, 353–54, 531*n10*; Kennan in, 560*n17*, 561*n19*; radio broadcasts from, 265, 559*n5*; U.S. and British embassies in, 45, 66, 221, 355–56, 522*n24*, 530*n7*, 566*n7*; *see also* Soviet Russia

Motion Picture Association of America (MPAA), 112
Mountbatten, Adm. Louis, 1st Lord Mountbatten, 349, 478
Mower, Barbara, 366
Mower, Jack H., 366, 367, 491, 561*n38*
Moyne, Walter Guinness, Lord, 61, 72, 76, 394
Mulcahy, Edward, 200
Munro, Gordon, 105
Murrow, Edward R., 379
Muslim Brotherhood, 325, 345, 430, 431, 478, 495
Muslims, 75, 113, 126, 130, 132, 310, 384, 404, 446, 478, 498, 507
Mussolini, Benito, 362
Mutual Aid, 34
Mutual Security Program, 334
My Silent War (Philby), 370

Nagasaki, atomic bombing of, 29, 155, 369, 377
Naguib, Gen. Muhammad, 358–59, 387, 430, 468
Nasser, Gamal Abdel, 359–60, 387, 430–32, 445, 447–49, 457–62, 464–70, 472–75, 477, 478, 487–88, 498
National Advisory Council, 98, 99
National Aeronautics and Space Administration (NASA), 514–15
National Economics University, 435
National Guard, U.S., 80, 552*n26*
National Health Service, British, 96, 174
National Iranian Oil Company, 318
nationalism, 64, 113, 148, 223, 305, 308, 324, 432, 434, 442, 498, 547*n30*; British, 169–70; Communist Chinese, 262; Egyptian, 57, 61, 196, 308, 319, 325, 344–45, 359, 430, 466–68, 497; German, 177; Iranian, 308, 311, 319, 393; Soviet, 4, 31, 65; in Vietnam, 242, 244, 405
Nationalist China, 79, 125, 182; *see also* Taiwan
nationalization, 309, 313, 314, 318, 332; in Britain, 24, 94–95, 106, 293; of Suez Canal Company's Lease, 317, 325, 345, 467, 469, 474–75, 544*n18*, 580*n8*

National Press Club, 169, 193, 490
National Security Act (1947), 122
National Security Agency, U.S., 370
National Security Council (NSC), 84, 122, 159, 214–17, 220, 308, 402, 406, 414, 417, 430, 435, 445, 501, 548*n37*; studies prepared and circulated by, 214–15, 221, 224–28, 232–35, 241, 254, 258, 263, 267, 302, 316, 382–83, 481
Navy, U.S., 84, 90–92, 121, 135, 144, 164, 197–98, 254, 259, 276, 296, 338–39, 342, 348, 401, 412, 421, 513, 531*n13*, 558*nn30, 34*; in Civil War, 580–81*n17*; Eastern Atlantic and Mediterranean Forces, 132; 5th Fleet, 511; Intelligence School, 531*n10*; Pacific Fleet, 290; Royal Navy cooperation with, 550*n51*; SEALS, 500; 7th Fleet, 437; 6th Fleet, 348, 454, 460, 474, 476, 498; War College, 531*n19*
Nazis, 11, 15, 27, 35, 64, 72, 84, 94, 96, 142, 158, 177, 231, 240, 243, 357, 388, 536*n35*; *see also* Hitler
"Negro Problem," 48
Nehru, Jawaharlal, 217–20, 244, 246, 254, 297, 322, 346, 382, 433, 434, 469, 475, 479, 488, 514
Nelson, Adm. Horatio, 57
Nene jet engine, 116, 117
Nenni, Pietro, 353
Nepalese Gurkhas, 288
Netherlands, 20, 189, 194, 259, 389, 519–20*n21*, 536*n26*
New Deal, 47, 93, 98, 107
Newfoundland, 29*n*, 50
New Guinea, 53
New Mexico, atomic bomb tests in, 23
New York, 33, 41, 194, 454; Cocoa Exchange, 51; Stock Exchange, 184
New Zealand, 44*n*, 50, 112, 122, 130, 154, 254, 259, 270, 284, 295–97, 363, 406, 411, 414, 432–34, 436, 475
Nicaragua, 207, 421
Nichols, Donald, 289, 552*n16*
Niebuhr, Reinhold, 177
Nigeria, 199–201, 365, 366
9/11 attacks, 168, 493, 506
1984 (Orwell), 28, 183, 264, 287, 520*n37*

Ninio, Marcelle, 570*n15*
Nitze, Paul, 186, 191–92, 215, 222, 225–27, 229, 246, 252, 263, 284–86, 324, 502, 541*n5*, 542*n21*, 545*nn28, 29, 31*, 561*n35*
Nixon, Richard, 4, 226, 242, 357, 404–406, 410, 417, 418, 423, 466, 477, 480, 487, 491, 501, 510
NKVD, 12, 31–32, 550*n49*
Nobel Prize, 21; Peace, 486, 579*n1*
Noel-Baker, Philip, 313
North African campaign, 61
North American Aviation, 118, 441
North American Newspaper Alliance, 371
North Atlantic Treaty Organization (NATO), 101, 167–70, 178–79, 182, 232, 252*n*, 253, 273, 295, 341, 406, 443–44, 484, 495, 511; Atlantic Command, 347, 348, 480; creation of, 159, 167–70, 174–75, 432; defense of overseas territories included in, 189, 198; demarcation line between East and West Europe provided by, 189, 351; European precursor to, 158; during Korean War, 280, 282; Middle East Command, 444; nuclear weapons options of, 333–34, 338, 436, 476; Snyder's role in U.S. participation in, 87, 334–35; trade with the People's Republic of China by members of, 392; and U.S. membership in other alliances, 363, 376, 427, 432–33, 442, 510; West Germany in, 429, 451, 470; *see also* Atlantic Pact
North Korea, 254, 255; *see also* Korean War
nuclear weapons, 5, 7, 273, 370, 413, 462, 493, 545*n31*, 549*n25*, 558*n32*, 573*n27*; U.S. plans for use of, 339–40, 397, 402, 413, 567*n26*; *see also* atomic bombs; hydrogen bomb
Nuclear Weapons and Foreign Policy (Kissinger), 226
Nutting, Anthony, 385, 460
Nyasaland, 199

Obama, Barack, 581*n19*
Office of Defense Mobilization, U.S, 445
Office of Strategic Services (OSS), 122, 123, 222, 356, 370, 371, 381, 560*n8*

Snyder, John Wesley (*cont.*)
93, *211*, 500; during Korean War,
271, 274, 283; Marshall Plan concerns
of, 99–100, 104; Marshall's friendship
with, 85, 86, 99, 527*n12*, 529*n43*;
National Advisory Council chaired
by, 98–99; NATO meetings attended
by, 334–35, 556–57*n12*; at NSC
meetings, 232; range of government
experience of, 85–87; in World War I,
99; during World War II, 144, 145
Sokolovsky, Marshal Vasily, 155
Somme, Battle of the, 361
Sophocles, 172
Sorbonne, 381
Souers, Adm. Sidney, 173, 214
"Sources of Soviet Conduct, The"
(Kennan), 101
South Africa, 44*n*, 154, 199, 218, 288,
366, 368, 389; Air Force of, 268
Southampton (England), 156–57, 171
Southeast Asia, 5, 80, 89, 91, 141, 189,
195, 215, 342, 353, 376, 403, 418–19,
427; World War II in, 305, 349;
see also specific regions and countries
Southeast Asia Treaty Organization
(SEATO), 432–33, 435, 442, 489,
495, 500, 510
South Korea, 105, 253, 254, 255, 433;
see also Korean War
South Vietnam, Republic of, 221, 433,
434; Diệm regime in, 435, 489–90;
recognition of, 247–49
Soviet Russia, 4–7, 18, 22, 27, 97, 132,
162, 168, 202, 220, 231*n*, 296, 329,
350–57, 363, 376, 380, 402, 403, 439,
451, 501, 520*n40*, 527*nn10, 18*,
531*n10*, 550*n51*, 566*n7*, 569*n60*;
airfields with potential to attack, 120,
155, 256–57, 263–64, 385, 440, 454;
Berlin blockaded by, 149–55, 157,
526*n23*; British arms sales to, 116–19,
469; and British economic instability,
49, 104, 182, 193, 222; Churchill's
hopes for summits with, 376, 386,
395, 397, 412, 419, 444; Churchill's
Iron Curtain speech on, 43–44,
46–47, 52, 68, 169, 171, 341, 342,
353, 377, 510, 544*n8*; clandestine
operations of, 31, 72–73, 276, 355,
370, 560*n12*, 579*n2*; collapse of,

505–506, 509, 513, 550, 578–79*n1*;
containment strategy for, 67, 101–102;
deterrence policy toward, 200, 253,
292, 335, 394, 437, 462–63; Eastern
European countries controlled by, 16,
30, 84, 142–44, 443, 519*n10*, 535*n9*;
Guatemala involvement accusation
against, 420–22; Hungarian uprising
against, 471, 474, 475, 480, 484, 491,
499; intercontinental ballistic missiles
of, 493–96, 499, 545*n29*; Kennan's
views on, 100–101, 123, 176, 178,
179, 252, 356–57, 384, 524–25*n17*,
535*n22*; in Korean War, 259, 263–67,
277–78, 282–83, 302, 351, 548*n2*;
London meeting with representatives
of, 461–62; Middle East instability
exploited by, 60–61, 63–66, 68–69,
135, 197, 200, 233, 311–14, 320–22,
345, 350, 441–42, 447–48, 458–61,
468–77, 485, 488, 531*n23*; Military
Marine Fleet of, 347–48; nuclear
arsenal of, 5, 195–96, 323, 392; Paris
Peace Conference representatives of,
76–77; the People's Republic of China
influenced by, 237, 437 (*see also*
Sino-Soviet bloc); Southeast Asia
influence of, 242, 247, 287, 290–93,
502, 545*n31*, 578*n57*; space program
of, 7, 493, 496, 514, 577*n41*; Western
nations' responses to threat of, 87–91,
95–96, 130, 140–44, 148–49, 157–58,
218, 226, 253–54, 261–63, 439–42,
527*n21*, 528*n23* (*see also* NATO); in
World War II, 11–16, 31–32, 63, 411
(*see also* Allied powers); *see also* Red
Army; Stalin, Joseph
Spaatz, Gen. Carl "Tooey," 85
Spain, 509, 580–81*n17*; Civil War in,
391
Spears, Edward, 575*n8*
Special Air Service (SAS), British, 73,
88, 288–89, 404, 506
Spellman, Card. Francis, 241, 353
Spender, Percy, 546*n21*
Sproul, Allan, 192
Sputnik, 7, 493, 496, 514, 577*n41*
Sri Lanka, *see* Ceylon
Stalin, Joseph, 45, 72–73, 125, 172, 184,
265, 337, 355–57, 361, 376, 377,
522*n24*, 530*n7*, 541*n4*, 549*n53*,

Updike, John, 510
U.S. Information Service, 360
U-2 reconnaissance flights, 473, 577*n41*
Uzbekistan, 30, 56

Vandenberg, Arthur, 59, 60, 65, 107, 137
Vandenberg, Gen. Hoyt, 155
Vanderbilt University, 98
van Oss, Hendrik, 290
Vatican, 352
Vaughan, Harry, 43, 169, 522*n19*
Venezuela, 309, 313, 581*n17*
Verdun, Battle of, 294
Versailles Treaty, 381, 491
Vickers-Armstrong Ltd., 201
Victoria, Queen of United Kingdom, Empress of India, et al., 24
Vietminh, 125, 129, 224, 230, 240, 242, 244, 249, 291, 295–96, 342, 405–409, 411, 416–17, 567*n19*; Chinese support of, 287, 288, 290
Vietnam, 22; American military presence in, 489, 500; Associated State of, 244, 248–49; *see also* South Vietnam
Vietnam, wars in, 6, 92, 240, 247–49, 290, 478, 496, 502, 532*n32*, 548*n44*, 553*n29*, 578*n57*, 580*n13*, 581*n18*; British position on, 404, 423, 428, 436, 503; colonial interests in Indochina threatened by, 243, 248, 364; French-Vietminh conflict in, 125, 129, 224, 230, 241–42, 249, 287–88, 290–91, 295–96, 342, 401, 405–13, 416, 417, 429, 431, 432, 434, 444; State Department resistance to involvement in, 363, 561*n35*; U.S. failure in, 4, 507, 508, 575*n62*
Vinson, Carl, 415
Vinson, Fred, 38, 47
Virginia Military Institute, 80
Vozhd (Supreme Leader), *see* Stalin, Joseph
V-2 long-range rockets, 115
Vyshinsky, Andrei, 12, 32, 77, 172, 278, 561*n19*

Wafd Party, 61
Wagner, Robert F., 71–72, 260
Wales, 298, 464
Walesa, Lech, 579*n1*
Wallace, Henry, 172

Wall Street, 19, 29*n*, 66, 70, 86, 94, 99, 102, 113, 145, 174, 490
War and Postwar Adjustment Policies (Baruch), 19
Ward, Barbara, 535*n21*
War Department, U.S., 80, 105
War Industries Board, 18
War Ministry, British, 433
War Mobilization and Reconversion, U.S. Office of, 86
Warren, Earl, 388
Warsaw Pact, 443, 484, 571*n37*
War Shipping Administration, 17, 94
Washington, D.C., 39, 43; British Embassy in, 16–18, 36, 39, 123, 146, 169, 476
Wasson, Thomas C., 133
Waterhouse, Capt. Charles, 465
Watry, David, 437
Watson, Bob, 140
Watts, Hugh, 74, 525*n35*
Webb, James, 173, 176, 180, 190, 191, 194, 225, 253, 271, 512, 514–15, 545*n26*
Wehrmacht, 541*n4*
Wells, H. G., 21
Westad, Odd Arne, 535*n22*
West Africa, 51
Western Union, 158
West Germany, 151, 168, 177, 231, 263, 299, 389, 429, 443, 451, 470, 482, 497, 536*n23*
Westminster Abbey, 160, 287, 388
Westminster College, *see* Fulton, Missouri, Churchill's speech in
Wheatcroft, Geoffrey, 517*n1*
Wherry, Kenneth, 166, 237, 240
White House Telephone Office, 191
Whitney, Jock, 225–26
Wiley, Alexander, 305, 307, 384, 394, 410
Wilford, Hugh, 580*n15*
Willkie, Wendell, 94
Wilson, Charles E., 402, 413
Wilson, Woodrow, 41, 159, 336, 491, 537*n6*
Winchell, Walter, 533*n52*
Wine and Spirits Wholesalers, 47
Wisner, Frank, 371, 424
Woodruff, Robert, 177, 178
World Bank, 47, 177, 185, 186, 530*n62*
World Trade Organization, 34, 513

A NOTE ABOUT THE AUTHOR

Derek Leebaert is the author of *Magic and Mayhem: The Delusions of American Foreign Policy*, *The Fifty-Year Wound: How America's Cold War Victory Shapes Our World*, and *To Dare and to Conquer: Special Operations and the Destiny of Nations*, and the coauthor of the MIT Press's trilogy on the information technology revolution. He has led a global management consulting firm for the past fifteen years and serves on the board of Providence Health System and other public service institutions. He is a former Smithsonian Fellow, a former professor at Georgetown University, and a founding editor of three enduring periodicals: the Harvard/MIT quarterly *International Security*, the *Journal of Policy Analysis and Management*, and, for investors and bankers, *The International Economy*. Leebaert is also a founder of the National Museum of the United States Army. He lives in Connecticut and Washington, D.C.

Visit the Knowledge Exchange: www.GrandImprov-KE.org.